ANDREW JACKSON

VOLUME THREE

THE COURSE OF AMERICAN DEMOCRACY, 1833–1845

ANDREW JACKSON

VOLUME THREE

THE COURSE OF AMERICAN DEMOCRACY, 1833-1845

Robert V. Remini

HISTORY BOOK CLUB
NEW YORK

For my granddaughter,
Caitlin Maureen Costello

When I review the arduous administration thro which I have passed, the formidable opposition I have met to its very close, by the combined talents, wealth, and power of the whole aristocracy of the Union, aided as they were, by the money monopoly, U.S. Bank, with its power of corruption, with which we had to contend, the result must be not only pleasing to me, but to every patriot. It shews the virtue and power of the sovereign people, and that all must bow to public opinion. It was the sovereign people that nobly sustained me against this formidable power, and enabled me to terminate my administration so satisfactory to the great body of the democracy of our Country.

—Andrew Jackson to Martin Van Buren
March 30, 1837

Contents

Photographs follow page 250.

MAPS AND FLOOR PLANS

Acknowledgments

IN WRITING THIS BIOGRAPHY of Andrew Jackson I have been extraordinarily fortunate in having at my disposal the immense resources of the Jackson Papers Project at the Hermitage, Tennessee. This project, conceived by Harriet Chappel Owsley, and handsomely supported by the Ladies' Hermitage Association, the Tennessee Historical Commission, and the National Historical Publications Commission, has assembled copies of the vast corpus of Jackson documents located in all parts of the United States and in many foreign countries. I must once again acknowledge my profound debt to the three successive directors of the project: Harriet C. Owsley, Sam B. Smith, and Harold Moser. They not only provided access to this rich collection but actively and personally assisted my research and writing of Jackson's life. And I can never begin to thank the Ladies' Hermitage Association for their encouragement and support. It never wavered even when sorely tried by my discussion of Jackson's marriage in volume one. Two members of this association deserve a special salute. Mrs. Fred Russell, regent of the association at the time the project was first proposed, lent her considerable influence in winning approval for the idea of collecting Jackson documents at the Hermitage. Without her active interest in the value and worth of the project it would have been impossible to achieve the necessary degree of support for this undertaking, since no university or research library seemed capable or willing to commit themselves to it at that time. Mrs. Harry A. J. Joyce, research coordinator of the association and member of the board of directors, seconded Mrs. Russell's efforts and provided essential aid at several critical moments. Both women have earned the lasting gratitude of Jackson scholars everywhere.

In preparing this final volume of the biography I was also fortunate to have at my disposal the splendid collection of Edward Livingston Papers maintained by the John R. Delafield Foundation. These papers have enriched my reading of the French spoliation controversy, among other things, and for permission to use this material I am profoundly grateful to John W. Delafield, Esq.

Essential to the final preparation of this biography have been the comments and criticisms from friends and colleagues in the profession who read all or parts of the manuscript and suggested needed changes or pointed out obvious and sometimes less than obvious mistakes. My colleague at the University of Illinois Peter J. Coleman read the entire manuscript in one of its earliest versions and gave me the benefit of his editorial skills and vast knowledge of American history. My friend John Niven of the Claremont Graduate School also read the entire manuscript in a later revision and provided me with telling criticism. Having just published a biography of Martin Van Buren, Professor Niven was particularly well qualified to catch all those small details that sometime threaten to slide into error. I am very grateful to him. As she did in volumes one and two of the biography, Harriet C. Owsley read selected chapters that touched on her expertise in Tennessee history and the Jackson family history. She has been my friend and staunch supporter since 1960, when I first walked into her office at the Tennessee State Library and Archives and asked to see all the Jackson manuscripts held by the library. There is no way I can properly thank her for all her many kindnesses over the past twenty and more years. Professor Mary Young of the University of Rochester read the chapter on Indian removal and wrote several pages of criticisms and suggestions. She alerted me to so many misstatements and foolish comments that she deserves most of the credit for whatever sophisticated parts can be found in that chapter. I only hope this acknowledgment does not jeopardize her good standing with her Native American friends and their allies.

Again, I wish to thank my friend John McDonough, manuscript historian of the Library of Congress, for his never ending help. He has watched over the progress of this biography since its inception and has gone out of his way to inform me of all new acquisitions of Jackson material both at the Library of Congress and at other repositories around the country. John H. Thweatt, senior archivist of the Tennessee State Library and Archives, has also provided every conceivable assistance in advancing this biography to its conclusion. My friends Wayne Cutler and Carese Parker, editor and associate editor of the James K. Polk Papers at Vanderbilt University, not only assisted me with information about relevant documentary materials but shared with me their considerable knowledge of national and Tennessee politics throughout the Jacksonian era.

Dr. William Seale provided the drawings of the White House rooms, which I revised very slightly in accordance with the findings of my own research. I am extremely grateful to him for his enormous help, and elsewhere in this book I have acknowledged my debt about details of White House activities during Jackson's administration. Annette Melville, art librarian at the Library of Congress, guided me in all three volumes of the biography in the selection of appropriate pictures and dust-jacket portraits of Jackson. Mrs. Allan Steele, chairman of the Museum and Relics Committee of the Ladies' Hermitage Association, made available copies of many pictures belonging to the association. And Betty C. Monkman, associate curator of the White House, not only allowed me to examine surviving pieces of service wear in the executive mansion from Jackson's administration but also provided copies of several pictures of Old Hickory in the possession of the White House.

Finally, I owe a special debt of gratitude to my editor and friend Hugh Van Dusen, who never realized what he was getting into when he first consented to publish this biography of Andrew Jackson. I trust he knows that I am very grateful to him for his faith in this project and his patience and counsel.

Preface

THIS THIRD VOLUME CONCLUDES my efforts at a comprehensive account of the life of Andrew Jackson. I first started writing the biography on April 11, 1970, and thought I could encompass Jackson's life in one hefty volume. Since my research into the Jacksonian era had begun more than two decades earlier—that is, when I first undertook a doctoral dissertation at Columbia University on the early political career of Martin Van Buren—I wrongly assumed that I could complete the biography in three to five years. Little did I know. The writing for the first volume alone took six years, interrupted on two occasions to complete other assignments. And the research never ended. As late as 1983 new collections of Jackson material were still turning up. The Duke University Library, for instance, recently acquired a small addition of Jackson letters, and the Library of Congress purchased a rather imposing addition to its Blair Family collection. I daresay that had I known when I started in 1970 that this project would involve a never ending tour of research and a twelve-year stint of writing and rewriting, I probably would never have undertaken it. Fortunately, I did not know, for the task has been one of the most rewarding and satisfying that I have ever attempted.

Even before I seriously considered a full-blown account of Jackson's life I had grappled with his biography. Back in the early 1960s I wrote a short, two-hundred-page statement that had a single and specific thesis to advance and avoided most other considerations. Thus, when I decided to write this big book on the General I had presumed that it would be a straightforward account which would narrate the important events and motivations of his life, as all biographies should, and pay careful attention to his character and personality. But it did not work out that way exactly

and ballooned into something far more encompassing than I ever anticipated. For Jackson was one of those unique American figures whose
life shaped the major historical movements of their time. As I wrote this
biography—and especially as I continued my research into his life—I
realized that he played an enormously vital role in three of the most
important developments in the history of the early Republic: its expansion, its struggle to preserve individual freedom, and its evolution into
a democracy.

During the early phase of Jackson's life he was directly associated with
American expansion, and indeed it had always been one of his goals to
assist that expansion. To protect the "Grand Republick" he was determined to drive the British and Spanish from the continent and remove
the Indians to a place where their presence could no longer hazard the
security of the nation. His achievements in establishing that security were
the central concerns of volume one. After his military career formally
ended, following his seizure of Florida, and he entered the political arena
as a candidate for the presidency, he became fiercely anxious over the
dangers to liberty that had resulted from the general corruption of the
postwar era. As volume two attempted to demonstrate, Jackson rode into
office in 1828 in the belief that he could wipe out the corruption and
reestablish the principles of republicanism through a policy of "reform
retrenchment and economy."

From the moment he began his administration President Jackson
sought to assert the single most important principle that guided his
political life, namely, the right of the majority to govern this nation. He
urged the people to express their opinions and wishes through state
legislatures, national conventions, elections, party caucuses, and other
such devices. And he argued that once expressed, the will of the majority
was absolute and that all officers of the government must obey that will
or resign their office. The course of American democracy was profoundly
influenced by Andrew Jackson. It was largely due to his efforts that many
of the fundamental doctrines of republicanism gave way to the doctrines
of democracy. "The substitution was underway by the 1830s," declared
Professor Marcus Cunliffe in a paper read before the American Historical
Association in 1982,[1] and this third volume of the life of Andrew Jackson
concerns itself principally with that substitution.

Some critics have resented my use of the biographical form to advance
a thesis, particularly those critics who wish to denigrate Jackson's importance in history or his claim to the affections of the American people.
Indeed, recent textbooks have all but dismissed Old Hickory, except to
level a few snide swipes at his Indian removal policy or to argue that he
opposed the reform movements of the period. Undoubtedly, the attempts to reduce Jackson from his position as "the Man of the People,"

[1]Marcus Cunliffe, "The Widening and Weakening of Republicanism in Nineteenth Century
America," paper read at the AHA convention, December, 1982, Washington, D.C.

a position accorded him by the Progressive and New Deal historians of the past, began with the publication of Richard Hofstadter's influential study *The American Political Tradition and the Men Who Made It* (1948). It was Hofstadter's contention that the leading Jacksonians were not champions of urban workers as Arthur M. Schlesinger, Jr., had argued in his *Age of Jackson* (1945), or of small farmers, as Frederick Jackson Turner and other Progressive historians had earlier suggested. Rather, according to Hofstadter, they were men on the make, entrepreneurs principally concerned with advancing their own political and economic advantage. And not infrequently, he claimed, they were captains of great wealth. Once this assault was launched there followed in many monographs an unending battering of Old Hickory that soon reduced him to what one recent historian summarized as "an inconsistent opportunist, a shady land speculator, a political fraud—and a strike-breaker to boot."[2]

Much as I admired Richard Hofstadter—as a matter of fact I wrote my master's essay at Columbia University under his direction and I regard him as one of the kindest and most gracious men I have ever met—and revere his work, I believe he was wrong about the Jacksonian movement and wrong about Jackson's place in American history. But it is not my intention here to attempt a refutation of the present claim of some historians that Old Hickory was an opportunist or a political fraud. I think the biography as a whole makes my position clear. I would simply state that I believe that the old man himself was scrupulously honest in all his financial transactions and that he tried to reform the government to root out corruption and provide the American people with a government of integrity and honor. As for his strikebreaking, that matter is treated in this final volume.

What I would like to emphasize—and what this book argues as part of its central thesis—is Jackson's right to many of the claims advanced for him by the Progressive and New Deal historians. He was in fact a Man of the People. In his own way, he did try to represent the American electorate. Indeed, he always insisted that as President he, and he alone, represented all the people and that he was responsible to them for whatever action he took. He actively attempted to advance democracy by insisting that all branches of government defer to the popular will. He even regarded the justices of the Supreme Court as subject to that will, and it is rather well known that he did not consider their interpretation of the Constitution as final or superior to that of the other two branches of government. Ultimate and final interpretation always rested with the electorate. Through proposed constitutional amendments, he repeatedly and unsuccessfully attempted to abolish the Electoral College in order to bring the people closer to the operation of their government. For he did

[2]Sean Wilentz, "On Class and Politics in Jacksonian America," in *The Promise of American History: Progress and Prospects,* Stanley I. Kutler and Stanley N. Katz, eds., *Reviews in American History* (December, 1982), X, 45–63.

not believe in the tenet of republicanism that tolerated the alteration of the popular will if it was judged improper by the legislature or some other representative body.

The evolution of American democracy during the period 1833–1845, therefore, is the major concern of this volume and the vital role Andrew Jackson played in shaping and directing it. Since Jacksonian America was transforming itself into a dynamic and industrial society, democracy seemed more suited to its needs in a modern world. The extent to which Jackson subverted the doctrines of republicanism by substituting the doctrines of democracy is also a central consideration of this book.

When Andrew Jackson spoke about the "people"—and he spoke about them constantly—he knew precisely whom he meant. When he said that he represented the people he made it clear that he was not talking about entrepreneurs, rising capitalists, or middle-class businessmen, as Hofstadter and others have suggested. In fact, many times he specifically noted that it was the wealthy capitalist who attempted to thwart all his efforts at fiscal and governmental reform. Rather, he repeatedly defined the great masses of people as workers and farmers. In the broad definition of farmers he included planters; but the term "workers" specifically referred to urban workers to a very large extent. Although Jackson himself was a wealthy man of high social standing in his own state (like the Roosevelt Presidents but without their social pedigree), who lived in a mansion and owned 150 slaves, his tone and style as President were distinctly populistic. He conducted himself with enormous dignity as befitted his station and he erected presidential trappings in the White House that bore monarchical traces, but he welcomed the attention and company of "the common man"—both inside and outside the White House. The tone and style of his public statements and appeals were genuinely democratic. They were not rhetorical mummery or "claptrap," as some historians have insisted.

This is not to imply that the Jacksonian movement as it developed across the country did not include many businessmen and rising capitalists in its ranks, even the enormously wealthy. The Democratic party has always had a share of corporate leaders. Nor do I wish to suggest a one-on-one identification of any economic or social class with a particular political party. But, as far as Jackson himself was concerned, "his" people, what he called the "great labouring classes" of America, were those who worked "by the sweat of their brow." They were not capitalists, entrepreneurs, or a moneyed class.

In the general assault upon Jackson and his works over the past few years it has been pointed out that he was an extensive slaveholder, as were many other leaders of the Jackson movement. But the criticism does not end there. It has also been asserted (wrongly) that the Democratic party itself was committed to the defense of slavery—that it came into existence to defend the "peculiar institution." As I read the documents it was never the purpose or goal of the Democratic party to defend slavery per se, nor did men like Martin Van Buren and other leaders construct the party in the late 1820s as a barrier against abolitionism. Jackson himself contended that those who sought to abolish slavery were intent on two things: destroying the Union (since they knew that southerners would never willingly agree to abolition), and destroying the democratic principle of majority rule. Abolitionists hated the democracy, he argued, and wished to restore a republican system in order that a "moneyed elite" could once more take control of the government to advance their economic interests at the expense of the common man.

In part, recent generations of Americans have ridiculed Jackson because he was a genuine hero, and heroes went out of fashion some time after World War II. His own generation did not see as well as we that he was a flawed hero, as most of that breed usually turn out to be when their lives are subjected to microscopic examination. Jackson also removed the Indians beyond the Mississippi River and for some that deed alone is so reprehensible as to condemn him for all time.

However, what needs to be taken into account in any final evaluation of General Jackson is that he loved the Union with a passion and that he sought to preserve it from those who would deliberately or unwittingly destroy it. Perhaps more than anything else, he believed in a virtuous people and was supremely optimistic about their capacity for self-government. He is in the true Jeffersonian tradition, only more emotional in his commitment to and affection for the great masses of people.

In sum, then, I regard Jackson's unquenchable love of the Union and his unshakable trust in democracy as the most admirable things about him and his great legacy to future generations of Americans.

Trailing after the old man for the past dozen years has been an exciting adventure that has taken me to strange and unlikely places around the globe. It has always been a great pleasure to accompany him on this journey, even at times when he was difficult and testy, arrogant and surly. In his company there was always a sense of excitement, and so it is with feelings of profound regret that I leave him. He has my respect and undying gratitude.

April 1983   ROBERT V. REMINI
Wilmette, Illinois

Chronology of Jackson's Life, 1833-1845

1833, January	Encourages alliance with Webster
1833, January 16	Force Bill message sent to Congress
1833, March	Prepares for removal of deposits
1833, March 2	Signs Force Bill and Compromise Tariff
1833, March 4	Pocket vetoes distribution bill
1833, March 4	Inaugurated for second term
1833, April 6	Meets Chief Black Hawk
1833, April 12	John Overton dies
1833, May	Reshuffles cabinet
1833, May 6	Assaulted by Robert B. Randolph
1833, June 6– July 4	Tours New England and Middle Atlantic states
1833, June 26	Notifies Treasury secretary of decision to remove deposits
1833, July 7	General John Coffee dies
1833, July 28– August 22	Vacations at Rip Raps
1833, September 18	Presents paper on deposit removal to cabinet
1833, September 23	Dismisses Duane
1833, October 1	Begins shift from national banking to deposit banking
1833, December 3	Forwards fifth annual message to Congress
1833, December 4	Explains pocket veto of land bill

1833, December 14	Rejects possible alliance with Webster
1833, December 27	Refuses Senate request for paper read to cabinet
1833–1834, December–March	Resists appeals to restore deposits
1834, January	Orders end of pension payments by BUS
1834, January 29	Orders troops against strikers
1834, February 5	Confers with Principal Chief John Ross
1834, March 28	Censured by Senate
1834, April 4	Grandson, Andrew Jackson III, born
1834, April 4	Bank policy approved by House
1834, April 15	Issues Protest over censure
1834, April 21	Issues codicil to Protest
1834, April 21	Proposes reform of currency and banking
1834, May	Threatens action against France
1834, June	Submits treaties with Siam and Muscat to Senate
1834, June	Takes no action against France
1834, June 16	Accepts McLane's resignation
1834, June 23	Nominates Taney as secretary of treasury and Butler as attorney general
1834, June 24	Appoints Forsyth as secretary of state and Dickerson as secretary of navy
1834, June 30	Signs Coinage Act
1834, July 8	Leaves Washington for Hermitage
1834, August 5	Arrives at Hermitage
1834, September 9	Leaves Hermitage for Washington
1834, September 30	Arrives in Washington
1834, October 13	Hermitage burns
1834, November 26	Joined by son's family
1834, December 1	Forwards sixth annual message to Congress and recommends reprisals upon French property
1835, January	Announces nation free of debt
1835, January 1	Personal indebtedness increases
1835, January 15	Nominates Taney to Supreme Court
1835, January 30	Escapes assassination attempt
1835, May	Demands Van Buren's presidential nomination
1835, May 1	Appoints Kendall as postmaster general
1835, May 29	Refuses to apologize to France

1835, July 2– August 17	Vacations at Rip Raps
1835, August	Learns of violence in South Carolina over abolitionist tracts
1835, August	Responds to demands of rioters in Washington
1835, October– November	Works to win Polk's election as Speaker
1835, December	Nominates Kendall as postmaster general
1835, December 7	Forwards seventh annual message to Congress and explains intentions toward France
1835, December 18	Second Seminole War begins
1835, December 28	Nominates Taney as chief justice
1836, January 15	Forwards special message to Congress over crisis with France
1836, February	Crisis with France resolved
1836, February 18	Nominates Andrew Stevenson as minister to Great Britain
1836, May 23	Proclaims removal treaty with Cherokees in force
1836, May–June	Orders military operation against Creeks
1836, June 15	Approves admission of Arkansas into the Union
1836, June 23	Signs deposit bill
1836, July 2	Signs Post Office Act
1836, July 10	Leaves Washington for Hermitage
1836, July 11	Issues Specie Circular
1836, August 2	Rebuilding of Hermitage completed
1836, August 4	Arrives at Hermitage
1836, August 23	Travels to Alabama
1836, October 1	Returns to Washington
1836, November 19	Suffers severe hemorrhage attack
1836, November 21	Passes crisis and begins slow recovery
1836, December	Appoints Andrew Jr. as private secretary
1836, December 5	Forwards eighth annual message to Congress
1836, December 19	Emily Donelson dies
1836, December 21	Sends Texas message to Congress
1837, January 16	Senate censure expunged
1837, January 19	Entertains Santa Anna in White House
1837, January 26	Approves admission of Michigan into the Union
1837, March 3	Pocket vetoes rescinding of Specie Circular

1837, March 3	Recognizes Texas's independence
1837, March 4	Issues Farewell Address
1837, March 4	Attends Van Buren's inauguration
1837, March 7	Leaves White House for Hermitage
1837, March 25	Arrives at Hermitage
1837, June 9	Grandson, Samuel Jackson, born
1837, September–October	Physical condition worsens
1838, January–February	Suffers severe hemorrhage attacks
1838, July	Quarrels with John Quincy Adams
1838, July 15	Joins Presbyterian Church
1838, September 16	Ralph Earl dies
1838, November 20	Andrew Jr. purchases Halcyon Plantation
1839, January–February	Defends accused slaves
1839, March–May	Sells Alabama properties to meet debts
1840, January 8	Attends Silver Jubilee of victory at New Orleans
1840, August	Quarrels publicly with Henry Clay
1840, September–October	Campaigns for Van Buren in Tennessee
1841, January 15	Andrew Jackson Hutchings dies
1841, July	Suffers an apparent heart attack
1841, August 18	Grandson, Thomas Jackson, born and dies
1841, December	Borrows $6,000 from General Plauché
1842, April–May	Entertains Van Buren at Hermitage
1842, May 31	Borrows $10,000 from Blair
1842, September 1	Writes last will and testament
1842, October 15	Sustains carriage accident
1842, December 10	Sells Hunter's Hill property
1842–1843, December–January	Assists research of biography
1843, January	Seeks to mediate Blair-Kendall dispute
1843, February 14	Restitution of New Orleans fine passed by Congress
1843, June 7	Revises last will and testament
1843, June 19	Grandson, Robert Armstrong Jackson, born
1843, November 11	Grandson, Robert Armstrong Jackson, dies

1844, May 13	Endorses Polk for President
1844, July	Convinces Tyler to withdraw from presidential race
1844, December	Urges Texas annexation
1845, April 30	*Globe* ceases publication
1845, May	Suffers massive edema
1845, June 8	Dies at Hermitage
1845, June 10	Buried in Hermitage garden

ANDREW JACKSON

VOLUME THREE

THE COURSE OF AMERICAN DEMOCRACY, 1833–1845

CHAPTER 1

Jacksonian America

A STAGECOACH RATTLED ALONG the Cumberland Road on its way to the nation's capital. It was a beautiful fall day and the countryside sparkled in the bright sunlight. Inside the coach sat the President of the United States, General Andrew Jackson of Tennessee, a long, bony shaft, looking like a "chafed lion" and staring glumly at the passing landscape. It was October, 1832, and the flaming colors of autumn only periodically roused Old Hickory from his brooding thoughts. His companions tried to buoy his spirits by predicting a great electoral triumph over Henry Clay in the presidential contest then nearing its conclusion, but the election hardly crossed the General's mind because he felt sure the American people would sustain him (as they did) and reelect him to office.[1]

No, not presidential elections, not even the malice of the Bank of the United States (BUS) in attempting to engineer his defeat at the polls, disturbed the President's thoughts. Rather, it was the continued defiance of South Carolina and Georgia over the rights of the states respecting the tariff and Indians that alarmed and worried him. To think, he rumbled to his companions, that corrupt demagogues would endanger the Union with threats of secession to satisfy their ambition and greed. He stirred in his seat as these morbid thoughts flashed through his mind. His hands fisted in his lap. *"The Union will be preserved,"* he growled at one point, "and treason and rebellion promptly put down, when and where it may shew its monster head."[2]

As the stage lumbered along the national road and Jackson stared at the gorgeous landscape and pondered the movements of the "scoundrels" who trifled with treason, he might have remembered back to the first time he journeyed from Tennessee to the nation's capital. That was

1

thirty-six years ago, back to another century, back to 1796, when Philadelphia was the capital of the United States. In the brief time span since his initiation as a freshman congressman, phenomenal changes had occurred throughout the country. A nation of fewer than 5 million people, jammed into a few narrow corridors along the Atlantic coastline, had tripled by the 1830s to 15 million spread across a vast continent. The purchases of Louisiana in 1803 and Florida in 1819 added millions of acres to the national domain and created a nation that stretched from ocean to ocean and along the northern rim of the Gulf of Mexico.

When Jackson took his oath of office on December 5, 1796, as Tennessee's first representative to Congress, there were sixteen states comprising the Union (Vermont, Kentucky, and Tennessee had recently been added to the original thirteen). Now, in 1832, with Jackson's triumphant reelection as chief executive, the Hero of the Battle of New Orleans presided over a Union consisting of twenty-four states. In the south and southwest, Alabama, Mississippi, Louisiana, and Missouri had achieved statehood; in the north, Maine, Ohio, Indiana, and Illinois had also won admission to the Union. The admission of Missouri had touched off a furious controversy over the right of Congress to restrict slavery in the territories, a controversy that ultimately produced the Missouri Compromise, which limited slavery to an area south of 36°30′ in the Louisiana territory. But what struck everyone as wondrous was the fact that Missouri lay totally west of the Mississippi River. It occupied an area beyond the original boundaries of the United States.

The nation was expanding rapidly. And the people with it. Following the Revolution, Americans scrambled over the Appalachian mountain range and swarmed across the fertile valleys beyond. Within a few years they reached Texas and California and Oregon. A surging, restless drive propelled them westward and they squeezed out Spaniards, brushed aside Britons, and murdered Indians. By the 1830s they seemed well on their way to fulfilling Jackson's old dream of empire, his desire that the United States should some day expand over "all Spanish North America." A society that only a few decades earlier had been confined to isolated communities in the east (and which honored close ties of family, church, and locality) had exploded, and its fragments flew across mountains and valleys and plains. By 1832 a totally different society had emerged which embodied strange new rhythms of motion and agitation.

"Go ahead!" That was the spirit of this new age. "The whole continent presents a scene of *scrambling* and roars with greedy hurry," exclaimed one foreign traveler. "Go ahead! is the order of the day." It is "the real motto of the country." Our age, pronounced the distinguished senator from Massachusetts, Daniel Webster, is wholly different from anything in the past. It "is full of excitement" and rapid change.

For one thing, Americans themselves were distinctly different from their forebears. They no longer seemed English or European in any way.

They had their own unique characteristics now that set them off as an individual people. In their speech they produced "strange" accents and inflections to the English language, and they no longer wore powdered wigs and silk stockings. They were restless and aggressive and highly mobile. More than anything else, they were consumed with a desire to be better off, to make money, to succeed in business. "No man in America is contented to be poor, or expects to continue so," insisted another foreign traveler. That might be acceptable in Europe, but not in this country. In America everyone must improve himself and find a better life.

And how could this be achieved? The answer was simple. Work! That was the first command of this new society. "Work," declared one, "and at eighteen you shall . . . live in plenty, be well clothed, well housed, and able to save." Pursuing this Puritan work ethic guaranteed the better life. And all other good things proceeded from it. "Be attentive to your work, be sober and religious, and you will find a devoted and submissive wife; you will have a more comfortable home than many of the higher classes in Europe."[3]

This formula for a successful life in Jacksonian America did not always bring uniform results, unfortunately. Some did not get ahead. Indeed, some fell behind, and their number swelled each year in most of the major cities. Women undoubtedly suffered the most. They had been far better off during the colonial age, when all members of the family cooperated in the process of survival. Now, with husbands off to business, the women stayed home to tend and educate the children and serve the needs of all the members of the·family. They were expected to be domestic, submissive, and dependent. Like it or not, they were commissioned the moral guardians of society.[4]

The attention to business and the dedication to work by the American male developed most strikingly after the War of 1812. Because of the war, the nation was forced to build its own internal economy and not rely as much on international trade as it had done in the past. Capital investments subsequently shifted from shipping and commerce into manufactures and industry. The factory system was introduced from Britain, and because of the nation's vast natural resources—water power, iron and coal—along with a steady growth of the labor supply through immigration, the Industrial Revolution quickly took hold. Within thirty years all the essential components for the creation of an industrial society were securely in place.[5]

The industrialization of America in the early nineteenth century was hurried along by a phenomenon called the transportation revolution. Again it was the War of 1812 that fomented this revolution, for the war demonstrated the perpetual danger of British invasions both northern, from Canada, and southern, from the Gulf. The need to dispatch troops rapidly—indeed Jackson's great victory over the British at New Orleans in 1815 was made possible in part by the haste with which he moved from

Florida to Louisiana—produced a demand for quicker and more efficient transportation. As a result, the nation inaugurated a spectacular building program of roads, bridges, highways, turnpikes, and canals. The Cumberland Road over which President Jackson traveled on his return to Washington in 1832 had been started in 1811, at Cumberland, Maryland. By the mid-1830s it reached Vandalia, Illinois, a distance of nine hundred miles. The Pennsylvania Turnpike and the Wilderness Road were also undertaken. New York began construction of the Erie Canal in 1817 and completed it in eight years. This 363-mile stretch linked the Hudson River with Lake Erie and opened up Ohio, Michigan, Indiana, and Illinois to the thousands of immigrants arriving yearly from Europe.[6]

After roads and canals came the railroads. Once invented, railroading quickly caught on in America. Its important history began in this country in 1828, with the construction of the Baltimore and Ohio Railroad. The man who lifted the first spadeful of dirt to start the construction of this road was Charles Carroll of Carrollton, the last surviving signer of the Declaration of Independence. Somehow it seemed appropriate that a man who had signed that noble instrument should be the person to turn the spade to signal the real beginning of the industrialization of America. The B&O was followed by the Lexington and Ohio Railroad, the Boston and Worcester, the Louisville, Cincinnati and Charleston, and others. Within a decade, over a thousand miles of track served eleven states.[7]

The transportation revolution not only aided Americans to trek faster and deeper into their continent, it also created new communities and new markets. Wherever the railroad stopped or changed direction or intersected with other forms of transportation, towns and cities sprang up. Cincinnati, St. Louis, Chicago appeared virtually overnight, while older cities such as New York, Philadelphia, Boston, Baltimore underwent spectacular growth. Railroads became the nation's arteries, pumping economic life to all the areas they served. Most important, they attracted foreign capital, and capital was the essential ingredient in building an industrial nation. By the beginning of Jackson's second presidential term, a free, rapidly growing domestic economy had been established within the United States.[8]

Naturally, industrialism sparked the rise of the trade union movement. These unions, besides demanding improved working conditions, also called for "enlightened laws" respecting imprisonment for debt, the auction system, and monopolies. They especially advocated improvements in general education. In July, 1828, the aspirations of labor produced the Workingmen's party in Philadelphia, which agitated against such abuses as legislative aid to those who monopolized "the wealth creating powers of modern mechanism." The party soon spread to Baltimore, Newark, New York, and Boston. It drew considerable support from middle-class capitalists as well as laborers, and during the course of its brief history tended to shift its political support from candidate to candidate, crossing political lines at will to gain the greatest possible advantage.⁹

The changes in America over the thirty-year span since Jackson's first trip to Congress as a freshman representative were positively breathtaking. Not only had the economy been transformed, but society itself registered significant alterations. The birthrate nose-dived, never to recover. The standard of living jolted upward. The conditions of life began to show signs of real improvement. For example, canning and refrigeration of foods commenced. Refrigeration, however primitive, meant that people could enjoy fresh food throughout the year. The ability to store food was vital to the growth of American cities where fresh food could not always be produced or grown.

The invention of canning and the gadgets to cut and store ice said something important about these Jacksonian Americans. They loved to tinker. They prized tools of all kinds that could make life more agreeable. "Where in Europe young men write poems or novels," commented one foreign observer, "in America, especially Massachusetts and Connecticut, they invent machines and tools." And during the Jacksonian age a prodigious number of important inventions appeared. Cyrus H. McCormick invented the mechanical reaper for harvesting grain in 1831; Samuel Colt produced the revolver in 1835; Charles Goodyear developed the process of vulcanizing rubber in 1839; and Samuel F. B. Morse conceived the telegraph in 1844. Perhaps no discovery matched in value and importance what a dentist by the name of William T. G. Morton gave the world: anesthesia, a discovery also claimed by at least three other Americans. What made these and other inventions and discoveries so important was that they revolutionized entire industries and professions or created new industries and processes that advanced the industrialization of the entire nation.¹⁰

Although it is true that Americans in the 1830s prized machines and tools, that did not keep them from writing poems or novels. Indeed, a flowering of American arts and letters occurred during the Jacksonian age. Such writers as Washington Irving, James Fenimore Cooper, Ralph Waldo Emerson, Henry Thoreau, Bronson Alcott, Theodore Parker, Orestes Brownson, Nathaniel Hawthorne, Margaret Fuller, Oliver Wendell Holmes, Henry Wadsworth Longfellow, James Russell Lowell, John Greenleaf Whittier, Edgar Allan Poe, Herman Melville, William Gilmore Simms, George Bancroft, Francis Parkman, William H. Prescott, and many others produced a vast literature of imperishable quality. In varying degrees their talents were matched by artists in other fields, including John James Audubon, Gilbert Stuart, Charles Willson Peale, Asher Durant, and George Inness. Such a staggering number of creative artists has never been duplicated in America.¹¹

Politics also changed. With all the profound social and economic transformations occurring throughout the nation, these changes were bound to affect, and be affected by, the political process. It was a new political world. The widening of the suffrage, the continued elimination of voting restrictions, the emergence of professional politicians who assisted the creation of mass political parties, the invention of ballyhoo techniques to delight the newly enfranchised and thereby capture sizable blocs of votes, the beginning of national conventions, the appearance of third parties like the Anti-Masonic and Workingmen's parties—all these constituted important political innovations that grew out of the economic and social ferment of the age and contributed to the ongoing democratization of American political institutions.[12]

All these changes, in whatever area, emphasized one important aspect of this new American society. The desire for equality. Not absolute equality—rather the equality of opportunity, the belief that no one should have special privileges that worked to the disadvantage of others. All should be treated evenhandedly and have the opportunity of achieving material success. It was up to the government, therefore, to make certain that the race for success was a fair contest. Government must serve as an honest referee among the various classes in society and prevent any one of them from gaining an unfair advantage over the others.

Privilege was anathema to Jacksonians. It was synonymous with "aristocracy," a term they held in the utmost contempt. If this nation was to be truly democratic, editorialized the New York *Evening Post*, then we must end "all privilege." Every democratic advance, argued the newspaper, came from "breaking down the privileges of a few."[13]

The Jacksonians also detested deference. It was akin to privilege and implied the existence of a "better" class. Where privilege usually connoted some specific advantage, such as money, deference involved something more subtle and therefore more pernicious. Jacksonians took great delight in deflating the pretensions of those who expected deferential treatment.[14]

Yet with all the talk about equality and the need to banish privilege and deference, it is obvious that equality did not apply to everyone. Certainly not to blacks, women, or Indians. Jacksonians arguing for equality simply did not think about these people. They had no understanding of such an expanded concept of equality. To fault them, therefore, for failing to appreciate what the modern world means by equality is an idle exercise. And it should be remembered that the attitudes they held toward blacks, women, and Indians extended well into the twentieth century.

Actually there were many Americans during the Jacksonian era who did concern themselves about the lot of these minorities, from abolitionists who demanded the emancipation of the slaves, to missionaries who labored to protect the rights of Indians, to all the men and women who fought for women's rights. The steady, unremitting drumbeat call for reform by Andrew Jackson at the beginning of his administration, in order to "cleanse the Augean stables" of government that had been corrupted during the Monroe and Adams administrations, contributed to the general demand for reform throughout a society that was seen as wallowing in materialism and indifferent to the poor and distressed. Organized efforts to correct social and economic abuses quickly formed. Over the next several decades groups of men and women banded together to improve education, promote humane treatment in penal institutions and insane asylums, achieve equality for women, foster peace throughout the world, and bring about the prohibition of the manufacture and sale of liquor in every state. In their search for a better society some Americans joined religious or secular associations that experimented in communal living. They founded settlements throughout the northeast and the old northwest. With the appearance of the Church of Jesus Christ of the Latter-day Saints (Mormons), such experiments reached across the plains and into the Rocky Mountains. The "demon of reform" had been loosed upon the land, claimed Ralph Waldo Emerson, and it possessed almost every aspect of American life.[15]

The ferment and excitement of this age, its commitment to equality, and its involvement with reform resulted in considerable measure from the industrialization of America and the democraticization of its political institutions. And all of it—the excitement, the ferment, the rapid institutional changes—seemed to come together in the person of General Andrew Jackson, the Hero of the Battle of New Orleans. He symbolized this age, both its positive and negative aspects, its democratic spirit and its driving and greedy ambition. His life and accomplishments typified American striving for improvement. An orphan at the age of thirteen, he had risen from a small cabin in the piney woods of Carolina to the majestic White House in Washington. He was a "self-made man," the personification of "Go Ahead" America. Most assuredly, this era deserved to be called the Age of Jackson.[16]

Apart from what he symbolized, and unquestionably more important than what he represented, was the fact that Andrew Jackson himself actively advanced the course of American democracy. His words, his actions, his beliefs—despite a number of contradictions along the way—contributed significantly to democratizing the processes of government. Throughout his presidency, this impossible Hero of the American people dedicated himself to the proposition that *"the majority is to govern."*

As he alighted from his carriage at the White House on Friday evening, October 19, 1832, after his long trip from the Hermitage in Tennessee, and prepared to face some of the problems generated by this restless, evolving, "Go Ahead" society, President Jackson looked weary and somber. The deepening lines on his face registered his growing concern over the problem of nullification with South Carolina. His agitation was palpable, for he sensed he was nearing a crisis in national affairs.[17] And it was a crisis on which hung the fate of the Union.

CHAPTER 2

"Nullification . . . Means Insurrection and War"

WHENEVER OLD HICKORY DECIDED upon a course of action, he pursued it with total commitment and with all the drive at his command—which was enormous. Upon his arrival in Washington he had hoped to address the problem of the Bank of the United States, now that the people had "nobly & triumphantly ousted [its] corrupt influence" by reelecting him to the presidency, but he was forced to confront the more frightening specter of disunion upon his return, the determination of South Carolina through nullification and the threat of secession to compel the federal government to accede to its demands to lower the tariff.[1]

Nullification! that wretched doctrine proposed by John C. Calhoun, that "abominable" claim that any state had a right to declare federal law null and void within its boundaries whenever it deemed such law (like the tariff) unconstitutional. And, if the federal government attempted to enforce the law, the state reserved the right to withdraw from the Union.

The President paced the floor of his study, muttering under his breath as he pondered his possible courses of action. One serious complication that troubled him was the situation in Georgia. The state was prepared to defy the Supreme Court's decision in the Worcester case over Cherokee Indian rights, and if Jackson enforced the court's decision, Georgia was certain to join South Carolina in support of nullification.[2] Bloody conflict would surely ensue. Fortunately, Jackson's overwhelming victory in the presidential election dampened the hopes of the Indians and their allies in Congress about challenging Jackson's determination to remove the Indians west of the Mississippi River. Faced with the defiance of South Carolina and Georgia, these congressmen understood the seriousness of the danger threatening the Union. With hardly a second thought they abandoned the Cherokees. They quietly informed the chiefs that the "best good" of the tribe lay in signing a treaty of removal with the United States government.[3]

As Jackson examined the options open to him to meet this fast-developing crisis, he was obliged to consider the use of military force as a real possibility. He did not shrink from it. But that possibility involved the necessity of asking Congress for the appropriate legislation, and once again that opened up the problem of Georgia. For if Jackson requested a force bill to coerce South Carolina, surely he could obtain similar authority to bring Georgia into line. "I can never consent to sustain him against South Carolina," insisted one congressman, "while Georgia maintains the attitude she does."[4] The one predicament virtually invited attention to the other.

Because of the seriousness of nullification and his own sympathy with Georgia's position on the Indian question, Jackson directed his attention to isolating South Carolina by placating Georgia. What he did was masterful. He worked (and ultimately succeeded) at winning the freedom of Worcester and Butler, the two missionaries whose violation of Georgian law had precipitated the conflict between the Supreme Court and the state. At the same time he assumed a posture of resistance against South Carolina, knowing that it would attract the support in Congress of many National Republicans—the opposition party—either out of their concern for the safety of the Union or their desire to prevent any harm befalling the tariff. Thus, simultaneously, Jackson prepared for a showdown with South Carolina, involving possible military action, and maneuvered to ease Georgia out of the line of fire.[5]

The ominous situation encouraged some men to assess the political opportunities. Amos Kendall, the fourth auditor at the Treasury and an important member of Jackson's Kitchen Cabinet, conjectured that the "National Republican party will be dissolved" and that its leaders will immediately cast about for a new combination. "All men of all parties in the northern, middle and western states," he contended, "may be united upon the question of *the Union against Nullification,* and an immense majority of the South may be rallied in the same cause. On this basis the National Republicans in the northern and middle states may be willing to unite with the friends of the administration." They will find, he added, that the measures of the administration and the Democratic party "are not so bad as in their excitement they had supposed." If they know that they will not be "repulsed," they might be induced to "array themselves under the republican banner."[6]

What Jackson hoped might result from such a reshuffling of political allegiances was the creation of a "moral force" throughout the country strong enough to demonstrate to the nullifiers a total support of the administration in its efforts to preserve the Union.[7] Such a demonstration might frighten the hotheads of South Carolina from precipitous action that could lead to bloodshed. Jackson's position was stated precisely by one of his closest advisers: "The greatest solicitude I feel is, that so strong a moral force shall be arrayed on the side of the administration, that the incipient treason of the South shall be awed into obedience without the shedding of one drop of American blood."[8] Over the next several months —and these were the months between his reelection to the presidency and his inauguration for a second term—Jackson encouraged various leaders of the National Republican party to join him in presenting a united front against the "nullies," and he even briefly considered the formation of a new party to accommodate a revised coalition.

With Congress about to reconvene in December, Jackson would have many opportunities to bridge the gap between the Democratic and National Republican parties, provided he displayed understanding, tolerance, and compassion. The creation of a "moral force" in the country to combat the forces of disunion was unquestionably the best solution to the present crisis and Jackson, more than anyone else in the country, had the resources, talents, and charisma to bring it about. And the more he worked at solving the problem through the application of moral force, the more he won the approval and admiration of the electorate. With each new crisis, wrote a New York politician, "Genl. Jackson . . . discovers his greatness." Everyone—even the President's enemies—could see it. "Those who but yesterday opposed your re-election with ferocity," the General was told, "now loudly profess their reliance on your saving the Union."[9]

The first public indication of Jackson's future direction came with his fourth annual message to Congress on the State of the Union. In referring to the crisis in South Carolina, he planned at first to soft-pedal it as much as possible, at least until he had a clearer idea of the state's intention. "As to nullification in the south," he advised his newly elected Vice President, Martin Van Buren, "I mean to pass it barely in review, as a mere buble, view the existing laws as competent to check and put it down, and ask merely a general provision to be enacted, to authorize the Collector . . . to demand of all vessels . . . where a state . . . resist the collection of the revenue, the duty to be paid in cash."[10]

As he maneuvered to isolate South Carolina in the country, so too Jackson pondered ways to isolate the nullifiers within Congress. He spoke to his Kitchen Cabinet about it and held several long conversations with his Tennessee friend Major William B. Lewis. In these talks, said Lewis, "I infer he will strongly advise" the Congress to reduce the tariff still further. "I *fear* he will leave Calhoun and his nullifying squad no ground to stand upon, if he goes on reducing the Tariff. It will be a pitty, as they will have no *pretext even* to dissolve the Union!"[11]

Jackson had his fourth annual message ready to present to Congress when the two houses convened on December 3 to begin the second (short) session of the Twenty-second Congress. The following day he sent it down. In it he exuded justifiable pride in the "highly prosperous state" of the nation's economy and predicted that the national debt would be "extinguished within the year 1833." He congratulated the Congress and the people for this "memorable and happy event" and took a small measure of credit in bringing it about.[12]

In view of this pleasing situation, he continued, and in justice to the interest of the various states, not to mention "the preservation of the Union itself," he recommended the gradual diminution of the tariff rates. He was now willing to acknowledge that the protective system tended to foster in the minds of the American people "a spirit of discontent and jealousy dangerous to the stability of the Union."[13] What it had done to South Carolina in particular had brought the nation to the brink of catastrophe.

This seeming alteration in his tariff policy was actually quite consistent with Jackson's minimal-government, reform-centered philosophy.[14] He had now arrived at the opinion that protection exploited the people, both worker and planter, concentrated wealth in the hands of the few, and produced "the germs of dependence and vice" so characteristic of monopolies and "so destructive of liberty and the general good." He had abided the system, he said, in order to collect enough revenue to pay the national debt. Now "the stability of the Union" dictated another course.[15]

"It is my painful duty to state," he went on, that opposition to the revenue laws had risen to such a height as to threaten "if not to endanger the integrity of the Union." He hoped that a peaceful solution to the problem could be found through the prudence and patriotism of the people and officials of South Carolina. Should moderation and good sense fail, however, Jackson promised to return to Congress with suggestions as to the best measures necessary to settle the matter once and for all.[16]

Then he turned to other matters: the Bank of the United States, public lands, internal improvements, and Indian removal. His last paragraph reiterated his basic philosophy of government: maintain peace at home and abroad, and prescribe laws on "a few subjects of general interest" not calculated to restrict individual freedom but to enforce human rights. "This Government will find its strength and its glory in the faithful discharge of these plain and simple duties," he concluded.[17]

Although Jackson fervently hoped that his annual message would not exacerbate the crisis with South Carolina, he did not minimize the danger. In a private memorandum which he entitled "Nullification in the South to be carefully watched," the President recorded the events that had occurred to date: how, "after playing off the farce for several years, Calhoun & Co at length" succeeded in forcing South Carolina to adopt the doctrine of nullification and declare the tariff laws unconstitutional. He then noted some of his own responses: how instructions had gone out to the collector of the Charleston port in South Carolina that the revenue laws were to be executed; how two companies of regular army troops had been ordered to reinforce the garrisons in the port; and how George Breathitt of Kentucky had been sent to South Carolina with instructions from the President to find the means to bring the crisis under control.[18]

Indeed, events in South Carolina had moved very swiftly during the last few weeks. On October 22, three days after Jackson's return to the White House, a special session of the South Carolina legislature met at the request of Governor James Hamilton, Jr. It subsequently called for a convention to meet at Columbia on November 19, 1832, to respond to the action of Congress in passing the Tariff of 1832. In turn, this convention, after it met, passed an Ordinance of Nullification on November 24, by a vote of 136 to 26, which declared the tariff laws of 1828 and 1832 "null, void, and no law, nor binding" upon South Carolina, its officers or citizens. After February 1, 1833, the Ordinance continued, "it shall not be lawful . . . to enforce the payment of duties . . . within the limits of this State." We are determined, said the members, to maintain this Ordinance "at every hazard" and "will not submit to the application of force . . . to reduce this State to obedience." If force is used, then the people of South Carolina "will thenceforth hold themselves absolved from all further obligation to maintain or preserve their political connexion with the people of the other States, and will forthwith proceed to organize a separate Government."[19]

News of the action of the Nullification Convention shot up to Washington and around the country with record speed. The defiance shocked and infuriated the President. As he prowled the corridors of the White House, he uttered all kinds of savage threats, but at no time did he allow his feelings to color his judgment or influence his actions. In moments of crisis he exercised absolute control over his normally volatile emotions.

Joel Poinsett, a South Carolina unionist who provided the President with reliable information on developing events in his state, immediately reported on the proceedings of the Convention. He also gave Jackson an account of the condition of the several military forts in the Charleston Harbor—just in case. Fort Moultrie, he said, was "in a very dilapidated state" but Castle Pinckney was "in fine order." Fortunately, Jackson's previous actions had prevented the seizure of these forts. Poinsett estimated that possibly 500 to 1,000 unionists could be mustered, provided they could be armed, but predicted that no violence was likely until February 1. After that date anything might happen. In the strongest possible terms, he reassured the President of the loyalty and dependability of the union men in South Carolina. "We had rather die," he wrote, "than submit to the tyranny of such an oligarchy as J. C. Calhoun, James Hamilton, Robt. Y. Hayne and [George] McDuffie and we implore our sister states and the federal govt. to rescue us from these lawless and reckless men."[20]

Jackson responded immediately. "I fully concur with you in your views of Nullification," he told Poinsett. "It leads directly to civil war and bloodshed and deserves the execration of every friend of the country." He said he had already anticipated some of the "precautionary measures" advised by Poinsett. Five hundred stand of muskets, for example, with "corresponding equipments," had been ordered to Castle Pinckney, and a sloop of war with a smaller vessel had been dispatched to Charleston and would reach the city momentarily. General Winfield Scott had been directed to take command of the entire operation. In addition, the commanding officer at Castle Pinckney would be instructed by the secretary of war to deliver the arms to the unionists in the state. Should circumstances so dictate, additional ordnance would be provided. "The Union must be preserved," Jackson reiterated, "and its laws duly executed, but by proper means." We must act, he went on, as "the instruments of the law." Poinsett was to tell the unionists "that perpetuity is stamped upon the constitution by the blood of our Fathers." Nothing could dissolve the Union. Nothing. Constitutional amendment was the process provided to secure needed changes or improve "our system of free Government." For this reason a state may not secede, much less "hazard" the Union. "Nullification therefore means insurrection and war; and the other states have a right to put it down."[21]

It is important to notice how careful Jackson was to act within the limits of the law. He talked tough but he had made up his mind to use force only if absolutely necessary and with extreme caution. He would bluster and threaten, but he moved slowly and carefully. He operated within the law, and, as one historian later commented, this was to be "the hallmark of his statesmanship during the Nullification Crisis." For example, he gave orders that the citadel on the mainland in Charleston was to be relinquished upon demand. Since South Carolina owned the building, prompt compliance would prevent an incident and head off any criticism that the federal authorities acted illegally. Besides, removal of these troops and their concentration at the forts would strengthen the military stance of the federal armed forces in Charleston. When in fact the South Carolina legislature demanded federal withdrawal from the building in early December, the troops quietly moved to the forts in the harbor and completely separated themselves from the South Carolina mainland.[22]

Events in South Carolina then began to move at a frightening clip toward confrontation with the federal government and possible civil war. The people of the state seemed to accept the Ordinance of Nullification with no perceptible concern. The union party, though respectable in character, was overwhelmed in the fall elections by an "immense, an almost silencing majority," completely sympathetic to the nullifiers. Robert Y. Hayne resigned as United States senator and John C. Calhoun resigned as Vice President of the United States. Hayne was elected to succeed James Hamilton, Jr., as governor. A new legislature, composed mainly of nullifiers, elected Calhoun to take Hayne's seat in the United

States Senate and then proceeded to pass the necessary legislation to carry the Ordinance into practical effect. For example, it authorized the governor to accept volunteers in case of invasion. Said Governor Hayne in his inaugural address: "If the sacred soil of Carolina should be polluted by the footsteps of an invader, or be stained with the blood of her citizens, shed in her defense, I trust in Almighty God that no son of hers* . . . who has been nourished at her bosom . . . will be found raising a parricidal arm against our common mother. And even should she stand ALONE in this great struggle for constitutional liberty . . . that there will not be found, in the wide limits of the State, one recreant son who will not fly to the rescue, and be ready to lay down his life in her defense."[23]

South Carolina rang with the rebel yell. Blue cockades with a palmetto button at the center appeared everywhere, on "hats, bonnets and bosoms." Then events turned ominous, for medals were struck bearing the inscription: "John C. Calhoun, First President of the Southern Confederacy."[24]

John C. Calhoun: the spoiler, the agitator, the traitor. That was how President Jackson saw the South Carolinian. That was how Jackson's advisers and closest friends also saw him. They spoke of the former Vice President as "the most wicked and the most despicable of American statesmen." They reckoned his nullification theory and his conspiracy to disrupt the Union as the consequences of a disappointed ambition. "He strove, schemed, dreamed, lived, only for the presidency," they contended. And when he failed to attain that office by "honorable means," he scrambled to rise upon the ruins of his country. That was Jackson's final judgment of the tormented southerner. He "lived and died in this opinion." On his deathbed, while reflecting upon his two terms as President, Jackson expressed his regret that he had not executed Calhoun for treason. "My country," he said, "would have sustained me in the act, and his fate would have been a warning to traitors in all time to come."[25]

There was another spoiler, another disappointed and mischievous malcontent: John Quincy Adams. The former President had returned to Congress as a member of the House of Representatives from his district in Massachusetts, and he was itching to create trouble. Anything to disrupt the councils of the nation. "He seems to carry within him a smothered fire," commented Frank Blair, editor of the Washington *Globe*, the mouthpiece of the administration, "that ever and anon, breaks forth like a volcano, accompanied by a stream of red hot lava. . . . His inspiration is fury and his energy that of a scolding old lady." Nothing would delight him more than to see discord and havoc attend the administration of his successor. He would even try to introduce in the House a debate on slavery—slavery no less!—to achieve his goal, not that he cared two figs

*This may be a reference to Jackson, who was born in South Carolina.

for the black man. "You will have seen that Mr. Adams, some days ago," reported one congressman, "offered a resolution, calling on the President to communicate to the House a copy of . . . the South Carolina Ordinance. This was an incendiary movement—had discussion been permitted, his resolution would have been a fire-brand. Mr. A. is a most mischievous old man—in a bad humour with the world." Fortunately, the House refused to consider the resolution by a vote of 106 to 65. But if ever this "mischievous old man" got hold of a really explosive issue and forced it to debate, he would shake the Union into a hundred fragments. As a matter of fact, not many years later, in 1836, Adams did find such an issue—the "gag" resolution, which was a proposal to lay all antislavery petitions to the House on the table—and almost fulfilled the prophecy.[26]

It was typical of Jackson to view the nullification controversy as a conspiracy of ambitious men. He always personalized quarrels. But in this instance, more than mere thwarted ambition was involved. The southern outrage over the tariff was real. They regarded it as a grievous impediment to their economic health. They reckoned the decline in cotton prices as one of the more disastrous results of tariff legislation. They argued that it was unconstitutional for the federal government to raise import duties to provide economic benefit to one section of the country at the expense of another. They felt wronged and provoked by such legislation which, they said, northerners deliberately and repeatedly rammed down their throats.

Many southerners and westerners (including Jackson) frequently railed at the east and north for supposed wrongs. There was a mounting alienation between the sections of the country over mostly economic issues that had begun decades before, and the tariff dispute only intensified it. By the 1830s the alienation was deep-rooted. As children, said Davy Crockett, "we have always been taught to look upon the people of New England as a selfish, cunning set of fellows, that . . . called cheatery mother-wit; that hung on to political power because they had numbers; that raised up manufacturers to keep down the South and West."[27]

And there was another growing cause of complaint between the sections: slavery. Not that it triggered the nullification controversy at this time or was directly involved in the events leading to the confrontation, even though it was essential to the southern economy.[28] Perhaps John Quincy Adams and John C. Calhoun might have hungered to raise it in order to foment further discord throughout the nation, but it did not come into serious discussion at this moment. In the early 1830s responsible officials generally understood and accepted the fact that any attempt by the federal government to interfere with slavery would constitute a frontal assault upon the freedom and property rights of those who were partners in the social compact. It has sometimes been suggested that the Democratic party in the 1830s was proslavery. That is nonsense. The

Democrats simply recognized that the question of slavery was not something they could freely decide one way or another. Not if they valued the
Union.

Still the slavery issue lurked constantly in the background, as though
waiting for the propitious moment to emerge from the shadows. From
time to time a few malcontents tried to drag it into national attention but
they were universally condemned as troublemakers.

The central question of the nullification controversy, raised by the tariff
dispute, was whether the states had the right to declare federal law invalid
within their boundaries (and, if necessary, to secede from the Union) in
order to protect their rights, particularly their property rights. And Congress could not provide the answer. The sense of the members as a group
was unclear and inexact. There were three distinct viewpoints: one class
of politician contended for the "inalienable & indefensible right of a state
to secede at pleasure;—another class, that there is no such right, consistent with the constitution, or theory of the Government—and a third class
seem disposed to admit the right to secede, but maintain the right of the
other states, on the first principle of self preservation, to whip the seced-
ing states into submission."[29]

Andrew Jackson had an absolutely clear conception of his position on
this question. It was simple, direct, and logical. It may not have been
historically accurate, but he sincerely believed it to be so. Most important,
it proceeded from his commitment to democratic principles. The federal
government, he said, was "based on a confederation of perpetual union"
by an act of the people. A state may never secede, and that was final.
Moreover, the people, not the states, granted sovereignty to the federal
government through the Constitution. They called the Union into existence, they created the federal government, and they granted federal
power. These actions, he insisted, were taken by the people at conventions that ratified the Constitution. And in ratifying the Constitution the
people automatically amended their state constitutions to accord with the
new arrangement.[30]

Jackson felt totally comfortable with this position. He believed it to be
the only one guaranteed to safeguard the liberty and rights of all. And
he was sure the American electorate supported his view.

One day he was visited by an old army comrade, General Sam Dale.
The nullification controversy clearly troubled the President, and he expressed his concern over what might happen if his theory of government
did not in fact command popular support. But the doubting thought was
instantly dismissed. "General Dale," Jackson said, "if this thing goes on,
our country will be like a bag of meal with both ends open. Pick it up in
the middle or endwise, and it will run out. I must tie the bag and save
the country."

Dale tried to reassure him by expressing the hope that things eventually would go right.

"They SHALL go right, sir," Jackson cried. And he reacted so passionately that he shivered his pipe upon the table.[31]

To make things "go right," Jackson prepared for immediate executive action. "As soon as it can be had in authentic form," he wrote in a private memorandum, referring to the Ordinance of Nullification, "meet it with a proclamation."[32]

A presidential proclamation to the people of South Carolina was what he had in mind. A bold, forthright statement of what nullification entailed in terms of inevitable bloodshed and civil war. More than that, the proclamation was meant to generate a "moral force" in the country to counteract the forces of disunion; it was meant to reach out to all Americans —not simply South Carolinians—and rally them to the defense of the Union and the Constitution.

Jackson had no way of knowing beforehand whether such a proclamation would actually create this "moral force" and unite the people behind him. But he sensed instinctively that this was the proper action for him to take. He knew precisely what he wanted to say in his proclamation. It was just a matter of finding the right words. Unlike his fourth annual message to Congress, which had soft-pedaled the issue and which some interpreted as "a complete surrender to the nullifiers," the proclamation must carry a strong and eloquent statement to excite the entire nation.[33]

Naturally, as he had done so often in the past, Jackson turned first for assistance to his Kitchen Cabinet, in particular Amos Kendall. The astute, energetic, and reform-minded Kendall was a vigorous writer whose previous efforts, such as the Bank veto, were much admired by the President. But on this occasion Kendall failed him. His attempt was too restrained, too muted, too similar to the annual message. Jackson wanted something more thrusting, something so eloquent as to "strike to the heart and speak to the feelings" of all Americans. So he turned to Edward Livingston, his secretary of state.[34]

A plain-looking man, but not unattractive, with a prominent nose and expansive forehead, Livingston was a brilliant scholar of the law. Among his friends and admirers he was known as Beau Ned because of the fastidiousness of his dress and the elegance of his manner. As a member of the cabinet, as a writer whose style frequently matched the grace and refinement of his bearing, and as one of the nation's outstanding constitutional minds, he could give the proclamation authority, grandeur, learning. But it must have fire. That above all.

Not that Livingston needed to provide the ideas for this proclamation. That the President would take care of himself. In fact Jackson closeted himself in his office and scribbled page after page of what he wanted said. Writing rapidly and with great emotion, he poured out his ideas about the Union, its preservation, and the rights of the states. His entire being vibrated with the intensity of his thought and conviction. After he had written fifteen or twenty pages, he was interrupted by a visitor who noted that three of the pages were still glistening with wet ink. "The warmth, the glow, the passion, the eloquence" of the proclamation shone bright on those still-moist sheets.[35]

Gathering these pages, along with the sheaves of notes and memoranda that he normally wrote on all major issues, Jackson presented them to Livingston and asked him to shape the proclamation into an authoritative and persuasive presidential paper. Livingston was honored, and said so. He took the sheets to his office, labored over them for three or four days, and then returned the finished product to Old Hickory.

In the quiet of his study, with no one to disturb him, Jackson scrutinized the finished product. As he read a look of disappointment flickered across his face. He was clearly dissatisfied. The work did not convey the full essence of his intent. Jackson fidgeted in his seat, he rose and paced the floor, and then he turned to Major Lewis's room to share his disappointment with his old friend.

Livingston had not correctly understood his notes, he complained. Parts of the draft did not express his views with the precision and passion that he wanted. After a moment's pause and a comment or two from Lewis, the President decided to ask for extensive revisions. He summoned Livingston and informed him that certain passages would have to be rewritten. He needed to rally public sentiment to the defense of the Union and the draft had not provided it. Livingston expressed his regrets over his failure and said he would try again.[36]

Jackson returned to his own room and struggled to find the exact words he wanted. On such occasions he worked long into the night with only a servant nearby to keep the fire going. On the evening of Tuesday, December 4, 1832, Jackson composed a conclusion to the proclamation and sent it to Livingston with his instructions. The document carried the full thrust of his intent.

for the conclusion of the proclamation

Seduced as you have been, my fellow countrymen by the delusive theories and misrepresentation of ambitious, *deluded* & designing men, I call upon you in the language of truth, and with the feelings of a Father to retrace your steps. As you value liberty and the blessings of peace blot out from the page of your history a record so fatal to their security as this ordinance will become if it be obayed. Rally again under the banners of the union whose obligations you in common with all your countrymen have, with an appeal to heaven, sworn to support, and which must be indesoluble as long as we are capable of enjoying freedom.

Recollect that the first act of resistance to the laws which have been denounced as void by those who abuse your confidence and falsify your hopes is Treason, and subjects you to all the pains and penalties that are provided for the highest offence against your country. Can the descendants of the Rutledges, the Pinckneys, the Richardsons, the Middletons, the Sumpters, the Marions, the Pickens, the Bratons, the Taylors, the Haynes, the Gadsdens, the Bratons [sic] the Winns, the Hills, the Kershaws, and the Crawfords, with the descendants of thousands more of the patriots of the revolution that might be named, consent to become Traitors? Forbid it Heaven!

Dr Sir-

I submit the above as the conclusion of the proclamation for your amendment & revision. Let it receive your best flight of eloquence to strike to the heart, & speak to the feelings of my deluded countrymen of South Carolina —The Union must be preserved, without blood if this be possible—but it must be preserved at all hazards and at any price yours with high regard

Andrew Jackson
Decb. 4th 1832
11 oclock P.M.

Edward Livingston Esqr—[37]

Jackson carefully noted the precise time of day that he signed this document. He knew the significance of his proclamation and appreciated its historic moment. In fact, on many of the documents and letters he wrote during the crisis, he carefully recorded the day, date, and time.

Livingston took Jackson's written conclusion and extensively revised it, eliminating most of the names of the distinguished South Carolinians that Jackson had laboriously included. But the fire and temper of the presidential piece was retained.[38]

At 4 P.M., Friday, December 7, 1832, Livingston returned with a second draft. After a slow and thoughtful reading, Jackson pronounced it satisfactory, although he asked for a few further changes in the final paragraphs. The opening sections needed nothing more and Jackson turned them over to Major Andrew Jackson Donelson, his secretary and former ward, and asked that they be copied. At this point Jackson emphasized speed. He was very anxious to issue the proclamation as quickly as possible. "The Message [to Congress] having been made public on the 4th," he explained to Livingston, "it is desirable, whilst it is drawing the attention of the people in South Carolina, that there minds should be drawn to their *real situation,* before their leaders can, by false theories, delude them again. Therefore it is, to prevent blood from being shed, & positive treason committed, that I wish to draw the attention of the people of South Carolina to their danger, that no blame can attach to me, by being silent. From these reasons you can judge of my anxiety to have this to follow the Message."[39]

These words clearly show how anxious Jackson was to avoid not only bloodshed but the accusation that he had failed to exert himself sufficiently to prevent the crisis from escalating. It was never his desire to seek a confrontation. He did everything in his power to avoid conflict because he knew how easy it was for such things to fly out of hand and lead to irreversible calamity.

As these final preparations for the publication of the proclamation took place, Major Lewis politely suggested to Jackson that he delete those portions of the message that might offend the "States-rights party." No need to antagonize them, he said.

The President glowered. "Those are my views," he rumbled, "and I will not change them nor strike them out."[40]

It was at moments like these that his colleagues in the cabinet recognized the true quality of Jackson's statemanship. "The President has much more sagacity in civil affairs," wrote one astute observer, "and a much fuller acquaintance with the principles and practice of the government than many of his opponents are willing to concede. He is very firm in his opinions—inflexibly upright—devoted to his public duties."[41]

The proclamation, dated December 10, 1832, was published on December 11. It is one of the most significant presidential documents in American history and has been frequently compared to Lincoln's inaugural addresses. It contains the subtlety of language to make its legal and constitutional arguments both impressive and persuasive. Yet it contains enough Jacksonian passion to give it spirit and life. Much of the wording and subtlety of expression should be credited to Livingston, but the ideas of government, the conviction of its sentiment, and the weight of its thought belong to Jackson.

The proclamation opened by declaring the actions of the nullifying convention inconsistent with the duty of citizens, subversive of the Constitution, and aimed ultimately at the destruction of the Union. To prevent this destruction and maintain the honor and prosperity of the nation and justify the confidence placed in the President by the American people, "I, Andrew Jackson, President of the United States, have thought it proper to issue this my proclamation" and state "my views of the Constitution" and its laws and declare the course this administration will pursue.[42]

"Strict duty" required "nothing more," the President said, than the exercise of his powers to preserve peace and enforce the nation's laws. Then he slammed head on against the argument of the nullifiers—and pronounced it false. "I consider, then, the power to annul a law of the United States, assumed by one State, *incompatible with the existence of the Union, contradicted expressly by the letter of the Constitution, unauthorized by its spirit, inconsistent with every principle on which it was founded, and destructive of the great object for which it was formed.*"[43]

In directing the publication of his proclamation the President personally ordered these words italicized. He wanted the people of South Carolina—indeed the entire nation—to appreciate the import of what he was saying.

The people of the United States, Jackson went on, formed the Constitution, acting through their respective states. "We are *one people* in the choice of President and Vice President." The people, he declared, not the states, are represented in the executive branch. This assertion culminated Jackson's efforts to redefine the presidency and the relation of the American people to their government. It was another appeal for recognition that it was the presidential office—not the legislature, no matter what Webster or Clay or Calhoun argued—that embodies all the people. The President is the representative of the American electorate and directly responsible to them. By his actions and words he articulates and executes their will.[44]

The Constitution, he continued, "forms a *government,* not a league," a government in which all the people are represented and which operates directly on the people themselves, not upon the states. A "single nation" having been formed, it follows that the states do not "possess any right to secede."

In addressing the question of secession and whether it was included among the rights of the states, Jackson was treading on very thin ice. And he knew it. Still he felt obliged as President to state his views since South Carolina had already declared that it would secede if force were applied to collect the tariff duties. "Surely then if the Proclamation were necessary to show the country what the Executive would do in the case of Nullification, it was also necessary to indicate his course in the event of secession." And the right of secession did not belong to the states, he argued. For if South Carolina could secede for Congress's levying tariff duties, then Rhode Island could secede "for taking them off," and that was absurd.[45]

Nor, the President went on, have the states retained their entire sovereignty. They surrendered "essential parts of sovereignty" in "becoming parts of a nation," such as the right to declare war, make treaties, and exercise exclusive judicial and legislative powers. The allegiance of their citizens was also altered. It was transferred to the government of the United States. Their citizens became American citizens and owed obedience to the Constitution and its laws.[46]

Again and again Jackson struck at the very root of the nullification argument. Again and again he stated his fundamental creed: The people are sovereign. The Union is perpetual.

Jackson's proclamation comes close, contends one modern historian, "to being the definitive statement of the case for perpetuity" of the Union. Among the many presentations decades later of the argument of a perpetual Union, the proclamation "stands above the rest for its incisiveness, coherence, and comprehensiveness." So complete is it, that the Supreme Court in 1869 could find no additional argument of any moment or significance.[47]

The Union is older than the states, Jackson declared. Its political character commenced long before the adoption of the Constitution. "Under the royal Government we had no separate character; our opposition to its oppressions began as *united colonies.* We were the *United States* under the Confederation, and the name was perpetuated and the Union rendered more perfect by the Federal Constitution."[48]

Here, then, is Jackson's unique contribution to a more profound understanding and appreciation of the American experiment in democracy and constitutional government. He was the first American statesman to offer the doctrine of the Union as a perpetual entity. His arguments and conclusions provide a complete brief against the right of a state to secede. In terms of constitutional arguments, Jackson's statement is far greater than Daniel Webster's more famous second reply to Hayne. Webster relied on a sentimental appeal, arguing for the Union "as a blessing to mankind." Jackson went beyond sentiment. He offered history and a dynamic new reading of constitutional law.[49]

Jackson's extraordinary understanding of what is meant by "the United States" did not arise from some profound intellectual exercise or a mastery of history and political science. Rather it was something that emanated directly from his background and education as lawyer, judge, legislator, military commander and politician. He simply knew as a fact, revealed by "common sense," that the people had called the Union into existence, and that only they could alter or dissolve it. To argue otherwise, he said, "reduces every thing to anarchy & strikes at the very existence of society."[50]

Having forcefully refuted the leading arguments of the nullifiers, Jackson concluded the proclamation with a direct appeal to the people of South Carolina. The mood and tone of the message changed dramatically, and here Jackson's own hand can be seen guiding the sentiment behind the words. Like a sorrowing but resolute parent, he warns his children of the consequence of their folly. It pains him to speak so harshly, he said, but he is determined that they behave like responsible and dutiful children. "Fellow-citizens of my native State," he began, "let me not only admonish you as the First Magistrate of our common country, not to incur the penalty of its laws, but use the influence that a father would over his children whom he saw rushing to certain ruin. In that paternal language, with that paternal feeling, let me tell you, my countrymen, that you are deluded by men who are either deceived themselves or wish to deceive you. Mark under what pretenses you have been led on to the brink of insurrection and treason on which you stand."[51]

Behold this happy country, he enthused. See the asylum where the wretched and oppressed find refuge. Look and say, "*We too are citizens of America.* Carolina is one of these proud States; her arms have defended, her best blood has cemented, this happy Union. And then add, if you can . . . this happy Union we will dissolve; this picture of peace and prosperity we will deface; this free intercourse we will interrupt; these fertile fields we will deluge with blood; the protection of that glorious flag we renounce; the very name of Americans we discard."[52]

This powerful nationalistic thrust, this appeal to sentiment and patriotism reached far beyond the people of South Carolina. It deeply affected citizens in every state. It rallied nationalists everywhere.

Then Jackson's tone darkened. The laws of the United States must be executed, he declared. "I have no discretionary power on the subject; my duty is emphatically pronounced in the Constitution." Let there be no misunderstanding of what is involved. Let the truth be known as to what will happen if the laws are disobeyed.

> Those who told you that you might peaceably prevent their execution deceived you; they could not have been deceived themselves. They know that a forcible opposition could alone prevent the execution of the laws, and they know that such opposition must be repelled. Their object is disunion. But be not deceived by names. Disunion by armed force is *treason.* Are you really ready to incur its guilt? If you are, on the heads of the instigators of the act be the dreadful consequences; on their heads be the dishonor, but on yours may fall the punishment. On your unhappy State will inevitably fall all the evils of the conflict you force upon the Government of your country. It can not accede to the mad project of disunion, of which you would be the first victims. Its First Magistrate can not, if he would, avoid the performance of his duty. . . . There is yet time to show that the descendants of the Pinckneys, the Sumpters, the Rutledges, and of the thousand other names which adorn the pages of your Revolutionary history will not abandon that Union to support which so many of them fought and bled and died. I adjure you, as you honor their memory, as you love the cause of freedom, to which they dedicated their lives, as you prize the peace of your country, the lives of its best citizens, and your own fair fame, to retrace your steps.[53]

The decision is yours, he concluded, "whether your sacred Union will be preserved and perpetuated." May the "Great Ruler of Nations" bring those who have produced this crisis to their senses and see their folly "before they feel the misery of civil strife."[54]

Jackson never so much deserved the trust and confidence and love of the American people as he did at this moment. It was a superb state paper. Little in it needed improvement. Indeed, Abraham Lincoln later extracted from it the basic argument he needed to explain and justify his intended course of action to meet secession in 1861. The proclamation is a major statement in constitutional law. It came about only because Jackson was a statesman of the first rank. And, as many Americans promptly acknowledged, they were fortunate to have him at the head of the government at this moment of crisis. "The dauntless spirit of resolution" presided over the nation in the person of General Andrew Jackson, protecting the Union and the people in his care.

CHAPTER 3

The Union Preserved

THE PUBLICATION OF THE PROCLAMATION produced cheers and welcome relief around the nation. Those who read it with fear and apprehension soon shed their anxiety over this clear and straightforward assertion of national supremacy. Even the opposition press approved. Union meetings were held in every large city and community in the north to express the public's endorsement of the President's position. Even southern towns proclaimed their support of Old Hickory. Faneuil Hall in Boston marked this "crisis in freedom" with a spontaneous rally of solidarity for the President's statement. Only Henry Clay seemed fretful. Some of Jackson's arguments are "entirely too ultra for me," he muttered, "and which I can not stomach." Most other National Republicans rejoiced. "The Presidents proclamation," wrote one, "gives great satisfaction to the liberal and patriotic of all parties, hereabouts. In my eyes, its merit, I confess, is the higher, from having been preceded by the wise moderation of his message. May it accomplish its good ends."[1]

Jackson himself radiated contentment and goodwill. He knew he had taken a firm and correct position, one the people would almost universally accept and applaud. He encouraged Democrats around the country to organize Union meetings and he alerted his partisan press to speak up for the principles he had so eloquently conveyed in his proclamation. He also polled the Congress to discover their reaction and was delighted with what he learned. "I am assured by all the members of congress with whom I have conversed," he reported to the Unionists in South Carolina, "that I will be sustained by congress. If so, I will meet it at the threshold, and have the leaders arrested and arraigned for treason."[2]

To his old and good friend General John Coffee, the President spoke

24

even more frankly and directly. Can anyone in his right mind, he asked, actually believe that a state has the right to nullify or secede, thereby destroying this Union and with it the liberty of the American people? "Then indeed is our constitution a rope of sand; under such I would not live." The people, he argued, joined together to form a "more perfect union" and granted to the government certain powers, at the same time reserving others to themselves. To change the form or system of government requires an amendment to the Constitution. Any other mode of change, he declared, "is revolution or rebellion." Showing a grasp of political reality far beyond many of his contemporaries, Jackson recognized what the American experiment in liberty had become. "The people are the sovereign," he preached, "they can alter & amend, and the people alone in the mode pointed out by themselves, can dissolve this union peacebly."

> Therefore when a faction in a state attempts to nullify a constitutional law of congress, or to destroy the union, the ballance of the people composing this union have a perfect right to coerce them to obedience. This is my creed, which you will read in the proclamation which I sent you the other day. No man will go farther than I will to preserve every right reserved to the people, or the states—nor no man will go farther to sustain the acts of congress passed according to the express grants to congress. The union must be preserved and it will now be tested, by the support I get by the people. I will die with the union.[3]

Perhaps no document reveals more clearly than this one Jackson's full commitment to the democratic philosophy of government. He believed totally in the concept of popular rule as expressed through the ballot box. No longer did he subscribe to republicanism with its fears and hesitations about democracy, fears that allowed the legislature or some other agency, such as the Electoral College, to "refine" or alter the popular will when necessary. Jackson insisted on democratic rule. He symbolized it. Only the people—no one else—had the final say. Henceforth his public and private pronouncements ring with the claim that the American government is anchored in democratic rule and not the slightest alteration of the system and its operation can be attempted without popular consent.

With this democratic creed as his justification and authority, Jackson "chaulked out" his plan to deal with the crisis: he would wait for South Carolina to pass the necessary legislation to raise an army, then he would go to Congress and ask for the power to call volunteers to serve as "the posse commitatus of the civil authority"; after that he would force open the federal courts which had been shut, obtain indictments against the leaders of the rebellion, arrest them, and turn them over to the authority of the law "to be prosecuted, convicted, and punished." If South Carolina raises an army of twelve thousand men, he boasted, "I will order thirty thousand to execute the law." Now is not the time "to temporise, or falter." Fortunately, his proclamation was receiving almost universal approval from the people. Since that is so, he declared, then the moment of greatest danger is past.[4]

Nevertheless, a grave danger persisted. Too many hotheads in South Carolina were spoiling for a fight. When Jackson's proclamation reached South Carolina it was greeted with "scorn & contempt as the mad ravings of a drivelling dotard."[5] Joel Poinsett praised the President for his "most able exposition" of the crisis but warned him to maintain his guard. "These men are reckless and desperate and I have little hope of a peaceful termination of this conflict."[6]

Fortunately, Jackson did not need the warning. Even before he got any reaction from South Carolina to his proclamation, he signaled an alert to the secretary of war, Lewis Cass. "We must be prepared for the crisis," he wrote. "The moment that we are informed that the Legislature of So Carolina has passed laws to carry her rebellious ordinance into effect, which I expect tomorrow, we must be prepared to act." He wanted three divisions of artillery readied, each one "composed of nines, twelves, and Eighteen pounders." He wanted assurances that troops could be moved within four days after such an order had been issued. He further demanded a full report from the ordnance division on the number of muskets, swords, pistols, ammunition, and brass pieces presently available for field service and where they were located. If a decision to march must be made, he wanted to move with speed and dispatch. When General Scott failed to get his troops to South Carolina with the haste he required, Old Hickory registered his displeasure. "The President has read with regret & astonishment," Jackson told Cass, "Genl Scott's letter of the 31st ult. wherein he states that the Troops that were to embark on the 10 or 11th ultimo had not reached Fort Moultrie on the 31st and had not sailed from Norfolk on the 24th. Punctuality is everything in military movements & the President requests the Secretary of War to inquire how this has happened & by positive orders prevent the like occurrence for the future."[7]

South Carolina did not plunge ahead with radical plans to implement the Nullification Ordinance as Jackson predicted, however, in part for fear of giving the President any pretense for military action that could appear justified to the rest of the nation.[8] Moreover, the nullifiers observed how well the proclamation had been received throughout the nation. They already felt the effects of the "moral force" that had been generated. Nonetheless, the legislature did authorize Governor Hayne to call out the militia, accept volunteers, and, if necessary, to draft ablebodied men between the ages of eighteen and forty-five. It also appropriated $200,000 for arms. Hayne responded by asking for volunteers. He also began the process of raising and training an army.[9]

The South Carolina legislature then passed a resolution requesting Hayne to issue a proclamation warning the people of the state against succumbing to the President's crude attempt to "seduce" them from their allegiance and to ask them to stand prepared to "protect the liberty" of South Carolina against whatever "arbitrary measures" were imposed by the "drivelling dotard" in Washington. Hayne happily obliged. And what he provided was "a most pugnacious document." He denounced Old Hickory's doctrines as "dangerous and pernicious . . . specious and false." If his doctrines become the foundations of a new system of government, Hayne warned, then there can "be no liberty," no security "either for our persons or our property."[10]

At the same time the nullifiers prepared for possible combat, the Unionists in South Carolina also armed. Poinsett labored to raise and equip a voluntary force. In this he had Jackson's total cooperation, for the President was anxious to avoid military action by the federal government at all costs. He was not itching to march through South Carolina, despite widespread fears to the contrary. His commitment to the Union and democracy did not mean that he had disavowed his belief in the integrity of the states or respect for their rights. Besides, he feared antagonizing other southern states if he appeared to be the aggressor. Moreover, he was very sensitive to the "military chieftain" charge that had been pinned to him since he first entered politics in the 1820s. If force had to be employed, he much preferred that it come from a civilian posse at the local level, what he called "a posse comitatus." Not that he would refuse to exercise his military authority if required; he just insisted that it be the last weapon to be used, and used only after intense provocation by South Carolina. Under no circumstances—and this he repeated over and over —did he want South Carolina to win sympathy or support from any other southern state, and certainly not as a result of any action of his. For this reason he authorized the collector of the Charleston Harbor to move the customhouse from the mainland to the federal forts at Moultrie and Pinckney if the nullifiers made any effort to obstruct the enforcement of the tariff laws.[11]

The Unionists even held a secret convention to decide upon a course of action. Jackson's proclamation was read to them and they responded enthusiastically. "It seemed to give them more life and spirit than any thing that had been said, though many very good speeches were made to nerve and strengthen their resolves." When the members realized that Jackson was not afraid to denounce nullification as "treason and rebellion," some cried out, *"Enough,* What have we to fear, we are right and God and Old Hickory are with us."[12]

Thus, although President Jackson was quite prepared to employ force if necessary—and he repeatedly threatened to apply it if provoked—he actually moved with remarkable restraint as he prepared to face down the nullifiers. Restraint characterized most of his preparations.[13]

What Jackson did supremely well during the following weeks was to keep up a barrage of public arguments, relayed to the people through the press, in which he sought to strengthen his moral force. In these arguments he insisted that the confederation of the original thirteen states was a "perpetual union," made more perfect by the establishment of the Constitution as the supreme law of the land.[14] When we look at that instrument, he declared, "we can find no reserved right to nullify or secede." Nullification was an absurdity, an absurdity "too great to be dwelt on."[15]

Martin Van Buren quite agreed with the President's argument as well as the position he had taken, but he questioned whether the mere passage of nullification laws constituted an act of treason that would authorize presidential action. "You will say I am on my old track—caution—caution," Van Buren counseled; "but my Dr Sir, I have always thought, that considering our respective temperaments, there was no way perhaps in which I could better render you that service which I owe you." What Van Buren did not fully appreciate was that Jackson allowed his words to freight his emotional intensity; his actions carried nothing but restraint.[16]

It soon became very clear that the danger of Charleston's "capture" by the nullifiers was increasing every day. Worse, the Unionists within the city found it impossible to raise a civilian posse of any consequence. This failure, of course, placed them in dire jeopardy if an army of nullifiers decided to march on Charleston. Poinsett pleaded with Jackson to authorize federal troops at the harbor forts to move immediately into the city proper if nullifiers began their march. But Jackson refused. To move troops would surely be interpreted as aggressive. It might even start hostilities. "Your own advice," he replied to Poinsett, "has been to do nothing to irritate." Extreme caution must be exercised in every action taken. The nullifiers, not us, have placed themselves thus far in the wrong, he said. "They must be kept there."[17]

Meanwhile, ugly signs mushroomed all over Charleston. Palmetto cockades were sported on hats and lapels, and it was reported that volunteer regiments of nullifiers adopted a red flag with a black lone star in the center as its ensign. The American flag appeared on public and private buildings and on steamboats flying upside down. (When Jackson heard about the steamboats he burst out in a stream of expletives. "For this indignity to the flag of the country," he reputedly said, "she ought to have been instantly sunk, no matter who owned or commanded her.") General Winfield Scott, in charge of military preparations, reportedly wrote to the secretary of war "saying that blood would be shed and that he did not believe any thing could prevent it."[18]

Jackson mobilized his cabinet to assist him in responding to these ominous developments. Legal and constitutional arguments and positions were debated; military strategy was analyzed; a mail express was established between Washington and Charleston in order to allow the delivery of information within four days from one point to the other; and further legislative action by Congress was charted. As Jackson explained to Van Buren in New York, "I must appeal to congress to cloath our officers and marshall" with the necessary authority to aid them in executing the laws and apprehending those guilty of treason. This call, he added, must be made well before February 1—the cutoff date for the collection of the tariff within South Carolina, according to the Nullification Ordinance—so as to give Congress enough time to act "or I would be chargeable with neglect of duty." And yet if he were to act independently on his own authority, he said, "I would be branded with the epithet, *tyrant.*" Jackson therefore planned to go to Congress with his requests on January 17, which would give the Congress two full weeks to act before the February 1 deadline.[19]

In addition, during these weeks, Jackson attempted several things at once: he continued building his moral force throughout the country; he maneuvered to prevent a head-on collision with the rebellious state; and he tried to create a volunteer force in South Carolina as a counterweight to the nullifiers in case the use of military power became necessary.

More immediate to the solution of the problem was the need to revise the tariff, as Jackson had requested in his fourth annual message to Congress, by gradually diminishing its rates. But rather than wait for a congressional committee to initiate the action, the President directed Louis McLane, his secretary of the treasury, to begin framing a suitable measure. McLane promptly obliged. By mid-December, just as events in South Carolina began to boil, a new tariff bill was ready to offer the Congress. It was turned over to the chairman of the House Ways and Means Committee, Gulian C. Verplanck of New York, with a plea to move it as quickly as possible. Jackson later referred to it as "the Tariff bill prepared by McLain under my view"; but generally it was known and cited as the Verplanck bill. It was introduced into the House on January 8, 1833, the anniversary of the Battle of New Orleans.[20]

According to this bill the tariff duties would be sliced in half. They would approximate the duties of the 1816 tariff as amended in 1818. A few duties were raised. Even fewer (like coffee and tea) were removed from the free list. The reductions were scheduled over a two-year period —half in 1834 and the remainder in 1835.[21] Although the bill did not completely fulfill Jackson's promise of reform, it did address South Carolina's grievance by erasing previous wrongs. It constituted a gesture of friendship, a willingness to accept South Carolina's complaint and redress it. But to protectionists in Congress the Verplanck bill struck them as a clear surrender to the nullifiers. And, indeed, it did involve a surrender. It obviously accommodated South Carolina with a downward adjustment of the tariff rates. But, at virtually the same time, Jackson sternly warned the state against persisting in its defiance by asking Congress for authorization to deploy the military to put down armed rebellion. On January 16, 1833, he sent his Force Bill message to Congress, something the *Globe* preferred to call "*a collection bill.*"[22]

The Force Bill message was written with the aid of Louis McLane. Part of it was first intended as a treasury report, since South Carolina's defiance involved opposition to the revenue laws, but the President at length decided to change its character and give it more significance. It was a bold message, yet reasonable and sane. No bluster clouded its content, no anger intruded. It was lucid and forthright, but also firm and determined. Jackson was intent on avoiding conflict, and most of his suggestions to Congress emphasized the need to prevent the use of force rather than the obligation to implement his authority to compel South Carolina to comply with the law. Again the President repeated that if it came to conflict, South Carolina must strike the first blow.[23]

The Force Bill message began by citing Jackson's last annual message, which had promised to notify Congress if the emergency worsened. The President then narrated the events that had brought them to the present crisis, quoting alternately from the Ordinance of Nullification and Governor Hayne's inaugural address and proclamation to the people of the state. In his opinion, said the President, the actions of South Carolina "are to be regarded as revolutionary in their character and tendency, and subversive of the supremacy of the laws and of the integrity of the Union." Jackson could not accept this. The right of the people of a single state, he said, to "absolve" themselves at will without the consent of the other states "and hazard the liberties and happiness of the millions composing the Union, cannot be acknowledged." Such action is "utterly repugnant" to the principles and goals upon which this government was founded. Jackson did not deny the "natural right" of rebellion when all effort to redress oppression had been exhausted. But all such effort had not been exhausted in the present instance, he insisted.[24]

Under the circumstances, then, the duty of the government was plain. The executive must execute the laws. The revenue must be collected. But an organized opposition to commence on February 1 might make it impossible to do so. Therefore Jackson asked that he be authorized to close any port of entry he deemed necessary and reestablish it at some other port or harbor. He also requested minor changes in the federal judiciary system in the area to protect United States property and jail lawbreaking nullifiers. Jackson was at great pains to explain how this request involved preexisting laws, that he was simply asking for congressional approval to exercise these laws. His scheme proved devilishly clever. By moving the customs he would force the nullifiers to go to considerable trouble to carry out their threats. They would have to travel a distance and invade federal installations, thereby engaging in blatantly hostile acts against the government. In effect, the President had reduced considerably the likelihood of armed resistance to the laws. As one historian has noted, "Jackson had outmaneuvered his foes."[25]

With respect to possible military action, the President's message was relatively tame. No Jacksonian fire scorched its outer edges. If South

Carolina resorts to force, he said, Congress need only make "a few modifications" of the law of 1792 as amended in 1795 for the President to call out the state militia and use federal ships and troops. "The ceremony of a proclamation" is unnecessary. Whenever he was officially informed by the courts or the authority of any state that the execution of federal law had been opposed by force, he had enough authority to respond to such aggression and save the Union from the "maddness and folly" of the miscreants who dared to assault it.[26]

Jackson then closed his message with an appropriate coda:

> The rich inheritance bequeathed by our fathers has devolved upon us the sacred obligation of preserving it by the same virtues which conducted them through the eventful scenes of the Revolution and ultimately crowned their struggle with the noblest model of civil institutions. They bequeathed to us a Government of laws and a Federal Union founded upon the great principle of popular representation. After a successful experiment of forty-four years, at a moment when the Government and the Union are the objects of the hopes of the friends of civil liberty throughout the world, and in the midst of public and individual prosperity unexampled in history, we are called to decide whether these laws possess any force and that Union the means of self-preservation. The decision of this question by an enlightened and patriotic people can not be doubtful. For myself, fellow-citizens . . . I have determined to spare no effort to discharge the duty which in this conjuncture is devolved upon me. That a similar spirit will actuate the representatives of the American people is not to be questioned; and I fervently pray . . . that our joint measures . . . [will] solemnly proclaim that the Constitution and the laws are supreme and the *Union indissoluble.*[27]

This wise and statesmanlike reassertion of the permanence of the Union was another broad appeal to all Americans to rally in defense of their country. It rejected secession in any form. And nullification was an abomination. Jackson labeled both pernicious. Many Americans at the time regarded secession as an intrinsic component of states' rights, and for them to surrender it would not only emasculate the states' rights philosophy but subvert individual liberty. Jackson divorced himself from these men with this message. He still retained his states' rights creed, but now totally shorn of any authority to tamper with the structure and integrity of the Union.

President Jackson marks an important break with the past. He is the first and only statesman of the early national period to deny publicly the right of secession. Secession was a doctrine no longer in keeping with a democratic society, no longer congenial to the idea of "a Federal Union founded upon the great principle of popular representation." Whether at some point in time it had any validity no longer mattered. It was a dead issue as far as Old Hickory was concerned, annihilated by the historical evolution of a democratic society.

Jackson not only insisted that the Union was indissoluble, but he argued that it had been formed by the sovereignty of the people, not the sovereignty of the states. It was not a confederation, not a banding together of individual states, but a permanent welding of the people.

Thus, by his words and deeds, Jackson continued to recast attitudes and perceptions of this nation and its operation. Republicanism was giving way to democracy, and Andrew Jackson was an important instrument in that change. Republicanism, with its emphasis on liberty, preached the need for strong states as a counterweight to the central government, but by the mid-1830s that philosophy could not accommodate the dynamics of an emerging industrial society. Protecting freedom in the modern world required a strong national government. Besides, the way to minimize the danger to individual rights was to fashion a government elected by all the people. In short, majority rule best protected freedom—not the states, and certainly not a hobbled or enfeebled central government.

Jackson's democratic impulses arose to some extent from his fierce concern for liberty. But far more important was his own character and personality. A shrewd politician, a forceful leader, and a political activist and innovator, he appreciated the full dimension of his popularity and the extent of his influence upon the electorate. So he repeatedly presented himself as "the representative of all the people" through whom the popular voice found expression. Democracy, obviously, dovetailed perfectly with his own conception of his presidential role.

Several months later Jackson and Nathaniel Macon of North Carolina exchanged a series of letters in which they discussed the President's drift away from the ideals of republicanism. What gave the exchange particular significance was the fact that Macon once acted as Jackson's ideological mentor when the young Tennessean first entered Congress. The conservative bent to Macon's thinking deeply influenced Jackson in the 1790s, and now, some forty years later, its potency had all but vanished and Macon was trying desperately to reactivate it. The older man did not approve Jackson's call for a Force Bill, nor did he surrender his belief that a state retained the right to secede. North Carolina's first ratifying convention rejected the Constitution, he argued; its second convention ratified the document. In calling the second convention, he said, the state "had the same right to have called a third and that might if it thought proper have rejected it again."[28]

It is not necessary to detail Macon's arguments in these letters, some of which commanded Jackson's agreement. After all, they both considered themselves adherents of the states' rights philosophy. But secession —that Old Hickory would not concede. That had nothing to do with states' rights. "In my opinion," he responded, "the admission of the right of secession, is a virtual dissolution of the union." To insist that secession is a reserved right, as Macon did, is to insist "that each state reserved the right to put an end to the Government" whenever it wishes. "I hold that the states expressly gave up the right to secede . . . when the present constitution was adopted to establish 'a more perfect union.' " The only right of secession is the right of revolution.[29]

To deny a state the right to secede, Macon shot back, reminded him of the old British doctrine, "once a subject always a subject." But despite your errors and miscalculations, he told Jackson in a final flourish, any administration that can pay off the public debt and win repayment of claims by American citizens against foreign governments is guaranteed everlasting fame and glory.[30]

The Force Bill message went down to Congress on Wednesday, January 16, only fifteen days before the February 1 deadline set by South Carolina. The clerk took an hour and a half to drone out the long, closely argued paper.[31] Among the lawmakers, as the newly elected senator from South Carolina, sat John C. Calhoun, his eyes black as coals and blazing with anger as he heard Jackson's "monstrous" assertions about the Union. Just a few days before he had sworn to uphold the Constitution when he took his oath of office, and many witnesses who heard him pronounce the solemn words could not help but feel "that he made a mental resolution that it should be as 'he understood it.' "[32] Now, as he listened to the President's words, he sat rigid and tense, ready to pounce to his feet the moment the reading concluded. "I perceived from its contents," he later wrote, "that it ought not to pass without a blow." The moment the clerk finished the reading Calhoun demanded the floor. He spoke for half an hour, but in that time he poured out all the fury and biting scorn that had festered inside him for the last four years. The words tumbled out with incredible speed, and he seemed transported by the exhilaration of their sound and fury. Silas Wright, Jr., of New York, who replaced William L. Marcy as Van Buren's eyes, ears, and voice in the Senate, told his Regency henchmen in Albany that Calhoun's performance was full of "passion and excitement."[33] It obviously signaled the beginning of a tumultuous session. With Henry Clay and Daniel Webster sitting nearby, waiting their turn to pronounce absolute truth, the Senate would no doubt reverberate to the conceits, eloquence, and intellectual power of these men over the next several months as the tariff bill and the Force Bill worked their way through Congress.

The same day he sent down his Force Bill message, Jackson forwarded a copy to Joel Poinsett and in an accompanying letter noted Calhoun's violent eruption. "Mr. Calhoun let off a little of his ire against me today in the Senate," he snickered, "but was so agitated and confused that he made quite a failure." In this same letter the President again reiterated his desire that the Unionists in South Carolina put down nullification themselves and not require federal intervention. But Poinsett warned him not to expect too much. "I ought not to disguise from you, that even if the case should arise of the *Posse Comitatus* being called out by the U.S. Marshall, there exists a disinclination on the part of the majority of the

Union party in Charleston to join in mortal conflict with their adversaries as a part of the Posse. There is scarcely a family wherein some member is not in the opposition ranks, and it is certain in such a contest father would be arrayed against son and Brother against Brother." In any event, he told Jackson that his Force Bill message was "admirable" and that they both entertained similar views on the subject. Still he worried over what might happen next. "I expect the next move will be secession and we must be prepared to resist it." In which case he asked Jackson how he wanted him to proceed. Of course, the Union men will "assemble . . . and protest and remonstrate and all that; but what active measure shall we take?"[34]

Just let me know the moment an armed force is illegally assembled, Jackson responded; I will then "issue my proclamation warning them to disperse" and if they refuse, "I will forthwith call into the field, such a force as will overaw resistance, put treason and rebellion down without blood, and arrest and hand over to the judiciary for trial and punishment, the leaders, exciters and promoters of this rebellion and treason." He expected to post from ten to fifteen thousand men in Charleston in ten or fifteen days at the most. If need be, "which god forbid," two hundred thousand men would be marched into South Carolina within forty days. Jackson then urged the Unionists not to lose heart, something he did in virtually every letter he wrote to them during this crucial time. "I repeat to the union men again, fear not, *the union will be preserved,* and treason and rebellion promptly put down, when and where it may shew its monster head."[35]

Jackson's proclamation and Force Bill message, with their powerful nationalistic thrust, appealed to southerners as much as they did to northerners.[36] Their patriotic fervor excited Americans everywhere. Since slavery itself was not involved in the nullification controversy, southerners outside South Carolina responded to Jackson's arguments with enthusiasm.[37] Their reaction would have been far different had slavery, in fact, been an issue in 1832 and 1833. Much more important to those who worried about Jackson's arguments concerning the Union was what those arguments meant in terms of maintaining freedom. They felt Jackson was insensitive to southern concerns or too prone to resort to force and less willing to agree to conciliatory reforms.[38] Some southerners saw the crisis as a direct consequence of Calhoun's fall from grace and from the succession to the presidency. Thwarted ambition, they said, generated this catastrophe.[39] Those who absolved Calhoun from wrongdoing tended to blame the tariff schedules or northern plots to revive the program of Federalists. John Randolph of Virginia feared the President had been "bound hand and foot" to his bitterest enemies, "the ultra federalists, ultra tariffites, ultra internal improvement and Hartford Convention men —the habitual scoffers at State-rights."[40]

Jackson, of course, had no difficulty in locating the cause of the crisis.

He regarded the "modern" doctrines of secession and nullification as the "mad theories of a few demagogues"—in particular "Mr. John C. Calhoun." He was sure the Verplanck bill was in trouble in Congress because of their "plots" and might be defeated. He told Van Buren that Richard H. Wilde of Georgia had given a speech to kill the tariff which "threw a firebrand into the House." "He is *wielded by Calhoun,*" said Jackson. "Last night the ire rages, it is said, beyond every thing ever heard before."[41]

Well, let them rage. Jackson sat in his study in the White House during the final days of January preparing an order to summon troops to defend the Union. Once South Carolina made good her threat to take action after February 1, federal soldiers would march.

Fortunately the need for this action quickly diminished once the provisions of the Verplanck bill arrived in South Carolina. The proposed new schedule proved so attractive that an enormous rally of nullifiers in Charleston on January 21 announced its willingness to postpone action on nullification until Congress had completed its deliberations on the bill.[42] Once this happened the pressure on Congress and the President eased considerably. Then the political jockeying began, and everyone had opinions as to what might happen next. "Now for my suspicions," reported Senator Silas Wright to the Albany Regency. "They are that Messrs Webster, Clay and Calhoun are at this moment in the most perfect harmony of aims to make mischief." Wright was certain that Calhoun would never permit the use of military force in his state and therefore would accept some "arrangement" with Clay. The Verplanck bill would be killed, predicted Wright, at the same time that an alarm would be sounded in the Senate that the use of force was imminent. At that point Clay would step forward with a "peace offering" in the form of a substitute tariff which Calhoun would immediately pronounce "an acceptable offering to S. Carolina." Then both forces would "join to put down the war [Force] bill as they call it." Thus Clay and Calhoun would get credit for having pacified the south and preserved the Union, while Jackson would be "scored" for having failed.[43]

Wright was not far off the mark as to the "arrangement" in progress. His only error was in thinking that Webster was part of it. Actually Webster took a very dim view of accommodating the South Carolinian, whose opinions on the Constitution and the Union he so heartily detested. His own nationalistic approach sharply conflicted with the nullifier's. So when Clay and Calhoun got together to make their "arrangement"—which occurred shortly after Calhoun's arrival in Washington in early January—Webster stayed clear. In fact it was widely reported that, at the first opportunity, he would come out in the Senate in favor of Jackson's proclamation and speak very pointedly and forcefully in support of the President. It was even rumored that Webster "would wage the war with Mr Calhoun" on the Senate floor.[44] Amazement gave way to absolute astonishment when Webster suddenly became a sought-after guest at the White House. "I dined at the Palace, yes, Palace, a few days since," reported Senator John Tyler of Virginia, "and found Mr. W. there in all his glory." The "arrangement" between Clay and Calhoun seemed matched by a "dalliance" between Jackson and Webster.[45]

Given the conflicting views of Calhoun and Webster on the nature of the Union, a verbal brawl on the Senate floor could hardly have been avoided. It came soon enough.

The Force Bill, now called the War or Bloody Bill, reached the Senate floor on January 28, when William Wilkins of Pennsylvania, chairman of the Judiciary Committee, introduced it. Wilkins spoke for two days, interrupted constantly by Calhoun. A long string of senators spoke in succession, most badly, a few brilliantly. John Tyler of Virginia gave a particularly effective speech in opposition to the bill, but his colleague, William Cabell Rives, recently returned from France where he headed the American mission and newly elected to the Senate, gave an even better speech in defense of the bill. One historian has rightly stated that the Force Bill debate far excelled the more famous Webster-Hayne debate. Not only were the speeches of greater intellectual power, but they occurred during a period of genuine national crisis.[46]

The excitement generated by the likely contest between the "giants" drew enormous crowds to the Senate chamber. Even when the upper house continued into evening sessions the audience did not slip away. Finally, on February 15, the glowering, resentful, angry, and bitter South Carolinian rose to speak. He stood at his desk, his gaunt figure hardly moving from his place. But his black, brilliant eyes roamed continuously around the room.[47] He denounced the Force Bill as a declaration of war against his state in total violation of the Constitution. He attacked the manner of its presentation and once more tried to explain his tortuous theory of nullification.[48]

The godlike Daniel followed. And he spoke to the heart of a nation that no longer believed in limited government as a means of ensuring liberty. A Union of people was his theme, and Webster gave it all the majesty of language that his great talent commanded. He made only one slip, in acknowledging that nullification might be justified if the Constitution was in fact a compact of states. Calhoun pounced on that admission and almost got the better of him. John Randolph, the addled former senator from Virginia, sat near Calhoun, and although he resented the South Carolinian and dismissed nullification as humbug, he was seen nodding his head in agreement as Calhoun spoke. A hat lying on a seat in front of him partially obscured Randolph's view of Webster. Suddenly his high, piercing voice could be heard throughout the chamber. "Take away that hat. I want to see Webster die, muscle by muscle."[49]

But it was not the Webster argument that was dying. Quite the contrary. Though he stumbled momentarily in the debate, Webster had the better of the argument as far as the rest of the country was concerned.

President Jackson totally agreed with everything Webster said, and it gave him great satisfaction to know that there was someone on the Senate floor —even though not of his party—who could defend the administration's argument and present a cogent case for the President's position. It pleased the old man to count Webster as an ally in this crisis. "Mr. Webster replied to Mr. Calhoun yesterday," he told Joel Poinsett, "and, it is said, demolished him. It is believed by more than one, that Mr. C. is in a state of dementation—his speech was a perfect failure; and Mr. Webster handled him as a child."[50]

The powerful debate between the opposing forces—a debate that cut across sections and party lines—climaxed with strong speeches, pro and con, from John Forsyth of Georgia and George Poindexter of Mississippi. Jackson hawkeyed every development and badgered his supporters in the upper house to drive to a final vote. On Wednesday, February 20, 1833, at ten in the evening, the vote was taken in the Senate, despite Calhoun's efforts to force an adjournment. The nullifiers, almost to a man, stalked out of the chamber. Only John Tyler remained to cast the single vote against the Force Bill. The final count was 32 to 1. Henry Clay and Thomas Hart Benton were among those not recorded.[51]

As a matter of fact both Benton and Martin Van Buren had doubts about the Force Bill. Van Buren had not yet returned to Washington, even though he had been elected Vice President the previous fall on the Democratic ticket with Jackson. Inauguration on March 4 still lay several weeks ahead. In moments of crisis he preferred to keep his distance from the seat of government lest he stumble into a situation that could jeopardize his future presidential aspirations. And frequently, as it turned out, he disapproved of the strong positions taken by Jackson. He worried over the President's constitutional grounds in condemning nullification and warned of the danger of inviting violence. When he read Jackson's Force Bill message he again whispered his concern and told the President that both he and Benton thought that the "military force part of the Bill is unnecessary to the administration."[52] Van Buren delicately put forth these views to Jackson and, after hemming and hawing about how he was not on the spot to have a full view of the whole ground, he nonetheless urged the President to back off. "If you can see your way perfectly clear in advising our friends in the house to waive for the present session the militia force part of the bill," he gently told Jackson, "it would I have no doubt instantaneously revive the kindest feelings in the South, and public sentiment coming on the back of it with a demand at the next session for a proper settlement of the disturbing subject of the Tariff, would redeem the Country and disappoint all sinister calculations."[53]

Van Buren's fears of a southern split from the party—a split that would severely damage his presidential ambitions—were well taken. Rives, for one, had already sounded the alarm. Thomas Ritchie, editor of the Richmond *Enquirer*, also expressed concern. And before long a number of states' rights southerners, led by John Tyler of Virginia, seceded from the Jackson party.[54] Tyler himself ended up running for the vice presidency with William Henry Harrison against Van Buren in 1840.

Jackson wearily shook his head over Van Buren's fears for party unity. In his mind the only question was saving the Union, and on that there could be no ambiguity or difference of opinion. Everyone must be told —no, everyone must clearly understand—that Andrew Jackson would not allow a so-called "peaceful" dismemberment of the Union. And if he must employ military force as a last resort, then so be it.[55]

The full terms of what Silas Wright had called the "arrangement" between Clay and Calhoun soon became apparent in Congress as pressure mounted on the South Carolinian to break the deadlock between the nullifiers and the administration. Jackson's resolute and unyielding stand could not be altered, and Calhoun realized that bloodshed might ensue and further ruin his cause not only in the north but throughout the south. "Calhoun is, (politically), a dead cock in the pit," exclaimed Senator William R. King of Alabama. "The father of nullification under no circumstances can even receive the support of the Southern States." As Representative Michael Hoffman of New York told the Albany Regency, the problem for "Calhoun & Co" was the danger that the governor of South Carolina wanted "to play war" and win glory, yet "shrunk from the responsibility of being hanged." Everyone seemed to realize that with Jackson in the White House "there is but one way of seperating or dissolving the union," and that was "by war." In that event "somebody may get hanged and some killed."[56]

Pressure also mounted on Henry Clay to step in and offer some form of "pacification." He knew the choice the moment he read Jackson's proclamation and the Force Bill message: civil war or a lower tariff. He came to a quick decision. Sometime in late January he got together with "Calhoun & Co" and offered to abandon the principle of protection and reduce duties gradually over a period of years to the revenue level, in exchange for which the South Carolinian pledged repeal of the Ordinance of Nullification.[57] Although Clay's offer came nowhere near the breathtaking reductions of the Verplanck bill, Calhoun willingly accepted this "compromise" in order to acquire Clay's support in preventing Jackson from scourging South Carolina with fire and sword.[58]

It was a self-serving arrangement. As Michael Hoffman told the Regency, this political alliance between "the head of Nullification and the head of the American system" provided Calhoun with an escape and Clay with power. It might even provide the Kentuckian with southern votes in his next bid for the presidency.[59]

Once the arrangement was accepted by both sides, Clay did not wait for the Verplanck bill to get to the upper house but immediately introduced his own "compromise" tariff. On February 9 he rose in the Senate and gave what Francis Granger of New York called a "mamby pamby" speech. Never had the Kentuckian delivered "so washy an affair." Granger said the bill itself was a "perfect death blow to manufactures."[60] Actually it was no such thing. Although Clay suggested lower rates in his bill, they would take effect in very slow steps. He proposed a ten-year period. The reductions would be minuscule in the beginning of the period and then take a sharp drop toward the end. In effect he proposed that by the year 1842 the duties would stand at a uniform 20 percent *ad valorem* and remain at that level. During this ten-year period a truce would be declared against lowering or raising tariff rates. They would be left alone. As for a free list, a few items would be added immediately—but many more in 1842. In effect what Clay offered the Congress was a choice between his own sharp drop in 1842 or the administration's sharp drop in 1833.[61]

No sooner did the Kentuckian sit down than John C. Calhoun rose to inform the Senate that he approved Clay's bill and would support it. All true lovers of the Union should join him, he said. And with that fatuous announcement the entire nation knew that Clay and Calhoun had reached an agreement to service one another's needs.

Upon the motion of Felix Grundy of Tennessee, a select committee of seven senators was formed to consider Clay's bill. Jackson sprang to attention and immediately moved to control the membership of this committee. He sent a note to his old friend Hugh Lawson White, the president pro tem of the Senate, and asked him to stop by the White House for a chat. White accepted the invitation, but before leaving the chamber he handed to the secretary of the Senate the names of the seven men he had decided to appoint to the committee and instructed the secretary to enter the names in the journal. The seven included Calhoun, Grundy, Rives, Webster, Dallas of Pennsylvania, Clayton of Delaware, and Clay as chairman. White then went immediately to see the President. Once the pleasantries were concluded, Jackson specifically requested that John M. Clayton not be placed on the list, that Clayton was hostile to the administration and unfriendly to Louis McLane, the supposed author of the Verplanck bill. White informed the President that it was too late, explaining what he had done before coming to the White House. But Jackson was not to be turned away so easily. He asked White to go back to the secretary that evening and substitute some other name before the journal was made up. White refused. It would be wrong, he said. And on that sour note, the interview ended.[62]

Jackson was furious, not only on account of White's refusal to honor his request, but at the persistent rumor he heard that there would be a motion offered in the Senate to lay the Force Bill—which had not yet passed the upper house—on the table until the tariff bill had been acted upon. "Surely you and all my friends," the President chided Senator Grundy, "will rush that bill thro the Senate— This is due to the country —it is due to me, & to the safety of this union and surely you and others of the committee who reported it will never let it slumber one day until it passes the Senate—lay *all* delicacy on this subject aside and compell every mans name to appear upon the journal that the nullifiers may *all* be distinguished from those who are in support of the laws, & the union." Furthermore, "I am mortified," over the composition of the select committee of seven. "Surely it was due to me" that at least a majority of the committee should be supporters of the administration. "It is a direct insult to me, & the Sec of the Treasury that such a man as Mr Clayton should be upon it."[63] That this occurred because of the direct action of Hugh Lawson White, his supposed friend, boded ill for the future.

To add to Jackson's "mortification," as well as seal the "arrangement" between Clay and Calhoun, the House of Representatives on February 15 elected as their printers Gales and Seaton, the editors of the Washington *National Intelligencer* and severe critics of the administration. Jackson had expected Frank Blair, editor of the administration's mouthpiece, the Washington *Globe,* to win the lucrative assignment. One vote made the difference.[64] Worse, the Senate then elected Duff Green, editor of Calhoun's organ in Washington, the *United States Telegraph,* as printer for the upper house. It was an unmitigated disaster. The Democratic leadership had surrendered control of their party by allowing members to vote their conscience. A combination of anger over demands for the prompt passage of the Force Bill and sympathy for southern fears over possible military intervention resulted in numerous disaffections. "Clay Webster & Calhoun," remarked Michael Hoffman, "aided by our disaffection elected Gales and Seaton printers to the House. I suppose the contract extended to the election of Green in the Senate."[65]

Jackson deserves a full measure of blame for this disaster. He was so preoccupied with winning passage of the Force Bill that he let everything else, including the tariff, go by the board.[66] Certainly in the Senate, the Clay-Calhoun combination seemed to be gaining the upper hand.

This Clay-Calhoun combination, or Clay's "great leap across the Potomac," as some called it, produced one fallout. Daniel Webster took angry exception to Clay's proposed tariff bill. He saw it not only as a sacrifice of New England's manufacturing interests but as an obvious deal with nullifiers to win their support. It is difficult even now to decide which bothered Webster more, the economic blow to his constituents or the offense to his nationalistic sympathies. Whatever it was, it drew Webster and the administration closer together. At one point Jackson sent his own carriage to convey Webster to the Capitol. At another he dispatched Edward Livingston to urge the Massachusetts senator to aid in the assault upon Calhoun and the doctrine of nullification. All of which deeply disturbed Henry Clay. "As for your friend, Mr. W.," wrote Clay to Nicholas Biddle, president of the BUS, "[since] he is determined not to allow me to consider him mine, nothing I can do seems right in his eyes; whilst others can do nothing wrong."[67] Not surprisingly, when Clay's tariff bill came before the Senate for debate, Webster condemned it and Clay was forced to reply.

It looked like a wild winter in the making. The political realignments in progress staggered the imagination. And no one could predict where it would all lead.

At this point Clay prevailed on his close friend in the House of Representatives, Robert Letcher, to move to strike out the Verplanck bill and substitute Clay's Senate bill. The move came so suddenly that the Jackson men were caught completely off guard. They looked about in amazement, their expressions registering their surprise. Then, before anyone realized what was happening, the substitute bill passed to a third reading. On the very next day, February 26, the Compromise Tariff of 1833, as it came to be called, passed the House by a vote of 119 to 85.[68] Scoffed Senator Thomas Hart Benton: the administration bill "was arrested, knocked over, run under, and merged and lost in a new one which expunged the old one and took its place."[69] Jackson was so busy worrying about the Force Bill that he let the tariff slip from his grasp. He had managed the tariff bill very badly because he had failed to manage it at all.

The sudden breakthrough in the House jolted the Senate into action. On March 1, after Calhoun delivered another speech detailing his objections to tariff regulations but reaffirming his commitment to vote for the compromise and work toward gaining acceptance for it throughout the south, the tariff measure passed the Senate by a vote of 29 to 16.[70]

On the same day, just a few hours earlier, the House of Representatives moved to a showdown vote on the Force Bill, which had already received Senate approval on February 20. Jackson never let up in his insistence that the Force Bill be passed. Every day he met with representatives and hounded them about it, particularly after he had bungled the tariff reduction. The President wanted both measures delivered for his signature. He would not take one without the other. When the final vote was tabulated on March 1, the Jacksonians sighed with relief. By the count of 149 to 48 the Force Bill passed the House.[71]

What an unparalleled triumph, crowed Jackson. "I say unparalleled because it has not happened, according to my recollection, in the course of our legislation, that any measure, so violently contested as this has been, has been sustained by such a vote." It was very important to Jackson that the passage of the Force Bill precede the tariff because Congress thereby fully demonstrated "to the world that she was not to be detered by a faction, which, if found in rebellion and treason, she was prepared to crush in an instant."[72]

Immediately after the passage of the Compromise Tariff, the Senate accepted amendments to a bill previously passed which appropriated for a limited time the proceeds of the sale of the public lands and distributed them to the states. The intent of this distribution bill was obvious. It was an effort by protectionists to limit the revenue and thereby force the government to seek adjustments in the tariff in order to regain lost income. The bill had been introduced by Clay, and since protectionists argued that it was really part of the compromise, the measure passed. Jackson killed it, however. He gave it a pocket veto.[73]

And he was unhappy with the tariff. It could have been better and should have been. Still he would let it stand. "The Bill which has passed is not of the exact character which I would have prefered, but it is hoped that it may have a good effect in the South as most, if not all of her prominent men gave it their support."[74]

On Saturday, March 2, 1833—the day after their passage—Jackson signed both bills, starting first (naturally) with the Force Bill. Two days later, March 4—which happened to be inauguration day—Duff Green in his *Telegraph* published the provisions of the Force Act in columns bordered in black for "the death of the Constitution." To many southerners it seemed as though the enactment of a "war bill" was a final act in the consolidation of power by the central government to suppress the states and the liberty of the American people.[75]

In fact the Force Act and Compromise Tariff ended nullification once and for all. Even South Carolina hotheads, like McDuffie and Barnwell Rhett, favored rescinding the Ordinance of Nullification. A convention was subsequently reconvened and the Ordinance repealed. But, in a symbolic gesture of defiance, the convention nullified the Force Act. "If this be no more than a swaggering conclusion of a blustering drama," commented the *Globe,* on March 28, "it will speedily be consigned to the contempt of an enlightened and patriotic public."

One factor compelling South Carolina's withdrawal from a stance of confrontation was the cool reception the doctrine of nullification received from other southern states. The Alabama legislature, for example, pronounced the doctrine "unsound in theory and dangerous in practice." Georgia said it was "mischievous," "rash and revolutionary." Mississippi lawmakers chided the South Carolinians for acting with "reckless precipitancy."[76]

Obviously, these states did not believe the issue of slavery was involved in the controversy. Certainly at the national level this issue did not intrude, although Jackson feared it could foment trouble in the future. "Nullification is dead," he declared to John Coffee, "but the coalition between Calhoun, Clay Poindexter & the Nullifiers in the South—intend to blow up a storm on the subject of the slave question—altho they know the east have no such views, still they will try to arouse the Southern people on this false tale. This ought to be met for be assured these men would do any act to destroy the union, & form a southern confederacy bounded, north, by the Potomac river."[77]

Although there may have been some hotheads in South Carolina who sought (or hoped) to divert the question away from the tariff issue and toward slavery, their efforts won little attention or support. One study in

Tennessee, for example, concludes rather decisively that the "slavery question simply was not an issue . . . in 1832 and 1833."[78] The same might be said about other southern states. Much of Jackson's success in handling the crisis was his skill in keeping the focus on the main question, namely, the right of a state to dissolve the Union. This he did brilliantly. He resisted all attempts to permit the tariff question to become the central issue. He insisted that the perpetuity of the Union was the overriding and central question.[79]

For Jackson, even the tariff was not important, although it obviously triggered the controversy. This may explain his failure to take a more active hand in winning passage of the Verplanck bill. "The tariff was only the pretext," he insisted, "and disunion and a southern confederacy the real object." Then he predicted what the next excuse would be, a prediction tragically fulfilled three decades later. "The next pretext," Jackson warned, "will be the negro, or slavery question."[80]

Although the administration had stumbled its way through the congressional session of 1832–1833 and had witnessed the formation of the Clay-Calhoun alliance, the final events of this session in resolving the nullification controversy probably constituted Jackson's greatest victory as President, according to one historian.[81] His policy—a combination of tariff reform and the Force Bill—was wise and practical. No other statesman at the time approached the solution of the crisis in quite the same way. They either plumped for one or the other. Clay and Calhoun (and Van Buren and Benton, it might be added) opposed the Force Bill and drove through their own tariff reform. But this tariff horrified a number of National Republicans, especially from the industrial states. Both Webster and John Quincy Adams disliked the Compromise Tariff and understood the political purposes it served. Of all the leading figures of the period, only Jackson had insisted on both measures as a combined package to solve the problem. And his "masterful statesmanship" played a crucial role in providing the final settlement that preserved the Union.[82]

Even more masterful was Jackson's ability to reassure the American people that in the White House sat a very determined President who knew what he was doing and had the means to prevent the breakup of the Union. No sense of impotence, drift, or indecision in Washington worried the electorate. If anything, some feared Old Hickory would seize any opportunity to act precipitously. But they soon saw how cautiously he proceeded, despite the strong tones of his public utterances, and how careful he was to avoid confrontation.

Only Andrew Jackson, as President of the United States, could calm the fears of the American people. Certainly not one or two congressmen, no matter how distinguished. The burden of resolution for this threatened castastrophe lay with the chief magistrate, and that Old Hickory triumphantly provided.[83]

But suppose the nullifiers had not backed off and had acted out their threatened secession, what then would he have done? A little later Barn-well Rhett asked him this question, and Jackson shot back: "In less than three weeks after the first overt act of Treason was committed by the nullifiers I would invade the State with upwards of fifty thousand volunteers, from the west, the north, and by water on the south."[84] Jackson later claimed that he "had a tender of volunteers, from Newyork, Pennsylvania Virginia &c &c, to upwards of one hundred & fifty thousand men" —more than enough to drive the nullifiers back to their "dunghills."[85]

Fortunately, calmness and reason prevailed at the time and a blood bath was avoided. The nation marveled. Even Europe applauded Jackson's superb handling of the crisis. "How nobly the President has borne himself in this crisis of the Carolina controversy!" commented one American foreign service officer. "What vigor! What wisdom! You should hear what Europeans say of us in order to feel—not vanity, but a just pride in the dignity of the American name."[86]

But Andrew Jackson had not only maintained the pride and dignity of the American name and preserved the Union from dismemberment; he had powerfully and successfully driven home the argument that the Union is perpetual.

CHAPTER 4

Reshuffling the Cabinet

THE NATION RESOUNDED WITH SUSTAINED CHEERS for all those responsible for saving the Union—not only Jackson, but Clay and Webster and the many other congressmen who had placed local and particular interests aside to labor for the preservation of the Union. Shy by a few weeks of sixty-five, Jackson stood at the very peak of his popularity. The American people loved him—and very nearly venerated him.

To many his first administration appeared to be a total triumph. The failures, the miscalculations, the wretched appointments, the moments of anguish and discord were mostly forgotten. Only the successes came to mind. His celebrated "reforms" were credited with revitalizing the American system of government: a nefarious bureaucracy replaced by one dedicated to service; the corrupting influence of the BUS halted; a national debt almost paid off; the tariff revised and nullification "knocked in the head"; extravagant public works suspended; and, most important of all, a democratic government committed to majority rule emerging and flourishing.

It was therefore intended that Old Hickory's second inauguration on March 4, 1833, should serve to remind the world not only of the President's universal esteem and success but also of the fact that popular government had arrived in the United States. Unfortunately, the weather did not cooperate. Unlike 1829, when the weather was springlike and pleasant, 1833 turned wintery and raw. On Saturday, March 2, two days before the inauguration, the temperature dipped to 6° above zero, the coldest day of the entire winter.[1] Snow covered the ground, and a driving northwest wind swirled it into tall mounds around the unfinished Capitol. Obviously the ceremony had to be held indoors, and that meant the

45

House of Representatives, the largest chamber available.

The disappointment was keenly felt, particularly for all the people who had hoped to fill the city and shout their approval of their Hero and his administration. A great many of them showed up anyway. They suffered the snow and biting cold to stand witness to their idol's triumph. But their chance of getting into the House chamber was virtually nil. This room ran ninety-six feet across at its widest. It was semicircular in shape and formed like an ancient Grecian theater. Still it could never accommodate the thousands of visitors to the city who vied for the privilege of witnessing the ceremony.[2]

Shortly before the inauguration, the newly elected Vice President, Martin Van Buren, finally arrived from New York. He went straight to the White House, where Jackson gave him quarters until he could arrange for something more permanent. He "sticks close to the President as a blistering plaster," sneered one observer. "Of this many of Gen. Jackson's friends complain loudly."[3] Even so, Jackson was delighted to see him again and have him close at hand as he began his new term in office. He relied on Van Buren for honest, if cautious, advice.

To demonstrate his regard and confidence in the "Magician," Jackson showed him his inaugural address. He had written it out in his own hand and it ran hardly more than a thousand words. It was a strong statement and contained many of Jackson's most cherished ideas and sentiments. Unfortunately, like his first inaugural address, a number of editors eventually laid rude hands upon it and they gutted its strength and diminished its power in favor of a weaker and more conciliatory statement.

The original address began on a note that combined a statement of republicanism with his own personal gratitude for the honor of reelection. "The will of the American people, expressed through their unsolicited suffrages," he said, "calls me . . . for another term of four years. . . . I find no adequate terms to express my heartfelt gratitude. It shall be displayed . . . in continued efforts, so to administer their government as to preserve their liberty, and promote their happiness."[4]

Then he turned to foreign affairs and acknowledged that his policy had been "crowned with almost compleat success, and has elevated our character among the nations of the earth."

In domestic affairs, he said that there were two objects that had been and would continue to be of utmost concern to him: the preservation of the reserved rights of the states, and the integrity of the Union. He swore he would protect the states in all their prerogatives and promised, if necessary, to refrain from the exercise of rightful powers in order to prevent "discontents and heartburnings among the people." But he wanted it understood that he would also protect the federal government in the exercise of its essential powers. "Without union our independence and liberty would never have been achieved, without union they can never be maintained." Let it be understood from this moment on, "the loss of liberty . . . must inevitably follow a dissolution of the Union."[5]

Jackson followed this by paraphrasing some of the things he had said in his Bank veto. He warned that legislation which is partial in its object or effect, which depresses one man or interest at the expense of another, "will ever lead to discontents, murmurings, dissention and revolution." Government, he said, "should treat all alike" and the way to do that "is to let all alone as far as is compatible with publick justice, peace and safety." To bring the American government to adopt and practice this principle, he pledged, "will continue to be the object of my increasing solicitude."[6]

The editorial committee who reviewed the address decided to silence the strident noises of the Bank veto. The conclusion of the nullification controversy was no time to stir up passions with allusions to the "monster" Bank. So his fine thoughts on what came to be called Jacksonian Democracy were deleted.

The final section of Jackson's own inaugural address gave vent to his nationalistic passion. It was a romantic outburst, an outpouring of devotion to the Union he revered. Naturally the committee suppressed it. "If, in madness or delusion," Jackson scribbled, "any one shall lift his paracidal hand against this blessed union . . . the arms of tens of thousands will be raised to save it, and the curse of millions will fall upon the head which may have plotted its destruction." For myself, he declared, when I approach "the sacred volume and take a solemn Oath" to support and defend the Constitution, "I feel in the depths of my soul, that it is the highest, most sacred and most irreversible part of my obligation, to *preserve the union of these states, although it may cost me my life.*"

It can be imagined with what speed the editorial committee in charge of sanitizing Jackson's written efforts struck out these phrases and sentences. Instead, they permitted him to promise to exercise no power not clearly delegated to the general government, to encourage simplicity and economy in government, and to raise no more money from the people than absolutely necessary.[7]

Once the committee erased all of Jackson's spontaneous enthusiasms, drained it of vitality, and corrected its spelling and grammar, the carcass was delivered to the printer for publication. And everyone thought it was grand—even his political enemies. "It is well done," recorded Philip Hone, a New York merchant prince, "not too long, and well adapted to the state of public affairs."[8] A copy of it was prepared for Jackson to read at the inaugural ceremonies.

So on Monday, March 4, the President and his new Vice President made their way to the Capitol to be duly sworn in. It was a cold day and windy. Indeed, the wind was so high that almost everyone was uncomfortable. Philip Hone said that "the severity of the cold [was] unmitigated." He arrived at the Capitol at 11 A.M. and found an immense crowd "who thronged the approach of every door." Because of the cold and the wind "the time spent in waiting was not particularly agreeable." Still that did not discourage a large crowd from swarming around the building, waiting to get inside and catch a glimpse of their Hero.[9]

At twelve o'clock the President and Vice President and their cortege arrived. Jackson wore a long and very full cloak, his usual apparel whenever he appeared in public. It added a small touch of majesty. And when he put on his tall beaver hat he was a man of imposing and commanding presence. Slightly over six feet, and weighing hardly 140 pounds, he carried himself with military stiffness and a sense of his own importance and power. But he looked wan and emaciated. "Exceedingly feeble" was the way Hone described him. What clothes belonging to the General survive show him a very narrow-chested man with long and skinny legs. Although everything about him seemed thin and frail, he nonetheless exuded great strength, particularly in public. Commentators invariably noted the force of his personality even when they described his feeble physical condition.

Shortly after noon the door of the House chamber opened and a "ruffian crowd," as Hone called them, swept into the hall.[10] Also present were the heads of departments, foreign ministers and their suites, the judges of the Supreme Court, the president and members of the Senate, the Speaker and members of the House of Representatives, the marshal of the District, and the mayor and corporate members of the city. Then General Jackson appeared. He walked slowly, but with a commanding stride, and took the seat of the Speaker of the House. Martin Van Buren trailed behind him and then took a position to the left of the President. Major Donelson stationed himself on Jackson's right. After a pause of a few minutes, so that everyone could get settled, the President rose from his seat and was greeted by the cheers of the entire audience. The cheering continued for several minutes, and when at last it died down, Jackson began to read his inaugural address. He whipped through it very quickly since the address was mercifully short. When he finally put down the last sheet he was again saluted with prolonged cheers and applause. As always, he bowed low to the "majesty of the people."[11]

The venerable chief justice, John Marshall, then stepped forward to administer the oath of office. Jackson picked up the Bible and pronounced the words with great care. There were handshakes all around and the crowd once more began cheering. The oath was also administered to Van Buren, after which both men retired. The crowd, naturally, headed straight for the President's "palace," as Hone called it, to attend the traditional "levee."

The celebration did not last long. The President was exhausted and compelled to retire after a few moments of handshaking. He looked awful. "I would bet large odds," said Hone, "that he does not outlive the present term of his office."[12]

Jackson did not attend any of the inaugural balls. But he was well represented by a large number of family and friends who were staying with him during the inaugural festivities. These included Andrew Jr. and his wife, Sarah; Andrew J. Donelson and his wife, Emily; Mary Eastin and her husband, Lucius Polk; Mary McLemore; and Ralph Earl, the painter. Of particular pleasure was the presence of General John Coffee and his daughter, Mary. Although he had never visited Jackson in the White House before, Coffee was his best friend, so his brief stay to help inaugurate the second term made the occasion even more memorable.

The White House was a happy place in the early spring of 1833. The laughter and shouts of children at play filled the many rooms. The Donelson's two children, Andrew Jackson Donelson, Jr., aged six, and Mary Rachel, three, formed the solid core. Soon a third child joined the family. Emily was pregnant and expected to deliver in May. Jackson's great favorite, of course, was his granddaughter, Rachel, who was nearing six months. He idolized this child and called her his "little Pet."

As new children joined the Jackson menage, older ones departed. Andrew Jackson Hutchings, whom the President had raised since the age of seven, had reached his majority and was anxious to start out on his own. There had been problems between the two men but nonetheless a close bond existed that grew stronger after their separation. "Whatever he may think," Jackson told Coffee, "I know I have performed all my pledges to his father on his dying bed, & to bring him into life, with a good education, pure morals, & a good estate, has been a subject of great attention, & much solicitude."[13]

As the young man headed for Alabama to take possession of the estate his father had left him and which Jackson had carefully guarded, the President offered him some sage advice. Old Hickory urged him to find a good wife who would keep an observant eye on his income and show economy and avoid extravagance in running his home, just as the sainted Rachel had for Jackson. "Live within your means," he counseled, "never be in debt, and by husbanding your money you can always lay it out well, but when you get in debt you become a slave, therefore, I say to you never involve yourself in debt, and become no mans surety. If your friend is in distress aid him if you have the means to spare. If he fails to be able to return it, it is only so much lost." Another thing. If you settle all your debts on the first of every year, you will know your means and can keep within it.[14]

Young Hutchings took the advice. Within a few months he became engaged to Mary Coffee, daughter of Jackson's friend, and married her on November 14, 1833. The President heartily congratulated him on his "judgment and prudence. . . . I view her as a treasure to your welfare and happiness in this world, and by her gentle conduct will lead you in the paths of virtue thro this life and prepare you for a better, beyond the grave."[15] From this point on the strong tie between the two men developed into a warm friendship and they corresponded frequently and intimately for the remaining years of Hutchings's life.

That other young people graced and enlivened the White House pleased Jackson immensely. He genuinely liked young people. Francis P. Blair's daughter, Elizabeth, was a frequent visitor and a great favorite. Mary Lewis, the daughter of the White House resident, Major William B. Lewis, always added sparkle to the surroundings, but when she met a young diplomat with the French legation, Alphonse Pageot, she consented to marry him and moved out of the White House. Jackson gave her a lovely wedding. The marriage of Cora Livingston, daughter of the secretary of state, in April, 1833, to Thomas P. Barton, a young foreign service officer, also produced a festive occasion in the White House and a handsome wedding gift from the President.

There were three marriages, for which Jackson was financially responsible practically in a row and they cost him heavily, especially when the receptions were held in the White House. Jackson tended to entertain sumptuously, and at these wedding receptions he was positively lavish. The redesigning and redecorating of the Hermitage also set him back several thousand dollars, and the new furniture purchased in Philadelphia to make Sarah feel at home came high. Furthermore, the loss of his new carriage, when the horses raced away and ended in an upset that "broke the body all to pieces," cost him another $1000.[16]

Nor was his plantation producing the record crop of cotton that he had anticipated. The previous summer he had replaced the overseer, Graves Steele, with Burnard W. Holtzclaw. He had had many complaints about Steele, ranging from poor management to mistreatment of his slaves, and he finally resolved the matter by bringing in Holtzclaw. The new man seemed enthusiastic and able. "I Git alongue With you Negrows Verer will indeede," he wrote the General in March, 1833. A short time later Major Lewis returned to Tennessee and looked in at the Hermitage and then gave the President a full report. "The farm is in pretty good order," he wrote. "The fences all look strong and good." The house, too, appeared "pretty much as it did when you were here last summer." Rachel's tomb needed repairs and Lewis suggested having a "neat little ironrailing" erected at a distance of four feet from the base of the monument and paved all around with flagstones. "This would not cost very much," he said, and would make it look "quite tasty and appropriate." About Jackson's work horses (enough to pull 19 plows), cows (82), hogs (300), and sheep (151), Lewis reported that they were "thriving." He also checked Jackson's prize race horses and said he "was much pleased and gratified at their appearance." On the whole, therefore, he told the President that if "Mr. Holtzclaw will hold out as he has begun I think he will make you a good crop . . . and take very good care of your stock." The only real problem he discovered was the mysterious death of a great many slaves. Lewis asked about it and Holtzclaw seemed to think that the cholera was responsible. Lewis doubted this. But he could offer no other explanation.

"I had heard at Nashville that Mr. Holtzclaw was very severe with the negroes, but from my own observation and what the negroes themselves told me while there I think, probably, he is not more so than is necessary. Where there are so many negroes, there must be a pretty rigid police." Holtzclaw assured Lewis that he had not been "severe" and the visitor reminded him that Jackson did not wish, nor would he permit, his "negroes knowingly to be treated with *cruelty.*"[17]

Jackson's behavior toward his slaves was what one might expect, considering his character and temperament. As long as they followed orders and acted like obedient children, he treated them reasonably well, indeed quite well. But if they ran away or disobeyed him, he could be exceedingly cruel, if not barbaric. The worst recorded example of his cruelty had occurred many years before when he advertised in the Nashville *Tennessee Gazette* on September 26, 1804 (and succeeding numbers), for a runaway.

Stop the Runaway

FIFTY DOLLARS REWARD.
Eloped from the subscriber, living near Nashville, on the 25th of June last, a Mulatto Man Slave, about thirty years old, six feet and an inch high, stout made and active, talks sensible, stoops in his walk, and have a remarkable large foot. . . . The above reward will be given any person that will take him, and deliver him to me, or secure him to jail, so that I can get him. If taken out of the state, the above reward, and all reasonable expenses paid—and ten dollars extra, for every hundred lashes any person will give him, to the amount of three hundred.

ANDREW JACKSON,
Near Nashville,
State of Tennessee

It is hard to believe that any civilized person could write such an advertisement. But that was thirty years earlier. Presumably, by 1833, Jackson's abominable disposition toward recalcitrant slaves had softened. In any event the tragedy of the deaths of his slaves genuinely disturbed him—and not on account of the financial loss.

Then came word of still another tragedy, "the death of my old and valued friend Judge Overton," on April 12, 1833. Some of Overton's last words and thoughts concerned Jackson. For one thing he directed that all their correspondence be burned and this, unfortunately, was carried out. "I regret he is gone," wrote the President, "but when I reflect he is beyond, where the wicked cease to trouble, and where the weary are at rest, altho I could lament in the language and feelings of David for Absalom, I am constrained to say, *peace to his manes.* let us weep for the living, and not for the dead."[18]

Morbid thoughts troubled Jackson throughout the spring. He worried about the ailing Sarah and her daughter, Rachel, "the d'r little pet." He urged his son to take them to Philadelphia to have them examined. Fortunately, his fears were unfounded. "Sarah has quite recovered," he sighed with relief, "and the little Rachel is growing finely having got over her little backset during Sarah's illness."[19]

As Jackson turned from the worries about his family and plantation to the cares of state at the start of his second administration, he was immediately confronted with one overriding problem: the "monster"; the corrupting hydra; the malevolent Bank of the United States. He must slay the beast, and the quicker the better.

In his message to Congress in December, 1832, Jackson had directed attention to the government's deposits in the BUS. He questioned the safety of the deposits and called for an investigation. "The hydra of corruption is only *scotched, not dead,*" he lectured James K. Polk, one of Jackson's floor managers in the House of Representatives and a member of the influential Ways and Means Committee. "An investigation kills it and its supporters *dead.* Let this be had—call upon the sec' of the Treasury who must agree with me that an investigation by Congress is absolutely necessary."[20]

The ostensible reason for Jackson's concern for the deposits was the behavior of the BUS with respect to the "three per cents." In March, 1832, the government had notified the Bank that it intended to pay part of the national debt in July from its deposits held by the Bank. Specifically it planned to redeem half of the outstanding 3 percent bonds amounting to $6½ million. Temporarily short of cash, the president of the Bank, Nicholas Biddle, requested and received a postponement of the payment for three months. Then he was informed that the government would make a second payment on January 1, 1833, and redeem the other half of the 3 percents, thereby paying off the national debt in toto, something Jackson had planned and desired since becoming President. In sum, the government asked for $13 million of its money within a three-month period. Biddle could not meet the demand[21] and dared not withdraw so much money from circulation during the presidential election of 1832. So he devised a scheme by which he would ask foreign holders of the 3 percents to hand over their securities to the BUS. The Bank would then pass them along to the government as evidence that the debt was paid. The Bank would simply borrow the principal for a year and pay an interest. To arrange this perfectly legal (if slightly devious) transaction, Biddle sent his aide, Thomas Cadwalader, to England to consult with the banking firm of Baring Brothers. But the final arrangement with the foreign bondholders turned out to be something quite different from Biddle's plan—and distinctly illegal, since it violated the Bank's charter. Because he had trouble convincing the holders to cooperate with the scheme, Cadwalader agreed to let Baring Brothers buy up the 3 percents for the BUS with the securities remaining in the hands of the original holders or the London bankers. This violated the charter because the Bank was prohibited from purchasing the public debt. Not only did this arrangement break the law, but it thwarted the government from achieving its declared policy of discharging the debt as soon as possible. When protests over Cadwalader's scheme developed, Biddle repudiated the agreement. But he could not understand the outcry and shrugged it off. "Supposing that the certificates are delayed for a few months, what harm does that do to anybody? The interest has stopped—the money remains in the Treasury; so that instead of depriving the Government of the use of its funds, directly the reverse is true, for the Government retains the funds and pays no interest."[22] Violating the charter obviously did not trouble Nicholas Biddle. He had been violating it for years.

But it troubled Jackson a great deal. Apart from everything else, it necessarily delayed the payment of the national debt, and probably for another twelve months.

Not that Jackson needed the incident of the 3 percents to convince him that the government's deposits were unsafe and should be removed. His spite against the BUS, grown more intense during the presidential election of 1832, provided ample excuse. Still he needed documentary evidence to justify the fateful action of removal and a congressional investigation made more sense than anything else. The Ways and Means Committee was chaired by Gulian C. Verplanck, who did not share Jackson's animus against the Bank. But with Polk an active member of this committee, the President believed that enough evidence of "corruption" could be uncovered to support his case for the removal of the government's deposits from the BUS. Without these deposits, and without a renewal of its charter, due to expire in 1836, the days of the life of the monster were numbered.

The investigation was eventually approved and began on January 31, lasting three weeks. The committee did not bother to go to Philadelphia to secure evidence, so Polk dispatched his confidential adviser, Reuben Whitney, to undertake a personal investigation for him. Whitney was a former Philadelphia merchant and Bank director who turned against the BUS when he was refused a loan. He made a very useful ally for the President because as a director he knew a great deal about the operations of the Bank. The committee interviewed the government directors of the BUS, along with Thomas Cadwalader, after which it issued a report on March 1 (subsequently approved by the full House by a vote of 109 to 46) that the government's deposits were indeed safe. A minority of three members of the seven-man committee dissented. Led by Polk, this minority issued a 170-page statement about the Bank's activities that both challenged the actions involving the 3 percents and suggested a good deal of impropriety in the management of the Bank's affairs.[23]

That was enough for Jackson. Incensed by the House's cool dismissal of Polk's report in its rush to adjourn on March 2, the President felt practically goaded into taking direct action himself against the Bank. He banged around the White House, grumbling and complaining. He closeted himself with several close advisers whose malice toward the Bank matched his own. He listened to Amos Kendall, who assured him that removal was imperative. He consulted with his attorney general, Roger B. Taney, about legal proceedings in the removal process. Since the law placed responsibility for removal in the hands of the secretary of the treasury and since that secretary, Louis McLane, opposed removal and would not do it unless commanded by the President to take the action, Jackson wanted to know the complete legal ramifications of his intended move.[24] The President also communicated with the government's directors of the BUS "relative to various proceedings of the Bank." He gathered as many facts as possible since he felt he must act very shortly.[25] Finally, and most important, he turned to his cabinet. He needed solid support from his official family if he seriously intended to launch this latest assault upon the BUS. Removal of the government deposits would surely rouse a storm of protest and the cabinet could lend valiant aid in meeting and subduing it. To prepare for the impending onslaught and gird his department heads for the attack, Jackson wrote out a questionnaire for his cabinet in which he posed five questions. He asked them to respond as quickly as possible and do it in writing. These were his questions:

1. Had anything occurred to lessen confidence in the safety of the public deposits?

2. Could the management of the BUS be trusted to carry out the government's "fiscal arrangements"?

3. Should the Bank be rechartered under any circumstances or with any modifications? And if with modifications, what should they be?

4. Should a new Bank be established? If so, "when and in what manner ought the suggestion to be made of my views on the subject. And upon what principles, and under what limitations and with what privileges" ought it to be formed?

5. Lastly, if the government's deposits were withdrawn, what system for their disposition should be established as to the places of their deposit and the manner of their distribution?

To this same questionnaire Jackson affixed "the results of my own reflection" on the various points he had raised, although he made no attempt to address the five specific questions.

1. "Under no circumstances and upon no conditions whatever" should the BUS be rechartered.

2. He would veto "any bill authorizing the establishment of a Bank out of the District of Columbia."

3. If he did assent to a new bank it would have to be located in the District and with many restrictions imposed by the states and the federal government "as security against the corruptions and evils which are now experienced from the uncontrollable authority of the present Bank."

4. There should be no national bank until the "experiment" of operating without one had been given a "full and fair" trial.

5. A system should now be devised for the deposit and distribution of the public funds through state banks.[26]

The responses by the cabinet officers to Jackson's questions came within a reasonable time, although a few (like those from Livingston and McLane) had to be pried loose. McLane was reluctant to admit how far from the President's thinking on the subject he stood. As secretary of the treasury, he should have had a leading role in the decision. But he had long since jeopardized his influence in the cabinet by pursuing policies unacceptable to the presidential will and temper.[27]

McLane delayed responding until May 20. He put it off as long as possible, ostensibly because a fire had completely destroyed the Treasury building. The fire occurred at half past two on Sunday morning, March 31, when smoke and flames on the main floor of the Treasury awakened neighbors who turned in an alarm.[28] Fortunately, a heroic effort to save the papers housed in the building kept the destruction of documents to a minimum, despite the loss of the entire building. Jackson immediately ordered an investigation, headed by the chief justice of the Washington circuit court, but not until 1836 were a former clerk, Richard H. White, and his brother arrested for the arson. It was claimed that they wished to destroy fraudulent pension papers. After four trials one brother was sentenced to ten years in prison; the other escaped conviction because of the statute of limitations.[29]

There is a delightful myth that Jackson chose the site of the new (and present) Treasury building in order to obstruct the view from the White House to the Capitol. Supposedly the sight of the Capitol offended him after a prolonged argument with the Congress over the location of the new building, so he walked over to 15th Street and at a spot directly between the White House and the Capitol drove his cane into the ground. "Put the damned thing right here," he commanded.

Actually the new building, designed by Robert Mills, was constructed on the site of the first Treasury building. Jackson preferred another site but acquiesced in the old one. Congress authorized construction on July 4, 1836, and the east wing, with its majestic colonnade, and the center wing of the present building were completed in 1839. During the interim the department moved into temporary quarters opposite Strother's Hotel on the south side of Pennsylvania Avenue west of 14th Street.[30]

When McLane finally got around to submitting his response to the questionnaire, he admitted his opposition to the removal of the deposits. Furthermore he claimed that only the secretary of the treasury was empowered to remove deposits since, in this instance, he was the agent of the Congress. In view of the strong vote in the House of Representatives at the end of the session declaring the deposits perfectly safe, he said that any tampering with the funds could cause economic catastrophe.[31] Some of the arguments were well taken and Jackson admitted as much.[32] Indeed they troubled him to such an extent that he turned over McLane's letter to Frank Blair and asked the editor for a reaction. Blair prepared a strong refutation which Jackson gratefully acknowledged.[33]

Quite obviously something would have to be done about McLane if the deposits were to be removed without causing a fuss. But Jackson had already been thinking about a number of cabinet changes. For the past six months he had mulled over a possible reshuffle. What he had in mind was the elevation of McLane to the State Department. For some time Edward Livingston had indicated a willingness to leave his present post and take an assignment abroad, specifically France. A complete Francophile, he was an authority on French law. His brother's greatest success had been as United States minister to France during Jefferson's administration when he negotiated the Louisiana Purchase, and for Livingston, at the age of sixty-eight, an assignment in France seemed an excellent way to close out his career. Besides, he longed to be "released from the labors and imprisonment of Washington."[34] At the same time, the current minister to France, William C. Rives, had long ago stated his decision to return home once he completed the treaty negotiations with the French over the spoliation claims. He returned to the United States in the fall of 1832, and it was at that time that Jackson began to think about reshuffling his cabinet.

As a matter of fact the President had already decided to ease Livingston out of the cabinet. Although he appreciated Livingston's legal acumen and literary gifts, Jackson repeatedly criticized his manner of handling people.[35] More important, he was bothered by the secretary's continued regard for the BUS despite the President's avowed hostility. So if Livingston wished to leave the cabinet and go to France it made sense to oblige him.

As for a replacement, Jackson immediately decided on McLane. Not only had McLane had a spectacular success in winning the opening of the West Indies from Great Britain in 1830, but he agreed enthusiastically with the President's foreign policy. Moreover he had provided strong support during the nullification controversy and had even approved Jackson's Bank veto.[36] As secretary of state, he might achieve distinction beyond what he had attained as minister to Great Britain. In all likelihood, therefore, Jackson had thought of elevating McLane sometime during the summer of 1832.[37] But the presidential campaign dictated that he wait until early winter. Then, when the nullification controversy escalated, Jackson put off the decision once again. Not until Congress adjourned in March, 1833, did he feel politically free to remake his cabinet.

So it was not a matter of "kicking McLane upstairs" in order to find a more willing Treasury secretary to remove the deposits. His elevation had been decided months before. The real problem that faced the President during these months between the initial decision to send Livingston to France and replace him at state with McLane and the final action involved in these multiple appointments, was the difficulty of finding someone as a replacement for McLane in the Treasury Department. With Jackson determined to kill the monster, he needed an able and willing partner in the Treasury. But, as he had so often in the past in making appointments, Jackson acted precipitously and unwisely. To a very large extent the trouble and turmoil that ensued resulted from the President's own folly.

Actually the President had someone perfect for the job sitting right there in his cabinet: Roger B. Taney, the attorney general. But Taney and McLane had had their differences over fiscal matters and such a choice might have been interpreted as an insult to McLane—and that Jackson would never allow. Besides, McLane "vigorously opposed" the appointment and so it was dropped.[38] Taney was undoubtedly miffed that his name apparently had never come up for consideration.[39]

There was another consideration. When he first decided to kill the Bank, Jackson had several ways to launch the assault: either he could remove the deposits and cause a lingering death, or he could obtain a writ of *scire facias*, a legal action to bring the Bank before the courts to determine whether its conduct dictated the forfeiting of its charter. If he decided on the writ, he wanted Taney to remain as attorney general. But Taney actually opposed obtaining this writ—and Jackson eventually agreed with him—because there were many things about the Bank's conduct which a President might act upon but which would be difficult to establish by "legal proof in a court of Justice."[40]

In deciding upon McLane's replacement there was considerable pressure on the President to appoint someone from Pennsylvania. After all the Bank was centered in Philadelphia, and if Jackson destroyed the institution then having someone from that state as Treasury head might deflect much of the political heat that was certain to be generated. Above all, however, Jackson needed someone of the highest ability. "The character must be one of high standing in the Nation," he told Van Buren; "he ought to be in constitutional and political views with us—opposed to the power of Congress to establish corporations anywhere except in the District of Columbia and opposed to the power of creating corporations the Government becoming a partner or shareholder." He should be "a man of integrity combined with talent," one devoted to harmony and unity within the administration to serve the entire nation. "Help me to search out such a character," Jackson pleaded. Or one as near to these qualifications as possible.[41]

Then, as he finished the letter, "a happy thought" struck him. William J. Duane! That was the man for the Treasury. It "flashed into my mind" quite suddenly, he told Van Buren.[42] What an inspiration! (And a great misfortune that he did not suppress it on the spot.) Duane's father, Colonel William Duane, had been the famous editor of the Jefferson party newspaper, the *Aurora*. If we appoint the son, argued Jackson, it would tend to link the Jefferson and Jackson parties in their anti-bank sentiments and unite them in the orthodoxy of republicanism.[43] Furthermore, the younger Duane had worked for the Girard banking interests in Philadelphia and therefore was "well acquainted with finances and commercial law." He was known to be anti-Bank and had served as chairman of a committee on banks of the Pennsylvania legislature. His appointment, the President gleefully argued, "will have a tendency to harmonize Pennsylvania and keep her with the Democracy of the Union."[44]

It is quite possible that the Duane name did not simply flash into Jackson's mind as he said. Rather it may have been planted there by McLane. According to Francis P. Blair, the President told him that "Mr. McLane had slapped his hand on his thigh after canvassing other Pennsylvanians, and named Duane as the very man for the place."[45] Of course, since Duane's appointment turned into a disaster, it is quite possible— indeed likely—that Blair was trying to fix blame for the appointment on McLane in order to exonerate Jackson.[46]

In any event McLane approved the choice, and without too much more thought the appointment was conferred—which was unfortunate and for which Jackson merits full blame. The President hardly knew anything about Duane. Since he expected his new Treasury secretary to remove the deposits from the BUS, the least he should have done was to have gotten a prior commitment that would bind Duane to the President's intended action. All Jackson knew was that Duane was anti-Bank; also that he was the son of a distinguished Jeffersonian editor. "A chip off the old block, sir," as Jackson himself was wont to say about his own son to fix a stamp of approval on some action or other.[47] It was probably an impetuous decision that seemed like an excellent idea.

On December 4, 1832—months before Jackson asked his five famous questions—McLane visited Duane and apprised him of the President's intention. Duane's first inclination was to refuse, but McLane urged him most forcefully to accept, fearful no doubt that Taney would get the nod if Duane rejected it. Duane's elderly father also recommended acceptance, and so on January 30, 1833, he capitulated and agreed to serve.[48] Several months earlier McLane had accepted the offer of the State Department, and he acknowledged that the final arrangements for his move had been "delayed only by the state of public affairs in the interval."[49]

So the cabinet was finally reshuffled ten months after Jackson had arrived at his initial decision. On May 29 Livingston submitted his resignation "with the sincerest gratitude for the confidence you have reposed in me—for the kindness and friendship with which you have been pleased to know me." On the same day Jackson accepted it, and he did so "with a deep sense of the very important aid which you have rendered." Since he would still enjoy the benefit of Livingston's service abroad as minister to France, "the regret which I would otherwise feel at your retirement from this station is greatly diminished." The appointment even pleased some of Jackson's political opponents. "I tender you my wishes for a happy & brilliant diplomatic career," wrote Webster to Livingston.[50]

One of the pleasant aspects for Livingston in going to France was the possibility of taking his daughter, Cora, and her new husband, Thomas P. Barton, a foreign service officer. Jackson agreed that young Barton might serve as secretary to the legation in Paris. And he performed the rite of appointment with a typical Jacksonian gesture of gallantry. "My dear Cora," he wrote, "Your kind letter with that of your dear husbands were duly received. I have postponed a reply, until by the hand of your father, I could enclose to you, his commission as secretary to the French legation, which I now do, & request that you present it to him with your own hand, and with it a tender of my high regard."[51]

The very same day that Livingston resigned, McLane was installed as the new secretary of state. The official announcement of his appointment, along with those of Duane and Livingston, appeared the next day, May 30, in the Washington *Globe*. Unlike the changes of the first cabinet reshuffle, this one produced hardly a murmur of comment. McLane's previous diplomatic success made his appointment seem highly appropriate and beneficial to the country, and everyone who knew him agreed that Livingston would perform admirably in France. Only Duane was relatively unknown. He was the question mark. And since no one had much information, it was simply assumed that Jackson knew what he was doing when he named Duane to this important and sensitive post at the head of the United States Treasury Department.

CHAPTER 5

"The Grand Triumphal Tour"

ON MAY 6, 1833, PRESIDENT ANDREW JACKSON, accompanied by some members of his cabinet and Major Donelson, embarked on the steamboat *Cygnet* for Fredericksburg, Virginia, where the President was scheduled to lay the cornerstone of a monument in honor of the mother of George Washington. Then it happened.[1] At Alexandria, where the steamboat made berth, Jackson retired to a cabin and had seated himself in a chair wedged between a long table (being set for dinner) and a berth. Major Donelson, Mrs. Thurston, wife of a Washington jurist, a Mr. Potter, clerk in one of the departments, Captain Broome of the marines, and several others were also in the room. Jackson was reading a newspaper and smoking his pipe with his right elbow on the berth and his left arm resting on the table. Mrs. Thurston sat immediately on his right. "Thus confined, and thus situated," he was interrupted by Robert B. Randolph, a former lieutenant in the navy, who had been dismissed for theft at Jackson's specific direction. "In a plain & supplicating tone," Randolph inquired if Jackson was the President. Old Hickory looked up from his newspaper and answered affirmatively. "Excuse my rising, sir," he said, "I have a pain in my side which makes it distressing for me to rise."[2]

Randolph said nothing but pressed forward between Mrs. Thurston and the table, pulling off the glove on his right hand as he moved. "Believing that he had a wish to shake hands with me, which is so common," Jackson later recounted, "I said to him, do not draw your glove."

"You have injured me," Randolph responded "in a soft tone" of voice.

"How?" asked the President.

And with that, Randolph "dashed his hand" into Jackson's face.[3]

"What Sir. What Sir," cried the President.[4]

Randolph attempted to strike again but Captain Broome seized him and pulled him away. A scuffle ensued and the table was overturned. Several of Randolph's friends, who had accompanied him aboard the vessel, grabbed him and rushed him off the boat. Poor Jackson had been so trapped behind the table that he could not rise with ease, nor seize his cane in time to defend himself. "Had I been apprised that Randolph stood before me," he said, "I should have been prepared for him, and I could have defended myself. No villain has ever escaped me before; and he would not, had it not been for my confined situation."

Blood was noticed on the President's face and he was asked if he was badly injured.

"No," he replied, "I am not much hurt; but in endeavoring to rise, I have wounded my side, which now pains me more than it did."

One of the shocked bystanders approached Jackson and offered to kill Randolph for the insult.

"No, sir," the old man responded, "I cannot do that. I want no man to stand between me and my assailants, and none to take revenge on my account. Had I been prepared for this *cowardly villain*'s approach, I can assure you all, that he would never have the timerity to undertake such a thing again."[5]

Jackson later told Van Buren that if he had been prepared and on his feet, Randolph "would never have moved with life from his tracks he stood in." Still more did he regret "that friends interposed, closed the passage of the door, and held me, until I was oblige[d] to tell them if they did not open a passage I would open it with my cane."[6]

Of course, Jackson soon decided that the attack was part of a political plot and that hostile newspapers were at the bottom of it. "The outrage attempted by that dastard Randolph, & *his associates in the conspiracy* upon my person, receives but few advocates except the Fredericksburgh Arena, the Richmond Whig, the Intelligencer, & Duff Green." But even more galling was the failure of Virginia justice to do anything about the attack. (Randolph claimed that he only pulled Jackson's nose.) This inability or unwillingness to deal with a criminal act, said Jackson, "is a disgrace to the old Dominion, and well calculated to disgrace our institutions abroad, and will compel us here, to go armed, for our personal defence." What a horrible prospect, he shuddered. Why, it could "lead to, what I would sincerely regret, & which never *shall happen* whilst I am in office, a *military guard around the President.*" The only safety now for goverl .ient officers, he declared, "is to be prepared & shoot down or otherways destroy those dastardly assasins whenever they approach us."[7]

Eventually, Randolph was apprehended and brought to trial, but by that time Jackson had left office and had no wish to participate in the "villain's" prosecution. "I have to this old age complied with my mothers advice," he told Van Buren, " 'to indict no man for assault and battery or sue him for slander', and to fine or imprison Randolph would be no gratification, and not being prosecutor, nor having any agency in it I cannot enter a *noli prosequi.*" He had one request, however. If Randolph was found guilty, Jackson asked for a presidential pardon and the remission of any fine. This, he said, "would be the better mode to close this prosecution." It "might have a good effect upon society."[8] And that ended the affair.

That Andrew Jackson should be the first President to be criminally assaulted is very suggestive. For one thing it says something about Jackson himself, the kind of man he was and the emotional passions he aroused in some people. But for another, and far more important, it says something about the age. It was a sign—one ugly and frightening—that the country was undergoing disturbing changes in its character, mood, and behavior. In forty and more years of the presidency, nothing like this had happened before. Regrettably, assaulting Presidents became a terrible fact of American life. And the thing that Jackson dreaded the most came about, namely the necessity of placing *"a military guard around the President."*

Although the Randolph incident "vexed him a good deal," Jackson appeared in excellent spirits upon his return to Washington. The incident seemed to "put his blood in motion."[9] But something else roused his energies and warmed his mood. Something else excited him. He had decided to make an extensive tour of New England with the hope of uniting the people after the long agony of nullification.

The very notion of such a tour demonstrated how far Jackson had matured as a politician. He wanted to stimulate nationalistic sentiments for the Union among the electorate—to enhance the moral force in defense of the Union—and he knew that nothing set off demonstrations of patriotic feeling quicker than the living presence of the head of state as he moved among the people. In deciding to undertake this tour Old Hickory had the wit and perception to appreciate how much it might help to unite the nation, strengthen the bond of union, and overcome the anxiety created by the recent trauma. He realized how much he might accomplish personally to restore the nation's sense of well-being.

In the early history of the United States, Jackson is one of the very few Presidents to take such a tour. Of the Presidents who preceded him, only George Washington and James Monroe traveled around the country. After Jackson, prior to the Civil War, John Tyler took one. No others did. Yet, in the twentieth century, these presidential excursions would become standard procedure for all Presidents who wished to maintain strong ties with the electorate.

Of the early tours, only Jackson's established a warm rapport between the President and the people. George Washington was too remote and forbidding to elicit more than respectful appreciation for his incalculable contribution to the nation's freedom, and the best that could be said about Monroe's tour is that it prompted one newspaper man to suggest that the President's arrival in Massachusetts marked the commencement of an "era of good feelings."[10] But Jackson's tour caused an emotional debauch. The delight, the happiness, the pure joy shown by the people in seeing their President had never been expressed in quite the same way before. It was as though the people needed to scream and shout in order to expel from their minds all the anxiety for the Union that had festered within them for the past six months.

And how they did demonstrate. The parades, the banquets, the toasts and addresses, the streets lined with people, the windows crowded with joyous faces, the roofs alive with people, the thundering artillery to salute the Hero, the mobbing to shake the President's hand or touch him, the baby-kissing—all these occurred during Jackson's tour of New England in the late spring and early summer of 1833. It was one long, ecstatic ovation.[11]

The decision to make the tour came early in the new year. Not only was it an obvious and astute decision, in view of the momentous events of the past several months, but it came as the result of a formal invitation. On February 5, 1833, a committee formed at a public meeting in Hartford, Connecticut, invited the President to visit New England and see for himself the cities, towns, churches, colleges, and industries of the region —in short to inspect her "institutions of Republican Freedom" and mingle with a "virtuous people" to get to know them better.[12]

Apart from strengthening the moral force in defense of the Union, the political wisdom of accepting this invitation was immediately apparent. Democrats did not fare well in New England as a rule. In 1828 Jackson carried not a single state in the area; four years later he captured two, Maine and New Hampshire, for a total of 17 electoral votes. But his popular vote in all the New England states between the two elections had increased dramatically. Perhaps a personal appearance tour at this juncture might cap this growth with a burst of popular enthusiasm that would swing New England to the Democrats. Moreover, there was much opposition in the region to Jackson's Bank policy and some misunderstanding of his tariff stance. Again, the magic of a personal trip might win converts to both his policies.

As always, Jackson conferred with his advisers in both the Kitchen and Parlor cabinets, although the final decision was always his, of course. All the members urged him to accept the invitation for national as well as political reasons. And they convinced him—rather easily. On March 7, 1833, he replied to the Connecticut committee and said he would be delighted to visit New England later in the year to view "the republican institutions which her sons have raised up with so much public spirit and success" and to savor "the satisfaction I should expect to derive from personal intercourse with the citizens themselves."[13] Word of the President's New England trip quickly spread, and immediately several legislatures and Democratic party organizations in the region inundated Jackson with requests that he include their state or city on his itinerary. The senate of Massachusetts adopted a series of resolutions asking the governor of the state to issue a formal invitation so that the commonwealth might accord the "chief magistrate of the union" its "customary hospitalities" and "respectful congratulations."[14]

Once Jackson made up his mind to accept the invitation, plans for the tour went forward with dispatch. Van Buren notified the Regency in New York to expect the President sometime about the first of June. Jackson will travel north and east as far as Portland, said Van Buren, then cut across to Burlington and head for Albany by way of Saratoga Springs. "This was the course suggested by me, but . . . it may be altered."[15]

The final arrangements, as they developed, charted a course for the President along the Atlantic seaboard with stops at all the major cities along the way. Generally speaking, Jackson decided to follow the route taken by President James Monroe in 1818. He was to be accompanied by Donelson and Earl from his own household, along with McLane and Cass. At New York, where the party would meet Van Buren, Cass would break away and head for Detroit on a western tour while McLane would continue with the party until they reached New Haven, after which he would return to Washington.[16]

Jackson waited to begin his tour until he completed his cabinet reshuffle. Once McLane took office on May 29 and William Duane was duly sworn in on June 1, the President felt free to leave Washington. But first he wanted to talk informally to Duane about the BUS since he had pretty much made up his mind to remove the government's deposits as soon as possible. Although he sensed that this was his proper course in the final act of slaying the "hydra," still he found it a "perplexing subject" and he needed to be absolutely sure he was embarked on the right course. Not only would he consult with Duane, but he thought he would like to talk to Van Buren about it in New York "before I finally act." What troubled him was the disposition of government funds after they had been withdrawn. It was not his intention simply to destroy the BUS and leave it at that. He wanted a substitute "system" as part of his general economic reform—a reform that included reducing government expenditures and paying off the national debt—but he needed "a system that will insure a solvent currency," he told Van Buren, "and a sure system for the fiscal operations of the Government."[17]

Amos Kendall, of course, argued long and hard for immediate removal. He wrote ahead to Van Buren to suggest a "system" for the proper disposition of the deposits after their withdrawal from the BUS. "I shall take it for granted that the deposits will be removed," he began. "Under the new order of things," a number of primary and secondary banks might be selected in the principal cities of the nation, Kendall went on, to receive the government's funds for their respective areas "upon their acceding to the terms proposed." These banks would make monthly reports to the secretary of the treasury and permit a regular inspection of their books. They would also handle most of the services presently provided by the BUS, such as the transfer of government funds from place to place.[18]

It was known that Van Buren had very negative feelings about the removal of the deposits from the BUS. He felt that any action at this time was imprudent. Because of these concerns and the fact that Jackson would consult with Van Buren when he arrived in New York, Kendall wrote his letter in the hope that it would quiet the Vice President's fears and win his acquiescence to the intended removal before he met with Jackson. "I beg you to consider what I have written," Kendall concluded, "and if you concurr with me, I hope your great influence may be exerted in every proper mode, to effect the desired object."[19]

But Kendall did not let the matter rest there. He and Reuben Whitney, who was then employed in the Treasury Department, went to see Duane on the day following his installation as Treasury secretary. Duane was informed that removal was a settled policy and that he would soon be directed by the President to transfer the government's deposits from the BUS to a group of selected state banks. As he listened to this announcement Duane's jaw dropped several inches. He was so startled by this information and the manner in which it had been brought to his attention —both Kendall and Whitney were his subordinates—that his face immediately registered his "mortification."[20]

Kendall caught the signal. He quickly changed the subject and took his leave.[21] But the incident nettled Duane and he complained to Jackson the next morning. It was an attempt, he said, "to reduce me to a mere cypher in the administration."[22] The President tried to reassure him. He denied sending anyone to instruct him on his duties, but admitted his inclination to remove the deposits. Since he was about to take off on his New England tour, Jackson did not feel it an appropriate time to discuss the matter in detail. Besides, he wanted Van Buren's opinion first. So he told Duane that he would send him his views from New York after consulting with the Vice President, along with the written opinions on the subject submitted by the other members of the cabinet.[23]

Jackson showed wretched executive management in this incident. He handled Duane very badly. He should have discussed the removal with him at length as soon as they met. There was no need to consult with Van Buren first—or if this was so imperative he should have kept it from Duane. But above all, he should have exerted greater efforts to convince his Treasury secretary that he was not a "cypher" brought in merely to execute a preordained decision.

So the removal decision was allowed to hang fire while Jackson set off for New England. Before leaving Washington the President saw Duane again and once more indicated that he had an open mind on the question. "He did not wish any one to conceal his opinions," said Duane, "and that all he asked was that I should reflect with a view to the public good."[24]

And off Jackson went, leaving behind a slightly disgruntled department head whose suspicions about the role he was expected to play in the cabinet were not altogether allayed. But Jackson did not dwell on it. The tour represented a marvelous opportunity to perform a real service for the American people and lift their spirits about the strength and permanence of their government. Although he suffered intense physical pain throughout the late spring, which worried his family and prompted them to advise canceling the trip, he thought it was too late to back out at this time. Too many plans and arrangements had been scheduled. Besides, he intended to visit the celebrated Dr. Philip Syng Physick in Philadelphia to see if the good doctor would provide him with something to relieve his constant pain and discomfort.

The presidential party set out on tour at nine o'clock in the morning of Thursday, June 6, 1833, and headed for Baltimore. The tone of the tour was immediately struck by the vociferous enthusiasm with which Jackson "was everywhere greeted."[25] Once the pandemonium began— and it began almost as the President stepped foot out of the door of the White House—it grew with each day and place he visited. It almost seemed as though a rivalry existed between cities to outdo one another in expressing their gratitude to the man who had done so much to preserve the Union.

The first day started with a grand adventure. For the first time in his life Jackson enjoyed the experience of a ride on a railroad train. At a point where the Washington Turnpike crossed the Baltimore and Ohio Railroad, about twelve miles outside Baltimore, the President was met by the Maryland Welcoming Committee, consisting of General Samuel Smith and James McCulloch. They escorted him to the train, or "Steam Carrs," as Jackson called it, for the ride into town. And "in a few minutes" he was whisked the twelve miles into Baltimore, arriving at half past two in the afternoon.[26] An immense crowd was waiting at the Three Tons Tavern on Brett Street to greet the Hero as he stepped from this new technological marvel of the modern age. Cheers rent the air and were repeated again and again. Indeed the President's three-day visit to Baltimore, recorded one touring Irishman, was the occasion for "an ear-splitting celebration."[27]

On leaving the railroad train, Jackson and General Smith seated themselves in an open barouche to drive to his lodgings at the Indian Queen Hotel. As the carriage passed through the streets the President "was greeted by masses of the people" who shouted to him, called his name, and then cried in unison, "Huzza! Huzza! Huzza!"[28]

It so happened that while Jackson was visiting Baltimore, the great Indian chieftain Black Hawk also arrived in town on exactly the same day. A year before, the warrior had led his people, the Sauk and Fox tribes, in a gallant but futile war against federal and state troops in northern

Illinois. The war lasted only a few months and ended with the final removal of the Sauk and Fox Indians across the Mississippi River. Black Hawk and some of his chiefs were "held as hostages for the future good conduct of the late hostile bands" and had been brought east and kept under heavy guard.[29] They were taken first to Washington, and on April 26, 1833, met President Jackson at the White House. Black Hawk was impressed by Old Hickory. "He looks as if he had seen as many winters as I have," the seventy-year-old chief said, "and seems to be a great brave." Jackson had little time for the Indians and told them that they would be temporarily incarcerated in Fortress Monroe. Black Hawk objected and said he would rather return to his nation. "You will go to Fortress Monroe," commanded Old Hickory, "and remain there contented until [I] give [you] permission" to return home. Their detention, he told them, depended on the conduct of the tribes and the dissipation of "all the bad feeling which had led to the bloody scenes on the frontier." The Indians remained silent. "I concluded," said Black Hawk, "it was best to obey our Great Father, and say nothing contrary to his wishes."[30]

Fanny Kemble, the celebrated English actress, visited the warrior in prison. She described him as a "diminutive, shrivelled looking old man" who exuded calmness and dignity despite his size. He wore a blue cloth "surtout," with scarlet leggings, a black silk neck handkerchief, and earrings. The cold dignity of the old chief, she said, expressed the indecency of his situation. To think of him, she wrote, "cooped up the whole horrible day long, in this hot prison-house full of people, made my heart ache."[31]

A month later Black Hawk was released from prison and was now being paraded throughout the eastern states. The object of this tour was to demonstrate to him the superiority of American arms and equipment, to let him see with his own eyes the extent and power of the American nation and the utter futility of resisting removal of his people beyond the Mississippi River. The great chief created quite a sensation everywhere he went. "He appeared melancholy & dejected," commented one, "never smiled, a most dignified look."[32] Baltimore was his first stop and he was again hauled before the President for final instructions before going forth to meet the American people.

Black Hawk arrived at Jackson's hotel with a small entourage. The President looked glum. "When I saw you in Washington," Old Hickory began, "I told you that you had behaved very badly, in raising the tomahawk against the white people, and killing men, women and children upon the frontier." Jackson's face grew stern as he spoke. "Your conduct last year compelled me to send my warriors against you, and your people were defeated, with great loss, and your men surrendered, to be kept until I should be satisfied that you would not try to do any more injury." During that meeting the President had promised to inquire whether the return of Black Hawk and the other chiefs would constitute a danger to the frontier and whether the Sauk and Fox tribes wished to have them back. The commanding generals on the frontier, Jackson continued, have approved your return, and the Indian people have requested it. "Your chiefs have pledged themselves for your good conduct, and I have given directions, that you should be taken to your own country."[33]

The chiefs showed no reaction to this announcement. "Major Garland, who is with you," the Great Father continued, "will conduct you through some of our towns. You will see the strength of the white people. You will see, that our young men are as numerous, as the leaves in the woods. What can you do against us? You may kill a few women and children, but such a force would be soon sent against you, as would destroy your whole tribe."

The chiefs stirred in their places. Jackson's voice now rose high and shrill. "We do not wish to injure you. . . . But if you again plunge your knives into the breasts of our people, I shall send a force, which will severely punish you for your cruelties."

"Bury the tomahawk," the President commanded, "and live in peace with the frontiers." Listen to the councils of Ke-o-kuk and the other friendly chiefs, "and I pray the Great Spirit to give you a smooth path and fair sky to return."[34]

General Jackson had a way with the Indians that both cowed and awed them. His manner was always stern, and slightly threatening. But he invariably held out the hope of a happy relationship if they obeyed his will.

Chief Black Hawk stepped forward. He looked squarely at the President. He spoke softly but with great presence and dignity. *"My Father,"* he said, "My ears are open to your words. I am glad to hear them. I am glad to go back to my people. I want to see my family. I did not behave well last summer. I ought not to have taken up the tomahawk. But my people have suffered a great deal. When I get back, I will remember your words. I won't go to war again. I will live in peace. I shall hold you by the hand."[35]

These words, as recorded by the American press, were undoubtedly doctored to reassure the reading public that the menace of Black Hawk had ended forever and that he would no longer disturb the peace. In any event Jackson was pleased with this verbal exchange and the willingness of the chief to accept a peace imposed on him by force. That evening both men attended a performance at the Front Street theater, and it was difficult to decide which of the two commanded the greater interest and attention.[36]

On Saturday, June 8, Jackson and his party left Baltimore for Philadelphia. They boarded the *Kentucky,* a Chesapeake Bay steamer, for Chesapeake City, where they transferred to a canal barge drawn by a team of horses. As the barge proceeded along the fifteen-mile course of the Chesapeake and Delaware Canal, Jackson sat on the upper deck to view the countryside and acknowledge the handwaving and shouting of the spectators on the shore. The canal ended at Delaware City, where the party again transferred to another steamer, the *Ohio*, which took them the rest of the way to Philadelphia.

There was one brief stop at New Castle, where Jackson met the governor of Delaware, Caleb Bennett. Jackson went ashore to meet him and as they walked down one street the President noticed a banner stretched across the road bearing the words, "The Union—It must be Preserved." The General studied it with pleasure. It showed that the American people understood the full purpose of his trip and approved.[37]

At Philadelphia the steamboat docked at the Navy Yard and a crowd estimated at thirty thousand greeted their Hero with long sustained cheers and huzzas. A barouche drawn by four white horses conveyed Jackson to the City Hotel, and the streets were so mobbed with people that a troop of cavalry was necessary to open a passageway. By this time the crowds bordered on frenzy. The warmth of their welcome, editorialized the *Globe*, proved that Philadelphia was indeed the "city of Brotherly Love."[38]

The following day, Sunday, Jackson attended services at the First Presbyterian Church. After the services, and before he could leave his pew, he was mobbed by the congregation, who extended their hands from every direction in the hope of clasping his. For some, just to touch him was enough. A master politician, Jackson waded into the crowd, but when he realized the potential danger and the ever increasing size of the congregation he quickly drew back and slipped out of the church by a private door.

Because of his health, the pain he constantly endured in his side, and the recurrent hemorrhages that prostrated him, Jackson planned to visit Dr. Physick during his brief stay in Philadelphia. The so-called "bleeding at the lungs" particularly distressed him. It went in cycles. Because the bullet fired by Charles Dickinson in 1806 lodged close to his heart it could not be removed. It subsequently formed abscesses which produced periodic flare-ups. There would be a period of repose during which the abscess remained stable or drained from his system without troubling him. But sometimes it would flare. Perhaps a coughing spell or heavy smoking would trigger an attack. Then he would start hemorrhaging. Chills seized him. Soon he was drenched in sweat. Frequently he collapsed. Finally, when the bleeding reduced the pressure on the abscess, he would slowly return to a "period of stability," although greatly weakened and several pounds thinner.[39]

The prospect of alleviating some of the worst aspects of his condition —even if the cause itself could not be eliminated without major chest and heart surgery—drove Jackson to see Dr. Physick. After a brief and pleasant introduction, the President explained his symptoms. He ended with a typical Jacksonian admonition. "Now, Doctor, I can do any thing you think proper to order, and bear as much as most men. There are only two things I can't give up: one is coffee, and the other is tobacco."[40]

The doctor was utterly captivated by his patient. For days afterward all Dr. Physick could talk about was Old Hickory. "He was so full of General Jackson, so penetrated with the gentleness, the frankness, the peculiar and indescribable charm of his demeanor, that he could talk of nothing else."[41]

Most of the doctors at the time usually recommended bleeding to treat difficult or mysterious problems. Even when the problem involved hemorrhaging—as it did with Jackson—doctors had no hesitation in calling for additional bloodletting. As the most distinguished member of his profession at the time, Dr. Physick apparently understood the impossibility of achieving any lasting improvement, and so he simply encouraged Jackson to keep up the good fight. "I have seen Doctor Phisic," the President informed his son, "who encourages me, and says my heart is not effected in any way, and the pain in the side can be removed by cupping.*"[42] He simply had to live with his condition, like it or not.

On Monday, June 10, the President and his party set out for Independence Hall. A large crowd of invited guests was introduced to Jackson at a reception given by the mayor at the Hall, but soon a mob forced its way into the building. For two hours they surrounded him and shook his hand. The air was stifling. Someone had enough sense to open the windows but then a "ludicrous scene ensued." People began tumbling out of the windows, falling a distance of six feet. Some jumped, others dove, still others simply rolled out.[43]

Though exhausted, Jackson showed no sign of it. He flattered the ladies, as usual, shook hands with their menfolk, patted the heads and cheeks of children, and even kissed babies. The scene horrified some. "The degeneracy of the age in taste, feelings, and principles," said one, was absolutely appalling. Jackson was led around by his party as though he were a wild beast on exhibition.[44]

At noon the President left the Hall, mounted a horse, and rode off to review a military parade. Cass and McLane flanked him, riding on the left and right and slightly behind. The parade lasted five hours; all the while Jackson sat bolt upright in his saddle. It should have drained him, yet he retained enough strength to attend a military ball that evening. Clearly he pushed himself. Already he had begun to wish the tour was over and that he might escape to the Hermitage. "I think it is the last journey, I shall ever undertake," he wrote his son. Still he had to admit that the size and adulation of the crowds proved the wisdom of taking this tour. "I shall not attempt to describe the feelings of the people," he declared, "suffice it to say that it surpassed any thing I ever witnessed."[45]

*Cupping is the method of drawing blood to the surface of the skin by creating a vacuum with a cup at the point where the cup is applied.

The following morning at 9 A.M. the party drove to the wharf, where they boarded the steamboat *Philadelphia*. Near Trenton they debarked and drove to the capital of New Jersey, where they dined and rested for the night. Meanwhile New York City geared itself for Jackson's coming. For more than a week preparations had been in full swing, with an official welcoming committee numbering four hundred people of the "highest standing and respectability." Even Philip Hone, who disliked Jackson intensely, considered it a distinct "honor" to be invited to join the escort aboard the steamer *North America*, which would accompany the President from Perth Amboy to New York City. "This has been a day of jubilee in New York," recorded Hone in his diary. "The Man of the People (for he is such in a greater degree than any who has gone before him) slept last night at Trenton and was to make his triumphal entry to-day [June 12]."[46]

The *North America* was convoyed by the *Ohio*, *Hercules*, and *Rufus King*, all filled with passengers. At eleven o'clock on Wednesday, June 12, the ships arrived at Perth Amboy. Two hours later the President arrived and the convoy set sail. The guests were then served "the most splendid dinner which was ever seen on board a vessel." The delicacies included "fourteen fresh salmon well cooked and in prime order." Niblo, of Niblo Gardens fame, provided the dinner, said Hone, "and the little man certainly covered himself with glory." As the ship entered the Narrows the two forts nearby began firing a salute. The sounds of their heavy guns broke up the dinner party and brought everyone on deck.[47]

Other ships of every size, shape, and description crowded the harbor. Those equipped to do so fired a salute. Governor's Island sounded its welcome with heavy firing. The landing of the presidential party took place at midafternoon on the wharf at Castle Garden. General Jackson was received by the mayor and escorted to a "great saloon" which had been handsomely prepared for the occasion. Everywhere people assembled to catch sight of the President. "The wharves and housetops and vessels were covered with people." Troops were drawn up on the Battery. Some one hundred thousand people jammed the area.[48]

At that time Castle Garden was separated from the Battery by water. A wooden bridge connected them. Immediately after the official greeting, Jackson mounted a horse and led the procession across the bridge. He had just reached the other side, followed by one or two others, when the Battery side of the bridge collapsed. Dignitaries of every age and shape plunged into the water. Cabinet members, presidential aides, governors, congressmen, mayors, and other celebrities tumbled into the shallow depths, all drenched, all frightened, and all struggling to regain solid ground. It was quite a sight. McLane escaped the dousing, but Cass, Donelson, and Levi Woodbury, the secretary of the navy, who had just joined the party, waded through four feet of water before clambering back to shore. Fortunately no one was seriously hurt, although dignities had been shattered and some sustained bruises and contusions.[49]

"Major Jack Downing," the pseudonymn for Seba Smith, had already begun to amuse the nation with hilarious accounts in the newspapers of the "Grand Triumphal Tour," and with this incident he claimed that "a hundred folks splashed into the water, all mixed up together one on top of t'other." He noted that Lewis Cass had lost his wig but he quickly reassured his readers that the loss created no problem. After all, the Indian tribes came within the jurisdiction of Cass's department and he would surely have no difficulty in finding "a scalp to suit him."[50]

While the dignitaries scrambled out of the water to dry themselves and regain their composure, Jackson waited for the preparations to be completed for a grand parade up Broadway to City Hall. Only a short time lapsed. Then the signal was given, the dignitaries, still dripping wet, took their places in line, and off they all went in a grand march up lower Manhattan, Jackson on horseback leading the way.

From the Battery to City Hall Park, Broadway was one "solid mass of men, women, and children, who greeted their favorite with cheers, shouts, and waving of scarfs and handkerchiefs." The President doffed his tall hat, still draped with a "weeper" in memory of his beloved Rachel, as he gestured his thanks and greetings to the people on both sides of the street. The outpouring of affection startled even those who remembered George Washington's arrival in New York to begin his administration in 1789. "The President [Jackson] is certainly the most popular man we have ever known." Not George Washington. Washington was too dignified, too grave for the popular tastes, and men could not approach him with familiarity. "Here is a man who suits them exactly. He has a kind expression for each—the same to all, no doubt, but each thinks it intended for himself. . . . Talk of him as the second Washington! It won't do now; Washington was only the first Jackson. . . . So huzza for Jackson!"[51]

All Manhattan huzza-ed for Old Hickory as he paraded up Broadway. People jammed every spot available—"a sea of waving and heaving and changing myriads." The uncovered head of the President was plainly visible to all as he bowed and waved his hat in response to "the enthusiastic and heart-felt greetings." "A freeman, a patriot, who had served his country, and who now was her chief magistrate, was come to visit his countrymen, and . . . had caused such a welcome as no monarch with all his pageantry had ever received."

Everyone commented on what they saw: a President waving to the people, shaking their hands, and kissing their babies. Not like the old days. The remoteness of a Washington, the shyness of a Jefferson, the hauteur of an Adams had vanished. Instead they had a President who mingled with the people and claimed to be their representative. And indeed he was. The country had become a democracy from the looks of things, and it was nowhere more visible than in the "office of the chief magistracy."

When Jackson reached City Hall, he was formally greeted by Governor William L. Marcy and his staff. Then, standing on a platform fronting the Park, the President received the marching salute of a corps of state militia. It was "truly a magnificent scene" and Jackson was deeply impressed. With "a quivering lip but a brightening eye," the General turned to Governor Marcy and said: *"Nullification will never take root HERE."*[52]

By this time the Vice President, Martin Van Buren, had joined the party, and when the City Hall ceremonies concluded the two men headed for the American Hotel, where a guard of honor awaited the General. As soon as he could excuse himself, Jackson soothed his aching body in a warm bath. He was subjecting himself to excessive physical punishment (which he realized) and he risked a complete breakdown. But the opportunity was so unique for binding the country together that he saw his punishment as a duty that must be endured for the sake of the Union. Besides, the people seemed so genuinely happy to see him that he felt he owed them as much time and attention as he could possibly muster. "I have witnessed enthusiasms before," he wrote his son two days after his arrival in New York, "but never before have I witnessed such a scene of personal regard as I have to day, and ever since I left Washington. I have bowed to upwards of two hundred thousand people to day—never has there been such affection of the people before I am sure been evinced."[53]

During Jackson's three-day stay in the city—which cost New York taxpayers about $9,000[54]—he took an excursion to Staten Island aboard a steamboat. As he stood on the deck he suddenly turned and swept the harbor with his piercing eyes. "What a country God has given us!" he murmured. "How thankful we ought to be that God has given us such a country to live in."

He paused a moment. Then he continued his paean. "We have the best country, and the best institutions in the world. No people have so much to be grateful for as we. But ah! . . . there is one thing that I fear will yet sap the foundations of our liberty—that monster institution, the bank of the United States! Its existence is incompatible with liberty. One of the two must fall—the bank or our free institutions. Next Congress, the effort to effect a re-charter will be renewed; but my consent they shall never have!"[55]

The monster Bank rarely left Jackson's mind, despite the hectic pace of the tour. So, at the first opportunity, he closeted himself with Van Buren to talk about the Bank, specifically the removal of the deposits. With him he carried a working paper, probably prepared by Kendall, which directed Duane to begin planning for removal. Jackson showed these "rough notes" to Van Buren and asked for his opinion. At the same time the Vice President received a letter from Louis McLane—who had left the party to return to Washington—urging restraint in any action affecting the deposits until Congress reconvened in December. For the next several days, whenever their schedule permitted, Jackson and Van Buren discussed the arguments pro and con concerning removal, and from time to time Cass and Woodbury joined the discussions.[56]

For his part, Van Buren probably favored the replacing of the BUS with a number of state banks such as Kendall had suggested. He had seen the success of the Safety Fund System of New York (which he helped to introduce), and he correctly gauged the temper of Jackson's thinking on the subject. But he was a cautious man and, like McLane, worried about the consequences of precipitously pulling the government's funds out of the BUS. Also, he worried about the effect of such an action on his own presidential hopes. He was heir apparent. No one could dispute that. But if the national party should be torn apart by needless conflict over the removal of the deposits, it would surely jeopardize his nomination at a party convention. If nothing else, he needed to exercise extreme care in allowing himself to become a pivotal figure in this developing controversy.

But the careful Van Buren did not reveal his hesitancy to Jackson, knowing how committed the old man was becoming to immediate removal. Instead he indicated his willingness to go along with whatever Old Hickory decided. Words of caution popped out of his mouth from time to time as they moved from city to city and continued their talks, but nothing that could annoy his chief. Nothing to upset him.[57]

The Grand Triumphal Tour proceeded northward into Connecticut after the visit to New York. It was noted with pleasure in the Democratic newspapers how careful Jackson was to shape "all his arrangements in such a manner as to avoid desecrating the Sabboth . . . which has been too often the case with our distinguished men." Not this President. With all the applause and cheers he had received he did not forget his obligations "to honor the institutions of heaven and in doing so to set a helpful example before the millions" he influenced. Moreover, he rekindled the patriotism of all who saw and heard him. "The smile—the grace—the manner of the President is very engaging," commented one newspaper. "He appeared to *feel* as a father surrounded by a numerous band of children—happy in their affections and loving them with all a parent's love.—Such are the impressions left by the visit of Andrew Jackson—'the Hero, the Statesman, the Patriot.' "[58]

At Bridgeport, Connecticut, the party paused for an hour and allowed the "Yankee gals" to express their affection for the President. At New Haven, Jackson attended a reception tendered by the governor and mayor, and visited Yale. On Sunday he participated in three church services—Presbyterian, Methodist, and Episcopal—and ran up a tavern bill estimated at $500.[59] While in New Haven he arranged for the repair of his carriage and its shipment to Washington.[60]

The party pushed on from New Haven to Hartford, leaving at six o'clock in the morning. Although the crowds along the route were not as large nor as demonstrative as those in New York, still they generated enough excitement to provide considerable political benefit for Democrats. The grand parade in Hartford was very colorful, for example, and no one remembered ever seeing such enthusiasm and excitement.[61]

No matter what town Jackson entered, the first thing he saw was an enormous sign stretched across the main street. Sometimes it simply said, "WELCOME" or "THE HERO OF NEW ORLEANS." But most often it read, "THE UNION MUST BE PRESERVED." In a number of New England towns the sign frequently quoted from Jackson's first message to Congress. The old man smiled broadly when he saw it: "ASK NOTHING NOT RIGHT—SUBMIT TO NOTHING WRONG."[62]

By the time Jackson reached Rhode Island his exhaustion was beginning to show, despite his efforts to hide it. Cannons boomed his presence everywhere he went and it was sometimes impossible to find a moment's rest. The receptions were constant, the speechmaking unavoidable. And the important state of Massachusetts still lay ahead. Jackson began to wilt.

Governor Levi Lincoln of Massachusetts had appointed Josiah Quincy, the son of the president of Harvard University, as a special aide-de-camp to accompany Jackson during his tour of Massachusetts. The young man waited at the Pawtucket Bridge as the presidential party completed its Rhode Island visit and prepared to cross the Pawtucket River, the boundary line between the two states. It was the morning of Thursday, June 20, when a solitary figure started walking across the bridge. In a moment Quincy realized that it was the President of the United States. The figure looked very slender to the young man, indeed cadaverous, "and very military-looking." Well behind Jackson walked Van Buren, Cass, and Woodbury. Then, as the group crossed from one state to the other, the Pawtucket artillery fired a final salute and in so doing broke practically every windowpane in Pawtucket, for which the state paid "a goodly bill."[63]

Quincy felt very uncomfortable as the President approached. His first task was to deliver an address of welcome, "and here was Jackson himself, advancing in solitary state to hear it." As the majestic figure neared, all kinds of fragmented thoughts swirled in Quincy's head. It suddenly became obvious to him that here "was, in essence, a knightly personage." Prejudiced, to be sure. Narrow, and mistaken upon many things. But clearly he was "a gentleman in his high sense of honor and in the natural straightforward courtesies" which were obvious at once and which were easily "distinguished from the veneer of policy." Quincy admitted that he was not prepared to be favorably impressed by someone who was "simply intolerable to the Brahmin caste of my native State."[64]

The lone figure crossed the bridge and now stood before the one-man welcoming committee. It was awkward for Quincy to make a formal speech to a single person. The military kept the crowds back on both sides of the bridge. Somehow Quincy got through his address and the

President made a suitable reply. They then walked to a barouche which was to serve them as transport for the length of Jackson's stay in Massachusetts. They stopped for breakfast at Attleborough and visited the jewelry factories for which the town was famous. The manager of one of these firms showed the President numerous cards of buttons stamped with the palmetto tree, the insignia of South Carolina. They had been ordered by the nullifiers as their badge, he said, but canceled by the President's forceful actions against them. Jackson laughed over the fact that treason in South Carolina had been turned to commercial value in Massachusetts.[65]

As they journeyed from one town to the next, Quincy slowly fell under Jackson's charm and seductive powers. The President talked constantly and frankly, both about events and individuals. Quincy was amazed at his conversational prowess. "His conversation," he said, "was interesting from its sincerity, decision, and point." Obviously, Jackson was not an ignoramus, as was so often claimed in Massachusetts, but an intelligent and articulate politician. Nor was he a man to accept differences of opinion with equanimity; but, said Quincy, it was also clear that because he was "honest and earnest, Heaven would not suffer his opinions to be other than *right.*"[66]

When they reached Roxbury at four in the afternoon they found a "triumphal arch" erected for the President's benefit. They were greeted by an orator who spoke glowingly of Jackson's noble deed in preserving the Union. "Sir," responded the President in his reply, "it shall be preserved as long as there is a nerve in this arm!"[67]

By the time the touring party neared Boston, Jackson was clearly in physical distress. Someone noticed that as he mounted his horse he fell forward upon the neck of the animal, as a tired old man would do. Then, like a shot, he bolted upright, sitting in the saddle in a stiff, soldierly fashion. It was the action of a determined man, but it was painful to see.

When Jackson arrived in Boston he was at a point nearing total exhaustion. Still there was no respite from the demanding schedule even though he had caught cold and desperately needed to rest. On the first day of his visit, June 21, he attended a parade, complete with fire engines; met the governor and received an official welcome in which he was praised for preserving *"the national sovereignty and independence"* against *"internal disaffection and disloyalty"*; and reviewed the Boston Brigade commanded by General Taylor.[68] During the review a tremendous blast from the artillery frightened the horses and sent them scurrying in all directions. Jackson quickly gained control of his mount and circled the troops and regained his position to receive the salute. But Van Buren, who was an excellent horseman, had neither whip nor spur and his horse began a series of retrograde movements in "a most unmilitary character" until it brought its tail up against a fence separating the Commons from the Mall.

"Why, where's the Vice President?" Jackson inquired.

"About as nearly on the fence as a gentleman of his positive political convictions is likely to get," joked Quincy in reply.

Jackson laughed out loud. "That's very true," he said; "and you've matched him with a horse who is even more noncommittal than his rider."[69]

Over the weekend Jackson continued to lose strength and on Monday, June 24, he took to his bed. Then he began hemorrhaging. It started with the cold, an abscess formed and then ruptured.[70] The hotel where he was staying, the Tremont House, was suddenly enveloped in silence. Extra carpets were laid in the halls of the floor to muffle all sound. Everyone tiptoed around the prostrate figure. The Quincy family physician, a Dr. Warren, was summoned, and the first thing he did was to bleed the President. When that procedure failed to gain results the good doctor bled his patient a second time.

While resting in bed after the bloodletting Jackson asked Quincy to read him the amusing articles in the newspaper by "Major Jack Downing." He rather enjoyed Downing's needling about the tour since they were done in good fun and so expertly. At one point Jackson interrupted Quincy's reading with a comment. "The Vice President must have written that," he chuckled. "Depend upon it, Jack Downing is only Van Buren in masquerade."[71]

After two days of rest, and after the doctor ceased his infernal bleeding, Jackson felt stronger. He forced himself to get out of bed. He willed himself to recover. Besides, he felt a duty to complete the draft of two communications to the secretary of the treasury regarding the removal of the government's deposits from the BUS. Andrew J. Donelson assisted him and both documents bore the date June 26. In the first Jackson announced that he had come to the conclusion that the removal "ought to be done as soon as we can get ready, and at furthest, by the 1st or 15th of September next." This would allow time to prepare a "new system" and have it in operation by the time Congress reconvened in December. To further this object he thought it "desirable" to appoint an agent from the Treasury Department—Amos Kendall, he said, would be a "proper person"—to proceed immediately to Baltimore, Philadelphia, New York, and Boston, and in these cities find "primary banks" to receive the government's deposits. Later other primary banks in the south and west could be selected, along with "secondary" banks that would assist in carrying out all the fiscal functions formerly performed by the BUS. Jackson, in this letter, chose his words very carefully. He did not order Duane to set removal in motion. "These views will be regarded by you as suggestions," he said. "It is not my intention to interfere with the independent exercise of the discretion committed to you by law over the subject."[72]

The second letter was a long, carefully argued presentation of the President's reasons for reaching his conclusion. It attempted to refute many of the arguments advanced against the idea, most notably McLane's, and ended by saying that he believed "the present and future interests of our country," the "purity of our Government and the liberties of the people," necessitated the action.[73]

The dispatch of these letters took a great weight off Jackson's mind. He felt a sense of relief. And, since the hemorrhaging had stopped, he decided he could resume his tour.

First off, he journeyed to Cambridge, where he was to be awarded an honorary degree by Harvard University. Young Quincy's father, also named Josiah, was the president of the university, and he felt obliged to confer the degree because of the precedent set when President James Monroe visited Boston. Also, a refusal to show the current President the same respect shown toward Monroe "would be imputed to party spirit." Since the American people had seen fit to elect this "frontiersman" President, the Harvard Corporation thought the honors conferred upon the man were "compliments" to the office he held.[74]

It was decided to confer the degree of Doctor of Laws. As a member of the Overseers of the corporation, John Quincy Adams was invited to be present for the ceremony. Adams was appalled. Not only on political grounds and the silent feud that existed between himself and Jackson, but on intellectual grounds. As "an affectionate child of our Alma Mater," he told Quincy, he could not witness "her disgrace in conferring her highest literary honors upon a barbarian who could not write a sentence of grammar and hardly could spell his own name."[75]

Adams's resentment and bitterness toward Jackson poured out as he wrote. He knew perfectly well that Old Hickory could both spell his name (which he always underlined) and write on occasion with enormous stylistic skill. True, his grammar and spelling lacked "refinement," but the problem had more to do with his indifference to them than anything else. On a single sheet he could spell a name or a word three different ways. They were all the same to him. But Andrew Jackson was no illiterate frontiersman, much less a barbarian. He combined grace of manner with impressive intellectual power.

It was a chilly and overcast day when Jackson entered his barouche at 10 A.M. for the short journey to Cambridge to receive the degree. As usual he was greeted with "acclamations" wherever he was seen. As he drove along the route he was full of conversation, his eye seemed brighter than ever, "all aglow with the mighty will which can compel the body to execute its behests." He seemed genuinely delighted at receiving the degree.[76]

When Jackson walked into the college chapel for the ceremonies, an emotional current surged through the witnessing crowd. Leaning on the arm of President Quincy, the General walked stiffly into the chapel. His appearance "instantly produced . . . something like admiration and respect" from the skeptical audience. He exuded a "mysterious charm upon old and young."[77]

The exercises, when they began, were conducted in Latin for the most part. President Quincy's address was certainly in Latin. Then, more Latin spouted from the mouth of young Francis Bowen, a student of the senior class, who was asked to deliver something appropriate. The degree itself was conferred in Latin, after which Jackson was expected to respond. According to one humorous account, the General looked out at the audience and said: *"Ex post facto; e pluribus unum; sic semper tyrannis; quid pro quo,"* and not a Latin scholar in the room could fault his grammar one iota.[78]

Actually Jackson mumbled something in the vernacular which nobody heard.

Major Jack Downing later embellished the story about Jackson's use of Latin. After giving a speech at "Downingville," the President was about to sit down when someone in the audience called out to him, "You must give them a little Latin, *Doctor.*" Whereupon Jackson replied, quick as lightning, "E pluribus unum, my friends, sine qua non!"[79]

The point of the story should not be lost. It was not a sly dig at Jackson. At least the American people did not interpret it that way. Rather it intimated that "a man of the people could triumph over the crafts and subtleties" of elitists.[80] It was the superiority of democracy over aristocracy, represented in the person of President Jackson, that the American people agreed was the point of the story.

After the exercises concluded, Doctor Jackson was taken to a parlor in the president's house where he received the students who passed before him and shook his hand. "I am most happy to see you, gentlemen," he said, "I wish you all much happiness." Or, to vary his greeting, "Gentlemen, I heartily wish you success in life."[81]

The General was very poised as he received the company. No barbarian, he. Old Hickory behaved with all the dignity and nobility of manner for which he was renowned. At first he shook hands with every student who approached him, but he soon found this effort strenuous and he desisted. However, when the two pretty children of Dr. Palfrey came up to him, the old man melted. He grasped their hands, lifted them up, and kissed them. It was, said young Quincy, "a pleasant sight. . . . This rough soldier . . . could kiss little children with lips as pure as their own."[82]

From Cambridge, the presidential party headed for Charlestown to view the Bunker Hill monument still under construction, receive two cannonballs as mementos of the famous battle, and hear an address from the long-winded Edward Everett.[83] Two hours of this, along with a procession around the town, and "the inevitable collation," wearied Doctor Jackson but he simply kept going. When someone suggested he cancel the afternoon events, he shook his head. "These people have made their arrangements to welcome me," he declared, "and so long as I am not on my back, I will gratify them."[84]

In his address at the Bunker Hill monument, President Jackson gave a short but intensely patriotic speech about the heroes who had fought and died at that spot to create a free and independent nation. Then, he went on to say: "And when to all these are added your moral, social, literary, and religious institutions—your happy equality of condition—your charitable establishments—your foundations for education—the general diffusion of knowledge—your industry and enterprise—and when we reflect that most of this is common to the New England states, you may well be proud of your native land, and our country may well be proud of New England."[85]

The cheers were deafening. Old Hickory, a master politician, had completely captivated his audience. His speech was reprinted all over New England.

The Grand Triumphal Tour pressed on. It moved to Lynn, Massachusetts, but by now Jackson could barely stand on his feet, and he was forced to take to his bed for several hours. After a short rest he struggled to his feet and rode on to Marblehead, a Democratic stronghold. Preparations for a "grand banquet" had been completed at Marblehead, but young Quincy decided that in view of the President's physical condition they should make all speed for Salem. Marblehead did not appreciate this discourtesy. Good Democrats all, they excused Jackson. But they warned Quincy not to show his face again in Marblehead.[86]

The drive to Salem produced some anxious moments. Quite clearly the President was getting weaker and weaker, and they thought he might faint. They rushed him to his hotel, tucked him in bed, and canceled all receptions. An elaborate procession had been planned, so Van Buren and Quincy rode in the presidential barouche in Jackson's place. Since it was getting dark no one was the wiser and the people cheered the carriage as it passed in the mistaken belief that they had seen the President. Quincy rode bolt upright; Van Buren bowed left and right and accepted the applause as his personal due.[87]

No one who had seen Jackson the night before as he slid into bed ever imagined that he could resume the tour the next day. But that is exactly what he did. "An exertion of the will of which only the exceptional man is capable," was the way Quincy explained it. And he hit it right on the mark. Jackson had long ago subjected his frail coil to a sovereign will, and it always responded to his command.[88]

On their way to Andover, Van Buren asked the President to relate what happened at the Battle of New Orleans. "It was, undoubtedly, the most interesting narrative I ever heard," admitted Quincy, so fascinating, in fact, that he failed to set down a single word of it in his journal. On only one point was his memory distinct. Jackson declared that the watchword "Booty and Beauty" had been given by General Pakenham himself.[89]

One of the things that Jackson and his nephew, Andrew J. Donelson, noted during their tour was the difference between New Englanders and southerners and westerners. What is different about New England, they both agreed, "is its order and habitual respect for those in authority."[90]

A principal stopover occurred at Lowell, the famed manufacturing town where man-made canals generated the waterpower to drive over 200,000 spindles. Of greater renown was its army of factory girls, who lived and worked in town under conditions that seemed utopian for the time. They worked in the mills, boarded in homelike dormitories, and were supervised by concerned and watchful guardians.

Jackson's arrival in Lowell produced a parade in his honor that "exceeded all anticipation."[91] It was about three o'clock in the afternoon when he arrived. The military escort consisted of a company of artillery, a company of riflemen, several companies of light infantry, and a procession of "young females" employed in the factories. It was quite a show. "The women and girls are crazy to see us," said Major Downing.[92] There were some five thousand of these young females, all under thirty and all dressed in snow-white dresses with sashes of different colors to designate their different manufacturing establishments. They were all hatless, their pretty faces "shining" up at Jackson as he passed. Each carried a parasol, most of which were green. They were massed four deep along the route and constituted a veritable *"mile of girls."* They waved the parasols at the President in graceful salute. Jackson was nearly beside himself with pleasure at the sight of these "self-respecting daughters of American yeomanry, who wrought so cheerfully with the machinery of the mills." When the President and his party arrived at the Merrimack Hotel they took a position on a platform and the whole procession of military and white-frocked young ladies passed in review before them.[93]

The townspeople of Lowell could not do enough to show their gratitude in having the President among them and their pride in their manufacturing establishments. The situation of the "young females" was repeatedly mentioned to the President. They were not the "oppressed, miserable, half starved females of an European manufacturing city, but well educated, well dressed females, perfectly independent of any control from the proprietors, at liberty . . . to leave it and seek any other employment that may produce more money." These were to be the "wives of virtuous, high-minded, independent citizens" and the mothers of future judges, legislators, and Presidents. "Does not the spectacle present, in a delightful aspect, the operation and effect of our truly republican institutions?"[94]

Jackson agreed totally, so much so that he asked to see a mill in operation, especially one that would demonstrate the "ingenuity of the machinery, and the immense power of the water-wheels." Although the mills had been closed down for the celebration of the President's arrival into town, at Jackson's request they were reopened.[95]

The operation of the mills fascinated the old man. He asked dozens of questions. How many people were employed in each mill? What was their average wage? How much cotton was "worked up" each day? How much cloth was turned out? The power loom especially attracted him, and to demonstrate its value one of the proprietors exhibited a piece of British cloth bought in 1813 for 85¢ a yard and then showed the President a piece of American cloth, recently produced and of superior quality, which sold for 14¢ per yard. "The president examined the fabrics attentively" and agreed that the American product was indeed superior. That its price was so significantly lower than the earlier British product truly amazed him.[96]

The President not only visited the mills but the print shops as well. Lowell took particular pride in these shops. And in their fire engines: the fire-fighting equipment represented the best in the country, and nothing less than a full demonstration for the President would do. Jackson stared with astonishment at the spectacle of the spraying water. The "immense power of the water wheels" attached to the equipment "was truly astonishing, covering the different buildings with water in a few minutes, by various pipes manned by the different engineers."[97]

Lowell dominated Jackson's thoughts long after he left the town. He spoke of nothing else during his ride to the state line. "What a country God has given us!" he kept repeating. "We have the best institutions in the world."

At the New Hampshire line, which they reached on June 27, young Quincy took his leave. Jackson was sorry to see him go, and the young man readily admitted that, despite his "Brahmin" upbringing, he had completely succumbed to this man of the people. "Come and see me at the White House," urged the President; "or, better still, at the Hermitage, if I live to return to it."[98]

The farewells over, the party headed immediately for Portsmouth, where the local Democrats planned to have an exclusive reception and keep the President all to themselves. But Jackson would have none of it. Such partisanship undermined the very purpose of the tour. He left the city as quickly as decency allowed and pushed on to Concord. By this time the President was out of sorts. He was exhausted by the travel and the endless receptions, parades, and celebrations. And he was offended by the mounting politicking he had to contend with at each stop along the way. His health began to worsen. Fatigue wore him down. He seemed to some in mortal danger.[99]

He reached his decision very suddenly. He would terminate the tour and return to Washington, and the reason given the public was his poor health. But John Quincy Adams had his doubts about the true reason. "Whether from real disease, crafty sickness, or the collisions of rival servility between the two parties in New Hampshire, is yet uncertain; perhaps a little of all three."[100] Perhaps.

The people in Maine, Vermont, and upstate New York were all deeply disappointed by the sudden cancellation of the tour, but they were reminded that he could no longer endure this steady drain on his strength. He "must hasten back to Washington," agreed Adams, "or he will be glorified into his grave."[101] Besides, he had already achieved the major objectives of his tour. And what with his poor health and the need to attend to the problem of the removal of the deposits, he should get back to the White House. So he turned around at Concord and returned through Lowell and Roxbury, avoiding Boston. He proceeded to Providence, where he caught a steamboat for New York, and from that point headed straight for Washington, arriving at ten o'clock in the morning of July 4. From Concord to Washington he traversed a distance of 474 miles in three days. Major Lewis was appalled at Jackson's appearance as he staggered into the White House. "I confess I was seriously alarmed at his feeble and emaciated appearance."[102]

The tour was a stunning political performance from start to finish. It accomplished everything Jackson desired. It stirred the patriotism of the nation, stimulated the notion of the Union as something perpetual, and raised the presidential office to new heights of popular esteem. For Jackson personally it strengthened his bond with the "ordinary citizens" of the nation. In effect he transformed formal presidential tours, such as Washington and Monroe had undertaken, into nationalistic, nonpartisan celebrations to quicken the nation's sense of well-being and remind it of its greatness and strength.

Not everyone applauded the Grand Triumphal Tour. The Richmond *Enquirer* worried about the attentions Jackson received. "They were more like the homage of subjects to their ruler, than of a free people towards their first magistrate." They resembled "the pomp of monarchy," and some bordered on "the vilest taste!" Still the *Enquirer* recognized that it was Jackson's extraordinary popularity and rapport with the people— rather than any defect in American institutions—that had produced these "attentions." "Amid all these superfluous, and many of them silly, descriptions, we cannot fail to perceive that the president has been received with a cordiality of kindness, and a sincerity of respect, which bespeak the great popularity of the man and his administration."[103]

"And so ends this magnificent tour," sniffed John Quincy Adams. It ended in personal triumph, in a strengthened Union, and in a happily exhausted but nearly prostrate President.

CHAPTER 6

Duane's Dismissal

WHEN PRESIDENT JACKSON STAGGERED into his room on the second floor of the White House he knew exactly what he must do to regain his strength and health. His chronic illnesses, extending back more than twenty years, had long trained him in the "arts" of self-medication. Frequently his nostrums were harmless. Sometimes they helped, but most times they only worsened his condition. He did believe in exercise and relaxation, both of which restored his energies. He also approved blood-letting, fasting, special diets, regular doses of calomel, the "matchless sanative," brandy, whiskey, and salt. He became so "expert" at medical treatment that he frequently suggested "cures" to his friends whenever they became ill. His good friend General John Coffee, for example, attended the second inauguration in Washington but on his way home fell ill with "dropsy in the lungs." Jackson immediately offered his "latest" medical prescription. "Permit me to suggest to you a dry diet," he wrote, "such as broiled beef on the coals, and ash cake bread, or hard biscuit, using as little liquids as possible. . . . If benefit is to result from it, & is worth the experiment—apply the flesh brush frequently, & freely, bathing your body in warm salt and water frequently, & your feet & legs in the same (warm) every evening, and rubing them with brandy or whisky, after they are well wiped—the spirits to be warm, and not wiped off. . . . Take as much exercise as you can, either on horseback, or in a carriage—and if any medicine is necessary, let it be calomel, after six hours, worked off with oil—no liquid but coffee used to give action to the medicine, & to work it off—salts are injureous to all dropsical habits. and calomel is the great cleanser of the blood."[1]

Because of his own "dropsical habits"—his feet and ankles sometimes

84

swelled to such a size that he could not stand without intense discomfort —"Doctor" Jackson took warm salt baths quite regularly. Indeed, as soon as he returned to the White House, he commenced a regular regimen of baths, exercise (mostly horseback riding), and calomel. He fasted a great deal as well, but that resulted more from his poor appetite than a planned diet.[2] His weight rarely exceeded 140 lbs. and sometimes fell below 130.

Fortunately for his mental health his mind was constantly diverted from his physical discomfort by the needs and concerns of his office. Upon his return to Washington several items awaited executive action, the most important of which was the question of the removal of the government's deposits from the "Golden vaults of the Mammoth Bank."[3]

Although Jackson had concluded that the deposits must be removed, he refrained from ordering Duane to execute the order. His reluctance was wrongly seen by Duane as a recognition of the right of the Treasury secretary to decide the question himself. Also, Duane foolishly assumed that any direction given the secretary on the matter must come from the Congress.[4] This was not Jackson's intent at all, but it was certainly one he unwittingly encouraged Duane to believe. Furthermore, Jackson did not wish to pull the government's funds out of the BUS in one sweeping executive action. Rather, as he explained to Duane, he preferred to withdraw the funds as the government needed them, until they were exhausted; meanwhile, new government revenues would be deposited in selected state banks.[5]

Soon after Jackson's return, Duane explained his opposition to removal in a detailed letter dated July 10. Although he did not approve renewing the Bank's charter, still he thought removal an act of vengeance and one "that might be regarded as extreme, if not utterly needless." Such an "arbitrary" act of replacing the BUS with state banks without the direction of Congress, he argued, would be unwise and improper.[6]

Obviously, Duane's behavior and attitude were distinctly at odds with the wishes of the President. And Duane knew it. Insisting that he, and he alone, was empowered to remove the deposits meant that sooner or later he was headed for a collision with the President. But he believed he was within his legal rights. The law creating the Treasury Department never called it an "executive" department. Also, the secretary was required to make his reports to Congress, not the President. Did that not suggest that the secretary had some special obligation to Congress, particularly since Congress controlled the purse strings? True, the President appointed the secretary, but the appointment needed the confirmation of the Senate. Although the President might dismiss the secretary, did he not have some obligation to obtain Senate consent to dismissal?

It was all somewhat vague. Under the circumstances, then, Duane felt he should stand his ground against any action that did not include congressional knowledge or consent. And if the President objected, so be it. Duane's pride and sense of independence had been severely damaged from the moment he took office and this was one way for him to recover his self-esteem. Although Jackson had tried to repair the damage he had needlessly inflicted, the secretary could not be mollified, as though he must prove his independence to the entire country.

Duane seemed oblivious to the fact that he was pitting his will against that of the President. He persisted because he believed it was his right. It never occurred to him that he was politicizing the issue to an extent that could only produce dangerous repercussions. Still, he stuck to his guns. He would not yield.

Jackson tried to be gentle. He acknowledged the Duane letter, noting with pleasure that the secretary concurred with him as to the impropriety of renewing the charter and the need for a substitute. And he also acknowledged that the secretary believed that Congress should decide on the substitute and that the substitution of state banks would be inexpedient. But, continued Jackson, you do not state what substitute you would advise the President to recommend to Congress. "The President therefore respectfully asks the Secretary of the Treasury to furnish him with his views upon that point, and to do him the favor to call on him on Monday morning to converse further upon the subject."[7]

On Monday, July 15, Duane presented himself before Old Hickory. As he walked into the room he noted his letter of July 10 lying on the President's desk. Jackson opened the conversation by remarking that he "feared" they did not understand one another.

"My object, sir," the General continued in as gentle a tone as he could command, "is to save the country, and it will be lost, if we permit the bank to exist. We must prepare a substitute, or our friends in congress will not know what to do."

Duane fidgeted. What really troubled him was the humiliation he had suffered at the very outset of his tenure. Within minutes he blurted out his anger over the visit of Reuben Whitney and how it had "mortified" him.

Jackson assured him that Whitney did not have his confidence. Duane responded that he was very pleased to hear it, and to prove it he took up his pen and struck out all references to Whitney in his July 10 letter.

Jackson smiled. He thought the worst was over. "Now we are friends," he said, "and should be so. If we differ in opinion, what of it? it is but opinion after all—and I like you the better for telling me frankly what you think."[8]

The remainder of their conversation was most cordial. Duane emphasized the fact that there was some doubt as to whether the state banks would agree to accept the government's funds out of fear of retaliation by Biddle. Jackson promised to look into it. They parted amicably.

What the President did immediately was to call in Amos Kendall and discuss the problem of possible retaliation. "They," said Jackson, meaning Duane and McLane, "tell me the State banks, through fear of the

United States Bank, which can crush them at will, cannot be induced to take the public deposits and do the business of the government."

Kendall's face twisted with sly amusement.

"Send me to ask them," he said, "and I will settle that argument."

"You shall go," declared the President.[9]

Subsequent meetings between Jackson and Duane were held on July 19 and 20. During their conversations, the President returned to the need for a substitute system of providing for the government's funds. "My wish is to meet Congress, with a declaration," he told Duane, "that we have a safe substitute, for the U.S. Bank. How can we do this, without inquiry. I desire Mr. Kendall to make that inquiry. . . . Information ought to be got even for congress; and it is through you, it should be collected. Now, do you understand me?"[10]

Once again an important decision had been made, after which the Treasury secretary was summoned before the President and informed of it. Considering Duane's low tolerance for such procedures, Jackson was creating needless trouble for himself.

When the President ended his statement the secretary just stared at him for a moment and then gestured comprehension and agreed on Kendall as the agent for the mission. With that, Jackson directed Duane to prepare a set of instructions for the agent.

But instead of obeying the order, the secretary wrote out a vague statement inviting the opinions of the state banks on the various financial possibilities open to the government. After reading what Duane had written, Kendall went immediately to Jackson and registered his complaint. He said he could not go under these instructions and if he did he would "return loaded with documents full of party bias, and virtually in opposition to the measure the President wished to adopt."

Jackson sighed. Then his head snapped upward. "Take the paper and modify it to suit your own views," he said.[11]

So Kendall took off on his trip, "virtually self-instructed." And it added one more incident to a growing catalog that isolated Duane and made him more recalcitrant and obstinate.[12]

Before Kendall left Washington, Jackson decided to prepare his own memorandum of instructions for his agent. In it, he said: "You will not consider yourself precluded by these instructions from making any other propositions to the said Banks for the purpose of ascertaining on what terms they will undertake the service refered to, and you are at liberty to receive any propositions from them which they may think proper to offer." That sentence alone gave Kendall very wide latitude. Jackson also advised Kendall to see the government directors of the BUS since they had reported on the misuse of public funds by the Bank. Then he rambled on about why the deposits should be removed.[13]

Kendall knew precisely what was expected of him. Unlike Duane, he completely agreed with the President's position and intended action.

"While I look upon the corrupt establishment [BUS] with detestation and loathing," he wrote to Jackson, "I cannot but feel some degree of exultation in seeing it compelled so soon to acknowledge its own dishonesty and confirm the aggravated charges of duplicity and fraud on the people which have been made against it."[14] Obviously, long before Kendall began his tour, the fate of the Bank and the future disposition of the deposits had been fairly well decided.

Kendall left Washington on July 28 and went immediately to Baltimore, where he stayed for a week.[15] Then he moved to Philadelphia, and on August 11 set out for New York, where he remained for four days before going on to Boston. Kendall claimed that he had two primary objectives in making the trip: first, to remove from Jackson's mind the doubt about state banks' being afraid or unwilling to become bankers for the government; and second, to ascertain the terms on which the banks would become the government's fiscal agents.[16] Actually he had a third purpose, and that was to find bankers who could qualify as loyal Jacksonians. To become one of the "selected banks"—or "pet" banks, as the opposition came to call them—it was essential that a prospective pet enjoy "friendly" relations with Democrats. Kendall was quite explicit on this point. In a letter to John M. Niles of Hartford, Connecticut, asking his views about banks to be approached in the New England area, he said: "With equal capital and character, those which are in hand politically friendly will be preferred; but if there are none such then we must take those which are in the control of opposition men whose feelings are liberal."[17] The second half of this sentence accounts for the later choice of some non-Jacksonian banks.

Kendall proved to be a most enthusiastic and zealous agent—exactly what Jackson wanted. He told Blair, just as he was about to leave for Boston, that four banks in Baltimore, another four in Philadelphia, and seven in New York had responded favorably to his invitation to assume the government's business. "We shall have a firm, zealous party," he enthused, "and shall have put down the Bank forever."[18]

Just before he left New York he was surprised to find at the breakfast table of his hotel two high-ranking officers of the Jackson administration: Louis McLane and Martin Van Buren. They were huddled together in deep conversation and when they spotted Kendall invited him to join them after breakfast. It soon developed what they were about. They informed Kendall that although they were both anxious to see a state banking system in operation as soon as possible, they did feel that the process of removal ought to be delayed until January 1, 1834. Such a postponement, they argued, would show proper respect for Congress. Then "the arrangement and reasons" for removal could be laid before Congress at the commencement of the new session. This would please the legislators and unite Jackson's friends behind his fiscal measures, they said.[19]

Apparently McLane talked Van Buren into going along with the idea. Even so, it appealed to the Magician because it had caution written all over it.

Kendall was wary of the suggestion. At bottom he opposed it. But he could ill afford to say so at the time because it might initiate a rift within the administration. For the sake of maintaining "union and harmony," therefore, Kendall agreed to write to the President in favor of the idea, provided the two men agreed to use their influence in Congress to win acceptance of the administration's decision to remove the deposits. He also felt that Duane should be enlisted in lobbying the Congress.[20]

That very evening Kendall wrote to Jackson and outlined the proposal. He told the President that if assurances of support could be given, such as he proposed to McLane and Van Buren, then "it may be better, for the purpose of avoiding other difficulties, to take the step suggested." By uniting the entire cabinet in favor of removal and coalescing their friends in Congress, the way would be cleared for an easy transition from the BUS to the state banks.[21]

Before this letter was written informing the President of the breakfast conference, Jackson had left Washington to take a short vacation at the Rip Raps in Virginia "to enjoy the fine sea breese and salt water bath" and thereby speed his recuperation from the debilitating effects of his tour that still afflicted him.[22] Late in July, he gathered his household together—his son, daughter, and granddaughter, Ralph Earl, Emily Donelson and her children—together with a few confidants, such as Frank Blair, and headed for his summer retreat. The party stayed at the Hygeia Hotel. Although his health was precarious and his feet and ankles badly swollen, he seemed in good spirits. His mind was constantly preoccupied with removal, but he exuded a sense of purpose and determination. He seemed quite sure of himself.[23]

Before leaving Washington the President had written to Van Buren and asked him once again for his advice. He did not wish advice about the removal itself, he wrote. That was decided; that was finished. What he needed was advice about when to do it. "I want your ideas *fully* on this point, as I am aware that there will be a diversity of opinion in the cabinet, and perhaps a majority against removing the deposits before the meeting of Congress."[24]

Van Buren stalled when he got this letter. Of course he answered it immediately, but he asked for an extension of time. "I want to see our friend Mr Wright before I answer your letter about the Deposits, but will do so in season."[25] The response slightly annoyed Jackson, but he had long since grown accustomed to Van Buren's wariness. Since he could expect to get an honest reaction from Van Buren—when the Magician finally got around to writing it—the President did not complain at this time.

As always, Van Buren worried about his presidential candidacy. Of course he must have Jackson's support—that above all—but he also needed a united party, and he was afraid to do anything that might jeopardize Democratic unity. The south had already begun to stir against many of the President's policies. To placate southerners and hold their support for the future, Van Buren hoped that McLane's proposal about delaying removal until January 1 might show respect and goodwill.[26]

There was another consideration that especially troubled him. If he came out in favor of immediate removal he could be accused of acting on behalf of New York financiers. Silas Wright spelled out the problem in a letter to Azariah C. Flagg, the Regency's financial brains. "I have recd. a summons from the magician to meet him . . . preparatory to his writing to the President about the Bank, which I suppose of course means about the deposits. I confess to you that that is one of the questions I am afraid of, and my fear wholly arises from the apprehension that some cursed Wall Street operation will be developed as having taken place in anticipation of the action . . . of the Government." You remember, he continued, I told you of a man in Washington who argued for "instantaneous" removal and gave as the reason "that he knew *friends of ours* in Wall Street" could make a financial killing. "From all such 'friends of ours', speculators upon the actions of government and upon its legislation, Good Lord deliver us!"[27]

The danger of removal being seen as a ploy to shift the financial capital of the country from Chestnut Street in Philadelphia, where the main headquarters of the BUS was located, to Wall Street in New York City was not lost on Van Buren or his Regency. That was one more reason for caution.[28]

In the meantime, Kendall's report on the McLane–Van Buren breakfast conference reached Jackson at the Rip Raps. But it only confirmed the President's mounting concern that his Vice President was not as firmly in place as he should be. So he wrote again to the Magician. Your behavior in holding back on removal until January 1 might injure "your popularity," the President slyly wrote. "It is already hinted that you are opposed to the removal of the Deposits, and of course privately a friend of the Bank. *This must be removed or it will do us both much harm.*"[29] So concerned was Jackson over Van Buren's possible alienation from the true faith that he urged Frank Blair to write the Vice President and add his words of admonition.

Blair was appalled at the idea of a postponement until January 1 and rightly blamed McLane as the instigator. "The fact is," he lectured Van Buren in his severest editorial tone, "disguise it as you may, Mr. McLane cannot be true to his own principles and to those of the President. He knows that the Bank power is the last hope of Federalism and he is fighting for it." Understand one thing: "The connection between the Bank & the Govt" must be severed once and for all—and the sooner the better.[30]

If McLane and Duane and Van Buren think they can "operate upon the President" to change his mind and delay the removal, they are sadly mistaken, said Reuben Whitney to Frank Blair. The decision to go ahead is absolute.[31]

It was during this sojourn at the Rip Raps that Jackson received the melancholy news of the death of his oldest and dearest friend—"my favorite friend," he called him—General John Coffee. Curiously, he was not staggered by the news, although he later told Andrew Jackson Hutchings that the "sudden shock" was "so unexpected" that "our philosophy fled & we were unmanned." But when he wrote the Coffee family to extend his condolences he seemed very philosophical about death. "He is gone from us, and we cannot recall him. we must follow him . . . and it becomes our duty to prepare for this event." It is religion alone, he said, "that can give peace to us here, and happiness beyond the grave." Only religion can support us in our declining years. All else is "vanity and vexation of spirit." On his dying bed, Coffee had expressed regret that he had not joined the church and he admonished his family not to follow his example. This "admonition," Jackson added in his letter to the family, "ought to be cherished by you all, and practiced upon." Apparently, Coffee had also asked for Jackson's prayers for his wife and children, and Old Hickory acknowledged that "they will be constantly offered up at the throne of grace for you all." Rely on "our dear Savior," he wrote; He will be father to the fatherless and husband to the widow. Trust in the mercy and goodness of Christ, and "always be ready to say with heartfelt resignation, 'may the Lord's will be done.' "[32]

These words had great meaning for Jackson. They were not simply pious utterances to console a grieving family. Intensely religious, a man who prayed often and attended church services on Sunday regularly, the President had long since resigned himself to "the Lord's will." Whatever happened, whether good or bad, must be accepted with resignation and understanding. Only through submission could one find peace in this world and eternal happiness in the next.[33]

Jackson also told the grieving family that had he known the extent of Coffee's illness he would have abandoned his northern tour and hurried to Alabama to offer him "all the comfort in my power." He promised to come to Alabama in the spring if his health permitted and pray "over his silent grave."[34]

Jackson remained at the Rip Raps until August 22, a stay of twenty-six days. Each day he went to "a little hut on the highest point of the Rocks looking out to the Ocean," and there with Blair he would go through his mail and talk over matters of state. It was here, said Blair, that Biddle tried to cannonade the "Old Chief" from every quarter of the Union.[35]

When the President departed the Rip Raps[36] there had been no response from Van Buren about removal. Not until September 4, after the Vice President had arrived at Albany and had heard from Silas Wright, did he finally transmit his opinion.[37] Wright had informed him that some of their friends approved immediate removal but that many others—including himself—preferred to wait until Congress reconvened in December. Van Buren therefore decided to adopt Wright's position. He wrote to the President and advised him to wait until January 1. Although he approved the idea of removal and the arrangements with state banks to negotiate the government's fiscal business, he thought there were valuable advantages to be gained by waiting until the first of next year. "But I am not so strenuous" on this condition, he concluded his letter, "as to feel, that I should be unable to sustain" immediate removal, "if, with a nearer and fuller view of the subject, you should find its adoption highly expedient."[38]

Jackson rejected Van Buren's recommendation. All the reports submitted by the Bank directors, all the reports from Kendall, and all the advice from Taney and Blair only convinced him that his instinct for immediate removal was sound.[39] Unless the deposits were removed, he argued, the Bank would bide its time, gird itself for a later battle, and then reactivate its drive for recharter. "Therefore to prolong the deposits until after the meeting of Congress would be to do the very act [the BUS] wishes," he wrote back to Van Buren, "that is, to have it in its power to distress the community, destroy the state Banks, and if possible to corrupt congress and obtain two thirds, to recharter the Bank."[40]

From the very beginning of his war against the Bank, Jackson understood his true object and goal. The nation was cursed with a Bank whose "corrupting influences" fastened "monopoly and aristocracy on the constitution" and made the government "an engine of oppression to the people instead of the agent of their will." Only the annihilation of the hydra could "restore to our institutions their primitive simplicity and purity." Only through purity and simplicity could freedom be preserved and republicanism fostered. Whenever the government identifies itself with "privileged joint stock Companies," like a national bank, or gets mixed up with the "log rolling system of Internal Improvements, Squandering the taxes raised on the whole people, in benefitting particular classes and maintaining a personal influence by partial legislation in congress," then corruption abounds, republicanism vanishes, and freedom is lost.[41]

Freedom! By which he meant "equality among the people in the rights conferred by the Government." This was something virtually unknown outside the United States. At the beginning of the nineteenth century "the great radical principle of freedom," as Jackson put it, was regarded in Europe as a dangerous and chimerical concept. Foreigners stood "waiting and watching" to see if Americans would fail with their experiment in liberty. To preserve freedom, therefore, was Jackson's prime responsibility. For if he failed, he said, then grasping individuals would play upon the "selfish, interested classes to aid in promoting an ambition

. . . to multiply the advantages and increase the strength of the predatory portion of the community." Then equality is gone and with it the freedom of the American people. "My great hope . . . arises from the prospect of being able to restore the equilibrium of the Government; equality in the condition of the people, so far as it depends on legislation."[42]

To restore equality he must quickly kill the Bank by removing the deposits. And with the restoration of equality the experiment in freedom would continue. The purity of American institutions would be reestablished and democracy would advance.[43]

A quiet certitude settled over Jackson during the waning days of the summer. He knew his duty, and he knew he retained public confidence. "Is it possible that your friends hesitate, and are overawed by the power of the Bank," he sarcastically wrote to Van Buren. "It cannot overawe me. I trust in my God and the virtue of the people."[44]

Van Buren hastily reassured Jackson that he held no firm conviction against immediate removal and that he was willing to abide by the President's wishes in the matter. He really had no choice. But he also understood the danger of any close association with the decision to begin removal immediately and so he informed the President that he would not return to Washington right away (as he once promised) but would tour New York with Washington Irving. "You know," he said, "that the game of the opposition is [to attribute] . . . the removal of the Deposits to the solicitations of myself, and a monied junto in N York, and as it is not your habit to play into the enemies hands you will not I know request me to come down [to Washington] unless there is some adequate inducement for my so doing."[45]

Jackson waved him off on his tour. Since the Magician could offer no real support, the President let him go. On this issue Van Buren no longer exercised any influence.

What Jackson planned to do, as it turned out, was to initiate removal immediately and then give "a full expose of the reasons that has induced it, and let, thro the Globe, be made unofficially, a statement of the causes and the facts that has induced it." This way he would "prepare the minds of the people for a full and official exposure, give strength to our friends, protect the State Banks, from oppression, and some from destruction, give them strength by which they can increase their loans to the commercial world as well as to the community at large."[46]

By law, actual removal belonged to the Treasury secretary, not the President of the United States. It was up to him to issue the order and then notify Congress of his action. Whether the secretary was obliged to follow the directions of Congress or the President when they conflicted, particularly on a fiscal matter over which Congress exercised control, had never been tested. No one seemed certain, although many argued that the secretary must obey Congress. Yet here was the President deciding the matter for the secretary as though the responsibility was his alone. A possible collision between the two men seemed unlikely, however, since Duane had promised Jackson during the summer that if he could not remove the deposits when directed to do so, he would resign his office.[47]

At this point Amos Kendall returned to Washington from his mission and immediately submitted his report to Duane. He glowed with excitement over his success in finding seven banks who were prepared to serve as depositories for public funds on the government's terms. Considering the likelihood and danger of Biddle's retaliating against any institution cooperating with Kendall, this initial expedition was reasonably successful. The daring seven included the Union Bank of Maryland in Baltimore, Thomas Ellicott, president; the Girard Bank of Philadelphia, James Schott, president; the Mechanics Bank of New York, John Fleming, president; the Manhattan Company of New York, Robert White, president; the Bank of America in New York, George Newbold, president; the Merchant Bank of Boston, Mark Healey, president; and the Commonwealth Bank of Boston, John K. Simpson, president.[48]

Kendall's report, along with the correspondence involved in the mission, was forwarded to the President by the secretary of the treasury. It was done pro forma, but privately Duane believed that "the mission of the agent was abortive, in all particulars." The banks most ready to become depositories, he said, showed the least ability "to pay their own responsibilities in coin." And yet, "it was into this chaos," he later argued, that he was being asked "to plunge the fiscal concerns of the country, at a moment when they were conducted, by the legitimate agent, with the utmost simplicity, safety and despatch."[49]

Feeling this way and convinced that his independence and stature as a member of the administration had been totally compromised, Duane decided that he would not remove the deposits. Nor would he resign. He knew his "rights." Since Congress had already declared its satisfaction with the BUS as the depository for government funds, and since the power of removal rested solely with him, he felt he must do what he thought proper for the good of the country. And that meant leaving the deposits right where they were.

Louis McLane—his natural ally in the cabinet if he had one—spoke to him early in September and asked him to consider removal after Congress reconvened. Again Duane refused. Unless he could convince himself that the deposits were unsafe with the BUS or he was ordered by Congress to remove them, he would not take action. He was beginning to dig in his heels. A streak of stubbornness was clearly visible.[50]

On Tuesday, September 10, Jackson called his cabinet together—it was his usual day for cabinet meetings—and all but the postmaster general, William T. Barry, attended. Once the members took their places, Jackson began to speak.

"Gentleman," he said, "I have got here the report of the agent on the deposite question, and I want to call your attention to it. . . . This is an important business. . . . How shall we answer to God, our country or ourselves, if we permit the public money to be . . . used to corrupt the people? Observe, I do not want immediate action, but I desire a day to be fixed. . . . I want harmony in my cabinet. . . . I want to go unitedly in this solemn duty." He said that he did not wish to "touch a dollar of the money" that was already in the BUS, but he did want new revenues to be put in a safe place. Kendall's report, he added, showed the readiness of a number of banks to accept the public money "and their ability and safety as substitutes for the present agent."[51]

Jackson paused a moment as he looked from one cabinet officer to the next. "Why, then, should we hesitate?" he asked. "Why not proceed, I say, as the country expects us to do? Here are the papers. When you have read them, let us come to an understanding."

Duane indicated his wish to speak. Jackson recognized him. The secretary thanked him and then said that he wished the other members to know that not until after he had assumed office did he discover that a removal of the deposits was contemplated without first hearing from Congress. That was all he wished to say.[52]

Jackson's brow wrinkled slightly but he said nothing. Then he distributed Kendall's report and the meeting broke up.

For the next several days the President consulted with each member of the cabinet individually. Only "Taney has been firm," Jackson said, "others wavering and major Barry not returned."[53] He told them quietly but definitely that he had made his decision and that it could not be altered: the deposits would be removed—immediately. He wanted a public announcement prepared with a date set for the start of removal. He also wanted the directors of the BUS to be told that any attempt to oppress the selected state (pet) banks or the community—any move against them whatsoever—and "the whole of the deposits" of the BUS would be removed forthwith. Otherwise the government would slowly withdraw its deposits as need dictated; new money, of course, would go into the pets.[54]

Because Jackson's mind was made up and because his Treasury secretary gave every indication of resisting removal, the President believed that Duane would resign. Certainly that was Jackson's wish. "If Mr. Duane will not agree to carry into effect these conclusions and remain, the sooner he withdraws the better—it is known what my determination is, and if he cannot act with me, on that determination, he ought to withdraw."[55]

In his ongoing discussions with the President, Duane complained of the abuse that had broken out against him in the Democratic press. This was the typical treatment Democrats suffered (especially from Blair) when they stepped out of line or took issue with the President. The "purity of his motives," Duane wailed, had been called into question by "persons" in the President's confidence. Jackson tried to reassure him. "It is impossible to describe the earnestness of the President's professions, in reply," Duane reported. He said he had the utmost confidence in his secretary and that he would prove it by offering the highest appointment then at his disposal once Duane stepped down as department head. What he had in mind was the appointment as minister to Russia. James Buchanan, who had been serving in that post since 1831, was returning in the fall and the President was quite prepared to offer it to Duane. By offering him this mission, the President hoped to make the transition and the decision as easy as possible for the Treasury secretary.[56]

But Duane would have none of it. He wanted no other office and he had no intention of resigning. He came away from his interviews, however, leaving the impression that he would stick to his promise to resign. And he knew this was what the President thought.[57]

It is really extraordinary how much latitude Jackson allowed his cabinet members in formulating opinions on issues facing his administration. Rather than bully them into accepting his own view, he gave them enormous leeway. He did expect them to support the administration's policy once he had formulated and publicized it, but until that time he permitted contrary opinions and disagreements. The Duane situation was a case in point. Moreover, the secretary of state, Louis McLane, and the secretary of war, Lewis Cass, also disapproved immediate removal. As did the Vice President. All this Jackson accepted without fuss. He encouraged his officers to think independently. He wanted them to make up their own minds and tell him honestly what they thought.

The following Tuesday, September 17, the cabinet reconvened and the President opened the meeting by expressing his hope that the members had thought carefully about the removal issue and were prepared to share their opinions with him and the others. Then, he turned to each member and asked for his judgment, starting with the secretary of state.

McLane came right to the point. Volatile and opinionated, he spoke in "an emphatic and lucid manner," reciting all the objections to immediate removal, about how the administration ought to wait for Congress, the constitutional difficulties that might be raised, the adverse effect on the country's finances, and the political dangers involved. It was a strong argument. Duane came next, and he simply felt that the matter should be left to Congress to decide. He had no faith in state banks, he said, and feared "serious evils" to the public if they plunged ahead as the President wished. Cass also opposed immediate removal and declared that it should be left to the secretary of the treasury. Woodbury waffled. He really opposed the measure but would support the President. So ambiguous were his words that Jackson regarded his remarks as favorable. Only Taney spoke unhesitatingly and enthusiastically for immediate removal. He had always favored such a step, "and was now more than ever for it." Barry was not present but later submitted a written opinion through Donelson and called for "prompt action." He told Jackson that he was "astonished at the course Mr. D. has taken."[58]

When all had spoken the President closed the meeting abruptly. "Gentlemen," he said, "I desire to meet you to-morrow, and will then make known my own views."[59]

His decision had long since been made. He would have allowed the cabinet to alter that decision only if they could convince him that the public good necessitated another course of action. But they had failed. What remained now was the presentation of the reasons for his decision. All summer long he had been working on them with Blair at the Rip Raps. Afterward he dictated a long statement cataloging his complaints. This working paper then went to Kendall for revision and later to Taney so it could be "given a calm judicial aspect, instead of that of a combative Bulletin." Jackson kept careful watch on all the changes to this paper and at one point instructed Kendall to examine the question of the constitutional right of Congress to create corporations and to cite "the impolicy & inexpediency of the measure, as well as its corrupting influence on the morales of the nation, and the absurdity of the power to create corporations."[60]

Taney was the last person to work on the paper. Then, on the night of September 17, following the cabinet meeting, he informed the President that he agreed with him on assigning an exact date for the change of the deposits to the state banks. "I think all the necessary arrangements can be made by the first of October." He had discussed it with Kendall and Thomas Ellicott, president of the pet bank in Baltimore, and they concurred that removal could be safely and expeditiously accomplished. "I am fully prepared to go with you firmly through this business, & to meet all its consequences."[61]

Jackson beamed. It was exactly what he wanted to hear. On the back of Taney's note he wrote: "To be filed with my private papers, As evidence of his virtue, energy & werth." He was also very pleased with the report that he would present to the cabinet the following day, and especially the legal arguments Taney had prepared for him on the "right & duty" of the President to order the Treasury secretary to remove the deposits. "Mr. Taney is a sterling man," Jackson told Van Buren. Such men as Taney and Kendall, he added, "are highly valuable to any cause, neither can be frightened, or bought." It was at this moment—if not earlier—that Jackson decided to replace Duane with Taney. "If Mr. Duane retires, I will have the able and hearty aid of Mr. Taney who is not afraid of the senate, or to meet with me, the question boldly."[62]

As scheduled, Jackson met again with his cabinet on September 18. He directed Major Donelson to read the paper that had been prepared since mid-July. It was a long statement, closely reasoned. It cataloged all of Jackson's complaints, conceits, and prejudices.

It began with a trumpeting declaration of strong presidential power: The voice of the people, heard throughout the land by virtue of the recent presidential election, commanded the extirpation of corruption and all other "sinister influences" which have seeped into the government. "The

President has felt it his duty," therefore, "to exert the power with which the confidence of his countrymen has clothed him." The Bank of the United States, from the moment of its inception, has steadily gained power and has become in itself a government against which the people can no longer contend. It has undermined republican ideals and promoted "aristocratical tendencies" within our institutions. "Too much vigilance and self denial cannot be exercised to restrain the sinister aspirations of wealth, and to check the growth of an authority so unfriendly to liberal Government and the just rights of the people." The "mass of people," Jackson went on, "have more to fear from combinations of the wealthy and professional classes—from an aristocracy which thro' the influence of riches and talents, insidiously employed, sometimes succeeds in preventing political institutions, however well adjusted, from securing the freedom of the citizen, and in establishing the most odious and oppressive Government under the forms of a free institution."[63]

It was a powerful statement and demonstrated all the skills of Taney, Blair, and Kendall—to say nothing of Jackson's. It then proceeded to discuss the constitutional question, as the President had directed, and listed the extraordinary privileges the Bank enjoyed. Jackson even referred to Biddle's handling of the French spoliation claims.

The question of the spoliation claims arose when a treaty was signed with France in 1831 by which the French agreed to pay 25 million francs in six annual installments for American claims against them arising during the Napoleonic Wars. The Bank attempted to obtain payment, even though the "money . . . was not wanted by the Government," and when the French failed to pay, Biddle charged the United States for this default, including principal, interest, cost of protest, reexchange, and damages at 15 percent. "The want of punctuality in the French Government," snorted Jackson, results in a penalty against the United States! "This is the fidelity of the Institution. . . . This is the gratitude with which the Government is requited."[64]

The incident of the 3 percents was also cited. Not only was the transaction improper and an explicit violation of the Bank's charter, but it deliberately thwarted the government's desire to pay off the national debt. The payment of the debt was set back nearly a year, fussed Jackson, because of Biddle's action. "If . . . the Bank can already venture to bring in the great Bankers of Europe as its allies in controlling the affairs of this Republic, it appears to the President that a new era may possibly arise in the progress of a few years in which the capitalist abroad may have an influence over the destinies of this country akin to that exercised by them in the States beyond the Atlantic."

Jackson closed the paper by stating that a continuation of the relationship between the government and the BUS "would tend to support its dangerous influence and abuses" and give to the Bank a strength "to defeat the will of the people and to secure a renewal of its Charter and a perpetuation of its power in the Government." Such a result, he concluded, is *"inconsistent with the duration of the happiness and liberties of the people."*[65]

When Donelson finished his reading, very little, if anything, was said. There was an almost inaudible shuffling sound as the members stirred in their seats. But the meeting was clearly over and after a moment or so they rose from their places and quietly left the room. Jackson was deeply disappointed in their obviously negative reaction. Duane hung back and approached the President. He asked if he might take and read the paper just read. Jackson gestured to Donelson to hand it over. Then Duane asked point-blank whether he was being directed to remove the deposits. Jackson replied affirmatively. But, he added, they should be removed on his, the President's, authority. He wanted that perfectly understood. This decision and this action were the responsibility of the President of the United States, no one else's. Then, with "great emphasis," he exclaimed that if Duane "would stand by him it would be the happiest day of his life."[66]

Duane withdrew, filled with doubts about his course of action. He had to consider, he later recorded, not merely whether he should obey the President and remove the deposits, but whether he should resign. "I was sensible that I had erred in giving any assurance on the latter point," he admitted. But what value is a man's promise when the good of the country was at stake. "Subsequent occurrences," he finally decided, had absolved him from his promise.[67]

As Jackson left the room his thoughts dwelt on the unenthusiastic response his cabinet had demonstrated. Not that it dissuaded him in the least. He knew his duty and he was determined to perform it. He ran into William B. Lewis in the corridor outside the cabinet room and unburdened himself. Lewis gave him no solace.

"It would seem to me," said Lewis, "that it would be much better to wait until Congress met, and let them legislate upon the subject." Unless, of course, Jackson thought the public funds in danger by remaining in the BUS.

"I do think so," Old Hickory responded. "Besides, I have no confidence in Congress."

"But, General," Lewis continued, "Mr. Duane would be assuming a very heavy responsibility in removing the public moneys from the custody of the bank, in the face of a resolution passed by the House of Representatives at its last session, by a very large majority, perhaps two-thirds, declaring them, in its opinion, safe."

"But," argued the President, "I don't want him to assume the responsibility. Have I not said that I would take the responsibility?"

Lewis agreed but wondered whether he could in fact assume that responsibility since the law quite clearly placed it with the secretary of the treasury.

Then Lewis asked his friend what he would do in the event that Congress, after it reconvened, passed a joint resolution directing the secretary to restore the deposits to the BUS.

"Why," he thundered, "I would veto it."

But suppose it was overridden—which might happen under the circumstances.

"Under such circumstances," Jackson declared, elevating himself to his full height and assuming a strong and dignified air as he spoke, "then, sir, I would resign the presidency and return to the Hermitage!"[68]

Jackson strode to his room to think over his intended course of action. The next morning he sent a messenger to learn whether Duane had come to a decision. But the secretary needed more time and said he would give his answer on September 21.

That was not good enough. Jackson sent Donelson to Duane to tell him that a public announcement of the decision would appear in the *Globe* the next day. Duane protested, but he was assured that the President meant every word. The announcement would appear, with or without the secretary's consent.[69]

And the very next day, Friday, September 20, the following notice appeared in the Washington *Globe:*

> We are authorized to state that the deposites of the public money will be changed, from the bank of the U.S. to the state banks, as soon as necessary arrangements can be made for that purpose . . . in time to make the change by the 1st of October, and perhaps sooner, if circumstances should render an earlier action necessary on the part of the government.

Duane was horror-struck when he read the statement. The humiliation that had begun on the first day of his tenure now culminated in this deliberate act of emasculation. At that moment Duane decided his course of action. He would refuse to obey the President's order, and he would not resign. He scratched out a statement and took it to Jackson.

"What is it?" asked the President as he glanced at the paper.

"It respectfully and finally makes known my decision," said Duane, "not to remove the deposites, or resign."

A flood of anger gripped the General. "Then you do not mean, that we shall part as friends," he said quietly.

"I must protect myself," came the response.

"But you said you would retire, if we could not finally agree."

"I indiscreetly said so, sir; but I am now compelled to take this course."

The words struck Jackson with stunning force. He could not believe them. That a man would violate a promise was inconceivable to Jackson, except a man without decency, without character, without honor.

Yet Jackson spoke quietly to his secretary. He had no wish to quarrel with him, much less dismiss him. They continued arguing but neither heard the other.

"We differ only about time," said Duane at one point, "—you are for acting now, I am for waiting for congress."

Jackson sighed. "How often have I told you, that congress cannot act until the deposites are removed."

"I barely desired a delay of about ten weeks," Duane protested, that was all.

"Not a day—" snapped the President, "not an hour."[70]

Since the secretary would not obey him and would not resign, Jackson had only one recourse: dismissal. But that opened up a problem that all previous Presidents had deftly avoided, namely, the right of a President to dismiss a member of the executive branch whose appointment had been confirmed by the Senate. Since Congress created all cabinet positions and since appointment to them required confirmation, did that not suggest that dismissal also involved legislative concurrence? Some thought so. It seemed especially true of the Treasury secretary because of his handling of public funds, which Congress exclusively controlled. But no one had ever tested the question. No previous President had ever dismissed a cabinet officer. They simply got an offender to resign. In that way they avoided the constitutional question of the extent of the President's removal power.

Jackson was the first President to hit the problem head on. He believed that all officials of the executive office fell totally and completely under his authority. They were to obey *him*, not the Congress. Here again Jackson established a new dimension of presidential power. He assumed total authority to remove all cabinet officers without notifying Congress, much less obtaining its consent. Today the power seems obvious. Not so in the early nineteenth century—not until Jackson decided it once and for all.

This was another example of the small but important actions Jackson took that added to the power of the presidential office. His success in undermining the equal but separate doctrine of the Founding Fathers and tilting power more toward the executive was the result of the changes that had taken place in the American system of government and American society since the beginning of the century. An expanding economy had produced a rising democracy and, as a consequence, the American electorate demanded a greater say in the operation of the government. Since Jackson had become their spokesman and symbol, they were quite prepared to accept him as their representative at the seat of government. What was happening, therefore, was something that everyone sensed and accepted, even if they could not describe or define it, namely, the slow, continuing evolution of the nation from a republic into a democracy. Jackson by his conduct as President and his relations to the American people was asserting his role as the tribune of the people. And the electorate genuinely saw him as their representative. Their will was now being exercised through him, not through the legislature as was true in

the past. The government had always been based on consent, right from
the beginning of the American experiment, but consent was indirectly
given through the legislature. Now, under Jackson, it was being expressed through the executive and in a very direct manner.

Contemporaries saw what was happening, and many expressed their
horror at the possibility of the nation converting to democracy. Some
resisted it, others warned of the consequences. The Washington *National
Intelligencer,* an antiadministration paper, regularly sounded the alarm
and predicted the rise of tyranny. "The true power of this government,"
preached one editorial, *"ought* to be to lie in the Congress of the United
States. . . . It was never contemplated that its deliberately expressed
opinions should be lightly disregarded—its well considered acts repeatedly rejected—and its legal authority overtopped by another and differently constituted power." But that is exactly what Jackson is accomplish-
ing, said the newspaper, and he claims to be doing it in the name of the
people. "Congress is the *democratic* branch of the government," the journal insisted, not the executive. "If power is safe anywhere in a Republic
it is safe with the representatives."[71]

Obviously much of the alteration of the American political system was
owing to Jackson himself. He was an aggressive, forceful, and dynamic
leader, accustomed to command, always prepared to expand his role to
achieve the goals he envisioned for the nation. He was the right man at
the most propitious moment in the ongoing development of American
democracy.

Not for a moment did Jackson doubt his authority to remove Duane if
he refused to go quietly. When his interview with Duane ended in a
stalemate he did not immediately discharge the secretary. He did not act
precipitously. He gave Duane another day or two to assess his situation
and determine how he wished to proceed. Of course he returned the
paper the secretary had left with him with a note that it was something
"I cannot receive." This only encouraged Duane to respond and attempt
once again to convince the President of his "rights." In an outwardly
courteous but provocative note he informed the President that Jackson
must dismiss him before he would leave the office. On September 23
Jackson obliged. In a short, curt letter he notified Duane that "your
further services as Secretary of the Treasury are no longer required." To
Van Buren, the President added, "I surely caught a tartar in disguise, but
I have got rid of him."[72]

"As the President is responsible for the manner in which the different
Executive Departments are conducted," Jackson wrote out in his private
memorandum book, "the power of appointment and removal is given to
him in order to enable him to fill them with competent and faithfull
officers." Only through the exercise of this power can the President be
certain "that the laws are faithfully executed and those measures adopted
which are best calculated to promote the public interest."[73]

From this point onward, Jackson moved swiftly. He immediately appointed Roger Brooke Taney as his new secretary of the treasury, gained his acceptance, commissioned him, and swore him into office. It was all done so expeditiously that "the business of the Treasury," said the General, "is progressing as tho Mr. Duane had never been born."[74]

As these events transpired, a possible danger began to develop that could have caused Jackson great embarrassment and possible loss of national support. Both McLane and Cass seriously considered resigning —and if they had done so it meant another shake-up of the cabinet, only worse than the one in 1831. When Jackson determined to remove the deposits without waiting for Congress, he rejected the advice and strong urging of McLane. Cass, too, had opted for delay—only less aggressively. Both men, therefore, felt their positions compromised, their usefulness dissipated, and their resignations imperative. By remaining in the cabinet, they said, they feared their presence might embarrass the President and themselves.[75]

Actually their departure would embarrass Jackson more. He dreaded the impact their resignations would produce on the Congress and the country. If the first cabinet dissolution had produced a constitutional crisis and seemed to shake the very foundations of the government, a second such "explosion" would surely produce turmoil. So Jackson exerted all his political skill and powers of persuasion to convince the two men to remain.[76]

What made it difficult was Jackson's desire to publish the paper Donelson read to the cabinet. Such publication might imply that Cass and McLane had capitulated to Jackson's position, something both men were known in Washington to have opposed. Publication, therefore, would tend to discredit them. Jackson got around this difficulty by agreeing to publish a statement in which he would declare that he took full responsibility for the action and that the decision was his alone. He spoke to Blair. "I am very willing to let the public know that I take the whole responsibility of this measure; Mr. Blair, I wish you would look out a place in the paper where I can put that in."[77]

Cass was still troubled, so he went to see Major Lewis. Cass thought he could confide in Lewis, as a close friend and someone who agreed with his position on removal. The major advised him to speak directly to Jackson. He gave McLane the same advice. McLane, it was whispered around Washington, was "very bitter against Taney & Kendall."[78]

On the morning of Tuesday, September 24, both secretaries waited on the President. They explained their position and their embarrassment. They said that they felt obliged to resign. To all of this, Jackson answered "kindly and firmly." The truth about their exact positions on the issue could be revealed, he said, and where final responsibility for the decision lay. He assured them that he wished no support from either "when their principles and opinions were not in accord" with his own. Jackson genuinely wanted them to remain. And he made this abundantly clear, not simply for political reasons but because of their talents and integrity and the services they could provide the country.[79] He simply wished them to attend to their departments, and when the opposition made an issue of removal to say and do nothing that would bolster the Bank's position.[80]

Both McLane and Cass were gratified by their interview with the President. Cass told Lewis that he had never seen the "President so kind, or more frank."[81] Moreover, the *Globe* duly announced that removal "was not to be considered a cabinet measure."[82] On the day following their interview, both men returned to the White House and informed the General that they had decided to stay. The President breathed a sigh of relief. Then he thanked them. "We are all united in our cordial friendship and confidence," he wrote Van Buren, "which on my part was never impaired."[83]

The dismissal of Duane, like so many other personnel actions taken by Jackson, was most unfortunate. The President did everything wrong. The manner in which Duane was appointed, the way he was treated upon taking office, the failure to reassure him, and the summary dismissal at the end were all characteristic of poor management and inept executive leadership. Not that Jackson did not attempt to repair some of the damage he had unintentionally inflicted. He did try to soothe Duane's wounded pride after the secretary's initial interview with Whitney and Kendall; he did seek to cajole him into agreeing to removal; and he did offer him the Russian post as an inducement to resign. Still, these were feeble efforts at best, and some of them came too late to have much effect. Jackson got just what he deserved. His bad judgment and mishandling of an unpleasant predicament combined to shake his administration and bring him grief.

But Duane is not without fault. When all is said and done, he placed his own judgment above that of the President. All because of wounded pride, he challenged not only Jackson's policy but his authority to make that policy. He was a small-minded, inconsequential bureaucrat, and he deserved to be sacked.

Fortunately, he was gone, and now Jackson prepared to move against the monster Bank. Now he felt secure in delivering the blow that would slay the beast and end the corruption that had so threatened the freedom of the American people. In arriving at this position he had strengthened his hand by moving Taney to a position of greater influence and strength and by demonstrating his absolute control of the administration and the entire executive branch. In removing the deposits, as he now planned to do, he was about to take one additional step that would further strengthen the presidential office. Moreover, it would strengthen the ideological position of the Democrats, provoke the creation of a new political party, and sharpen the lines of division between the two parties. Finally, and most important of all, it would further advance the democratization of American institutions.

CHAPTER 7

Panic!

ALL DURING THE DAYS OF THE REMOVAL DECISION Jackson felt quite unwell. He became feverish, particularly at night, and only the excitement of crisis kept him going. "Incessant labour with the prevalance of billious disease occasioned by the unholsome miasma from the vegetable deposit thrown up by digging the canal thro the swamp of the tiber,* that has rendered our city very sickly, has visitted me for the last ten days," he wrote on October 1.[1] Fortunately—since the major contest with the Bank still lay ahead—the fever left him after a few days and he slowly regained his strength.

The demands on his time mounted steadily over the next several weeks. To start the process of removal required the preparation of directives and the marshaling of the government's machinery to initiate and direct the necessary action. Several moves were imperative: the final selection of the state depositories; the preparation of new orders for the distribution of government funds; and the announcement of arrangements concerning funds presently deposited with the BUS.

Almost as soon as Taney assumed office as the new Treasury secretary, he appointed Kendall as special agent for the removal. Together, and with the help of Levi Woodbury, who, in a single day's time, became an ardent advocate of the presidential policy, they prepared an order dated September 25, 1833, which officially announced the government's switch from national banking to deposit banking.[2] The order stated that commencing October 1 all future government deposits would be placed in selected state banks and that for operating expenses the government

*The Tiber was a small stream in Washington that disappeared with the building of an underground drainage system for the city.

would draw on its remaining funds from the BUS until they were exhausted.

To decide the selection of additional state banks and arrange details of the proposed operation, Jackson summoned his cabinet together and invited Kendall to attend. No objections were made to any of the original seven selections.[3] The next important question was what to do about the BUS in case it retaliated. The behemoth might easily force the selected banks into bankruptcy by "making a run on them" to an amount that could collapse the deposit banking system before it got started. As a precaution, therefore, it was decided to place in the possession of some of these banks—and do it "confidentially"—a considerable number of transfer warrants for government deposits held by the BUS, which were to be used against the monster only to counteract any hostile action it might attempt.[4]

Another precaution involved the Post Office Department. Because of gross mismanagement, the Post Office had encountered severe financial problems, and some state banks had offered to help solve them. To provide these banks with government funds, therefore, might be seen as an effort to bring them under government (Post Office) control. So it was decided to do two things: to exclude these banks (with one exception) from receiving government deposits; and to require pledges that the Post Office would never ask "accommodations" from any of the selected (pet) banks. The postmaster general, William Barry, gave his pledge to both Kendall and Jackson. And he was commended for his loyal support. Except for incompetence and general lack of administrative ability, Barry proved to be everything Jackson wanted in a cabinet officer.

The "experiment" in deposit banking began with the seven institutions Kendall had selected on his summer tour. By the end of 1833, the original number had increased to twenty-two. Over the next three years some ninety-odd banks were added to the system, and in each case those selected were regarded as "friendly" to the Democratic creed, or, if not friendly, at least "liberal." By December 13, 1833, the public funds held by the BUS were practically drained away. And in implementing Jackson's policy, Taney sent a half million dollars in warrants to the Bank of America in New York and another $100,000 to the Union Bank of Maryland in Baltimore. They were instructed to use these warrants only "in difence and to avert injury."[5]

Taney's energy and skill in instituting deposit banking—all the while attending the business of the Attorney General's Office until a replacement could be found—commanded Jackson's unbounded admiration and respect. It almost seemed as though he had found a replacement for the absent Van Buren. Taney was particularly careful in selecting the pets, for he realized that one miscalculation could ruin the entire system. He tried to get the best advice possible, and he did not rely exclusively on Kendall. He was totally committed to Jackson's reform program, and he threw himself diligently into the task of making this "experiment" in deposit banking a total success.[6]

Jackson marveled. "Mr. Taney is a host," he exclaimed, "his energy combined with his clear views will enable him to carry into effect the change." Taney has taken proper precautions against the BUS, the President said. "A good general will always keep his enemy in check. We have the Bank now check mated, will treat her gently if she behaves well."[7]

The shift from national to deposit banking provided another boost to the growing power of the President. The new system gave Jackson almost "complete executive control" in arranging the government's fiscal operation, a responsibility welcomed by Jackson because it necessarily removed it from the hands of the BUS.[8] Permitting complete executive discretion in the selection of the pets virtually stripped the Congress of its preeminent position in the control and disbursement of public moneys. In short, deposit banking represented an enormous extension of executive authority.[9]

The elevation of Taney necessitated finding a new attorney general. And, as usual, Jackson turned to Van Buren for advice. The Magician promptly advised him to go slowly, for the last thing Jackson needed was yet another bad appointment.[10]

Of necessity, Jackson wanted someone of superior legal talents. But he also wanted someone who would be "right upon the Indian and Bank questions."[11] Everyone told him that the selection should come from the south because of the late unpleasantness with South Carolina and because that area was not represented in the current cabinet. Jackson personally was indifferent to location, but of course he was quite prepared to do what was politically necessary. So the first choice fell to Peter V. Daniel of Virginia. Unfortunately, his appointment was announced before he had given his consent.[12] After a long conversation with the President, Daniel decided to decline the offer for family and personal reasons. Still the unfortunate error in releasing Daniel's name prematurely worked to Jackson's advantage, for his choice pleased the south and then freed him to select the best man he could find without reference to geographic location or any other political consideration. He ultimately made an excellent choice in Benjamin F. Butler of New York. A member of the Albany Regency and Van Buren's longtime friend and former law partner, Butler combined superior legal skills with dedication and hard work. Although his appointment further weighted the cabinet toward the north and increased Van Buren's influence, it added needed strength to that body in terms of talent, loyalty, and commitment.[13]

But Van Buren had to exert all his influence on his friend to get him to accept the job. The salary only came to $4,500, and it meant relocating his family and probably commuting a great deal between Washington and New York. What finally convinced Butler to take the position, however, was its importance to his career. "Although you are not a slave of mad ambition," Van Buren told him, "you are, as you ought to be, tenacious of your professional standing. This cannot be increased at home, and can only be made *National*, by becoming identified with National concerns."[14]

At a subsequent interview Butler impressed Jackson straight off. The President particularly admired his diligence. After accepting the office, Butler arrived in Washington on a Saturday, received his commission, was sworn into office on Monday, examined and signed all the patent papers on his desk, dined with Jackson and the cabinet, and left for Baltimore on the nine o'clock stage to attend court. "This is dispatch," wrote the astonished Jackson. "He has left us *all* favorably impressed with his amiability and fine talents."[15]

With his cabinet now complete and in reasonable harmony, Jackson was ready to complete the banking reform he had started years before. Now if the monster would just lie still, he would swiftly administer the lethal blow of extracting all the government's deposits. With "one million and a half of coin" to be used in case the beast put up a fight, the President felt confident and exhilarated. "We act solely on the defensive," he said, as though it were true, "and I am ready with the screws to draw every tooth and then the stumpts." If I am not mistaken, he went on, we will have "Mr. Biddle and his Bank as quiet and harmless as a *lamb* in six weeks."[16]

Some lamb. The roar that echoed out of Philadelphia in the fall of 1833 sounded more like a raging tiger. Nicholas Biddle could hardly be expected to stand by without murmuring while Jackson slaughtered his Bank. He had already begun to take defensive actions during the summer on hearing rumors that the deposits might be removed. He slowly reduced the Bank's lending operation. Then, when the signal was finally given to begin the shift to deposit banking, Biddle counterattacked. He called a special meeting of his board of directors on October 7 and won their approval for a general curtailment of loans throughout the entire banking system. He swelled the Bank's liquid assets by refusing to increase discounts and restricting discounted bills of exchange to eighty days. Western branches of the BUS were ordered to purchase bills of exchange payable solely in eastern cities. This would apply an economic squeeze that could shatter western growth and expansion. It marked the beginning of a bone-crushing struggle between a powerful financier and a determined and equally powerful politician. Biddle understood what he was about. He knew what he needed to achieve to save his Bank. If he brought enough pressure and agony to the money market, only then could he force the President to restore the deposits. He almost gloated. "This worthy President thinks that because he has scalped Indians and imprisoned Judges, he is to have his way with the Bank. He is mistaken."[17]

What made the situation all the more precarious was Jackson's ignorance of financial matters and his total lack of appreciation for the BUS and its importance to the American economy. (He continued, however, to conduct his private financial operations through the BUS even after he had ordered the deposits removed.[18]) The Bank was interlaced with the economy. To damage it of necessity would devastate the financial and business community. Moreover, the men associated with Jackson in this perilous "experiment" were equally ignorant. And a few of them were guilty of conflict of interest. Roger Taney, for example, had ties to the Union Bank of Maryland, and Reuben Whitney to the Girard Bank in Philadelphia.[19] Fortunately, Taney was a man of integrity and devoted to the success of deposit banking. He quickly overcame his ignorance during the short period he served as secretary of the treasury. He learned immediately that the system would never work without financial stability on the part of participating institutions and so he devoted his considerable talents and energies to achieving that end.[20]

But the storm unleashed by the Treasury Department order hit the administration with stunning force. The business community erupted with howls of complaints and condemned the order as endangering the entire economic fabric of the community. They labeled it a "naked, barefaced act of usurpation and mischief . . . a Proclamation of War."[21] This intrusion of the government into the financial operations of the nation was a violation of basic republicanism, the very thing Jackson had promised during his presidential campaign in 1828 to terminate. By this order he had outfederalized the Federalists.

If the outcry from the business community was severe—and it grew in severity over the next several months when the full effects of Biddle's curtailment policy took hold—the political outcry was even worse. Jackson was again branded a tyrant, for "tyranny is a disregard of the law and the substitution of individual will for legal restraint." His bold expansion of executive power foreshadowed the onslaught of despotism, cried the opposition press, and the end of republican government.[22] A political battle soon raged around the country over the constitutional powers of the executive, and even Democrats were devastated by the reaction it provoked.[23] Many of them had doubted the wisdom of the Bank War from the moment of its inception. Still they rallied behind Jackson over his Bank veto when Clay, Webster, and Biddle prematurely pushed for recharter. But removal!—that was something else. That endangered the very financial structure of the nation, and with it the American experiment in freedom and democracy.

It soon became obvious that removal could split the Democratic party almost down the middle. And mass desertions could throw control of Congress into the hands of the National Republicans, damage the organization of the party, and ensure Democratic defeat at the next general election. "I consider that every movement which throws off a fragment from the Jackson party," wrote Duff Green, editor of the Washington *Telegraph*, "promises to swell our numbers. . . . You must see that every shock breaks loose some interest and that which our opponents lose we gain—We are in the field we must grow in strength."[24]

The very thing that Van Buren feared the most—the fragmenting of party strength—seemed imminent. The greatest danger involved the loss of southern support because of southerners' fierce commitment to states' rights and their concern that Jackson was undermining that philosophy with his powerful thrusts by the federal government. Said Duff Green: If we can unite on a southern candidate, we can beat Van Buren in 1836.[25]

So total was the devastation to all but the staunchest Jacksonians that even Daniel Webster, who had slid away from many of his previous associates over nullification and nearly entered a political alliance with Old Hickory, eventually scrambled back into the opposition fold. Jackson's removal policy totally alienated him.[26]

The removal of the public deposits could never have been accomplished by anyone other than Jackson himself. It took monumental self-confidence in the need and importance of the action and incredible popularity with the electorate to accomplish it. When, for example, Major Lewis sent him newspaper articles or pamphlets or other public statements that questioned the wisdom of removal, Jackson dismissed them with a sneer. "I have cast my eyes over the piece marked in the newspaper you handed me," he scribbled to Lewis. "I would like to be informed why it was sent for my perusal—I never trouble myself *with dead Ducks or madmen*—or even those who are not made, when their plain object is to draw the public mind from their own debasement."[27] Politicians around the country, both those who hated and those who idolized the President, agreed that none but a political colossus could engineer such a feat. Only a man completely identified with the people could summon the support necessary to take such a bold action.[28] "When will our friends at Washington be made sensible enough," Old Hickory was told, "that you understand public sentiment infinitely better than themselves"; so if you say the deposits must be withdrawn, the people will readily accept it, despite the supposed agony inflicted upon the business community.[29] "If the people approved the veto," wrote Isaac Hill, "how much more will they approve the withdrawing of the Deposites—an act which will the more redound to the credit of the President since in its accomplishment he had not only to encounter the opposition of his political enemies but the coldness of friends."[30]

One important reason for popular acceptance of Jackson's decision to remove the deposits was the fact that in his hands (whether he did it consciously or not) the Bank issue became infused with moral overtones, namely, the struggle of honest working people against evil aristocrats who were scheming to rob and exploit them. It must be remembered that whenever Jackson spoke to the people about the Bank they *always* heard these overtones—and responded just as he expected them to do.

Over the next several months Nicholas Biddle intensified the political and economic havoc that enveloped the country. He steadily increased the pressure of his squeeze. His curtailment of loans came with such suddenness and severity that it pitched the country into an economic panic reminiscent of the breakdown of 1819. He wanted to bring about a depression—and the deeper the better. "The ties of party allegiance can only be broken," he declared, "by the actual conviction of existing distress in the community." And such distress, of course, would eventually put everything to rights. "Nothing but the evidence of suffering abroad will produce any effect in Congress. . . . Our only safety is in pursuing a steady course of firm restriction—and I have no doubt that such a course will ultimately lead to restoration of the currency and the recharter of the Bank."[31]

This murderous squeeze caught the country at a particularly vulnerable moment. Business was enjoying rapid expansion; it craved credit; and it sorely needed an abundant supply of cash. In addition, the tariff duties came due at this time. Business required a steady increase in the credit and currency supply but, instead, faced near-total constriction of both. Thus, a general prosperity suddenly sustained a crippling setback. Within two months the Bank reduced its loans by more than $5½ million. In the next five months the total curtailment reached $18 million. To make matters worse, the Bank demanded payments of all imbalances by state banks in specie, and to meet this demand the state banks were required to collect from their borrowers and curtail their own loans. It was a spiraling recession that threatened to carry the nation into a major economic collapse.

By the opening of the new Congress in December, 1833, a general cry of distress was beginning to be heard around the country. Newspapers reported the alarm and angry letters from manufacturers inundated congressmen. The merchants of New York, declared James A. Hamilton, "are really in very great distress nay even to the verge of General Bankruptcy." Biddle was delighted to hear such doleful news, especially from his New York correspondents, who told him that "things are getting worse and worse here." Every major city sustained a number of business losses; wages and prices sagged; workingmen were discharged. By the end of January, 1834, the pressure was reported "as great as any community can bear." The following month, Senator John Tyler of Virginia insisted that "Bankruptcy to the North is almost general." One man who had traveled to Baltimore, Pittsburgh, Wheeling, Cincinnati, Frankfort, and Louisville found "great despondency pervading the trading part of the people." The distress among the merchants, said another, 'is truly appalling."[32]

Jackson himself was bombarded with these cries of distress and complaint. But he paid them little heed. The country was sound, he argued, and the panic artificial. Once Biddle's monster breathed no more, business conditions would return to normal.

Still the cries of distress added to Jackson's general indisposition during these panic months. He sounded very crotchety for weeks at a time and snapped at servants without provocation. When asked what troubled him, he naturally cited Biddle's curtailment policy, the constant pain in his left side, and the new pain "in my right shoulder and side." But then, with a sigh, he admitted the truth. The greatest pain of all was the loss of his son's family. They had returned to Tennessee after vacationing with him at the Rip Raps. The President especially missed "our sweet little Rachel," his "dear little pet." She is "so good," he said, "running all over the house." Oh, he wistfully wrote, "I wish I could see her walk, and hear her begin to prattle—it would be a great consolation for me." He consoled himself by looking at the likeness of the child that Ralph Earl had painted and which now hung in his bedroom. Jackson had not wanted his family to leave him, but his son insisted. "I dreaded the long travel for our sweet little pet," he told his daughter-in-law, "fearful that it . . . might get sick & no doctor near—but when I reflected that she, as well as you & Andrew were under the protection of the phician, our Saviour & our god, my fears vanished."[33]

His little pet had come to mean so much to the President that the mere thought of her during these months of anguish and turmoil brought tears to his eyes. "She is given to us as a blessing," he told the child's mother, "let us be thankful for the boon, but never for one moment be unmindful of that gratitude we owe to god, for this precious gift." After his family left him, "everything appeared silent & in gloom about the House." He could not rest and frequently he roamed the corridors at night, peering into the empty rooms and moaning over the departure of his loved ones. "When I walked into your room," he told Sarah, "found it without its occupants—everything changed, the cradle of the little pet without it, and its little waggon there—my feelings were overcome for the moment." His mind wandered to the Hermitage and he luxuriated in the thought that they were safe at his plantation. With that, "my mind became calm & reconciled to my fate—saying with calm resignation, the 'Lords will be done.'" Then, in a burst of emotion, he told Sarah how much she meant to him and how good she had been to him. "I remember my promise— that so long as you would be a loving daughter to me, I would be a tender father to you, you have thus far my dear Sarah fulfilled your part—and I trust I have and will perform mine."[34]

Although these closing months of 1833 were especially trying for Jackson, he managed to shake himself out of his depression and nostalgia for home. He had an obligation to the people and the nation, and he never let duty drift for long from his mind. Besides, other crises cropped up with mounting frequency in the fall of 1833, and they diverted his attention from his family, the Hermitage, and his nagging bodily pains. For example, it appeared as though another nullification crisis might develop in Alabama when local citizens seized public land—in violation of a treaty with Creek Indians—and refused to vacate when ordered to do so by the federal government. Instead, they appealed for assistance from their governor, John Gayle, and he promised to protect them. Federal troops were under orders to remove the squatters if they remained on the land after January 15, 1834—and to use force if necessary. For a brief moment it looked as though another head-on clash between state and federal authorities was in the offing, despite the example of South Carolina just a few months before. "I thought the Presidents Proclamation of Last December, had completely destroyed the Southern Hydra," wrote Major Lewis; "but it seems another head has shot up in a neighbouring state. To demolish this, however, the powers of Hercules will not be required —Governor Cass seems to be fully competent to the task." Secretary of War Cass did indeed perform his duties most competently. But even more effective in ending the crisis was the lack of enthusiasm by Alabamians for the governor's flirtation with Jacksonian wrath. When he found that "his *people* will not stand by him," Gayle quietly retreated. That ended the matter. As an excuse and apology, the President was told that Gayle "had taken to *hard drinking*."[35]

With the return of Congress in early December, Jackson totally regained his combative mood. He had little time to brood about home and retirement and his "little pet." The Congress required his full attention. And, without anticipating it, the removal agony brought him a number of benefits. First of all, it unified the executive branch. Taney emerged as a strong and capable administrator. McLane, who resented Taney's triumph, faded into the background. He no longer opposed or criticized the President's policies. He kept mum. Woodbury was converted into an ardent advocate of removal, to such an extent that when Taney left the Treasury Woodbury became the obvious choice as successor. Cass, too, rallied behind the President. Even Van Buren capitulated unconditionally. He knew the fight would be rough and that he could not stand quietly on the sidelines. He had to stand with Jackson. And to gain political merit required that he give wholehearted support. "You see how the wind blows at Washington," he wrote James A. Hamilton, "and that we who cannot but be in the fight will have a rough sea. So be it. What cannot be cured must be endured." He even praised Taney's published exposition of the reasons for removal, so much so that John Quincy Adams suspected that he wrote it, "or a great part of it," himself. Perhaps the ultimate capitulation came from Major William B. Lewis, a longtime supporter of the BUS. "That ill fated establishment now has a heap of vices," he wrote. "It has fallen by its own hand and will perish without the sympathies even of its own friends."[36]

Removal also strengthened the ideological position of the Democrats. It provided them with an easy rhetoric that found great appeal with the people. They could revile aristocrats, the money power, and foreign domination of finance. They could load their accusations with enough moral outrage to frighten their opposition into silence. Democrats became very adept at exciting the passions and prejudices of workers and farmers. They identified themselves with the masses against aristocracy and wealth. They spoke of the people as good and wise and just, whose will must always be obeyed.

In particular, removal strengthened Jackson's hand as party leader and head of the government. That he could take such a controversial issue and force its acceptance upon his party and the people measured the extent of his leadership and the force of his personality. To oppose removal meant opposing Jackson, and congressmen did so at their peril.

Jackson remained relatively calm throughout the turmoil. He was supremely confident that once he had tightened the screws to draw every tooth of the BUS and then the "stumpts," the recession of 1833 would fade and the country return to normal. He reassured his cabinet. He reassured party leaders. If they would simply listen to him and do as he asked, they had nothing to fear. Even businessmen got the Jackson treatment. Whenever they came to him to complain about economic conditions and the terrible price they had to pay for his policy, he quietly directed them to Nicholas Biddle as the source of their problem and their only recourse for relief.

One such group of "great bankers and great merchants," headed by James G. King, the son of Rufus King, former senator from New York, brought the President a petition bearing six thousand signatures. They found Jackson seated at a desk with a long clay pipe in his mouth, the bowl of which rested on the table. Enormous clouds of smoke gushed from the blackened bowl. Hearing the deputation enter the room, the President looked up.

"Excuse me a moment, gentlemen," Jackson said as he half rose from his chair and bowed to the group. "Have the goodness to be seated."

Ever the gentleman and courtly commander, Jackson hurriedly finished what he was writing, pushed the paper away, and rose.

"Now gentlemen, what is your pleasure with me?"

The deputation broke out in a torrent of complaints. They begged him to rescind his removal order. They described their distress. They feared insolvency.

"Insolvent do you say?" replied Jackson. "What do you come to me for, then? Go to Nicholas Biddle. We have no money here, gentlemen. Biddle has all the money. He has millions of specie in his vaults, at this moment, lying idle, and yet you come to me to save you from breaking. I tell you, gentlemen, it's all politics."[37]

Jackson continued talking like this for fifteen minutes, excoriating Biddle and the Bank for the harm they had done the country and its institutions. Gradually he worked himself into a towering rage. He ranted; he paced the room; he gestured with wide sweeps of his arms; he pointed at the deputation and swore that his decision was irreversible and that he would never restore the deposits. Let there be no mistake on this point, he thundered, let it be understood distinctly and "explicity that the name of Andrew Jackson would never be signed to a bill or resolution to place the Public money in the Bank of the United States or to renew the Charter of that Bank."[38]

At length, he paused. The harangue ended quietly. Silence gripped the deputation. The verbal bombardment had totally immobilized them. They rose to leave and the President escorted them to the door with the "utmost politeness."

As the deputation descended the staircase, a messenger caught up with them and asked their leader to return to the President's office. When he did so he found Jackson chuckling over the result of the interview.

"Didn't I manage them well?" he laughed.

The old rascal had staged the tantrum. He was not one whit as angry as he pretended. But he got his message across with stunning force and clarity: under no condition would he rescind his order and restore the deposits.[39]

Other deputations beseeched him. To all he replied with the same tone and language: "In the name of God, sir! what do the people think to gain by sending their memorials here? If they send ten thousand of them, signed by all the men, women, children in the land, and bearing the names of all on the grave-stones, I will not relax a particle from my position."[40]

As he always said, once he had made up his mind, Andrew Jackson was immovable.

CHAPTER 8

Jackson's "Revolution"

WITHOUT DOUBT, JACKSON NEVER RECONSIDERED his decision to kill the Bank. His conviction on the matter was absolute. "After having resolved upon a thing," said Major Lewis, who knew the President as well as anyone, the General "never looks back." He goes forward. He plans for the future.[1]

The immediate future revolved around the return of Congress on Monday, December 2. And Jackson had two concerns: the composition and organization of the Congress; and the preparation of his fifth annual message on the State of the Union.

With respect to the makeup of Congress and what that might mean in terms of his Bank policy, the President feared that the Bank's friends would attempt "to bring back, by joint Resolution of both Houses, the public deposites to that Institution." It was up to him to block that resolution, for "if they fail in this there will be no further attempts made, at least for the present," to win recharter for the BUS.[2] Jackson knew that his great problem centered in the Senate, where a majority favored recharter. In addition, the Bank enjoyed the unrivaled talents of Clay, Calhoun, and Webster, each of whom was prepared to speak for hours and days, if necessary, to assault the White House and raise fears of approaching economic doom. Only Thomas Hart Benton on the Democratic side could match the triumvirate in eloquence, biting sarcasm, and staying power. As it turned out, Silas Wright, Jr., of New York, a member of the Regency, Van Buren's closest friend and recently elected to the Senate to replace William L. Marcy, added enormous strength to the Jackson forces. His style of oratory might not match the best efforts of Webster, but his intelligence, shrewdness, parliamentary and committee

116

skills placed him among the leading legislators of the day. When he spoke his colleagues listened with attention, not only because the voice of Van Buren and Jackson could be heard in his words but because his thoughts had precision and substance and power.[3]

Not the least important in Jackson's calculation about the composition of Congress was the recognition that the newly elected Vice President, Martin Van Buren, would preside over all important debates in the Senate. Although he had no vote, unless it became necessary to break a tie, his very appearance each day lent an aura of presidential presence in the chamber.[4] Handsomely turned out in the latest fashion, coiffed in excellent taste, and exuding charm in all directions, the Little Magician provided a unique style to the legislative proceedings, one he used several times to deflate the opposition.

Unfortunately, Van Buren did not arrive in Washington until Saturday evening, December 14, a good two weeks after Congress had reconvened. Jackson sent for him immediately. When the little man got to the White House, he found Senator Grundy of Tennessee in close conversation with the President. After a cordial exchange of greetings, Jackson told Van Buren that the organization of the Senate had been delayed by Grundy, supported by Daniel Webster—mark that, said the President—despite Henry Clay's desire to press for the appointment of the standing committees. Webster was still trying to capitalize on his good relations with the White House, relations that had improved considerably during the nullification controversy but had soured recently on account of the removal issue. Van Buren looked glum as he listened but did not interrupt. Grundy then explained to the Vice President that he believed "an arrangement could be made with Mr. Webster and his friends" to win control of the committees for the administration. At that point Van Buren jumped to his feet. These prospects for an "arrangement" had Webster's presidential ambitions written all over them, the Magician exclaimed. Anyone could see that. The words tumbled from his mouth in a rush. He spoke with great feeling and considerable vehemence, citing the senator's involvement and commitment to the Bank and the "antagonistic position which the President and Mr. Webster had always occupied." He admitted that the administration would have trouble in the Senate during this session, but said he was ready for it and "would enter upon it in the full conviction that the people . . . would carry us, as on many previous occasions they had carried us, triumphantly thro' the crisis."[5]

As Van Buren pronounced these sentiments, the President looked intently at him, one hand resting on the mantel. He saw the anguish in his friend's eyes. Then, after pondering a moment, he turned to Grundy and told him to drop the matter. Grundy nodded his assent and withdrew. And that, says Webster's most recent biographer, was as close as the Massachusetts senator ever came to being elected President of the United States.[6]

Although the National Republicans and their allies held a majority in the Senate, it was a very narrow one and certainly it could never muster a two-thirds vote to override a presidential veto. But in the House the situation was far different. Here the Democrats held a clear majority, and it was here that Jackson expected to influence the course of legislation. The strategy for this campaign had been determined months before.

To begin with, it was essential to elect a Speaker who was loyal and dedicated to Jacksonian principles, since the Speaker appoints all committees and exercises enormous influence on the conduct of business. The current Speaker, Andrew Stevenson of Virginia, had been offered the post of minister to Great Britain and he was anxious to take it. Tall, impressive in appearance, and hardworking, he seemed ideal for the position. But with the decision to remove the deposits and the danger that Congress might demand their restoration, Jackson and his advisers determined to delay Stevenson's appointment as minister and return him to the House as Speaker. The only other problem was whether Stevenson had the votes for reelection. Jackson decided to leave nothing to chance. He instructed his liaisons with Congress not to bring Stevenson forward for the Speaker's position "unless he can be *surely* elected." A careful check confirmed the presence of the necessary votes and so Stevenson was duly nominated and elected.[7]

It was also decided to revise the membership on key committees to strengthen the President's hand. Gulian C. Verplanck of New York, for example, had shown himself a "weak reed" during the last session, and the New York party replaced him in the House with a more dependable Democrat. That opened up the all-important position of chairman of the Ways and Means Committee. Since Jackson's Bank policy would be the central issue of the session, the chairman of that committee advanced in fact to the position of unofficial floor leader of the administration. The choice of that chairman, then, became immensely important to Jackson's determination to kill the monster. For that reason the President decided to tap James Knox Polk of Tennessee for the post. His strong friendship for Polk went back almost ten years, ever since the young man won a seat in Congress by defeating Andrew Erwin, a leader of the anti-Jackson forces in Tennessee. Ambitious, introverted, and iron-willed, Polk exuded just enough passion and power to captivate the old man. His large, restless, steely-grey eyes, set in deep sockets, gave him a formidable appearance. And because he had proved to be a dependable and energetic congressman he now inherited the chairmanship of the powerful Ways and Means Committee. As early as the previous summer Jackson had made this decision, and to prepare Polk for his new assignment the President had forwarded to him all the anti-Bank propaganda he thought the congressman should have. Aside from Jackson's essential decision in the matter, the selection seemed completely appropriate to other Democrats in view of Polk's "yeoman services" in the Bank War during the previous session.[8]

The other members of this vital committee were also selected with care. Some of the best Jackson men in the House were added to the committee to bolster Polk's position. These included Churchill C. Cambreleng of New York City, whom John Q. Adams called "utterly unprincipled";[9] John McKinley of Alabama, Polk's personal friend; Henry Hubbard of New Hampshire; Isaac McKim of Maryland; and George Loyall of Virginia. The opposition was allotted only three places on the committee, but the men assigned were also talented.[10]

To support his forces in Congress, Jackson called on his enormous propaganda machine to generate popular approval for removal. The newspaper organs of the Democratic party, under the leadership and guidance of the Washington *Globe*, poured out a steady stream of editorial venom aimed at the Bank and its president. Charges of corruption and violation of the Bank's charter filled daily issues. But infinitely more important, the Democratic press expressed Jackson's action against the BUS in moral terms, specifically a struggle of honest workers against corrupt aristocrats, between the laboring poor and those who would exploit them. Thus, from the beginning of its history, the Democratic party rested on a moral base. It pledged its allegiance to the disadvantaged, and this was one of Jackson's great legacies to the political life of the nation. The Democratic party, at Old Hickory's direction, committed itself to the concerns of the masses of American people. So successful were his efforts that the "middling and lower classes," it was observed, had developed "a radical and deeply seated hostility to the Bank."[11]

Moreover, removal became the central issue of the decade. No other approached it in importance. It was the "President's own measure, conceived by him, carried out by him, defended by him, and its fate dependent upon him." Not until slavery replaced it in the minds and emotions of Americans was any other issue debated in Congress "with so much ability, bitterness, and pertinacity." Not only did it provide Democrats with a moral cause, but it produced extraordinary political realignments and the rise of the Whig party. In forcing removal upon Congress and the nation as his final act in slaying the monster Bank, Jackson performed an act "high and daring, and requiring as much nerve as any enterprise of arms, in which the President had ever been engaged."[12]

The stage was therefore set for what many predicted would be a monumental battle in Congress over removal. In preparing for the great contest during this "Panic session," as it is sometimes called, Jackson set to work on his fifth annual message to Congress and had it ready by the end of November. He turned it over to Blair but gave him strict instructions about it. He wanted no one to see it until it was delivered to Congress. He had learned his lesson from last year, he said, for if "Joe Gales," editor of the Washington *National Intelligencer,* were to get his hands on it, "the Bank will have an answer ready prepared."[13]

The message went down on December 3, the day after Congress reconvened, and it provided much of the ammunition that went into the opening round of the long battle between the pro- and anti-Bank forces. The message began on a happy note by proclaiming the country's prosperity at home and abroad. It detailed foreign problems and reiterated Jackson's now famous slogan of seeking nothing that was not right and submitting to nothing that was wrong. With respect to France, the President noted the problem of the debts owed to Americans on account of the Napoleonic Wars. The secretary of the treasury had tried to collect the first installment of this payment by means of a draft upon the French minister of finance. The draft was drawn in favor of the BUS, and the French government was informed of this action by the American chargé d'affaires in Paris. However, the French Chamber of Deputies had not passed the necessary appropriations to cover the draft and so it went unpaid. But "I have received assurance" through our own chargé and the French minister in Washington, he continued, that the king and his ministers will abide by the treaty and that measures will be presented at the meeting of the Chambers to obtain the necessary appropriations. To move things a little faster, he had designated Edward Livingston as the new American minister to France; Livingston had left on his mission in August and had been presented to the king early in October.[14]

After reviewing relations with other nations—particularly the status of the payments owed by them to the United States—Jackson said that his diplomatic policy was simply one of "aiming at no exclusive advantages, of dealing with all on terms of fair and equal reciprocity, and of adhering scrupulously to all our engagements."[15]

Jackson then moved to the question of the finances of the country and noted with particular pride that the revenues from taxes, customs, and the sale of public lands ran to more than $60 million. As a consequence, the national debt had been reduced to $4,760,082.08. Which means, he crowed, that the debt could be completely discharged during the coming year. "I can not refrain from expressing the pleasure I feel at the near approach of that desirable event." And he could not resist taking a measure of credit for this happy prospect. It is evidence, he bubbled, not only of the abundant resources of the country but of the "prudence and economy with which the Government has heretofore been administered": we shall have the "proud satisfaction" of bequeathing to the next generation "the rare blessing" of a sufficient revenue "raised without injustice or oppression of our citizens."[16]

Again, he called for economy in the appropriation of funds. "We are beginning a new era in our Government." One without debt, so let principles be practiced that would be an example for the future. "I can not too strongly urge the necessity of a rigid economy and an inflexible determination not to enlarge the income beyond the real necessities of the Government" nor its appropriations "by unnecessary and profuse expenditures."[17]

Finally, he got to the removal of the deposits. He had taken the step, he said, "upon the high considerations of public interest and public duty." The secretary would soon report directly to Congress on this action and present the reasons for the action, all of which Jackson himself approved. He pronounced the Bank an "electioneering engine" which used its money to influence the election of public officers. It was therefore a simple matter of whether there would be a democracy or a moneyed aristocracy, "whether the people of the United States are to govern through representatives chosen by their unbiased suffrages or whether the money and power of a great corporation are to be secretly exerted to influence their judgment and control their decisions." Notice the distress the Bank had recently produced in the country by a curtailment of its loans, he continued, "even while it retains specie to an almost unprecedented amount in its vaults." Through this means the Bank expected to force a restoration of the deposits and a renewal of its charter.[18]

Jackson then moved on to the question of the Indians and their ouster to the west. He noted that relations with the Indians had been peaceful since the conclusion of the Black Hawk War. As to their transfer beyond the Mississippi River, he said: "My original convictions upon this subject have been confirmed by the course of events for several years, and experience is every day adding to their strength." These tribes "have neither the intelligence, the industry, the moral habits, nor the desire of improvement" to allow them to maintain continual contact with United States citizens. Circumstances had placed them in the midst of a "superior race," and without going into the reasons for their "inferiority," Jackson said, they must disappear "ere long" unless their destruction could be prevented through their removal to the west. "The experiment which has been recently made has so far proved successful." It should be noted how often Jackson called his policies "experiments"—at least in their initial stages. This usage tended to underscore the reform aspect of his programs.

With respect to the ouster of the Indians, Jackson's hideous, not to mention racist, judgment was stated flatly without the slightest realization that it was hideous or racist. Quite simply, it was typical of American thought in 1833.[19]

Then Jackson hearkened back to his old request for a constitutional amendment respecting the election of the President. He felt that it was important "to the future quiet and harmony of the people that every intermediate agency in the election" should be removed—specifically the Electoral College—and that eligibility should be limited to a single term of four or six years. Such an amendment, he believed, would advance the democratization of American political institutions. And on that note he ended. He promised, moreover, to cooperate with the Congress in every way possible.[20]

The very next day Jackson followed up this message with an official notification that he had vetoed the land bill passed during the closing days of the previous session. Actually he had pocket vetoed it. Now he was informing the Congress, in a long and labored paper, why he had decided to kill it. Among other reasons, he cited the deliberate effort to keep the price of land high. Like Jefferson, he opposed the use of public lands as a source of revenue. They were meant for settlement and development, he said. Those unsold after a period of years should be abandoned to the states and "the machinery of our land system entirely withdrawn." Such a surrender would promote the general interest, he declared.[21]

At one time Jackson thought that the distribution to the states of a surplus resulting from land sales would be a good idea. It could be used for education or internal improvements. But over the years he had seen how politicians distorted the distribution idea to increase the power and revenue of the government. For example this land bill which he had just vetoed. Instead of assisting the people, the government was hindering them in their search for security and economic independence. Besides, what was the point of the government's retaining land within the states for which it had absolutely no need or interest. Best to get rid of it—first by reducing its price and allowing the cost of the land to be gradually paid off by the buyer, and second, by returning what remained to the states for whatever purpose they might have for it.

This pocket veto directly challenged Clay's American System. It reiterated the Jeffersonian concern for people, rather than the economic need to stimulate national expansion.

Following these messages, Jackson sent down for confirmation the names of his nominees for the government directors of the BUS. And, as expected, his nominations touched off a skirmish with the Bank forces in Congress. Four of them—Henry D. Gilpin, John T. Sullivan, Peter Wager, and Hugh McEldery—were obnoxious because they had supplied the President with information and copies of the board's minutes with which he documented his case of mismanagement in the operation of the Bank's affairs. The Senate expressed its displeasure in these nominations by rejecting all four.[22]

But the scene really got tense when Taney sent down his report justifying removal. This occurred on the day after Congress reconvened. The report made a strong case for Jackson's decision and cited the following reasons for the removal: the use of Bank funds to influence elections; Biddle's personal control of the Bank's funds; loans to congressmen and other such "corrupting practices"; interference with the payment of the public debt; demand for damages over the government's draft on France; and the exclusion of the government's directors from real control of the Bank's affairs.[23]

Without wasting a moment, Henry Clay rose to the bait. His manner in the beginning of this debate was sly and insinuating, but over the next several months it became sharp and biting. At this point he cooed his concern that something might be amiss in the Treasury. The Senate should act immediately, he said, by investigating in depth the reasons for the removal. And it should be done by the entire Senate, not a committee. He suggested that perhaps the President had exercised a power over the Treasury not granted him by law and "dangerous to the liberties of the people." He went one step further and offered a resolution requesting that Jackson lay before the Senate a copy of the paper he had read to his cabinet on the removal. The paper had in fact been published and widely disseminated, but Clay was not satisfied with that.[24] After all, it was up to the Senate to decide whether that paper "be genuine or not." Although Senators Forsyth and Benton objected, the resolution carried by the vote of 23 to 18.[25]

Jackson responded the next day. He rejected the request out of hand. The Senate had no right to call for it or call for any other communication he might make to his cabinet, whether written or spoken. To the American people, he would always explain himself; not to the Senate, however, unless it involved anticipated legislation. Jackson stood on his rights. "The call was a wrong step," said Benton, "and gave the President an easy and a graceful victory."[26]

He had no such easy victory in the House, however. In that chamber, where he felt confident of his support, Jackson believed Taney's report would be forwarded to Polk's Committee on Ways and Means where he expected a gentle reception that would result in a series of resolutions condemning the Bank's conduct, rejecting recharter, and approving removal of the deposits. He also expected this committee to initiate legislation for regulating the pets. But Jackson did not reckon with Polk's miscalculation. George McDuffie, acting on a suggestion by Clay, requested that Taney's report be taken up by the committee of the whole, and Polk unwittingly went along. Once the request was approved, McDuffie then proposed unlimited debate on the President's authority to remove the deposits, a debate the Democrats fervently sought to avoid.[27]

Jackson fumed. The mismanagement by his friends was inexcusable. Still he kept his temper. Quietly and calmly he lectured Polk on what to do, telling him that the "time for full discussion is when the committee collect the facts and report them to the House." Once they presented these facts to the full House Jackson expected all serious opposition to his position to crumble. The facts would speak for themselves. The embarrassed Polk hardly knew how to respond to the President's rebuke except to say that he had been tricked.[28]

Under Jackson's prodding, Polk tried to maneuver the House to reconsider its decision, but the motion was debatable and debate could not be terminated except by passing the previous question, always a difficult and treacherous procedure. Once again Jackson intruded. He thought he spotted a parliamentary slip and hastened to tell Polk "to call for the previous question." Here is evidence that the intent is to block an investigation of the Bank, he said, "and ought to be met promptly by the previous question."[29]

Polk tried his luck—and failed by three votes. As unlikely as it sounds, considering their majority, the Democratic leaders could not control the proceedings of the House. Because of their bumbling they had opened up a debate and provided the opposition with a public forum to frighten the nation about the evils of the President's policies. And throughout the session the situation worsened. Several times the leaders had trouble holding the Democrats in line. On at least one occasion a general stampede away from the President seemed imminent. As the economic panic became more intense around the country and petitions and memorials favoring the BUS swamped the Congress, Democratic unrest and confusion swelled. Felix Grundy predicted that the administration would find itself in a minority in the House before the session ended.[30]

Richard Wilde, one of the strongest pro-Bank members of Polk's committee, declared that the debate was proceeding handsomely against the majority. But he warned "if they have not the V.O.T.E. there is little doubt we should have the V.E.T.O." In the Senate, Silas Wright reported a similar situation. "Mr. Clay is captain and he trains his troops daily and constantly. . . . How long this will be so we know not. Mr. Calhoun seems ambitious only to follow and obey and Mr. Webster looks black as a thunder cloud and seems to go heavily."[31]

As the battering of the administration intensified in both houses and Biddle continued his policy of contraction, a sense of paralysis and anxiety gripped the Congress. And the real pyrotechnics had not yet begun. "Clay opens his battery in the Senate on Thursday," December 26, reported Representative Wilde. "I have no doubt he will make a strong argument. He has prepared himself with care."[32]

Indeed he had. He planned to speak at length and send a thundering condemnation of the President reverberating around the nation. He proposed to haul Jackson before the bar of congressional justice and censure him for improper conduct. His method of achieving his end consisted of presenting two resolutions for action by the Senate: the first censured Jackson for his arbitrary dismissal of the Treasury secretary and the subsequent removal of the deposits in direct defiance of the legislature; and the second declared the reasons offered by Taney for the removal "unsatisfactory and insufficient."[33] The object of these resolutions was not simply to demonstrate senatorial displeasure in order to recall the President's action. According to Senator Benton, they were introduced "purely and simply for popular effect. Great reliance was placed upon that effect. It was fully believed . . . that a senatorial condemnation would destroy whomsoever it struck—even General Jackson."[34]

The chamber was packed when Clay rose to speak. Everyone knew that he would launch a mighty effort against the President and that much energy and forethought had gone into the preparation of the speech. The atmosphere was electric. Tension mounted as Clay stood and waited for the murmuring to subside. He enjoyed the emotional anxiety he had created, savoring every delicious moment of it. He glanced quickly around the room. Then he began. He started off by accusing the President of "open, palpable and daring usurpation." It was not a matter of banks and charters and money, he said, but the rapaciousness of the executive in seeking to expand the powers of his office and assume responsibilities and rights not granted by the Constitution and the laws of the nation and dangerous to the liberty of the American people. "We are," he thundered in his first display of emotion, "in the midst of a revolution, hitherto bloodless, but rapidly tending towards a total change of the pure republican character of the Government."

A revolution? Indeed—and bloodless, just as Clay described it. The nation under the guidance of a popular and dynamic leader was moving further away from the "pure republican character" of the political system as originally established by the Founding Fathers and toward a more democratic system that insisted on greater representation of the people and greater responsiveness to their will. The executive, not the legislature, was now seen as best embodying the will of all the people. He was their tribune.

Of course Clay interpreted the "revolution" differently. He saw the change as moving from pure republicanism into something approaching despotism, not democracy. What the nation was witnessing, he contended, was "the concentration of all power in the hands of one man." The President had paralyzed the powers of Congress through "an extraordinary exercise of the executive veto, not anticipated by the founders of the constitution, and not practiced by any of the predecessors of the present Chief Magistrate." The constitutional participation of the Senate in the appointing power "is virtually abolished" and reduced to "an idle ceremony."[35]

Jackson's "rage for innovation," he continued, extended to the judiciary. "Decisions of the tribunals, deliberately pronounced, have been contemptuously disregarded, and the sanctity of numerous treaties openly violated," as witnessed by what had happened to the southern Indian tribes. In addition, the currency was deranged, internal improvements "crushed beneath the veto," the tariff soon to be abandoned, and the government by March 3, 1837, "will have been transformed into an elective monarchy."

Until the last session of Congress, Clay moaned, there had been one remnant of congressional authority left untouched. The purse strings. The constitutional power of Congress over the treasury had never been questioned or contested. And yet within sixty days of the close of the last congressional session, the President of the United States "in utter contempt of [Congress's] authority" had assumed control of the Treasury and ordered the removal of the government's deposits from the United States Bank. The real question before the Senate, therefore, was whether the protective barriers of civil liberties would "be prostrated and trodden under foot, and the sword and the purse be at once united in the hands of one man."

The President, said Clay in a voice rising in pitch and volume, "neither by the act creating the treasury department, nor by the bank charter, has any power over the public treasury. Has he any by the constitution? None, none." At this point Clay was shouting and the anger of his words animated his face. But he seemed to be enjoying himself thoroughly as he pressed on. He relished every dramatic moment of it. The President, he continued, had the temerity to claim that his rights devolved upon him by virtue of the Constitution "and the suffrages of the American people." Since when had there been a "double source" of executive power? "By what authority does the President derive power from the mere result of an election?" Sir, Clay cried, "I am surprised and alarmed at the new source of executive power which is found in the result of a presidential election. I had supposed that the constitution and the laws were the sole source of executive authority . . . that the issue of a presidential election was merely to place the Chief Magistrate in the post assigned to him." But General Jackson obviously thought otherwise, he said. The President proposed "that if, prior to an election, certain opinions, no matter how ambiguously put forth by a candidate, are known to the people, those loose opinions, in virtue of the election, incorporate themselves with the constitution, and afterwards are to be regarded and expounded as parts of the instrument!"

Here then was the fundamental difference between Jackson and his opponents in Congress. Old Hickory actually believed that power was derived from the people directly and that by the exercise of their suffrage they granted the President the right to speak in their name. It was not so much a mandate (that is, an instruction to perform a specific act) that Jackson claimed. Rather he argued that he, and he alone, was the spokesman of all the people by virtue of his national election. Government exists, he contended, to accomplish the public will, and the presidential office functions as the instrument to express and execute that will.

Clay closed his speech with a thumping peroration. "The land is filled with spies and informers, and detraction and denunciation are the orders of the day. People, especially official incumbents in this place, no longer dare speak in the fearless tones of manly freemen, but in the cautious whispers of trembling slaves. The premonitory symptoms of despotism are upon us; and if Congress do not apply an instantaneous and effective remedy, the fatal collapse will soon come on, and we shall die—ignobly die—base, mean, and abject slaves; the scorn and contempt of mankind; unpitied, unwept, unmourned!"[36]

The galleries erupted in applause and shouts of approval when he finished, so much so that order was restored only after the visitors had been ejected from the chamber. The speech took Clay three days to deliver, ending on Tuesday, December 31, but it was one of his best. And what he demanded was nothing less than Jackson's censure by the full Senate, believing that it would completely "destroy" the President and rescue the nation from impending doom.

The speech sent Jackson into a towering rage. "Oh, if I live to get these robes of office off me," he seethed, "I will bring the rascal to a dear account."[37] He later likened the Kentuckian to "a drunken man in a brothel," reckless, destructive, and "full of fury."[38]

After he had calmed down, Jackson assumed a more philosophical air. In fact he was rather amused, if not proud, that the opposition termed his efforts a "revolution." He would keep records, he declared, "for the benefit of the future historian, whose pen may be employed in recording the events of the present day, or as the opposition say, *'the revolution.'* It is a revolution from a destructive corrupting and demoralising paper system that makes the rich richer, and the poor poorer." His revolution, he said, was aimed at providing equality for all Americans by converting the nation from a paper to a specie currency. If ordinary citizens could get rid of "ragg money" and switch to gold and silver, they would advance equality and democracy throughout the nation. Leave the rags to bankers and merchants, he wrote. A metallic currency "will give prosperity to our country, by giving to labour a fair and stable reward, and in keeping pauperism from our doors." That was the "revolution" he espoused, and such a revolution, he exclaimed, "must be hailed by posterity, *as a glorious revolution.*"[39]

Clay's denunciation of executive despotism in the Senate was buttressed by Calhoun and Webster in speeches of heroic length and intensity that took days to deliver. "Mr. Calhoun, if possible, surpassed Mr. Clay in the vehemence of his denunciations." He adopted the Kentuckian's "leading ideas of revolution" and "of a robbery of the treasury."[40] The plundering of the Roman treasury by Julius Caesar was an act of virtue compared to Andrew Jackson's recent conduct, said Calhoun. At least Caesar's seizure was done openly by an intrepid and bold warrior. "The actors in our case are of a different character—artful, cunning, and corrupt politicians, and not fearless warriors. They have entered the treasury, not sword in hand, as public plunderers, but, with the false keys of sophistry, as pilferers, under the silence of midnight."

"With money and corrupt partisans," declared Calhoun, looking straight at the presiding officer, Martin Van Buren, "a great effort is now making to choke and stifle the voice of American liberty . . . by corrupting the press; by overawing the other departments; and, finally, by setting up . . . a national convention, which, counterfeiting the voice of the people, will . . . dictate the succession; when the deed will be done, the revolution be completed, and all the powers of our republic, in like manner, be consolidated in the President, and perpetuated by his dictation."[41]

Daniel Webster, who came within an ace of entering an alliance with Jackson in 1833, now officially and publicly re-joined Clay and his friends and lent his considerable verbal support to the pro-Bank forces. As a reward for his decision against bolting the National Republican party he was chosen chairman of the Senate Committee on Finance, whose membership also included Tyler of Virginia and Willie P. Mangum of North Carolina, both Calhoun supporters, and Thomas Ewing of Ohio, a Clay partisan. It was at this time that Webster wrote his notorious letter to Biddle in which he informed the banker that his annual "retainer" had not been "renewed or *refreshed* as usual. If it be wished that my relations to the Bank should be continued, it may be well to send me the usual retainers."[42] And this was the man who would chair the Senate Finance Committee!

Although Webster argued forcibly against the removal of the deposits and scored many telling constitutional points against the President's position during the censure debate that lasted practically throughout the Panic session of 1833–1834, he did not resort to vituperation and personal attack as did Clay and Calhoun. He could not bring himself to that. He stood with the President on nullification and the preservation of the Union. For that reason he muted his language. The arguments hit their mark on several occasions, but they never overstepped Jackson's narrow threshold of anger.

The relentless pounding of the President by the Senate's "great triumvirate" to win Jackson's censure for removing the deposits was answered by equally lengthy and eloquent speeches by Democrats, most notably Thomas Hart Benton—"Old Bullion" as he came to be called—and John Forsyth of Georgia, one of Van Buren's close friends. Responding almost immediately to Clay's call for censure, Benton took four days to "batter" the Kentuckian. He returned sarcasm for ridicule, stinging rejoinder for biting accusation. "The senator from Kentucky," Benton sneered, "calls upon the people to rise, and drive the Goths from the capitol. Who are those Goths? They are General Jackson and the democratic party—he just elected President over the senator himself, and the party just been made the majority in the House—all by the vote of the people. It is their act that has put these Goths in possession of the capitol to the discomfiture of the senator and his friends; and he ought to be quite sure that he felt no resentment at an event so disastrous to his hopes, when he has indulged himself with so much license in vituperating those whom the country has put over him." He contended that Clay's censure motion charged the President with an impeachable offense, a matter for the House to consider, not the Senate. "The senator wishes to know what we are to do? . . . I answer . . . to leave this impeachment to the House of Representatives . . . and to those who have no private griefs to avenge."[43]

Other Democrats chorused their derision of pro-Bank congressmen by citing their willingness to approve the corrupting power of the BUS, which owed no direct responsibility to the American people, yet condemned the exercise of presidential authority, derived from the Constitution and augmented by popular support. They could stomach Biddle's despotism but not Jackson's attack upon it. They ranted about "King Andrew" but never once mentioned "Czar Nick."[44]

In the midst of this ongoing debate (and almost as though the President were intent upon proving the opposition's argument about his despotic intentions), Jackson again exercised his presidential powers early in 1834 in a unique and unprecedented manner. Labor violence on the Chesapeake and Ohio Canal had erupted near Williamsport, Maryland, in mid-January, 1834. Local authorities appealed to the state legislature which, in turn, asked Jackson for military assistance. The request was transmitted by Governor James Thomas on January 28, 1834. The President immediately directed the secretary of war to order "such military as will be able to aid the civil authority of Maryland to put down the riotous assembly." He directed "at least" two companies of regulars to be dispatched and "with as much expedition as possible."[45] In sending federal troops to put down a strike—for that was precisely what he had ordered —Jackson acted "in accordance with his own conception of the enlarged powers of the presidency." He responded to his perceived duty to maintain "law and order." He was the first President, therefore, to use federal troops to quell a disorder "which had not arisen out of a violation of federal law or a defiance of the federal government."[46] It was another sign that the country and its political system had changed dramatically.

Jackson felt he had a responsibility as the chief executive to maintain order throughout the entire country, no matter the circumstances; and that was especially true when his aid was requested by the lawful authority of a state. He ordered federal troops to put down civil disorders on more occasions than any previous President. But he paid a political price. He was again assaulted for illegally expanding the powers of his office. He was pilloried for violating the rights of the states. And, as the contest between the pro- and anti-Bank forces grew more vituperative, as the economic panic initiated by Biddle worsened, as memorials and complaints from all sections of the nation poured into Congress and demanded relief, and as more and more nullifiers, states' righters, old strict constructionists, and Jackson-haters joined the opposition, Democrats panicked.[47] There was nearly "a breaking up of old parties," reported one congressman. "The Terrors of popular displeasure in members from Jackson regions, the timid, the wavering, the . . . fear of being in a minority at home, all presented obstacles, that required all our prudence, forbearance, indulgence, perseverance and spirit to ensure us success."[48] Rumors swept through Congress alleging that a majority of House members favored a restoration of the deposits and that if the President did not accede to their wish his majority in the House would dissolve. Amos Kendall declared that "some of the truest members seemed on the point of yielding." One of them stopped and exclaimed: "We cannot resist this tremendous pressure; we shall be obliged to yield."

"What!" retorted Kendall, "are you prepared to give up the Republic? This is a struggle to maintain a government of the people against the most heartless of all aristocracies, that of money. Yield now, and the Bank of the United States will henceforth be the governing power whatever may be the form of our institutions."[49]

Although some of his partisans weakened, Andrew Jackson grew increasingly resolute. No amount of pleading or cajoling or intimidating— much less threatening—could shake him from his purpose. He would kill the monster if he had to do it alone with his bare hands. "The President remains inexorable," reported Senator Samuel Bell of New Hampshire, "but many of his partizans are in much distress under the impression that his lawless and reckless conduct and his obstinacy will prostrate the party."[50]

Jackson caused the Democrats even greater fear when he decided early in 1834 that the way to weaken the BUS and its friends in Congress even further was to order an end to the Bank's operation of paying pensions to Revolutionary War veterans. It was a political masterstroke. In January, 1834, the President instructed Secretary of War Lewis Cass to order Biddle to relinquish all the funds, books, and accounts relating to pensions to the War Department's commissioner of pensions. Biddle indignantly rejected the order. The Bank would not be intimidated by such transparent and highhanded political tactics.[51]

Upon Biddle's refusal to obey the President's order, the secretary of war suspended pension payments. Again a howl of protest erupted from the nation as veterans suffered this latest battle wound in the continuing Bank War. Jackson immediately referred the matter to Congress, protesting that the Bank not only defied the government but inflicted needless misery on the nation's patriotic heroes. In the House the President's complaint was referred to the Ways and Means Committee, which predictably returned a majority report rebuking the Bank for causing the suspension of pension payments. In the Senate, however, the majority voted its agreement with the Bank for refusing to obey an improper order.[52]

And so it went, a running battle between the branches of government. But this latest evidence of Biddle's power and contempt for the well-being of the American people sent a new charge of anger and resentment throughout Democratic ranks. Their newspapers rang with denunciations of the "hydra of corruption" which gorged itself on the pitiful pensions snatched from the veterans of the Revolution. This was not General Jackson's doing. Who could believe that he would deny these heroes their rightful due from a grateful nation. Only the Czar of Chestnut Street, who instigated havoc at will, was capable of such wanton cruelty.[53]

So potent was this propaganda that even Webster urged Biddle to relinquish the pension money. He granted that the government's argument was flimsy. "But, after all, it is a bad subject to dispute about. The pensioners will not believe [that Jackson] is the cause of keeping back their money," and furthermore they will agree with the President that the Bank has proved itself to be a dangerous monopoly and must be destroyed. Several other friends of the BUS seconded Webster's appeal, but Biddle would not listen. He would not be bullied. The veterans could rot for all he cared. A greater duty compelled him to meet this challenge with defiance.[54]

Biddle may have had justice on his side, but politically he was headed for destruction. By his inept responses to Jackson's deadly thrusts he was surely and rapidly losing public support. Without realizing it, without intending it, he was assisting Jackson in the annihilation of his Bank.

CHAPTER 9

The Rise of the Whig Party

THE SENATE WAS PACKED TO OVERFLOWING. A spectacle was in progress that held each person in the chamber utterly enthralled. Henry Clay was in the process of baiting the Vice President and his words dripped with sarcasm and ridicule. He teased and mocked. He purred and petted. Then he pounced.

Intercede with Jackson, he implored Van Buren. "Go to him and tell him, without exaggeration . . . the actual condition of his bleeding country." Everyone knows how great is your influence over him. He will listen to you. Tell him the nation is nearly ruined and undone by the measure he has put into operation. "Tell him of the tears of helpless widows, no longer able to earn their bread, and of unclad and unfed orphans. Tell him that he has been abused, deceived, betrayed, by the wicked counsels of unprincipled men around him. . . . Entreat him to pause and reflect that there is a point beyond which human endurance cannot go, and let him not drive this brave, generous, and patriotic people to madness and despair."[1]

Some guests in the galleries chortled, others burst into gales of laughter. The Little Magician just smiled. He hardly moved a muscle. He waited until Clay completed his bravura performance and then leisurely gestured another senator to take his seat as presiding office. He hopped down to the floor and then, instead of leaving the room, he walked straight across the chamber toward Henry Clay. The galleries gasped. It suddenly seemed as though a brawl might ensue right there on the Senate floor between the Vice President of the United States and the distinguished senator from Kentucky. Everyone froze.

Seeing Van Buren approach, Clay slowly rose from his seat. He stared ahead, watching in hypnotic fascination as the figure came steadily toward him. Could it be that the Vice President, that soul of courtesy and amiability, was about to do or say something violent or ugly? At last Van Buren reached Clay's side. But instead of rebuking the senator by word or act, the Vice President bowed. Then, in a mocking voice, he said: "Mr. Senator, allow me to be indebted to you for another pinch of your aromatic Maccoboy."

The words dissolved the tension in the chamber and the Senate breathed a sigh of relief as Clay, flabbergasted, waved his hand toward the gold snuffbox resting on his desk. He was too dumbfounded to utter a sound. Van Buren took a pinch of snuff, applied it deftly to each nostril and then leisurely returned to the Vice President's chair, smiling triumphantly at the other senators as he went.[2]

The incident unnerved Clay, as Van Buren intended. All during the session the senator had seized every opportunity to bait the Vice President and the practice had begun to irritate. Even the senator's supporters took offense at some of his antics.[3] Clay made much of the fact that Van Buren had not arrived in Washington until December 14, two weeks after Congress reconvened.[4] He constantly poked fun at the little man. But these gambols provided such entertainment that spectators demanded daily performances. And they drew a packed chamber. "The Senate chamber is now the centre of attraction," claimed Mrs. Samuel Smith, "not only of political interests, but of the fashionable world likewise. It is daily crowded by all the beauty and fashion of *our* great world—crowded almost to suffocation."[5]

Although Van Buren and Clay jousted with each other in public they had enough political sense not to allow it to spoil their social intercourse. Each time Clay spotted the little man at a party he would joke with him about how Jackson's revolution would soon bring an end to their freedom. Van Buren gave as good as he got and generally laughed off the senator's dire predictions of doom.[6] But a great many other congressmen shared Clay's fears. Their immediate concern was what would happen to the currency and credit of the nation once the BUS disappeared. It was all very well to put an end to the Bank's corruption, but what kind of financial and banking system would follow. A national banking operation was indispensable, in the minds of many, and no amount of political claptrap could alter that fact.

With regard to money, Jackson believed in only one kind: specie. That was real money. It was the only instrument to pay laborers for their honest work. It would provide a "fair and stable reward" for their services, the value of which could not be manipulated by dishonest jobbers, and would end price fluctuations and the boom and bust economy that had characterized the nation's economy since the inception of paper money.

As for a banking system, Jackson might conceivably have been talked into another national bank, once the wreckage of Biddle's corporation had been hauled from the scene, but he first insisted that his "experiment" with deposit banking receive a fair trial to discover whether the nation could successfully adapt to it. To each alarm he heard about the imminent collapse of his "experiment" he countered with the argument that more time was needed to give his system a fair opportunity to prove its worth. When he was warned that state banks "of good standing" could not be found in some areas to receive the government's deposits, Jackson retorted that in such instances the "Secretary of the Treasury will prepare orders to the Collector to receive the Deposits & keep them in an iron chest."[7]

But a number of Jackson's supporters in Congress were unwilling to wait out a period of experimentation with deposit banking. There were "more than thirty members" of the House of Representatives alone, reported Congressman Robert T. Lyttle of Ohio, "who voted with us, & will throughout against restoring the Deposits and also against the present Bank who are *decidedly* in favour of a *New one.*" Other Democrats agreed. "Our friends," recalled Richard M. Johnson of Kentucky, "were divided during the Panic Session upon *the Bank & a Bank.*" Van Buren worried that this widespread feeling among Democrats could produce much mischief. He told Jackson that the danger "is not from *the* Bank but from *a* Bank." Still talk continued in Congress that the only way to escape the panic and save the party was to create another national bank.[8]

The Democrats ran into trouble when they tried to define the sort of bank they wanted. To replace the BUS with an exact replica managed by Democrats would never get Jackson's blessing. So there was much speculation on what was feasible. Some Democrats suggested a much smaller version of Biddle's company and under tighter government supervision. They proposed an institution with a $10 million capital stock located in Washington and with such modifications of the charter as to avoid Jackson's constitutional "scruples." Another group advocated what they called a "people's bank," in which the stock would belong to the several states as well as the United States. Still a third group argued for a bank in the District of Columbia that would merely serve as a "fiscal agent" for the government with no power to grant loans. Of all the schemes, perhaps this last one came closest to winning Jackson's approval if deposit banking failed.[9]

Most of these Democrats who wanted another national bank were prompted by political or economic fears—or prospects of a financial killing—and most seemed certain that deposit banking would ultimately go under. Besides, they were apprehensive about its popular reception. "If State Banks will do," Congressman Johnson explained to Blair, "I am better satisfied than with any National Bank—but if time should not convince the people of this & we all see it I feel confident that you & myself will concur in the course."[10]

This loose talk about starting up another national bank among Democrats disturbed Jackson to such an extent that he decided to put an end to it. And he had a quick and easy way to do it. He instructed editor Blair to carry an editorial in the Washington *Globe* to state his position unequivocally. He wanted no confusion on where he stood. As instructed, Blair prepared the editorial for publication in the February 11 issue of the *Globe* after first getting Jackson's approval of its wording. "An effort is made, in secret whispers here," Blair wrote, "that the President . . . is opposed only to *the* Bank of the United States, but not to *a* Bank." We are authorized to state emphatically, he continued, "that all reports to the contrary are mere inventions of the enemy—*and that the President is firmly resolved to adhere to his plan of the State Banks."*

Jackson's precise position on the money question was best explained by James K. Polk in a little-heard speech in the House (most available audiences generally crowded the Senate chamber) and amplified in a lengthy report in early March by his Ways and Means Committee. The administration's principal object of legislation, said Polk, is to increase the specie on which the circulation of the state banks would depend for their support. As conceived by the administration, the deposit banks would cease issuing or receiving bank notes under five dollars. This would necessarily create a demand for gold and silver coins. Later, in easy stages, they were to prohibit notes under ten dollars, then under twenty dollars. This would force the banks into keeping ever larger stocks of coins in their vaults and thus ultimately to restore the country to specie currency. His ideas, Jackson told James A. Hamilton, would "give a more uniform currency than any United States or National Bank ever has, or can do, and introduce a metallic currency throughout the Union sufficient for the laboring class by putting out of issue and circulation all notes under *twenty dollars."* Thus everyone can trade on their own credit and capital "without any interference by the general Government; except using its power by giving through its mint a specie currency, and by its legislation a standard value to keep the coin in the country." At long last, then, "a uniform and sound currency" would be established, just as Jackson had promised in his first message to Congress in 1829.[11]

Jackson's major concern was the protection of "the laboring class." He firmly believed that a system of paper currency enabled the rich to exploit the poor, and it was that exploitation he felt obligated to terminate.

Jackson's total commitment to hard money (under $20) was another shattering experience for the Democrats. It was bad enough to get rid of a national bank and substitute deposit banking, but widespread use of precious metal seemed like lunacy. Benjamin F. Butler, the new attorney general, tried to reassure his banking friends in New York. "In respect to the *hard money* proposition," he told Thomas W. Olcott, the cashier of the Mechanics and Farmers Bank in Albany and the Regency's chief banker, "which I perceive has excited some apprehension among our friends who are interested in the local Banks, I . . . assure you that he [Jackson] entertains no such Utopian dreams as the opposition presses have ascribed to him. If he were enabled to regulate the whole matter precisely as he could wish, he would proceed to high amounts, but not ultimately to an amount higher than $20. If there are any persons who wish to go further, it is enough to say that their number is not only very small, but that there is not the slightest *possibility* of carrying any such project into effect."[12]

Because amounts higher than $20 did not directly affect "the laboring class," nor involve their possible exploitation by greedy bankers, Jackson consented to proceed no further than $20 in his hard-money reform. The consequence of his bank policy, starting with his veto of recharter and continuing through removal of the deposits and the establishment of the deposit banking system with its emphasis on hard money, together with his aggressive and innovative presidential style, finally set in motion a realignment and reordering of party structure and loyalty. What resulted was not only a dramatic change in the Democratic party but the appearance of a new political party, the Whig party, as a counterweight to the Democrats.

The old parties of the 1820s (the National Republicans and the Democratic-Republicans) "reformed" themselves by 1834 to constitute two new parties, the Whigs and Democrats. Although the Democratic party retained the first half of its old name—the term "Republican" continued to be used by some on account of its association with Thomas Jefferson, but less and less frequently—its membership and ideology underwent considerable change. And Jackson was the catalytic agent. Those former Democratic-Republicans who could not abide his reform program or presidential style deserted to Clay and his friends. By and large these "deserters" included nullifiers and states' rights ideologues. (To a lesser extent, a few National Republicans switched over to the Democrats, attracted by Jackson's intense nationalism as demonstrated in the nullification controversy.) What remained in the Democratic party still constituted a very large number of American voters, for Jackson's program and personality attracted adherents from every profession and class and section in the country. With respect to ideology, Jacksonian Democrats steadily drifted away from the strict "republicanism" of an earlier period. They no longer tolerated a begrudging sufferance of popular opinion, the sort of thing that allowed the legislature to alter public judgment when deemed necessary, such as happened in 1825 when John Quincy Adams was chosen President over Andrew Jackson. Now the Democrats preached an absolute observance of majority will. The people were wise and good and must be obeyed. As Jackson himself said: *"the majority is to govern."*[13]

As for the Whig party, the forces producing it had been in train for a number of years, but under the pressures of the Bank War and Jackson's insistence on a new fiscal policy, it finally emerged during the late winter and early spring of 1834—the Panic session—as Congress battled the President over the removal of the deposits. National Republicans, Bank men, nullifiers, high tariff advocates, friends of internal improvements, states' righters, and—most particularly—all those who abominated Jackson or his policies, slowly converged into a new political coalition that quite appropriately assumed the name "Whig." Derived from British politics, the name signified opposition to the monarchical party which advocated strong executive leadership. Also, the name was associated with the patriotic cause in the American struggle for independence against the British crown just a few decades before. To men like Clay, Webster, Adams, Calhoun, and others, Andrew Jackson represented in American government the same sort of arbitrary authority that was associated in Britain with the crown. In their minds, Jackson presumed monarchical powers, powers that were unconstitutional and abhorrent to the American experiment in liberty.

Perhaps Philip Hone, the New York merchant, first invoked the name to designate the new coalition. According to one source, James Watson Webb, editor of the New York *Courier and Enquirer*, used it at Hone's suggestion.[14] In any event it quickly caught on and seemed to those who assumed it as appropriate as calling Jackson "King Andrew." Did not his vetoes, contempt of the Supreme Court, "spoils system," his claim as a coequal with Congress in lawmaking, and his reiterated argument that he alone represented all the people—did these not justify its use?

What gave the name wide currency was a speech delivered in the Senate on April 14, 1834, by Henry Clay. In using the term in his speech, Clay not only signaled its acceptance by the leadership of the anti-Jackson forces but triggered a public response from the Democrats. On April 22, in reply to Clay's speech, the Washington *Globe* noticed the new designation in an article entitled, "Principles of the Alias Party." Said Blair in this editorial: "It is the custom with all offenders when they have disgraced one name by their crimes to assume another." He charged that the new party actually consisted of none but Tories, Federalists, National Republicans, and Nullifiers who had banded together under the auspices of the monster Bank and "boldly resolved to take a name directly opposite to that which belongs to the founders of their party." By way of "metempsychosis," he sneered, the "ancient TORIES now call themselves WHIGS." No matter. "By whatever false names the enemies of the Democracy may choose to be known they fortunately never fail to furnish us with a clue to their true sentiments."

Because of the concentrated assault on Jackson as a tyrant and despot by the Whigs, the Democratic press made a special effort to justify the President's actions and remind Americans of the circumstances that had brought him to power. He was elected, they lectured, to "bring the Constitution back to what it was under Jefferson" by casting off the doubtful powers which had been assumed by preceding administrations. By his vetoes, they said, he had ended the extravagant waste of the taxpayer's money; by his efforts at a strict accountability he had rid the government of official delinquency and provided a rigid economy in the disbursement of public money. And his veto of the Bank recharter bill terminated one of the greatest threats that had ever arisen in the country to the freedom won by the Founding Fathers against the Tories who now call themselves Whigs.[15]

Later in the spring the Democrats invariably alluded to the new coalition as the "Wig" party, since everyone knew that aristocrats wore wigs and that honest, God-fearing Americans had long ago stopped wearing them or tieing their hair in a queue. This new age rejected anything having to do with "ques and Wigs." Let the whole world know what this antiadministration party really is, jeered the *Globe.* "The Modern Wig— a cover for bald federalism."[16]

The Washington *National Intelligencer,* along with many other newspapers formerly committed to the National Republican party, immediately adopted the Whig name, its leadership, and what these newspapers called its antiexecutive, antiauthoritarian ideology. They applauded the "heterogeneous quality" of their party, particularly after the Democrats accused them of attracting every disaffected and elitist group in the nation. True, confessed the *National Intelligencer,* we are composed of diverse elements. We include "all parties in the country save only that whose sole article of faith is executive infallibility—the Yezedies of the political church." The concurrence of such opposite materials in a common cause, the paper went on, "proves that the public grievance must be great indeed and truly alarming which could produce" such a union.[17]

In terms of ideology, the Whig press declared that the new coalition represented the supremacy of representative government over dictatorial rule. The President had paralyzed the powers of Congress through an "extraordinary" exercise of the veto, they insisted. Never had there been such rapaciousness on the part of the executive to expand the authority of his office. The veto power "is not to be exercised upon the mere will and pleasure" of the executive, but "upon sufficient reasons" which the President must assign to Congress every time he resorts to it. "This President is *answerable,* therefore, to Congress for the veto when he applies it. The Senate is not in any matter as answerable to him but entirely independent of him in regard to their share of the power of appointment to office." And that was the basic difference between the Democratic and Whig parties: the one would rule by executive fiat, the other by legislative mandate.[18]

Democrats hooted at this "fake" distinction. In a modern society, with modern instruments of production and transportation reshaping America, the discussion of a contest between branches of government was an idle waste of time. The real contest, the Democrats contended, was the one defined by Andrew Jackson in his Bank veto message. "He has drawn the just distinction," declared the *Globe*, "between those classes of society that labor and those that do not; those that earn their living by the sweat of their brow and constitute the bone and muscle of the country, defending it in war and supporting it in peace—and those who live by their interest in the stocks and the various speculations that are favored by extension of bank credit."[19] The President has shown that the burden of the present system falls almost exclusively on the working class. He has endeavored to alter that system to free labor from this unnecessary, devastating, and unfair burden. Therein lies the difference between parties, the difference between those who live by the "sweat of their brow" and are represented by Democrats, and those who live by speculating in the stock of banks (and other such moneyed corporations) and are represented by the Whigs.[20]

The great advantage that the Democrats exploited throughout the Jacksonian era was the recognition that society was changing and that the important question of the age involved the rights of individuals and classes to achieve the promises of American life and not the manner of government and the relative power or authority among its several parts. The Whigs, unfortunately, hearkened back to an earlier time that worried over the distribution of powers within and between governments. In the Jacksonian age the Industrial Revolution was redirecting the country toward a more urban and industrialized society where the standard of living was rising rather rapidly, where a widened suffrage gave hundreds of thousands more white men the right to vote and hold office, where great fortunes were in the process of being made (and even greater poverty was becoming more apparent). With all these revolutionary changes taking place, the Democrats sensed the importance of responding to the needs and interests of the great mass of the electorate rather than an elite minority who could protect their own interests. Politics was groping toward a more overtly social and economic orientation. And in their appeal to the electorate, the Democrats, with Jackson as their leader and symbol, moved right along with it.

But, because Jackson and his party repeatedly declared their concern for "those that earn their living by the sweat of their brow," that did not mean that Democrats challenged or rejected capitalist values. Quite the contrary. Their propaganda against a corrupt aristocracy and in support of the virtuous mass electorate actually facilitated the union of entrepreneurs (who, among other things, sought an end to legislative ties to banking) with wage earners and farmers, thus cutting across existing lines of occupation and wealth. In short, their appeal attracted a wide range of voters who stood squarely with Jackson in his contention that *"the majority is to govern."* Many Democrats around the country probably agreed with Representative Aaron Ward of New York when he said that Andrew Jackson "is now the great champion and Bulwark of the rights of the People, not only of this Country but of the world: for I do most firmly believe that on the result of this great struggle [over the Bank] depends the future fate of free principles both here and every where."[21]

As for issues, the Whig party pretty much adopted Clay's American System for their program. By and large they favored a national bank, strong credit and currency facilities to assist the ongoing industrial revolution, and federally sponsored public works. Most of them also advocated tariff protection, but on this issue they could not expect support from southerners, particularly nullifiers. As a group, Whigs tended to be socially conservative, economically venturesome, and politically hostile to "Jacksonian equalitarianism." According to one modern Whig historian, they distrusted the "city rabble, the backwoodsmen, the illiterates in general." They mostly included industrialists, bankers, "go-ahead" businessmen, and conservative farmers from all sections.[22]

Both Democrats and Whigs included men of recent wealth, the upwardly mobile, but to what proportion is still debatable. Both included party professionals who contrived the ballyhoo to create voter appeal, who pursued office to satisfy their own ambition, and who rewarded loyalty and hard work for the party organization. Together, both parties effectively destroyed the old-fashioned dynastic or "family" parties (both national and local) that had typified the political systems of the past.

The realignment of parties during Jackson's administration generated a tremendous amount of political excitement, both in Washington and around the nation, which accounts for the wild scenes in Congress and the commotion in the country about the panic, the removal of the deposits, the censure resolutions, and the course of American freedom and democracy. Even those men who understood the political game and played it with care and finesse could sometimes find themselves embroiled in agitated scenes of confrontation with their opponents. Henry Clay, for example, happened upon Martin Van Buren outside the Senate chamber one day and somehow got tangled in a verbal contest.

The Magician began the exchange on a light and jocular note, which was his wont in such situations. He bantered about the approaching spring elections in the country and offered to bet Clay a suit of clothes that in New York and Virginia the Democrats would trounce the Whigs.

Clay bridled. It was as though Van Buren had struck him in the face. Suddenly he poured out his anger in a torrent of words that escaped his lips before he could ponder them. It was one thing to abuse Van Buren on the floor of the Senate—that was part of the political game—but quite another to do it in private. That was hardly his style. As he spoke he could barely contain himself. He told Van Buren "that if the people entertained the Administration in its late measures, I should begin to fear that our experiment of free Government had failed; that he [Van Buren] would probably be elected the successor of Jackson; that he would introduce a system of intrigue and corruption, that would enable him to designate his successor."

Van Buren just stared at the senator, hardly believing his ears. Clay ended his outburst by predicting that "after a few years of lingering and fretful existence, we should end in dissolution of the Union, or in despotism."

At that, Van Buren burst out laughing. He chided Clay for his "morbid feelings."

His laughter broke the tension. A trifle amused at his own foolishness, Clay smiled. Then, in a half-serious tone of voice, but "with good nature," he added that he "deliberately and sincerely believed" what he had said.

The look of amusement drained from Van Buren's face. He turned and walked away.[23]

CHAPTER 10

Censure and Protest

THE SOCIAL AND POLITICAL TURBULENCE that occurred in the United States during the opening months of 1834 was unprecedented. "I have never known the country so generally and so deeply excited as they are upon the recent measures of the administration," wrote one man. Huge gatherings of the electorate occurred in many cities. One in New York was "said to be the largest ever known in this country." At these meetings, "inflammatory harangues, cannon firing, great feasts" took place. It will be difficult for people "in after times," wrote Senator Benton, "to realize the degree of excitement, of agitation, of commotion which was produced by this organized attempt to make panic and distress."[1]

"We have had," reported Representative Churchill C. Cambreleng to his friend Edward Livingston, who had recently arrived in Paris to begin his duties as United States minister, "one of the most extraordinary" congressional sessions in memory. The "most bitter and violent denunciations—with cries of ruin, panic and despair" characterized the proceedings and "have succeeded in producing an excitement in the country which you have probably seldom seen even in times of embargo or of war." The Whigs "vainly hoped," he continued, "that by distressing the people they could revolutionize public opinion—forgetting the lessons of all past history. . . . You who have had so much experience in public life, will wonder how old politicians could commit such a blunder as to suppose they could gain the confidence of the people by espousing the cause of a great monied institution. . . . They forgot one thing—that in every contest between avarice and patriotism, the latter has hitherto in this country uniformly triumphed—they also forgot that when a whole people were roused the relative strength of the democracy was increased and that is our present condition."[2]

One of Jackson's greatest contributions to this nation, so Cambreleng seemed to be saying, was that he roused the people with his cry against the monster of Chestnut Street and in so doing strengthened the relative power of the mass electorate within the American system of government. First he raised his voice with his veto; then, he raised it again with the removal of the deposits. And each time he sounded his cry the democracy responded and rushed to his support, swelling in numbers with each response. Summoned to perform their duty as freemen, they rallied themselves with Old Hickory in the "contest between avarice and patriotism."

Put another way, President Jackson had loosed the power of the masses, something never done before. To Whigs, this was frightening in its implications; to Democrats, it was awesome and wonderful. "Genl. Jackson," said one congressman, "now stands at the head of the democracy & if he triumphs as I feel a prophetic confidance he will, in this great struggle for the liberties of the human race, there is not a man in our annals . . . that will be more dear to all future time."[3]

Throughout the controversy over the removal of the deposits, Jackson "relentlessly" insisted (and his Democratic press echoed it around the nation) that "this great struggle" for liberty "was between the monied aristocracy of this country thro the power of the U.S. Bank, and the people." Democracy versus aristocracy, the laboring class against the "speculative class." The outcome would decide, he declared, "which shall govern this now free & happy country."[4] If the deposits are restored, he argued, the Bank will be rechartered with its present powers intact and "then indeed is our liberty gone & we will be doomed to be governed by a corrupt monied aristocracy until put down by another revolution." By removing these funds and hastening the destruction of the BUS, the great bulwark of free government, based on the popular will, would be reinforced.[5]

Although removal complicated and intensified the Bank War, it advanced the course of democracy in Jackson's mind and that realization encouraged him to greater efforts. The battle absolutely invigorated him. His spirit never seemed brighter. "You would be surprised to see the General," reported Major Donelson. "This Bank excitement has restored his former energy, and gives him the appearance he had ten years ago. Even the opposition, who in some form or other have had a closer view of him latterly, begin to admit that he is not in need of a *Kitchen* Cabinet in as much as he seems to speak understandingly and able."[6]

Not even the General's poor health slowed him down, although he suffered severe lung congestion early in 1834, accompanied by chest pains and a hacking cough. To alleviate the symptoms he put on a "medicated Hare skin" prepared for him by its inventor, a man named Schnider, and which was to be worn "for affections of the chest, and pulmonary complaints, Astma, coughs, colds, and dispyspepsia etc."[7] His only real concern—and it was one that periodically disturbed his mind and drained his energies—was the welfare of his "little family." He worried especially about his son, Andrew Jr. The young man had no head for business, and the more the father guided and instructed him the more the son committed monumental errors of judgment. Either Andrew was stupid or he just did not care. Probably both. At times it almost appeared as though he resented his father's efforts to teach him how to survive in the modern world and the skills necessary to run a plantation.

Jackson had badgered his son for years about his poor business sense and his indolent habits. The boy never seemed to complain or answer back. He offered excuses and then went right back to his old habits. At times he drove his father to distraction. And the situation did not improve after Andrew married. If anything it got worse, and it reached a climax in 1834.

On his way back to the Hermitage in 1833, Andrew Jr. stopped off in Philadelphia and purchased a chest of tools for use on the plantation. He entrusted the purchase to an agent. As a result tools worthy of a professional cabinetmaker were delivered, not those "well suited to a negroes work shop." Jackson dutifully paid the bill. Then he tried to teach his son an important lesson. "I trust that it will hereafter admonish you to purchase your own Tools for the farm and not entrust it to an agent. remember my advice my son, never purchase any useless article, those that are needful for your comfort . . . purchase always as far as you have the means, and be always certain, if you wish to die independent, to keep your wants within your means, always when you have the money, paying for them when bought."[8] This was one of Andrew's cardinal sins. He bought things he did not need—even when he was out of pocket. And he hardly seemed to mind the consequences of his act since his father never failed to bail him out.

A worse problem was Andrew's business naiveté—to put the best light on it. To some he behaved like the proverbial village idiot. A helpless lamb among ravenous wolves could not have been more easily victimized than young Andrew whenever he entered the marketplace. The elder Jackson warned him repeatedly about his weakness. Hardly a year passed without the lecture.

> I have said before and now repeat—the world is not to be trusted. Many think you rich, and many you will find under false pretentions of friendship would involve you, if they can, strip you of your last shilling, and afterwards laugh at your folly, and distress. Real charity always (when you have the means) relieve it, and providence will smile upon the act, provided it is done in the way pointed out by our saviour in his sermon on the mount which I beg you to read.[9]

But Andrew never learned, no matter how many times he was fleeced. And he was one of those singular individuals who could smile through any adversity and reassure himself that the fault lay elsewhere. He was incompetent, lazy, weak, and unlucky. Apart from drinking and an occasional extramarital fling, he most enjoyed hunting. He wasted much of his life pursuing the sport and died prematurely in 1865 at the age of fifty-seven when he accidentally shot himself in the hand while climbing a fence.[10]

On this homeward journey in 1833, Andrew went on a buying spree. In addition to the tools, he purchased a young black girl and child from George Hibb and paid for them with a promissory note. This, despite the fact that his father had given him $800, which was more than "sufficient to pay for the wench and child, and to cover all expences home." Worse, Andrew failed to remit full payment when he arrived home, as he had promised. Jackson groaned. Not only had his son disregarded his explicit instructions about signing notes, but he jeopardized his credit and business standing as well. And if Andrew did not have the means to pay for the "wench and child" why had he failed to ask his father for the money? "Altho heavy drafts of late have been made upon me," wrote Jackson to Andrew, "I should have paid with pleasure, rather than you should have injured your credit, or that Mr. Hibb should have had cause to complain of your want of punctuality." Then followed another lecture.

> Why will you not my d'r Andrew, attend to my admonition about your money matters—never incur debts when you have the money to discharge your contracts, and in this instance there was no necessity to have left any unpaid. You had my advice to buy the girl, and if you had not the means in cash, which I thought you had, you ought to have drew on me, notifying me thereof. . . . hereafter my son, recollect my admonitions—buy nothing on credit when you have the cash to pay for it, buy nothing on credit that is not absolutely necessary for your comfort, or that of your family.[11]

Andrew always had a lame excuse. ("At the time I was lying sick," was a favorite, knowing his father would be solicitous.) And he invariably promised to do better. He was full of promises.

Late in 1833 he had good news. The farm had yielded upwards of 50,000 lbs. of cotton which had been shipped to Maunsel White, Jackson's broker in New Orleans, and when all of it was ginned the total would come to 100 bales. But not only was this information sent belatedly, Andrew neglected to report the weight of the bales, the handling charges, or whether the cotton had been sold or simply shipped. So the good news had little meaning. Without these figures Jackson could not calculate his balance sheet, he said, particularly since he had no idea what debts had been incurred on the farm.

Jackson hated nagging his son, but he feared for his future. He tried to explain that he wanted to free Andrew and the farm from all debt so that "after I am gone, you and your family" will not be burdened with financial need. "Hence it is, and was, that I was and am so solicitous to be furnished with the full information on all the points required of you."[12]

Andrew did not answer. The father repeated his request again and again about the weights and the sale of the cotton.[13] It was exasperating. Then Andrew committed an even worse blunder. He entered into negotiations with Harry R. W. Hill for the purchase of Baldwin's Hill, adjoining the Hermitage, for $10,000. It included 563 acres at approximately $17.75 per acre. "I could get it for no less," said Andrew, "or lose it—and father Mr Hill is to give me an answer in a day or two, whether he will, or will not, extend the payments to three years, I think I can get him to do it. . . . What think you of it."[14]

Old Hickory thought the price too high. And he warned against extending the time to make payment: "no farmer can pay six percent for mony, nor ought any farmer to be in debt, and anticipate his crops, and rely upon that, alone, to meet it. a blast comes, the crop fails and then the estate must go to meet it." There followed still another admonition:

> My dear Andrew, attend to my advice, it is that of a father—let us econo-mise until we are again clear of debt, then by laying up your cash from your productions, you can always purchase land or other things at a fair price.[15]

But Andrew had already agreed to the purchase. All Jackson could do was hope for the best. He felt uncomfortable about Hill and warned his son about any dealings with him. "He is a very keen man, and do nothing with him but what is reduced to writing." No matter the size of the contract, whether large or small, get it in writing, he begged. To be sure nothing was amiss he asked his son to send him the contract he had executed for the land.[16]

Two months passed. No word from Andrew. Repeatedly Jackson asked to see the contract and to know the other debts he had incurred. *"Put it in writing,* that I may know really what it is that I have to provide for. . . . I pray you my son to close this business on the receipt of this if not done before; and learn to close your contracts allways spedily and in writing."[17]

In late March Jackson received word from his New Orleans broker, Colonel Maunsel White, that the cotton had arrived and that the proceeds of the sale would be assigned to N. and J. Dick, the New Orleans agents of Harry R. W. Hill. "I would like to be informed how the Messhrs. Dick, has had any thing to do with the proceeds," asked Jackson of his son. Did Andrew not know that Dick was "my deadly enemy," "unworthy of trust," and dishonest in his private and political dealings? "Is it possible you have given Mr. Dick, a power to receive the proceeds of our crop?"[18]

Things were worse than Jackson ever imagined. The Dicks were connected to Hill, and Andrew had made an agreement with Hill on terms the President knew nothing about. "I am fearful you have been dealing too loosely with Mr. Hill" and unless everything is in writing in very

precise terms "you will have *trouble.*" "My son, attend to your fathers
advice, and it will keep you clear of law and lawsuits which you ought by
all precaution to avoid." In any event, he pleaded, send me the contract![19]

Apparently Andrew had no contract, at least not in his own possession.
And he had indeed consigned the proceeds to Dick, who turned them
over to Hill in accordance with his agreement with Andrew. Nothing
could be done about it. Fortunately the price of cotton had risen on the
Liverpool market. Maunsel White was an honest agent and he sold the
cotton at an average of 11¼¢ per pound. The crop totaled 37,800 lbs.,
not 50,000. White told Jackson that some of the cotton was of poor
quality, but that the second shipment had been better and he had gotten
a higher price for it. Had it all been of the finer quality he could have
obtained several more cents per pound. All told, Jackson realized
$3,918.05 for the cotton, almost half of what Andrew had originally led
him to expect.[20]

Eventually Jackson also learned the terms of the agreement with Hill:
$5,000 payable in May, and another $5,000 next January. Jackson sagged.
He feared that after paying all expenses in running the farm, the return
from the cotton sale would leave them very little. As for Hill, "I fear you
would find but little favour" from him, and it may be that "the Hermitage
with the premises purchased might be sold for the debt." But Jackson
exaggerated. Probably he wanted to frighten Andrew and impress upon
him what his folly could cost them. "My dear Andrew, the looseness with
which you have attended to this business, has occasioned me much trouble and writing, and I do hope it will be a lesson to you thro' life."[21]

Fortunately, Jackson had a handsome salary of $25,000 a year as Presi-
dent to fall back on to ease the pressure of his indebtedness and meet the
first payment of the debt. But he was something of a spendthrift himself.
Each year his salary slipped through his fingers. Most of it went toward
meeting the costs of entertaining and purchasing furniture. His dinner
parties, held frequently, were sumptuous. Also he regularly opened the
drawing rooms of the White House each week during the congressional
session to receive visitors, normally on Thursday at 8 P.M. On special
occasions, like New Year's Day, the drawing rooms were opened to the
public from noon until 3 P.M. These receptions—or levees, as they were
usually called—attracted huge crowds, so that each room was "literally
crammed with the most singular and miscellaneous assemblage" imagin-
able. Tradesmen and farmers with their wives comprised the largest
number in attendance, but generals and commodores, public officers,
foreign ministers and members of Congress—"in short, every trade,
craft, calling, and profession"—put in an appearance. One visitor from
Britain registered his dismay at the sight of this motley crowd. "There
were present at this levee," he wrote, "men begrimed with all the sweat
and filth accumulated in their day's—perhaps their week's—labour.

There were sooty artificers, evidently fresh from the forge or the work-shop; and one individual . . . whenever he passed, left marks of contact on the garments of the company." The visitor spotted President Jackson in one room shaking hands "with men whose very appearance suggested the precaution of a glove. I must say, however, that under these unpleasant circumstances, he bore himself well and gracefully."

At these levees, punch and lemonade were normally served. But no sooner were they brought into the saloons by the servants than the mob rushed for the trays and the contents were seized "by a sort of *coup-de-main.*" After the first serving the butlers usually armed themselves with "shillelahs" to beat off "the predatory horde" in order to move freely from one room to the next.[22]

But Jackson thoroughly enjoyed entertaining. Besides, he felt his office required it. The mansion belonged to the people, he said, and they had a right to see it. In addition to these levees he gave numerous dinner parties, some of which numbered hundreds of guests. More often they consisted of twenty or thirty individuals. At a typical gathering for dinner the group consisted of the President, his hostess, Emily Donelson, and her husband, Ralph Earl and any other Tennessee guest in the house, the Vice President with one of his sons (usually Major Abraham Van Buren), and then members of the cabinet, Congress, officers of the diplomatic corps, visiting politicians, society leaders, and local officials of the District of Columbia, Maryland, or Virginia. The guests normally arrived around five o'clock and stayed until 10 or 10:30 P.M. Dinner began at 6:30 P.M.[23]

Although Emily Donelson proved to be a most excellent "First Lady," since she was "a very agreeable woman" and had been raised to entertain large numbers of guests, Jackson sometimes wished that Sarah could serve as his hostess.[24] Then his "little pet," his "sweet little Rachel," would remain at his side throughout the year. He doted on this child with a passion, and he worried about her constantly as she went through all the dangerous stages of early childhood. She was now a year and a half old, and very susceptible to colds. But he was assured that she was "growing and improving finely, running all over the house and begins to talk, and is very sprightly." She had learned a great many new words, "and is continually calling for Grandpapa." That tickled the old man and intensified his longing for the Hermitage. Virtually every day his thoughts flashed to Tennessee and his "little family." Sarah was expecting again and due to deliver at any moment. He feared for her safety. Fortunately, despite occasional illnesses, she came to a safe delivery and presented her husband "with a fine son" on April 4, 1834. The couple named the child after his grandfather: Andrew Jackson III.[25]

The birth of his first grandson, the President said, more than compensated for the verbal abuse he suffered throughout the Panic session of 1833–1834. It almost took his mind off Clay's censure resolutions which still commanded the attention of the Senate and the fascinated interest of the nation. There seemed to be no pause in the opposition's determination to explore all the avenues of Jackson's "improper" conduct as chief executive—his so-called revolution. Even Democrats sometimes worried about the President's behavior. "Our politics are in a wretched condition," wrote one. "The powers of the Constitution have been too severely taxed:—we have been made too familiar with modes of action which were designed to be last resorts." It was never intended by the Founding Fathers that the government should operate in the manner prescribed by Jackson; he has stretched its powers beyond safe limits for a healthy republic.[26]

Jackson's extension of the powers of his office obviously reflected the sort of man he was. But it also reflected his intuitive understanding that the nation was shifting from republican ideals (which specified limits to government and suffrage to protect liberty) to more democratic ideals, which encouraged an enlarged suffrage and greater "solicitude" for the rights of the laboring classes of the country. According to Blair in the *Globe,* Andrew Jackson's "motto is: Let labor have security, prosperity will follow—all other interest rest upon it and it must flourish if it flourishes."

Jackson may not have been so epigrammatic but he did believe that government had been improperly directed to benefit the "speculative class" and that it was his duty as President to right the balance and see that the laboring class find equal opportunity. And if that meant using presidential powers to bring it about, so be it.

But many feared that such behavior "too severely taxed" the Constitution. In Congress, Clay called it a revolution and demanded the President's censure. Other senators amplified his argument. The senator from Kentucky, said Calhoun at one point, contends that "we are in the midst of a revolution." He agreed most heartily. "Yes, the very existence of free governments rests on the proper distribution and organization of power; and, to destroy this distribution, and thereby concentrate power in any one of the departments, is to effect a revolution." He disagreed with Clay only about the time at which it commenced. Clay stated that it began shortly after the commencement of the present session, but Calhoun placed its beginning with the tariff restrictions and the termination of its first stage with the passage of the Force Bill, which "absorbed all the rights and sovereignty of the States, and consolidated them in this government."[27]

Other Whig senators lambasted the President over his claim of popular support for his "revolution." "We are told," snorted Senator Peleg Sprague of Maine, "and it is constantly reiterated in our ears, that in all these assumptions and claims of prerogatives, the President is sustained by the people. . . . But they are not infallible." They are susceptible to hero worship. A military chieftain, "having wrought real or fancied deliverance by successful battles," can easily take advantage of it, for history abounds in instances of just such calamities. "In the paroxyms of their devotion they are ready at his shrine to sacrifice their rights, their liberties, their children and themselves." Therefore, they must be protected against themselves by the legislature.[28]

Sprague was speaking about old-fashioned republicanism, namely the right of the legislature to disregard the "will of their constituents" when they fall victim to devotional "paroxyms." He rejected the Jacksonian claim that the will of the majority was sovereign and that legislators must always obey it or resign their office.

During a period of approximately one hundred days, while a "phalanx of orators and speakers" daily pounded him and demanded his censure, while hundreds of newspapers incessantly assailed him, while a stream of committees bemoaning the distress poured through the White House to beg for relief, while public meetings held in all sections of the country berated him for his reckless disregard of their happiness and prosperity, and while "a nation seemed to be in arms, and the earth in commotion against him," President Andrew Jackson grew stronger in his determination and his conviction that he led a struggle for greater democracy in America. "Never could it have been said with as much truth," wrote Van Buren, "that heaven & earth & the other place too are rained to defeat him."[29] Senator Benton saw Jackson often during these hectic days, usually at night. And, said Benton, "I . . . never saw him appear more truly heroic and grand than at this time. He was perfectly mild in his language, cheerful in his temper, firm in his conviction." Benton had observed him in many perilous situations, he said, "both civil and military," but never had he seen him more confident or trusting in the people than at this time. Each day, late at night, Benton would drop by the White House and provide a résumé of the activities in Congress, the status of the contest over the censure resolutions, and the chances of their eventual victory. Each day Jackson would say, quietly and simply: "We shall whip them yet. The people will take it up after a while."[30]

But time was running out as the Senate, under Clay's prodding, moved steadily toward a vote on the censure resolutions, the resolutions that could presumably "destroy whomsoever it struck—even General Jackson." Indeed, in the House, one member drew up a resolution proposing the impeachment of the President. He jotted down notes for a speech to introduce the resolution and on the sheet of paper expressed the belief that the story about Jackson having been slashed on the head and wrist by a British soldier during the Revolutionary War was pure invention, a tale told for electioneering purposes, to win public sympathy and support. These notes fell accidentally to the floor of the House and came into the hands of Frank Blair, who showed them to Jackson.

"The d———d, infernal scoundrel!" Old Hickory roared. "Put your finger here, Mr. Blair," he commanded as he lifted his hair and pointed to the long dent in his head. Blair obeyed and found that the wound had been far deeper than he had supposed. He could place a whole finger in the scar.[31]

In the midst of the censure debate a series of tragedies occurred that seemed to some congressmen like the "tolling bell of doom," warning of the nation's probable fate under its present tyrannical rule. From time to time during the session the proceedings in Congress were abruptly interrupted to announce the deaths of General Lafayette, William Wirt, John Randolph of Roanoke, and Charles Carroll of Carrollton, the last surviving signer of the Declaration of Independence. And while in the very act of announcing the death of Randolph in the House, James Bouldin of Virginia suddenly stopped speaking and fell lifeless to the floor. Shortly thereafter, Representative James Blair of South Carolina, the only member of the House from that state who was not a nullifier, put a pistol to his head and blew his brains out.

As Representative Cambreleng said: "We have had one of the most extraordinary" congressional sessions in memory, one now about to be climaxed by a vote in the Senate to censure the President of the United States. Something like this had never happened before. It was unthinkable—indeed "disgraceful"—and yet Clay and the other Whig leaders insisted that it be done. Besides, they were sure they had the votes, and they expected by that vote to "destroy" General Jackson.

The resolution was read once more on the Senate floor:

> *Resolved,* That the reasons assigned by the Secretary of the Treasury for the removal of the money of the United States deposited in the Bank of the United States and its branches, communicated to Congress on the 4th of December, 1833, are unsatisfactory and insufficient.
>
> That the President, in the late executive proceedings in relation to the public revenue, has assumed upon himself authority and power not conferred by the Constitution and laws, but in derogation of both.[32]

Having debated this resolution for months, having explored all of the implications of Jackson's "revolution," the senators prepared to vote on the censure. The question was called. On March 28, 1834, by a vote of 26 to 20, the Senate passed the resolution of censure against the President of the United States. Earlier, on February 5, by a vote of 28 to 18, it rejected Taney's reasons for the removal of the deposits.

Of the twenty-six senators to vote for censure, Clay, Calhoun, Webster, Poindexter, Benjamin Leigh of Virginia, Sprague, and Theodore Frelinghuysen of New Jersey were obvious and expected. Also, nullifiers and strong states' rights advocates, such as Mangum of North Carolina, Tyler of Virginia, Preston of South Carolina, and Waggaman of Louisiana, could have been anticipated. Presumably the others were deeply disturbed by Jackson's "revolution." Among those voting against the resolution were the stalwarts, Benton, Hill, Wright, Forsyth, White, Grundy, Tallmadge of New York, and Wilkins of Pennsylvania.[33]

The censure, an unprecedented action by the Senate, was a savage blow to Jackson's pride. Ever the protector of his fame and always the defender of presidential authority, he resented the insulting demonstration of "spite and envy." He reacted immediately. He had no intention of accepting this rebuke of his conduct without a stiff, formal, and official reply and protest. Although it would be improper to defend himself on any particular charge made by the Senate, he told Amos Kendall, at least he could state what he did and why he was authorized to do it. He could explain that because of the Bank's "corruptions and violations of the charter" it would have been "criminal in me" not to remove the deposits. All of this must go into a written reply. Point by point Jackson explained to Kendall what he wanted said. He indicated the emphasis the reply should take. He identified the motivation behind the censure. "It must . . . be by this false clamour," he declared, "to endeavour to degrade the Executive in the minds of the people and destroy the confidence of the people in him, and thereby procure a re-charter of the Bank of the U.S. Against all such unauthorized, unprecedented, unconstitutional conduct by the Senate I do protest."[34]

The President also set Roger B. Taney to work on his "Protest" and virtually wore him out with the pressure of the assignment. Even Kendall wilted under the strain, although he helped polish the final version. Because Jackson wanted an elaborate defense of his legal and constitutional rights, he asked his new attorney general, Benjamin F. Butler, to write a major portion of the paper. Indeed, it was generally understood that Butler contributed the greatest part of the Protest, with the others infusing what "strength" they could muster into the finished product. But the ideas that informed the document emanated almost entirely from Jackson.[35]

The Globe, of course, wasted no time in registering its outrage. The perpetrators of this "shameless libel," Blair raged, were the "notorious stipendiaries" of the Bank and would have been "hissed out of the Senate if the voice of the people had been truly uttered by the members of that body." This action is nothing more than "the triumph of perfidy."[36] Without trial, without a chance to answer the accusations, without regard to constitutional and legal forms, the "purchased" opposition has vilified and condemned the chief executive. Is this the proper mode for legislative behavior? the Globe asked. Is this just? And will the people allow such a flagrant disregard of the law to go unpunished? "We say then to the People of the United States, is it not worthy of consideration to provide an amendment to the Constitution, limiting the senatorial term to four years and making the office elective by the People of the several States?" The "aristocratic" Senate, Blair predicted, must in time be made subject to the will of the "People." The Congress must become totally democratic.[37]

Although Jackson constantly stood by the side of his team of writers, explaining the direction his Protest should pursue and urging them to its swift completion, they needed over two weeks to finish the statement to Jackson's satisfaction. On Friday, April 18, it was done. The President then handed it to his private secretary, Andrew Jackson Donelson, and asked him to deliver it personally to the Senate.

At the Capitol the message was anticipated, for an "unusually early audience of both sexes" gathered in the Senate galleries. They knew that the President had prepared a strong rebuff to the censure, but what they heard absolutely stunned them. Its doctrines challenged the entire concept of Whig ideology. It boldly reasserted presidential powers. And it advanced the argument that the nation had become a democracy.

The Protest was dated April 15, and Jackson wasted no time at the very outset in registering his complaint. "Without notice, unheard and untried, I thus find myself charged . . . with the high crime of violating the laws and Constitution of my country." He deemed it an imperative duty, he said, to maintain the "supremacy . . . and the immunities" of his office and to that end "I have caused this my *solemn protest*" against the censure to be transmitted to the Senate.[38]

Jackson then lectured the members about the division of powers under the Constitution, the rights of his office, and the necessity of a formal impeachment proceeding, initiated by the House, when presidential actions are to be called into question. The resolution of the Senate, he said, was wholly unauthorized by the Constitution and in derogation of its entire spirit in assuming the right "to take up, consider, and decide upon the official acts of the Executive." The President, therefore, was accused and found guilty of an impeachable offense without following the exact and explicit directions of the Constitution.

After this long and involved discussion of the constitutional and legal implications of the Senate's action, Jackson got down to specifics. He began with the question of his removal of Duane. The power of appointment, he said, resides with the President; the Senate may neither nominate nor appoint. Moreover, Jackson continued, all executive officers are removable at the President's will. Jackson was at pains to argue this point and to include specifically the officers of the Treasury Department. The custody of the public property had always been considered an appropriate function of the executive department, he said, and "every species of property belonging to the United States" (whether land, munitions, buildings, merchandise, clothing, provisions—or public money) is in the charge of officers appointed by the President, responsible to him, and removable at his will.[39]

Congressmen sat bolt upright in their seats when they heard that incredible assertion. Jackson was dead wrong in the matter and later beat a hasty retreat.

There could be no doubt, the President continued, that it was the legal duty of the secretary of the treasury to transfer public funds from the Bank of the United States whenever there was sufficient reason for making the change. Since that officer was subject to his direction, Jackson went on, and since he had determined that sufficient reason did exist, he ordered the removal. "So glaring were the abuses and corruptions of the bank, so evident its fixed purpose to persevere in them, and so palpable its design by its money and power to control the Government and change its character, that I deemed it the imperative duty of the Executive authority . . . to check its career and lessen its ability to do mischief, even in the painful alternative of dismissing the head of one of the Departments."

In accordance with "a solemn decision of the American people" expressed in the recent election—he never failed to make this point—and in view of the "exposed abuses and corruptions" of the Bank, he had concluded that it was his "right" and "duty" to take the appropriate action and appoint a secretary of the treasury whose "opinions" agreed with his own. Jackson noted that of the twenty-six senators to vote for the censure, four of them (from Maine, New Jersey, and Ohio) had acted in direct contradiction to the expressed will of the legislatures that elected them to office. In other words, these senators had censured the President for an action which their own states formally approved. Once again legislators demonstrated that they did not intend to be "palsied" by the "will of their constituents."[40]

Then Jackson formally proclaimed what had been implicit in many of his previous actions and messages, namely that the President is the representative of the American people and responsible to them. No President had ever made such an assertion. No President assumed such a remarkable relationship with the electorate. When the words were spoken, the atmosphere in the Senate was palpable with excitement. Each word uttered sent shock waves around the chamber.

"The President is the direct representative of the American people," Jackson declared. The secretaries are not. They become responsible to the people only because they are subordinate to the chief executive. If the secretary of the treasury were in fact independent of the President in the execution of the laws dealing with the public moneys, as the Whigs contended, then there would be "no direct responsibility to the people in that important branch of the Government." It would mean that it was within the power of the BUS, or any other corporation, to induce the secretary to promote its views, and through him to control the whole action of the government in defiance of "the Chief Magistrate elected by the people and responsible to them."[41]

Responsible to the people! That was Jackson's claim, and that was totally novel. It was a modern idea in keeping with the democratic spirit of the times, but it was certainly not one the Whigs could approve with their philosophy about legislative government constituting the basis of republican rule. They insisted that the President was responsible to Congress.

But Jackson did not argue the point. He simply stated it, as though it needed no argument. The truth of his words was beyond the need for defense. Even so, he did not end his statement without implying that this relationship with the people was his, and his alone. It in no way included the members of Congress. For this reason he was obliged to protest *"solemnly"* an action calculated "to concentrate in the hands of a body not directly amenable to the people a degree of influence and power dangerous to their liberties and fatal to the Constitution of their choice."[42]

Jackson closed the message by expressing personal offense over the imputation that his Revolutionary War wounds were imaginary. "In vain do I bear upon my person enduring memorials of that contest in which American liberty was purchased," he pointedly remarked, if any doubts could be entertained "as to the purity of my purposes and motives." Then, in a flight of eloquence and deeply felt commitment to a duty he had kept before him from the day he entered the White House, he said that his one ambition, the one that informed all his actions and intentions, was

> an anxious desire and a fixed determination to return to the people unimpaired the sacred trust they have confided to my charge; to heal the wounds of the Constitution and preserve it from further violation; to persuade my countrymen, so far as I may, that it is not in a splendid government supported by powerful monopolies and aristocratical establishments that they will find happiness or their liberties protection, but in a plain system, void of pomp, protecting all and granting favors to none, dispensing its blessings, like the dews of Heaven, unseen and unfelt save in the freshness and beauty they contribute to produce. It is such a government that the genius of our people requires; such an one only under which our States may remain for ages to come united, prosperous and free.[43]

No sooner did the last words of this Protest fall "from the lips of the secretary of the Senate," than George Poindexter of Mississippi rose to his feet, his face contorted with anger and outrage, and addressed the chair. "In indignant tones," he denounced the message and declared that it could not be considered an executive message because it did not pertain to any of the public occasions on which the President is authorized by the Constitution to address himself to the Senate. He considered it an "unofficial paper," merely signed by one "Andrew Jackson," and since it evinced nothing but disrespect to the Senate he moved that it not be received. A foolish and ultimately unsuccessful debate on the motion went on for hours and lasted until five o'clock in the afternoon. The motion was supported by Frelinghuysen and Southard of New Jersey and Sprague of Maine, and opposed by Benton and King of Alabama.[44]

Observers remarked that there was a huge crowd in the chamber during the reading of the Protest and the lengthy debate that followed. Nearly half the members of the House of Representatives deserted their own hall to attend the proceedings. At one point the galleries broke out into prolonged applause and they were ordered to be cleared. One or two spectators were arrested for rowdyism but they were released upon adjournment.[45]

The opposition press agreed that Jackson's statement about his rights and his relation to the American people had "produced everywhere as great a sensation as within the halls of Congress." Said the New York *Daily Advertiser:* "I wish to draw your attention to a passage in the Protest of the President and to a parallel passage to it in modern history." The President's passage was the remarkable assertion that "the President is the direct representative of the American people." The parallel passage, said the newspaper, can be found in January, 1814, when Napoleon, impatient with the rebuke he received from the French legislative body, "summoned them before him . . . to prorogue them." Let us forget the Bank issue for the moment, continued the newspaper. "Every man must now give his opinion whether Andrew Jackson is our agent or our master. That is the real question and the real and urgent business before Congress."[46]

Although the opposition press expressed their horror at the ideas contained in Jackson's Protest, the most devastating assault came in the Senate—and without wasting a day. Daniel Webster, now regarded as the "Great Expounder and Defender of the Constitution," opened a blistering attack in the Senate to answer Jackson's "outrageous contentions." Again, visitors packed the galleries. They hung on every word.

Webster stood for a moment and gazed at his audience, the deep-set eyes staring out from under bushy eyebrows. Then he began. "Again and again we hear it said," he rumbled in his magnificent voice, "that the President is responsible to the American people! that he is responsible to the bar of public opinion! For whatever he does, he assumes accountability to the American people! . . . And this is thought enough for a limited, restrained, republican government! An undefined, undefinable, ideal responsibility to the public judgment!" Webster paused for a moment to let his words sink in. "I ask again, Sir. Is this legal responsibility? Is this the true nature of a government with written laws and limited powers?" Obviously not, he asserted.

Then Webster confronted Jackson's "revolutionary" (Whigs invariably used this pejorative word) idea that the chief executive was the direct representative of the people, that he was, so to speak, the "tribune of the people." Again, Webster denied it. "Connected, Sir, with the idea of this airy and unreal responsibility to the people is another sentiment, which of late we hear frequently expressed; and that is, *that the President is the direct representative of the American people.*" Webster's face darkened as he spoke these words. "This is declared in the Protest," he stormed. "Now, Sir, this is not the language of the Constitution. The Constitution no where calls him the representative of the American people; still less their direct representative. It could not do so with the least propriety." Just look at the manner of his election, said Webster. "He is not chosen directly by the people, but by a body of electors, some of whom are chosen by the people, and some of whom are appointed by State legislatures. Where, then, is the authority for saying that the President is *the direct representative of the People?* . . . I hold this, Sir, to be a mere assumption, and dangerous assumption."

Webster then brought the entire speech to a thunderous close. "And if he may be allowed to consider himself as the SOLE REPRESENTATIVE OF ALL THE AMERICAN PEOPLE, then I say, Sir, that the government (I will not say the people) has already a master. I deny the sentiment, therefore, and I protest against the language; neither the sentiment nor the language is to be found in the Constitution of this Country."[47]

With unparalleled eloquence the Massachusetts senator had expressed the feelings of a majority of his colleagues who feared that Jackson was embarked on an illegal and unconstitutional course to restructure the American government to the advantage of the chief executive. Unless stopped dead in his tracks, it was the beginning of presidential despotism, or, as Webster put it: "ONE RESPONSIBILITY, ONE DISCRETION, ONE WILL!"[48]

Some Democratic newspapers, especially in the south, were just as disturbed as Webster by Jackson's arguments. The President is already strong enough, protested the Richmond *Enquirer,* "and in some cases too strong." It would be particularly unfortunate if a bad precedent were set by so popular and respected a man as Andrew Jackson. "Bold and bad men may come after him who may abuse his example. We should regard it as one of the greatest misfortunes which could happen to us if the confidence of his countrymen were shaken in the democratic principles of a Jackson." If carried too far, Old Hickory's doctrines could lead to a fatal undermining of American freedom.[49]

The *Globe,* of course, had no such fears. And it ridiculed Webster for finding meanings in the Protest that only "a Bank debtor or attorney" could conceive. "The speech of Mr. Webster against the Protest," said Blair, "places him at the head of the self-named *Wig party.* He has thrown Mr. Clay and Mr. Calhoun entirely into the background. They must hereafter be considered '*the lesser lights'* in the galaxy of disinterested worthies who maintain the cause of Bank power."[50]

But Calhoun quickly emerged from the "background." He too berated the President in a long and closely argued speech. "Why all this solicitude on the part of the President to place himself near the people?" he asked. "Why this solicitude to make himself their sole representative . . . ? The object cannot be mistaken. It is preparatory to further hostilities—to an appeal to the people . . . to enlist them as his allies in the war which he contemplates against this branch of the Government." Previous Presidents understood that the seat of government was the Congress, Calhoun continued, and acted as the head of a coordinate branch of that government. But "this President" now claims to be the head of the entire government and the spokesman of all the American people. Surely this is revolutionary doctrine, Calhoun insisted; it is the destruction of tripartite government, the triumph of despotism, the end of republicanism.[51]

Jackson's ideas as promulgated in the Protest did indeed spell the end of republicanism. But the reliance upon legislative government as the equivalent of representative government had long been eroding. To some, like Jackson, the Congress had sacrificed its position as the centerpiece of the republican institutional structure when it held a caucus in 1824 and tried to force its candidate upon the country as the next President. In that single act the Congress proved it could not be trusted to guard republican forms and institutions. Then, after the election, when the House of Representatives placed John Q. Adams in the White House, in total disregard of popular will and through a "corrupt bargain," Congress further demonstrated its inability to protect the people's rights and their freedom.[52] Congress could no longer be trusted to preserve liberty, claimed Jackson. Only a "virtuous people" can protect it. And, in the operation of government, they must place at its head—that is, in the presidential office—someone who respects and obeys their will, who reveres them for their virtue, and whom they trust.

Andrew Jackson liked to believe that he was just such a person. In his Protest, he seemed to be telling the people that they must now look to the President to find real representation. And it was that very claim that senators cited as revolutionary.

Senator Benjamin W. Leigh of Virginia labored throughout a long speech, reported Frank Blair, "to prove that the President by his Protest makes an appeal to the people and in effect proposed *revolution* as a means of redress for the wrong which the Senate has done him." Blair sneered that it was the first time he had ever heard it argued that an appeal to the people meant "invoking a revolutionary remedy."[53]

While the senators hammered at the President, the Vice President quietly slipped away to the White House to express his own concern over some parts of the Protest. He feared that as published the Protest might give people the wrong notion about Jackson's claim to control public funds and he further feared that some of the ideas in the document might be interpreted as violating the Constitution. He urged the General to write a second message and disclaim any intention of denying the right of Congress to provide for the custody, safekeeping, and disposition of the property and public money of the United States. At one point Van Buren got himself very worked up about the danger, worrying about its effect upon their supporters and allies. Their friends were leaving them, he wailed.

The President remained calm. "Mr. Van Buren," he replied, *"your* friends may be leaving you—but my friends *never* leave *me.*"[54]

In any event, the wisdom and concern of his friend—and probably a fear that the "revolutionary" statements about his relationship to the people could be jeopardized without a modification of the point Van Buren had raised—convinced him to write a *"codicil"* as requested.[55] Although he was well satisfied that nothing in his Protest could be misconstrued about Congress's right to control the public funds, nevertheless when taken out of context some passages could be misrepresented. In his second message, or "codicil," he did not claim the right to dispose of public property except under authority provided by law, nor to interfere with any person having control of such property unless he be an officer whose conduct is the President's responsibility under the Constitution. Furthermore, he repudiated the notion that he had claimed for himself and his successors any power or authority not clearly granted by the Constitution and the laws to the President.[56]

It was a substantial retraction. After having made his "revolutionary" pronouncements, he now hastened to assure everyone that by no means did he intend to assume unconstitutional authority. However, he did not repudiate his claim of being the representative of the people. That stood, and that was the most significant statement of his message, for it permanently changed the relation between the President and the people and between the President and Congress.

Obviously the codicil also dissatisfied the Whigs. Poindexter immediately moved that it too be rejected. He again called on the Senate to condemn the Protest as a breach of the privileges of Congress.[57] Another two weeks lapsed while the Senate lashed the President for his outrageous claims and despotic behavior. Then it voted. By the count of 27 to 16 the Senate of the United States upheld its censure of the President's conduct.[58]

Jackson's novel concept about the President representing the people found immediate acceptance with the electorate. Perhaps the very fact that it had been stated simply and forcefully, but not argued, made it easier to gain acceptance. Clearly, its timing was perfect and eventually even the Whigs capitulated to it. Sighed Senator Leigh: "Until the President developed the faculties of the Executive power, all men thought it inferior to the legislature—he manifestly thinks it superior; and in his hands the monarchical part of Government (for the Executive is monarchical . . .) has proved far stronger than the representatives of the States." The President, not Congress, had become the instrument of popular will.[59]

In introducing and ultimately winning acceptance of his interpretation of presidential powers, Jackson liberated the chief executive from the position of prime minister responsible only to Congress. With Jackson, the chief executive no longer served simply as the head of a coordinate branch of the government; no longer was he restricted in his actions by what the Congress would allow him. Henceforth he could assert himself as the spokesman of the people and by the skillful use of his powers force the legislature to follow his lead. This did not free him from the political necessity of working with Congress to accomplish the public will, but it did allow him to assume greater control of the government and to dominate and direct public affairs.

It was this very sense of domination and direction that so agitated the Whigs. What made it worse was the precedent Jackson was setting for future Presidents—whether they followed the precedent or not. It was there. It was waiting to be used.

All of which meant that Jackson saw himself as the head of the government, executing the popular will, and responsible only to the electorate. He truly believed himself a servant of the people—and that, in the end, is how the people saw him. They believed him "honest and patriotic; that he was the friend of the *people*, battling for them against corruption and extravagance, and opposed only by dishonest politicians. They loved him as their friend."[60]

This mutual attitude of love and respect—amounting to a bond—between a President and the electorate was something totally novel in American history. It did not exist with Washington or Jefferson or any President previous to Jackson. And out of this special relationship forged between Old Hickory and the American people a sense of mutual dependence and commitment emerged which changed the tone and style of the government to something publicists had started to call a democracy.

CHAPTER 11

"The Bank Is Dead"

ALTHOUGH JACKSON MAINTAINED AN AIR of calm throughout the verbal mauling he suffered during the Panic session of Congress, he did not sit still. He intruded his presence in the House and Senate at every opportunity. He asserted his leadership both as head of the government (a rank he accorded himself) and as head of the Democratic party.

From the beginning of his term as President, Andrew Jackson had steadily increased his involvement in all the operations of government, whether executive, legislative, or judicial. Perhaps such intrusion might be expected from someone of his temperament and military background, from one accustomed to command. But there was more involved. Over the years Jackson had improved his political skills, and increasingly he employed them to nudge the Congress to do his bidding. With the help of an enormous propaganda machine, which he directed through the columns of the *Globe,* and with the formidable support he enjoyed from the mass electorate, he commanded unassailable advantages which few congressmen could disregard or dismiss. What aided Jackson tremendously in his vigorous assertion of presidential power was the existence of an explosive political issue which he had raised and around which he had drawn very precise and impenetrable lines. He had decreed the destruction of the BUS. By removing the deposits he forced congressmen to come to terms with the issue and either join him in killing the monster or remove themselves from Democratic ranks. It was one or the other. Jackson established a hard line on the Bank issue from which he never deviated. To all who begged him to end the economic panic by restoring the deposits he replied calmly but "explicitly that the name of Andrew Jackson would never be signed to a bill or resolution to place the Public money in the Bank of the United States or to renew the Charter of that Bank." As the congressional session progressed and the economic suffering sharpened, Jackson's language became more explicit—also more colorful. "Were all the worshippers of the gold Calf to memorialise me and request a restoration of the Deposits," he told Van Buren, "I would cut my right hand from my body before I would do such an act. The golden calf may be worshipped by others but as for myself I serve the Lord."[1]

If nothing else, therefore, the Bank issue effectively tightened Jackson's control of the party and the government—despite the Senate's censure and a worsening economic crisis.

What intensified the apprehension within the administration about the consequences of the panic was the fear that the experiment with state banking would fail. Already there were rumors that the pets could not sustain themselves under Biddle's squeeze, and these rumors gravely worried Kendall, Taney, Blair, and the other White House stalwarts. Kendall begged the Baltimore pet to hang on. "The responsibility of your situation is *immense,*" he wrote. "We can stand the stopping of other Banks, but if the *'Pets'* begin to go, it is impossible to appreciate the consequences. . . . For Heaven's sake, fortify yourselves so that you *can stand amidst ruin.*"[2]

But even these rumors of disaster did not weaken Jackson's resolve. He repeated again and again that he would not abandon deposit banking. He would not end the experiment. "I read your letter to the President," Van Buren told Theodore Sedgwick, "who was not a little amused at the idea that any one could apprehend any thing like giving way on his part."[3] And the message was carried around the country when the *Globe* categorically declared the President's "final determination" was to have done with national banking. We want to "put an end" to all "doubts and misgivings," reported Blair, by announcing that the President will never abandon the state banks.[4]

Because Jackson appreciated that pressure must be applied to Congress and that the most effective kind came from the country at large, he diligently undertook the task of mounting that pressure. Specifically, he called for mass meetings, caucuses, and conventions—all selected "by the people themselves and charged with their instructions" to express "popular" sentiment about the Bank. "Get up meetings and memorials," Jackson ordered the party leaders in the states, and "let the U.S. Bank turn its screws" to its everlasting shame.[5]

One of Jackson's most important objectives in directing this action, it will be noted, was his effort to gain general acceptance of the idea that the people in convention or meetings can "instruct" the government on a particular issue. Moreover, he argued, the government was obliged to obey the popular will. The right of instruction was absolute in Jackson's thinking.

To his summons several states immediately responded. Ohio, North

Carolina, Tennessee, Maine, Maryland, New Jersey, and New York (in various ways and forms) condemned the Bank in vigorous language. They approved the removal of the deposits, expressed outrage over the curtailment policy, and demanded the release of veterans pensions. They also conveyed their shock over the Senate's disrespectful treatment of the President by its censure.[6]

Anything to do with the shaping of public opinion increasingly excited Jackson's interest and prompted his involvement. Under the circumstances his interest was natural, given his commitment to the "doctrine of instruction." Senator Hugh Lawson White of Tennessee said that as Old Hickory's administration progressed he "became more and more open and undisguised in his interference to influence and control public opinion. I am well acquainted with his signature," White declared, "and have seen many newspapers and other publications sent under his frank to individuals, and to members of assembly, calculated and intended to injure, in public estimation, those who were unwilling to act in accordance with his wishes."[7]

With congressmen during this Panic session, Jackson was unusually attentive and active. Frequent White House meetings were called. Polk and Benton reported daily to the President and received encouragement and advice. Andrew Stevenson, the Speaker and "intimate" of Roger Taney, got both presidential direction and up-to-the-minute information on the Treasury Department's operations with the pets. Congressional delegations heard regular pep talks. Sometimes the old man purred at them, sometimes he bared his claws. The Pennsylvania delegation, which reportedly led a movement toward desertion from the Democratic party, received a "frightful" mauling. "I am told," reported one Pennsylvania Whig, "that he absolutely rode with whip and spur over our delegation who were so overwhelmed that they had nothing to say for themselves."[8]

One problem that Jackson handled most expertly in Congress was the persistent rumor that the Bank War had been devised and plotted by New York politicians for the purpose of benefiting Wall Street financiers at the expense of their counterparts on Chestnut Street in Philadelphia. It was not enough for the administration to deny the rumor; the denial must come from the New Yorkers themselves—and from the very highest level. Consequently Jackson asked Van Buren to request Silas Wright, Jr., the Regency's most able spokesman in Congress, to deliver a speech in the Senate which would end once and for all the rumors about a New York conspiracy to make Wall Street the financial capital of the country. Coming from Wright, the repudiation would be seen as originating with Van Buren and bearing the approval of the Regency.[9]

As directed, Wright delivered the speech with his mentor perched in the chair of the presiding officer. He presented the resolutions of the New York legislature which Jackson had initiated condemning the Bank and supporting removal. But as he spoke, other senators immediately sensed the significance of his speech, and several of them, including Webster, moved closer to Wright to catch each word. Clay paced nervously around the chamber, pausing every so often to stare at the speaker, register some reaction, and watch reactions among his colleagues. Calhoun, all the while, stirred restlessly in his seat, sometimes rocking back and forth as though mesmerized.[10]

Among many things, Wright unequivocally repudiated any and all desire by New York to take advantage of the Bank War to advance its financial position. So well did Wright argue this point that Van Buren detected a definite change among both Whig and Democratic congressmen. "The current is now fast setting the other way," he told Theodore Sedgwick. "The successful effort of Mr. Wright to force out the true issue has given a right direction of public sentiment." The attorney general, Benjamin F. Butler, agreed, but he also credited Jackson with this happy development. It was not until "the strong language of the President & the explicit assertions" of Wright "that the administration were *really* & in *good faith,* desirous to test" the deposit banking system "and that there was no intention to set up a new Bank for the benefit of New-York, that the democracy of Pennsylvania rallied in support of the President. For the last five or six weeks, the public mind in that state, and in the whole South, has been highly excited, and the opposition to the Bank has been daily gaining strength."[11]

Shortly after Wright's speech, and just as several states began to respond to the President's urgings that they express their outrage over Biddle's behavior, the current of popular opinion on the issue turned irreversibly away from the Bank and toward Jackson. For one thing the economic panic began to ease—or, rather, merchants suddenly realized that the distress was simply "Biddle-created" and not as deep and as widespread as they originally feared. Also, the pets were holding their own, despite Biddle's determined efforts to drive them into bankruptcy.

The slow, steady cracking of opposition to the President's "experiment" with deposit banking finally widened into an unbreachable chasm when the pro-Bank governor of Pennsylvania, George Wolf, reversed his position and denounced the BUS in his annual message to the state legislature on February 26, 1834. When a state bond issue failed to find subscribers, Wolf blamed the Bank and charged it with bringing "indiscriminate ruin" upon the community. The effect was devastating—and immediate. The state senate passed resolutions castigating the institution for its unconscionable actions; the state's Democratic party completely endorsed the President's actions; both U.S. senators stated publicly that, like Wolf, they were reversing themselves and would no longer support the Bank; and virtually the entire Pennsylvania delegation in the House abandoned the stricken institution. Most of these Pennsylvanians had decided that the financial distress of the past several months had not been caused by *a* national bank, but by *the* Bank of the United States.

The BUS was doomed. Deserted by its own state, the corporation was shunned and ostracized. Once Pennsylvania signaled its discontent, a yapping pack of opportunists pounced on the Bank and howled their demand for its immediate destruction.

Andrew Jackson glowed. The message of Governor Wolf sent him into a state of euphoria, although he did not display it publicly. He wrote to Wolf privately and expressed his own thanks and that of the country for "the exalted and truly patriotic stand you have taken in the defence of public liberty."[12]

Congressmen, state legislators, and governors quickly imitated Wolf's condemnation. One of the most important came from New York. The Regency governor, William L. Marcy, wrote a powerful attack upon the Bank in his annual message. More significant, he helped break the back of the financial pressure by recommending to the legislature that it permit the issuance of four or five million dollars of state stock to be loaned to the state banks to meet the emergency. The legislature complied by creating $6 million of 5 percent stock. The effect of this action in easing the panic was felt almost immediately.[13] Van Buren, speaking for the President as well as himself, sent Marcy an enthusiastic letter of congratulations for having "nailed the flag of New York to the mast on the side of the great principle that our Government is only Republican so long as it conforms to, & executes the regularly expressed will of the people. That it may be kept so nailed to the mast as long as there is a single rag of it left, is my sincere prayer." Everyone now appreciates, he said, that "by means of public & private distress" Biddle sought "to force the people" to acquiesce in the continuance of a monopoly they did not want. It is difficult to determine, Van Buren went on, "whether the weakness or wickedness of the attempt is the most striking." This "Reign of Terror" will only serve to prove that there exists "a spirit," even in this country, as eager to make "hewers of wood and drawers of water" of their fellow men as any in the world.[14]

The general reversal of attitudes within the business community about the culpability of the Bank in creating the present distress was reflected in the many newspapers that had previously defended the BUS. Where they had once pleaded for a restoration of the deposits to end the panic, now they excoriated the Bank for instigating it. Public outrage around the country was also noted. "There is by all accounts a great revulsion or rather awakening in public sentiment," claimed Van Buren. "The bankites are thunderstruck," noted Nathaniel Green, editor of the Boston *Statesman*, "at this uprising of the people."[15]

This mounting public pressure, coupled with Jackson's firm leadership and resolve to kill the monster and make a go of deposit banking, awakened the Democrats in Congress to a sense of their actual and growing strength. Finally they properly organized themselves in the House, where they held a majority, to give Jackson the support he needed. Polk labored hard to achieve this result. After several mishaps he at length engineered the referral of Taney's report to his Ways and Means Committee. Once he had his hands on the report he was ready to move.

For the past several weeks Polk had been working on his own report upholding removal. Now, with a strong sense of popular support behind him, he pressed for a showdown with the Bank. In his enthusiasm he even invited Taney to draft the report himself but the cagey secretary wisely declined. Even so, the two men conferred almost daily, and as a consequence the finished draft presented a very strong case for both Jackson's removal action and the entire hard money policy.[16]

Not only did this report argue the right of Taney's power over the public funds but it also upheld the reasons he had given for the removal. It cited the exclusion of the government's directors from the operation of the Bank, the loans to congressmen, the interference that delayed the payment of the public debt, the veterans pensions, and the Bank's demand for damages because of France's failure to honor the government's draft under the Treaty of 1831. More important, thanks to Taney's help, the report suggested the direction of Jackson's social and economic goals once the Bank had been obliterated. It provided the first "official hint" of the President's latest reform.[17]

The principal goal, said the report, would be the enlargement of the specie on which the state banks would rely for support. This would provide the sound currency that Jackson had demanded in his first message to Congress and would rescue the country from the sudden expansions and contractions of paper currency that had plagued it since the inception of national banking. This "reform"—again Jackson wanted the public to know that this effort was part of his overall program of "reform retrenchment and economy"—would be accomplished by banning small notes under twenty dollars from circulation. In turn this would create a demand for specie and force banks to keep the coin in larger quantities in their vaults. It was Jackson's belief that only specie would protect the laboring masses from the greed of the aristocracy by freeing them from the tyranny of a paper system that was manipulated by the rich. Thus, his economic policy had far-reaching social implications.[18]

For a month the House debated the report. Finally the Democrats decided to test their strength and attempt a knockout blow that would end the Bank War once and for all. After first checking with the administration and the other House leaders, Polk called for a vote on a series of resolutions which had already been approved by his committee and which were aimed at nullifying the action of the Senate by registering the House's total approval of the President's Bank policy. On April 4, 1834, the questions were called. By a vote of 134 to 82, the House declared that the Bank of the United States "ought not to be rechartered." Then, by the count of 118 to 103, it agreed that the deposits "ought not to be restored." Next, by a vote of 117 to 105, it recommended that the state banks (the pets) be continued as the places of deposit. And, lastly, by the overwhelming vote of 175 to 42, the House authorized the selection of a committee to examine the Bank's affairs and investigate whether it had deliberately instigated the panic.[19]

That did it. That, in effect, ended all hope of the Bank's survival. It seemed only a matter of time before the Democrats would assemble enough evidence from an investigation to prove that Biddle had wantonly and irresponsibly brought economic havoc to the country in order to get his charter. Biddle's very ruthlessness killed the Bank, for he drove away prospective supporters and forced the Democrats to "an inflexible anti-Bank position."[20] He had convinced the public that he was an irresponsible and ungovernable force in American economic life. Even the business community eventually admitted that he had behaved improperly and by the spring of 1834 they forced him to ease the financial pressure.

"I have obtained a glorious triumph," Jackson crowed. If nothing else the votes in the House completely scuttled the efforts of the Senate to disgrace him by forcing a restoration of the deposits and a recharter of the Bank. Without the approval of the House, neither action by the Senate, with or without the intimidating tactic of a censure, could be enacted into law. "The overthrow of the opposition in the House of Representatives by the vote on the resolutions," wrote Jackson, ". . . was a triumphant one, and put to death, that mamouth of corruption and power, the Bank of the United States." The attorney general concurred. "The Bank is dead," Butler informed the Regency.[21]

The growing impotence of the Senate on account of the determined stand taken by the House was clearly demonstrated several weeks later. Two resolutions passed by the upper house in early June declaring Taney's reasons for removal unsatisfactory and demanding the restoration of the public money to the BUS went to the House for action. In rapid-fire order the Democratic majority ordered that they lie on the table, which killed them as "dead" as Jackson could have wished.[22]

Still one more nail was hammered into the Bank's coffin. And the hammerer was Biddle himself. The investigating committee authorized by the House resolution arrived in Philadelphia armed with subpoena powers and anxious to examine all the Bank's books. The investigators found Biddle as truculent as ever. He refused permission to examine the books or the correspondence with congressmen relating to personal loans from the BUS. (Not much later Daniel Webster requested that his accounts be moved "out of the Bank, & all its branches" so that during the next congressional session he could "say that I neither owe the Bank a dollar, nor am on any paper discounted at the Bank, for any body, to the amt. of a dollar."[23]) In addition, Biddle steadfastly refused to testify before the committee. He was clearly in contempt of Congress, to say nothing of his obligations under the terms of the charter. But, from the beginning of its history, the Bank had regularly violated its charter, and

Biddle saw no reason to alter that tradition. Back in Washington, after the futile and frustrating trip to Philadelphia, the committeemen demanded a citation for contempt. Taney supported the action, as did several members of the Kitchen Cabinet, most notably Blair and Kendall. But many southern Democrats opposed this extreme action and refused to cooperate.[24] As Biddle bemusedly observed, it would be ironic if he went to prison "by the votes of members of Congress because I would not give up to their enemies their confidential letters." Although Biddle escaped a contempt citation, his outrageous defiance of the House only condemned him still further in the eyes of the American public. His latest action, commented William C. Rives, proved "to the people never again to give themselves such a master."[25]

Now that the Bank of the United States lay bleeding to death, with no hope of resuscitation, Jackson was anxious to move forward with his hard money and state deposit schemes in the expectation of providing a regulated, responsible banking system. He had in mind a complete economic reform program, something first hinted at by Polk a few weeks earlier. The President acted swiftly. On April 21, 1834, he proposed a series of measures that would provide a general reform of currency and banking. The measures were contained in a report submitted to the House Ways and Means Committee by Secretary Taney.[26] The proposals included the following: that the selection of pet banks be left to the secretary of the treasury; that he be permitted to remove the deposits from any bank after submitting his reasons to Congress; that banks submit monthly reports of their condition; that the government have the right to examine the books and records of the pets; that gold be revalued to bring it to a parity with silver; and that the deposit banks be required to cease issuing notes under five dollars. Later, the prohibition against paper would be extended to all notes under twenty dollars. In this way the country would be restored to coin for its regular transactions and bank notes would serve commercial purposes only.[27]

According to Taney's report, the currency reform would follow three stages: first, the total destruction of the BUS; second, the revaluation of gold; and third, the implementation of a full deposit system throughout the country.[28] As a condition to receiving the government deposits, the pets must cease issuing or receiving notes under five dollars. Taney did not go so far as to require gold or silver for the payment of government debts, much as he might like to do so, but he did oppose making the notes of deposit banks receivable for all government dues.[29]

It was too late in the congressional session to expect all of these proposals to be enacted into law, particularly as they applied to deposit banking, but in terms of the first two steps of currency reform, considerable progress was made: the BUS was prostrate and barely breathing; and the revaluation of gold was accomplished before Congress adjourned.

The first Coinage Act had been passed in 1792 and decreed the minting of gold and silver coins at a ratio of 15 to 1. A more exact ratio, in keeping with commercial rates, would have been 15.5 to 1. Consequently, this Coinage Act tended to drive gold out of circulation. A $10 gold eagle coin, for example, was really worth about $10.66⅔. By revaluing gold upward, therefore, Jackson believed that the metal would be drawn back into circulation. So he requested that it be done. "The drops of sweat which fall" from the farmer's brow, the President said through the columns of the *Globe,* will be turned into gold and silver. "His bushels of corn, wheat etc. will not be resolved into a dirty rag in the corner of his pocket promising to pay what the insurers have not the means of paying." Let the merchants have their banks and rag money. They can take care of themselves. "But let the people and the Government of the People beware of them."[30]

The gold currency bill, or the Coinage Act of 1834, passed on June 28, 1834, with wide bipartisan support, including Calhoun and Webster. It went into effect on July 31 and raised the ratio between gold and silver to 16 to 1. Now silver was undervalued, but at least a gold eagle would pass at $10, a half eagle at $5 and a quarter Eagle at $2.50.[31] Jackson was delighted at the speed with which the gold eagle made a reappearance. Some people had never seen one, he said.[32] This reappearance, crowed the *Globe,* "is one of the first fruits of the great measure of removing the deposits and rousing a continent to its energies against the oppressions of the lawless and gigantic moneyed power. . . . Let the country rejoice. There is no longer a plea for federal bank notes! Gold is a good enough *national* currency for the republicans of the United States!"[33]

A short time later the *Globe* proudly announced that "Dr Benton's yellow lozenges"—a recognition of Senator Benton's efforts at currency reform—in the shape of $5 coins had just been minted in Philadelphia.[34] And Jackson declared that for their good work in killing the Bank and initiating deposit banking, Benton, Polk, and Taney "deserve not only golden medals, but the gratitude of their country."[35] Of course, any number of people recognized that there was little gold in the country— maybe a million and a half dollars' worth—but with the favorable ratio established by the new law it was expected that by September "it will be coming in plentifully, and will begin to have a sensible influence on the general currency."[36] The opposition press sniffed at the claims of the Democrats about the new coinage law. "A golden eagle is a pretty thing," sneered the *National Intelligencer,* "but a good $10 bank note is a more useful one from the facility from which it can be transferred and remitted." Besides, the ratio is too high in favor of gold, the paper argued. The "exact proportion" should be fixed at 15.865 to 1.[37]

It was not long before all circulating specie was called "Jackson money." The Democrats, naturally, applauded the name, and the Whigs, just as naturally, argued that he was undeserving of this recognition since the gold bill was really introduced and supported by them. "If there be any credit attached to the introduction of what is slavishly termed Jackson money," asked the *National Intelligencer,* "to whom does this credit belong? TO THOSE WHO OPPOSE ANDREW JACKSON!!"—that's who.[38]

The President was positively ecstatic about "Jackson money" and he urged all his friends and supporters to load up on the golden eagles and present them for payment whenever they traveled, just as he would do. "The importance of a circulating gold coin at as early a day as possible to society & particularly the labouring classes, in the present crisis," Jackson wrote his secretary of the treasury, "is so obvious, that I cannot omit pressing it upon your recollection. . . . You know my anxiety on this subject in the present crisis of our affairs, and I show your particular attention to it."[39] Indeed, Jackson became single-minded in his efforts to convert the country to gold. "The President is determined not to die," reported Van Buren, "until he sees the country full of Gold & then he is ready to give up the Ghost, office & all."[40] At first Democrats seemed eager to cooperate with Jackson's currency reform, but they soon discovered how burdensome it was to carry around gold and silver coins when traveling. It was enough, noted Mrs. James K. Polk, "to show you how useful banks are."[41]

With the congressional session rapidly drawing to an end and the Bank War just about over, Jackson thought he could at last submit his most recent cabinet appointees to an unfriendly Senate with a reasonable expectation of getting them confirmed. For months he had held off. Despite repeated demands that he lay the names of Taney and Butler before the Senate for its approval, Jackson had wisely refused, knowing what their likely fate would be. During the heat of the debate over the removal, several senators pointedly noticed that half the executive department heads had not yet received the approval required by law. In effect, they questioned whether the actions of these officials—such as Taney's in removing the deposits—had the full force of law since their appointment procedure had not yet been completed. Whether this was true did not disturb Jackson one whit. He was taking no chances, and so for months the operation of the Treasury Department continued with a head who, in the eyes of some, had no legal right to his office. The failure to submit Taney's name was seen as one more instance of executive usurpation of power. Jackson's appetite for control of the government seemed insatiable.[42]

So the senators bided their time. Sooner or later Jackson would have to come to them and they would be waiting. Much as the President might have preferred to duck a showdown over Taney's appointment, he could not avoid it indefinitely. Of course he knew that the senators would tear into the nomination like ravenous wolves to get revenge for the removal of the deposits and poor Taney would be made to bear much of the pain and humiliation. But what finally forced Jackson to send down the nominations, other than the approaching close of the session and a flickering hope that they might escape unscathed, was the decision of Louis McLane to resign the office of secretary of state.

The resignation had been coming for some time. In fact McLane thought seriously of it at the beginning of the year but had allowed himself to be talked out of it because of the administration's troubles with the Senate. But when Jackson chose to disregard his advice about the developing problem with France over the spoliation claims, he felt he had to leave, and so on June 16, 1834, he submitted his resignation. He and Jackson parted friends.

McLane had taken over as secretary of state on May 29, 1833, after Congress had adjourned. His appointment should have gone before the Senate when it reconvened in December, 1833, but it had been delayed because the appointments of Taney and Butler would also have to be submitted. Jackson knew he might get Butler and McLane safely through the Senate, but he also knew that Taney would surely get shot down. So he sat on all three appointments, hoping that time would dissipate the animosity against Taney. And he had time, for recess appointments without confirmation are permissible until the last day of the next session of Congress.

Of course, none of the heat and animosity dissipated as Jackson had hoped. And, as June 30 approached, the day fixed for the adjournment, the President was obliged to submit the names of his growing list of appointees. It should be mentioned that there was genuine fear by some that he would disregard the Senate altogether and go through an endless process of reappointing whomever he pleased during succeeding recesses.[43]

The senators, throughout the session, regularly scolded the President for his obvious ploy to delay confirmation. They declared it unconscionable—and unconstitutional. Daniel Webster, John Tyler, and others berated the President for his misbehavior.[44] And the situation worsened. Not only was a majority of the cabinet unconfirmed, but a lengthening list of ministers to foreign countries also lacked Senate approval. To add insult to injury, the administration asked for appropriations to the Russian and British posts even though no appointments to these posts had been made since Van Buren's rejection as minister to Great Britain in 1832 and James Buchanan's resignation as minister to Russia in 1833. It was becoming ridiculous. Jackson's problem with his appointees to foreign posts fell under one of two categories: either they failed to stay at their posts for any length of time for a variety of reasons (like Van Buren, Randolph, and Buchanan), or they resigned and came home after a successful mission (like McLane and Rives). Every few months the President had an empty mission to fill.

Eventually time ran out. Jackson had to act. So he slowly fed his long list of nominees to the waiting Senate shredding machine, and, as expected, some of them got chewed up and spat out, while others passed through virtually unscathed.

On Monday, June 23, Jackson submitted Taney's name as secretary of the treasury. On Tuesday it was rejected by a vote of 28 to 18.[45] The next day the *Globe* blasted the Senate for its "indecent haste to immolate this excellent man on the altar of mammon." With a loud voice, the *Globe* said, the majority cried, *"Crucify him. Crucify him!"* They merely carried out the decree of the Bank. *"But he will rise again!"* prophesied the *Globe*. And let no one doubt that the man to succeed him will be as inflexible as Taney, for General Jackson will entrust the department to *"none other."*[46]

Taney resigned his post immediately and McClintock Young, the chief clerk in the department, was appointed acting secretary ad interim. But Jackson wasted no time in tossing in another nomination for secretary of the treasury, shrewdly calculating that the Senate had no stomach for rejecting a second name. At first the President could not decide on Taney's replacement—whether to give it to Levi Woodbury, who desperately wanted it and had Van Buren's active support, or Thomas Hart Benton, who was so close to his own ideas about money and banking.[47] At length, discretion prevailed, and Jackson awarded the Treasury to Woodbury, moving him up from the Navy Department. Woodbury was close with Van Buren and had strong backing from that quarter, but more particularly he was known to be fiercely anti-Bank and would carry out the President's directions without question or hesitation. Balding, heavy-set, and regularly plagued by presidential fever, Woodbury had a keen mind and strong administrative skills. He was tight-lipped and tactful and generally proved to be an excellent Treasury secretary—one of Jackson's more notable appointments.

As the President had anticipated, Woodbury's nomination was confirmed unanimously on June 29. "Nothing marks the hand of Mr. Biddle in the Senate more plainly than the rejection of Mr. Taney by every vote the Bank can command in that body," editorialized the *Globe*, "and the confirmation of Mr. Woodbury's nomination by a unanimous vote." But the Senate should know that Woodbury approved of the removal as well as the Protest. Not only did he endorse the principles of the Protest but he advised Jackson to assert the right of the President to maintain his independence. Why, then, was Taney rejected and Woodbury confirmed? "There is no reason . . . *but that the Bank had willed it.*"[48]

The rejection of Taney deeply offended Jackson. He saw it as a personal insult, directed at himself, and one in which he must somehow win retribution no matter how long it took or in what manner. For his "virtue and patriotism," Taney had been sacrificed to the cause of liberty and free government. But Jackson was philosophic. "I have however the great consolation in the support of the great body of the people, and the pleasure to know that this corrupt majority cannot be gratified in the recharter of the Bank. its days are numbered."[49] In moments of deep disappointment, Old Hickory invariably roused himself by remembering that the people remained faithful because he was motivated by "truth & principle" to perpetuate the "public good."[50]

The *Globe* commented on Jackson's concern for his friend. Like the President, the paper said, Taney had been a foe of corruption and a "fearless champion of Liberty against Money." He fought those who would reduce the masses of American people to "hewers of wood and drawers of water." His name and that of the President would be forever linked, and therefore Jackson felt a special obligation to see that Taney was vindicated for his loyalty and courage.[51]

On the day that Taney was rejected by the Senate, Benjamin F. Butler was confirmed. But then the upper house handed Jackson a second defeat. By the close vote of 23 to 22 it rejected his nomination of Andrew J. Stevenson to be minister to Great Britain.[52] Stevenson had decided to resign from Congress when the spring elections showed his district in complete disagreement with him on the question of the removal of the public deposits. Like William C. Rives, who had resigned his Senate seat for the same reason,[53] Stevenson recognized the right of the people to instruct him on a matter of national importance and his duty to obey that instruction or resign. As good Jacksonians, both Stevenson and Rives felt that that was the true meaning of democracy.[54] Jackson applauded Stevenson's manly dedication to "just principles," and as a reward for his loyal and excellent tenure as Speaker of the House, the President nominated him as minister on May 22, 1834. When word of the possible appointment reached Philadelphia, Nicholas Biddle urged Webster to work for Stevenson's rejection. It would be, he said, "the greatest moral and political lesson, which the Slaves of the Executive could receive."[55]

At the time of the nomination, Stevenson had not yet resigned either as Speaker or as member of Congress, in part because of the administration's need to agree first on his successor as Speaker. So the Whigs in the Senate delayed action on the nomination. They insisted on his resignations before they would move.

Stevenson obliged on June 2, and immediately the House set about selecting his successor. James K. Polk, who had so valiantly defended the President during the removal fight, coveted the post and had Jackson's blessing. But he ran into opposition. John Bell, his colleague from Tennessee, who had remained silent on the Bank, hoped to attract support from the Whigs and the anti–Van Buren (mostly southern) Democrats. For his part, Polk expected the administration men to vote for him, along with a substantial body of nullifiers who believed that Polk opposed Van Buren's succession to the presidency. Like Calhoun, these nullifiers loathed Van Buren with a passion and would support no one connected with his presidential candidacy. In an effort to unify the Democratic forces in the House, Jackson called the various contenders to the White House on May 19 for "a confidential communication." But he failed to break the deadlock and the House was forced to start its balloting for Speaker without a clear favorite in the running.[56]

Then the Whigs outfoxed the Democratic leadership. Instead of supporting an obvious candidate, like a northern Whig, they placed their favor on Richard H. Wilde of Georgia, a nullifier. The ploy was obvious. Polk instantly saw his strength crumbling. He appealed to Senator Willie P. Mangum of North Carolina, a close friend of John C. Calhoun, to rally the nullifiers behind his candidacy. But the cautious Mangum could not be rushed. Instead he watched the face of the enemy, Martin Van Buren, who presided over the Senate. As the House balloted, bulletins were hurried to the Senate with the results, and each time they arrived Mangum studied the Vice President's reaction. On the eighth ballot, John Bell showed a big gain in votes. An expression of concern flickered momentarily across Van Buren's face and in that instant Mangum knew that Polk was the Magician's candidate. Word of it shot over to the House. The nullifiers bolted en masse to Bell. The Whigs dropped Wilde and switched to Bell. On the tenth ballot Bell won a majority and was elected Speaker.[57]

Jackson was flabbergasted. It was a bitter defeat—and one he deserved for failing to exercise sufficient leadership to prevent it. Moreover, it was a double loss. Not only had his friend been defeated, but an important position was lost. The Whig strategy had beaten him soundly and he took his defeat with little grace. He had planned a big celebration and even instructed his official carriage to stand ready to bring the new Speaker to the White House for refreshments and congratulations. Now the President stared glumly out the window of his study. The festivities were abruptly canceled. When visitors came the next day to call, Patrick, the doorkeeper, told them that "if they would take his advice, they would as soon put their fingers into a candle, as to go [to the President's room], for he was in a miserable bad humor."[58]

Another aspect of this defeat rankled. A Tennessean had been party to it. Lately a number of Tennesseans had deserted him and joined the Whigs or aided them in their efforts to recharter the Bank and force a restoration of the deposits. Old friends and neighbors they were, and yet they acted like "traitors." John Bell, Davy Crockett, and Hugh Lawson White were some of the men who gave comfort to his enemies—and the mere thought of it sent Jackson into a passion. Especially White's defection. "How sorry I am to see my old friend judge White permitting his name to be prostituted for such wicked purpose in his old age." The Whigs only used him. They cared nothing for him. He did not see that "our republican government" would be lost to a "monied despotism" unless the Bank was destroyed. No President or member of Congress would ever be elected without its consent. But, sighed Old Hickory, Judge White "has permitted Mr. Bell Crockett & Co, to make a bed for him, &

he must sleep in it." Unfortunately, he had shaped "his course without consulting any of his *old friends.*"[59]

And there were other disappointments and rejections. Earlier in the session Jackson's nominations for reappointment of the four government directors of the BUS had been rejected—not once but twice. "Nicholas Biddle *now* rules the Senate," Jackson grumbled to Edward Livingston in Paris, "as a showman does his puppets." The Stevenson defeat for the London mission also embittered him. On two successive days he visited his nominee and swore to him that he would not yield to the Senate or abandon the nomination. Then, at the very end of the congressional session, as another sign of its spite, the Senate elected George Poindexter of Mississippi as its president pro tempore. This was a deliberate slap in the face. Few men stood lower in Jackson's estimation than George Poindexter.

One of Jackson's most annoying problems with the Senate was the constant sniping by some of its members at the Post Office Department. This sport had been going on for years, and with good reason. The postmaster general, William T. Barry, was simply incompetent. Sooner or later they were bound to catch up with him, but for a long time his loyal support of the administration during the Eaton imbroglio saved him from dismissal. Eventually the Senate Committee on the Post Office decided to examine the most serious charges leveled against Barry, and on June 10, 1834, Senator Thomas Ewing of Ohio reported his committee's findings. Among other things the committee discovered that the department was insolvent to the amount of $803,625; it accused Barry of borrowing sums of money without authority; and it charged him with assigning mail contracts on a political basis.[60] Of course the Whigs tried to connect Jackson with these charges, particularly the misappropriation of funds. They said the President was fully aware of Barry's incompetence and yet retained him and covered up his malfeasance.

Because Congress was close to adjournment, the Whigs demanded a continuation of the investigation by an interim committee which would report when Congress reconvened in December. The Democrats countered by suggesting that responsibility for the investigation be shifted to the President, but the Whigs laughed that idea right out the chamber door. Instead, they jammed through a resolution keeping the investigation alive throughout the summer and fall, all of which further soured Jackson's mood and disposition.

Two other nominations worried the President during these closing days of the session. He still needed to appoint the secretary of state and secretary of the navy. And the situation at the State Department especially distressed him. When McLane decided to resign because of a difference of opinion over the direction of foreign affairs, he faulted his old friend Martin Van Buren, who failed to support his position with the President. And this failure offended McLane, offended him so deeply, in fact, that he did not inform Van Buren of his decision to resign.[61] The Vice President learned of it quite by accident in a conversation with Mrs. McLane. The news came as a shock. Then he realized its impact on Jackson and what must be going through the President's mind about his own involvement in the decision. "My omission to speak to him in relation to a matter of so much delicacy," Van Buren later recounted, about which they had previously held so "many embarrassing and painful consultations," would very naturally cause Jackson "much uneasiness." The General might even have "misgivings as to the steadfastness of my devotion to his policy and to his person."[62]

Van Buren raced to the White House. He found Old Hickory "lying on a sofa, quite alone and evidently jaded and despondent—a condition to which his naturally elastic and self reliant spirit rarely succumbed." The Magician began speaking as he entered the room. He swore he knew nothing of the resignation, for he would have tried to prevent it. Certainly he would have discussed it with Jackson. Surely the President understood this, surely he knew his friend would never hide essential information.[63]

The General brightened when he heard these words. A great weight of doubt and uncertainty was lifted from his shoulders. He realized that the resignation had been prompted by Van Buren's failure to support McLane's position and had been made without his knowledge. The two men practically embraced. With that Jackson asked Major Donelson to read McLane's letter and his own answer to it. Then he asked Van Buren's opinion. The Vice President did not like the answer and said so frankly. He thought the President had gone further than the occasion required "or than justice to himself allowed." He feared that Jackson's answer might "be construed as conceding errors on his own part." Van Buren pointed out the offending phrases, whereupon Jackson asked him to make the necessary changes and then give them to Donelson so he could prepare a final copy.[64]

That off his mind, the President took up the question of a successor. Van Buren suggested his friend John Forsyth, the senator from Georgia. Without a moment's hesitation, as though rewarding Van Buren for his faithfulness, Jackson gave his consent. Among his many virtues, Forsyth had in the past provided outstanding support on Indian removal and the Bank question. He had spoken over seventy times during the present session alone in favor of Jackson's fiscal policy. He had also helped reduce the danger of nullification in his state. All things considered, Forsyth was a competent and dependable official, not brilliant in any way but genial and pleasant to work with. A thin, sensitive man, he looked aristocratic and exuded an air of aloofness. He was an "easy-going, amiable man," said one, ". . . conservative and opposed to all extremes."[65]

So the office of secretary of state was filled with little more than a few moments of thought on the part of President Jackson. Small wonder he made so many wretched appointments. Forsyth's nomination shot through the Senate without a whisper of opposition on June 27, 1834, and Forsyth assumed his new duties on July 1, the same day he resigned his Senate seat.

To replace Levi Woodbury in the Navy Department, Jackson again followed Van Buren's suggestion and appointed Mahlon Dickerson of New Jersey. The President wanted to head off men he disliked, such as Joel B. Sutherland of Pennsylvania, who had his eye on the Navy Department. Dickerson was a "fussy" sort, frequently ill and a bit testy at times. A former governor and senator from New Jersey, he had been originally slated for the Russian post as a replacement for James Buchanan. But Dickerson balked at the suggestion, so William Wilkins of Pennsylvania was dispatched to Russia in his place. This shuffling back and forth resulted because the political situation in Washington was "highly volatile" and therefore all diplomatic appointments had become a means of "liquidating political debts or purchasing political aid." At the moment Pennsylvania was thought to require a "sop" on account of losing the Bank. Sutherland and Wilkins were put forward for anything Jackson might have to offer. Since the President would not accept Sutherland, the appointments of Wilkins and Dickerson were therefore engineered to keep both Jackson and Pennsylvania happy.[66]

But Dickerson had other claims on the President. He had an outstanding record on the Bank and tariff issues. Most important he had repeatedly proved himself a loyal and dependable Jacksonian in Congress, obeying instructions from the White House to the letter. Unfortunately, he proved to be a careless and indolent administrator. Nonetheless, his nomination stirred no opposition in the Senate, and Dickerson was confirmed on June 28, the day the President submitted it.[67]

With these confirmations Jackson completed his cabinet and never changed it again, except for the postmaster general, which was not strictly a cabinet post at this time. Forsyth, Woodbury, Cass, Dickerson, and Butler remained in office for the remainder of Jackson's second term and continued (with the exception of Cass) into the next administration. But none of this can hide the fact that in a little more than a year there had been a spate of cabinet turnovers: three secretaries of state; four secretaries of the treasury; two secretaries of the navy; and two attorney generals.[68] A remarkable and pitiable record for any administration.

June 30 was the last day of the congressional session and Jackson was extremely happy to see the members pack up and leave. On this final day, Benton rose in the Senate and introduced a proposal to "expunge" from the record the resolution censuring Jackson's conduct. The other senators quickly rejected it, but Benton announced his determination to "expunge" no matter how many times he had to introduce it. Each session of Congress thereafter he called for its passage and it became one of the major points of violent argument between Democrats and Whigs.[69]

Despite the censure, the loss of the Speakership, and the humiliation of Taney, the important victories of this Panic session all went to Jackson. And everyone knew it. "Our cabinet is not quite as strong as heretofore," wrote George Dallas, "—but public opinion seems setting with resistless force against the Bank and the opposition. The passage of the Gold Bill and the dextrous dispersion of a considerable quantity of quarter-eagles, with a decided improvement in our foreign exchange, have had a powerful influence. Panic has gone by—men are beginning to be ashamed of their bug-bear and its terrors—and our Fourth of July celebrations have turned out overpoweringly democratic."[70]

Although Jackson suffered a few losses, some of which were important, like the Speakership, he exerted renewed leadership over the nation and the party by virtue of his victory over the BUS, and he breathed new power and authority into the presidency. Far more important, the Bank War provided a powerful assist in moving the Republic further down the road to democracy. The war was constantly described by the Democratic press as an effort to stop the few from robbing the many. Quite simply, they said, it was a contest between democracy and aristocracy. Whatever the truth of this assertion, the American people came to believe that the destruction of the BUS did indeed constitute a momentous victory for majoritarian rule. Furthermore, Jackson claimed that his reelection as President in 1832 represented "a solemn decision" by the people to have done with the Bank. As far as he was concerned, the electorate through his reelection had directed the Bank's overthrow because of its corrupt influence on society. Since government must execute "the regularly expressed will of the people," the President and the Congress had no choice but to obey. As Jackson declared at the start of his administration, *the majority is to govern.*" "All must bow to public opinion."[71]

By contrast the Whig leadership could not match Jackson's accomplishments. It was virtually impotent. Van Buren called it "a burnt out Volcano."[72] The coalition of Clay, Calhoun (who was technically not a Whig but a cooperating nullifier), and Webster could make fearsome noises as it pummeled Jackson for his aggressive use of presidential power, but when it moved beyond that vocal display of histrionics to win either recharter or the restoration of the public deposits, it fell apart. Each man went his separate way in proclaiming what should be done. As a result the Whig party could mount no effective resistance to Jackson's program of reform.[73]

Old Hickory emerged from the Bank War battered and bloodied. But the people saluted him as their champion, who loved and respected them, and who had won a great victory for democracy.[74]

CHAPTER 12

The Hermitage Fire

ADDED TO ALL HIS POLITICAL MISERIES, Jackson suffered intense physical discomfort throughout the spring of 1834. So when Congress finally adjourned, Old Hickory wasted little time in packing his trunk and heading west to Tennessee. By early July Washington had become unbearably hot and muggy—"indeed . . . the hottest weather we have had for many years"—and it was essential to get the children out of town, especially during what Jackson called the "sickly season."[1]

As the great carriage pulled away from the White House on July 8 and passed through the new entrance gates that Jackson had built, the party went immediately to the home of William C. Rives in Virginia to drop off Emily Donelson and her three children so that they could spend the summer at Warrenton Springs. The party encountered a great many difficulties crossing the state of Virginia, what with "heavy rains, unusually hot weather, & bad roads." Also, Jackson suffered a severe attack of "hillions collic" along the way, consequently they did not get to Abington at the western end of the state until July 25.[2] So many exasperating and amusing things happened to them on the road that Old Hickory wished he had time to write down a few anecdotes for the *Globe*. He told one, however. At Gordonsville he spotted Senator George Poindexter of Mississippi seated in a stagecoach. Poindexter also caught sight of Jackson lounging on the porch of a tavern. Rather than tempt fate, the senator stayed in the stage out of sight until the horses were changed and the passengers had taken breakfast. Major Lewis, to whom the President recounted the anecdote, said that Poindexter "was afraid to encounter the *flashes* of his *eye.*" In any event, when the coast was clear, Poindexter finally got out of the stage and had breakfast. In the meantime, reported

Jackson with malicious delight, "the stage drove off & left him." The story was repeated widely in Washington, "and is a source of much amusement to our friends," Lewis later reported.[3]

Despite the slow homeward journey, Jackson was heartened by the "enormous" crowds that came out to see and applaud him. And he found their reaction to the gold bill and a specie currency remarkably good, indeed "doing wonders." Everywhere he went he paid his bills in specie, having gotten a large supply before leaving Washington. "I found on my whole journey every thing to cheer us," he said, "prosperity every where, and all gratified and happy on the prospects of a circulating and stable metalic currency, and particularly the gold coin which many had not for years seen a piece." These cheering observations had a noticeable effect on his health. He recovered so quickly from "his last confinement" during the first ten days of their trip, said Major Donelson, that they were able to step up their rate of travel to thirty-five miles a day and therefore hoped to get to the Hermitage by early August.[4]

The country was indeed prospering. Biddle's panic quickly subsided during the spring months. The passage of the gold bill almost immediately improved the nation's foreign exchange and exerted "a powerful influence" on the economy. Meanwhile, Biddle slowly loosened his financial squeeze. Pressured by businessmen and criticized by some of his staunchest supporters, he was forced to give way. Then, in July, 1834, the Bank's board of directors voted unanimously to end all curtailments.[5]

By the time Jackson arrived at the Hermitage on the evening of Tuesday, August 5, he had seen numerous signs of the country's economic recovery. And they enhanced his sense of victory over the Bank. Although he was "worn down" and near total exhaustion, he beamed with "happy pride" and "brightened spirits" as his family rushed from the house to greet him and welcome him home. Only his "little pet" held back. She was shy and had not seen her "Grandpapa" for months. But she quickly overcame her shyness when he held out the present he had purchased for her. "I brought her a little doll which was the only thing that induced her to come to me," he said. She soon had the old man cooing. Ah, he wrote, she is "as sprightly as a little fairy and as wild as a little partridge."[6]

The President went immediately to see his new grandson and he marveled at his size. He was heavier, said Jackson, than little Rachel; he "is a very large fat boy well fed by the spoon as well as the breast." Jackson found the rest of his "household" reasonably well—he always checked on the health of his people before anything else—except for a few servants. Sarah was only slowly recovering from childbirth and suffered several "relapses." She nursed her infant son as often as her strength allowed. "But indeed he is a Hercules," exclaimed Jackson, "and feeds well, will swallow a large spoonful of pap at once, but must be nursed at night to put him to sleep." Sarah would not permit the child to be nursed by anyone else, even when she "had a severe attack" that confined her to bed a few weeks after Jackson's arrival. During Sarah's illness, little Rachel clung to Jackson every waking moment for security, and the old man loved it. "My little pett Rachel, since the confinement of Sarah has become quite attached to me," he gloated. "I take her once a day to see her dear mama, she kisses her and calls then for her nurse which she calls Mamee, and goes away cheerfully."[7]

No sooner did Jackson arrive at the Hermitage than a committee from Nashville attended him to present the resolutions of a recent Democratic meeting and to invite him to a formal dinner. Jackson was exhausted and wished to decline, but "I was compelled to yield," he said, "as I was confidentially advised it was the sincere wishes of all, that an opportunity might be given to promulgate the sentiments of the people (by toasts) around the board." Jackson was particularly susceptible to requests couched in populistic terms, and although he had been "labouring from the moment of my arrival," reading and answering his mail, greeting visitors and Democratic delegations, he cheerfully agreed to attend the dinner.[8]

"Upwards of fifteen hundred of my friends" turned out for the dinner on Saturday, August 13, all of them "well dressed and truly Republican." Most of these men were attending a convention in Nashville to revise the state constitution. A parade preceded the dinner, complete with band, the firing of guns, and the ringing of church bells. At the dinner everyone present tried to reach the President and shake his hand. Some of the leading political lights of Tennessee attended, including James K. Polk, John Bell, Cave Johnson, Felix Grundy, and their friends. Bell feebly protested his loyalty to the President but Jackson said he expected him to "come out boldly against a Bank as well as the Bank" if they were to maintain cordial relations. Everyone in the room who spoke to Old Hickory congratulated him on the prospect of a stable metallic currency, "instead of rags." This was the true path, the President responded, by which "the morals of our people and our free institutions" might be preserved.[9]

To the disappointment of the assembled crowd only two toasts were permitted by the committee on arrangements, one of which toasted the President's health. Jackson naturally responded—which he came prepared to do. In a strong voice he called out:

> The true Constitutional currency, gold and silver coin.—It can cover and protect the labor of our country without the aid of a National Bank, an institution which can never be otherwise than hostile to the liberties of the people, because its tendency is to associate wealth with an undue power over the public interests.

Bell's friends paled. They wanted a national bank. The toast, said Jackson, "came upon the ears of the Bank aristocracy with as much surprise as the toast I gave at the Jefferson dinner in Washington." Bell himself cursed, and Ephraim H. Foster, who had been defeated by Grundy for the Senate, bawled: "We are broke down. Grundy & Polk are to rule this State, the Bank will have to go down."[10]

Jackson vigorously denied that his toast was intended specifically for Bell. "I am Bells personal friend, he is mine," the President protested; "I am also his political, if he will adopt what I believe the true policy for the safety and interest of the country." Bell needed to understand that Jackson opposed not only *the* Bank but any national bank. "For if we burn the old Phenix, and foster a young one from its ashes, the young will grow as hateful and injurious as the old one." Once a complete metallic currency became operative around the country, he said, they could relax because then the behavior of banks with their "over issues and sudden withdrawalls" would not affect "the vallue of labour, or of the property of the country." The mint was presently casting half eagles to the amount of $20,000 a day; when the die for the eagle was ready, said the President, the mint would issue $40,000 a day, or 4 million every hundred days.[11]

The first half eagle coined at the Philadelphia mint was sent to Jackson at the Hermitage. He wrote to the director of the mint, William Findlay, and acknowledged receipt. Then he asked Findlay to assure Adam Eckfeeldt, the "chief coiner," that he would "treasure" it as a souvenir in recording the events of the present day, "or as the opposition say, '*the revolution.*'" It is a revolution, he went on, from "a destructive corrupting and demoralising paper system that makes the rich richer, and the poor poorer," to a metallic currency that will give prosperity to all, especially the working class.[12]

One additional reason for Jackson's concern over Bell and his friends was their determination to block Van Buren's succession to the presidency if at all possible. They expected to capitalize on southern distaste for the Little Magician. At first they planned to support Judge John McLean; then they shifted to Richard M. Johnson, and finally settled on Judge Hugh Lawson White of Tennessee. White's candidacy made a lot of sense to the Bell crowd because he was popular with both voters and politicians in Tennessee. And he was not afraid of Andrew Jackson. The President, of course, looked upon this movement as divisive and personally offensive. But he had to exercise care in demonstrating his displeasure lest anyone accuse him of dictating the choice between his two friends and interfering in the people's right of "free suffrage." Also, he was not about to offend White, since White himself was not directly responsible for the movement.[13]

The developing danger to his candidacy was not lost on Van Buren. Although separated by a thousand miles he wrote regularly to Jackson to record his devotion and loyalty, for without Old Hickory's active and determined support he could never aspire to the White House. He wrote every week, sometimes twice. These were long, detailed letters containing news, information, advice, expressions of affection, and protestations of undying loyalty. When in Washington, he explained in one letter, and we are together, there is no time to indulge "personal feelings." It is only when separated "that I have an opportunity to give full vent to those feelings, and then they come upon me with irresistable force. . . . Believe me that whatever you do, that can by possibility bear upon me, I always take it for granted (although I may not be able to comprehend it at the time) is intended for my benefit, and sincerely entertaining the conviction that your foresight and judgment in such matters is superior to my own, I am quiet, and content."[14]

So politics did not allow Jackson much rest or peace at the Hermitage during his short "vacation." Even though he planned to stay only a month at home, the demands of his office and position as head of the Democratic party intruded constantly. He sincerely wished he could remain longer. He was much troubled by conditions at the Hermitage, and he was reluctant to return to Washington before the fall harvest because he could not trust his son to execute his orders faithfully or to keep him fully informed of everything transpiring at the farm. Because of a late spring frost he knew the cotton yield this year would be half of normal; in addition, it had been necessary to get rid of the overseer, Holtzclaw, and replace him with Edward Hobbs. Under the circumstances, therefore, conditions at the Hermitage would be uncertain for a while and so Jackson pleaded with his son to write him at the White House at least twice a month and give him complete information about what was going on. It was very stressful for him to sit in his study in Washington and not know what was happening in Nashville.

Of course young Andrew promised to do as his father asked, assuring him that his failures in the past had been occasioned by unforeseen developments. He swore that things would be different hereafter. What troubled Jackson more than anything else was his son's penchant for endorsing the debts and obligations of friends and relatives. This simply could not go on, and over and over Jackson repeated his admonition to his son to decline every appeal to lend his signature as a guarantee for a loan. "I therefore repeat to you, my dear Andrew, not to involve yourself any more by indorsements, or creating debts except for the family and farm, but say to all and every one that I have absolutely enjoined you not for any one."[15]

Sarah's protracted recovery from childbirth and the infant's sudden illness in early September also worried Jackson. But his fierce sense of duty to his office and obligation to the American people took precedence over everything else. On the morning of September 9, following breakfast, he and Andrew J. Donelson set out for Washington in the hope of arriving at the capital by October 3. (Actually they arrived on September 30.) He wrote to Major Lewis to arrange to have the White House in readiness. "Say to the chamber maid to have all our beds clear of bedbuggs."[16]

Jackson was hardly gone a day when he experienced terrible anxiety for his family and wrote to Andrew of his fear and concern. "I did not suppose that my anxiety for Sarah & the dear little ones would have been so great as it is. I shall be uneasy until I hear that she & the dear little babe is intirely recovered." He then ended his letter on a note of intense piety, an impulse that had become habitual with him over the last few years:

> I have not time to write Sarah—kiss her and the dear little ones for me, and say to her let nothing disturb her mind, that I nightly offer up my prayers to the throne of grace for the health & safety of you all, and that we ought *all* to rely with confidence on the promises of our dear redeemer, and give him our hearts, this is all he requires & all that we can do, and if we sincerely do this, we are sure of salvation thro' his attonement.[17]

On his way east, Jackson met a steamboat commander who agreed to freight the Hermitage cotton to New Orleans for $2 a bale. This agreement would save "upwards of one hundred dollars," so Jackson informed his son of the arrangement and directed him to make certain that each bale weighed 500 lbs. or more. He also expressed his concern for the health of Sarah and her child and begged his son to write to him at Salem, Virginia. "It will reach there before me, as I cannot reach there before the 20th or perhaps the 22d instant. I will be uneasy until I hear from you all."[18]

Andrew never wrote. The President searched in vain at every stop along his route through Virginia for some news from home. His concern mounted. Even in Washington he found nothing from Andrew. He waited nearly two weeks to hear from his son before writing him again and conveying his deep chagrin and disappointment.

> *My son,* Thirty days has elapsed since we left the Hermitage, Sarah on a sick bed & the babe not recovered from its attack. I left them with great anxiety for their restoration to health, but I resigned them to the protection of that allwise providence who holds us all in the hollow of his hands, in confidence he would preserve them. Still I had your promise my son, that you would write me how they were, and I am now, even now, without one line from you. I am wearied with anxiety and disappointment. I have daily since my arrival here expected to receive a letter from you, and with each day, a disappointment. . . . I am at a loss to conclude, and am still at a greater loss to account for your silence, after the charge I gave you, and your promise to write me.[19]

Jackson's apprehension that something was wrong was well founded. For when word finally arrived from home—and it came first from friends and neighbors—it brought catastrophic news: the Hermitage had burned. His beautiful home was in ruins.

The fire occurred at four o'clock in the afternoon of Monday, October 13. Young Andrew was in the fields at the time and Sarah rested in the house. Apparently the roof was ignited "by sparks or soot of the chimney" in the dining room and since a stiff northwest wind was blowing, the fire quickly spread. Within minutes several servants noticed the blaze and sounded the alarm. Two of them, Charles and Squire, attempted to get a ladder and climb to the roof but none could be found. Besides, "the roof was so steep which would have made it hard to get up to the fire."[20]

Joseph Reiff and William C. Hume, two carpenter-contractors, who were constructing the Tulip Grove home nearby for Andrew J. Donelson, spotted the blaze and rushed to take charge of the efforts to extinguish the fire. They ordered the servants to save as much of the furniture in the house as possible. Most of the downstairs belongings were pulled clear, although many pieces of furniture were "broken and otherwise injured in getting it out." The upstairs furniture did not fare as well. Virtually all of it was partially damaged or burned and included the loss of a considerable number of letters written by Rachel Jackson. Sarah "acted with firmness," reported Stockley D. Donelson to Jackson, "and gave every necessary direction to save the furniture."[21]

Through determination and agility, Joseph Reiff managed to climb to the roof of the dining room, which extended as a wing from the house itself, and finally put out the fire. He had the assistance of William Donelson's servants, who were working nearby, along with the laborers and hands who were building Tulip Grove. Fortunately they were all standing on the grounds outside the house when the roof fell in. No one was hurt.[22]

Quite characteristically, Andrew faulted the servants for the calamity. "Oh had I been there," he wrote, "it might have been prevented. The cursed negroes were all so stupid & confused that nothing could be done until some white one came to their relief." But Robert Armstrong reported to Jackson that "on the whol I expect, every thing was done that could be done, and I have no doubt it was purely accidental."[23]

Andrew, Armstrong, and Stockley Donelson each reported to Jackson on the disaster and all tried to minimize the extent of the damage to the house and its furnishings. All agreed that the walls of the house were sound and that the Hermitage could be rebuilt on its original site. "Some of the petition walls and arches over the window, and some other repairing of the walls" needed work, said Stockley Donelson, "all of which Mr. Austin can furnish brick to do by deferring the building of some of Maj Donelson back buildings. It can all be covered in before winter sets in, which it will be necessary to do, if the House is to be rebuilt in the same place etc; as the walls would be much damaged by being exposed to the winter rains." Armstrong told Jackson that his papers, letter books, valuables, and most of the furniture had been saved. But he greatly underestimated the loss, although he did acknowledge that the upstairs wardrobe and large bedstead had been badly damaged. The smoke damage was considerable, which no one recognized at first. Armstrong estimated that the house could be rebuilt for approximately $2,000 or $2,500 and he recommended that Jackson stick with the old site. Andrew thought it would take "3 or 4 & perhaps 5 thousand dollars to repair every loss— but I think not more than 3 or 4—that is to rebuild it & furnish every thing again."[24]

Poor Sarah was distraught by the catastrophe. The family moved immediately to the Baldwin place at Hunter's Hill and Andrew reported that they were very comfortable. Within two days, a large work force set about preparing the house for renovation, at least until they had final word from Jackson as to whether they should rebuild on the old site or not. Three or four whipsaws were started and the workmen began to cover the house completely to protect it from further damage by the weather.

On October 23, the President learned of the fire. "The Lords will be done," he sighed. "It was he that gave me the means to build it, and he has the right to destroy it, and blessed be his name." Since neglect was imputed to no one and it appeared to be an accident, Jackson accepted his loss with Christian resignation. "I will have it rebuilt," he said. "Was it not on the site selected by my dear departed wife I would build it higher up the Hill, but I will have it repaired." His only worry concerned Sarah. "I am fearful that the fatigue & alarm may be injurious to our dear Sarahs health—let not the loss trouble you & her for one moment," he told his son.[25]

Since the walls and foundation of the Hermitage had been declared "safe & good," Jackson directed that they be "covered in before the heavy frosts & winter rains injure it" so that the house could be restored in the spring. Meanwhile he started to make plans for the rebuilding. He told his son he would arrange to have tin shipped up for the roof to cover a house 80 feet by 44. He wanted the windowsills made "of good hewn stone—if it can be got in time" and he suggested hiring the workman who did Major Donelson's window and door sills. He authorized Armstrong to draw on him for $1500 to meet the initial expenses and he asked Andrew to "make a contract with some solvent & responsible workmen to undertake the whole job." He also asked for a detailed accounting of the loss of furniture and wondered about his wine cellar and Emily Donelson's china. With all the confusion and commotion, Jackson added, do not forget to harvest and house the cotton. Have it ginned, baled, and sent to market. "It becomes us now to act with oeconomy, and use industry to repair and regain the loss."[26]

Unfortunately, young Andrew was not the man to deal with emergencies or cope with financial and administrative problems. Within a week his father was reciting again his old complaints. Edward Hobbs, the new overseer, alerted Jackson to the fact that they were without wheat seed and the slaves without shoes. In a weary voice, Jackson lectured Andrew about dressing the slaves properly and he added "one remark my son for your guidance hereafter, never be without seed raised on your own farm of every thing you cultivate, it is a wretched mode of farming & shews careless management wherever it happens."[27]

Poor Jackson was desperate for his son's help in running the farm. He got little. If the cotton was of good quality and they could gin 70 bales of 500 lbs. each, as Andrew claimed, and the price kept up between 14¢ and 16¢, then, said Jackson, "I trust I will be able to pay Hill for the land, meet my other engagements and rebuild my house—but you must aid me, have the useless stock sold, and the blood stock well attended, and a good crop next year if a good season, planting as much cotton as the hands can in moderation attend & pick out." He urged his son to hurry the cotton to market; he asked for regular reports and an immediate accounting of the cotton shipped to market so that he could figure his expenses and plan for the future. He reminded his son about maintaining an accurate "cotton book," one kept each day during the "picking season" which would enable them to avoid overestimating the weight of the cotton crop and misjudging future revenues.[28]

Fortunately, Jackson had Colonel Robert Armstrong, postmaster at Nashville and a former comrade in the Creek War, to rely on to look after the repairs of the Hermitage. Armstrong reported on November 4 that in short order contracts would be let, repairs started, and the cost (with luck) kept around $2,500 to $3,000. Major Lewis, who had returned to Tennessee shortly after Jackson arrived back at the White House, also helped. He visited the Hermitage to inspect the damage and survey the operation of the farm. He had also been commissioned by the President to present a pair of shoes to the "little pet." Lewis presented the shoes with a flourish, and the child's mother asked Rachel who sent them.

"Grand pa-pa," Rachel piped up.

Lewis beamed at the child. Where is your "grand pa-pa?" he asked.

"City," came the reply, for she could not pronounce the word *"Washington,"* said Lewis, "owing I suppose to its length."[29]

After consulting with Andrew and Armstrong, Major Lewis suggested to Jackson a number of alterations that would improve the style of the Hermitage and increase its size and the number of people it could accommodate. The President said he would have been content to restore the house to its former condition "but as I know I shall [not] be long on earth to enjoy its comforts in retirement," he left it to Andrew to exercise his own discretion about the proposed alterations, "provided it does not add too much to the expence of the repairs." All I want, he said, "is a good room to which I can retire if I am spared to live out my irksome term here, and I am sure I shall not want that room long."[30]

Because of Sarah's delicate health, the youth of the children, and the difficulty of living at Hunter's Hill for the winter months, it was decided to send Sarah and the children to Washington to live with the President at the White House. Andrew would join them after the house had been covered for the winter and the cotton shipped to market. Major Lewis agreed to escort the fatherless family from Tennessee. "Sarah, like a good wife," reported Lewis to Jackson, "says she is willing to do whatever her husband thinks is for the best." They left Nashville on November 12. Immediately the old man began to worry. "I shall be uneasy until they reach me," he fussed, ". . . but my prayers are nightly offerred up for their safety, & under his care they are safe. . . . I trust in god they will reach me in health and safety."[31]

The Hermitage disaster was announced by the newspapers around the country and Jackson received many expressions of sympathy and offers of aid. A subscription, for example, was gotten up in New Orleans to raise a fund to rebuild the house which would be offered to the country at large and with no contribution larger than 50¢ so that *"every man"* who might wish to do so could tender Jackson "this complimentary mark of public gratitude." But the President rejected the offer. "I respect as I ought the feelings that dictated the generous feeling in the proposition but cannot accept the boon. I am able to rebuild it, and hope whatever generosity the good people of Neworleans intended to bestow on me as a memento of their regard for my services may be applied to some charitable institution." Jackson was a proud man, but he also felt it improper for a President to take advantage of his position and popularity to feed on public generosity.

The little family arrived at the White House at 11:30 P.M. on Wednesday, November 26. Sarah was exhausted "and a little complaining," so Jackson gave her "a dose of phesic" which seemed to bring her around by morning. The "little pet" flung herself into Jackson's outstretched arms when she spotted him. "Grandpa," she cried, "the great fire burnt my bonnet, and the big owl tryed to kill Poll [her parrot], but papa killed the owl." The old man hugged the child. "She is very sprightly," he boasted, "and the son is a beautiful and fine boy. I am happy they are safe with me." Sarah and the "sweet little ones," he told his son, send you a kiss. *"I will take care of them* until you Join us."[32]

Unfortunately, Andrew did not take as good care of his father. The $5,000 note that Andrew had promised to pay Harry Hill on January 1, 1835, was not met and started to draw interest at 6 percent. The last words Jackson had written him just a few short weeks before concerned this debt: "I must close for the mail," wrote Jackson on December 7, "but I beg you in conclusion to recollect the debt due to Hill & how injurious it is to pay interest upon a debt, when the farm does not produce three percent in the capitol."[33] And so began Jackson's long descent into the hell of mounting indebtedness created by his son.

The contract for the rebuilding of the Hermitage was signed on January 1, 1835. Colonel Charles J. Love, a close friend and business associate for many years, helped supervise the preparation of the contract. Earlier, Jackson had called him in to participate in the negotiations and arrangements over the restoration. "Every care has been taken to have the Contract made so full and plain that it cannot be misunderstood," Love told Jackson. The "Col'ol and myself will keep a strict look out that the work is done agreeable to contract." Other bids had been much higher, and of course, the "house is large." In any event, "we got the best bargain we could" for a price of $3,950, which did not include painting or decorating. It was further agreed that the rebuilding would be completely finished by December 25, 1835.[34]

Work on the house began almost at once. And, naturally, problems immediately arose. Labor was scarce and it was difficult to secure enough hands to keep to the original schedule. In addition, changes were suggested to improve the appearance and size of the house. Lewis felt that the stories of the house should be made higher and Armstrong agreed. The size and arrangement of the windows were also altered to make them more decorative and in better proportion to the rest of the house. Jackson himself had a hand in some of the alterations. "I would reduce the roof somewhat," he instructed his son, "but not to make it too flat." He much admired the portico he had built for the White House, designed many years before by Benjamin Latrobe, as well as the Mount Vernon portico. This feature reflected the fashionable Greek revival style at the time with its templelike columns and pure white color. The monumental portico style had a powerful influence on American architecture. It certainly excited the imagination of President Jackson. So he decided to add a colossal colonnade to his home in Tennessee, just like the one he had in Washington. To do this, the house itself was made taller—which is why he agreed to Lewis's suggestion—and this meant adding a "false" or "fake" front to the building in order to allow for columns big enough to provide the desired effect. It was all done so expertly that even today few people looking at the Hermitage realized that the front of the house is fake and serves merely as a setting for the columns.[35]

Because of the changes in design, the difficulty of obtaining sufficient laborers, and the normal delays in building operations, the Hermitage was not completed until the summer of 1836, approximately eighteen months after construction had started. The final accounting of the costs of the restoration was presented to Jackson by Colonel Armstrong on August 2, 1836. [See page 190.]

These costs,[36] virtually double the original estimate, did not include the household furnishings lost or damaged in the fire. To replace wardrobes, bedsteads, dressing bureaus, tables, chairs, rugs, drapes, and sundry other articles of furniture came to $2,303.77, purchased from seven Philadelphia merchants. And these expenses did not include personal items lost, such as little Rachel's "bonnet." To replace these items, Sarah went on a shopping spree shortly after she arrived at the White House and ran up a $345.80 bill, all of which the President paid.[37] Dear Sarah was picking up some of her husband's less attractive attributes.

Jackson turned the task of refurbishing the Hermitage over to Sarah

August 2, 1836

Estimate of Bills of the Hermitage House, with the Amount Paid and
  balances due 1 June

For amt. of Rieff and Hume bill pr. agreement contract			$ 3950.00
For Extra work done upon change of Plan			239.00
For work done on west wing and New Kitchen finding every thing..			186.00
For the full length two story Porch added finding every thing..			750.00
			$ 5125.00
To cash paid Rieff and Hume at sundry times per receipts		2285.00	
"ditto paid 25 april		1000.00	
"ditto paid by A Jackson in work		513.00	
"ditto paid June 24th..		500.00	4298.00
			827.00
For Amt Bill Higgins Plastering		$ 900.00	
To Cash paid Higgins in part	500.00		
"ditto paid do June 24	225.00	725.00	$ 175.00
		400.00	
For Amt Bill of Painting, Paints, oil etc			
To Cash paid Horn and Wells (Horn 100.00)	188.00		
"Do paid Horn	50.00		
"Do paid Wells	25.00	$ 263.00	$ 137.00
"Do Paid Horn. 2d of August 1836. pd by A.J. jr			$ 85.00
			$ 52.00

and Major Lewis. Since Lewis had experience in outfitting the White
House, especially the East Room, the President asked him to accompany
Sarah to Philadelphia to select the furnishings. Jackson's only suggestion
was a practical one, namely that beds with plain (rather than carved) posts
be purchased since they would be easier to clean. Once selected the new
furniture was shipped from Philadelphia by coastal vessels to New Orleans, and then transported to Nashville via river steamboats. Jackson's
agent in Philadelphia was Henry Toland, and the items purchased were
consigned by Toland to Maunsel White, the New Orleans factor, who
arranged for the shipment to Nashville.

Unfortunately, a good portion of these newly purchased furnishings
were lost in another fire when the *John Randolph* burned at the wharf in
Nashville on March 16, 1836. This second conflagration did not overly
perturb Jackson—nor shake his confidence in divine providence. He accepted the disaster as "the Lords will." But, as a result of this latest

misfortune, he was forced to offer for sale some of his land in the western district for $5 an acre—provided he got cash. The lost crates of furniture were all replaced even though it drove him deeper into debt. "The burning of my house and furniture has left me poor," he wailed.[38]

He exaggerated, of course. But, despite the losses and cost, what eventually rose out of the ashes was a beautiful house, majestic in size and appearance, and totally appropriate to the manner, style, and presence of its master, the man many people would later call the "Sage of the Hermitage."[39]

CHAPTER 13

The Most Dangerous Moment

AT THE VERY START OF HIS ADMINISTRATION in 1829, when Jackson announced his intention of instituting reforms in the operation of government, he made it clear that his intention included foreign as well as domestic affairs. Shortly after his inauguration he called to the White House the various ministers representing foreign countries and told them that he had no designs on the safety of other nations and that his policy was simple and straightforward. It was a policy he later defined more precisely in his first message to Congress: "to ask nothing that is not clearly right, and to submit to nothing that is wrong." When they heard it, the American people applauded the sentiment. Throughout his New England tour his words constantly appeared in newspapers and on banners and signposts. Like his slogan "Our Federal Union, It Must Be Preserved," his admonition to the world that the rights of the United States would be respected stirred the patriotism of his countrymen.[1]

In terms of foreign affairs, Jackson's first administration had been a smashing success. He won the opening of the West Indian ports from Great Britain, secured several most-favored-nation treaties with foreign nations, and collected millions in debts owed by foreign countries. The American people marveled at his diplomatic skill. Even foreign governments acknowledged his success in settling long-standing American indemnity claims against them.[2]

By the end of his first term in office, therefore, Jackson had gained a large measure of respect for American rights around the world. And it was based almost solely on his alert response to any foreign action that bore the slightest semblance of contempt toward American rights. The incident that occurred at the port of Quallah Battoo in Sumatra is a case

192

in point. Unfortunately, its resolution necessitated the use of American military force.

On February 7, 1831, the American vessel *Friendship*, engaged in the pepper trade, was attacked and plundered by Sumatran natives. Specie, opium, stores, and instruments were taken. Word of the attack sped to Washington and Jackson responded at once. The frigate *Potomac*, captained by John Downes, was dispatched to the scene with instructions to negotiate with the ruling king for restitution and indemnity. Failing that, Downes was authorized to take appropriate punitive action. But Downes exceeded his instructions—or rather reversed them. On the morning of February 6, 1832, he attacked the port of Quallah Battoo, drove off the natives, and fired the town. Then he proceeded to negotiate, and he eventually worked out a peace agreement after assuring the native chiefs and rajahs of swift American reprisal for any future attacks or raids.[3]

Jackson reported the initial outrage by the Sumatran natives in his 1831 message to Congress and followed up on July 12, 1832, with a special message on the subject. The opposition press was shocked by the barbarity of the reprisal. Furthermore, they pilloried Jackson for making war without a formal declaration from Congress. They cited it as yet another example of executive despotism. How stupid to argue, responded the ever watchful *Globe*, that it takes the special permission of Congress to exterminate pirates and lay waste their lairs. Americans should be proud, the newspaper said. "The Maylas on the other side of the globe were chastened in the name of Andrew Jackson and the American ensign became a safe passport among the remotest nations."[4]

The President's response to the initial (and piratical) attack by the natives was perfectly appropriate. Unfortunately, his instructions to Downes to negotiate first were disregarded. Some Americans surpassed even Old Hickory in the intensity of their nationalism. Difficulty arose because the President's representative failed to follow orders, and this was a problem that Jackson faced repeatedly.

Indeed, his only public diplomatic failure during his first administration had been the appointment to Russia of John Randolph of Roanoke, who stayed at his post for a very brief period and then returned home without so much as a by-your-leave. Van Buren had been responsible for this unfortunate appointment (as he was for many of Jackson's worst appointments) and was motivated into recommending Randolph for political reasons.[5] At the time he seemed to think that because United States relations with Russia were "simple and friendly little harm would be done if it should turn out that we had made a mistake in the selection of the Minister."[6] It was expected that a commercial treaty would be signed with Russia, after which the envoy would probably return home. Sending someone as quixotic as Randolph abroad may have made excellent political sense to Van Buren but it also demonstrated his ignorance—and

Jackson's as well—about how to improve United States relations with foreign nations.

Randolph was replaced by James Buchanan of Pennsylvania, and again partisan politics was the deciding factor in the choice. Foolishly, Jackson permitted most of his diplomatic appointments to serve purely political ends.[7] In the case of Buchanan, the appointment came about with Samuel D. Ingham's dismissal from the cabinet in 1831. It occurred to both Jackson and Van Buren that if they got rid of Buchanan by sending him abroad they could remake the political leadership in Pennsylvania by encouraging more proadministration men to assume command of the Democratic party in that state. But Buchanan knew little French and was reluctant to take the post when it was offered.[8] He much preferred the mission to Great Britain. Besides, he held out hopes of winning the vice presidential slot on the Jackson ticket in the 1832 election. But when all those hopes collapsed he decided to take what he could get and so he dutifully trotted off to St. Petersburg.[9]

Buchanan was instructed by Edward Livingston, who succeeded Van Buren as secretary of state, to secure a commercial treaty as his first priority and then, if possible, a treaty for the protection of neutral rights in wartime.[10] He arrived in Russia on June 2, 1832, and toward the end of October reported to Livingston that "there is, at present, the fairest prospect of speedily concluding a Commercial Treaty with this Government."[11] Through constant prodding, a certain amount of tact, and appeals to personal interests, Buchanan finally talked the Russians into agreeing to a treaty which he signed on December 18, 1832, along with Count Nesselrode, the Russian foreign minister. The day was the czar's birthday and Buchanan had suggested it as an appropriate signing date. This most-favored-nation treaty placed the ships, crews, and cargo of each nation on a basis of reciprocity, with each country receiving the same treatment it was accorded in its home port.[12] This was the first such treaty the Russian government had ever signed, and the Russians' acquiescing to it was due almost solely to the czar's appreciation of American handling of reports concerning his treatment of Poles. The czar was extremely sensitive to criticism on the matter. The western press excoriated him. Even the *Globe* got in a round of sharp criticism but abruptly halted it in the fall of 1832 on command from the White House. Jackson had been alerted to Russian sensitivity and by his action provided Buchanan with the means of explaining away the *Globe*'s initial criticism. Thereafter the newspaper simply emphasized the importance of United States–Russian friendship.[13]

Buchanan had done his job well. But he had a strong assist from the administration. He notified Livingston of his success, adding: "I congratulate the President, that after the many fruitless attempts which have been made by our Government to conclude such a Treaty, it has at last been accomplished." The difficulties were such, he said, as "to inspire me with a stronger resolution to accomplish, if practicable, the wishes of the President." However, he failed to gain the treaty over neutral rights. The Russians dismissed the idea as too idealistic.[14]

The many and spectacular diplomatic successes of the early Jackson administration encouraged the President to pursue an even more vigorous foreign policy in winning recognition of American rights, and for a time it looked as though the northeastern boundary between Maine and Canada might be settled. The Treaty of 1783 which ended the American Revolution called for a boundary in the northeast which was described so inexactly in the Treaty that it could not be run. A convention in 1827 named the king of the Netherlands as arbitrator, and in 1831 he suggested a line that Jackson was willing to accept. Not only would it avoid possible hostilities with Britain, but the President did not think the American claim for a larger portion of the disputed territory could be substantiated. The king proposed a compromise that essentially split the difference between the two countries.[15]

Van Buren thought it might be a good idea to offer an indemnity to Maine as an inducement to accept the proposal, since the Constitution forbids altering the boundary of a state without its express consent. After considerable negotiations, a secret agreement was reached in 1832 whereby Maine would be awarded the proceeds from the sale of a million acres of federal land in Michigan in return for the surrender of all claims to the disputed territory bordering Canada. The agreement was signed by officials of Maine and the administration. So it looked for one bright moment as if an important and long-standing dispute was close to solution. Unfortunately it foundered because of another atrocious appointment to a ministerial post suggested by Van Buren and accepted by Jackson, one arranged without so much as a second look at the candidate's abilities or qualifications.

William Pitt Preble, a former assistant to Albert Gallatin when Gallatin served as minister to England in 1826, was chosen minister to the Netherlands. Since Preble came from an influential Maine family, it was anticipated that his appointment would encourage Maine to accept whatever solution to the boundary dispute the Jackson administration eventually worked out. More important, Preble's appointment was expected to strengthen the Democratic party in New England, where it desperately needed strengthening. But had Van Buren or Jackson the wit to consult Gallatin about their intended choice they would have learned that Preble was an incompetent, vain, abrasive hothead, and a self-righteous prig. As it turned out, Preble not only resisted any genuine compromise of the conflicting claims after he became minister, but he sacrificed national interests to the special claims of his state. His subsequent denunciations of the compromise proposed by the king caused Maine to change its mind and protest the settlement. And there matters sat.[16]

Jackson called his cabinet together to see what could be done. Livingston, McLane, and Cass attended, along with Nicholas Trist, who at the time served as Jackson's secretary and worked in the State Department. During the discussion Livingston asked for a ruler to draw some lines on a map that lay on the table. As Trist returned to the room after obtaining a ruler he heard Livingston express a word of caution to the President. Livingston ventured that any attempt to adopt the proposed settlement without Maine's consent would probably raise a public clamor. Jackson glanced up at Livingston, a surprised look on his face.

"I care nothing about clamors, sir, mark me! I do precisely what I think just and right."[17]

As he spoke Jackson's forefinger came down hard on the map. All the men in the room snapped to attention. And they knew he meant what he said.

Nonetheless, the cabinet united in their opposition to the settlement. The rejection by Maine had already stirred strong feeling in the Senate. Better to work for another agreement altogether, they urged, or else leave it to the Senate to resolve. Much as he hated to do it, Jackson took the advice. "I had determined to accept the award made by the King of Holland," he later insisted, ". . . but my whole cabinet remonstrated against my decision recommending me, as the senate was in session, to lay it before them. I yielded to this recommendation, but sincerely have I regretted it since."[18] Most probably he yielded to prevent political damage to the party in New England.

For the remainder of his term as secretary of state, Edward Livingston tried to renegotiate the terms of a boundary settlement with the British government. But his efforts were frustrated by the lack of a conciliatory attitude by all the parties involved.[19]

Jackson had more success elsewhere. Because of the Quallah Battoo incident in Sumatra, the President recognized the need for formal treaty agreements with Asiatic countries, and he therefore commissioned Edmund Roberts, a sea captain and merchant, as a special envoy to draw up commercial treaties with Cochin China (present-day Vietnam), Siam, Muscat, and Japan. By this action Jackson initiated diplomatic relations with nations of the Far East. The mission was intended to extend the commerce of the United States into areas hitherto unexplored. Roberts failed with Cochin China because he refused to authorize an alteration of Jackson's letter of introduction to the Emperor to permit a tone of supplication in the salutation.[20] This "breach of etiquette" doomed the mission. So he proceeded to Bangkok, where he enjoyed better results. On March 30, 1833, he concluded a Treaty of Amity and Commerce with the Siamese government. From there he went to Muscat and signed a treaty with that government on October 3, 1833. Both treaties opened these nations to American trade on a most-favored-nation basis, and they were ratified by the Senate in June, 1834.[21] These were the first treaties between the United States and Far Eastern countries. What made the Muscat treaty especially valuable was the fact that the sultan of Muscat ruled the spice-rich island of Zanzibar off the east coast of Africa as well as the kingdom of Oman on the coast of Arabia.[22]

Jackson was so pleased with these results that in April, 1835, he authorized Roberts to begin negotiations to open Japan to the West. He also authorized him to renew his attempts at a commercial treaty with Cochin China. Unfortunately, the envoy died at Macao on June 12, 1836, before reaching his destination. And although Roberts signed only two treaties with Asiatic countries, the information obtained about commercial advantages in the Orient later prompted a steady expansion of American trade in the Far East.[23]

Commercial treaties were also concluded with several South American countries. Colombia and Chile signed a series of treaties in 1831, 1832, and 1833 that extended reciprocal trade concessions to the United States. Indeed, when Jackson took office there were few commercial treaties with European and South American countries. By the close of his administration agreements had been concluded with Turkey, Russia, Morocco, Great Britain, Mexico, Colombia, Chile, Venezuela, the Peru-Bolivia Federation, Siam, and Muscat. This attention to improving commercial opportunities around the world provided another dimension to the economic expansion of America during the Age of Jackson.

Through diplomatic channels the President also hoped to demonstrate to other nations, particularly South America, the meaning of his brand of democracy, namely his belief that the people of all countries have the right to govern themselves. He was especially solicitous of Simón Bolívar, the Great Liberator, and expressed the delight of the American people in Bolívar's efforts to establish in Colombia a "liberal" government. The President's interest in South America even led to an investigation of the possibility of American involvement in a canal route across Central America.[24] Jackson also upheld the right of Americans to participate in fishing off the Falkland Islands. And that almost landed the United States in a mess of trouble.

The Falkland Islands, off the coast of Argentina, were claimed by Great Britain but in 1820 were colonized by Argentina, then known as the United Provinces of La Plata. The islands served as depot for whalers, sealers, and other fishermen. Louis Vernet, governor of the colony, in an effort to assert Argentine authority over the Falklands, seized three American ships in 1831 on the pretext that they violated Argentine law. The captain of one of the vessels escaped and reported the incident to George W. Slacum, the American consul at Buenos Aires, who protested the seizure. Jackson bridled when he heard about this "gross violation of American rights" and later informed Congress in his third annual message that he had dispatched a warship directly to the islands. An American vessel, the U.S.S. *Lexington,* had already taken up a position near Montevideo, and its captain, Silas Duncan, proceeded to the Falklands and on January 1, 1832, destroyed the sparse settlements. At the request of the residents Duncan agreed to escort them to Montevideo.[25]

Jackson immediately dispatched Francis Baylies of Massachusetts as chargé d'affaires to Buenos Aires. A skilled lawyer and former congressman who also spoke Spanish, Baylies was instructed on personal orders of the President to protest the seizure, demand reparation, and negotiate a most-favored-nation treaty which would specifically recognize the right of American citizens to fish off the Falklands and in the inshore coastal area.[26] But, infuriated by Duncan's foray, Argentina refused to disavow Vernet's action or make restitution for the seizure. Instead, Argentina demanded reparation for Captain Duncan's deportation of its citizens. The negotiations promptly collapsed. Baylies demanded his passports and departed the country on September 3, 1832.

The situation could hardly have been worse, and Baylies told Livingston that the Argentinians ought to be taught a lesson or the United States would suffer the contempt of all South America.[27] The tension eased considerably, however, when Great Britain decided to reassert its claim to the islands and reoccupied them in 1833. Under the circumstances, Jackson decided not to invoke the Monroe Doctrine in connection with the occupation. He was not anxious to quarrel with the British. He had other concerns closer to home. Besides, American fishing rights were adequately protected under British rule and Jackson saw no strategic value in the islands for the United States. He was therefore relieved that the incident could be ignored and then forgotten. Not much later full diplomatic relations with Argentina were restored.[28]

If Jackson chose to disregard Argentina's seizure of American property, he was infinitely less indulgent with European powers. Following the successful conclusion of a treaty with France to pay United States claims arising out of the Napoleonic Wars, Secretary of State Livingston urged the American ministers to Portugal, Naples, and Spain, where similar debts were owed, to begin immediate negotiations to secure like treaties with those countries. The example of France provided a hefty boost to American claims and it was used with telling effect. A treaty with Portugal was the first to be concluded. It was signed at Lisbon on January 19, 1832, although payment was delayed until 1837. This delay in no way sparked a presidential tantrum because Jackson understood Portugal's continuing financial distress and was willing to cooperate in any way to help bring about full payment as soon as possible.[29] Jackson had no complaint with a foreign nation that showed goodwill. It was only the arrogant dismissal of United States claims that drove him to threats and angry outbursts.

The Kingdom of the Two Sicilies proved more difficult. Several unsuccessful attempts had been made by previous administrations to obtain payment for losses by Americans in Naples during the Napoleonic Wars. In his third message to Congress, Jackson called a halt to United States forbearance. He promised to secure an indemnity and, to that end, he sent as his chargé d'affaires to Naples, the capital of the kingdom, a young Maryland supporter, John Nelson. Livingston instructed Nelson to assure the king of the President's goodwill and desire for friendly relations; but he also said that such goodwill could result only from the kingdom's prompt recognition of United States claims.[30] Nelson, on his arrival, soon learned that the Neapolitan government had the means to pay its debt if it wished; he also got a taste of Italian indifference and discourtesy as soon as he pressed his arguments. By his fourth dispatch to the secretary of state, Nelson openly declared that the only means of speeding prompt recognition of United States rights was for Jackson to obtain congressional authorization for the use of naval force. Anything less, he said, would invite another act of discourtesy and dismissal of the American demand.[31]

At this point Jackson himself took a direct hand in the negotiations. He penned a note for Nelson and sent it to Livingston with orders to have it transmitted immediately. The note contained very specific instructions:

> despatch for Mr Nelson—forthwith on the receipt of it to make it known to the Govt. of Naples, that unless within 20 days from the delivery of his note they explicitly promise to admit our claims, and enter upon an adjustment for their final payment, that he is instructed to ask his passports, assuring that Government, that this notification & demand is for the express purpose on the refusal, to enable the president to put into execution all his powers to coerce justice to be done to our merchants—That this step would have been taken on the receipt of the despatches by the Antonio,* had it not have been from the assurance in the ministers note that on the return of the minister, whose absence was occasioned by great emergency & who would return in a few days, that answer promised should be given.[32]

Livingston rewrote the note in more acceptable diplomatic language and dispatched it to Nelson. It was dated June 11, 1832, and delivered to Nelson by the frigate *United States*. The presence of this American warship in the harbor, with its black cannons staring at the city, coupled with General Jackson's thinly veiled threat, jolted the Italians into coming to terms. An offer was proposed to effect a compromise by the payment of a lump sum. As expected, the Italians bid low, but after a few weeks of haggling an agreement was finally reached. According to the treaty signed on October 14, 1832, the Kingdom of the Two Sicilies agreed to pay 2,119,230 Neapolitan ducats, or approximately $1,755,450, which Nelson accepted as payment in full. The settlement also included provision for payment in nine installments with an annual interest of 4%—all of which were paid on time.[33] The Senate ratified the treaty on December 17, and the exchange of ratifications between the two countries took place in Naples on June 8, 1833.

Through a separate arrangement in 1836 and the payment of an addi-

*Antonio Statella, Prince Cassaro, minister and secretary of state for foreign affairs of the Kingdom of the Two Sicilies.

tional 1,500,000 ducats, this treaty paid claimants about 95 percent of their claims—again providing another spectacular success for a popularly supported administration. Forcing recognition from foreign nations for debts owed the United States when previous, more elitist, administrations had failed was proof, claimed the President's friends, of the merit and strength of democratic government. Again Americans responded with nationalistic pride over Jackson's extraordinary accomplishment.

Another diplomatic success involved the British. Early in 1831, the American ship *Comet,* en route to New Orleans from the east coast and carrying 164 slaves, was wrecked on the Bahama banks. British officials forthwith freed the rescued slaves, whereupon the Jackson administration, in December, 1831, asked for compensation for the owners. A similar incident arose in the wreck of the *Encomium* in 1833. The British were reluctant to make restitution, but Secretary Livingston pointed out that the idea that slaves automatically win freedom when shipwrecked on British soil was a doctrine "too dangerous" to be tolerated by the United States. The British ultimately acquiesced and paid the claims in 1836.[34]

Still another diplomatic achievement came with the acceptance by Spain of a treaty that spelled out her obligations for indemnity to American citizens over claims from illegal seizures of ships during the South American wars of independence. The treaty, in which Spain agreed to pay $600,000, was signed in Madrid by Cornelius Van Ness, the American minister, on February 17, 1834. This amount was less than half of what the United States had originally demanded, but with the death of King Ferdinand VII in late 1833, and the resulting civil strife of the Carlist wars which sent Spanish affairs into lasting confusion and disorder, the Jackson administration decided to take what it could get and count itself lucky to do so well under the circumstances. The new secretary of state, Louis McLane, tried to move beyond indemnity claims and win improved trade with Cuba as well as force Spanish recognition of the independence of its lost South American colonies, but in this he had no success.[35]

More promising at first was a commercial treaty signed with the new Kingdom of Belgium, another sign of the administration's continuing efforts to expand the nation's foreign markets. On the American side everything went well and even included immediate Senate ratification. But the Belgian government decided that its minister to Washington, Baron Désiré Behr, had exceeded his instructions, particularly in agreeing to define legal blockades. Since England and France were presently defending Belgium against the Netherlands by a blockade that the treaty deemed illegal, the Belgians naturally refused to ratify the instrument. Secretary of State McLane offered to extend the period for ratification to make adjustments, and this was done, but the treaty never won final approval. A United States–Belgium treaty was therefore postponed for almost twenty-five years.[36]

The continued success of Jacksonian diplomacy through three succes-

sive secretaries of state, in almost as many years, says something significant about the role played by the President. The foreign policy of the
United States from 1829 to 1837 was Jackson's policy—just as it should
have been. No secretary of state took the lead in determining the conduct
of American foreign affairs. All of them advised United States ministers
abroad that Jackson reserved to himself final judgment in most matters.
Typical was the following dispatch to a minister from the secretary:
"What course it may be proper to take in this view, I am unwilling to
indicate, without further instructions from the President."[37]

If Jackson merits much of the credit for the diplomatic successes of his
administration, he also bears the blame for the disasters. And one came
soon enough. It involved the spoliation claims against France and almost
led to an act of war. In the minds of some it even jeopardized the struggle
against the Bank of the United States, and it certainly brought out some
of the worst attributes of Jackson's character. The entire episode was so
unfortunate that Roger B. Taney later called it "the most dangerous
moment of Genl. Jackson's administration."[38]

The United States minister, William C. Rives, concluded a treaty with
the French on July 4, 1831, in which France agreed to pay 25 million
francs in six equal annual installments. France also agreed to lower her
tariff duties on long-staple cotton imported from the United States. In
return the United States consented to reduce its duties on imported
French wines. The ratifications were exchanged in Washington on February 2, 1832, and Congress fulfilled the pledge to reduce the wine duties.
His mission crowned with glorious success, Rives returned home in September, 1832, and Nathaniel Niles, who acted as chargé d'affaires, took
over the American legation in Paris. Secretary of State Edward Livingston
notified Niles on February 8, 1833, that he should inform the French
government that the secretary of the treasury had drawn a bill on the
French minister of finance for the first installment of the indemnity along
with interest on the remaining installments. The draft, dated February 7,
1833, was sold to the BUS and transferred to the Bank's agent in France
for collection.[39] Niles dutifully informed the minister of foreign affairs,
the Duc de Broglie, who expressed shock and dismay at the action of the
American government in drawing a bill through the BUS and not waiting
to collect the money directly from the French government. However,
Broglie haughtily assured Niles that the French government had no intention of reneging on its commitment. It was simply a matter of obtaining the necessary appropriation from the Chamber of Deputies. Fair
enough, but unfortunately, the Chamber neglected to authorize the first
installment at its next session—a payment that by then was long past
due.[40]

At this point Jackson once again reshuffled his cabinet. Livingston was
sent to France as minister and McLane was shifted from Treasury to
State. Since McLane's own action as Treasury secretary had precipitated

the predicament in the first place, he felt a bit testy toward the French over their failure to live up to their responsibility. Jackson, too, was nettled. "Unless that government makes . . . strong assurances that satisfactory arrangements will be made," he told Van Buren, ". . . I will recommend to the next congress to increase the duties on their Brandy, wine & silks."[41] His anger turned to cold fury when Nicholas Biddle presented a bill to the President for 15 percent damages because of the French nonpayment. Jackson absolutely refused to pay it. So Biddle coolly deducted it from the dividends paid on the government's stock in the BUS.[42]

Jackson boiled. The humiliation of the French failure to meet its commitment was compounded by Biddle's demand for this penalty fee. The more the President thought about it the more he understood the necessity of getting Livingston to France as quickly as possible to learn "the *real causes* of the delay, and the *real source* of the opposition" to meet the American request for the first installment. And he would not permit the French to excuse their own delinquency by complaining about his decision to draw a bill on the minister of finance, rather than wait on the French government. It was Livingston's duty, therefore, to make certain that the French understood the American government's determination to bring about the "prompt and complete fulfilment" of the terms of the Treaty.[43]

Livingston tarried in New York for a longer period than Jackson felt appropriate. "He ought to have been at Paris some weeks ago," the President grumbled in a letter written on July 30. But Livingston was at the point of closing his career, not beginning it. He was sixty-nine years of age and preparing for retirement. He no longer had the ambition or vigor to sustain a long and difficult struggle with the tightfisted French. Still he commanded impressive strengths. An experienced diplomat, he was well versed in jurisprudence, enjoyed a background in French law, and understood and appreciated the French language and culture. His wife spoke fluent French and corresponded with her husband in that language. Livingston, in fact, seemed ideal for the post. To accompany him on the mission, he took along his recently acquired son-in-law, Thomas P. Barton of Philadelphia, to serve as his secretary.[44]

After what seemed like an interminable delay, Livingston finally left New York in mid-August and arrived in France the second week of September. He received a cordial welcome from King Louis Philippe and, like Niles before him, he was assured that the necessary appropriation of money would be passed at the next session of the Chambers. He received similar assurances from the Duc de Broglie, who went so far as to promise that the government would formally request the appropriation from the Chambers the day after that body reconvened—which was scheduled for December 22, 1833.[45]

The President finally took formal notice of this disagreeable development in his fifth annual message to Congress delivered on December 3, 1833. Within moments of the opening phrase, Jackson expressed his deep regret that the important articles of the treaty remained unfulfilled. A draft upon the French minister of finance had been drawn, he declared, "to avoid the risk and expense of intermediate agencies." It was drawn at Washington five days after the installment was payable at Paris. Not until that moment did Jackson realize that an explicit appropriation for the purpose was required from the Chambers. He had received numerous assurances—most recently from the newly appointed American minister —that the appropriation would be forthcoming from the Chambers at its next session. "Should I be disappointed in the hope now entertained," Jackson concluded on this matter, "the subject will be again brought to the notice of Congress in such manner as the occasion may require."[46]

The only concern Jackson expressed in the message was the failure of the French to provide the necessary documents which the American commissioners would need to determine individual claims to be paid from the indemnity. For a time Jackson believed that this was the reason for the French delay, but he soon learned otherwise.[47] In any event there was nothing threatening in his message. Nor was the tone quarrelsome. Jackson simply expressed his regret over an unpleasant occurrence and said he hoped it would all be amicably resolved in the immediate future. If his hopes went unrealized he would return to Congress in due course.

In fact Jackson showed extraordinary restraint. His advisers and ministers suggested stronger measures, but the President moved cautiously. Livingston, for example, suggested that the French needed a little shove. After all, he said, they hate to part with money and would do anything to avoid it. As a consequence, they might fail to realize how determined the administration was to collect the indemnity. And such a misapprehension could needlessly worsen the relationship. Better to nudge them, he counseled. Suspend the reduction in the duty on French wines which the Congress had already enacted until they paid what they owed.

But Jackson rejected this advice. He would do nothing to agitate the French. He relied on their sense of justice to bring the matter to a speedy end. "The President," McLane told Livingston, "could not adopt your suggestion." Besides, he added in a slightly ominous tone, it might not be strong enough to do the job.[48]

So Jackson waited. And nothing happened. Not until January 13, 1834, was the appropriation bill introduced into the Chambers and then it went straight into committee, where it reposed like a corpse for two months. Perhaps a little nudging might have been in order at the very beginning, just as Livingston had suggested. After all, he knew the French better than anyone and the sort of persuasion that would encourage them to act. Anyway, nothing was done. Finally, on March 10, 1834, the committee unanimously urged the Chambers to pass the appropriation. Debate on the motion began on March 28 and after five days of intensive and often brilliant argument, the motion to pay the indemnity was defeated by a vote of 176 to 168.[49]

Jackson was thunderstruck. He could not imagine a more stunning defeat, nor a more studied insult. The French had administered a savage blow. And they should have known that Andrew Jackson was not the man to take it lightly.

His anger mounted the more he thought about it. His initial reaction was to do something dramatic—and preferably violent. His sputterings could be heard in the columns of the Washington *Globe.* The total number of deputies, explained the newspaper, is 460, and yet on a matter involving the mutual harmony and good understanding between France and America only 344 members took the trouble to attend and vote. Over 100 members stayed away. Appalling. Was France deliberately baiting the United States? Did it wish to rupture relations? This nation, said the *Globe,* did not take kindly to such behavior. It was shocked and dismayed.[50]

The action of the French Chambers not only angered Jackson but embarrassed the Duc de Broglie, who had practically guaranteed approval. He put up an able and vigorous argument to the deputies for payment, and when that plea was rejected he felt he had no alternative but to resign. His place was taken by Henri Gauthier, Comte de Rigny.

The rejection of the appropriation bill, of course, resulted from several causes, a number of which were intertwined. Some of the deputies thought the indemnity too high, that it would offend the French people and encourage other nations to demand restitution for alleged wrongs. Others, especially monarchists, hated the Untied States because of the American Revolution and its impact upon French life and thought. And still others, mainly republicans, disliked the king and his government and therefore seized any opportunity to embarrass it.[51]

Livingston, in his several dispatches to McLane, tried to account for what had happened. To a large extent he credited the determination of many deputies to pull down the ministry. He had not yet received an explanation from any member of the cabinet, he reported on April 3, but he felt that the United States should do something quickly "to show that they will no longer be trifled with. The President will recommend such as he thinks most effectual for that purpose" but he thought it proper to make a suggestion. "I do this with great diffidance," he said, "but with a sincere desire to promote the interest and assert the honor of my country. First I think the minister should be recalled."

Livingston was obviously very agitated himself. He went on to explain his reasons for this drastic action, but after scribbling several lines he paused. He thought over what he had just written and then crossed it all out. He obviously had second thoughts. Instead he proposed that the President prohibit the importation of any article produced or manufactured in France. "This would at once make them feel the folly of their course in the most vital parts."[52]

Livingston calmed down even further after speaking with the king. He was assured that His Majesty regretted the action taken by the Chambers, that nothing could be done until a new session was called, "that this would take place very soon and that he hoped nothing would in the meantime be done to alter the relations of the two countries." Moreover, the king said that the action had caused him "the greatest embarrassment" by the breaking up of his cabinet. He felt it had happened on account of "prejudice and misstatements" which he was in great hopes would be removed by the next session.[53]

Livingston also spoke to Broglie, who blamed himself for having mistaken the temper of the deputies and forced a vote. But Livingston rather suspected the lack of support by the other members of the ministry who used this opportunity to get rid of Broglie. "That the vote was lost," he informed McLane, "by the want of exertion on the part of the ministry is manifest."[54]

During all these discussions the French seemed genuinely concerned about the course Jackson would take in response to the Chambers' action. Livingston did not speculate on the matter but he advised McLane that the French were very apprehensive. Show them we mean business, he urged. If the President will embargo all French products he will deliver a clear and forceful message that will surely get results.[55]

The President did indeed intend to take bold and decisive action, one appropriate to the dignity of the American nation. In this he had the strong support of McLane, who, as a former Federalist, wasted no affection or understanding on the French. But some of the other members of Jackson's cabinet were not as anxious to see the President engage in what they were certain would result in a shouting match with the French. Something dreadful might happen. Roger B. Taney later remembered seeing Jackson "indignant & somewhat excited at this open breach of faith" but thought the President would eventually make allowances for a government in which the treaty-making power lay with one branch of government and the power of appropriations to execute the treaty with another.[56]

Shortly after news of the action by the deputies arrived in Washington, Jackson called a meeting of his cabinet. He walked into the room looking solemn and determined. The members came quickly to attention and Jackson told them what he had on his mind. He proposed to communicate to Congress by special message the refusal of the French government to carry out the terms of the treaty and to ask authority to issue letters of marque and reprisal to attack French shipping.

Taney blanched. He was horrified by the announcement. He was then in the midst of "removing the deposits" and he instantly saw what this retaliatory act might provoke in terms of the Bank War. He was even "more surprized & startled" when McLane agreed to the proposal in "earnest & decided terms." In addition, Secretary of War Lewis Cass approved the action. Both men agreed that strong measures were needed to reassert the American posture of sovereignty and power.

Taney spoke up. He proceeded cautiously in expressing his opposition to the proposal. He knew, he said, how sensitive Jackson was "upon questions which he thought concerned the honor of the United States—and that on such occasions he was apt to be prompt in decision & prompt in action: and did not always stop to calculate the difficulties in his way —or the forces that might be arrayed against him." (Although he did not say it, Taney was also sure that Jackson had discussed the matter with McLane before the cabinet met and he feared it would be impossible at this time to divert the President from his chosen course.) Nonetheless, Taney felt it his duty to express his opinion on the subject and how this decision might affect the Bank War. At the moment the country still reeled from Biddle's panic. Confidence in the government had been shaken, Taney argued, "credits cut off—bankruptcies occurring every day among leading merchants and the whole country suffering under the severest pecuniary pressure & distress." The revenue had fallen off precipitously, he reminded them, with not enough cash available to meet ordinary expenses. The people believe the country will go bankrupt, he cried, or at least be compelled "to resort to direct taxation" to pay its bills.

"We [are] in no condition to go to war if it can be avoided," he declared. "France [is] . . . greatly superior to us in her naval armament ready for action, & would probably blockade our harbors & bombard our commercial cities before we could be prepared to meet them." However unjustifiable the action taken by the French Chambers, it did not constitute a "national insult" requiring "immediate hostile action to maintain our honor"; we must exhaust "pacific measures & frank remonstrances" before we assert our rights by force.[57]

McLane vigorously rebutted this argument. He thought that the king and his ministers had not made sufficient efforts to obtain the appropriation and were hoping in the end to avoid paying it altogether because the French people disliked seeing their money spent for such humiliating purposes. The indemnity, said McLane, would endanger the "popularity & influence of the ministry at home" and therefore they had decided to withdraw their support from it. Even without the appropriation, he continued, the ministry had the power to meet the bill drawn by the secretary of the treasury if the French truly intended to abide by the terms of the treaty. He said he regarded the action of the Chambers as not only offensive "but almost a defiance—and that this country was called upon to take some step that would shew that we did not mean quietly to submit to this refusal to execute the Treaty."[58]

Did he propose a declaration of war? No, not that, said McLane; but he advised "an immediate application to Congress for authority to issue Letters of Marque & Reprisal" since by the "law of nations" the United States had a right to redress itself in this manner. Such behavior did not constitute an act of war, he said. It was the exercise of a right and "would give no just ground for war or complaint by the French government." McLane then cited a number of authorities on the subject and reminded the cabinet that France herself had resorted to this procedure when Portugal neglected or refused to pay an indemnity. Since France herself had recently exercised this right without bringing about hostilities, "she could with no consistency or question, complain of its exercise on our part."[59]

Taney sharply differed with this interpretation. While letters of marque did not constitute a declaration of war in the technical sense, still any nation that felt itself strong enough to resent an insult and vindicate its honor would not tamely submit to such an indignity. Maybe France applied it to Portugal, but that did not mean that she would allow anyone else to practice it on her. "Nor would the French government hazard its existence," he ventured, "by permitting such a wound to be inflicted upon the national pride, without resenting it by a declaration of war—or immediate hostilities."[60]

All during this exchange the President listened very intently. A few times he interrupted but he expressed no decided opinion on the points raised one way or the other. He reserved judgment on the main question for later decision. None of the other members of the cabinet, with the possible exception of Cass, added much by way of substance to the discussion. It was clear to Taney, however, that although the President reserved comment on the principal issue he was "strongly inclined to adopt the advice of Mr McLane & Genl Cass and upon the ground stated by them."

When the meeting ended, Taney left the room, he said, in a "state of great anxiety & alarm, than I have ever felt at any other moment in my public life." He realized he had completely failed to win over the President and, as a result, open hostilities seemed inevitable. Although he was confident that Congress would never authorize the letters of marque, when requested, a declaration of war could easily ensue. The Bank had already persuaded a great many in the nation that Andrew Jackson was responsible for the financial "distress and ruin which pervaded the country" and this latest action would only prove "that he was a rash & reckless man acting generally from the impulses of passion." Even those Democrats who still supported the President "were becoming uneasy & alarmed at the state of things—and were beginning to doubt whether the removal of the deposits was not a rash & ill advised measure." Worse, "it seemed to me perfectly manifest," wrote Taney several decades later, "that if in the midst of such distress & anxiety and upon such a cause of quarrel he recommended a measure which if carried out would inevitably lead to immediate hostilities with France, public confidence in his prudence & discretion would have been greatly shaken—and the panic & pressure become so intense—& spread so widely that his administration would be overthrown in less than a month—and the Bank with all its arrogance & open corruption fastened immoveably upon the country." France would not even wait for a decision of Congress about the letters of marque, but would declare immediate war.[61]

These fears were all rather extreme and prompted totally by Taney's concern over the Bank War. Clearly he resembled a man in shock. But he believed passionately in what he said and felt he had a duty to do everything "in my power to avert these dangers."

He turned to Martin Van Buren, the Master Magician. They had not discussed the subject beforehand but Taney was sure that the Vice President's "calm & sound judgment" would alert him to all the dangers inherent in McLane's argument. Jackson would listen to Van Buren "& weigh well" what he advised. Then, once "his own good judgment" came into play, the President would surely see "the dangerous consequences that must inevitably follow" if he prepared the special message. So Taney decided he must see Van Buren immediately and win his active support. An interview was arranged for the following day. "I acted promptly," Taney later recalled, "because I felt that the danger was immediate & no time should be lost."[62]

The two men met in Taney's private office. Great clouds of cigar smoke swirled around Taney's head as he explained his purpose and, as he guessed, Van Buren agreed totally with him. Among other reasons, the little man clearly saw the political danger to his presidential hopes at the next election. Now they must convince Jackson. Van Buren consulted with William C. Rives, who had obtained the treaty with France, and learned that he too objected to anything precipitous but felt that some action must be taken (preferably commercial, such as placing heavy duties on French silks) which would "mark the sense entertained by our government of the conduct of the French Legislature." In any event, he said, "I think it is absolutely necessary, both in the interest of peace & our own honor, that something should be done to close this controversy with France, as speedily as possible."[63] He also reminded Van Buren that it was extremely unlikely that Congress would accede to Jackson's request for authority to issue letters of marque and that the French were probably counting on this reaction since they knew all about "the violent spirit of faction, at present existing in this country." Which was one reason why the deputies were so "emboldened" to take the course they did. If the President and Congress should disagree over the appropriate action, Rives continued, then "the effect would be decidedly bad." It would be wise to learn from Congress prior to sending a special message "what may be done, before the President recommends to them any measure."[64]

This last point made enormous good sense and it was not lost on Van Buren. Nor would it be lost on Jackson. So the Vice President went immediately to see the President and they had a long talk in the White

House. As always, Van Buren came well prepared and presented his arguments in legalistic fashion and never strayed from his point. Jackson just listened—although he occasionally interrupted with a question or a comment. At the end of the discussion the President was persuaded to hold off on a special message. Although the force of the objections by his two most valued advisers no doubt carried great weight, it is most probable that after an initial show of anger and the hurling of potentially lethal threats, Jackson quietly calculated the effect of a sudden strike at France in terms of his war against the Bank and his relations with a difficult and temperamental Congress. Another thing—he had just been censured by the Senate, and the possibility of his winning congressional approval for authorization to issue the letters of marque was about as likely as Henry Clay's declaring against the Bank of the United States. And although he knew that he could win the American people to his cause, he was afraid that a divided government with the President ranged on one side and Congress (or at least the Senate) on the other would play straight into the hands of the French. What added the final argument was the information Jackson received from Livingston at this time that a corvette of the French navy was being sent with dispatches to Louis Barbe C. Sérurier, the French minister at Washington, to explain the "sentiments and intentions of the French Government" on the matter. Surely wisdom dictated that he wait until Sérurier received these dispatches and communicated their contents to the American government.[65]

In any event, Jackson turned away from his aggressive stance. He instructed the secretary of the navy to have a frigate prepared at Norfolk to stand by to take dispatches to Paris. What the dispatches to Sérurier contained, he said, "will determine us on this matter." A little later he ordered the secretary to inspect all "ships in ordinary & in dock and report their conditions so that . . . should an emergency occur we may be prepared for it."[66]

Fortunately, the corvette crossed the Atlantic at a slow pace, arriving in early June. Sérurier spoke officially with Secretary McLane on June 5. McLane had expected Jackson to send his special message to Congress in late May, for he advised Livingston that the debates in the Chambers were being printed to accompany the President's message.[67] But the special message never went to Congress. Jackson decided to stand fast for the moment. He heeded the advice of Taney and Van Buren and chose to follow a moderate course. But that did not mean that the French could continue their defiance. He would simply give them more time in the expectation that they meant to acknowledge their obligation and meet all the terms of the treaty.

The French dispatches expressed a regret that the Chambers had failed to appropriate the first installment of the indemnity. It also conveyed the belief that the attitude of the deputies had changed in the interim and that a better regard for treaty obligations could be expected at the next session. The government promised to make every "loyal and constitutional" effort to win passage of the bill.[68]

Jackson's reply to these dispatches was not delivered for three weeks. Although he had determined against a special message he wanted the French to fret a little over what course he might take. He also wanted to give them a little more time to make a satisfactory settlement. The reply, as delivered to Sérurier, stated that the President was willing to wait for the government's appeal to the next Chambers but that he would present the matter to Congress, as his duty required, at the opening of the new session in December, "*to announce at that time* the result of that appeal, and of his Majesty's efforts for its success."[69]

Jackson's decision to give the French more time and hold back on a special message to Congress was more than Louis McLane could abide. It was bad enough that the President had ignored his advice about the Bank and the deposits, but when Jackson overruled him on a major question of foreign affairs in favor of Taney's recommendation, he felt he must resign. Without telling Van Buren, who had once been his strong supporter and confidant, McLane abruptly submitted his resignation to Jackson on June 16, 1834. He was replaced with Senator John Forsyth of Alabama.

And so Jackson locked himself into the Taney–Van Buren position, although he momentarily feared that Van Buren had left him out on a limb by not alerting him to McLane's decision to resign.[70] In the opinion of Taney he had agreed to "take a calmer & more deliberate view of the whole subject." He abandoned a course, said Taney, that would have "resulted in the overthrow of his administration" and maybe war with France. It surely would have led to a recharter and victory for the Bank, a possibility that made Taney shudder. It could not have been more perilous. It was a "crisis," he later recorded, which appeared to be "the most dangerous moment" of General Jackson's entire administration.[71] Fortunately the President had the wisdom to see it and back away.

CHAPTER 14

"Permit Nothing
That Is Wrong"

ALTHOUGH JACKSON TEMPORARILY RETREATED from taking direct action, he nonetheless remained determined to make the French pay what they owed. Throughout the summer of 1834 he kept in close and direct contact with Edward Livingston, acknowledging that he had been "obliged to forbear for the present," but affirming his readiness to implement his resolve with strong measures. He expected the Chambers to be summoned immediately after the conclusion of new elections to appropriate the necessary funds. He supposed that they would be called together in September "or in due time that we can have the information to communicate to Congress at the first of their next session."[1]

But, if the French fail us again, the President wrote his minister, "you will find me speaking to Congress as I ought—I cannot recommend a war thro' the Custom Houses," such as Livingston had recommended. "This cannot protect our national character, and must at last lead to war—the only way to preserve our honor is to carry into effect my maxim 'Ask nothing but what is right and permit nothing that is wrong.'"[2]

Just how he would carry his "maxim" into effect, Jackson did not say. But it is important to understand that he had a clear sense of his direction. This maxim constituted the President's basic policy in regard to his conduct of foreign affairs, and he expected Livingston and all his other ministers to remember it and use it as their guide. As applied to the present crisis over the spoliations, the maxim meant that the President would not permit France to insult this nation by reneging on its treaty obligations. He was willing to provide more time for them to attend to the matter, but he wanted it understood that he expected to go to Congress when it reconvened in December with definite information as to what France proposed to do.

211

What troubled Jackson, as it did Livingston, was the recognition that Western Europe really disliked the United States. Indeed, a certain amount of animosity intruded into all negotiations between Europe and America. The problem centered on European fear and envy. Because the United States was a free nation based on a broad suffrage that tolerated an expanding democracy, there was considerable resentment abroad. Democracy represented a danger to the crowned heads of Europe. If the American democratic "experiment" succeeded, it would serve as a guide and an encouragment to the more liberal and radical factions in Europe. Monarchies might be swept away—as happened in France during the Revolution. And everyone knew the bloody consequence of that catastrophe. So there were many in Europe who, believing that democracy was the worst of all possible forms of government, wished the United States ill and hoped the "experiment" would fail.

Livingston discussed this situation several times with Jackson. "Every effort is making to discredit our institutions here," he wrote in early summer, "and chiefly in the Governments calling themselves liberal when the progress to a really free form of Government is considered as the greatest of evils because of the most imminent and the most destructive of the monopoly of power now possessed by the very few who have usurped it, and keep the great mass of the nation without any share in the management of its affairs." This was particularly true in France, he said. There is little personal security and no political influence among thirty of its thirty-two million people. And this melancholy fact was not likely to change. The "Yoke is so firmly fixed" that there was small chance of its being shaken off in the foreseeable future. "Yet they fear our example and seize on every occasion to represent our Government as on the point of Dissolution, reprinting both in France and England, extracts from the nullifying and bank presses, to prove the fact."[3]

Because of the Europeans' resentment, because of their malice, and because of their contemptuous prediction of democracy's certain "Dissolution," Jackson became all the more determined to command respect for American rights. His "maxim" took on greater significance in his mind as his administration advanced, and he referred to it more frequently in his letters and public statements. He placed particular emphasis on the latter half of the maxim, which spoke about tolerating nothing that was patently wrong.

Jackson returned to the Hermitage during the summer of 1834 and waited out the time for the Chambers to reassemble. He soon suffered a rude shock. After receiving the President's instructions, Livingston notified Comte de Rigny that inasmuch as Sérurier had given "assurances" that no time would be lost in settling American claims, General Jackson intended to place the matter before Congress in December and recommend such measures as "justice and the honor of the country may require." The President, said Livingston, interpreted the note presented by Sérurier to the secretary of state as a pledge that these just claims would be forwarded by the government to the Chambers in the summer session, beginning July 31, or else that the deputies would be called into special session early in the fall. "The President will feel the utmost concern," Livingston advised Rigny, ". . . if I should not be enabled by your Excellency to inform him that the projet de loi would be presented at this session, or that the chambers will be convened again at a day early enough for them to consider the subject . . . before the first of December when Congress will meet."[4]

Comte de Rigny wasted no time in setting Livingston straight. It was impossible for the matter to come before the Chambers during its short summer session because its only business was organizational. Every country "regulated by a Representative System," he lectured, suspends its parliamentary labor during this time of year. "I regret therefore that on that point, it is out of the power of H.M.'s Government to comply with your request." As to the "demand" that the Chambers be summoned in the autumn, the government could not possibly enter into any "positive engagement to that effect." But as soon as it is "convenient" to do so, he continued, "you may rest assured, that one of the first questions submitted to their deliberations will be that of the Treaty."[5]

Obviously, then, nothing would be done before Congress reconvened in December. Since the President was determined to discuss the matter in his next message to Congress on the State of the Union, Rigny simply hoped that Jackson would do it in such manner "as to induce that body, to place a full reliance in the purity of our intentions & to guard them against a disposition to adopt measures, the more to be regretted, as they would tend to injure here the Solution" of the question.[6]

Livingston was exasperated. He appealed to the king. He even showed the monarch Jackson's private letter.[7] Again he got nowhere. However much the king and his minister wished to see the indemnity paid, there was nothing they could do to hurry it along. And both men disagreed with Livingston over the alleged "pledge" given by Sérurier, since the king could not bring it up during the summer session and could not call a special session in the fall. At this point Livingston began to suspect that the French government would be impotent even when the Chambers reconvened in January.[8]

Obviously this situation was developing in a manner that alarmed those who best understood Jackson's mind. Sérurier had spoken in such a way as to indicate the desire of the king's government to honor its commitment and a determination to do so as quickly as possible—certainly before Congress met in December when the President would be forced to make a statement about it.[9] Because of Sérurier's "pledge," Jackson had postponed any immediate action. He had agreed to "take a calmer & more deliberate view of the whole subject." Now he was about to learn that nothing would be done—at least not before he reported to Congress. And who knew what that might provoke?

The situation then started to move out of control. For on July 31 the Chambers met and listened to the king's speech, after which they were prorogued until December 29. That was nearly a month after Congress was scheduled to reconvene and hear the President's State of the Union address.

The arrival of the news of the action (or rather lack of it) by the Chambers, along with Livingston's dispatches of his diplomatic failure, had the expected effect on Jackson. Livingston worsened the report by telling the President that the king would not put the Chambers to the *"great inconvenience"* of meeting during the "hot season." Jackson's eyes "blazed" when he read that statement. "What! the personal inconvenience of the members put in competition with his private pledge, as well as the pledge of the national faith by his own act in ratifying the Treaty." Can I remain silent any longer? he roared to Van Buren. I must speak to Congress and "it must be in langu[a]ge of truth." I must ask Congress to take appropriate action. Obviously the ploy is now for the French to delay until Congress adjourns before we know the result. For, mark my words, "that result will be . . . another rejection" unless "overawed" by the action of Congress.[10]

Well, what did Van Buren have to say for himself? Did he still counsel inaction and forbearance? Jackson thought his Vice President ought to return to Washington from New York, where he was spending his vacation, and help with the composition of his congressional message. He meant to make it one that would jolt the French into compliance and respect for American pride and honor.[11]

Van Buren tried to calm Jackson down. But he was in no hurry to return to Washington. He had been consulting with William Rives for the past several months and even forwarded some of Rives's letters to the President. The former minister still opposed vigorous measures because he believed the French would repudiate the treaty in defense of their honor and this in turn might lead to war. He blamed Livingston for the present lamentable situation. "Some of my friends in France," he told Van Buren, "write me that . . . Mr. Livingston is in very bad health & bad spirits, that he has been very little in France of late, having been travelling in Belgium, England & elsewhere for the benefit of his health, & that he was not in Paris during the late session of the chambers even." Again, Rives urged commercial restrictions as the only judicious action for the government to take.[12]

Jackson rejected Rives's opinion about Livingston as misinformed. His minister remained in Paris until the Chambers had been prorogued, he retorted. Not only did Livingston speak to the king and Rigny but "did every thing that could be done" to induce a settlement. True, the minister was not well and suffered a "strange fever" that had sent him to Savoy for a cure, but that was after the Chambers had been prorogued and Paris "entirely deserted by the Ministers of the crown, and all the Diplomatic Corps." Concluded the President: "Surely Mr. Rives has not weighed the subject well."[13]

Once Jackson returned to Washington from his visit to the Hermitage his mounting irritation with the French government was communicated to Sérurier by the new secretary of state, John Forsyth. In an interview on October 22, the secretary warned that Jackson was not the sort of President to sit quietly and indefinitely while France dawdled about honoring her commitment. Sérurier counseled discretion. To this Forsyth replied that Jackson was "deeply mortified" and was determined to state the case to Congress when it reconvened. The Frenchman appreciated that a definite course of action had been determined by the President and could not be changed. He hesitated for a moment and then said, "What do you wish, Monsieur, a collision between us, or the execution of the treaty?"

"The execution of the treaty," Forsyth replied, "but the President owes to the people of the United States and to their Representatives, an account of his proceedings and of the state of this affair."[14]

After several more interviews with the secretary of state, the French minister felt compelled to inform his government that Jackson's message to Congress would likely be "very painful." The government of France could expect a very "hostile tone in the President's message."[15]

Indeed, Jackson was determined to deal very sharply with the French in view of their callous disregard—if not contempt—of American rights and sensibilities. "You may take it for granted," Van Buren informed Rives, "that a strong (but I trust prudent) statement of the injuries we have recd. from France will be made. It cost the President a great effort to allow the matter to pass by last Winter, & the French government have behaved very badly."[16]

Jackson's strong feelings were bolstered by Livingston in a dispatch written on November 22—but too late to affect the drafting of the annual message—that urged a forceful statement from the President. It is "[my] firm persuasion," he wrote, "that the moderate tone taken by our Government when the rejection was first known was attributed by some to indifference or to a conviction on the part of the President he would not be supported in any strong measure by the people." The delay on the part of France, he averred, was due to an expectation that the President's message might arrive before the Chambers began their discussion and "contain something to show a strong national feeling on the subject. *This is not mere conjecture; I know the fact.*" On the tone of the message, he concluded, "will depend very much, not only the payment of our claims, but our national reputation for energy."[17]

General Andrew Jackson hardly needed this sort of encouragement.

While Old Hickory sat in the White House no one would insult the "Grand Republick" and get away with it, least of all a foreign nation, even a traditional ally. This upcoming annual message would have his special care and attention. Each word would carry his imprimatur. Nothing in it would escape his attention.

As usual, the department heads were asked for contributions to the message. Certain favored individuals, like Van Buren and Taney, were invited to submit suggestions. All of these went into the mill that slowly ground out the presidential view of the State of the Union. The cabinet was consulted and shown portions of the completed text when it was ready. Particular secretaries known for their felicity of expression were given passages to edit and polish. At one point Forsyth, who was especially adroit in his use of language, decided to change a passage dealing with the French question, only slightly altering Jackson's meaning. The alteration was prompted by Forsyth's desire "to make the message more diplomatic in terms and more conformable . . . to peaceful and courteous national intercourse."

When the entire message was ready to go to the printer it was brought to Jackson for final approval. John C. Rives, who had just become a full partner in the operation of the *Globe,* was present at this reading. The only other person in the room was Andrew J. Donelson. While the General paced the room and smoked his long clay pipe, Donelson read from the proof sheets of the message. Rives sat quietly to one side.

Donelson knew about Forsyth's slight modification of the text and decided to say nothing about it. When he came to this change he read it as quickly as possible and nearly slurred some of the words.

Jackson stopped in his tracks. His head turned toward Donelson. "Read that again, sir."

Donelson obeyed, only this time he read it carefully and distinctly.

"That, sir, is not my language," Jackson exclaimed; "it has been changed, and I will have no other expression of my own meaning than my own words."

The offending passage was erased and Jackson's stronger language reinserted. Donelson was obliged to read through the message again and when the President finally satisfied himself that it said precisely what he wanted he handed the text to Rives. As he did so, he warned the printer, "at his peril," not to let it out of his hands until it was printed as corrected and until the President's permission had been granted. He even forbade Rives to be seen with the message in his hands.[18]

Jackson's sixth annual message to the Congress was dated December 1, 1834, and within four sentences (which welcomed the members back and acknowledged "Divine Providence" for the nation's general prosperity) the message took off on a review of foreign affairs. The successes of the administration in winning acceptance of its policy to ask only what is right and permit nothing that is wrong were enumerated, nation by nation. Then Jackson delivered the blow everyone expected. "It becomes my unpleasant duty to inform you," he said, "that this pacific and highly gratifying picture of our foreign relations does not include those with France at this time."[19] He next narrated the events that led to the treaty of 1831, followed by a long and detailed exposition of the subsequent negotiations to bring about the execution of the treaty. The results had been very frustrating, he admitted. "Not only has the French government been thus wanting in the performance of the stipulations it has so solemnly entered into with the United States, but its omissions have been marked by circumstances which would seem to leave us without satisfactory evidences that such performance will certainly take place at a future period."[20]

When the French Chambers defeated the action to pay the indemnity, Jackson went on, the President could have notified the Congress and asked for appropriate action commensurate with the interest and honor of the United States. But along with the news of the action of the Chambers came the "regrets" of the French king and information that a corvette was on its way to America with instructions to its minister to give the most "ample explanations" of what had happened and the "strongest assurances" of future good relations. The "pledges" given by the minister, said Jackson, assured him that as soon as the new Chambers convened, an appropriation bill would be laid before them, that the king and his ministers would exert all their constitutional powers to win approval of the bill, and that the result would be made known early enough to be communicated to Congress at the commencement of its present session. Relying upon these pledges, Jackson continued, and upon "that sacred regard for the national faith and honor for which the French character has been so distinguished . . . I did not deem it necessary" to come before Congress with a complaint at that time.[21]

But the pledges had not been "redeemed," the President growled. When the new Chambers met, there was no attempt by the king to procure an appropriation. This could have been overlooked if the Chambers had not been prorogued until December 29, thereby making it impossible to affect a settlement before the present Congress adjourned. As matters stand, Jackson continued, the executive has exhausted all his authority and the Congress must now decide what further steps should be taken. We are a peaceful nation, he argued. Friendly intercourse with all powers is our desire. "But these objects are not to be permanently secured by surrendering the rights of our citizens or permitting solemn treaties for their indemnity, in cases of flagrant wrong, to be abrogated or set aside."[22]

We could cut off trade, he went on. But that action would hurt our own citizens. Also, it would set off another internal controversy over tariff schedules. True policy, he said, dictates that the issue be kept "disencumbered" by such tactics so that the "whole civilized world" can see and pronounce France a culprit of international wrongdoing.

It is my conviction that the United States ought to insist on a prompt execution of the treaty, and in case it be refused or longer delayed take redress into their own hands. After the delay on the part of France of a quarter of a century in acknowledging these claims by treaty, it is not to be tolerated that another quarter of a century is to be wasted in negotiating about the payment. The laws of nations provide a remedy for such occasions. It is a well-settled principle of the international code that where one nation owes another a liquidated debt which it refuses or neglects to pay the aggrieved party may seize on the property belonging to the other, its citizens or subjects, sufficient to pay the debt without giving just cause of war. This remedy has been repeatedly resorted to, and recently by France herself toward Portugal, under circumstances less questionable.[23]

Seize French property! That struck the members of Congress squarely in the face and they turned and stared at each other as the words came tumbling from the mouth of the clerk.

If France does not appropriate the money for the indemnity at the next session of the Chambers, the message continued, it may be assumed that the treaty has been repudiated and therefore "prompt measures" by the Congress will be both "honorable and just" and have the "best effect upon our national character." To be specific, Jackson recommended the enactment of a law authorizing reprisals upon French property. Such a measure, he declared with straight face, ought not to be considered by France "as a menace." After all, "nothing partaking of the character of intimidation is intended by us." Rather she should see it as evidence only of an "inflexible determination" by the people of the United States to insist upon their rights. If, however, France attempted reprisals or continued her intransigence, then she would simply add violence to injustice and expose herself to the "just censure of civilized nations and to the retributive judgments of Heaven."[24]

It really was an incredible statement. It was an obvious threat, and Jackson thought by simply denying that fact that he could make it disappear. He wanted it both ways: to threaten France, and yet not have it taken as a threat.

Jackson ended this section of his message by restating Congress's right to take whatever action it thought could best protect the rights and maintain the honor of the country. Whatever it did, he concluded, the President would faithfully enforce the decision to the extent that he was authorized to do so.[25]

The remainder of the message contained happier information. The best of it concerned the national debt. As of January 1, 1835, after satisfying all the government's operating obligations, the national debt would be totally extinguished and the Treasury would carry a balance of $440,000. No national debt. Not a cent owed to anyone. What an extraor-

dinary accomplishment. What a proud boast. As Roger B. Taney had said
to Jackson just a few months earlier, "it is I believe the first time in the
history of nations that a large public debt has been entirely extinguished."[26] Jackson himself could not help crowing about this accomplishment, although he rightly credited it to the industry and enterprise
of the American people, despite the rude financial shock of last winter
inflicted by Nicholas Biddle.

> Free from public debt, at peace with all the world, and with no compli-
> cated interests to consult in our intercourse with foreign powers, the pres-
> ent may be hailed as the epoch in our history the most favorable for the
> settlement of those principles in our domestic policy which shall be best
> calculated to give stability to our Republic and secure the blessings of
> freedom to our citizens.[27]

Such an accomplishment was especially pleasing in that it demonstrated to the world the value and superiority of republican principles of
government. It showed the monarchs and despots of Europe the true
worth of freedom. Those who wished America ill could stew in their envy
and resentment.

Jackson himself deserves much of the credit for this extraordinary
achievement. Not only had the elimination of the national debt been an
object of his presidential reforms from the beginning of his administration, but he worked earnestly and persistently to achieve it. He watched
congressional appropriations with a miser's eye, vetoing legislation that
he deemed extravagant and a waste of public money.[28] He also tried to
keep administrative expenses under tight control. And he instituted a
program of reform to discharge any federal employee guilty of misappro-
priating and mishandling federal funds. The elimination of the national
debt did not happen simply because the country was prosperous and
expanding. It happened because Andrew Jackson was determined to
make it happen and he did everything within his constitutional power to
bring it about.

The heady effects of this long-desired and unusual event prompted
Jackson to deliver a lecture on the blessings of republicanism. No longer
can it be doubted, he told the Congress, that "simplicity" in government
and "rigid economy" in its administration should be regarded now "as
fundamental and sacred." We should abstain entirely, he said, "from all
topics of legislation that are not clearly within the constitutional powers
of the Government and suggested by the wants of the country." Every
diminution of the tax burden, he continued, "gives to individual enterprise increased power" and furnishes everyone with "new motives for
patriotic affection and support." It was because of the debt that the taxing
power had been brought into extensive operation. It even produced the
disturbing quarrel over the tariff.[29]

Jackson rounded out his message with a final shot at the BUS, a nod of approval over Indian removal, a discussion of the troubled Post Office Department, and a tortured analysis of his attitude toward internal improvements.[30] He announced his veto of the Wabash River Navigation Act sent to him at the close of the last session. He regretted vetoing the bill, he said, but he had no choice. "I am not hostile to internal improvements," he declared, but they must be enacted properly and legally. He did not think the Constitution authorized such appropriations, so if the people really wanted public works they could amend the Constitution.[31]

And on that note Jackson closed his message. The immediate reaction to it in Congress was predictable. The Whigs hated it. Some of them hated practically every word. The Democrats, of course, could not say enough in its praise. By and large the people loved it because they concentrated on the part dealing with France and felt that Jackson's words were everything they should be. Americans were a free, united, and proud people, and it was good to know that their representative in Washington never forgot it nor would he let anyone else forget it either.[32]

Even some Whigs secretly admired Jackson's vigorous language in dealing with the French. "Dr. Jackson, who can make his patients swallow anything, has, by the aid of his regular-bred practitioners in the study, and the green-apron boys below," confided Philip Hone to his diary, "managed to give the body politic enough to ensure tolerable regularity until his next regular visit." And, on the French matter, Hone admitted that "the message is quite satisfactory; its explanations are clear, its language dignified, and its sentiment manly and patriotic."[33] Maybe too patriotic, worried some Whig newspapers. The old soldier was reverting to type, they feared, and he might provoke a needless war. They further insisted that Jackson's tone of "intimidation and menace" did not represent the true views of the American people.[34]

The *Globe* responded to these "unpatriotic" effusions with an official comment from the White House. The President had simply reported to Congress in pursuance of his constitutional obligations. His message was not a response to the French government. It was, so to speak, an exchange of ideas within the family, and nothing more. France was not to read it in any other light.[35]

Which was nonsense. Everyone knew the French would both read and study the President's message. Sérurier not only sent the message home but also included detailed reports on the military and naval readiness of the United States since he assumed that war was a genuine possibility.[36]

The French section of the message was referred to the appropriate committees in both houses of Congress. The Senate Committee on Foreign Relations consisted of a majority of rabidly anti-Jackson Whigs: Henry Clay, Willie P. Mangum, and Peleg Sprague. The French ministry, said the *Globe*, could hardly find in the government three men more determined than these to thwart and harass the intentions of the Jackson administration.[37] Although the House Foreign Affairs Committee dawdled over Jackson's recommendations, the Senate committee, prodded by Clay, submitted a report on January 6, 1835. But Clay's principal object was to quiet French fears, not challenge Jackson. The report agreed substantially with what the President had reported, but it went on to suggest that no action be taken by Congress until the Chambers had reassembled and had determined what they planned to do.[38] Clay then proposed a resolution, which the Senate unanimously passed, declaring it "inexpedient at present" to pass any legislation with regard to US-Franco relations.[39]

Neither Jackson nor the Democratic leadership in Congress objected. The fact that the resolution had such overwhelming support indicated a strong inclination in Congress to wait and see what France would do next. The prevailing mood seemed to imply that the problem should be settled through diplomatic channels if possible. No one in Congress wanted to foment a confrontation.

Jackson accepted that. He sensed immediately that any attempt to push matters further along would provoke more opposition than he cared to handle at the moment. Even the *Globe* withheld objection to the Senate resolution. Everything was locked in a waiting position. The next move belonged to the French.

At a dinner party given at the height of this tension, the Vice President, who had recently arrived from New York, the secretary of state, several foreign ministers, and judges of the Supreme Court attended, and all engaged in an analysis of the French question. Van Buren seemed a trifle nervous throughout the evening, although he tried his best to cover his obvious disquiet. Then, suddenly, the "gamster" appeared. Henry Clay strode into the room, looking smug and complacent. He obviously enjoyed the discomfort of the Democrats as they watched him circle the room and greet the various ministers and judges. The conversation soon centered around the favorable or unfavorable disposition of the French and English governments toward United States interests. Since several gentlemen present had been abroad recently, they ventured the opinion that American interests were best served with Tory ministries in both England and France.

Clay instantly saw his opening.

"With your permission," he said to the Vice President as he lifted his glass to propose a toast.

Van Buren gestured his approval with a nod of his head.

"I propose," smirked Clay, "Tory ministries in England & France and a *Whig* ministry in the U. States!"

The company burst into laughter. Even the Democrats laughed, despite themselves.

Van Buren smiled wanly, but carefully set down his glass.[40]

CHAPTER 15

"No Apology"

THE PRESIDENT SAT IN HIS STUDY staring at the fire, smoking his long-stemmed pipe and silently chuckling to himself. He was exceedingly pleased with his message. Everything about it tickled him. The sections on the French problem, the Bank issue, and the question of internal improvements had conveyed his thoughts and wishes precisely, and he had a sense that the people strongly approved them. Best of all the message gored the Whigs in all the places that gave them maximum pain. How they writhed over what he had said about the Bank. How they choked and sputtered over his internal improvements pronouncement. Many of them had already responded with cries of outrage. Others just hung their heads and sighed. "My political enemies appear quite chop-fallen," Jackson gleefully recounted to his son. "I have had a triumph over them."[1]

Apart from this triumph over his "political enemies," a major cause of Jackson's buoyant spirit during the opening weeks of 1835 was the "glorious" accomplishment of extinguishing the national debt. The last installment of that debt was paid in January, 1835. It was one of the "reforms" for which Jackson had struggled over the last four years. It was an accomplishment for which he took justifiable credit.

Jackson's view of the national debt was terribly naive—but it was a naiveté of the ordinary citizen. Ridding the nation of indebtedness was virtually synonymous with paying off the mortgage on the old homestead. It was a mark of individual achievement, a badge of freedom, a symbol of success. For the nation as a whole, the obliteration of the national debt proclaimed the triumph of American republicanism and the constitutional system. It demonstrated the blessings of democracy to the entire world.

This unique and happy event added to Jackson's personal distinction and honor. Ordinary citizens credited him with having achieved the impossible, of having run the government so efficiently and honestly that he had scored the spectacular feat of actually conducting the nation out of debt.

"Out of debt!" The words sent a charge of "exultant joy" through the entire country. "Out of debt!" Every "honest citizen" felt the "magic of the words."[2]

Because the final payment of the debt nearly coincided with the anniversary of the Battle of New Orleans, the Democratic party felt it auspicious (and politically advantageous) to combine the two events into one great celebration. It was twenty years since Jackson had annihilated a British army and proved the power and might of American arms; now, in 1835, he had proved the vitality and strength of American political institutions. As the *Globe* declared: "New Orleans and the National Debt —the first of which paid off our scores to *our enemies*, whilst the latter paid off the last cent to *our friends*."[3]

On January 8, 1835, a banquet of "extraordinary magnificence" was held at Brown's Hotel in Washington at 6 P.M. A dinner was provided "in the very best taste," and nearly 250 persons attended. The room was festooned with evergreens, a portrait of George Washington hung from one wall and a portrait of President Jackson from the opposite wall. "On no occasion," reported the *Globe*, "did we ever before witness so much grandeur of scenery calculated to elevate the feelings of patriotic exultation." A band struck up "Hail to the Chief" as the company marched into the hall. Thomas Hart Benton, "Old Bullion," presided. No one had a better right, for no one had done more to aid Jackson in killing the monster Bank and asserting the supremacy of specie, or working toward paying the debt. Assisting Benton on the occasion and serving as vice presidents were James K. Polk, Silas Wright, Jr., William R. King, Henry A. Muhlenberg, Isaac Hill, John Y. Mason, and E. K. Kane.

It was a glittering affair, just as the *Globe* reported, but President Jackson declined to attend. The purpose of the occasion was to celebrate a momentous event and he did not wish to subvert it by his presence. He wanted no personal glorification. It was far more important that the nation remember its heroic past and celebrate its deliverance from economic bondage. In that, and that alone, Andrew Jackson would have all the satisfaction and honor he needed.

In Jackson's place, Vice President Martin Van Buren attended as distinguished guest. More and more he was seen as the General's hand-picked successor and this celebration pointedly served to identify him with the triumphs of the Jackson administration. The entire cabinet also attended, along with the Speaker of the House, many members of Congress, and high-ranking officers of the army and navy.

The ceremonies began with a divine blessing invoked by the chaplain of the Senate, the Reverend Mr. Hatch. Then Senator Benton rose to address the gathering and at once the affair became more lively and spirited. The evening was a rare opportunity for him to boast about the financial predictions he had sounded over the past four years, and he made the most of it. As he got to his feet his face glowed with pride and enthusiasm. He quickly warmed to his main point.

"The national debt," he exclaimed, *"is paid!"*

"Huzza!" the crowd roared.

"This month of January, 1835," Benton continued, "in the fifty-eighth year of the Republic, ANDREW JACKSON being President, the NATIONAL DEBT IS PAID! and the apparition, so long unseen on earth, a great nation without a national debt! stands revealed to the astonished vision of a wondering world!"

Again the crowd interrupted with *"Great Cheering!"*

"Gentlemen," Benton went on as he prepared to give his toast, "coming direct from my own bosom, will find its response in yours:

"PRESIDENT JACKSON: *May the evening of his days be as tranquil and as happy for himself as their meridian has been resplendent, glorious, and beneficent for his country."*

Everyone in the room had risen as Benton began this salute to their great chief, and when he concluded they burst into a long round of applause.

It was this sort of thing that Jackson feared the occasion might become and why he chose to stay away. But the Democrats could not help themselves and they heaped lavish praise upon him as, one after another, they rose to offer a toast.

After the Committee of Arrangements offered their salute, the Vice President spoke. It was not one of his better efforts and, as usual, he went on too long. Several of the honored guests could not quell their loquaciousness and spoke in paragraphs.

Then, Levi Woodbury rose. *"The President of the United States,"* he said simply. "Venerable in years—illustrious in deeds."

Silas Wright offered: *"The Citizen Soldier.* The strength and security of free government. WASHINGTON, LAFAYETTE, and JACKSON have personified the character."

Mahlon Dickerson, the new secretary of the navy, toasted: *"The Eighth of January, 1815.* An important era in the history of America—second only to the 4th of July, 1776."

Felix Grundy saluted: "The Constitution of the United States, administered upon the principles of Jefferson, Madison, and Jackson."

Jackson himself sent a toast to be read in his absence. It said nothing about himself or the 8th of January. It simply focused on the important deed of extinguishing the debt.

"The Payment of the Public Debt," he proclaimed. "Let us commemorate it as an event which gives us increased power as a nation, and reflects luster on our Federal Union, of whose justice, fidelity, and wisdom it is a glorious illustration."[4]

After dozens of other toasts, the evening ended with the singing of "The Altar of Liberty," a song especially written for the occasion. When it was all over, the Democrats shook hands and patted each other on the back in recognition that they had helped celebrate one of the most "unique and glorious" events in the history of the United States.

The event was advertised around the country, and Blair gave it special attention in his *Globe.*[5] Later the proceedings were printed in pamphlet form and some ten thousand copies were published and distributed. It made a remarkable souvenir of something special in the progress of American democracy.

Small wonder Jackson glowed with goodwill and happiness during these opening weeks of 1835. He positively radiated contentment. Another reason for his continued buoyant mood was the presence of his son's family in the White House, particularly his "little pet." The child's antics always found a place in his frequent letters to his son. "The dear little Rachel [is] as sprightly as a little lark." She "is speaking quite plain." And "the dear boy," meaning Andrew III, "had an attack of croop, but is quite well & cheerful."[6]

As good an example as he set about writing letters, Jackson could never get his son to show the same courtesy and interest. And it made the old man furious. Andrew always promised to reform, but nothing changed. Even now when Andrew's family lived at the White House one would think the frequency of his letters would increase. But no, not even his wife was favored. It seemed that young Andrew rather enjoyed the status of "single-blessedness." He liked being disentangled from family responsibilities.

What bothered the President particularly was his desire to know more about the condition of the Hermitage and how it weathered the fall rains and winter freezes. He was forced to rely on Colonel Love and Colonel Armstrong to transmit his instructions, although he always deferred to his son on any question or "any change in the height of the walls, or in the interior, that maybe by you thought advisable, that will not increase the expence beyond my means. . . ." He authorized Andrew "with the advice of Col Armstrong & Col Love [to] make such changes as you may believe will be best for you & Sarah & family hereafter . . . therefore my son, arrange it as you may think best for you & Sarah and your families convenience."[7]

Despite his recent "triumph" over his political enemies, the payment of the national debt, the continued progress of his reforms, and the success of the democratic system he so grandly presided over, Jackson saw his term of office as an "irksome" burden and he longed to get back to the Hermitage to finish out his life in peace and quiet. He thought about death a great deal. He did not believe he had many years left— although he had been saying that for the last ten or more years. Of course, in the 1830s death was an ever present phenomenon that regularly struck all ages, the young, middle-aged, and old. Infant mortality was particularly frequent, and no amount of preparation or forewarning ever lessened the shock and pain.

It was especially distressing when the firstborn child of Mary and Andrew Jackson Hutchings died late in 1834. Hutchings had not always measured up to Jackson's expectations, but his marriage to Mary Coffee gave promise of better things to come. When he learned of the child's death, Jackson was deeply saddened. He tried to write a comforting letter to the parents but what resulted was a curious mixture of condolence, puritanical fundamentalism, Christian fatalism, and a genuine personal belief in a jealous and vengeful creator. It was pure Jackson.

Washington
January 25th 1835—

My Dear Hutchings,
    Your letter convaying the molancholy intelligence of the death of your dear little babe, has been some time recd—I tender to you and your dear Mary my heartfelt condolence on this sad & mournful occasion. I am truly happy to find that you both have met this severe bereavement with that christian meekness & submission as was your duty. This charming babe was only given you from your great creator and benefactor, it is probable you doated upon him too much, to the neglect of him who gave the boon, & he has taken him from you, to bring to your view that to him your first love is due, and by this chastisement, to bring you back to your duty to god— it is to him we owe all things—it is he that giveth, and he has a right to take away, and we ought humbly to submit to his will, and be always ready to say, blessed be his name. We have one consolation under this severe bereavement, that this babe is now in the boosom of its saviour, a sweet little angel in heaven, free from all the temptation, pains & evils of this world and we ought to prepare to unite with him & other sorts [saints?] who have gone before us to those mansions of bliss, where the weary are at rest—Then let us not mourn for the dead but for the living, and prepare to follow him to the mansions of bliss.[8]

Thoughts of death came forcefully to his attention early in 1835 when Jackson was nearly killed in an assassination attempt. It was the first time a President had been attacked with intent to kill. Unhappily, it was also another sign that something powerful and frightening was operating in the country which was changing its character and mood. The nation had come through forty years without such an experience. Six Presidents had administered the country during periods of stress and calm, through war and peace. Still nothing like this had ever happened before. Never had an American citizen dared to approach the chief executive and attempt to alter the course of history by pointing a loaded pistol at him and firing it.

Then, and later, some thought that the cause of this monstrous deed lay with the personality of Jackson himself, that he was just a little too strong, too controversial, too dominant a character, and therefore an obvious target for the demented in society. Recently there had been several threats against his life.[9] Later there were more.

Brower's Hotel, Philadelphia, July 4, 1835

You damn'd old Scoundrel . . . I will cut your throat whilst you are sleeping. I wrote to you repeated Cautions, so look out or damn you I'll have you burnt at the Stake in the City of Washington

Your Master
Junius Brutus Booth

You know me! Look out![10]

No doubt the forceful personality of Jackson did indeed attract lunatics everywhere. But as some suspected at the time, a deeper and more troublesome factor may have been involved. American society itself was undoubtedly at fault. Since the beginning of the nineteenth century the American way of life had changed dramatically—sometimes for the better and sometimes for the worse. The industrial revolution, the transportation revolution, the increased migration westward, the steady rise of the standard of living, the increased momentum in the democratization of political institutions, and the social and economic mobility that visitors instantly noticed—all these had produced marvelous improvements in the quality of life in America. But they also produced hideous side effects. Poverty, urban crime and violence, blatant and vulgar materialism, the disparity of wealth and privilege spawned by the industrial revolution, racial and religious bigotry—these, too, increased. Social conditions fell to such a depth that reform movements had already begun. These were organized attempts to change and better American society, to extirpate materialism, to raise the quality of education, to advance the rights of women, to free the slaves, to ameliorate working conditions, to improve penal and mental institutions, and to establish temperance as a national virtue.[11] The assassination attempt, therefore, was only one more indication that something was terribly amiss with American life and needed attention and healing. It was "a sign of the times," editorialized the New York *Evening Post* on February 4, 1835.

The incident occurred during the funeral of Representative Warren R. Davis of South Carolina. The services took place on Friday, January 30, in the House chamber. Both houses, the President, and his cabinet attended. The chaplain gave a long and witless eulogy, something about the uncertainties of life. Throughout the service, the President looked feeble, although he presented a figure of commanding presence. "There sat the gray-haired president," recounted Harriet Martineau, "looking scarcely able to go through the ceremonial."[12]

The rites concluded, the congregation filed past the bier and then proceeded to the east porch of the Capitol, the House members first, then the Senate, with the President following behind. Waiting at the entrance of the rotunda of the east portico stood a thirty-year-old man, his face hidden by a thick black beard. As the President with Woodbury and Dickerson reached the rotunda, the young man stepped up to him, drew a pocket pistol, and aimed it directly at Jackson's heart. He stood only two and half yards away. He squeezed the trigger and an explosion rang out. Some said it sounded like a rifle shot. Senator John Tyler, who had stepped out of the line of procession, said it reminded him of an "ordinary cracker."

Jackson instantly reacted. Instead of ducking away, as most rational men might do, he started for the assailant, his walking cane raised high.

The young man dropped the pistol and produced a second one which he had held ready-cocked in his left hand. By this time several witnesses realized what was happening and tried to seize the would-be assassin. But before they could wrestle him to the ground he took dead aim at the President and pulled the trigger.

A second explosion thundered through the chamber. Jackson hesitated only a split second and then continued his lunge at his assailant, ready to thrash him with his cane. The young man ducked away. Woodbury "aimed a blow" at him and Lieutenant Gedney of the navy finally knocked him down. "The President pressed after him until he saw he was secured."[13]

In both instances the caps had discharged but failed to ignite the powder in the barrel. The day was very damp, said Senator Tyler, "a thick mist prevailing" and the pistols were loaded with the "finest powder. It is almost a miracle that they did not go off."[14]

Immediately after the attempted assassination, there was a general rush to get the President to safety. "Boiling with rage," the General kept trying to club the young man but was finally hustled to a carriage and sped to the White House. Once away from the rotunda, Jackson quickly regained his composure. He acted as though nothing had happened. Indeed, his outward calm in moments of crisis always amazed his friends. Martin Van Buren, who followed him to the White House and expected to witness an outpouring of Jacksonian wrath, was stupefied to find Old Hickory "sitting with one of Major Donelson's children on his lap and conversing with General Scott, himself apparently the least disturbed person in the room." Outside the White House a sudden thunderstorm broke, booming and raging and threatening; inside the house an old man quietly played with a child and shrugged off the seriousness of what had happened to him.[15]

The would-be assassin turned out to be one Richard Lawrence, an unemployed house painter. He was quickly hurried off to "civil authorites" and incarcerated. When the House sergeant-at-arms asked him why he attempted to assassinate the President, Lawrence replied that Jackson had killed his father three years ago. He also muttered something to the effect that he was the legitimate heir to the British throne and that Old Hickory had impeded his succession. Inasmuch as his father, an Englishman, had died a dozen years before it seemed clear to the authorities that Lawrence was deranged. "There is nothing but madness in all this," said John Tyler.[16]

But some Democrats, including Jackson, believed that Lawrence was a political assassin, commanded by Whigs. And they had some justification —or so they thought. During a medical examination, when asked whom he preferred as President, Lawrence answered: "Mr. Clay, Mr. Webster, Mr. Calhoun."[17] "It seems he has been a furious politician of the opposition party," wrote Francis Scott Key, "& is represented by some as a very weak man, easily duped or excited." Blair suspected an assassination plot and openly insisted that "a secret conspiracy had prompted the perpetration of the horrible deed." These fears intensified when Judge Cranch, the chief justice of the District, set bail at a paltry $1500. "There is much excitement among our friends," Taney was told, "on account of the smallness of the sum required." But as soon as it became clear that Lawrence could not meet his bail the tension among Democrats quickly dissipated. Lawrence was subsequently brought to trial. On April 11, 1835, he was found not guilty because "he was under the influence of insanity" when he attempted the assassination. He was immediately committed to an asylum.[18]

Because Jackson was a religious fatalist he could not help but see the hand of "providence" in protecting him from what seemed like certain death. When the king of England expressed his concern, Jackson acknowledged that "a kind providence" had been pleased "to shield me" against "the recent attempt upon my life."[19] Others agreed. "The circumstance made a deep impression upon the public feeling," wrote Senator Benton, "and irresistibly carried many minds to the belief in a superintending Providence, manifested in the extraordinary case of two pistols in succession—so well loaded, so coolly handled, and which afterwards fired with such readiness, force, and precision—missing fire, each in its turn, when levelled eight feet at the President's heart." The attack did indeed have a profound effect upon the public. And it produced political gain as well. It "warmed up the love of his friends," Major Donelson was told, ". . . and has given him new friends and advocates." It generated genuine concern and affection for the old man in every section of the country.[20]

To many Americans, Jackson's escape from near-certain death resulted from "a special interposition of Providence." The President had been spared in order to continue serving his country—especially during this time of mounting crisis with France over the indemnity claim.

Jackson himself believed that a special grace protected this country. But he did not rely on "Providence" to prevent an international disaster. In all crises, he trusted himself—now more than ever.

Supported by the House Committee on Foreign Relations, chaired by Churchill C. Cambreleng, Jackson obtained a resolution from that committee which empowered the President to act in any emergency that might grow out of the crisis, particularly after Congress adjourned.[21] The full House unanimously endorsed the resolution and accordingly inserted into the general fortification bill an appropriation of $3 million authorizing the President to make such military and naval preparations as might be required during the congressional recess.[22] Although the House passed this appropriation, the Senate took no action and the bill died when Congress adjourned.

Jackson snorted disapproval. "You will see from the papers sent you by the Secretary of State," he informed Edward Livingston, "the disgraceful course of the faction of the Senate the evening of the adjournment of Congress and the unprotected state in which they have left our seaports and towns." Then, after thinking a moment, he added: "I will defend them."[23] One reason for Jackson's agitation was his concern that should his message receive a "hostile reaction" in France, after it got there, he had no "contingency" by which to respond quickly to this "emergency."[24]

The President's message arrived in Paris at two o'clock in the morning of January 8—the anniversary of Jackson's military triumph at New Orleans. "The contents being soon known caused the greatest sensation," reported Livingston to Forsyth. The excitement "is at present very great." The pride of the deputies "is deeply wounded by what they call an attempt to coerce them by threats." This sentiment was fostered by American newspapers, such as the Washington *National Intelligencer* and the New York *Courier*, which had been sent to Paris by troublemakers and declared to be the sentiments of a majority of Americans. If war should break out, Livingston added, these newspapers can share the blame. But whether Jackson's strong language will be cited by the deputies in order to continue their intransigence remains to be seen. "It has certainly raised us in the estimation of other powers," Livingston continued, "if I may judge from the demeanor of their representatives here." Since Rigny wanted to see the message as soon as it arrived, Livingston himself carried it to him on the morning of the eighth. However, no further discussion ensued between the two men in order to give Rigny time to read and study Jackson's language.[25]

Livingston was beginning to have great doubts about the ultimate success of his mission. Already there were too many elements in play that might coalesce to form a powerful opposition in France to prevent any payment whatsoever. "I have hopes," he told George Dallas, "but no very sanguine expectations of success. The leaders of the three opposition parties have united" on a mode of attack and "their joint force" may swing a great many votes in the Chambers.[26]

These doubts intensified when Livingston was summoned to the foreign ministry on January 13. He began his discussion with Rigny by expressing "regret" that the President's message "had been so much misrepresented . . . as to be construed into a manner of hostilities." As Jackson himself had earlier indicated, Livingston went on, the message was "part of consultation" between different branches of the American government and the President was merely doing his duty in presenting the facts to Congress as he knew them. The President was simply offering different "modes of redress"[27] allowed by the "law of nations" to avoid hostilities. In passing, Livingston commented that it was most unfortunate that an earlier call of the Chambers had not been sent out in view of "Mr. Sérurier's promise" that it would be done. Rigny reacted sharply to this statement and Livingston recognized at once that "this was the part of the message that had most seriously affected the King." Rigny insisted that the crown had acted in good faith and the intimation in the message disputing that fact was not true.

The interview was a long one and ended with both men "lamenting that any misunderstanding should interrupt the good intelligence" between their respective countries. As Livingston took his leave he again expressed the hope that "the excitement would soon subside and give place to better feelings" all around.[28]

Late that same evening Livingston was stunned by a notification from Rigny informing him that the king had ordered Sérurier home. Livingston was offered his passports if he so desired. Although the French government had decided to go ahead and ask the Chambers for an appropriation to pay the indemnity, nevertheless it felt itself "wounded" by Jackson's groundless "imputations." The king could no longer tolerate having "his minister exposed to hear language so offensive to France." Sérurier, therefore, was recalled.

Livingston sat staring at the notification for many minutes after reading it. He could scarcely believe his eyes. After all that had happened earlier in the day, he later wrote Forsyth, "you may judge of my surprise" when at ten o'clock in the evening this note arrived.

The following day the Baron Lionel N. Rothschild called on Livingston to offer his considerable skills in an effort to prevent a complete rupture between the two countries. He assured the American minister that Rigny's note was not intended as a request for Livingston to depart the country but rather a form of protocol in view of Sérurier's recall. Livingston should not leave until so ordered. If he stayed, then the burden of ordering his departure would be thrown back to the French government and would force it to come to a definite decision about the indemnity. Livingston mulled over Rothschild's advice. "[I must not] give to the French Government the advantage," he declared. He must keep them at a disadvantage. So he decided to "remain but keep aloof until I receive your directions," he told Forsyth.[29]

Livingston penned a seventeen-page "note" to Rigny in which he offered all the explanations of American behavior that he felt the French government had a right to expect. Dated January 29, 1835, the note encompassed most of the arguments advanced by his government and attempted to demonstrate that the complaints against Jackson's message were groundless.[30] Its argument was superb as only a sharp constitutional mind could devise, and when Jackson saw a copy he pronounced it excellent. "I have read" it, he later said, ". . . with delight, it is full and compleat." The only omission he felt that Livingston might have made was reference to McLane's letter to Sérurier informing him that in view of the "assurances" given by the king "that I would withhold from making the promised communications to Congress until the next session, when I would be able to lay before them the final action of the chambers on the subject of the treaty."[31]

The news of Sérurier's recall hit the United States with devastating force. "A strong sensation" was felt in the House of Representatives, recorded John Quincy Adams in his diary, and many members wished to adjourn forthwith as a gesture of protest. Gloomy old Adams was sure the French Chambers would reject the government's bill to pay the indemnity and this would be followed by "some rash and foolish act of President Jackson." If the two countries are to be saved from war, he grumbled, "it seems as if it could only be by a special interposition of Providence."[32]

A war hysteria of sorts gripped some parts of the country after the recall became known. A New York City contingent of national guards offered their services to the President, but Jackson assured their commanding officer "that the dangers of a rupture between us and our ancient ally . . . will soon pass away."[33]

News of the recall arrived in Washington by express in fourteen hours from New York City at about 1 P.M. on February 20. Representative Aaron Ward of New York went immediately to see Jackson to confirm the report. He told the President that the news had "created much excitement—the members of both Houses seemed disinclined to attend to business and all seemed anxious to hear the news." What agitated everyone was the sense that the United States, the innocent party in the dispute, was made to look guilty of some wrongdoing. If any minister should be recalled it should be Livingston. Jackson responded that he had received no official information. His only recent letter from abroad had come from Aaron Vail, the chargé in London, who said it was "rumoured" that Sérurier had been recalled and that Livingston had his passports "tendered to him." Ward was deeply concerned about the consequences. "Should the news prove true," he told John Sing, "you will have occasion to prepare your armour for the battlefield."[34]

Official word of the French action came in due course. Livingston informed the secretary of state and the President what had happened and why he had decided to stay put. "I [am] here by your direction," he explained to Jackson; "I ought not Voluntarily to leave my post without your orders."[35]

Three days after the news of the recall first reached Washington, Sérurier notified Forsyth of his intended departure and presented Alphonse J. Y. Pageot as chargé d'affaires. For months Sérurier had acted coolly toward the President, refusing several invitations to dine at the White House on the grounds of ill health. "His indisposition was partly real," commented Van Buren, "& partly produced by the Message."[36] What made the situation even more disagreeable now was the fact that Pageot was married to Mary Lewis, the daughter of Major William Lewis, and their young son had been christened "Andrew Jackson Pageot" in the White House.

In taking his departure, Sérurier presented to Forsyth a detailed defense of French policy, just as he was instructed to do by his government. This would have been perfectly usual and appropriate, except that one phrase in the statement—*"prétendu non-accomplissement"* *—conveyed the idea that Jackson deliberately communicated to Congress a statement about French policy which he knew to be untrue. This attack upon the President's integrity was intolerable and Livingston was instructed to secure adequate explanations. It was just one more irritant to worsen relations between France and the United States. Livingston was also ordered to demand his passports and return home if the French persisted in their refusal to pay the indemnity.[37]

On March 8, Jackson summoned Forsyth and Van Buren to the White House for a discussion of Livingston's conduct. At the outset of the meeting the President said that he approved what his minister had done. Van Buren assured him that all true Democrats agreed. Forsyth then produced Livingston's letter of January 29 to Rigny and the three men "went through it very delibertely," only regretting that McLane's note to Sérurier had been omitted. But do not worry about this, Van Buren assured Livingston in a private letter. "You know the Genls. fidelity to his friends & those who seek to injure you in his estimation without grounds that are palpably well founded only destroy themselves." After further

*The full sentence reads: *"Les plaintes que porte M. le Président contre le prétendu non-accomplissement des engagements pris par le Gouvernement du Roi."* The official translation: "The complaints which the President brings against the pretended non-fulfillment of the engagements taken by the Government of the King." The rub was whether or not "prétendu" meant "pretended."

discussion, the trio decided that the appropriation bill might pass the Chambers after all, despite Sérurier's recall. If only the king would "send us a plain, sensible, sincere & liberal minded man," Van Buren wistfully wrote, then there would be no difficulty in maintaining "friendly & beneficial relations between the two countries. The Genl. thinks he has, as he certainly has, strong grounds for complaint & in such cases he moves strongly—probably sometimes a little more so than is necessary, but he is you know not implacable and returns to the relations of amity (when he can do so honorably), with sincerity & alacrity."[38]

Immediately after the meeting Jackson wrote to Livingston to assure him that his "course is fully approved." Had the United States minister left Paris, the President wrote, "I should neither have been surprised or disapproved the step—still as you could reconcile it to yourself to remain it is better. France has been in the wrong in all this matter and we will keep her in the wrong." Stick to your post, he counseled, and do what you can to bolster American contentions and demands. The U.S.S. *Constitution* will sail for France about the middle of March, he added, and will bring further dispatches.[39]

An appropriations bill to indemnify the United States was finally introduced into the Chamber of Deputies by the French minister of finance on January 15, 1835. It was immediately referred to a committee for a report. Then, a change of ministry occurred on March 13 which returned the Duc de Broglie to the head of the department of foreign affairs as well as head of the ministry. This change was seen abroad as a favorable sign for the payment of the indemnity.

The committee report on the appropriations bill was returned to the full Chambers on March 28. It noted Jackson's message to Congress and attributed his unfortunate statements to a misunderstanding of the constitution of France and suggested that an acceptable explanation of his remarks ought to be demanded before France paid the indemnity. In a speech to the Deputies, Broglie contended that Jackson's message was not an official act of the United States and therefore not subject to any consideration whatsoever by the French government. Sérurier had been recalled. What more did French honor require? Nothing, Broglie answered himself, so let us approve the bill.[40]

The debate on the measure began in earnest on April 9 and continued for nearly ten days. "The opposition is very violent," Livingston reported to Jackson, but the strong support of the ministry ought to overcome it and win passage of the bill.[41] Very little in the way of new information or arguments was presented during the debate, but it soon became clear that a majority strongly resented Jackson's language and felt they should do something about it. At length an amendment to the bill was proposed by E. B. A. Valaze which required "that the money shall not be paid until the Government of France shall have received satisfactory explanations of the Message of the President of the Union dated the 2 Decr. last." The bill with this amendment then passed the Chambers on April 18, 1835, by a vote of 289 to 137.[42]

Livingston was chagrined. The amendment, he informed Forsyth, "I think will render the whole bill nugatory." To comply the United States must acknowledge the right of France to demand explanations about communications between different branches of its government. This was preposterous, and "so humiliating that I have not hesitated to consider it as equivalent to a rejection of the treaty and I shall therefore in obedience to your instructions ask for my passports."[43]

Before leaving France, Livingston delivered one last dispatch to Broglie which again denied that Jackson's message had impugned the good faith of the French government or contained a "menace" to win passage of the appropriations bill by the threat of reprisals. He then turned over the ministry to his son-in-law, Thomas P. Barton, who served as chargé d'affaires. Barton was instructed to remain in Paris until the bill was presented to the Chamber of Peers and passed, after which he was to follow Livingston out of the country. "I take for my guide in breaking up the Legation," said Livingston, "not only the general direction so to do when the law be rejected which I think it virtually is . . . but more particularly the instruction contained in your Despatch No 57 when you directed me to apply for my passport if no answer is given to my note in eight days."[44]

As for the explanation demanded by the Deputies, Livingston thought that in all likelihood they would be satisfied with nothing "unless it in Effect Declares that the President did not intend to call in question the good faith of the French Government or to suppose that they would be influenced by menace."[45]

Livingston left Paris on April 29. He said he could not remain in Europe because that might be interpreted "as evidence of a wish to resume my mission." On May 5 he sailed from Le Havre for home aboard the U.S.S. *Constitution.*[46]

The news of the passage of the indemnity bill by the French Deputies arrived in the United States on May 26. The first reaction was one long shout of thanksgiving. Once again the Jackson administration had triumphed and forced a European nation to pay its legitimate debt to this government. Once more a democratic President, elected by the "free choice of the people," had scored a diplomatic victory. Even John Quincy Adams offered something approaching praise—although he quickly tempered it by criticizing the diplomacy involved. "The victory of President Jackson's Administration is complete," he wrote, "and will sweep away every fragment of opposition to the remainder of his term. His experiment was a hazardous one, and the management of the negotiation by his Cabinet has exhibited great maladresse." But Whig opposition was worse, he confessed. It was typified by much "blundering, and has proved excessively unpopular."[47]

The "great sensation" produced by the unexpected triumph was modified somewhat by the realization that an explanation of Jackson's message was required before the indemnity would be paid. This, said Adams, "throws an awkward obstacle in the way of a final settlement." But most Americans thought it a face-saving device that meant little. I hope, said William C. Rives, "that the silly condition" imposed by the French will not prove serious. "Ministers found it necessary, I suppose, to assent to it as a sort of salve to the national pride." Even opposition newspapers made light of it. The Washington *National Intelligencer* said that France should accept Jackson's disclaimer that "nothing partaking of the character of intimidation" was ever intended by the United States. This should be repeated in the next State of the Union message and accepted as a full explanation.[48]

But it remained for the White House to pass judgment on what the French had done. And it came almost immediately. The Washington *Globe* on May 29 announced Jackson's reaction to the demand for an explanation. It was abrupt and needlessly aggressive—but it said exactly what the American people were thinking and saying. "France will get no apology," blared the *Globe*, "—nothing bearing even such a remote resemblance to one, that it can be palmed off upon the world as such by all the vaunting and gasconading of sputtering Frenchmen."

"No apology." That was Jackson's response. And that was final.

CHAPTER 16

Democratizing
the Government

JACKSON'S BUOYANT MOOD AT THE BEGINNING of the year soured with each passing month. The winter was long and cold, the negotiations with France protracted and barren. And the General's personal financial situation was getting worse each month. The $5,000 debt owed to Harry Hill could not be paid on January 1, 1835, and it began to draw interest at a staggering (for Jackson) 6 percent. In addition, for "the first time I have had to buy corn and forage to sustain my stock" and support "my farm this spring & summer." With the rebuilding of the Hermitage, and "my heavy expences here" in Washington, "I find my funds nearly exhausted."[1]

These financial burdens were intensified by his son's incompetence. Jackson had no choice but to rely on him and trust him. But Andrew regularly disappointed him. His judgment was bad, his resolutions to improve worthless, his drinking becoming a problem, his laziness exasperating, and his reliability problematic. Jackson showed his son infinite patience. He lectured him constantly—which probably did more harm than good—but the old man felt it was his duty.

> You must, to get thro' life well, practice industry with oeconomy. never create a debt for any thing that is not absolutely necessary, and when you make a promise to pay money at a day certain, be sure to comply with it, if you do not you lay yourself liable to have your feelings injured and your reputation destroyed with the just imputation of violating your word. Nothing can be more disgraceful, or more injurious to a mans standing in society, than the charge truly made that he has promised to pay money at a day certain, and violating that promise. I therefore repeat, create no debts, our real wants are but few, our imaginary wants many, which never ought to be gratified by creating a debt to supply them.[2]

237

Of course, a constant burden for Jackson was his wretched health. Much of the winter he felt unwell and could not explain the cause. "I have been severely attacked with pains," he wrote, but the nature of the pains and their location he did not specify. Just pain. Constant pain. Almost every day he suffered excruciating headaches. "I shall when my head gets better write you more fully," he frequently scribbled at the end of his letters. In the late spring his nose became inflamed, and to make matters worse his old problem of "costiveness" returned. "My bowels are become quite torpid,"[3] he told William Lewis, "and I have grown weary of taking medicine so frequently. I postponed it too long, having passed over three days without a passage." He would then resort to a high cathartic, usually Dr. Rush's "Thunderbolt." That would bring on nausea and severe diarrhea which could totally prostrate him.[4]

His ill health tormented him to distraction. But even harder for him to bear was the illness or indisposition of his grandchildren. Infant and childhood mortality being so high in the early nineteenth century, any sickness in children carried the threat of immediate tragedy. When little Rachel became ill in the spring of 1835 nothing would do but that she be taken to the celebrated physician Dr. Philip Syng Physick, in Philadelphia. When the doctor cured Rachel of her illness, the grateful grandfather wrote him a heartfelt letter of appreciation.

> My dear Sir, By Mr. Toland I presented my deep sense of gratitude for your kind attention to my dear little grand daughter Rachel. She is now I may say perfectly recovered and to your skill and kind attention, under a kind providence, we are indebted for the restoration of our beloved child, for which I owe you a debt of gratitude that I am sure I never can repay, but will always be remembered with the most grateful and lively recollections. With the assurance of what pleasure it will [give] me to have it in my power to serve you or yours,
>
> *Andrew Jackson*[5]

Fortunately, at the time of Rachel's sudden illness she was already in Philadelphia, for Sarah had gone to stay with her sister Emma during her sister's confinement. But this, too, distressed poor Jackson. "I have been very lonesome since Sarah left us," he wrote. Another convalescent in the White House was Andrew J. Donelson. He came down with "an attack of congestive fever" in January and it stayed with him for the remainder of the winter. This increased the President's burden because it meant he had to forgo the services of his trusted secretary. In April Donelson returned to Tennessee for a short visit to help him shake off the lingering aftereffects of his illness.[6]

Still, there were moments of pleasure. The early adjournment of Congress on March 3 brightened Jackson's spirit, along with several stunning electoral victories in Connecticut, Rhode Island, and Virginia. Slowly the Jackson magic was working itself deeper into New England and carrying

Democrats into local, state, and national office. The old warrior seemed to forget his infirmities as the results of these spring elections reached his desk. He sent copies of the *Globe* to his son to tell him about these victories. "You will see that the democracy of the country is triumphant everywhere." Show the *Globe* to Major Donelson when you are done with it, he added, "I know it will give him joy."[7]

What gave Jackson particular joy, however, was the unanticipated promise from his son that he would take the pledge to stop drinking. Jackson could hardly believe it. He was ecstatic. "May I rejoice in the sentiments you have expressed with regard to your future course of life —my son it is one that will lead you to respectability here, and a happy immortality—I have the utmost confidence in your pledge on this subject, and I am happy, because in your reputation, my future fame depends.— when I am in the silent grave it is in you, & yours, that my name is to be perpetuated,—and to you, & yours, propriety of conduct is my name to be connected." It was very important to Jackson that his name be "perpetuated" and this explains in part his tolerance of Andrew's many character defects. Also why Jackson thanked him and blessed him over and over when he spotted any signs of improvement. "I thank my god you have taken this resolution," he wrote, "—it insures your happiness here and hereafter and makes me happy." The President sent the resolution to Sarah because he knew that "she will rejoice to receive it."[8]

So strongly did Jackson feel about the abuse of alcohol that in 1834 he agreed to sign a declaration prepared by a temperance organization. The declaration also included the signatures of two former Presidents, James Madison and John Quincy Adams.

DECLARATION

Being satisfied, from observation and experience, as well as from medical testimony, that ardent spirit, as a drink, is not only needless, but hurtful; and that the entire disuse of it would tend to promote the health, the virtue, and the happiness of the community, we hereby express our conviction, that should the citizens of the United States, and especially ALL YOUNG MEN, discontinue entirely the use of it, they would not only promote their own personal benefit, but the good of our country and the world.

JAMES MADISON
ANDREW JACKSON
JOHN QUINCY ADAMS[9]

Jackson himself never completely gave up alcohol, although he occasionally abstained for days and weeks at a time.

In between the moments of joy, Jackson wrestled with his many complaints. Sometimes he lacked the strength to cope with all his problems and infirmities and he took to his bed. These sieges lasted a very short time but they spared him worse relapses. At such times he meditated on his future happiness when he could return to the Hermitage at the conclusion of his term in office. "I am counting the days of my captivity here & every *one* that passes, console myself that it is shortened 24 hours."[10]

One of Jackson's persistent problems, if not one of the direct causes of his "excruciating" headaches, was the Post Office Department. That office had given him nothing but trouble virtually from the day he appointed the postmaster general, William T. Barry. And the fault was entirely Jackson's because he had appointed an incompetent. Worse, he had been warned about Barry and yet he chose to disregard the warning. His old friend John Pope, former senator of Kentucky and recently appointed territorial governor of Arkansas by Jackson, wrote to the new President at the start of his administration and told him what a dreadful mistake it would be to appoint Barry to office. "He and his friends have lost us the state administration," Pope told Jackson on February 19, 1829, "and had nearly lost you the state. He is not fit for any station which requires great intellectual force or moral firmness."[11] That should have given Jackson pause—and maybe it did—but it did not last long enough to prevent the appointment. The General exercised poor control over his cabinet selections at the beginning of his presidency and this one slipped out of his hands before he fully apprehended the danger.[12] Once appointed, Barry proved a loyal friend, if an incompetent administrator. He established friendships with Major Lewis and Van Buren, and gave Jackson unstinting support during the Eaton scandal. That alone was enough to cement Jackson's misplaced loyalty as well as ensure Barry's tenure even when the first cabinet was dissolved in 1831.

The Post Office Department steadily deteriorated. Corruption seeped through its operation. Debts mounted—both to banks and to contractors. Charges of inadequate service, "reckless" operations, and outright theft were all too common. Perhaps Barry himself was honest, said Amos Kendall, but even his "best friends could readily comprehend how he might have been misled by corrupt men about him."[13]

The situation got so bad that many cities were publicly complaining about the lack of mail service that sometimes stretched from weeks to months.[14] Contractors regularly defrauded the government and thought nothing of raising their rates by more than a thousand percent. Eventually the Congress decided to investigate and both houses established committees. The House committee, with a Democratic majority, was chaired by Henry W. Connor of North Carolina; the Senate committee, with a Whig majority, was chaired by Thomas Ewing of Ohio. Both committees returned reports that excoriated the department for its gross deficiencies and failures.

The central problem was management—or rather the lack of it. Related to this was the corruption of the contractors and the inability of the department to deal with them. The investigating committees also cited "recklessness" in the handling of the department's finances, the awarding of contracts to friends and relatives of department employees, the concealment of facts, extravagance in printing costs, and the allowance of "straw" (fictitious) bids that permitted the department to hand out substitute contracts without readvertising.[15]

The Senate report came on June 9, 1834, and said that the affairs of the department were "in a state of utter derangement" occasioned in some instances by a "total disregard" of the law.[16] This report stirred up a storm of abuse against the administration during the summer of 1834 and forced Jackson to take note of it in his next message to Congress.

Although the Senate report could be dismissed by Jackson as biased because it represented Whig prejudice, no such excuse could explain away the House report, submitted on February 13, 1835. This report represented a Democratic majority and came complete with documentary evidence. It concluded that the finances of the department had been managed "without frugality, system, intelligence, or adequate public utility." Every principle of "enlightened economy" had been ignored, the report went on. Ignorance prevailed throughout the department and expenses had not been kept within the bounds of income.[17]

In other words, everything for which President Jackson stood—reform, retrenchment, and economy—had been violated by this single department. Corruption of every variety operated within his administration and, like so many other disasters that occurred during his two terms in office, this one could be laid directly at Jackson's feet because of his inadequate administrative control, his poor appointments to key positions, and his mistaken notion about loyalty and friendship when it came to running the government. The one thing Jackson prided himself about was honesty. It was the one virtue he demanded of his department heads in the operation of their offices. But, as was frequently pointed out, Barry was not so much corrupt himself as lacking in "moral firmness" so as to avoid entrapment by the corrupt men associated with him.

Long before the House report became public knowledge Jackson had decided to take action. It obviously meant the removal of Barry. But the General was reluctant to dismiss him since there was no evidence of his own misconduct. Instead he decided to shift him to another post—perhaps out of the country where he would be out of sight and out of mind.

As a replacement, Jackson immediately thought of Amos Kendall. Almost from the first moment of their meeting in early 1829 the President had resolved to award the former editor an important position within the administration. Kendall chose the position of Fourth Auditor in order to help institute Jackson's reforms; and he also provided invaluable assistance in the founding and editing of the Washington *Globe*. Now Jackson wanted him as postmaster general.

He spoke to Kendall in midsummer 1834, although he did not mention the exact position he had in mind. Kendall played coy. "Be assured that I feel satisfied whether the occasion may arise in which your kindness can be made effective or not," he wrote Jackson; "and I beg you not to think of me for any place when you believe another would better perform the service or give more strength to your administration. That you should close your eventful career with success and honor, is a consideration more dear to me than any personal gain or convenience."[18]

In the fall Jackson got more specific. In writing his State of the Union message he invited Kendall's help and spoke to him about needed reforms in the Post Office Department. Kendall allowed that a better control of post office finances was essential and that a revenue of $3 million ought more properly to be controlled by the Treasury. "I should place the matter," he told Jackson, "on the ground where were I president or postmaster general I'd call on Congress to put an end to so dangerous a system." He would also have the money pass through the hands of the comptroller as well as the auditor. "Having 14 or 15 clerks whose business I cannot examine in detail, I should feel the responsibility of an auditor to be fearful, if their work were not overhauled and revised in a comptroller's office." Instead of dispensing with these offices they should be "strengthened and made more efficient," he said.[19]

By now Jackson had definitely decided to appoint Kendall to Barry's position. Not only did Kendall's suggestions and comments exude enthusiasm about reforming the post office, but he had already demonstrated his capacity to do an efficient job in the auditor's office. As for Barry, the President would quietly ship him out of the country.

Sometime during the short 1834–1835 congressional session, probably around the time of the House report, Jackson offered the post to Kendall. He said that a change in the leadership of the Post Office Department was absolutely essential and asked his friend to take it. But Kendall initially hesitated, both for personal and political reasons: for one thing the Senate might reject his nomination; for another he had a large family and found it increasingly difficult to provide for them in public life.[20] Still Jackson persisted. "There are many men who would be glad to accept the Department," he said, "and I suppose would put everything right there; but *I know you will.*"[21] What could Kendall say? Eventually he acquiesced. He simply requested that the appointment be delayed until immediately after the close of the short session of Congress and that his formal nomination to the Senate be held off until near the close of the next long session. Jackson agreed.

The change of leadership was scheduled to take place on May 1, 1835, and was duly announced. But Barry proved recalcitrant. Initially he had agreed to go abroad but then "certain parties" who resented Kendall's climb to cabinet rank convinced Barry that he had been "banished." Jackson denied this and probably reassured him by promising a seat on the Supreme Court in due course. In any event, Old Hickory "found means to obviate the difficulty," and on June 1, 1835, the shift in personnel took effect: Barry went abroad as minister to Spain (although he died in England on his way to Madrid), and Kendall assumed the office of postmaster general.[22]

Although some of the President's own friends (like Taney) worried at first about the Kendall appointment and how it would be received, they later changed their minds. "You are aware," Taney said to Van Buren, "that I entertained some apprehensions about the manner in which Mr. Kendall's appointment as Post Master General would be received. I am now convinced that I was entirely mistaken. The appointment is popular —decidedly popular—with the great body of the people."[23]

The reason for his popularity was the speed with which Kendall improved the operating efficiency of the department. He immediately established a set of work rules for his staff.[24] He swept out the top administrators and replaced them with his two best clerks from the Fourth Auditor's office, Robert Johnson and Joseph Perry, with Johnson in charge of accounts. He appointed Preston S. Loughborough, "a man of superior talents," he said, as chief clerk. But far more important was his own close involvement with the operation of the department. "I superintended the operations of the system myself," he later wrote, "and carried on a large portion of the correspondence." He roamed the halls of his offices. He became acquainted with the officials and clerks and learned about their specific duties. "I visited their rooms," he recalled, "examined their books, and asked all needful explanations." Where he spotted fraud, corruption, or suspicious procedures, he "rotated" the offenders out of office. Since contractors were one of the main sources of corruption (through favors mostly), he announced to his subordinates that the acceptance "of any present of value from any mail contractor or a free ride in stage lines, steamboats, or railroad cars carrying the mails" would be cause for instant dismissal. When gifts and free rides were sent to Kendall himself he returned them with "polite letters." So energetic was his supervision and control of the department that within months he established a record of efficiency and honesty that won public respect and acclaim.[25]

Equally important was his reform of the finances of the department. Kendall found the post office confused and disorderly and deeply in debt. He left it solvent and organized, efficient and under tight administrative control. The department owed money to both banks and contractors, running into the hundreds of thousands of dollars, and was "subjected to continual embarrassment in devising ways and means to meet its engagements."[26] Kendall acted immediately. He ordered a moratorium on all payments upon obligations incurred before the coming quarter. Incoming funds were used to pay current expenditures. "Extra allowances" were suspended; and any draft on department funds was automatically refused except by special arrangement.[27] Within two and a half months, Kendall had paid all debts of the preceding quarter; and, in addition, he had amassed a sizable surplus. Obviously, the department always had the money to operate properly; it was simply mismanaged under Barry. Thus, by mid-August, 1835, "the Department was disembarrassed."[28] A surplus of over $100,000 in current operations existed and Kendall could now begin to pay off the "old debt" owed to banks and contractors. By the spring of 1836 this "old debt" was completely liquidated.

On April 1, Kendall proudly marched into the President's study and informed him that the Post Office Department was entirely cleared of debt. Jackson's pain-etched face broke into a broad smile. He rose from his desk, warmly grasped Kendall by the hand, and shook it vigorously.[29]

To sustain this economic efficiency, Kendall instituted new accounting and auditing procedures and halted the system which allowed the expenditures of huge funds with few and sometimes inaccurate records to document the transactions. In addition, he established the "Inspection Office" to control field operations and check on contractors and local postmasters. He appointed special agents to exercise a rigid system of supervision over the accounts of postmasters and the performance of contractors.

Kendall went further with his reforms. He reorganized the department's entire operation. All those things pertaining to the establishment, supervision, and discontinuance of post offices were assigned to the "Appointments Office," supervised by a first assistant. All things pertaining to mail routes and performance of contracts for carrying the mails were assigned to the "Contract Office" under a second assistant. And all things pertaining to the performance of mail service under contracts were assigned to the "Inspection Office" under a third assistant. The supervision and control of all financial matters and "mail depredations" came directly under the postmaster general himself, through this chief clerk.[30]

Reordering the department's financial operation required congressional approval and action. Accordingly, a new Post Office Act was passed on July 2, 1836, which incorporated most of Kendall's reforms. The measure was a "masterpiece" of loophole plugging, according to one historian.[31] It rectified every source of mismanagement that Kendall and the two investigating committees had uncovered in 1834 and 1835. As for the financial operations, they were brought into conformity with the standard practice of other departments, and the unchecked fiscal responsibility of the postmaster general was terminated. Revenues collected were paid directly to the Treasury; the postmaster general estimated his expenses annually and these were appropriated by Congress, supplemented from general funds when necessary. Furthermore, the act of 1836 spelled out the responsibilities and duties of the postmaster general, and those postmasters whose commissions earned $1,000 became presidential appointees requiring confirmation by the Senate for four-year terms.[32]

The reform act of 1836 not only provided efficiency and greater honesty in the running of the post office at the department level, it also resulted in better mail delivery throughout the United States. There was a dramatic improvement over past performances in mail service which had profound implications that no one at the time suspected. In business alone such a marked improvement in communications around the country accelerated the already rapid industrialization of the nation. It constituted a small part of the developing communications revolution that included the expansion of the railroads and the (coming) invention of the telegraph.

Amos Kendall ranks as one of Andrew Jackson's most intelligent and best appointments. He brought to the government service a dedication to Jackson's program of reform that was unmatched by any other official. Combined with this were his energy, attention to duty, administrative talent, and intelligent understanding of public service. "I have set out," he told Caleb Butler in May, 1835, "upon the principle of not suffering any party . . . to promote the removal of good, faithful and quiet men whatever may be their political opinion, and I mean to persist in it. Brawlers of any party who make politics instead of attention to their official duties, their constant occupation, I mean to cut adrift from the public service, if I cannot otherwise conquer that propensity. All of support I ask for the administration from Postmasters is, a faithful, polite and obliging performance of their public duties." Kendall's reform of the post office was an important achievement of the Jackson administration. It is one important reason why Jackson's term in office ranks high on a list of *least* corrupt administrations in American history. The determination of the President to extirpate corruption, matched by the dedication, energy, and skill of his cabinet officer, produced this remarkable accomplishment.

The President supported and encouraged Kendall along every step he took to reform the department. Even before Kendall officially notified him of the new regulations he had established, Jackson had seen them and read them "with attention." Although he was vacationing at the Rip Raps at the time, the General wrote to Kendall and told him how pleased and excited he was about them. "I have no doubt but much good will flow from them," he said, "and produce faithful performance of duty by both contractors and postmasters, which was much wanted. . . . These regulations fully meet my approbation, & must all impartial men, & will enable Congress to legislate upon the intricate subject more beneficially & understandingly."[33]

As important as Kendall's reforms were to Jackson's purpose of restoring the government to virtue and honesty, they came at a price that no one at the time fully realized. They encouraged a fearsome swelling of the government's bureaucracy. Kendall's decision to institute three separate offices to run department affairs, each with its own assistant postmaster general, reflected what was happening throughout the entire governmental apparatus during Jackson's administration. In order to tighten control at the top and thereby ensure efficiency and honesty, new offices and bureaus were being set up with specific duties and responsibilities that freed the department head from administrative details so that he could supervise the entire operation and run it according to the guidelines adopted by Jackson at the beginning of his administration.[34]

But that created another problem that worried and offended the President. It produced a huge bureaucracy. It launched a new army of government employees. It swelled the size and operation of government. And this struck at the very heart of Jackson's republican philosophy of reform.

Of all the particulars cited by Jackson in his efforts at "reform retrenchment and economy," none was as important as restoring honesty to government and reducing the size of government in order to protect the freedom of the American people. The Jackson administration did much toward getting rid of corrupt individuals, although it made monumental mistakes such as appointing Samuel Swartwout as collector of the custom's house in New York.[35] But in the matter of reducing government, Jackson completely failed. He simply could not have it both ways: he could not reform the government by tightening the administrative process to root out corruption without approving the establishment of bureaus in each department to investigate and oversee operations. Moreover, Jackson could not prevent the expansion of governmental operations even if he tried. The amount of government business simply ballooned during the 1830s. It reflected an expanding economy and a mobile people. Like the business of America, the business of government boomed. In fact, according to a Senate committee investigating this phenomenon, the expenditures of the government doubled in just a few years, rising from $11,490,460 in 1825 to $22,713,755 in 1833. "The entire character and structure of the Government itself," warned the Senate report, "is undergoing a great and fearful change."[36] Take the land office as an example. It alone did so much business that it generated two tons of official paper in 1833 which was stored in bundles "in the utmost confusion" in the attic of the Treasury building. The immense volume of government business necessitated administrative improvement if the department heads expected to have any control over the operations of their departments.

And Jackson insisted on such control.[37] He kept after his cabinet officers to institute "reform"—his word—which would improve service and eliminate corruption and waste. For example, he regularly sent a list of complaints brought to him about the "dissopation and intoxication" of personnel in the various bureaus of the departments. "The Secretary of the Treasury is charged to cause strict inquery to be made into the above," he wrote on one occasion, "and also into the habits of all the clerks in the Treasury Department, that all given to dissapation reported, that they may be dismissed from office & the Executive Dept relieved from the imputation of having men of dissopated habits in their employment."[38] The President also noted that particular individuals in the War and Post Office departments were seen at the "streets grog shops & billiard rooms" and that other clerks and their wives received books and other presents. If inquiries into these charges proved true, he said, the offenders were to be removed immediately.[39]

Jackson appreciated that his constant surveillance of the bureaucracy did not sit well with officeholders, but he considered this "an honorable testimonial for my administration." It proved his worthiness of public trust. "I have long since perceived that no administration will ever command the affection of the office Holders which seeks to extirpate abuses and which acknowledges the right of the people to reach through the election of the Chief Executive, every subordinate officer, and thus to remove all who shall have given dissatisfaction to the public."[40]

Because of Jackson's personal vigilance and insistence, all the departments underwent some form of reorganization to improve their operations. What resulted, as a consequence, was the creation of new bureaus that tightened and strengthened central control of the department by its head. These bureaus provided professional supervision of departmental operations and improved the field service. They drastically cut down the paperwork and attention to minutiae that had been the lot of cabinet officers in the past.[41]

An example of this bureaucratic growth can be seen in what happened to the State Department. Jackson had called for its reorganization, and three times, in 1833, 1834, and 1836, new bureaus were added. Under Secretary McLane a structure was established in which a chief clerk functioned as undersecretary who supervised all bureaus. There were eight such bureaus: the diplomatic bureau with three subdivisions, two for Europe and one for North and South America; the strategic (consular) bureau; a home (authenticating certificates) bureau; a bureau of archives; a bureau of pardons; copyrights and the library; a disbursing bureau; a translating bureau; and the Patent Office. Similarly, the War Department was reorganized in 1832 and 1833, as was the Navy Department, and, of course, the Post Office in 1836.[42]

Frequently these bureaus appeared from nowhere and just grew. Before long they became monstrosities, not only in size but in cost and operation, and they had to be subdivided. A case in point was the Patent Office. This office was set up by President Thomas Jefferson in 1802 within the State Department and assigned a clerk. The granting of patents was a presidential function on advice of the secretary of state and therefore the secretary's office was intended to help with the paperwork. Before long the clerk of this office started calling himself the "superintendent of patents," a title that the Congress formally recognized on April 23, 1830. The enormous number of patents requested during the 1830s (reflecting in one respect the vitality and growth of American life and institutions) could sometimes take Jackson half a day to process. So Congress passed a bill on March 3, 1836, establishing the Office of Commissioner of Patents within the State Department. The commissioner was authorized to superintend and perform all acts dealing with patents, and he was appointed by the President with the consent of the Senate. The presidential signature was no longer required on patents, and this lightened Jackson's administrative responsibilities considerably. The same thing happened with land grants. Thus, a onetime clerk was elevated to the status of commissioner and assigned a chief clerk and subordinate examiners and clerks of his own.[43] And it was only the beginning.

This natural devolutionary process played havoc with Jackson's avowed intent to reduce the size and operation of government. But there was absolutely nothing he could do about it—not without destroying the purpose of government and its needed functions. Andrew Jackson presided over the country during a time of unprecedented expansion, prosperity, and growth. The government simply kept pace with that phenomenon.

One obvious advantage of this bloated bureaucracy for Jackson was the expansion of executive patronage. That meant he could exercise better control of his administration, the government, and the party. And in turn that meant an increase in presidential power. All of which sent shivers down the spines of Whigs. On January 6, 1835, John C. Calhoun introduced a resolution into the Senate that a select committee be formed to inquire into the extent of the executive patronage, the causes of the great increase, and the expediency and practicality of its reduction. As chairman of that committee, Calhoun made a long report on February 9 and locked horns with Senator Benton in a "very sharp and spicy debate." Among other things, Calhoun revealed that 60,294 persons were employed by the executive branch of the government, and when pensioners were added to that figure a total of 100,079 individuals were directly dependent on the public treasury. In less than ten years the number employed by the executive had doubled.[44]

Surely Jackson delighted in some of the advantages that accrued to him on account of these changes. He certainly took pride in the benefits resulting from the reorganization of the departments. On account of the bureau system, reported one official, "order and system have been established. Economy in expenditures and efficiency in service" had been achieved. "And, above all, the department now knows what is done," and what is not.[45] More than that, said Jackson, the people can now reach into the government, through their President, and pluck out the subordinate officer who had proved unfaithful and unsatisfactory.[46]

It has been noted many times (and forgotten as frequently) that Jackson's presidency inaugurated an era of "creative administration." Indeed. Since the inception of the government under the Constitution there had been only two formal administrative reorganizations. Under Jackson virtually every federal department was "reformed," and the Post Office and Land Office, which employed more than three-fourths of the civilian personnel of the entire government, underwent major overhauls.

As the operation of the government expanded and changed, so did its physical appearance and arrangement. No longer did the executive office buildings—State, Treasury, War, Navy—cluster about the White House as they once did. They had scattered to new locations to find more spacious quarters to accommodate their ever burgeoning operations. The State Department moved to G Street as did the Treasury Department and the Land Office. When the Post Office building went up in flames in December, 1836, a new location was found on 14th Street. Suddenly, like the country at large, the capital had expanded in every direction. It provided mute but visible testimony that a new and modern age had begun.

With all this growth and change in Washington there was one enormous benefit that surpassed all others: the democratization of the institution of government. Through the expansion of employment, a large work force was introduced into government service, and under Jackson that employment opened up to citizens of every class and section of the country. Running the government was now something in which all Americans could participate. It was not reserved for an elite. Jackson's principle of rotation in order to promote popular government was really achieved through this natural process of growth rather than a system of removals and replacements.

It has been argued by one modern historian that Jackson's appointees, in terms of their social, economic, and education backgrounds, were not much different from those of his predecessors. Thus, government service was not really opened to the masses but rather remained with the same class of bureaucrat that had always controlled it.[47] Even if this argument is true, it must be remembered that the perception of Americans at the time was quite different. They believed a democratizing process had occurred. As tens of thousands of new faces joined the government service, Whigs naturally assumed that a massive execution of incumbent officeholders had taken place and that their positions had been filled by political hacks and mindless partisans. "A Reign of Terror" had been instituted, they wailed, and Jackson's "spoils system" (as they called his rotation policy) introduced the riffraff of society into the operation of government. Public service had been debased. "The government, formally served by the *elite* of the nation," complained one man, "is now served, to a very considerable extent, by its refuse."[48]

The very fact that Jackson's policy became widely known and accepted as a "spoils system" reinforced the perception that the "elite" had been replaced by the "masses." This perception in turn convinced Americans that Jackson had firmly (and everlastingly) established the principle that government service was open to all, not just the few. The protracted debate over rotation publicized and popularized Jackson's contention that "no one man has any more intrinsic right to official station than another." Henceforth, government office would be open to all; and the argument over the wisdom of that principle only added to the general climate of democracy that characterized Jackson's administration.[49]

It was the establishment of the principle—rather than the actual type of individual appointed—that ultimately advanced the democratic process. By throwing open government service to all citizens (whether or not Jackson actually did choose his appointees from the same class as his predecessors), he brought "endless sources of vitality" to the "body administrative" from the "body politic," according to another historian.[50] Thereafter, the relationship between the people and their governmental operation was never again seen as a process best left in the hands of the rich, powerful, and wellborn—even when the rich, powerful, and wellborn were actually appointed, as they continue to be to this day.

The establishment by Jackson of the principle that government service is open to all was unquestionably the most important result of his efforts to "reform" the Washington bureaucracy. It constituted an important milestone in achieving self-government for the American people. It further strengthened the bulwark of freedom.

This sensitive oil of Jackson in profile was possibly painted from life by Matthew Harris Jouett, a Kentucky artist. *Ladies' Hermitage Association.*

Refusing to wear his dentures, Jackson sat for this minature portrait by Samuel M. Charles in 1835. *White House Collection.*

Bloated, grumpy, formally attired, and propped against a pillow, Jackson posed for this daguerreotype on April 15, 1845, just weeks before his death. *Library of Congress.*

"City of Washington, from Beyond the Navy Yard, 1833" by George Cooke is presently hanging in the Oval Office of the White House. *White House Collection.*

Jackson's "Grand Fantastical Tour" of 1833 as drawn by Hassan Straight-shanks "under the immediate superintendence of Maj. Jack Downing." *Library of Congress.*

Sarah Yorke Jackson proved a great consolation to Jackson during his final years and together they joined the Presbyterian Church. *Library of Congress.*

Andrew Jackson, Jr., had one interest in life, as this picture indicates, and it ultimately killed him. The portrait is attributed to Ralph E. W. Earl. *Ladies' Hermitage Association.*

The "Great Father" and his Indian "children." On the wall can be seen a picture of Columbia standing triumphant over the prostrate form of Great Britain. *William L. Clements Library.*

The bombastic, tumultuous "Old Bullion," Senator Thomas Hart Benton of Missouri, Jackson's ablest and most vocal supporter in Congress. *Library of Congress.*

The elegant and aristocratic Nicholas Biddle, "Czar Nick" as the Jacksonians liked to call him, as drawn by J. B. Longacre about the time that his bank came under presidential attack. *National Portrait Gallery, Smithsonian Institution.*

This sketch of the first attempt upon the life of a President was supposedly drawn by an eyewitness. *Library of Congress.*

Roger B. Taney. With the exception of Van Buren's election to the presidency, nothing gave Jackson greater pleasure than raising Taney to the position of Chief Justice of the United States. *Library of Congress.*

The learned and fastidiously dressed Edward Livingston, whom his friends and admirers called "Beau Ned." *Library of Congress.*

John Forsyth was the last and least competent of four secretaries of state during Jackson's administration. *Library of Congress.*

Louis McLane never learned the art of serving Jackson's needs in the cabinet and consequently his political career came to an abrupt end. *Library of Congress.*

Levi Woodbury, one of Jackson's more capable and industrious appointees to the cabinet. *Library of Congress.*

Benjamin F. Butler astounded Jackson by the speed with which he took control of the attorney general's office and mastered its duties and responsibilities. *Library of Congress.*

Henry Clay, whom Jackson called "that roaming, lying demagogue," among other things, is regarded by many as the greatest senator in American history. *Architect of the Capitol.*

CHAPTER 17

A Question of Freedom

AN OLD WOMAN FEARED THE DEMOCRACY was headed for destruction and damnation. Her woeful cries finally drove her granddaughter into writing the President and conveying her deep sense of apprehension and anxiety. "The late arrival of catholicks to our peaceful and happy land" was the cause of her forebodings. And a rumor alleged that Andrew Jackson was himself at "heart a Roman," that he intended establishing "an *Inquisition* in the United States," and that together "with the blood thirsty priest" he would drench his "native land with the blood" of his countrymen. Oh, say this is all a dreadful lie, the granddaughter pleaded in her letter, and spare an old woman the miseries of "these poignant fears."[1]

Jackson's response was gentle. He was not in the habit of responding to such letters, he said, but in order to give the old grandmother some "peace of the mind" he offered her a statement of his religious faith.

> I was brought up a rigid Presbeterian, to which I have always adhered. Our excellent constitution guarantees to every one freedom of religion, and charity tells us, and you know Charity is the reall basis of *all true religion,* and charity says judge the tree by its fruit. all who profess christianity, believe in a Saviour and that by and through him we must be saved. We ought therefore to consider all good christians, whose walks correspond with their professions, be him Presbeterian, Episcopalian, Baptist, methodist or Roman catholic. let it be always remembered by your Grandmother that no established religion can exist under our glorious constitution.[2]

Thoughts about religion periodically reminded Jackson of his pledge to Rachel to join the church once he left office and could not be charged with playing politics. As soon as his term in office ended and he retired

251

to the Hermitage he vowed to profess his faith in a formal declaration of commitment. But before he could retire the matter of the presidential succession must be resolved, and that necessitated the convocation of the Democratic party at a national convention and the formal nomination of a candidate.

Not that Jackson doubted who that candidate would be. Martin Van Buren had long ago won his support and allegiance, and if the President of the United States had anything to say about it, the next President would be the Little Magician himself. But already there were forces at work to block that succession, forces that expressed not only their dislike of Van Buren personally but their resentment and anger at what Jackson had done to the country and the principles and ideals he had engrafted upon the Democratic party.

His "revolution" infuriated some men. Despite Jackson's commitment to republicanism and states' rights, he had done more than any previous President to strengthen the central government, especially the executive branch. He advanced the doctrine of direct representation of all the people by the President. He sought to provide executive leadership of Congress, to control the Treasury, and to determine legislation by a judicious use of the veto. Whigs—and some Democrats as well—detested these things. They feared the drift of the nation under his leadership toward a popular democracy. And they positively abhorred his policies on the Bank, tariff, and internal improvements, as well as his handling of the French indemnity claim. The thought of these policies and practices continuing under the presidency of a hand-picked successor quickened their determination to do something to prevent it. "The agitating questions which have for the last two years given so much bitterness to the disenssion in Congress," reported Major Donelson, "are now displayed with all their force upon the Presidential canvass."[3]

The dissatisfaction, especially within his own party, proved stronger and wider than Jackson ever anticipated. He regarded Democratic opposition to Van Buren's elevation as nothing more than a combination of nullifiers and Bank men who hoped to disrupt the party and ensure the election of Henry Clay. As usual, he sniffed out a conspiracy, one hatched by Clay for his own benefit, and directed by John C. Calhoun, John Bell, and other dissidents. To his shock and surprise he soon learned that a number of old friends also verged on open revolt and would not submit to a rubber-stamped candidate.

The rebellion flared first in Jackson's own home state and it was led by "John Bell, Davy Crockett and Company." They prevailed on Judge Hugh Lawson White to seek the presidency in open defiance of Jackson's expressed wish. Bell's purpose, according to Old Hickory, was "that he might secure his re-election to the speakers chair, and recharter the U. States Bank."[4] He is "a very ambitious gentleman," said David Campbell.[5] As for Crockett, there was no way to account for the antics of that strange loon. Bell and Crockett reportedly first approached Richard Johnson of Kentucky, but when he rejected their advances they turned to White.[6] Because he had become increasingly disenchanted with the President's policies and cordially and actively disliked Van Buren personally, Judge White succumbed to Bell's seductive appeal. Accordingly, a majority of the Tennessee congressional delegation in the House of Representatives held a meeting in December, 1834, and nominated White for President. They rejected Van Buren in part because of his supposedly "malevolent" influence on Jackson, but in greater part because of Van Buren's connection with Lewis and Eaton, who were opposed by the Carroll faction in Tennessee, which had engineered Eaton's defeat for the Senate in 1833.[7]

Jackson was mortified by this development. That Judge White, an esteemed and valued friend, would league himself with such malcontents to bring discredit on his leadership and administration deeply offended the old warrior. The very fact that it was done "in opposition to a national convention" showed how underhanded, conspiratorial, and antidemocratic it was. "You will find from information every where that the opposition, and particularly the nullifiers, are taking him up," the President wrote to Alfred Balch, one of Van Buren's oldest supporters in Tennessee, "and Mr. Bell and Co. are more intimate with Duff Green and the nullifiers than with the friends of the administration." He likened them to Aaron Burr and said they would soon be denounced as "Traitors to the Democratic republican cause." Their object is "to destroy this administration" and "build up a colossal monied power to corrupt and over shadow the government." All the "opponents of popular rights," he said, are invited to support White in order to " *'destroy the landmarks of party.'* This suits precisely the views of the ever vigilant enemies of the cause of Republicanism." They conspire against me, he ranted, but all I have ever tried to do was preserve the identity of the Republican party as embodied in Jeffersonian principles based on the rights of the people and the states. "I have labored to reconstruct the great Party and bring the popular power to bear with full influence upon the Government," to maintain "democratic strength unbroken" and to "perpetuate" the power of the people.[8]

Bring popular power to bear upon the government! That was Jackson's great object as President. He genuinely strove to advance the course of democracy in America. And he believed the Whigs would deprive the people of the right to elect their President if at all possible. They therefore encouraged White's nomination to strip Van Buren of southern support and thereby throw the election to the House of Representatives, where Clay would be chosen President. "The idea that he [White] is popular in the south," wrote Major Donelson, ". . . was well suited to the taste of Whigs and Nullifiers."[9]

White's "betrayal" gnawed at the President throughout the winter. It "is a mortification to me," he kept muttering. Did White not realize that this conspiracy was designed "to destroy me, and all the effects of my administration, and hand me down to posterity as an old dotard, ruled by corrupt office holders, and corrupt office seekers." He was so distraught that he even spoke to White's new wife and urged her to inform her husband that "he had got into a false position, & if he did not snatch himself from it, he was politically lost."[10]

Apparently Jackson was correct in arguing that Clay plotted to encourage as many candidates as possible and thereby send the election to the House of Representatives. "I concur with Mr Clay," wrote Senator Benjamin W. Leigh of Virginia, "that in the actual state of things, it is as well, and perhaps better, that there should be as many competitors in the field against Mr Van Buren as can be brought out with a hope of getting a single state—tho the actual state of things I deplore as desperately evil."[11] *"Divide and conquer,"* cried Jackson, that is the Whig strategy, and once again they would deprive the people of their right to choose their President and hand it over to corrupt politicians in the House of Representatives. "Remember this prediction," he warned, "and look out for apostates in Tennessee."[12]

Jackson also plotted. He liked to pretend that he had not attempted in any way to control or influence the presidential choice of the Democratic party. He believed that the selection belonged solely to the national nominating convention. But he also believed that the convention would —indeed, it must—nominate Van Buren. No other choice was acceptable. And now, with the endorsement of the "apostate" White by "professed former friends," it had become necessary to head off other possible nominations by calling a national convention as soon as possible. In fact, immediately.

Moreover, the Whigs gave every indication that they would not (some said "could" not) hold a convention. For one thing, their strategy called for a House decision and that could best be achieved by encouraging the states to put forward many candidates, both Democrat and Whig. For another, they feared a free-for-all between Clay, Calhoun, and Webster at a convention that would tear the party to bits. "We are commencing a singular schism," laughed Churchill C. Cambreleng, "—the prostrated condition of the opposition— . . . they must now I think divide—Clay and Calhoun will try and keep together and Webster will probably hang himself on his own hook—They are talking of Judge White or of any body against Van Buren but its idle work—the battle has been fought and won, thanks to the able tactics of the triumvirate."[13]

As predicted, no convention of Whigs was held. They "cannot agree upon any one man," declared Joel Poinsett. Possible candidates were left to their own devices in seeking nomination. Naturally the party reverted to the stand-by tactic of allowing different states to propose favorite sons. In due course the Whigs in Massachusetts put forward Daniel Webster at the same time that Alabama announced her support for Judge White. Clay, however, dropped out of the contest when Ohio rejected him in favor of a favorite son, Justice John McLean. Without strong western support, Clay recognized the hopelessness of his cause.

As events subsequently revealed, the principal Whig candidate turned out to be General William Henry Harrison of Ohio, nicknamed "Old Tippecanoe" because of his victory over the Indians in 1811, who was expected to win western votes (especially after McLean withdrew from the race) and the support of those who preferred military heroes as presidential candidates. What remained of the old Anti-Masonic party also swung behind Harrison. Jackson gave a loud snort to "Tip's" nomination. He dubbed him, "Clay's stool pidgeon."[14]

The Democrats convened in Baltimore on May 20, 1835. Jackson predicted that it would be "filled by high talents and more than ever attended any previous convention." Since there had only been one previous Democratic convention, that prediction was not hard to make. And, indeed, the showing was impressive. More than six hundred delegates showed up from all the states but Alabama, South Carolina, Tennessee, and Illinois. "I am amazed at the prodigious turnout of Democratic Volunteers assembled here," wrote Blair (who was covering the convention for Jackson and the *Globe*) to the President. "If you had sounded your trumpet to put down Nullification, more enthusiasm would not have been inspired than I now see manifested to put down the machinaticns of the *blue* and *white* whigs."[15] Jackson was humiliated that there would be no representation from Tennessee. "My heart bleeds," he told Blair, "to think that my native & adopted states are the only ones unrepresented."[16] Eventually an obscure Tennessean, Edmund Rucker, who happened to be in Baltimore at the time, was corralled into attending the convention as a delegate and he delivered Tennessee's entire slate of 15 votes to Van Buren. It was an exceedingly stupid thing to do, for it provided the opposition press with ammunition to taunt Democrats over their "Ruckerized Office-Holder's Convention."[17]

The delegates assembled at ten o'clock at the Fourth Presbyterian Church in Baltimore and selected Andrew Stevenson of Virginia (recently rejected by the Senate as minister to Great Britain) as permanent chairman. He urged the crowd in his speech on assuming the chair to choose a candidate who would carry out the principles and reforms of the Jackson administration.[18] After two days of organizing themselves and writing resolutions, the members unanimously nominated Jackson's choice, Martin Van Buren, as their candidate for President.[19] When the result was announced the delegates broke into "loud and enthusiastic" cheering that continued for some time. The only problem that worried the managers of the convention at first was the split in the Pennsylvania delegation, representing the rivalry between the Wolf and Muhlenberg factions. Happily, both sets of rival delegates voted for Van Buren.[20]

The selection of Vice President, however, did not go as well. Since Van Buren headed the ticket it was obvious that the second place would have to go to someone from the west or the south. The south wanted William C. Rives of Virginia, but the west preferred Richard M. Johnson of Kentucky. Indeed, there had been talk that the west would even try to push Johnson for the presidency. "I hope the West will not insist upon their Richard," worried Joel Poinsett, "Col Johnson may be an excellent man and a brave indian warriour, yet I do not enjoy thoughts of his being the chief of this great nation."[21] Supposedly Johnson had killed the Indian chief Tecumseh during the War of 1812, but that did not concern the delegates as much as Johnson's open "association" with a mulatto mistress. "The idea of voting for him is loathed beyond anything that has occurred with us," Jackson learned from a Tennessee friend. "I pray you to assure our friends that the humblest of us do not believe that a lucky random shot, even if it did hit Tecumseh, qualifies a man for Vice President."[22] But Jackson did not react to these warnings. He was gratified that another westerner would find favor with the party, and since Johnson came from Kentucky and had strong western backing the General offered no complaint.

The convention in Baltimore went on to nominate Johnson over Rives by a vote of 178 to 87. Johnson's count barely reached the required two-thirds vote needed for nomination. What made the difference was the 15 Tennessee votes provided by Rucker. Virginia was scandalized. Just before the voting began, John Mason of Virginia rose to announce that his state could not support any one who could not "maintain and carry out the political principles" that Virginia held sacred.[23] When Johnson received the nomination in spite of this threat, the Virginia Democrats declared that they had no confidence in Johnson's principles or character and therefore would not support him.[24]

The convention adjourned at 9 P.M., Friday evening May 22, after selecting a committee to write an address to the electorate. What finally resulted, according to a recent historian, was a long statement "similar to the platform of a modern convention, setting forth Democratic principles, past accomplishments, and future policies."[25] The committee issued the address on July 31. It emphasized Jackson's oft-repeated contention that the Whigs were intent upon a policy of "divide and conquer" to subvert the popular will, just as in 1825. And this election was "one of the most important that had ever occurred in our country," since it involved not only the fate of the party and republicanism, "but the continuation of that wise course of national policy pursued by Gen. Jackson, and upon which his administration has been based." The statement specifically cited those measures relating to foreign affairs, the tariff, internal improvements, and the Bank of the United States. Then it trumpeted the virtue and patriotism of the party's leader, Andrew Jackson.

There is not a liberal or candid man who does not and ought not to feel proud and exalted, at the spectacle which his country now presents, both at home and abroad. When was it ever more, if indeed so prosperous? When was public or private credit more stable? Prices so high? The People so happy? When did it ever progress so rapid in wealth, in arts, and useful knowledge, and public spirit, or national character? When so erect among the nations of the earth? Never. Have we not then a right to say, that these are the blessings of a President and Republican administration? These are the generous triumphs of Democracy? And what else but the union of the Republican Party and confidence in the virtue and patriotism of Andrew Jackson, the Chief Magistrate of the People's choice, could have done this? And when the political and ambitious men of his day, who have assailed and calumniated him shall be mingled in the dust, with the thousands whose examples they have imitated; when no record shall be found of their memories, or any recollections of their services, this Patriot will be the admiration of every American, and the highest example of political virtue.[26]

It was wise to confine the address to Jackson's character and achievements, for in them the committee could expect to command an enthusiastic public response. It was in the growth of American democracy under Andrew Jackson that the electorate recognized the ever unfolding success of their experiment in freedom. His achievements, his character, and his commitment to liberty and democracy comprised the guarantees for the nation's continued progress and happiness. The statement was little more than an evocation of praise for the name and works of Andrew Jackson.

Old Hickory himself greatly admired this statement of principles and accomplishments not only because it heeded his warning about the Whig strategy to throw the election into the House where the will of the people could be subverted, but also because of its generous acknowledgment of his continuing battle for the rights of the people against the greed and avarice of ambitious demagogues.[27]

Once the convention nominated Van Buren as his successor, Jackson breathed a deep sigh of relief, even though a long campaign lay ahead before the electorate would register its will. But Jackson always had confidence in the public, in their virtue and in their ability to sense the right political course to follow. The sole danger arose from "apostates" whose "conspiracies" menaced freedom and jeopardized popular suffrage. He only hoped that the worst danger lay behind them now that the Democratic party had officially named its presidential candidate.

On Monday, July 6, Jackson decided to flee the heat and oppression of Washington and escape "for retirement and ease" to the Rip Raps, his favorite vacation spot.[28] With him he took Emily Donelson and her children, his son and family, Ralph Earl and, for the last ten days, Major Donelson, along with six servants. He decided against returning to the Hermitage since the house was still undergoing repair. Major Lewis, who returned to Tennessee in the spring, reported favorably on the progress of the rebuilding. The foundation was in excellent condition, he said, and the walls "perfectly sound." New windows had been installed and they were "of very pretty size and proportion and will look much better than the old ones." The roof had just gone up and with any luck the house should be ready for occupancy in the fall. There was nothing Jackson himself could do to advance the work and so he was urged to try and get some rest and relaxation at the Rip Raps.[29]

The President did try to relax. But in vain. "Business and company follow me every where," he complained. His excruciating headaches never let up, even out of the White House. In addition, he had swollen feet, a pain in his side, a hacking cough, and his eyeglasses needed adjustment. The strain and pressure of his duties aggravated his weakened condition and instead of diminishing at the Rip Raps, as expected, they suddenly worsened. For, without warning, he was abruptly alerted to a situation that portended something truly frightening and dangerous. Amos Kendall notified him of the circumstances shortly after he had arrived at the Rip Raps. It seemed that civil disorder had broken out once again in South Carolina.[30]

On July 29, 1835, a steamboat entered Charleston Harbor carrying a cargo of mail which was duly delivered to the city's postmaster, Alfred Huger. As he supervised the sorting of this mail, Huger discovered thousands of antislavery tracts addressed to the city's most prominent citizens. The American Anti-Slavery Society, founded in Philadelphia in 1833 by Lewis and Arthur Tappan, William Lloyd Garrison, and Theodore Dwight Weld, among others, had begun an intensive propaganda campaign to convince the nation (and southerners in particular) that slavery was an abomination and should be terminated immediately.[31] The society marked the beginning of a momentous reform movement that would vastly overshadow in importance (as well as obscure) all of Jackson's mighty efforts at reform.

Huger was dumbfounded by what he saw—and quite at a loss as to what he should do. So he wrote an express letter to the postmaster general in Washington and requested instructions. Meanwhile he planned to keep the material safely locked away. Unfortunately, word of its presence quickly spread through Charleston and by evening an angry mob, numbering over three hundred, formed in the streets and started to march upon the post office. But along the way they were met by the city guard and persuaded to return to their homes. A few of them, however, waited in the dark for several hours and then broke into the post office and seized the abolitionist tracts. The next evening, July 30, 1835, amid wild scenes of rejoicing, a bonfire on the Charleston parade grounds consumed the "incendiary" material, fed also by effigies of Garrison, the Tappans, Weld, and other abolitionists. Although it was an act of public disorder, several leading South Carolinians declared the action necessary to prevent such dangerous propaganda from freely circulating "in a community full of uneasy planters and restless slaves."[32]

The situation worsened when a committee of five was formed, headed by former Governor Robert Y. Hayne, to inspect all incoming mail steamers in cooperation with Huger, and to burn any materials the committee found objectionable. An illegal elite, appointed by a mob, now ruled a terrorized city.[33] And they presumed the right to censor the mail.

Kendall responded immediately to Huger's urgent letter. He said that the inflammatory materials should be intercepted but he wanted it done "with as little noise and difficulty as possible." He was genuinely afraid of creating a larger incident over the matter, and so he decided that the best course of action was to give no instructions at all but to allow each postmaster individually to act on his own. He told Huger that after a careful examination of the law, "I am satisfied that the postmaster general has no legal authority to exclude newspapers from the mail, nor prohibit their carriage or delivery on account of their character or tendency." But, he continued, "I am not prepared to direct you" to deliver the tracts. The post offices exist to serve the people in all the states and are not to be used "as the instrument of their *destruction.*" Although he had not seen the material himself, Kendall said he was prepared to believe Huger's description that they were in character "the most inflammatory and incendiary—and insurrectionary in the highest degree." Never knowingly, therefore, would he aid in the circulation of such tracts. "We owe an obligation to the laws, but a higher one to the communities in which we live." If the laws be perverted to destroy the communities, then, he said, "patriotism" dictates that we disregard the laws.

So Kendall threw the decision back at Huger: "I cannot sanction, and will not condemn" what you have done. You must evaluate the character of the tracts and then decide yourself what is best.[34]

Before anything else, Kendall feared the political consequences of his act. That gave him pause. Since a presidential election was approaching and the Democrats had already named their candidate, he did not want to jeopardize it by a move that could trigger a major domestic squabble. Besides, his own confirmation as postmaster general awaited the return of Congress in December. And there was always the fear, given the temper of South Carolina and the temperaments of its leading politicians, that the specter of nullification would be raised again. Who knew what bloody consequence might then ensue?

Even so, the incident involved a question of freedom, the right of individuals under the Bill of Rights to free speech and a free press. And that question demanded appropriate attention by the administration.

Kendall wrote immediately to Jackson at the Rip Raps for direction. He enclosed copies of his correspondence with Huger and admitted that his response had been dictated by his desire to avoid creating a clamor. He added that he had given orders to the Washington postmaster not to deliver such tracts "except to such persons as claim them as actual sub-scribers. I think these steps carried out will pacify the South."[35]

Jackson replied by return mail. He expressed his sorrow and regret that such men live in this country "as to be guilty of the attempt to stir up amongst the South the horrors of a servile war." If they could be reached, he said, they ought to be made to atone for their wicked deed with their lives. But, he allowed, "we are the instruments of, and executors of the law; we have no power to prohibit anything from being transported in the mail that is authorized by law." The only thing that can be done, he continued, is to deny delivery to anyone except those who really sub-scribe to them, just as Kendall had directed in Washington. Once the subscribers are known, they will be shunned by "every moral and good citizen" in the community and this will shrivel circulation and settle the problem. Obviously Jackson believed that all right-minded citizens would condemn abolitionist propaganda because it fomented slave uprisings.[36]

Jackson deeply regretted the attack on the Charleston post office nonetheless, and particularly the seizure by force of the abolitionist tracts. Defiance of law always provoked him. And it was becoming fright-eningly prevalent during the 1830s, another sign of the disturbing changes occurring throughout the United States. "This spirit of mob-law is becoming too common and must be checked," he declared, "or ere long it will become as great an evil as a servile war." And the instigators of such violence must be punished, "or we will soon have no safety under our happy Government and laws."[37]

Thus the President admitted that neither he nor the postmaster general had the right to interfere with the delivery of mail authorized by law. Therefore, until Congress reconvened and could pass appropriate legis-lation to outlaw the delivery of abolitionist tracts to protect public safety, "we can do nothing more than direct that those inflamatory papers be delivered to none but who will demand them as subscribers." And in each instance, Jackson said, the names of these subscribers should be taken down and "exposed thro the publik journals as subscribers to the wicked plan of exciting the negroes to insurrection and massacre."[38]

Jackson's position placed him between the two extremes created by the event since he disapproved using the mails to distribute inflammatory materials to foment civil strife and abhorred the method taken by the Charleston mob to prevent distribution. He thought public pressure could intimidate subscribers until such time as Congress altered the law to authorize postmasters to confiscate the material. It was always clear in Jackson's mind that Congress had the authority to act to preserve public order and that only federal authorities could "dispose" of the mail.

But Jackson's position raised any number of problems. Who should decide what constituted "inflammatory" materials? What role should the states play? Surely what South Carolina regarded as inflammatory could be vastly different from what New York might find objectionable. In the matter of slavery, for example, did it not make sense to allow the state some voice in determining what might lead to mob violence among her own citizens? Furthermore, did the senders of the tracts have the right to send their propaganda to whomever they pleased? And what about the right of southerners to be spared the offense of receiving this objectionable material? Also, did subscribers have the right to keep their identity secret since the publication of their names might place their lives in jeopardy? And on and on.

For Jackson, the matter was simple and the solution obvious. The law must be obeyed until such time as it is changed. Kendall, on the other hand, appealed to a "higher" law and used it as a basis for giving postmasters virtual freedom in deciding upon a course of action. In any event, his hands-off policy calmed the hotheads in Charleston and undoubtedly prevented an even greater crisis. Throughout the summer and fall a number of southern communities passed resolutions forbidding the distribution of abolitionist tracts and in some places vigilante committees were formed to make sure these resolutions were respected.[39] Kendall chose not to interfere and finally established the policy, as stated in his 1835 annual report of his department, that postmasters should obey any state laws forbidding the circulation of incendiary printed materials. Jackson did not approve this policy—namely, allowing the state to determine the execution of federal law—but he chose not to interfere with the administration of the Post Office Department. Instead he went to Congress.

In his seventh annual State of the Union address, delivered on December 7, 1835, the President called on Congress to enact legislation which "will prohibit, under severe penalties, the circulation in the Southern States, through the mail, of incendiary publications intended to instigate the slaves to insurrection."[40] But John C. Calhoun and other nullifiers in Congress objected to Jackson's approach. They wanted a law that forbade delivery of abolitionist tracts in any state or territory where local law forbade such material. In effect, the controlling hand in the matter of delivery would be local. This Jackson would never allow. So neither position became law. Instead, the Post Office Act of July 2, 1836, forbade postmasters from detaining the delivery of mail. Unfortunately, southerners regularly violated this law and chose to believe that federal authority over mail ceased at the reception point.[41]

Jackson's attitude and response to this incident have been unfairly criticized. For one thing he has been charged with calling abolitionist tracts "unconstitutional and wicked."[42] He did no such thing. He called the attempt to foment insurrection and servile war "unconstitutional and wicked." Moreover, Jackson's position was correct as far as it went: the law must be obeyed. If the law is wrong it must be changed through due process; but no mob, and certainly no state authority, can change federal law. Where Jackson can be severely faulted is in his failure to enforce the law after its passage on July 2, 1836,* and in his lack of precision in pinpointing which federal authority decides the "incendiary" character of abolitionist propaganda, and then providing for an appeal. As William Leggett, editor of the New York *Evening Post,* declared: "If the government once begins to discriminate as to what is orthodox and what heterodox in opinion, what is safe and what unsafe in tendency, farewell, a long farewell to our freedom." And, as a future attorney general later decided in 1857, a postmaster may refuse to deliver mail of an incendiary character but it is up to the courts to decide what is and what is not incendiary.[43]

Jackson did not provide strong leadership in this matter. He let it drift out of any legal (and federal) control. He did so because he feared provoking civil strife at a time when the French question still boiled. And he was also concerned about Kendall's confirmation. He was enough of a politician to sense the need to leave the question alone and go along with Kendall's easy solution.

Furthermore, like most Americans in the early nineteenth century, Jackson lacked any deep and abiding sense of civil rights. With all his concern for freedom and the need to defend the individual against arbitrary government, he could not advance beyond the limitations of his age and grapple with the larger question of personal civil rights at the heart of this problem. Nor was he disposed to leave the matter to the courts for decision. Jackson had a low opinion of judicial review, given the decisions rendered in the Bank and Indian cases. Since he had no ready solution himself, and worried over the dangerous consequences of another confrontation with South Carolina, he chose to leave the matter to whatever compromise his postmaster general could work out.

In effect, then, the government preserved the right of abolitionists to distribute their tracts through the mails. In so doing it reaffirmed the principle of free access to the mails uncensored by the government. But by turning its head and pretending not to notice, the government also permitted local postmasters to stop the mail to oblige the laws of southern states. Jackson did not command Kendall to pay attention to these violations, for, unlike the nullification crisis of 1832–1833 when South Carolina flagrantly defied the established law of the land, the incident in 1835 did not involve a specific law. It involved jurisdiction, about which there was conflicting interpretation.

But it also involved freedom of the mail, which supposedly Jackson was trying to protect; and it involved the right of the individual to protect himself against a government telling him what he could or could not read or subscribe to. For Jackson to force delivery of the mail every time it was stopped in the south was certain to provoke conflict without settling the essential question of freedom. Obviously the answer to the problem had to be found in the courts, but neither the President nor the Congress was

---

*It should be pointed out that Jackson's term in office ended on March 4, 1837, a little over six months after this law was enacted.

willing to take that route. Jackson should have guaranteed the delivery of the mail without any interference from the states—and stood firm on it. That was in fact his position. But he would not enforce it. And he would not enforce it because he was not ready to apply to the courts when the question about the character of the pamphlets came into question. His reluctance was typical of most Americans at the time. Application for judicial decision of political and private rights—even when involving conflicting interpretation—was not accepted procedure in the early nineteenth century. That developed only in time and after many crises and controversies, including Civil War.

Jackson's instincts were good. He knew what should be done, but he could not see how enforcement was possible without inciting a confrontation that could lead to bloody conflict. With the spoliations question still pending and with the French currently strengthening their military posture in the West Indies to blockade the southern coast in case of hostilities with the United States,[44] Jackson chose to pursue a prudent course at home and thereby avoid division and discord. Once again he showed how cautious he could be when circumstances dictated. Once again he indicated a willingness to overlook provocations from quarrelsome states when a larger danger to the country threatened. Once again he demonstrated the dimensions (and limitations) of his statesmanship.

CHAPTER 18

"The Republic Has Degenerated into a Democracy"

THE U.S.S. CONSTITUTION SAILED INTO NEW YORK HARBOR on Tuesday, June 23, 1835, and was welcomed by a cheering crowd who had come to the wharf to greet the retiring minister to France, Edward Livingston. Their happy cries brought a great sense of relief to Livingston. His fears that he might somehow be blamed for the disaster in France immediately vanished. The crowd noisily followed him to his lodgings in the city and massed around City Hall at the public reception given in his honor. Ten days later at a Fourth of July dinner, Livingston gave an intensely patriotic speech, at the conclusion of which the audience shouted in unison, "No apology!" "No explanations!" and "Hurrah for Jackson!"[1]

Livingston explained to the press that his return should not be misinterpreted as an "evil omen." Rather he felt that the President needed to know his views more fully about the situation and that a personal interview was the only satisfactory way to do it. The press almost universally praised him for his diplomatic efforts, particularly after his last letter to Broglie of April 25 was published in the newspapers.[2] They called it an extraordinarily able state paper. "Thank you, thank you, my dear Sir, a thousand times for your valedictory letter to the Duke de Broglie," wrote George Dallas to Livingston. "There are parts of it which will be immortal in the diplomacy of America:—the whole of it, in argument, style, and patriotism, is admirable. If you had done nothing for your country abroad but the penning of this single epistle, I should say that you had done enough for fame and for universal affection."[3]

In accounting for his actions abroad, Livingston prepared two reports: one for Forsyth dated June 21, and the other to Jackson. In the report to Forsyth he explained that he left France "in order to show more

264

decidedly the serious light in which this condition would be considered in the United States." And in his letter to Jackson, he said he was extremely anxious to know that he had the President's approval for his conduct, especially his decision to come home.[4]

Livingston wasted no time in getting to the White House. Old friends were disappointed in not having an opportunity to see him as he flashed down the East Coast. On June 26, only three days after his arrival in New York, he stood before Jackson and received the approbation he so desperately needed to hear. Indeed, the President was unusually effusive, and Livingston later thanked him again for his "kind and affectionate reception."[5]

Livingston formally resigned his post on June 29. He felt he had completed his mission and that his "services can no longer be useful to my country." Forsyth accepted it but said that the President could not let him go without an expression of his "regard and respect, the result of many years of intimate association in peace and war." Although there had been differences "on some points of general policy" between Livingston and the administration, Forsyth noted, the President had always valued his minister's "singleness of purpose, perfect integrity, and devotion to your country." It was an appropriate but not an overly flattering letter, and George Dallas felt it inadequate to Livingston's outstanding diplomatic efforts. "I only wish that I had been the writer of the letter in reply to your resignation," he wrote: "it does not meet the case." If the letter was indeed less fulsome in praise than expected, perhaps it reflected the administration's disappointment that the indemnity still remained unpaid.[6]

On the basis of Livingston's report to the secretary and the President, new instructions were prepared for Thomas Barton, the chargé in Paris. He was told to remain at his post but not to take any action. The President had authorized the Rothschilds to receive the indemnity, should it be forthcoming, and would so inform the French government without demanding its payment. "For yourself," the instruction read, "you will, if the bill of indemnity is rejected, follow Mr. Livingston to the United States." If the money was made conditional, he was to await further orders but maintain "a guarded silence."[7]

Once these new instructions had been dispatched to Barton, the President went off on vacation to the Rip Raps. Jackson felt that the next move belonged to the French. Everything was in place to receive payment; if it was refused then he would take further action. "The French matter only remains," he wrote Kendall, after disposing of several items of business with him, "and if she does not pay the debt before next Congress, I will then speak to Congress the language of a true American and of truth, and show that from her equivocation and dishonorable subterfuge, all intercourse ought to be closed with her until she complies with her Treaty; and recommend Letters of Mark and reprisol until the debt is made.

Think on this and let me have your views." Then he added: "Still I am of the opinion that France will pay the money without apology or explanation; from *me she will get neither.*"[8]

While on vacation Jackson received word that the chief justice, John Marshall, had died on July 6, 1835, after serving on the high court for thirty-five years. It meant that Jackson would have a real opportunity to shape and influence the Supreme Court just as decisively as he had the other two branches of government. He had already added several men to the court, none of whom were distinguished. His first appointment was John McLean at the very outset of his administration. The position originally had been slated for William T. Barry, but after Barry agreed to take the post office, the seat went to McLean.[9] Then Justice Bushrod Washington died in 1829, after serving thirty-two years, and Jackson replaced him with Henry Baldwin of Pennsylvania. Baldwin was a longtime friend and a popular congressman who had helped bring Pennsylvania into the Jackson camp. The Senate overwhelmingly approved the choice on January 6, 1830, by a vote of 41 to 2.[10]

The seven-man Supreme Court remained relatively stable for the next five years. Then Justice Wayne Johnson of South Carolina died and was replaced by James M. Wayne of Georgia, who was confirmed by the Senate early in 1835. By this time Jackson was having increasing difficulty in getting his nominations through the Senate, especially when the triumvirate of Clay, Webster, and Calhoun took after him and raised serious objections to his choices. His nominations for the Treasury and the Court of St. James's (Taney and Stevenson) were both turned down.

The resignation of Justice Gabriel Duval of Maryland set the stage for yet another confrontation between the President and the Senate. Since Duval came from Maryland and since Jackson was very anxious to reward Taney for his loyalty and past services, the President decided to nominate him to replace Duval. He did so on January 15, 1835. The Senate waited to the last day of their short session—which ended on March 3—to take any action. It was the same day that Jackson awaited Senate action on the fortification bill. So great was his expectation that he sat in an antechamber in the Capitol until 1 A.M., Wednesday morning, March 4, signing bills as they were hurried to him. At length the Senate refused to pass the fortification bill and postponed Taney's confirmation, which was tantamount to rejection. Instead they voted to do away with Duval's seat and reduced the court to six members. But the House refused to go along with this scheme and the bill failed. When the secretary of the Senate brought the news of Taney's defeat to Jackson, the old man threw down his pen, growled that it was past midnight and that he would sign no more legislation from scoundrels. And with that, he strode out of the building.[11]

Now the Chief Justice was dead and two places on the court remained to be filled. For the higher position many distinguished members of the bar hoped that Associate Justice Joseph Story would be named since he was perhaps the most outstanding jurist in the country. But Jackson could not abide his political or constitutional principles and that ended Story's chances. Webster had a passion for the seat but he, too, was dismissed. Some mentioned Thomas Hart Benton, but Benton made it clear that he "should not take it if it was offered to me. Taney is my favorite for that place, and P. P. Barbour next." He added that the man selected should add grace and dignity to the post, instead of hanging on until he stumbled or was carried off.[12]

There probably was never any doubt in Jackson's mind whom he would appoint as chief justice and how he would get his nominee safely through the Senate. Taney was his choice. No one else. And Taney he meant to have.

To win Taney's confirmation, Jackson engaged in some careful calculations. He reckoned that the past few months had vastly improved his chances of controlling the upper house. Several factors contributed. First of all the spring elections had gone against the Whigs in a number of states, especially North Carolina and Virginia. The fall elections were very likely to go the same way and that might add several Democrats to the Senate. As it happened, the sudden death of two opposition senators, one from Connecticut and the other from Illinois, also improved Jackson's strength in the upper house. Second, he expected to win the admission of the Michigan Territory into the Union as a state, thereby adding two seats to the upper house. Unfortunately, the Democratic majority in the Territory had been "rather hasty in their movements" and organized their government before they were authorized to do so by Congress and that delayed Michigan's admission.[13] Third, the Supreme Court had two vacancies and it was unthinkable that they would be left unfilled because of a difference of opinion between the President and the Senate. Finally, Jackson had over the years taught the opposition that when they rejected one of his nominees he tended to leave the position vacant. Or, if possible, he appointed someone even more objectionable. As he later said in offering advice to another President: "I could recommend to Mr. [John] Tyler to do as I did, whenever the Senate rejected a good man, on the ground of his politics, I gave them a hot potatoe, and he will soon bring them to terms, and if not, if they leave the office not filled, the vengeance of the people will fall upon them."[14]

Jackson's "hot potatoe" in 1835 consisted of a package. What he planned was the appointment of Taney to Marshall's place and Philip P. Barbour of Virginia to succeed Duval. Both would be proposed together —one tied to the other. And since Marshall and Duval came from Virginia and Maryland respectively, Jackson's appointment of two men from the same states eliminated any objection to them on the grounds of geography. (The switched places was the only difference.) Then, to really ram his appointees down the throats of the senators, he proposed to renominate Andrew Stevenson as minister to Great Britain, even though Stevenson had already been rejected. The post had been vacant since Van Buren's rejection in 1832 and this renomination served notice that it would remain vacant unless Stevenson was confirmed.

Except where friendship was involved, most of Jackson's appointments became "means of liquidating political debts or purchasing political aid." His appointments to the courts also fell within this political rubric. And his nominations to the Supreme Court carried the additional consideration of the candidate's place of residence. Jackson always tried to maintain an even geographic distribution for the high court. Since friendship, politics, and geography constituted the President's total criteria for appointment, most of his selections were predictably substandard. To wit: McLean turned Whig and forever schemed to win a presidential nomination; Baldwin lacked judicial experience and repeatedly demonstrated marked bias in favor of the Bank of the United States; Wayne harbored opinions contrary to Jackson's regarding states' rights, even though he came from Georgia. The record so far was abysmal, as many critics noted. "He has not yet made one good appointment," declared John Quincy Adams. "His Chief Justice will be no better than the rest." As it subsequently developed, his only outstanding appointment to the Supreme Court was Roger B. Taney as chief justice. And Taney's appointment more than made up for the rest.[15]

These appointment problems, to be decided when Congress reconvened in December, the uproar in South Carolina over the abolitionist tracts, the French indemnity matter, and other official duties commanded Jackson's thoughts and attention at the Rip Raps during the summer of 1835 and dashed all hope of finding relaxation and rest.[16] He vacationed for forty-one days and paid a total of $576.87 for lodgings for himself, five other adults, two children, and six servants.[17] Fortunately, his headaches disappeared, so he counted the vacation a great success. On August 17 he returned to Washington while his son and daughter continued on to Philadelphia to purchase furniture for the Hermitage to replace what had burned.[18]

Once he was back in the White House Jackson's headaches started up again, for the city verged on total chaos, "a scene of horrible disorder." Rioting had flared intermittently for nearly a week and considerable property had been destroyed. What started it off, according to the local press, was the appearance of an emissary from one of the abolition societies, a Reuben Crandell, who distributed "incendiary publications among the negroes of the district" which were "calculated to excite them to insurrection and the bloody course" that led to the Nat Turner Rebellion in 1831.[19] Crandell was arrested in Georgetown and jailed, but several free blacks, "having incendiary publications in possession and giving vent to insolent expressions," were set upon by a mob of some forty or fifty men. Once whipped into a frenzy, the mob attacked both property and persons. On Wednesday night, August 12, three houses within half a mile of the White House "were pulled down" and then set ablaze "amidst the yels of infuriated madmen." What intensified the violence, according to Secretary of the Navy Mahlon Dickerson, was the rumor that one of Jackson's "hired domestics," a mulatto man named Augustus, had "rec. some inflamatory papers from the North" and was distributing them to other "persons of color." The mob threatened to enter and search the White House even when informed that the "felon" had fled. It will not happen now or later, said Dickerson, "without the loss of some lives."[20]

The riots paralyzed the black community with fear for their safety. These riots were not uncommon in the Jacksonian age and reflected many underlying currents that touched on economic, social, and psychological disorders that afflicted this fast-changing society.[21] An older generation could not believe the havoc that had been set loose in the past few years. Not only were Americans shooting at their President, they were rioting and burning and looting. A wholly different society—and an intensely frightening one—seemed to be emerging. "We grieve to report these things," commented the Washington *National Intelligencer:* Clerks garrisoning public buildings; United States troops posted at their doors; the windows barricaded to defend them against the citizens of Washington. "We could not have believed it possible."[22]

Jackson laid a "severe censure" upon the Washington authorities for not suppressing the riots immediately. However, once he returned to the capital, the midsummer madness seemed to abate. Shortly after his return a deputation waited upon him and demanded that Augustus be dismissed from his position.

Jackson glared at them. "My servants are amenable to the law if they offend against the law," he growled, "and if guilty of misconduct which the law does not take cognizance of, they are amenable to *me.* But, I would have all to understand distinctly that they are amenable to me *alone,* and to no one else. They are entitled to protection at my hands, and this they shall receive."

He dismissed the deputation with a wave of his hand. A little later a secretary reminded the President that Augustus could read and write and that Jackson's enemies might induce the servant to steal his papers and reports in order to broadcast false information.

"They are welcome, sir, to anything they can get out of my papers," the General replied. "They will find there, among other things, false grammar and bad spelling; but they are welcome to it all, grammar and spelling included. Let them make the most of it. Our government, sir, is founded upon the intelligence of the people; it has no other basis; upon their capacity to arrive at right conclusions in regard to measures and in regard to men; and I am not afraid of their failing to do so from any use that can be made of any thing that can be got out of my papers."

But fragmentary information does not provide the whole truth, said the secretary, and might give the people a false impression.

"Well," said the President, "if they can't know all, let them know as much as they can. The more they know of matters the better."[23]

This optimistic view of the people, this belief in their goodness and wisdom, this trust in the masses "to arrive at right conclusions"—this was what was wrong with the country, cried the Whig press, and has fomented the civil disturbances of the past several years. In noticing the summer riots in Washington and the riots in other cities relating to the presence of blacks in society, these newspapers blamed it all on the fact that the masses had risen to political power, that *"the Republic has degenerated into a Democracy."* So said the Richmond *Whig,* and this contention was immediately endorsed by other Whig journals.

What has brought about "the present *supremacy of the Mobocracy?"* asked the Richmond paper. The answer is plain. Andrew Jackson and his "demagogue adherents" have been in hot pursuit of the majority for over ten years. "They have classified the rich and intelligent and denounced them as aristocrats; they have caressed, soothed, and flattered the heavy class of the poor and ignorant, because *they* held the power which they wanted." Practicing the maxims of Robespierre, they have "unblushingly and atrociously" drawn a line in society, proscribing the business classes and "directing the hatred of the multitude upon them as Aristocrats and their *foes;* and they have deeply stirred for their base ends, that unworthy, that nearly universal sentiment in the human mind, the jealousy which the poor feels towards the rich." We appeal to the columns of the *Globe,* continued the Richmond *Whig,* for the truth of what we say, and "to the State Papers of Gen. Jackson himself; not one of which is exempt from the reproach of an artful appeal to the passions of the poor and ignorant." Small wonder, then, that mobs terrorize cities, burn buildings, and assault citizens. They are encouraged by the President and his "demagogue adherents."

"The Republic has degenerated into a Democracy," wailed the Richmond *Whig,* and democracy has produced nothing but wretched government and civil disorder.[24]

A great many people agreed with this assessment. They had seen a popular war hero ride to power on the enthusiasm of mobs. They had watched his so-called reforms produce a spoils system, the destruction of the nation's currency and credit system, the annihilation of republican government, and the establishment of executive despotism. And it all began with the rise to power of ignorant people whom Jackson and his friends called virtuous and wise.

The Democratic press—particularly the *Globe*—quickly responded to this attack. The people are hated by the rich and the monopolists, said these newspapers, because they have terminated elitist power in the country by electing a government devoted to principle and justice. Because the people will not support the ideas and tolerate the greed of the rich, they have been denounced and accused of producing every evil in society. But if the truth be told, it is the rich who deliberately foment discord and discontent in the nation in order to discredit the democracy.

"Who endeavored to spread panic and madness and violence through the land?" asked the *Globe*. Who brought about the recent panic? "Were they not the . . . Bank leaders and the whole band of disappointed politicians and speculators who invoke through the public prints the unsheathing of swords, the flashing of dirks, and the aid of firearms, to put down the Democracy which has gained its victories by appeals to the public intelligence sustained by the popular suffrage of the country?"[25]

To put down the Democracy! That was the objective of these "Bank leaders" and speculators. And it was to be achieved through "panic and madness and violence"—anything. Then, with democracy gone, Jackson and his works would tumble with it and the aristocracy would reassert their mastery over the people.

Now there was a new source of discord "rearing its ugly head" across the land, the *Globe* contended—a danger of catastrophic proportions, "tending to civil war and disunion, which is always held in reserve to supply excitement" when every other device failed the Whig leadership. "Who is the great propagator of the SLAVE EXCITEMENT, which has already produced mobs in many of the cities and villages of the North as well as the South; which . . . has driven the father, the husband, and the master, to rush beyond the laws to destroy the instigators of a servile war . . . ? It is ARTHUR TAPPAN, the president of the abolition associations —the archenemy of the present Administration—the devoted instrument of an opposition which invariably draws on his magazine for the elements of civil commotion, when all the ordinary political firebrands have been extinguished."[26]

Just look at the urban riots that had taken place recently at so many different locations around the country—in Pennsylvania, Maryland, Mississippi, and even the city of Washington. Did not the public see the connection between this violence and the antislavery agitation? "Behold ye Liberators, Emancipators, Abolitionists, the fruits of your extravagance and folly, your recklessness and your plots against the lives of your fellow man! Behold!"[27]

Put simply, abolitionism was nothing more than a concerted plot to destroy the democracy, insisted the *Globe*. And who were the abolitionists?—the rich, the elite, the privileged. They were the disappointed politicians with no popular support who therefore sought influence and power through violence. They were not motivated by concern for the slave. They hated and feared the black man. They simply wanted to regain their lost power—lost because of the advent of democracy. They desired the destruction of the people and so they sponsored havoc and hoped to bring the whole country to civil war. Then, when they had reduced the nation to ruins, they would reestablish their oligarchic rule and make this a land of the rich and powerful.

"Yes, Democracy is the cause of all this fury on the part of the aristocratic faction," pontificated the *Globe.* And all because "it will not suffer a minority to rule. It will maintain the rights of the People. It will not consent that the Government shall succomb to a Bank monopoly. It will not surrender the Constitution to factious incendiaries, and hence it is chargeable with all the crimes which those enemies of the country commit."[28]

Ironically, commented one newspaper, many of the agitators are slave-owners themselves. They are the nullifiers, malcontents like Calhoun, McDuffie, and Duff Green, who use the slave question to promote sectional jealousies. Their ultimate aim is the dismemberment of the Union and the establishment of a southern slavocracy. "Who agitate the slave question?" was the editorial query of one Democratic paper. "Who seek to produce sectional parties, founded on local jealousies, to obliterate the great landmarks of party founded on principles?" Surely the entire country "must have observed that the active instruments of Mr. Calhoun, especially Mr. McDuffie and Duff Green, immediately set to strumming on this sensitive chord in the South" now that the tariff question had been laid to rest by the administration. And they found cooperation from their northern allies. "The Northern Bank Aristocrats now see their only hope is, breaking the ties which heretofore united the Northern and Southern Democracy, and this may only be effected by encouraging a sectional feeling." This was the reason, argued the Democratic press, that these "Northern Bank Aristocrats" encouraged the nomination of Hugh Lawson White for the presidency. "They secretly rejoice at the activity of their abolition friends in the North, as it contributes to this end, and at the same time affords them an opportunity . . . to render a Bank candidate acceptable . . . to the Southern opposition in the House of Representatives if they shall succeed in subjecting the presidency to its disposal."[29]

By the mid-1830s it dawned on such Democrats as Jackson, Blair, Kendall, Taney, Benton, Van Buren, and others that the rise of democratic government under the aegis of Andrew Jackson had generated such fears and anxiety from its opposition that a counterattack had been launched in which an ingenious array of issues was employed: first the Bank issue, then nullification, and now slavery. In their desperation, the opposition had even resorted to civil disorder and the destruction of private property. By raising the slave issue and provoking urban violence, these malcontents in the north and south hoped not only to put an end to popular government but to the Union itself.[30] The "stupid" will of the people would be hushed in the convulsions brought on by a fraternal struggle between the north and south. Thus does democracy breed its own destruction.[31]

Jackson and other like-minded Democrats genuinely saw abolition as an evil force dedicated to the dismemberment of the Union and the discrediting of the democracy. They labeled it a violation of law, a threat to property rights, and an assault upon liberty. Only madmen and cowards would deliberately raise the slave issue and bring it into prominence. Only those intent on the termination of the American experiment in liberty encouraged abolitionist agitation. The *Globe* warned of what might happen next. It predicted that the question of slavery would be formally raised in Congress at the commencement of the next session. This was "an object pressed by the opposition in several States. . . . They are getting up memorials precisely upon the plan of the Bank panic politicians, to produce excitement upon the subject, ultimately to connect it with political movements against the Administration." The enemies of democracy would thus drag the dangerous and explosive problem of slavery into national attention with the object of provoking bloodshed and civil strife. And after the conflagration, warned the *Globe,* the plutocrats would rule the land.[32]

Still, with all his concern about the tactics invented by demagogues to subvert the democracy and disrupt the Union, Jackson remained steadfastly optimistic about the future. His belief in the Union and his faith in the inevitability of popular rule never wavered. "Our government," he reiterated many times, "is founded upon the intelligence of the people." "I for one do not despair of the republic; I have great confidence in the virtue of the great majority of the people, and I cannot fear the result."

Jackson's optimistic thoughts were conveyed in the columns of the *Globe:* "There is an infinite advantage even in the salutary fear inspired by the knowledge the people have obtained of their own power. . . . Democracy shows not only its power in reforming Governments, but in regenerating a race of men—and this is the greatest blessing of free governments."[33]

CHAPTER 19

"To Demand the Respect of All Europe"

WITH URBAN RIOTS BECOMING ALMOST COMMONPLACE, with the rising agitation of abolitionists producing violence and bloodshed, and with the mounting conspiracy between "Bank Aristocrats" and nullifiers intent on discrediting the democracy, Andrew Jackson returned to the White House in the late summer of 1835 gravely disturbed by what was happening in the country. "I was counting on a state of ease and quietude for the ballance of my term," he told Colonel Love, "but the extraordinary attempt to divide the Democracy & republican party will keep me in troubled water the Ballance of my term." With a sigh he envisaged the approaching end. "I am now within 18 months of freedom, & if providence permits me to live I will be a happy man on that day—for I am sure The great Democratic republican party will sustain me, against all attempts of the opposition to destroy my administration, and my fame with it."[1]

Of nagging concern to Jackson was the persistent problem with the French, and he was becoming increasingly determined to put an end to it. Fortunately, events in Europe began moving in Jackson's favor. The deteriorating situation in Spain, the danger of another invasion of Belgium by Holland, the reluctance of Britain to intervene to halt the invasion, and especially the developing hostility of Russia toward France—all converged to convince the Duc de Broglie that he must disengage France from the conflict with the United States. Furthermore, the Chamber of Peers had approved the indemnity bill, albeit with a condition. So Broglie prepared a note, dated June 17, 1835, to his chargé in Washington, Alphonse Pageot, the son-in-law of Major Lewis, which struck a very conciliatory tone and simply asked the President to indicate that he had never meant to assume "a menacing attitude" toward France.[2]

Pageot received the note the last week of August and since Forsyth was still out of town on vacation, he went to see Asbury Dickens, the chief clerk. Pageot told Dickins what he was about and specifically requested that the Broglie note be read. In effect, the United States would receive a communication from a foreign power that was not official. (It was simply a note from the head of the ministry to a deputy.) That bothered Dickins, so he contacted Jackson for instructions. Since the President had already decided to take a more direct hand in the "French matter" and bring it to an early decision, he sent back specific orders. The letter was not to be read, he commanded, or received. "We were ready to receive any written communication from the French Government which Pageot was instructed to make," Jackson said, "but that we could *receive* nothing and *hear* nothing that was not officially communicated by the French Government." Moreover, Dickins was told that if Pageot handed him any official communication querying him about Jackson's message to Congress he was "to meet it by a very laconic note informing him that this Government could not recognize the right of France to require the explanation asked for—that in the official communications between the coordinate branches of our Government we could not permit a foreign interference &c &c."[3]

Meanwhile, Jackson began preparing instructions for Barton in Paris. In essence, as the President explained to Donelson, he ordered Barton to inquire whether Pageot had informed the French government that an agent (the Baron Rothschild) had been appointed to receive the indemnity. If not, he was to communicate this information and add that the agent was ready to receive the money. If the money was not *immediately* forthcoming, Barton was instructed to ask "respectfully" when payments could be expected. If no satisfactory answer was given he was then to demand his passports, leave Paris, and inform the French government that its course was "a violation of the Treaty." If Broglie demanded "an explanation or apology" before releasing the funds, Barton was told "to say that he is expressly forbidden to discuss this subject."[4]

Jackson's handwritten note was dated September 14. The only change he incorporated from what he had told Donelson was to give the French government three days to respond to Barton's initial inquiry and five days before asking for his passports in case of a negative response to the demand for payment.[5] These instructions were prepared in a note by Secretary Forsyth, who had returned to Washington the previous week, and reiterated to Pageot on September 11. The President took great care with the Barton instructions and they showed marked attention by him to every possible detail that could hurry the negotiations to a conclusion. He was particularly anxious to get a definite response from Barton in time to add it to his annual message to Congress in December. "The President especially directs," Forsyth told Barton, "that you should comply with these instructions so early that the result may be known here before the meeting of Congress, which takes place on the 7th of December next."[6]

Barton followed his instructions to the letter—at least in the beginning. He obtained an immediate interview with Broglie on October 20 and was received promptly and cordially. After the usual diplomatic pleasantries, Barton asked when the United States could expect payment.

"Tomorrow, to-day, immediately," replied the Frenchman, in a bright tone of voice, "if the Government of the United States is ready on its part to declare to us . . . that it regrets the misunderstanding which has arisen between the two countries; that this misunderstanding is founded upon a mistake, and that it never entered into its intention to call in question the good faith of the French Government nor to take a menacing attitude toward France."[7]

After some minutes Barton rose. "In a short time," he said very solemnly, "I shall have the honor of writing to your excellency."[8]

Nearly three weeks later—on November 6 to be exact—Barton requested his passports. This was much later than the President had directed. Another three weeks transpired before Barton left Paris for home. Because of these long delays Barton had disrupted Jackson's timetable and later the President took great exception to the young man's failure to follow his instructions more precisely. It meant that the annual message to Congress would have to be prepared with no clear information about French intentions.

Still, Jackson's own position was absolutely firm. "It is high time that this arrogance of France should be put down," he wrote to Amos Kendall, "and the whole European world taught to know that we will not permit France or any, or *all* the European Governments to interfere with our domestic policy, or dictate to the President what language he shall use in his message to Congress." The President must communicate to Congress the condition of the Union and recommend appropriate measures that he may deem proper. My message of 1834, he said, "faithfully" complied with this requirement, "and it would be disgraceful to explain or apoligise to a foreign Government for any thing said in a message. it is the summit of arrogance in France, and insulting to us as an independent nation to ask it, and what no american will ever submit to."[9]

In Jackson's mind the situation had reached its climax and must now be resolved, one way or another. He waited each week for some news from Barton to tell him whether the French had agreed to pay or had decided to face him down in a final confrontation. The waiting was maddening.

Of course he realized that Congress could give him a great deal of trouble if the "malevolence" of Clay, Calhoun, and Webster in the Senate and "Bell, & Company" in the House joined in an all-out assault on his administration. So he took particular care to prepare for the return of Congress on December 7. He began by contacting key administration leaders to discuss with them the organization of each house. He sent them propaganda in the form of newspapers, pamphlets, and reprints of articles. "You must be here some days before the meeting of congress," he told James K. Polk, his leading spokesman in the House of Representatives, ". . . there must be a meeting of the friends of the administration and select the candidate for speaker and elect him on the first ballott." Bell must be defeated for reelection as Speaker. That above everything.[10] Jackson also insisted that his friends in Tennessee get the legislature to instruct Tennessee's senators to vote in favor of Benton's resolution to expunge the censure passed against Jackson in 1834. It was not vindication that Jackson was after. Rather he wanted to shift the political battle in Tennessee from one between Van Buren and Judge White to one between Jackson and Clay, which Old Hickory knew he could not lose. It was a clever stroke. Even if it failed it would weaken the Bell-White forces in Tennessee, and therefore in Congress.[11]

At length, Jackson began to prepare the final draft of his message. And still no word from Barton. Only a few thin notes arrived from the chargé to the secretary of state and these gave the administration little to go on. Soon a rumor got abroad that Barton had been recalled, but even this portentous news generated additional support in the country for the President's position. "There is something about General Jackson," wrote one Pennsylvania politician, "that it is impossible not to like and respect: —and his lofty and immoveable sense of national honor in this case, beset as he is with every temptation to qualify and bend, fills me with gratitude. You remember Shakespeare said,

> Rightly to be great
> Is not to stir without great argument,
> But greatly to find quarrel in a straw
> When honour's at the stake.

To me, this has been the exact course of the President."[12]

The presidential message, when completed, had its usual number of writers and editors. Only this time Jackson himself took a more direct hand. He researched various parts, particularly the section dealing with the indemnity, and sent them off to Kendall so that "the whole ground may be before you" for the final rewrite.[13] He even attempted to compose the entire section on France himself. The words came painfully to him. "I regret to inform you," he scratched at the top of the sheet, "that we have received no official information from France, since my last message to Congress." A bill had been passed by both the "chambers and peers" and approved by the king which provided payment but included a proviso "as insulting to us, and degrading to her, thus heaping insult upon injury."[14]

Jackson could not resist uttering these bitter words. They conveyed his resentment and anger and failure. He retraced the history of the relations between the two countries over the last four years and concluded that the

French acted in "bad faith." "What disgraceful and dishonorable attitude has france by this proviso placed herself? . . . How degrading such conduct as this to that proud and chivalric nation? would this have been the conduct of her Frances the first, her Henry 4th, or her Boneparte, or even any high minded honorable Frenchman." Jackson reiterated his right to speak to the Congress without having to justify himself to foreign countries. "And is this degradation to be submitted to, that the President must submit his communications to the agents here of foreign Governments and know from each whether it is worded, pointed and made suitable to eachs palate before he sends it to congress. there cannot be an individual american that would yield to such arrogant presumption in a foreign government, and if there are, he is unworthy of the name, and unworthy to live under blessings of freedom our Government affords."

Just how bitter he was could be read in his reference to the failure of Congress to appropriate the necessary funds for defensive purposes. Because of this failure the French could claim that the President lacked the support of the Senate "and therefore they may trifle and sport with our national character and honor, violate her treaty, insult us by demanding apology for pretended insult when none was offered or can be found, and that she will not comply with her treaty until a change of the Executive is made."[15]

It was an incredible document—full of anger and fury and certain to worsen the already fractured relations with France. It was an act of self-indulgence, something Jackson had to get out of his system. But that he ever thought such expressions could be inserted into a presidential message reveals the extent of his sense of failure and frustration. Fortunately, there were a number of advisers and friends who gently moved him away from these disastrous outbursts and toward something the French might read as conciliatory.[16]

While the message was still undergoing final revisions the members of Congress slowly returned to Washington. Although his mind was diverted by sudden flareups of headaches, coughing spells, and even small hemorrhages, Jackson forced himself to attend to the business of getting the House of Representatives organized under strong Democratic control. To Old Hickory's mind, that meant winning James K. Polk's election as Speaker. Over the past few months this election had grown in importance in Jackson's thinking. Not only did it involve the defeat of John Bell but it represented an important comeback after the failure of his friends in Tennessee to block White's formal nomination by the legislature or to win passage of instructions to Tennessee's senators to expunge the censure resolutions.[17]

Jackson worked diligently throughout the fall to ensure Polk's selection by the Democrats and his election by the full House. Through Levi Woodbury and Isaac Hill, he cultivated support from New England; he secured votes in Indiana and Illinois; and Richard M. Johnson helped bring Kentucky into line. At first there was danger that the Democrats might choose John Y. Mason of Virginia or Joel B. Sutherland of Pennsylvania as their candidate in order to bolster Van Buren's presidential prospects in those states. But Jackson would not hear of it, and he put heavy pressure on Blair to make it widely known that Polk's election was a test of the administration's strength in Congress.[18] Bell had much to lose by a rival Tennessean's victory and everyone knew it. Bell, therefore, redoubled his efforts to encourage Mason and Sutherland to run. But both men had more sense than to risk their future in a direct confrontation with Jackson, and both withdrew. The election was held on December 7 and Polk won on the first ballot by a vote of 132 against Bell's 84 and a few scattered votes for several others. It was an impressive victory —and one the President found very gratifying. He congratulated Polk and all the administration men who had worked to bring about this victory.[19] It began the congressional year on as satisfactory a note as Jackson could have wished.

With the twenty-fourth Congress in session and organized, Jackson sent down his seventh annual message, dated December 7, 1835. It was an unusually long message, running in excess of 15,000 words. He opened as usual by again noting the extraordinary prosperity and growth of the nation. But then he quickly switched to foreign affairs and sped through most of the European and South American nations to address the French matter. Once more he provided a "brief recapitulation" of what had happened to date. With restraint and delicacy (so unlike his own memorandum written a few weeks earlier) he justified his actions and reviewed the behavior of the French government. Then he spoke the words that caught everyone's immediate attention. "The conception that it was my intention to menace or insult the Government of France is as unfounded as the attempt to extort from the fears of that nation what her sense of justice may deny would be vain and ridiculous." He defended his message and denied that any nation had a right to question it. He alluded to the several occasions in the past when France took exception to presidential messages which he had uncovered in his research. In each instance the exception was dismissed as improper.[20]

At this point Jackson deliberately aimed his following words over the heads of the members of Congress and directly to the American people:

> The honor of my country shall never be stained by an apology from me for the statement of truth and the performance of duty; nor can I give any explanation of my official acts except such as is due to integrity and justice and consistent with the principles on which our institutions have been framed. This determination will, I am confident, be approved by my constituents. I have, indeed, studied their character to but little purpose if the sum of 25,000,000 francs will have the wight of a feather in the estimation of what appertains to their national independence, and if, unhappily, a different impression should at any time obtain in any quarter, they will, I

am sure, rally around the Government of their choice with alacrity and unanimity, and silence forever the degrading imputation.[21]

Jackson ended this portion of his message by outlining his final instructions to Barton. "The result of this last application has not yet reached us, but is daily expected." When it arrived it would be transmitted to Congress immediately in a special communication.[22]

Turning to other matters, the President announced with immense satisfaction that "the condition of the public finances was never more flattering than at the present period." The national debt had been liquidated completely and a surplus of about $19 million was expected by the close of the year and $20 million more in 1836. He proposed some national public works, such as improvements in the navy yards, but did not suggest lowering the tariff because that would "disturb" the principles on which the compromise tariff was based. Another great source of revenue was the sale of public lands, which amounted to the "expected sum" of $11 million during 1835. Both the enormous surplus piling up annually and the general system of land sale needed congressional action, he said. In passing, he mentioned that he still held the opinion that "it is our best policy" to promote the speedy sale and settlement of the land.[23]

Next he turned to the Bank of the United States and pushed it deeper into its grave by calling for a final windup of its affairs. The BUS was but one of the "fruits of a system" which distrusts "the popular will as a safe regulator of political power" and whose "great ultimate object . . . is the consolidation of all power in our system in one central government."[24]

The United States government had functioned nicely over the past year "without the agency of a great moneyed monopoly." The state deposit banks had done a very creditable job of collecting and disbursing the moneys of the United States. But a "practical reform in the whole paper system" was vital, he continued, and to that end he urged "the suppression of all bank bills below $20" and the substitution of gold and silver as the "principle circulating medium in the common business of the farmers and mechanics of the country." Jackson went on to deny that his actions in removing the deposits of the BUS were motivated by consideration for executive power. On the contrary, he felt that in the matter of public moneys the President should be "ever anxious to avoid the exercise of any discretionary authority which can be regulated by Congress."[25]

The President next considered the military posture of the country and again expressed his displeasure over the failure of the fortification bill to win passage in the Senate. This subject naturally brought him to the problem of the Indians and he announced that their removal approached its "consumation." "All preceding experiments for the improvement of the Indians have failed," he declared. "It seems now to be an established fact that they can not live in contact with a civilized community and prosper." Regardless of the treaty stipulations into which the United States had entered with the tribes, no one could deny the "moral duty" of the government to protect and (if possible) to preserve and perpetuate "the scattered remnants of this race." Most of the Indians had already removed or were about to go. With the exception of two small bands living in Ohio and Indiana, not exceeding 1,500, and, of course, the Cherokees—who had not yet signed a treaty of removal but would do so within three weeks—all the tribes on the eastern side of the Mississippi River and extending from Lake Michigan to Florida had "entered into engagements which will lead to their transplantation."[26]

The removal of all Indians from "civilized" society was almost complete, Jackson pridefully told the Congress: we have accomplished something monumental and everlasting.[27]

Turning to cheerier matters, Jackson noted the improved condition of the post office, along with the surplus recently accumulated, and the likelihood that its debt would be liquidated within another quarter or two. But he completed this section of the message on a less happy note in detailing the circumstances of the South Carolina seizure of abolitionist tracts. Finally, he addressed a subject that he had raised in his first message, namely the need to amend the Constitution to make the election of the President more democratic by the removal of all "intermediate" agencies between the people and their chief executive. Although he did not mention it specifically, the alleged ploy of Whigs to wrest control of the presidential election in 1836 from the people and hand it to the House of Representatives was the cause of Jackson's return to this subject.

> However much we may differ in the choice of the measures which should guide the administration of the Government, there can be but little doubt in the minds of those who are really friendly to the republican features of our system that one of its most important securities consists in the separation of the legislative and executive powers at the same time that each is held responsible to the great source of authority, which is acknowledged to be supreme, in the will of the people constitutionally expressed. My reflection and experience satisfy me that the framers of the Constitution, although they were anxious to make this feature as a settled and fixed principle in the structure of the Government, did not adopt all the precautions that were necessary to secure its practical observance, and that we can not be said to have carried into complete effect their intentions until the evils which arise from this organic defect are remedied.

The people—not the legislature—have a right to elect their highest officers, the President asserted, and "some stronger safeguard" to protect that right must be engrafted upon the Constitution.[28]

And with that injunction, Jackson closed his message. All in all, it documented the extraordinary progress and prosperity of the nation. The blessings of America seemed to be shared by all, in some degree, and the President simply acknowledged what was generally known and appreciated around the country. "Never had any country before made such rapid strides," wrote Edward Livingston to his brother-in-law, Auguste Davezac, "towards wealth happiness and good Government. Without a shilling of Debt we have 20,000,000 in the treasury—more than 100,000 seamen are employed in most lucrative commerce, our manufactures increase, our farmers growing rich & the whole population becoming well educated and well informed of their rights & bred up to Defend them—and especially of that administration under which it has attained this Degree of prosperity." Because Livingston had just returned from abroad he was forcibly struck by "this Degree of prosperity" and by the nation's success in advancing democracy.[29]

Jackson was seen as personally responsible for promoting democracy during his term in office—and with good reason. Although some worried at the moment about the French unpleasantness, they were united behind Jackson, no matter what happened. They were grateful for his efforts on their behalf. They believed in him and revered him as they never had done before with any political leader. Most Americans, therefore, gave his annual message their near-unanimous approval and support.[30]

But before the crisis with France was brought to a satisfactory conclusion, one more bit of nastiness took place that nearly signaled the beginning of open hostilities between the two countries.

Alphonse Pageot, the French chargé, was so certain that Jackson's message would be found offensive to his government that he refused to attend a reception given by the President the following week to members of the diplomatic corps. Worse, on December 1, Pageot sent to Forsyth a copy of the Broglie note (which the secretary had already refused to receive) and asked that it be shown to Jackson so that he might incorporate "all the facts" about the French attitude in his message. Again, Forsyth rejected it, only this time he chided Pageot for pursuing this tactic. The President's position, lectured Forsyth, "remains unchanged." No unofficial communication to this government would be received.[31]

Pageot expressed "astonishment" that mere "form" took precedence over "substance" in trying to resolve the differences between France and America. He now believed that a complete rift was unavoidable. A month later he received word from his government that Barton had been recalled and he was instructed to "lay down the character of chargé." He notified Forsyth of his government's command on January 2, 1836, thereby severing the diplomatic relations between France and the United States. It was an ominous sign.[32]

And still no word from Barton. Jackson's nerves were almost totally frazzled by this time. "I have been in bad health for some days," he wrote. He did not know how much longer he could stand the suspense, despite the "demi-official" word from Le Havre that the French ministry would make arrangements "either absolute or conditional" to pay the indemnity this winter. Once more his combative mood resurfaced. Once more he needed to shake his fist at the French and bellow at them for daring to insult the American people. "The Duck," he wrote in his own inimitable style of spelling, referring to Broglie, "knows nothing of me . . . if he does not know that neither apology, or what is the same, explanation will ever be given by me—If Mr. Barton returns,—the mony not being paid,—I will speak to congress as I ought,—of this fact you may rest well assured."[33]

But nothing further could be done until he heard from Barton. Finally, after a long and difficult voyage across the ocean, the young chargé's ship landed in New York on January 12, 1836. Two days later he appeared in Washington. His father-in-law was waiting for him. Together, they headed immediately for the White House, picking up the Vice President and secretary of state along the way. Outwardly, Van Buren appeared calm but inwardly he suffered great apprehension. "His outward appearance is like the unruffled surface of the majestic river which covers rocks and whirlpools," commented one New Yorker, "but shows no marks of the agitation beneath." Forsyth, too, was deeply concerned.[34]

"Well, sir," the secretary said at length, addressing Barton, "what are you going to tell the President."

"I am going to tell him the whole truth, as I understand it," came the fatuous reply.

The agitation on the faces of the other three men intensified. The "whole truth" might produce a gargantuan Jacksonian explosion.

They were now standing near the steps of the White House under the north portico. Seeing the alarm written on the faces of his companions, Barton stopped and turned to them.

"Gentlemen, do you want oil poured upon the flames, or water?"

"Oh, WATER, by all means," they chorused.

"That," responded Barton, "will be the effect of the little that I have to say."

The four men entered the mansion and were greeted by the porter. They hurried to Jackson's study. The General looked up from his desk as they were ushered into the room and he immediately spotted Barton.

"So, sir," barked the President, looking squarely at Barton and ignoring the others, "you have got here at last, have you!"

Van Buren paled, and Forsyth and Livingston looked extremely uncomfortable. It was an "ominous beginning" to the interview and they feared the worst.

Barton hastened to explain the reasons for his long delay—the weather, the negligence of a pilot—and this seemed to mollify Jackson. Then, in a very solemn voice, the President asked what was on his mind: "Tell me, sir, do the French mean to pay that money?"

All the members in the room held their breath.

"General Jackson, I am sorry to inform you that they do not."

The President stiffened. He rose from his chair and addressed the other three men.

"*There*, gentlemen! What have I told you, all along?"

He paced the room in a state of extreme excitement. No one said a word. Suddenly he stopped and turned again to Barton.

"What do they say about it, sir? What excuse do they give?"

"General," Barton replied, "I am exceedingly desirous to make you acquainted with the state of affairs in France, as far as I myself understand it; but to do this effectually I must beg to be allowed to tell my story in my own way."

The President looked thoughtful, then slowly nodded his head. "Right, sir," he said, and with that he seized a chair and threw his weight into it with dramatic force. "Go on, sir."

"I verily believe, General," Barton began, "that down to a recent period, the French government was trifling with us."

Up sprang the President when he heard the words "trifling with us."

"Do you hear that, gentlemen? *Trifling with us!* My very words. I have always said so."

But Jackson quickly calmed down and resumed his seat.

"I mean by trifling with us," Barton continued, "that they thought the treaty a matter of no great importance, and one which was not pressing, and would not be pressed by the United States. It could be attended to this year, or next year—it was of small consequence which."

Barton went on to say that popular opposition to the payment of the indemnity before the President had apologized was so great that it could topple any ministry—even the king himself—should an attempt be made to meet American demands. Everyone seemed anxious to avoid a collision with the United States but the people made it clear that the honor of the nation demanded an explanation before any money changed hands.[35]

His narration at an end, Barton looked extremely doleful. After a moment's pause the President rose from his chair and dismissed the chargé with his usual mark of courtesy and friendship. The other members filed out of the room but as they left, the President signaled to Livingston his wish to consult further with him.

Jackson had already begun to prepare his report or special message to Congress even before he heard from Barton. The draft had been shown to Livingston several days before and his comments invited. The tone of the draft worried the former minister. "The message about to be delivered," Livingston wrote the day before Barton landed in New York, "is one of no ordinary importance: it may produce war or secure peace." The draft "you did me the honor to show me would make an admirable manifesto or a declaration of war; but we are not yet come to that. The world would give it that character; and, issued before we know the effect of the first message, it would be considered as precipitate."

Now, standing in the President's study, Livingston again counseled Jackson to go easy. The tone and mood of the message, he suggested, should be one of "moderation and firmness," not anger or violence. "Our cause is so good, that we need not be violent. Moderation in language, firmness in purpose, will unite all hearts at home, all opinions abroad, in our favor." To assist the President further, Livingston had presumed to draft a "hasty" statement which he said he knew Jackson, "with your usual discernment," would decide whether "it suits the present emergency."[36]

Actually, Jackson had already decided on a moderate course because he knew that "our cause is so good" that any intemperate language of his would jeopardize world opinion of the justice of the American claim—which explained why he was so quarrelsome in the interview with Barton. He used the occasion to let off steam, having already written a message that blended moderation with firmness. Such behavior was quite usual for Jackson, especially during moments of great tension and anxiety. Everyone remembered the emotional scenes and later reported them, and they account for Jackson's overblown reputation for violence and anger.

The revised draft was shown to Livingston, Forsyth, and Van Buren. Probably Kendall also had a hand in crafting some of the paragraphs. Whatever trace of "violence" still remained in any passage was smoothed away in the final discussions the President had with these advisers and with his cabinet. The message itself, as approved and transmitted to Congress, was dated January 15, the day following the interview with Barton. However, it was delivered on Monday, January 18.[37]

The message was relatively short and included the correspondence between Barton and Broglie. From the language used in the correspondence, Jackson declared, it is "a preemptory refusal to execute the treaty except on terms incompatible with the honor and independence of the United States." Does France expect a declaration that we had no intentions of obtaining our rights by an address to her fears rather than her sense of justice? She has already had it. Livingston's note of April 25, 1835, to the French foreign minister, which I formally approved, explicitly gives it. Does France want "a degrading, servile repetition of this act" in terms which she will dictate? "She will never obtain it. The spirit of the American people, the dignity of the Legislature, and the firm resolve of their executive government forbid it."

Under the circumstances, the President felt it would be appropriate for the United States to retaliate by prohibiting French products and French ships into American ports. Also, in view of French naval preparations in the West Indies, Jackson urged "large and speedy appropriations" for the increase of the navy and the completion of coastal defenses. "Come what may, the explanation which France demands can never be accorded, and no armament . . . will, I trust, deter us from discharging the high duties which we owe to our constituents, our national character, and to the world." Not only would he preserve the monetary interests of the country but its independence and honor as well.[38]

It was a strong statement but nowhere near a call to arms. The reaction to it in Congress was predictable. The Democrats rose to praise its tone and spirit. Several of them lambasted the French. Thomas Hart Benton blamed the Senate for not passing the defense bills of the previous session and thereby inviting the subsequent insult from France. On the other hand, the opposition strongly condemned the President's message. Calhoun warned that if the Congress followed Jackson's recommendation "we instantly made war: it is war," and the opprobrium would fall entirely to the United States. Webster, naturally, defended the Senate in its previous action concerning defense, while Henry Clay sought to hustle the message off to his Foreign Relations Committee, where he could more properly maul and beat it to death.[39]

At this point in the controversy, Great Britain decided to step in and assist in the resolution of the problem between her two potential allies. Her own national interests dictated the intervention. To start, the movement of the French in the West Indies had the prospect of causing a blockade of American ports, which would mean an interruption in the supply of cotton to English textile mills. More important, the threatening posture of Russia, particularly over Turkey, coincided with a growing sense of mutual need between England and France. Thus, if war should break out between England and Russia, it would be "frightfully" inconvenient for the British if France was engaged in hostilities with the United States.

The unsettled conditions in Europe also worried the French, and the possibility of mediation by the English to settle the American dispute seemed like an excellent means of extricating themselves from a bothersome annoyance. In a complicated and involuted diplomatic procedure[40] it was finally arranged for Great Britain to make the offer of mediation without appearing to be prompted by their French ally. Charles Bankhead, the British chargé in Washington, was notified, and on January 27, 1836, he officially and formally offered British mediation in a note to the secretary of state.

Britain had "witnessed with the greatest pain and regret," said the note, the progress of the misunderstanding between France and the United States. Britain was united by the closest ties with both nations: an active alliance with one and "by community of interests and by the bonds of kindred" with the other. If both antagonists would agree to this mediation, the note concluded, "means might be found of satisfying the honor of each" without resorting to the great evils which war would certainly bring.[41]

After consulting with Jackson, Forsyth replied on February 3 and thanked Bankhead for Britain's concern. He mentioned that the President's last message to Congress, as well as his special message of January 15, certainly demonstrated the desire of the United States to restore friendly relations with France. But he explicitly denied the right of any country to demand an explanation for a presidential message to Congress. The United States can not yield on this principle, said Forsyth, and the President will not "subject this point to the control of any foreign state." However, if after this "frank avowal" by the President of his position and the "explicit reservation of that point," Great Britain still believes it can assist in resolving the dispute, the President had instructed Forsyth to inform Bankhead that "the offer of mediation made in his note is cheerfully accepted."[42]

Jackson officially notified the Congress of his formal acceptance of mediation on February 8. He suggested that nothing be done about French commerce until the efforts at mediation became clearer, but he repeated—and "I can not too strongly repeat," he said—his recommendation that the Congress strengthen the nation's military defenses.[43]

Both administration and opposition newspapers applauded the intervention of the British.[44] Even if nothing came of mediation, at least it eased the tension between France and the United States and seemed to diminish the possibility of war. Philip Hone recorded in his diary on February 1 that the "war of etiquette" appeared to be averted. "God grant that it may be so; and I cry for William the Fourth and Andrew Jackson, the *mediator* and the *mediatee!*"[45]

The French themselves had formally accepted the British offer of mediation on December 27, 1835. Once Jackson accepted, it had been the intention of the British to propose one of Livingston's notes to Broglie —that of April 25—as the basis for a settlement of the dispute. The British seemed to think that this note contained all the explanations the French needed or could expect and that they had not given proper attention to it.[46] However, when Jackson's message to Congress of December 7, 1835, arrived in Paris on December 31, the French rushed along the process of settlement. They decided not to wait for U.S. acceptance of British mediation. They declared that Jackson's message gave full satisfaction to their demands and that they would now pay the indemnity. They took the passage where Jackson had said that he did not intend to menace or insult the French as sufficient explanation to justify releasing the money. No doubt they were gently prodded by the British into adopting this interpretation,[47] and on February 15, Bankhead notified the American government that the French had accepted the President's "explanation" and removed the difficulties which had prevented payment. The first installment of the indemnity, he said, would be paid whenever demanded by the United States government.[48]

Jackson notified Congress on February 22 that the controversy had ended. "It is a matter of congratulation," he wrote, "that the mediation has been rendered unnecessary." He hoped that what had happened would produce only "a temporary estrangement" and that time and the respect and esteem the two nations held for one another would "soon obliterate from their remembrance all traces of that disagreement." But Jackson could not close this happy announcement without reminding Congress of its failure to provide for the national defense. Once again he recommended that the means be provided to repel aggression; for if we wish to avoid insult we must be ready to resist it, and if we desire peace it must be known "that we are at all times ready for war."[49]

The nation at large broke out in one long shout of praise for President Andrew Jackson. Even the Whigs admittedly found it difficult to deny him full credit, although a few of their newspapers preferred to congratulate the country at large on its triumph rather than the administration.[50] This splendid outcome, predicted Martin Van Buren, will bring "an increase of reputation abroad & of strength to the administration at home."[51]

Jackson himself was ecstatic over his total victory and he believed it would help to achieve his overall diplomatic goal of gaining the world's respect for American rights and claims. "I was shewn a letter yesterday," he wrote to Edward Livingston, "stating that I never stood so high in Paris as I do now with all parties and particularly with the Chambers, what may be the feeling of the Duc DeBrolio I cannot say, but we occupy a high standing in all Europe, and will now take our stand on a level with the greatest powers of Europe, and have a durable peace with all the world —My object will be to place our defences on such a footing as to demand the respect of all Europe."[52] Actually, this goal—"to demand the respect of all Europe"—had always been Jackson's objective. In his first message to Congress he had said that "it is my settled purpose to ask nothing that is not clearly right and to submit to nothing that is wrong."[53] But the motive underlying this "settled purpose" was to achieve the respect of the world.[54] And this he did.

Still, he was faulted for his methods, that his diplomacy consisted of the stick and the threat, of employing tactics and language that were far stronger than needed, thus endangering the peace and safety of the country. The criticism is well taken. But there are a number of extenuating circumstances, at least as far as the French controversy goes. First, the French acted very badly. They had agreed by treaty to pay the indemnity and then defaulted, not by accident (as is sometimes claimed) but because they did not really want to pay the debt. It was considered excessive, and it was known to be unpopular. And, as William C. Rives, the former minister to France, always said, the French hated to part with money. "Nothing can exceed the reluctance of a *Frenchman,* or of the *French* government, to pay money," he wrote.[55] So, strong measures were called for to make them fulfill their pledge, and Andrew Jackson was just the sort of President to respond enthusiastically to that kind of need. Moreover, Edward Livingston, who had an outstanding reputation at home and abroad as an intelligent and skillful lawyer, advised the use of strong measures. Jackson would have been extremely unwise had he acted differently to what his own minister, who was on the spot, advised him to do.

In any event, Jackson's handling of the controversy produced something that was very important for the United States. It increased European respect for America, as the President wished, and it strengthened the ties between the United States and Great Britain. It also reordered the relationship between France and the United States. Heretofore France simply presumed that America owed her something because of her assistance in the Revolution and that therefore she could do whatever she pleased and get away with it. She knew better now. And that made for a healthier relationship. France would think twice in the future before offending the United States or initiating an action that could provoke an incident. What Jackson had produced, therefore, was saner and more conducive to good diplomatic relations.

But, in the long view of history, perhaps the most important result of the spoliation controversy was the success of President Jackson in facing down European scorn of the American experiment in liberty and forcing a recognition of American rights as a free and independent nation. As Livingston constantly reported, Europe feared the United States lest the American system of democratic government prove irresistible to European peoples and encourage them to cast off their monarchical rulers. Even a longtime ally like France behaved in a contemptuous manner, to the point of refusing to honor its pledge and pay a legitimate debt. As far as Jackson was concerned, France and the rest of Europe needed to be taught that the United States must be treated at all times like any other sovereign and independent nation, no more, no less. To do otherwise risked grave consequences.

In sum, then, Jackson proved extraordinarily successful in his conduct of foreign affairs, not simply because he forced European nations to acknowledge their financial obligations to this country or the impressive number of commercial treaties he concluded, but because he strengthened the position of the United States throughout the world. Through a vigorous diplomatic policy that had specific and honorable goals to achieve, he advanced this nation's claim to the dignity and respect it rightfully deserved. "Our venerable President," wrote Aaron Vail, the American chargé in London, "occupies a higher place than ever in British estimation. His firm and manly tone, the unquestionable justice of the claims he advocated, and the strength of his position upon every point of the dispute, are themes of unanimous commendation, and the American name is on higher ground than I ever knew it since I have resided here."[56]

Once Jackson notified the Congress that the spoliations controversy had ended, only one small misunderstanding between the two countries remained unresolved: the phrase *"le prétendu non-accomplissement des engagements"* that Sérurier had used in his note to the secretary of state. The official translation, which indicated that Jackson had acted in bad faith and deliberately deceived the Congress and the American people, was obviously faulty, claimed Bankhead and several other diplomats. *Prétendu* meant "alleged," they said; even the French government disclaimed any intention of implying that Jackson believed the allegation was true. The American government found this explanation totally acceptable and official notes were exchanged with the French which put it all in writing.[57]

The United States government immediately began proceedings for the execution of the treaty, and on March 19, 1836, the French ministry ordered payment of the first installment. The rest of the money came very quickly, and on May 10, 1836, the President officially notified the Congress that the four installments had been paid to the American agent.[58] With all the indemnity money that Jackson was bringing into the country from France and Naples, "Old Bullion" Benton expressed the hope that *"every dollar . . . will come to us in gold."*[59]

All that now remained to end this unpleasant haggle over an indemnity was the resumption of normal diplomatic relations. Forsyth asked whether the reappointment of Livingston would be acceptable to the French (since Livingston had indicated a willingness to resume his mission), but in the same breath declared that Sérurier must not return to the United States.[60] The French forthwith rejected Livingston. Then the British suggested that both countries appoint entirely new diplomatic representatives and this seemed to satisfy everyone. Whether the rejection of Livingston would have touched off another all-out defense of a friend by Jackson never will be known because Livingston died suddenly on May 23, 1836. The President wrote his widow and extended "the condolence of a sincere and old friend."[61] Jackson nominated on June 28, in Livingston's place, Lewis Cass, the then secretary of war whose one outstanding qualification for the post was his ability to speak the French language. The President also agreed to accept Edouard Pontois as the minister from France.

Unfortunately, in the reestablishment of diplomatic relations, Jackson again mismanaged the appointment process when a third (and interested) party interfered for personal reasons and dictated the choice of a chargé. This time the appointment involved the French chargé, Alphonse Pageot, and the presumption of Major Lewis to bring him back to America despite the agreement to appoint totally new diplomatic personnel.

The "intrigue" developed when Lewis asked the newly appointed minister to France, Lewis Cass, to query the President about his "sentiments" toward Lewis's son-in-law, Alphonse Pageot. General Jackson subsequently admitted to Cass that he "had nothing but the kindest and friendly feelings to Mr. Pageot individually." His only complaint—he assumed that all Pageot's actions had been dictated by Paris—was the chargé's improper efforts to get Broglie's note of June 17—the one Jackson refused to receive—into the public prints. Because Pageot presumed that publication would aid the French cause, he showed the note to Henry Clay and the editors of the *National Intelligencer*. Clay succeeded in forcing a resolution through the Senate demanding a copy of the note, but his efforts were sidetracked when Barton returned home and public attention shifted to the President's anticipated special message to Congress of January 15. Just before Pageot sailed for home the newspapers published the note. Under orders from Paris, the young man had handed a copy of it to a New York newspaper.[62]

Still, the spoliation problem ended happily and Jackson was pleased to forget about Pageot's "indiscretion," especially when he learned through the new British minister to the United States, Henry Stephen Fox, that Pageot had acted upon the orders of his government. Cass related all this in a letter —including the information supplied by Fox—to Major Lewis who promptly sent the letter to his son-in-law in Paris. Then he added as a postscript, the astonishing information that the President had no objection to Pageot's coming back to Washington as chargé. Obviously, Lewis was desperate to bring his daughter and grandchild back to America.[63]

Pageot immediately showed the letter to the king—which meant that the confidential information Jackson had received from Fox about Pageot acting under orders in publishing Broglie's letter had been compromised. In any event, the king thought as an "act of friendship" toward Jackson that he would return Pageot to the United States as chargé. When the young man reappeared in Washington, the President was clearly annoyed since the appointment violated the decision that the two countries would appoint totally new diplomatic representatives. When he was informed of the circumstances that had produced this result, Jackson came within an ace of recalling Cass. He was shocked and embarrassed. He was placed, he later informed Lewis, "in a very humiliating situation, and would, had it not been my friendship for you and your family, produced the immediate recall of Govr. Cass, but for friendship sake, I brooked the humility, and passed it over in silence except to yourself."[64] Again, friendship blinded him to his duty. Not only should he have recalled Cass, but he should have sacked Lewis from his position in the Treasury and sent him back to Tennessee.

With Cass, the President was particularly and justifiably furious. "I have never blamed Mr. Pajoet, nor have I you for your attachment to your children," Jackson wrote in a memorandum to Lewis, "but, I never can but blame Govr. Cass." By divulging the confidential information the President had received from the British minister, which was eventually relayed to the king of France, Cass had acted with "great impropriety." The knowledge he had obtained from cabinet meetings and private conversations with the President had been spilled halfway around the world. Oh, Jackson cried, "I have a right to exclaim, keep me from such advisers, as Govr. Branch, Mr. McClain, and Governor Cass."[65]

Pageot was permitted to remain in America, Lewis had his daughter back with him again, and Cass went off to France to improve his diplomatic skills. And Jackson once more paid a high price for fumbling the appointments process.

CHAPTER 20

Twilight of the Indians

JOHN ROSS, THE BLUE-EYED, BROWN-HAIRED PRINCIPAL CHIEF of the Cherokee Nation, stood before the blue-eyed, white-haired Chief Magistrate of
the American nation. Ross was a Scot with only a dash of Cherokee blood
in his veins—one eighth to be exact. But he considered himself an Indian
—and Jackson did too. In fact Jackson considered him a very bad Indian
—"a great villain," to quote him[1]—because he had actively and successfully impeded the President's determination to remove the Cherokees
west of the Mississippi River.

Ross had served with Jackson at the Battle of Horseshoe Bend during
the Creek War in 1814. He was a wily and able Indian leader who could
match the skills of any of the commissioners sent by the American government to treat with the Cherokees. He was rich, lived in a fine house, was
served by black slaves, and virtually controlled the annuities paid by the
United States to the tribal government for former land cessions.[2]

In many respects Ross and Jackson were much alike: both tough and
persistent, a sign perhaps of their Scotch background; both dignified;
both polite; and both attentive to the interests and affairs of their people.

Ross had requested the meeting and the President had graciously
designated the noon hour of Wednesday, February 5, 1834.[3] When the
Principal Chief arrived, Old Hickory gestured him to a chair. The two
chiefs went through a few minutes of polite conversation, but both maintained an extraordinary degree of reserve. They were each playing a
political game, although the odds were clearly in Jackson's favor, and
both men probably knew it.

The Cherokee Nation, more than any other tribe, had valiantly resisted
the President's determined effort to expel them from their ancient

haunts. They fought and argued and finally sued in the Supreme Court.[4] In vain. Time had run out and the Cherokees were subjected to enormous pressure by the President and the state of Georgia to sign a treaty exchanging their lands in the east for a new domain west of the Mississippi River. Already a so-called Treaty party among the Cherokees had been formed. The members of this party appreciated Jackson's inflexible position and decided to end their resistance and try to get the best treaty possible for their people. The leaders of the Treaty party were able and dedicated men and included Major Ridge, his son, John Ridge, Elias Boudinot, the editor of the Cherokee *Phoenix,* and his brother, Stand Watie, as well as John A. Bell, James Starr, and George W. Adair. These men risked their lives in acquiescing to removal, and all of them were subsequently marked for assassination. Not many years later, Elias Boudinot and John Ridge were slain with knives and tomahawks in the presence of their family and friends, while Major Ridge was ambushed and shot to death.[5]

The leader of the party opposed to removal was John Ross, and he easily deduced Jackson's game, which was to play one faction off against the other. This was what had brought him to Washington: to make sure that the President understood that he must contend with Ross's opposition party as well as the Treaty party. But Jackson was no fool. He had no intention of allowing Ross to set the rules for their encounter. As a matter of fact he very reluctantly agreed to see Ross. He much preferred negotiating with the Ridges and Elias Boudinot. At least they were flexible and willing to listen to "reason." Unlike Ross, they seemed to understand that Andrew Jackson had determined to remove the Cherokees and nothing under heaven would change his mind.

One important reason for Jackson's intense dislike of Ross and preference for Ridge and Boudinot was his belief that Ross headed a mixed-blood elite intent on centralizing tribal power and revenue to satisfy their own economic self-interest. The Ross party, according to Jackson, was the Indian equivalent of the pro-Bank aristocrats in white society. The "real" Indian, the *full-blooded* brave, said Jackson sarcastically, was an individualist, a hunter, who wanted no part of this modern Cherokee state which sought only to satisfy the corrupt values of mixed-bloods. "Real" Indians, like Ridge and Boudinot, understood Jackson's genuine concern for the welfare of his red children and saw that further resistance to removal would surely result in the complete debauchery of the Cherokees and their ultimate annihilation.[6]

In addition, whenever he came to Washington, Ross "often proposed to make a treaty for mony alone," Jackson claimed, "& not Land." Moreover, he would "let the Cherokees seek their own country beyond the limits of the United States—to which," said Old Hickory, "I always replied we were bound by treaty to keep our Indians within our own limits."[7] So Jackson not only disliked Ross, he distrusted him and convinced himself that the Principal Chief was nothing more than a greedy little potentate who cared nothing for the moral interests of his people. Despite his feelings, however, the President showed his adversary every respect and courtesy when they met at the White House. He listened carefully to what the Chief said; he did not try to bully him; and he did not lose his temper.

What especially concerned Ross on this occasion was the rumor that Jackson had commissioned the Reverend John F. Schermerhorn, an ambitious cleric who had been helpful in obtaining a removal treaty with the Seminoles, to treat with the Ridge faction and see what could be done about obtaining a treaty. In alarm, Ross requested permission to submit a proposition for a treaty himself.[8] Jackson readily agreed. His "game" of playing one side against the other had already begun to work. He therefore directed Schermerhorn to suspend negotiations with Ridge and the Treaty party.

Unfortunately for Ross, he was not Jackson's match in political maneuvering. He lacked finesse and he overplayed his hand. He began the discussion by making impossible demands. He insisted at first that the Nation be permitted to retain some of their land along the borders of Georgia, Alabama, and Tennessee, as well as a small tract in North Carolina. He then required the United States to give assurances that the Indians would be protected in their new and old settlements by federal troops for a period of no less than five years.

Jackson stared blankly at Ross for a few minutes. Then, in a calm voice, he said very quietly that nothing short of an entire removal of the Cherokee Nation from all their lands east of the Mississippi River was acceptable.

Ross took another tack. In that case he wanted $20 million for the Cherokee Country East, plus reimbursement for all losses sustained by the violations by the United States of former treaties. Also, he demanded an indemnity for claims under the 1817 and 1819 Cherokee treaties.

The President's calm and soothing voice had apparently not conveyed Jackson's proper meaning to the Principal Chief. So he tried again. His voice hardened, his eyes registered his displeasure, and the muscles of his cheeks twisted his face into a stern and forbidding mask. He rejected the "preposterous" demands and accused Ross of insincerity and filibustering. He would not be trifled with, he warned. If this was the best the Chief could offer, then there was no purpose to any further discussion.

Ross protested his sincerity. He came to see the President to work out a reasonable solution to the problem, he said. To prove it, he offered to abide by any award that the Senate of the United States might recommend. Jackson had always assured the Cherokees that in concluding a treaty he would grant terms as liberal as any the Senate might offer. Of course it was generally known that the President and Senate were on very bad terms, and perhaps Ross hoped they might outbid each other in some kind of competitive contest. Or perhaps he was bluffing. If it was a bluff, Jackson called it. He accepted the offer and assured the Principal Chief that he would "go as far" as the Senate. And on that conciliatory note, the interview concluded.[9]

No doubt Ross expected Jackson's enemies in the Senate to provide highly acceptable terms to the Cherokees for their removal and thereby thwart what Ross thought were the President's plans to punish the Indians for their intransigence and cheat them out of a fair price for their lands. But to make certain the senators fully understood the position of the Cherokees, petitions and memorials were hastily obtained and presented. These, of course, were referred to the Senate Committee on Indian Affairs, chaired by John P. King of Georgia, who gave them short shrift. In less than a week the Principal Chief was informed by Secretary of War Lewis Cass that the Senate was not prepared to offer more than $5 million for the Cherokee lands.[10] It was a devastating blow.

Jackson had won the game. He had faced down Ross's demands and forced the Chief into a verbal agreement. Now the President charged the Indian to keep his word and negotiate a treaty on the basis of a $5 million payment.

Ross demurred. He could not accept such a trifling amount and maintain his credibility with the Cherokees. So he insisted he had been misunderstood. He absolutely refused to negotiate for such a paltry sum. He was so angered and outraged that he even approached Mexican authorities about transporting the Cherokee Nation to a province of Mexico, but nothing came of it.[11] He returned to his people full of bitterness and remorse.

With Ross deftly disposed of, Jackson turned back to the Treaty party. He ordered Schermerhorn to reopen negotiations. Since both sides readily acknowledged the wisdom of a speedy removal, a "draft treaty" was arranged with minimal difficulty and signed on March 14, 1835. John F. Schermerhorn, among others, acted on behalf of the United States, and John Ridge, Elias Boudinot, and a delegation of chiefs for the Cherokee Nation. The treaty provided that the Nation cede and relinquish to the United States their rights and titles "to all lands owned, claimed and possessed" by the Cherokees, including lands reserved for a school fund, east of the Mississippi River, in return for which they would receive $5 million. This amount, in the opinion of one modern historian, represented "unprecedented federal generosity."[12] A program of removal was also provided, along with scheduled payments for subsistence, claims and spoliations, blankets, kettles, rifles, and the like. After due notice, the treaty was to be submitted to the Cherokee National Council assembled at New Echota, Georgia, for their approval, and for the approval of the President with the advice and consent of the Senate.[13] American newspapers jubilantly published the terms of the treaty, and everyone seemed so anxious to get rid of the Cherokees that even Whig journals declared that "these allowances with their distribution appears to us to be exceedingly liberal to say the least of them."[14]

The treaty plucked from the Cherokees an enormous domain of choice land in western North Carolina, northern Georgia, northeastern Alabama, and eastern Tennessee, comprising approximately 7 million acres.[15] It was an acquisition of staggering proportions. Small wonder American newspapermen gloated over it and reckoned the spectacular benefits for the country. Cherokees were aghast at the loss of their country and pledged to fight it at New Echota. Some of them appealed to Jackson for better terms. They assured him that the treaty could never win approval. They predicted death for those who had signed the document in the name of the Cherokee Nation, and they reminded Jackson of the many services they had provided him personally, going back to the Creek War in 1813. They said they were sure he would heed their supplications and do justice to his "red children."

As always, Jackson accorded Cherokee delegations marked deference when they visited him at the White House to make this appeal. He treated them as dignitaries of a foreign nation, although he would never acknowledge anything remotely resembling independence or sovereignty. And, as usual, he gave them one of his famous "talks," a talk usually distributed among the Cherokee people and published in the newspapers.

"Brothers," the Great Father said to a delegation on one occasion, "I have long viewed your condition with great interest. For many years I have been acquainted with your people, and under all variety of circumstances, in peace and war." Because he was such a superb actor in such situations, Jackson frequently paused during his talk to watch the reaction his words produced. He carefully played to his audience. "Your fathers were well known to me, and the regard which I cherish for them has caused me to feel great solicitude for their situation. . . . Listen to me, therefore, as your fathers have listened. . . ."

For a long moment Jackson grew quiet. The Indians normally stood in a circle around him and he used the opportunity to turn around and make certain they all heard and understood him. After a few moments he began again.

> You are now placed in the midst of a white population. Your peculiar customs, which regulated your intercourse with one another have been abrogated by the great political community among which you live; and you are now subject to the same laws which govern the citizens of Georgia and Alabama. You are liable to prosecutions for offenses, and to civil actions for a breach of any of your contracts.

Jackson wanted this point clearly understood. State laws applied to all. No one was exempted, not even Indians. He had been hammering at this since the question of removal first arose. He repeated it over and over.

Most of your people are uneducated, and are liable to be brought into collision at all times with your white neighbors. Your young men are acquiring habits of intoxication. With strong passions, and without those habits of restraint which our laws inculcate and render necessary, they are frequently driven to excesses which must eventually terminate in their ruin. The game has disappeared among you, and you must depend upon agriculture, and the mechanic arts for support. And, yet, a large portion of your people have acquired little or no property in the soil itself, or in any article of personal property which can be useful to them. How, under these circumstances, can you live in the country you now occupy? Your condition must become worse and worse, and you will ultimately disappear, as so many tribes have done before you.

That last threat of inevitable extinction was one of Jackson's oldest ploys and it invariably produced a devastating effect upon the Indians. The idea of their eventual disappearance from the race of men caused the tribes great anguish and sorrow.

Another Jackson ploy was his arrogant presumption that he was speaking to untutored aborigines who still lived in the stone age. He probably did this because of its political effect on American white people in convincing them of his wisdom in advocating removal. But the Cherokees were in fact highly civilized according to the white man's standards, and to prove it they had "offered censuses of their wealth, descriptions of their dress, housing, furniture, tableware, and work habits; copies of their constitutions and laws; and enumerations of their Christian converts." They mirrored both the best and worst in white society.[16]

In his talk to this particular Cherokee delegation, the President went on to tell them that for the past eighteen years he had urged their removal as the only means of saving the Indians from extinction. But they never heeded him, he said. Instead, the Cherokees went to the courts for relief. They turned away from their Great Father. And what was their reward? After years of litigation the Supreme Court gave them little satisfaction and in the process the Nation had earned the enmity of many whites.

I have no motive, Brothers, to deceive you. I am sincerely desirous to promote your welfare. Listen to me, therefore, while I tell you that you cannot remain where you now are. Circumstances that cannot be controlled, which are beyond the reach of human laws, render it impossible that you can flourish in the midst of a civilized community.

Today this outburst sounds outrageously racist. Actually it was a very realistic statement of what Cherokees would suffer if they lived among whites, given the disposition of Georgia frontiersmen and the legal liabilities imposed on persons of color in that state. It was an opinion common to virtually all Americans at the time.

"You have but one remedy within your reach," the Great Father intoned. "And that is, to remove to the West and join your countrymen, who are already established there." And the sooner it is done, he said, the sooner you can begin "your career of improvement and prosperity." The United States has assigned the tribe "a fertile and extensive country, with a fine climate, adapted to your habits." In addition, he continued, the Nation would receive $5 million, a sum which divided equally among all the Cherokees—assuming (incorrectly) their number came to ten thousand—would give $500 to every man, woman, and child.

"The choice is now before you. May the great spirit teach you how to choose. The fate of your women and children, the fate of your people to the remotest generation, depend upon the issue." The President reminded them of the fate of the Creeks and how reduced in circumstances their lives now were because they had resisted his will and violated the law. "Think then of all these things. Shut your ears to bad counsels. Look at your condition as it now is, and then consider what it will be if you follow the advice I give you."[17]

Thus ended the Great Father's talk. The Cherokee delegation turned away subdued, and maybe shaken, but still unconvinced about the wisdom of surrendering their land. Other delegations followed, and each one got the same reception and message. Soon the General was telling the delegations that "the present is the last proposition that he will make to them while he is in office; and they must abide the consequences of its rejection."[18] Jackson never could resist a not-so-subtle threat when he spoke to "obdurate" Indians.

These talks convinced few Cherokees outside the Treaty party. In fact the National Council of the Cherokee Nation formally rejected the treaty in the fall of 1835. Nor did it help the President's cause when the Principal Chief, along with his house guest, John Howard Payne, the playwright and composer of "Home, Sweet Home," were arrested in November, 1835, by the notorious Georgia Guard and carried off. Even the American press was outraged and called the seizure an act of "lawless banditti."[19] Although both men were soon released it severely hampered Jackson's efforts to induce the Cherokees to move west. Fortunately, he had the wit (or luck) to appoint Schermerhorn as a commissioner to treat with the Cherokees, along with William Carroll of Tennessee. Carroll was ill and contributed little to the negotiations, but Schermerhorn more than compensated for Carroll's indisposition. With the zealousness of a religious fanatic, including a fire-and-brimstone manner of harangue, Schermerhorn lived among the Indians for over six months and exhausted every means to win their approval for their removal. Finally, he called "a council of all the people" to meet at New Echota during the third week in December, 1835, and he arranged to have a large contingent of the Treaty party present. The fact that the National Council had already rejected a treaty of removal troubled him hardly at all.

Ridge and his supporters arrived at New Echota on December 19, followed by three hundred others a few days later. Most Cherokees boycotted the meeting. On December 22 the meeting was convened. The "draft treaty" signed the previous March was discussed and a committee of twenty was formed to consider the details of its provisions. Ridge, Boudinot, John Gunter, and their friends were members of this committee. Ross was conspicuous by his absence, having gone to Washington to plead with Jackson for better terms.[20]

On December 28, what came to be called the Treaty of New Echota—it basically repeated the provisions of the "draft treaty" approved in March—was brought to the assembled Cherokees. The committee of twenty announced its acceptance of the terms of the treaty. A vote was taken and the treaty approved by the count of 79 to 7.[21] This incredibly low number represented few Cherokees, certainly not the elected government of the Nation and certainly not the thousands of Indians who should have participated in the ratifying process. No matter. The treaty was approved and signed. Then a committee of thirteen was designated to carry the treaty to Washington and empowered to act on any alterations required by President Jackson or the Senate of the United States.

It was chicanery, pure and simple. The ratifying process was a fraud, an act approaching highway robbery. Nonetheless, it produced a removal treaty, and the power of the Cherokee Nation was broken at last.

Ross protested with every skill and device at his command. He gathered signatures of fourteen thousand Cherokees to accompany his complaint. He memorialized the Senate and documented the fraud that had produced the New Echota Treaty. Of the thousands of Indians who should have participated in ratifying the treaty, he said, fewer than a hundred were involved. (According to Schermerhorn, some three to five hundred Cherokees attended his meeting, but he clearly exaggerated the number.) Ross stayed on in Washington throughout the spring of 1836 in the hope that he could muster enough opposition in the Senate to kill the treaty. He begged Jackson to see him, but the Chief Magistrate informed him through the secretary of war that he did not recognize any existing government among the eastern Cherokees.

What drove Ross to near fury was Jackson's refusal to deal with the duly constituted authority of the Cherokee Nation as established under the Cherokee constitution of 1827. But Jackson argued that a duly constituted authority of the Nation did not in fact exist. The Cherokee constitution of 1827 called for an election in 1832 and it had not been held. Instead, the Principal Chief filled positions on the National Council with his friends. Thus, according to Jackson, when the National Council rejected the "draft treaty" in the fall of 1835, it acted illegally and Schermerhorn was totally justified in disregarding this action and calling a new council at New Echota. At least such a council would represent "all the people" according to their "ancient customs."

To President Jackson, the Principal Chief resembled nothing so much as an antidemocratic aristocrat, similar to an American Whig, and interested solely in his own power and prestige. Ross was greedy for money, according to Jackson; he cared nothing for his people; he violated the constitution by failing to hold an election in 1832; and he filled offices with his friends in order to subvert the will of the Cherokee people and prevent them from seeking a home beyond the Mississippi River. (It is very possible that Ross's actions reminded Jackson of his own rejection as President by the House of Representatives in 1825 and the "misuse" of the patronage power by President John Quincy Adams throughout his term in office.) To make matters worse, Ross had predicted better days for the Cherokees if Henry Clay defeated Jackson for the presidency in 1832. All in all, according to Democrats, John Ross was an evil influence among the Cherokees. "What is there [in him]," editorialized the *Globe*, "but an utter recklessness of character, a shameless disregard of the truth, and a wild and ill-regulated ambition."[22]

In any event, the Treaty of New Echota barely squeezed through the Senate. Henry Clay spoke powerfully against it and tried to show great sympathy and understanding for the benighted Cherokees. But the Democrats sneered at him and reminded the public how he had once declared that the disappearance of the Indians from the "human family will be no great loss to the world."[23] Edward Everett, Daniel Webster, Henry Wise, and others also delivered long and fervent appeals against the treaty, but on the final vote it won approval by a single vote. A two-thirds majority was required, and on May 18, 1836, a total of 31 Senators voted for it; 15 voted against. Had the "stool pidgeon,"* as Jackson always called him, Hugh Lawson White, chairman of the Senate Committee on Indian Affairs, voted against the treaty, as he told the Cherokees he would, the treaty would have been lost. But he knew he could never survive the outrage of Tennesseans had he opposed the measure and so he reversed his position and betrayed his promise.[24]

The President immediately added his signature and proclaimed the Treaty of New Echota in force on May 23, 1836. Although a petition signed by fourteen thousand Cherokees denounced the treaty, still the President and Senate accepted it as expressing the will of the Cherokee people.[25] Jackson was determined to remove the Indians, and he convinced himself that the action at New Echota by the consenting Cherokees was a legal action binding on the entire Nation. Besides, he regarded the petition containing the fourteen thousand signatures as the work of Ross's mixed-blood elite, the sort of petition that Nicholas Biddle concocted to block the removal of the deposits and win recharter, and totally unrepresentative of the popular will. The President also recognized that there was little opposition to the treaty by the American electorate—and that was a controlling consideration. The debate over ratification in the Senate did not begin to compare with the verbal brawl unleashed by the

---

*The *Globe* defined "stool pidgeons as candidates who are willing to be used as decoys, set up as People's candidates, but nominated to draw the election from the People to the politicians in the House." *Globe*, September 9, 1835.

debate over the Removal Bill in 1830. Although the New Echota Treaty was a worse violation of Cherokee rights than the Removal Act, it did not produce a sense of moral outrage on the part of the religious community in the country. Indeed, the American Board of Commissioners for Foreign Missions, whose object was the "civilizing" and the Christianizing of the Indians, made no real effort to prevent the treaty's ratification.[26] The Board was more concerned about winning the approval of the War Department to set up new missions among the Osage and Chippewa tribes. The Cherokees were virtually abandoned.

The Treaty of New Echota was almost identical to the "draft treaty" signed in Washington on March 14, 1835. It provided that the Cherokee Nation cede all its remaining territory east of the Mississippi River to the United States for a sum of $4.5 million and a joint interest in the country occupied by Cherokees who had already moved beyond the Mississippi River. The Cherokees would be paid for their improvements. They would be removed at government expense and maintained by the United States for two years. Removal was to take place within two years from the ratification of the treaty, that is by May 23, 1838.[27]

And so began one of the most disgraceful and heartrending episodes in American history. The Cherokee Nation was forced to comply with a treaty it never approved. It was made to act out the fraud perpetrated upon them by greedy and determined white men. Unfortunately, the Principal Chief would not accept the hopelessness of the situation and he encouraged and led the Cherokees in blocking the execution of the treaty. Although some few hundred Indians resigned themselves to their fate and headed west, the vast majority would not budge from their homes during the two-year grace period allowed by the treaty for their removal. They listened to John Ross and they trusted him. The "great villain" persisted in his defiance, but it was simply a matter of time. Once the deadline for their evacuation was reached and they still resisted, then the federal government took action and applied force. The Indians were rounded up, herded into prison camps, and then sent west along what the Cherokees came to call "The Trail of Tears."

The militiamen sent into the Cherokee country were not disposed to treat the Indians kindly. With rifles and bayonets, they flushed the Indians out of house and cabin and locked them in stockades specially erected for the purpose. Indian families at dinner, wrote one observer, "were startled by the sudden gleam of bayonets in the doorway and rose up to be driven with blows and oaths along the weary miles of trail which led to the stockade. Men were seized in their fields, women were taken from their wheels and children from their play." When the captured Cherokees turned for one last look at their homes they saw them in flames, set ablaze by the lawless rabble who followed the soldiers. These outlaws looted and raped and desecrated graves.

By the thousands the Indians were herded into stockades where many sickened and died. In June the first contingent of about a thousand Cherokees were sent down the Tennessee River by steamboat on the first leg of their westward journey. Then they were boxed like animals into railroad cars for the second part of their journey, and again many died because of the oppressive conditions. The Cherokees walked the last leg of "The Trail of Tears" until they reached their final destination in the Indian Territory beyond the western boundary of Arkansas. In all it was an 800-mile journey.

It has been estimated that some 18,000 Cherokees were removed, of whom 4,000 died as a result of their capture, detention, or westward journey.

No one can deny the incredible suffering endured by the Cherokees. Yet it is important to point out that genuine efforts were made to prevent this tragedy. General Winfield Scott, who commanded the operation, issued specific orders to his troops to treat the Cherokees with humanity. Furthermore, he delayed the emigration of most of the tribe in response to their pleas, and the removal itself was carried out by the authorities appointed by the Nation under a contract Scott made with the Cherokee representatives. In addition, he tried to obtain as much medical assistance for the Indians as possible. Many other white men, like Scott, acted humanely during the removal. But they simply could not contend with the scope of such an operation.

Jackson himself had retired from the presidency when the Cherokee exodus was set in motion and he deeply regretted the torment the Indians endured. Still he shares much of the blame for this inhuman deed. He was so anxious to expel the red man from "civilized society" that he took little account of what his inflexible determination might cost in human life and suffering. And the suffering was truly horrendous. "Oh! the misery and wretchedness that present itself to our view in going among these people," wrote one man. "I fought through the Civil War," said another, "and have seen men shot to pieces and slaughtered by thousands, but the Cherokee removal was the cruelest I ever saw."[28]

This cruel and bloody resolution of the Indian problem was applied to other tribes during the waning years of Old Hickory's administration. The Creeks had long ago submitted to Jackson's will. But their removal did not go smoothly—or peacefully. For one thing, a formal treaty of removal was never obtained. The acquisition of Creek lands, therefore, involved many frauds and created such a stench of corruption that the smell of it wafted clear up to Washington. Jackson was embarrassed and infuriated when he got a whiff of the stench. He ordered an immediate investigation. Defrauding the tribes had never been his intention; removal was meant to preserve Indian life and customs and these Native Americans were supposed to receive adequate recompense both for their land and its improvements. Jackson directed Secretary of War Lewis Cass to investigate vigorously and to apprehend and prosecute the perpetrators. Then, just as the investigation was getting under way, the Creeks rose up in their wrath and frustration and began killing whites. These attacks occurred in May, 1836, and were probably instigated by "a few unprincipled and wicked contractors."[29] The fury of the Indian assaults and the panic among whites living in Alabama and Georgia brought an immediate end to the investigation. Instead, Cass ordered General Thomas S. Jesup to subdue and then remove them. Thus began the so-called Creek War of 1836. Over 10,000 troops operated against the Creeks. After several bloody encounters in July, the troops captured Jim Henry, "the most redoubtable of the Creek chiefs," and with that accomplished, the "War" was declared at an end.[30] Sixteen hundred Indians, some of them handcuffed and in chains, were carted off to the west. A week later another thousand Creeks were rounded up and removed. After that it was a steady stream of frightened, starving, sick, and desperate Creeks who were forced to leave their homes and find refuge in the Indian Territory. All together, 14,609 Creeks were removed during the summer and fall of 1836, and their journey became one long chronicle of horror.[31] So what could not be accomplished by treaty was achieved by the gun.

Upon the arrival of one group of Creeks at Fort Gibson in the Indian Territory an old chief addressed a white leader of the removal operation. "You have been with us many moons," he said. "Our road has been a long one. . . . On it we have laid the bones of our men, women, and children. . . . You have heard the cries of our women and children. . . . Tell General Jackson if the white man will let us we will live in peace and friendship."[32]

An even greater agony accompanied the removal of the Seminole Indians—an agony both for the Indians and their white tormentors. A series of treaties had been concluded (in particular, Payne's Landing in 1832, and Fort Gibson in 1833) which provided for the removal of the Seminoles from their reservation in Florida to the Indian Territory. Pressure for their removal became intense after 1834 because a mounting number of runaway slaves found refuge among the Seminoles. Probably there were several hundred black slaves living among the Indians, although their number was invariably exaggerated by southerners. In any event the cause of red and black people was joined against whites in this unique situation.

In October, 1834, President Jackson sent the Seminoles one of his "talks" and expressed his displeasure that the Indians had not yet begun to remove. Though he said he did not believe that any of his "red children" were "so dishonest and faithless as to refuse to go," still there was much foot-dragging and this made the Great Father very angry.

The chiefs in council responded with appropriate words of obeisance. "My Brothers!" said one. "Our father in Washington says we must act like good and honest chiefs, and go without any trouble. Let us show our father that his red children are honest."

INDIAN REMOVAL—SOUTHERN TRIBES

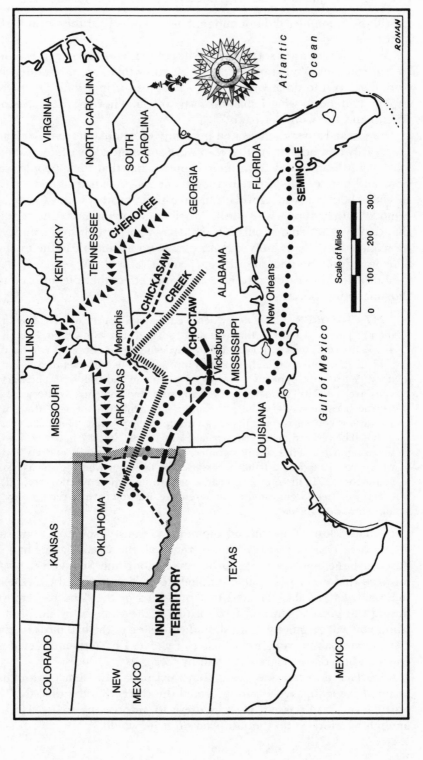

COLORADO

KANSAS

NEW MEXICO

OKLAHOMA

INDIAN TERRITORY

TEXAS

MEXICO

MISSOURI

ILLINOIS

ARKANSAS

Memphis

Vicksburg

MISSISSIPPI

LOUISIANA

New Orleans

KENTUCKY

TENNESSEE

CHEROKEE

CHICKASAW

CREEK

CHOCTAW

ALABAMA

GEORGIA

VIRGINIA

NORTH CAROLINA

SOUTH CAROLINA

FLORIDA

SEMINOLE

Gulf of Mexico

Atlantic Ocean

RONAN

Scale of Miles

0   100   200   300

Still the Seminoles did not budge. Four months later the Great Father sent another talk.

"My Children: I am sorry to have heard that you have been listening to bad counsels. You know me, and you know that I would not deceive, nor advise you to do any thing that was unjust or injurious. Open your ears and attend to what I shall now say to you. They are the words of a friend, and the words of truth."

The Great Father then recited his litany of complaints and demands. He wearily reminded them that they were surrounded by whites, that the game had disappeared from their country, and that their people were poor and hungry. He also reminded them that they had signed a treaty to cede their lands in Florida and, like their brothers, the Creeks, to remove to the country west of the Mississippi. Furthermore, he recalled that they had added a stipulation that they wanted their new country to be scouted by certain chiefs to make certain it was suitable to their needs. This was done, he said, and the agreement ratified.

"I now learn that you refuse to carry into effect the solemn promises thus made by you. . . .

> MY CHILDREN: I have never deceived, nor will I ever deceive, any of the red people. I tell you that you must go, and that you will go. Even if you had a right to stay, how could you live where you now are? You have sold all your country. You have not a piece as large as a blanket to sit down upon. What is to support yourselves, your women and children? The tract you have ceded will soon be surveyed and sold, and immediately afterwards will be occupied by a white population. You will soon be in a state of starvation. You will commit depredations upon the property of our citizens. You will be resisted, punished, perhaps killed. Now, is it not better peaceably to remove to a fine, fertile country, occupied by your own kindred, and where you can raise all the necessaries of life, and where game is yet abundant? . . . If, therefore, you had a right to stay where you now are, still every true friend would advise you to remove. But you have no right to stay, and you must go.

Then Jackson's tone turned ominous. Because "some of your rash young men" might forcibly oppose removal, the Great Father had ordered a large military force to be sent among the Seminoles. I have directed that every reasonable indulgence be shown you, the Great Father said. I have also directed that one-third of the tribe be removed during the present season. If you listen to the voice of friendship and truth, you will go quietly. "But should you listen to the bad birds that are always flying about you, and refuse to remove, I have then directed the commanding officer to remove you by force."[33]

After Jackson's talk was read, General Duncan L. Clinch, who commanded the troops, rose and informed the chiefs that the time for "expostulation" had passed. He was there to enforce the treaty. He had enough warriors to do the job. And do it he would.[34]

His manner was needlessly abrupt and offensive. He almost seemed anxious to provoke a confrontation. Then it happened. Suddenly the platform on which the dignitaries of both sides were sitting gave way. The occupants tumbled to the ground, a distance of ten feet. Many of the Indians, suspecting a trap, started howling and headed for cover. Others doubled over with laughter. When order was restored the remaining chiefs chose not to take offense over Clinch's manner and asked for a postponement of their meeting, after which they promised to gather a council that would truly represent the entire tribe.[35]

The governor of the Florida Territory, John H. Eaton, the former secretary of war and Jackson's longtime friend, warned the administration that any show of force to achieve removal would be met with fierce opposition. The use of military pressure would surely provoke war, he said. Avoid needless provocation. Besides, a new and potentially dangerous Indian leader had emerged in the past few months, a mixed-blood by the name of Osceola, whom the whites called Powell. He was bold and dashing, a handsome man about thirty-five years of age, who had declared himself unyieldingly opposed to removal. He favored "proscribing" every Indian who obeyed the Great Father's command.[36]

To prevent Osceola from infecting other Indians with his venom against removal, the federal troops seized him in late spring 1835 and placed him in irons. For hours the Indian raged like an animal. He frightened all who watched his antics. Then he quieted. His mind slowly determined upon a course of action and this had the effect of calming him down. He cooperated with his jailers. He even signed a document certifying the validity of the Treaty of Payne's Landing. So subdued did he seem that the federal authorities freed him. But he was now more dangerous than ever. He breathed a hatred for whites so intense that he shook with passion every time he thought of his internment.

A series of running battles then broke out which flared into serious trouble by the early fall. The plans Osceola conceived in jail were beginning to take hideous shape in the wanton killing of anyone favoring removal. In keeping with the advice of Governor Eaton to avoid provocation at all cost, President Jackson invoked the Intercourse Acts of 1802 and 1834 which decreed that no person might enter the Indian reservation without a pass issued by the War Department or the Indian agent. But such orders were nearly impossible to enforce and so the killing and raiding and stealing escalated. One chief, Charley Emathla, understood the Great Father's determination and prepared to remove. He sold his cattle and was about to depart for the west with a small party when Osceola and his supporters surrounded them. An argument ensued. Then Osceola shot the chief and left his body to decay on the trail. He took the money in Charley Emathla's pockets and flung it in every direction.[37]

The militia tried to put an end to this steady intensification of hostilities, but its very presence virtually guaranteed bloodshed. When a small detachment of soldiers separated from the main body of troops to escort a baggage train at Kanapaha, Osceola ambushed and seized the train. This action occurred on December 18, 1835, along the rim of the Alachua Savannah and marked the official beginning of the Second Seminole War.[38] It worsened two weeks later at the Battle of Withlacoochee, and because of the impossible terrain across much of Florida—the swamps in many places were impenetrable—the war showed signs, right from the start, that it might go on indefinitely. To make matters worse, the President and his war secretary gave the situation little heed at first because they were preoccupied with the French crisis; in addition, two of the highest-ranking generals of the army, Winfield Scott and Edmund Pendleton Gaines, were bitter enemies. All of these factors—not simply the swamps of Florida—conspired to produce a vicious, bloody, and protracted war.

Within days after the Battle of Withlacoochee, General Scott was ordered to take command in Florida. He was summoned to the White House to receive directions and advice from an old Florida campaigner who had not forgotten his experiences during the First Seminole War. The President had much advice to give. First off, he said, find out where the "Indian women were collected" and "proceed at any hazard & expense" to it. This would draw Osceola—or "Powel," as Jackson called him—out of the swamps and into a position where he could be attacked. Also, the President continued, "have two good spy companies immediately organized, led by gallant men, acquainted with Indian cunning and treachery, and good woodsmen." Nothing compares to good spies, he declared. Jackson then advised Scott to pass through South Carolina and Georgia on his way south and muster the militia into service. By that time you will know where the Indian women are located, he ventured. Take eight days' rations strapped to the backs of your men, he continued, and by forced marches head directly to "the deposit of women and children" where you will "find all the warriors" and where with "one blow" you can put an end to the war. Jackson admonished Scott against entering the swamps with wagons, "telling him that if he did he never would find an Indian."[39]

Unfortunately, this straightforward strategy got mangled in army protocol and procedures. The dividing line between the eastern and western army commands passed through the Florida combat zone, and Scott was directed to disregard that line. Of course, General Gaines, through whose command Scott now operated, was infuriated. The resentment and quarreling between the two generals began almost immediately and became so public that even the newspapers commented on it. "The old question of the relative rank of these distinguished officers," editorialized the Washington *National Intelligencer*, "has already led to unfortunate results which may in the end be disastrous. The collision of the authority of these officers has been accidental and we trust it may be amicably resolved."[40]

Scott performed very poorly in battle against Osceola. He was neither trained nor temperamentally suited to this sort of warfare. When Scott reached the depot of provisions, Jackson later recalled, he waited several weeks with the militia for the arrival of wagons. He planned to deploy "three grand columns" in a circling action. But "to surround what!" Jackson barked, "—the Indians—no—for . . . Gen'l Scott had no positive information where the Indian women and children were." At length Scott took the field with his three columns. And got lost. The three grand columns never did meet—not until they arrived at Tampa Bay, and they never found a single Indian. With the advance of summer, or what Jackson called "the sickly season," Scott abandoned the campaign and took up residence in St. Augustine.[41] He was forthwith removed from command and sent against the hostile Creeks in Alabama. Ultimately, both Scott and Gaines were summoned before a court of inquiry for their failures, although both escaped punishment.[42]

There followed a long period in which the Florida command remained very ill defined. At different times the new governor of the Florida Territory, Richard Keith Call, a former aide to Jackson during the Creek War, was authorized to conduct the military operation. An exchange of letters between the President and the governor failed to clarify the matter,[43] for Call was told that Scott had been directed to turn over the command to General Clinch, but that if Clinch declined it then the command belonged to Call—unless, of course, General Thomas S. Jesup should arrive in Florida, in which case he would assume command. This was lunacy. How or why Jackson permitted this madness defies understanding. Probably the reasons involved a combination of bad health, distraction over other problems, both foreign and domestic, and his perennial difficulty in separating friendship from all questions of policy; for he hated to disappoint his old friend Call, whose heart was set on acting as both governor and commander of the Seminole War.[44]

Still, Jackson hesitated. His instincts seemed to warn him away from turning the military command over to the governor. In response, Call whined and complained. Then Old Hickory rebuked him. "For the Lord's sake take some energetic stand," he bawled, "raise your people to action & energy, pursue & destroy every party of Indians that dare approach you. . . . You must act promptly & regain the military fame lost by the wretched conduct of Gen¹ Gaines & Scott, instead of complaining. . . . I expect you to act with energy, or you will loose your military fame."[45]

Did this mean that Call had the command? No one knew for certain. The matter came to a head several days later when Jackson received from Call a plan of action which promised to defeat Osceola and bring the war to a speedy end. The President jumped at it. According to this scheme, the Withlacoochee would be used as a supply line, and after a feint by horsemen against hostile villages to cover the movement of men and equipment up the river, an all-out assault would crush Seminole resistance. Whatever the merit of the details of this scheme, Jackson approved them. He seemed desperate. Any show of energy excited him. He scribbled on the back of Call's letter that the plan "will redeem us from that disgrace which now hangs over us."[46]

Governors were not normally given command of a field army, but within a month after the President received his letter, Call got the command he so desperately desired. Still, he failed. He could not bring the Seminoles to heel. He found it easier to maneuver troops on a sheet of paper than through the wet and marshy terrain of Florida. He could not force the Indians to battle. They just vanished into the everglades. Thus Call's promised offensive ended with his army turning around, hungry and rebellious, and coming back to the place where they had started, without so much as engaging in a single major battle.

Jackson seethed. Call had promised to lead an offensive and end the war. Instead he marched to the very edge of Seminole country and then turned back. In his anger and frustration, the President administered another tongue-lashing to the hapless governor. Through the acting secretary of war, Benjamin F. Butler, Old Hickory expressed his "disappointment and surprise" that Call had conducted such an atrocious campaign. The governor was accused of moving his troops without first obtaining adequate supplies from the various depots which were under his direct command. Worse, he was castigated for approaching the enemy "with so large a force within so short a distance of the enemy" and then retiring without making the slightest show of military strength. "This disappointment and regret are greatly increased by the consideration that these retrograde movements will probably have the effect to expose the frontiers to new invasions by marauding parties, and to encourage the Indians in their resistance, thereby increasing beyond what might otherwise have been needed, the severity of the measures which will now be required to subdue them." In view of everything that has happened, the letter concluded, and for "fear that the state of your health" will not permit you to finish the campaign, "the President deems it expedient to relieve you from the command." Major General Thomas S. Jesup will take over.[47]

Jackson also wrote a personal letter to Call and mocked him for failing to end this "Punic War" after all his promises.[48] It was a crushing rebuke and Call never fully recovered from it. Call blamed Jackson for his disgrace. He demanded a court of inquiry, but it was never granted. And so a twenty-three-year friendship slowly disintegrated and Call drifted out of the Democratic and into the Whig party.[49]

"I am sorely mortified," Jackson confessed to General Jesup on giving him the command. He begged his general to defeat Osceola "before Congress meets."[50] The "late retrograte," as he called the governor's retreat, at least forced the President to give the Seminole War more serious attention. "I have been confined to my room all this day taking medicine," Jackson groaned to his acting secretary of war. "I have been brooding over the unfortunate mismanagement of *all the military* operations in Florida, all which are so humiliating to our military character, that it fills me with pain, & mortification—the sooner that a remedy can be offorded the better."[51] He therefore directed that Jesup begin a vigorous campaign against the Seminoles at once, attack their strongholds along the banks of the Withlacoochee, and penetrate the entire country between the Withlacoochee and Tampa Bay. You will, Jackson commanded his general, establish posts at or near the mouth of the Withlacoochee, at Fort King, and at Volusia, and you will take the "proper measures for securing through them, the safety of the frontier." Jesup was also directed to make permanent arrangements for procuring "sufficient and regular supplies." As soon as these "dispositions" were complete, he was to proceed "without delay" to cross the Withlacoochee and capture the position now occupied by the Seminoles, "attacking and routing them" wherever they might hide. Engage the Indians in battle, Jesup was instructed, and their total submission would surely follow. But if they run away, as usual, then push forward to the south of Volusia and to the east and south of Tampa Bay so as to force their "speedy and effectual subjugation." This direction to attack the enemy in all their strongholds, the President declared, "you will regard as a positive order." In all matters Jesup was instructed to exercise sound discretion calculated to protect the frontiers and bring about the subjugation and speedy removal of the Indians.[52]

Jesup lasted nearly eighteen months. During that time he captured nearly 3,000 Seminoles and had them removed. He also captured Osceola by violating a flag of truce. In late October, 1837, Osceola had come to Jesup's command post under the flag to negotiate the release of three chiefs who had been captured in the vicinity of St. Augustine. While yards of white cloth floated over the camp, Jesup ordered the place surrounded. Osceola was seized, interned at Fort Marion in St. Augustine, and then at Fort Moultrie off Charleston, where he died a few months later, on January 31, 1838.[53] In April, Jesup was relieved of his command and General Zachary Taylor replaced him.

These latter events occurred months after President Jackson retired from office in March, 1837. He grieved over the protracted struggle in Florida and raged at the imbeciles who could not bring the war to a speedy end. And part of the blame, interestingly enough, he assigned to Floridians. In an interview with the retiring territorial delegate, Joseph M. White, the President vented his anger in a most remarkable scene. White had commented on the strain the war had placed upon the people of Florida, to which Jackson retorted that the territory had never yet put a brigadier general's command in the field.

"Let the damned cowards defend their country," he bellowed in a sudden explosion.

As he roared, Jackson became more agitated. Why, he said, with "fifty *women"* he could "whip every Indian that had ever crossed the Suwannee." The people of Florida, he fumed, had done less to end the war or to defend themselves "than any other people in the United States." If they had been "men of spirit and character," he cried, they would have crushed the Seminoles in a single blow. Oh, I tell you, if five Indians had set foot into the white settlements of Tennessee or Kentucky, he went on in this furious and passionate outburst, "not one would have ever got out alive." Jackson was literally beside himself at this point. He said that the male Floridians ought to go out and let the Indians shoot them, then at least the "women might get husbands of courage, and breed up men who would defend the country." At the height of this insanity the President declared that there never were more than 600 Indians in the territory!

Finally the tumult ended. Jackson grew quiet and eased himself into a chair. White waited a moment and then risked another explosion by asking why "your Army and all your Generals," who have been in the field for over a year, had not conquered these 600 Indians. "Why are the people of Florida thus reproached," he continued, for not doing what "all your regular troops, and Tennesseans, have failed to accomplish?" To drive the knife deeper, White declared that Jackson's vaunted Tennesseans had had a great deal of difficulty in getting their wounded off the field at one recent battle.

The figure in the chair rumbled. He reared up. His eyes blazed. "It is a lie!!" Jackson boomed.

White backed off. He was not present at the battle, he said, and could not vouch for the report. The wild-eyed President slunk back into his chair.[54]

This ghastly scene portrays perfectly the depth of Jackson's anguish over the war. He left office burdened with the agony generated by the Seminole War and for years he could not shake it from his mind.[55] In Congress the opposition mocked him over the financial burden of the continued hostilities and what it did to his efforts to reduce the cost of government and ease the burden of the taxpayer. By the time Jesup departed from his command, the cost of the war neared $10 million, or approximately $458,000 per month. The American people could thank Andrew Jackson for this bloodletting, said Caleb Cushing of Massachusetts, both the loss of treasure and the loss of lives.[56]

The Second Seminole War continued until 1842 before the last battle was fought. By that time, nearly 4,000 Seminoles were removed to the west and the few who remained in Florida escaped into the everglades. By the middle of the twentieth century maybe 1,000 Seminoles still resided in Florida and nearly triple that number lived in Oklahoma.[57] Some 1,500 regular soldiers died during this war out of 10,000 who participated. There is no way to calculate accurately the mortality among volunteers or among Indians.

The Second Seminole War marked the fiercest and bloodiest and cost-

INDIAN TERRITORY

MISSOURI

ARKANSAS

KANSAS

TEXAS

OSAGE

CHEROKEE

Fort Gibson

Arkansas River

CREEK

OTO

PAWNEE

IOWA

SAC
AND FOX

KICKAPOO

POTAWATOMI

SEMINOLE

Canadian River

CHOCTAW

CHICKASAW

Red River

North Canadian River

Scale of Miles

0   20   40   60   80   100

liest opposition to Jackson's policy of removal. But it could not deter it or bring it to an end. The so-called Five Civilized Nations of the South —the Choctaw, Chickasaw, Creek, Cherokee, and Seminole—had all been expelled to the west. But removal did not end with these tribes. The Black Hawk War accomplished the permanent relocation of the Sauk and Fox Indians from Illinois. The Quapaws, the Appalachicolas, the united tribes of Otos and Missouri, and the four confederated bands of Pawnees of the Platte signed treaties of cession that removed them from "civilized society." The Chicago Treaty of 1833 with the Chippewa, Ottawa, and Potawatomi provided valuable land to whites in Illinois, Michigan, Wisconsin, and Iowa. During the closing years of Jackson's administration treaties with the Miami, Caddo, Wyandot, Menomini, Saginaw, Kickapoo, Delaware, Shawnee, Osage, Iowa, Pinkeshaw, Wea, Peoria, and other tribes brought additional territory in Arkansas, Louisiana, Kentucky, Indiana, Illinois, Ohio, Kansas, Michigan, Iowa, Minnesota, and Nebraska.[58]

By the close of Jackson's eight years in office approximately 45,690 Indians had been relocated beyond the Mississippi River. In addition, a number of treaties had been signed and ratified (but not yet executed) that would raise that figure by several thousand. According to the Indian Office, only about 9,000 Indians, mostly in the Old Northwest and New York, were without treaty stipulations requiring their removal when Jackson left office. The operation, of course, provided an empire. Jackson acquired for the United States approximately one hundred million acres of land for about $68 million and thirty-two million acres of western land.[59]

The removal of the American Indian was one of the most significant and tragic acts of the Jackson administration. It was accomplished in total violation not only of American principles of justice and law but of Jackson's own strict code of honor. There can be no question that he believed he acted in the best interest of the Indian, but to achieve this purpose countless men, women, and children suffered deprivation and death. Jackson's humanitarian concerns—and they were real concerns—were unfortunately shot through with ethnocentrism and paternalism that allowed little regard or appreciation of Indian culture and civilization.

Andrew Jackson left office bowed down by the stupefying misery involved in removal, but he left knowing he had accomplished his goal and that thousands of Indians had found what he considered a safe haven west of the Mississippi River.[60] He left believing he had saved the Indians from inevitable doom. And, indeed, he had.[61]

CHAPTER 21

"A Bomb Thrown
Without Warning"

JACKSON'S SUCCESS IN REMOVING THE INDIANS was matched by his mounting political successes in Congress and around the country. And he promptly took advantage of this opportunity and formally nominated Roger Brooke Taney as the chief justice of the United States on December 28, 1835. At the same time he forwarded the name of Philip P. Barbour of Virginia for the position of associate justice. Both nominations went to the Senate Judiciary Committee and were reported out on January 5, 1836. The recommendation urged that the nominations lie on the table.

Fortunately, Jackson's strength in the Senate gained with each passing month, reflecting his gains throughout the country. Connecticut, Illinois, and Louisiana each sent a new representative to the upper house whose loyalty to the party and the President proved unshakable. Furthermore, when the Virginia legislature instructed its senators to vote in favor of Thomas Hart Benton's resolution to expunge the censure of Jackson from the Senate journal, John Tyler resigned rather than submit to dictation. He was replaced by William C. Rives, former minister to France and (at the moment) a loyal Jackson Democrat. He took his seat on March 14, 1836, and his arrival in the Senate encouraged Taney's friends to force a showdown on the nomination.[1]

On March 15 the Democrats girded themselves for a test of strength. After several futile efforts by the Whigs to delay confirmation and move adjournment, the Senate proceeded to take up the two nominations in executive session behind closed doors. Taney came first, and by a vote of 29 to 15 he was confirmed. Clay, Webster, Calhoun, and the "stool pidgeon" voted "nay." The Senate then turned to Barbour's nomination

315

and, after beating off a motion by Daniel Webster to postpone action until the House had voted on a new judiciary bill that would rearrange the judicial circuits and increase the Supreme Court from seven members to nine, confirmed him by the vote of 30 to 11.[2]

Flexing their newly developed muscles, the Senate Democrats then rushed forward the nomination of Amos Kendall as postmaster general. And they really meant to humiliate the Whigs with this one. Jackson had submitted Kendall's name in December, 1835. Again, the Democrats displayed their ever mounting strength and won confirmation on March 15, 1836, with a margin of 25 votes before the disgusted Whigs could force an adjournment.[3]

The *Globe* gloated over these triumphs. When the *National Intelligencer* lamented that so many senators missed these crucial votes because of the "lateness of the hour," Frank Blair sneered. "And when was it," he editorialized, "that the opposition ever let the shades of night prevent them sitting, when they wished to record their votes against a cabinet minister? Did they not sit as late to put them on record against Mr. Stevenson? They put their veto on Mr. Taney last year, after one o'clock at night."[4]

To top off this series of victories, Jackson sent back to the Senate on February 18, 1836, the nomination of Andrew Stevenson as minister to Great Britain. It went immediately to the Committee on Foreign Relations, whose chairman, Henry Clay, brought in a recommendation two weeks later that the nomination be rejected. On March 16, the day after the confirmation of Taney and Barbour, the Senate confirmed Stevenson by the vote of 26 to 19. Clay, Calhoun, and White voted against him, while Webster chose to absent himself. Thus, after more than four years—a really disgraceful delay—the nation now had an accredited minister to the Court of St. James's. It was almost two years since Stevenson had been rejected in 1834. During that time the Senate had undergone thirteen individual changes in membership, out of a total of forty-eight men, and of those thirteen, ten voted to confirm Stevenson.[5]

Jackson had gained the day. These votes measured the distance of his increased political strength in Congress. Of course, he may have skewered the republican system just a bit, but he insisted that he had acted in the best interests of the American people. His tenacity as well as his loyalty to friends and party supporters brought cheers from Democrats around the country. But Whigs described the President's conduct as viciously partisan—the cantankerous schemings of an arrogant, misguided, and stubborn old man.[6] Jackson always figured that he could wait out the Whigs because he knew the people would rally behind him. Sooner or later, he declared, the will of the people would be felt by his enemies.[7]

Because Jackson identified himself totally with the people and believed that his will represented theirs, he became increasingly intolerant of opposing political views. He labeled them conspiracies to disrupt the processes of democracy. He also presumed to interpret the Constitution for the people, and when his opinions clashed with the courts he appealed to the electorate to resolve the matter. They constituted the final court of appeal, he said. Surely, no one seriously believed that "four men who form a majority of the Supreme Court" should have "dominion . . . over the rights of the states and the rights of the majority of the people of the United States." The people rule; they decide the government they want; and all must submit. The idea of unrestrained judicial review—such as exists today—horrified him.[8]

Jackson's constitutional views proved untenable, but they were genuinely democratic. What he did, of course, was further subvert the doctrines of republicanism. Central to the constitutional system was the notion of checks and balances, but Jackson made a shambles of that notion by insisting on his primacy as President in interpreting and executing the law because he—and he alone—represented all the people. Andrew Jackson was the great advocate of democracy. Majoritarian rule was the only thing that mattered in his thinking about the operation of government. But the democracy he practiced reduced to near ruin the kind of republic conceived by the Founding Fathers. He tilted the tripartite system in favor of the executive. In circumventing the Supreme Court, in thwarting the will of Congress and insisting on his right to direct legislation, and in riding roughshod over the claim of any state to assert its sovereignty against the collective rights of the nation, he reshaped the constitutional system into something more appropriate to a modern, democratic state, which requires strong executive leadership. He functioned under the self-imposed limitations of a laissez-faire libertarian. But self-imposed limitations hardly promote balance between three separate and equal branches of government. Within the parameters of law, if the only check upon the President is the popular will, then majoritarian democracy may have been achieved but that is not the structure of government as originally conceived. And it is certainly not republicanism as understood by Americans of the early nineteenth century.

But clearly the Americans of the Jacksonian age had advanced beyond the concerns of an earlier generation that feared popular rule. They wanted the kind of democracy their President advocated because it placed them at the very center of the governmental process. Andrew Jackson not only symbolized their age but he served as their leader and guide to a more representative society. And the final years of Old Hickory's administration witnessed the almost total victory of the forces cooperating with him in devising a more democratic government, even though many Whigs—and the great triumvirate in particular—denounced it as "revolution."

Not only did the old man force acceptance of his nominees during the final year of his administration, but he completed his "experiment" in reforming the banking and currency system of the country and even converted some Whigs in the process into supporting the deposit banks.

Two considerations brought the matter of the final reformation of the currency to a head. The first was the lack of any legislation regarding the deposit banks since Jackson had arbitrarily and ruthlessly removed the government deposits from the BUS and placed them in selected pet banks. The action represented a colossal assertion of executive authority and Jackson was quite willing to go along with this ad hoc arrangement, except that the deposit system really needed the support of law. Several efforts along these lines had been attempted, but the Whigs invariably piled amendments on top of the proposed legislation in order to emasculate the system. So the matter just drifted from session to session, and after a while some Democrats seemed content to leave it at that.

The second problem was the existence of a mounting surplus. The general prosperity of the country, the lack of a national debt, and the "strict economies" practiced by the Jackson administration had produced an embarrassment of riches. What to do with this surplus? Jackson himself had suggested to Congress in his first message that once the debt had been liquidated the surplus might be distributed among the states, according to representation, to be used for public works and education. If there were constitutional objections to this proposal—and he knew there were many states' righters who would object—then he suggested that a constitutional amendment might resolve the difficulty. He returned to the scheme of distribution in his second message as the best way to address the need for internal improvements. After all, he had vetoed the Maysville Road bill and distribution looked like the only way to reconcile his veto with the clamor for public works. By the time he got to his third message, delivered on December 6, 1831, Jackson seemed less keen on distributing the surplus and more intent on reforming the tariff, which was a principal cause of the growing surplus. It was far more desirable, he said, "to relieve the people from unnecessary taxation after the extinguishment of the public debt."[9]

Mention of tariff reduction produced howls from many Whigs, especially Henry Clay. Ultimately, a tariff compromise was arranged in 1833 that provided some reduction of the duties over a ten-year period. Rather than disturb this compromise—particularly since the tariff quarrel had generated a nullification crisis—the question of further reductions of import duties was considered improper and so discarded. But, of course, that meant the surplus continued to swell. Henry Clay finally put his head to the problem and came up with a different kind of distribution plan. He proposed to distribute the proceeds from the sale of public lands. In presenting his bill, Clay went out of his way to state that the distribution of the *revenue* was unconstitutional, but not the distribution of the proceeds from land sales.[10] To his mind, the virtue of his land bill was that it would block the administration's efforts to lower the price of land (then established at $1.25 per acre by the Land Law of 1820) and consequently limit internal improvements projects. What Clay suggested was a bill in which 10 percent of the land revenue would go to states in which the land lay and the rest be distributed among the states according to their congressional representation. By this scheme, money would be made available for internal improvements, and it freed the tariff money for use in meeting the normal expenses of the federal government. In this single package, Clay protected his tariff, advanced internal improvements, maintained the current price of land, and distributed the surplus. But his scheme would effectively close "the door of opportunity" to the great masses of the people, according to Clay's most recent biographer. His policy catered to the immediate interests of the wealthy and opposed the wishes of the American democracy.[11]

Clay's land bill passed the Senate in 1832 but failed in the House. It came up again the following year and passed both houses during the closing days of the congressional session. Jackson pocket vetoed it. When Congress reconvened the following December, he sent the reasons for his veto to the Senate in a message dated December 4, 1833. "The public lands are the common property of the United States," said Jackson in his message, "and the moneys arising from their sales are a part of the public revenue." No distinction can be made as to source when expending or distributing it, as Clay had attempted to do. The object of this bill, he went on, is not to return to the people an unavoidable surplus of revenue which they have paid, but to create a surplus for distribution among the states so they can engage in activities they might not otherwise be able to afford. "It seizes the entire proceeds of one source of revenue and sets them apart as a surplus, making it necessary to raise the moneys for supporting the Government and meeting the general charges from other sources." In fact it compels the taxpayer to contribute to the creation of a surplus for distribution to the states. "If this principle be once admitted," the consequences are clear: the states will always look to the federal government for handouts. Eventually all their funds will come from the federal Treasury. Without assuming any new principle, said Jackson, the Congress need go but one more step to "put the salaries of all the State governors, judges, and other officers, with a sufficient sum for other expenses, in their general appropriation bill."[12]

A more direct road to the total consolidation of government and federal intrusion into every aspect of American life cannot be devised, Jackson declared.

> Money is power, and in that Government which pays all the public officers of the States will all political power be substantially concentrated. The State governments, if governments they might be called, would lose all their independence and dignity; the economy which now distinguishes them

would be converted into a profusion, limited only by the extent of the supply. Being the dependents of the General Government, and looking to its Treasury as the source of all their emoluments, the State officers, under whatever names they might pass and by whatever forms their duties might be prescribed, would in effect be the mere stipendiaries and instruments of the central power.[13]

Money is power! Whoever pays the bill sets the rules. And in government, such an exercise of power would mean the destruction of liberty and the creation of an absolute state. "It was not for territory or state power that our Revolutionary fathers took up arms," Jackson exclaimed; "it was for individual liberty and the right of self-government."[14]

The preservation of individual liberty had always been President Jackson's goal. He knew only one certain means to that end: the perpetuation of the minimal state.

The intelligent people of our nation, Jackson continued, are too wise not to see the dangers inherent in amalgamating all political power in the hands of one centralized agency, of establishing "one mass of common interest and common feeling." Such a calamity would rob us of the blessings we now enjoy "from our happy Union."[15]

As for the public lands, Jackson took the Jeffersonian position that they should be surveyed and sold to benefit individuals seeking a homestead. Let the land be made available to those who would occupy and farm it. Let its price and its availability suit the convenience and needs of the American people. It is not in the interest of this nation that the public land be used as a means of making money for the government. "I adhere to the opinion," Jackson stated, ". . . that it is our true policy that the public lands shall cease as soon as practicable to be a source of revenue." Already the price had been reduced from $2 an acre to $1.25. The price should be reduced still further, he declared, so that all the people, not just the rich, can own landed property. "While the burdens of the East are diminishing by the reduction of the duties upon imports, it seems but equal justice that the chief burden of the West should be lightened in an equal degree at least." This would have a "harmonizing" effect on all the sections of the country and "add another guaranty to the perpetuity of our happy Union."

Jackson ended his veto message by declaring his regret that he must disagree (once again) with the Congress over their legislation. But he assured its members that any future legislation on this subject which would be compatible with the "Constitution and public faith shall have my hearty concurrence."[16]

Still the problem of distribution remained. And the surplus kept growing. Once the national debt disappeared, the excess revenue in the Treasury climbed to $36 million within a year. Soon states and politicians itched to dig their fingers into this largesse. Some complained that this handsome sum should be circulating in the marketplace, stimulating industry, creating jobs, and adding to the general welfare and the pursuit of happiness, not salted away among the pet banks. The eagerness to get at this cash mounted so alarmingly and so precipitously that Jackson risked a stampede among Democrats away from his leadership if he continued to block the congressional desire for distribution.

The sharp-eyed Clay saw his opportunity. In the present circumstances he realized immediately how he could garner political capital as well as embarrass the administration and divide Democratic ranks. He introduced his land bill once again. It was similar to the one Jackson had already vetoed but Clay revised the figures to give 15 percent of the sales —what tempting bait!—to the states in which the land was sold. The rest of the sales would be divided equally among all the states.[17]

Once more Jackson signaled to the Democratic leaders in Congress that he would veto Clay's bill. Despite this warning, and not unexpectedly, the Senate approved the bill. But if Jackson would not go for the distribution of land sales, grumbled the Democrats among themselves, perhaps something else which would appeal to the President could be substituted to rid the government of its unwanted fortune. What the Democrats finally proposed was a distribution bill tied to a system of regulating and controlling the deposit banks.

At first it was not certain that Jackson would go for a double-headed bill, and a number of congressmen, including Richard M. Johnson, spoke to him about it. What Jackson wanted to do, of course, was institute a general reform of the nation's currency and banking, not hand out monetary prizes to the states. His suggestions along these lines had been submitted to the House Ways and Means Committee on April 21, 1834, in a report prepared by the secretary of the treasury.[18] Unfortunately, they failed to gain congressional approval when initially suggested, but Jackson kept returning to them at every opportunity. And once the ratio between gold and silver was readjusted, the President seemed determined to substitute specie for paper. "The President with his respects to the Secretary of the Treasury," he wrote to Levi Woodbury on April 30, 1836, "and brings to his view the propriety of writing to the Deposit Banks to supply themselves with Specie (Gold) whilst it can be done by buying bills on Europe the exchange being now in our favour—the best mode is to urge the Banks to lay in a good supply of Gold."[19] Not only was Jackson intent on encouraging the use of specie in normal business and private transactions, and attracting as much of it into the country as possible,[20] but he actively intruded into the banking business to destroy its paper-issuing operation and force a wider adoption of specie. For example, as the time approached for the charter of the BUS to expire, Jackson instructed Woodbury on June 13, 1836, to "prepare a notification for Monday next that no notes of the United States bank are receivable in the public dues after the 13th instant . . . and add that no notes of any bank, except bank notes payable on demand, or presentation, in specie, made so by their charter, will be received in payment of the public dues."[21]

Quite obviously Jackson was determined to have his way about reforming the currency and banking in the country, and the longer the Congress failed to legislate on the question the longer Jackson would continue to exercise broad presidential powers to force the banking operations in the country to comply with his fiscal views. For the Democrats in Congress it meant that they must endure the incessant complaints of the Whigs about "executive usurpation" and Jackson's uncontrolled authority over public funds. So, at length, the House Democrats came up with a scheme to do two things: distribute the surplus and regulate the deposits of the public money. They figured that Jackson would swallow his dislike of distribution in order to get the regulation of the deposit banks. And to make distribution more palatable to him, they specified that the revenue from all sources would be distributed, not simply the revenue from land sales. As for the deposit features, the bill sharply curtailed the Treasury Department's discretion in the selection of the pets. Each state must have at least one deposit bank located within its boundaries, provided certain stipulated conditions were filled. The measure limited the amount of federal money to be held by each bank by forbidding a deposit bank from holding government funds in excess of a sum equal to three-fourths of its capital stock actually paid in. This single regulation, as subsequently enacted into law, necessitated the immediate increase in the number of deposit banks, and they soon mounted from twenty to ninety. As a result the best feature of the deposit system was severely weakened. No longer did the government deal with a small number of specially selected banks whose fiscal soundness and reliability could provide real strength to the system. Once the number of pets shot up to ninety it was impossible for the Treasury to exercise any real control over them. This delighted enterprising capitalists around the country who soon discovered that without restrictive controls they could engineer more speculative and more profitable financial deals.[22]

For Jackson the best part of this bill was the provision requiring the deposit banks to redeem all their notes in specie on demand and to issue no notes for less than five dollars after July 4, 1836, nor receive any note under five dollars in payment of an obligation owed to the United States. Later the amount would be increased to ten dollars and by March 3, 1837, to twenty. The bill also provided that whenever the deposit in any bank exceeded one-fourth of the capital stock of the bank, the deposit bank was required to pay the United States an interest of 2 percent on the excess.[23]

Attached to these deposit provisions in the bill was the distribution of the surplus. This section stated that all money in the Treasury as of January 1, 1837, in excess of $5 million, would be turned over to the several states in proportion to their respective representation in the House and Senate. The money would be distributed in four installments:

January, April, July, and October, 1837. In return, the states would provide the secretary of the treasury with negotiable certificates of deposit. These certificates could be sold by the secretary if necessary. When negotiated, they would bear an interest rate of 5 percent.[24]

When Jackson first saw this "two-headed monster" he was tempted to inform his friends in the House that if the bill passed and came to him in its present form he would bounce it back to them with a resounding veto. He had repeatedly asked for a banking system that could be regulated, one consisting of a small number of banks whose strength could wisely influence other banks. Instead, what they offered was a collection of unregulated banks holding more money than these institutions could properly handle. Making matters worse was a distribution bill piggybacked on top of it. Did they think him an idiot? He knew what they were about.

But Jackson kept his counsel. He desperately wanted a deposit bill and he particularly liked the paper-issuing restriction of the present one. So he consulted his many advisers and asked for their opinion. Blair strongly opposed the measure and counseled him to veto it if it passed. Taney also had his doubts, and although he was now the chief justice he willingly provided Jackson with an opinion. Because Taney's arguments were very persuasive, the President asked him to commit his ideas to paper so that they might form the core of a veto message should he decide to refuse his consent to the present bill.

Early in June, 1836, the deposit bill passed both the House and the Senate.[25] At the same time Taney presented Jackson with the paper he had been commissioned to prepare. Taney wrote it as a veto, speaking as though he were the President addressing the Congress. In it he said that the bill went beyond his expectations. Had the measure been a deposit bill only he would have approved it, despite several limitations. But the distribution of the surplus caused a serious problem. This provision had nothing to do with the rest of the bill. "In my judgment," wrote Taney, speaking as Jackson, "Congress have no power to raise money in order to appropriate it to the uses contemplated by this part of the Bill." What it amounts to in effect is a loan to the states. And that is unthinkable, for it would establish a relation of debtor and creditor between the states and the United States. "The feelings which such a state of things must necessarily create would in a short time shake this Union to its very foundation and destroy the brightest hopes of the friends of freedom in every part of the civilized world."[26]

Everyone agrees, the paper continued, that the government of the United States is a limited one. "I have always belonged to that school which holds that it can exercise no powers but those which are granted in express terms by the constitution." So vital is this concept, so "essential to the freedom and perpetuity of our institutions," that nothing can induce me to exercise any doubtful power by the federal government.

Thus, the question comes down to this: can the United States raise money for the purpose of lending it to the states? Certainly no express power is provided in the Constitution and nothing about it falls under the "necessary and proper" clause. I am convinced that the taxing power can be used for national purposes only. "We have no right to go further." We must not burden the people with taxes beyond the amount we need to run the national government. If we do otherwise, we assert for this government "an unlimited power of taxation and appropriation" with no regard for the purposes for which it is intended.[27]

Had Jackson known that federal income would outstrip expenses he would have advised a reduction of the tariff duties, although he really had no wish to disturb the compromise hammered out in 1833. Because of "the prosperous state of our finances," the increased revenue could be used for coastal defense, he said, and to build up the navy.[28]

It was a strong paper and probably reflected Jackson's own views very precisely since he and the chief justice had had a long talk about it before Taney prepared the paper. Even so, if he vetoed, the problem of the surplus would remain. And the problem of regulating the deposit of public funds would also remain. That gave him pause and nudged him toward giving his approval. Another compelling reason for signing the bill was the need to move the country further along in the use of specie. Besides, what were his alternatives once he vetoed the bill? He could opt for another national bank. But that course ran counter to everything he believed about the currency and banking. He did consider the establishment of a Bank of Deposit and Exchange in Washington and told Amos Kendall about it. Such an institution, he said, might set an example for other states and prove beneficial to the "safety of our currency . . . and check the paper system & gambling menace that pervades our land & must if not checked ruin our country & our liberty."[29] But this was a pious wish. It was really too late now to undertake new projects with vast and uncertain implications. His administration was nearly over and time was fast running out. In addition, this was a presidential year and it was very important to Jackson that Van Buren succeed him. For a Whig to succeed, or the election go to the House, as it did in 1825, was more than the old man could bear.

In the final analysis it was a political consideration that determined Jackson's decision. Rather than jeopardize Van Buren's election, he would sign the deposit/distribution bill. Such a vast outpouring of federal money into the coffers of the states was certain to enhance Van Buren's electoral chances. It was an opportunity he could ill afford to let pass by. So, with a wistful sigh of regret and "a repugnance of feeling and a recoil of judgment," Jackson informed the Democratic leadership in Congress that he would accept the bill provided they made a few alterations. He wanted section 13 amended which dealt with the manner funds would be returned by the states. It was very important to Jackson that everyone understand and accept the fact that the money was a deposit, not a loan to the states.[30]

The Democrats in Congress were elated. Not only had they escaped the predicament posed by Clay's land bill, but they foresaw enormous political benefit in providing the states with a monumental gift of cash expected to be in excess of $20 million.[31] The amendment to section 13 was duly introduced by Representative Joseph B. Anthony and passed overwhelmingly by a vote of 123 to 50. "I have never witnessed such rejoicing, as I have this day among our friends," Richard M. Johnson told Jackson after he had conveyed the President's message to the other members of Congress; "as soon as I gave assurances to most of them, that you would approve of the deposit principle . . . the amendment embracing your suggestions went like wild fire, or the fire in the prairie."[32] When the entire bill came up for a final vote on June 22, 1836, it passed the House by a count of 155 to 38. The Senate also passed it by a vote of 40 to 6, and Jackson affixed his signature on June 23, 1836.[33] Almost immediately thereafter Congress adjourned and headed home.

But many Democrats around the country—especially ideologues— were distinctly unhappy about the distribution portion of the Deposit Act. From a party point of view, wrote Thomas Hart Benton at a later date, it was the "commencement of calamities" that ultimately pitched the Democrats into the electoral debacle of 1840. The Richmond *Enquirer* growled its complaints and was joined by the Albany *Argus*. "The distribution bill is universally condemned," wrote one Regency member. "I have not heard an opinion in favor of it expressed by any one." The *Globe*, too, voiced its fears and predicted that distribution would divide parties just as banking, internal improvements, and the tariff had done in the past. "Money is the agent of the class that would establish wealth as the sovereign power of the Republic," editorialized Jackson's mouthpiece. "That class will never cease its efforts to make Government a machinery to draw from the great mass of the community all its surplus means to convert the accumulation into a fund to prostitute to the Aristocracy all who may be trusted by the people." It is the duty of the Democracy, the newspaper went on, to make certain that each state treats the surplus as a "sacred deposit" and have an "honest intention" to return it whenever the federal government requires it. If, on the other hand, the Whigs succeed in getting up among the states an appetite for annual handouts from Congress, then the great principles of the Constitution will have been lost and the Democracy transformed into an Aristocracy controlled by a moneyed elite.[34]

The Whig press applauded the measure. "The Deposit bill has given very general satisfaction throughout the country," noted the *National Intelligencer.* But this endorsement only further agitated the Democratic press. It is quite remarkable, snapped the *Globe,* how solicitous the Whigs have become of the deposit banks. They never felt that way before.

Obviously they plan to seize the "corrupting largesses" to subvert the Democracy. What the government really should do, said the *Globe*, is distribute the money among the people. "This can be done only by REDUCING THE TAXES. Reduce the taxes; reduce the price of the public lands to actual settlers; let each and all be reduced so as to keep the revenue within the expenses of the Government."[35]

Such complaints and criticisms troubled Jackson because he feared his action might be interpreted as an abandonment of principle.[36] But Blair reassured him of his constancy and Taney wrote to say that he was justified in signing the bill once Anthony's amendment to section 13 had been passed in the House. "However objectionable the bill is on the score of policy," he said, "yet there is no constitutional difficulty in the way, and no sufficient ground for a veto."[37] But Taney's reassurance lacked conviction, for he had to admit that the policy involved in distribution was "a most unfortunate and mistaken one." Once the general government can raise money beyond its wants and place the money wherever it chooses, then "I see no limitation whatever to the powers of the General Government." This was Jackson's position precisely, and it profoundly disturbed him that he should be the President to begin a practice that would end with the government giving money to states, individuals, and corporations and then prescribing the rules by which they must behave. As he said many times, such a national calamity spelled the culmination of American freedom.[38]

But Jackson was naive, if not downright foolish, in thinking that politicians and businessmen would subscribe to any fiscal view that collided with their ambition and avarice. The nation was in the throes of vast social and economic changes. It was expanding along two broad fronts: centrifugally in space across a wide continent; and centripetally toward the city and the factory. The American people were continuing their evolutionary progress toward a capitalistic, industrial, modern, and democratic society. The speculative boom worsened during the 1830s as inflation took hold and swelled with each passing year. Because state banks operated without any real control, and because the deposit banks failed to provide any guidance or strength in achieving sound currency and credit, the country was soon inundated with a fresh supply of paper money. Even though bank notes under five dollars had been prohibited as early as September, 1835, by the secretary of the treasury, the financial boom of the mid-1830s moved too fast to stem the flood of paper. The very thing the President had sought to prevent was now running out of control. By the fall of 1836 there were clear signs that a crash was not far off.[39]

Land speculation was particularly bad, and here Jackson felt there was something he could do to ease the speculation and stop the proliferation of paper money. The General Land Office was doing a fantastic business, so much so that "doing a land office business" entered the national vocabulary. Land sales reached nearly $25 million in 1836; by the time

Jackson decided to do something about it, the sales were running up to $5 million each month.[40] Worse, fraud in land sales occurred everywhere and kept increasing. "Associations of individuals" tried to monopolize the operation, buy land cheaply, drive the price up, and then sell it to settlers beyond its real value. It was even reported that the public money in the deposit banks was diverted for this notorious operation. The situation soon verged on chaos. The quantity of paper money had reached an astronomical figure; it had swollen by more than 50 percent in the last eighteen months. Moreover, the opportunity of converting this "shadowy paper" into real estate was so tempting, and the means of obtaining loans so easy, that something had to be done before disaster struck.[41]

Jackson rose to the need. His decision was swift and bold. He decreed that henceforth only gold and silver would be accepted for the purchase of public lands. He summoned his cabinet to inform them of his decision. Straight off a majority of them objected. They knew that Congress (then in session) would balk at this further exercise of executive power and might even pass legislation to countermand it. That was a real danger. The President spoke to Senator Benton about it since Benton had unsuccessfully attempted several times in the past to introduce a resolution in the Senate to halt the speculative mania in land. Benton confirmed the danger. So Jackson decided to wait until Congress adjourned and then issue his order. He had the "nerve which the occasion required," Benton gleefully recorded, even though it was certain to produce a howl of protest from Whigs around the country to say nothing of the bellows of outrage the Congress would sound when it reconvened the following December.[42]

Again the cabinet was summoned. The President informed them of his intended action; after expressing their fears and disapproval, they quietly accepted the inevitable. Major Donelson was then directed to prepare a draft of the order and Senator Benton was invited to lend his aid in the preparation of the document. When a rough draft was ready, Jackson took it to his cabinet for their final comments and suggestions. Then he signed and released it.[43]

The Specie Circular, as it was called, was issued immediately upon the adjournment of Congress on July 11, 1836, through the secretary of the treasury. It ordered that from August 15 onward, nothing but specie would be received for payment of public land, except from actual settlers, who were permitted to use bank notes. It was issued under the authority of the resolution of 1816, which gave the secretary of the treasury discretionary authority to receive or reject the notes of specie-paying banks in revenue payments.

The Specie Circular was another forceful exercise of executive authority. It marked, said Benton, "the foresight, the decision, and the invincible firmness of General Jackson."[44] It also showed a marked disregard for the will of the Congress and the opinion of a majority of the cabinet. But

Jackson felt justified. He knew that most congressmen (as well as the members of his cabinet) were themselves deeply engaged in land speculation. They were not about to approve an order that would interfere with their own financial plundering.[45] So, motivated by the need to end the spiral of inflation, Jackson plunged ahead with his order and brought a jarring halt to the speculative land mania that had run out of control.

The Specie Circular caused a sensation. It was a "tremendous bomb thrown without warning."[46] Millions in bank paper on its way to land offices was turned back. "The disappointed speculators raged. Congress was considered insulted, the cabinet defied, the banks disgraced."[47] Still it did the job. And the "great mass of the people applauded it," according to Martin Van Buren, "as an attack upon the speculators whom they dislike." They believed implicitly that Jackson would never have issued the Circular "if it had not been for the public good."[48]

The Whigs erupted. They ranted and sputtered and swore. The *National Intelligencer* rightly denounced the Circular "as a measure of the same arbitrary character as the removal of the public deposits in 1833, emanating from the imperious will of an irresponsible Magistrate, the execution of which will not only effectually cripple the deposit banks, but produce a derangement of all the business of the country."[49] Other Whig journals had more specific complaints. The *National Gazette* of Pennsylvania and *Stone's Commercial Advertiser* of New York saw the Specie Circular as part of Jackson's continuing attack upon the commercial and mercantile classes of society. The *Commercial Advertiser* called the Circular another Jacksonian war against "the natural laws of trade."[50]

Henry Clay chimed in. He could hardly resist such an inviting target. He called the Circular "a most ill-advised, illegal and pernicious measure"—just what a dictator might be expected to do. In response, Blair accused Clay of trying to set off another panic, just as he and his Bank friends had done in 1834. The pattern of his pronouncements, said Blair, was always the same: first a speech of alarm, including a denunciation of the President for a so-called illegal order; then the prediction of ruin. He is obviously trying to affect the coming presidential election, Blair went on, but his tactics will not work because no single measure during Jackson's entire administration has met with more popular acclaim. Only "the speculators and those who are the advocates of the *rag currency* cry out against it."[51]

And the cry grew louder with each passing month. The demand for specie in the west prompted easterners to hoard it. Pressure for hard money mounted in the cities, and businessmen expressed their alarm over the possible consequences. The *Globe* tried to soothe these fears by announcing the appearance of a "new dollar" to be issued by the mint in the near future. For thirty years the coinage of the American dollar had been suspended. Not since 1805 had there been such a coin. Now it would be made available to all. The face of the coin would show a full-length figure of Liberty seated on a rock, holding a spear and a shield, the classic emblem of the liberty cap on her head. On the reverse side the American eagle on the wing would be depicted. Other coins would be issued with this design, said the *Globe,* as soon as it was practical to do so.[52]

The issuance of the "new dollar" and the Specie Circular demonstrated one thing, argued the Democrats: Andrew Jackson had restored "real money" to the country. And the benefits were sure to be felt by all classes and in all sections of the country within a very short time. Nonetheless, the pressure grew worse over the next six months, despite these reassuring words, and some Democrats began to mutter that Jackson had better provide some relief from the strictures of his Specie Circular and his "lunatic" insistence upon specie as the medium of exchange. But those who made these demands did not know Old Hickory. He would never back away from his hard money principles. Once he had fixed his course, it was virtually impossible to budge him. "The old Chief is unwilling to admit that the government has by any act contributed to the present pressure in the money market," said Congressman Aaron Vanderpoel of New York. "His doctrine is, that it has its origin in the mischievous expansion of the paper system, and the mad speculations and overtrading of the last eighteen months. You know too that the President is *in one respect like Revolutions. He never goes backwards.*"[53]

So forward Jackson went, urging all to follow him and assuring them that once the "mad speculations" ceased and the salubrious effects of specie trading had entered the normal operations of public and private business, the pressure would ease. But it did not. It steadily increased. And after a while some men began to predict that before long there would be a terrible economic collapse.[54]

CHAPTER 22

Jacksonian Democracy

ONCE THE "SLY" OLD MAN HAD PULLED HIS "SNEAK" TRICK on the Congress and issued his Specie Circular after the adjournment, he was ready to go home for a visit and a rest. He had not seen the Hermitage since the fire two years ago. There had been a number of delays in rebuilding the house, most of them resulting from the difficulty of getting skilled labor during an inflationary period. Also, the cost of reconstruction had escalated beyond anything Old Hickory expected. But the house was now very near completion and he had been told it looked handsome and elegant. He was anxious to see it for himself.

Besides the inevitable delays in building a spacious house, numerous changes, suggested by his son and daughter-in-law and by Major Lewis, among others, had been introduced into the overall design and these further delayed completion and added to the costs. And there had been another disastrous fire. The steamboat carrying eighteen crates of furniture and furnishings from Philadelphia to the Hermitage had burned in the river at Nashville just a few months earlier. As John Eaton observed to Jackson, "fire of late has become your great foe."[1]

The cost of rebuilding and refurbishing the Hermitage totaled nearly $10,000 before everything was completed. The initial estimate for the rebuilding alone had been given at somewhere between $2,500 and $3,000. In the final bill presented on August 2, 1836, to Jackson, the total cost came to $5,125, which included the changes made to the windows, the west wing, and kitchen, along with the addition of a full-length two-story (double) porch, front and back. New furnishings, shipped on three steamboats, cost $3,700, exclusive of what was lost in the steamboat fire.[2]

Anxious to see his home again and even more anxious to escape Washington after a long, grueling congressional session, Jackson left the city on the night of July 10, accompanied by Major Donelson.[3] He was in reasonably good health, but he ran into such bad weather (and worse roads) that his nerves soon had him edgy and uncomfortable. At one point it took seven hours to travel ten miles. It had been raining steadily for two weeks. In many places, he said, it took a team of ten horses to pull one wagon through the mud and bog.[4]

When Jackson finally reached Jonesborough at the eastern end of Tennessee he was welcomed with an enormous reception. For it was in Jonesborough that he had first settled in Tennessee nearly fifty years before. He stayed only a few months when he first arrived, but it was his introduction to the west, to the frontier, and to Tennessee. That was back in 1788.

Because of the size and enthusiasm of the crowd to greet President Jackson, the old master lost no opportunity to remind his listeners of their long devotion to the Democratic party and the need of maintaining that devotion through the election of Martin Van Buren in the fall. Even though Judge White was a Tennessean and someone they all knew and admired, still Jackson told them that the Judge had betrayed his party, principles, and friends and therefore did not deserve their support. Some of the farmers in the crowd informed the President that only a few days before, White, Bell, Peyton, and Wise had held a public dinner in Jonesborough at which Jackson and his administration had been assailed as threatening "the freedom and purity of the elective franchise and our liberties." These farmers said they were concerned about White's charges and wanted to know about the reputed "misapplication of the public funds and the official patronage."[5]

The old man responded "with his usual frankness" and courtesy. He spoke "the truth" to them, according to the Democratic press, and explained at length his efforts at reform and how difficult it had been to root out "corruption in Washington." It was very important to Jackson that the people of his own state understand the objectives and principles of his administration. And it was important to him that they demonstrate their approval of his record by voting for the Democratic presidential candidate in the fall. But he knew the election would be a struggle—an uphill struggle all the way. Not because Tennesseans had lost their affection for Old Hickory—quite the contrary—but because of their dislike and distrust of the Little Magician, Martin Van Buren. There were great fears among Democrats that Tennessee would bolt the party for Judge White.[6]

So, even though the trip home across the state was a hard one for the old warrior, particularly in view of the sharp criticism he heard about his foisting the Vice President on the nation, Jackson was determined to lend every aid he could to support the Democratic ticket.[7] During his entire visit to Tennessee, the President actively campaigned for the regular ticket as much and as often as his health and the dignity of his office allowed.

At Nashville the Democrats prepared a great reception to welcome him home. A committee of 100 had arranged the details. Resolutions had been passed that hailed his accomplishments and the magnificent qualities of his mind and character. These resolutions were typical of the usual outpouring of gratitude and devotion that Jackson now received from virtually every section and state of the Union. The praise was always extravagant but genuinely felt.

"This is the man who should be loved by every true American. For us he fought —for us he risked his fortune—for us he risked his life, and for us he has labored from youth to old age. The People never have—the People never will forsake or forget him."[8]

By the time Jackson reached home on the evening of August 4 he was totally exhausted. But then he saw the Hermitage, his newly built mansion, and the weariness and exhaustion of his long trip immediately slipped away. What he saw in the dim light was a beautiful and stately house rising majestically before him. It seemed to tower to an enormous height—certainly well over two stories. A handsome portico supported by six fluted columns added a touch of elegance, but the double porch softened the look and made it appear like a comfortable plantation home, not a public building. Two wings of a single story each, and projected forward a distance of ten feet, added approximately forty feet to the width of the original house. The left or west wing was the dining room with a service pantry and a storage pantry behind it, and the right or east wing served as Jackson's study and library.[9]

The double porch extended ten feet forward from the house. Each column rested on a stone and brick foundation. The column itself was made of wood but the capital at the top was fashioned from cast iron designed in the Corinthian mode.

The first floor of the house was then, and is today, divided by a large central hallway running the entire length of the building. At the far end of the hall a magnificent staircase sweeps upward in a flowing spiral to the second floor. The walls of the central hallway were covered with a wallpaper imported from Paris and, in four scenes, depicted the adventures of Telemachus on the island of Calypso while on journey in search of Ulysses. To the left of the hall were the front and back parlors separated by folding doors; to the right a passageway ran to an exit at the side of the house. Several bedrooms opened off the passageway. The General took the front bedroom; his son and daughter occupied the back bedroom, which had an adjoining nursery. Jackson's bedroom connected directly with his study next door. From this study Jackson had an exit built leading immediately to the front portico outside.[10]

The second floor was divided into four large guest rooms, one of which was reserved for the painter Ralph Earl.

It is very probable that the restoration of the Hermitage borrowed much from George Washington's home at Mount Vernon, especially the monumental colonnade and the shape of the driveway leading to the front portico. Jackson frequently took the steamboat trip down the Potomac to Mount Vernon, where he liked to visit with Martha Washington's granddaughter, Nellie Custis Lewis, who lived close by. Jackson was deeply impressed by the beauty and serenity of Mount Vernon.

The restoration of the Hermitage meant that the General could retire in comfort and a degree of luxury appropriate to the nation's first citizen. His retirement from public office in a little over six months now seemed all the more appealing. But the cost of rebuilding this imposing house, plus the necessity of liquidating the $5,000 debt to Harry Hill, combined with the staggering losses he suffered from another crop failure, left Jackson in dire financial straits.[11] This had been the second crop failure in as many years. Some blame for the disaster belonged to young Andrew, for once more he demonstrated how poorly he understood his responsibilities and how little he could be trusted with the financial management of the Hermitage properties. The young man simply lacked the necessary interest in farming and shifted many of his duties to the shoulders of the new overseer, Edward Hobbs. Then, when Hobbs disregarded instructions, Andrew let it pass without saying a word. In vain did Jackson attempt to educate Andrew about his duties. "My son," the President wrote, "you must assume energy; & command how our concerns are to be attended to by Mr. Hobbs & let him know, you must be obayed." Jackson had to remind his son not to forget to have the south pasture sowed. "We must seed well or we never can reap well." He was shocked to "discover all oats, hemp, & millet has been badly & slovenly sowed."

The financial strain of all these mishaps, plus the mismanagement of his plantation, forced Jackson to sell off some of his property. The loss of his furniture was the final blow. "This catastrophy will make it necessary that I should have more means," he told his son. Since Andrew had informed him that there was a prospective buyer who would pay $5 an acre for 400 acres in the western district, Jackson agreed to the sale. "If you can get that for it in cash, I authorize you to sell it. You can with truth say that I had declined taking that offer for it, because it was too low, but the burning of my house, & now my furniture, makes it necessary to me to sell."[12]

To make matters worse, Jackson's many physical ills began acting up again. Because of the dampness and rain he experienced on his route home, he caught a bad cold, which triggered violent spasms of coughing. This, in turn, activated the pain in his side and made it very uncomfortable for him to ride or sit for any period of time. "I fear I will have to use the lancet soon," he told Frank Blair. Such bloody episodes prostrated him for a few days but then he always managed to rally. A little

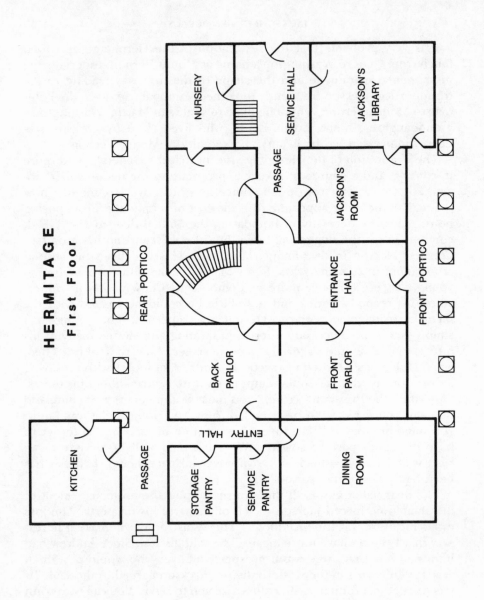

HERMITAGE
First Floor

REAR PORTICO

NURSERY

SERVICE HALL

JACKSON'S LIBRARY

PASSAGE

JACKSON'S ROOM

ENTRANCE HALL

FRONT PORTICO

BACK PARLOR

FRONT PARLOR

ENTRY HALL

KITCHEN

PASSAGE

STORAGE PANTRY

SERVICE PANTRY

DINING ROOM

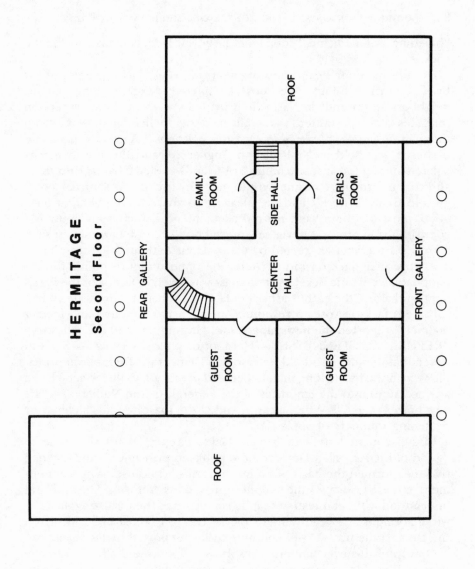

HERMITAGE
Second Floor

ROOF

REAR GALLERY

FAMILY ROOM

SIDE HALL

EARL'S ROOM

CENTER HALL

GUEST ROOM

GUEST ROOM

FRONT GALLERY

ROOF

"bleeding and medicine," commented Andrew Donelson, usually did the trick.[13]

Despite his poor health and his financial woes, Jackson enjoyed his brief sojourn at home. The house completely delighted him, and his neighbors and friends in Nashville provided a welcome-home reception (once his health permitted) that reaffirmed their belief that he was indeed the man *"who should be loved by every true American."* A great dinner and barbecue was held in Nashville on August 20, and the President circulated among the vast assemblage of friends to shake hands with them and chat informally. "I came here to meet my friends on Saturday last," he told Blair, "where I had the pleasure to shake by the hand at least 4000, most of whom were my old acquaintances, their sons & my old companions in arms—I never saw more good order & harmony in such a crowd. I was met & greeted by the matrons & their daughters."[14]

At this affair Jackson did not miss the opportunity to politic for the national Democratic ticket. After a toast was given in honor of the President, and after "the enthusiastic shouts of approbation" to this toast had subsided, Jackson rose to respond. "In his usual dignified and feeling manner," reported the newspapers, Old Hickory intoned the following: "REPUBLICAN TENNESSEE:—Her motto, *'principles not men'*—She will never abandon her good old Jeffersonian Democratic Republican principles which she has so long maintained and practiced, to throw herself (on any occasion) into the embraces of the Federalists, the Nullifiers, or the new born Whigs."[15] When Jackson ended the toast he was "cheered by deafening thunders of applause."[16]

In subsequent letters to friends Jackson repeated his reference to "good old jeffersonian Democratic republican principles," and claimed that they formed the basis of all his "reforms." Because of his commitment to these principles the people approved his "reforms," he said, and understood without question that he championed their cause against the wicked designs of a wealthy aristocracy.[17] His "great measures," declared the Democratic press, "will continue to be supported by *the people.*"[18]

On top of this ever mounting display of support and affection by the American people, Jackson received very cheering news from the secretary of the treasury. All four installments of the French indemnity had arrived, reported Woodbury, and "every dollar of this money has been received in gold." Furthermore, the third installment due from Naples had "also been punctually paid & . . . that likewise is in gold." As an aside, Woodbury remarked that the Specie Circular seemed to have been "well received by most of our friends."[19] Jackson had reason to hope that his administration would end on a note of total—one might even say "golden"—triumph. And, as always, he yearned that it would come soon.

On August 23 the President started for Alabama to visit the family of his deceased friend General John Coffee. He felt a deep obligation in this regard, and he had postponed the trip longer than he ever intended.

Along the way down to Florence, Alabama, where the Coffee family lived, he again attracted immense crowds to whom he repeated his message of the need for loyalty to the Democratic party. He campaigned almost every day as he headed south. James K. Polk, the hardworking leader of the state organization and Speaker of the House of Representatives, persuaded Jackson to alter his plans a trifle and come to Columbia for a large party rally. Some five thousand persons attended. They came to see their President and affirm their continued support of his administration. At the rally, General Pillow, on behalf of the citizens of the Columbia community, gave a lengthy and flattering address. Then the President stepped to the speaker's rostrum. "You have said that my election was depicted to the country as a worse calamity than war, pestilence or famine." Jackson smiled as he spoke. "The feelings which employed such language were not prompted merely by a wish to injure me. They had a higher ambition to gratify. They aimed at the prostration of the principles which the country had decided should be brought into operation." Our country is a democracy, he cried, and the government is expected to represent the will of the people. It is the destruction of our democracy that these partisans hope to accomplish. But the virtue of the people has in the past and will in the future annihilate these efforts. "Such charges pass by me as the idle wind. They are but the devices of an exposed and disappointed ambition and cannot but benefit the cause they intended to destroy."[20]

To Andrew Jackson and the American people at large it seemed obvious and incontestable that the nation was indeed a democracy. Perhaps they believed it had always been one. But under Jackson the concept of popular or majority rule really took hold. The Democrats trumpeted the rights of the people; they called the people wise and good and virtuous; and they insisted that the will of the people must in all instances be obeyed by their representatives. They denounced elitism and the pretensions of aristocracy. And although Jackson called this old-fashioned republicanism—or, to use his exact words, "jeffersonian Democratic republican principles"—it would later, and more properly, be called Jacksonian Democracy. The transformation of the United States from a republic to a democracy was a slow process that had begun long before Jackson came to office. But more than any other single individual he contributed to and symbolized the arrival and acceptance of that concept. His charisma, popularity, and accomplishments made it all possible.

Historians generally have tended to deny that Jackson held any firm philosophy of government that guided his actions. They choose to believe that he was principally motivated by private animosities and deep-seated prejudices, by passion and pride. They do him a grave injustice. Actually Jackson not only subscribed to a definite philosophy of government but he imposed that philosophy on his party and because of it markedly hurried the democratizing process.

To understand the thrust and direction of Jackson's political thinking it is necessary to remember the single, central event that shaped many of his ideas about government, to wit the "stolen election" of 1825 when John Quincy Adams and Henry Clay entered a "corrupt bargain" and elevated Adams to the presidency in defiance of the popular will. To Jackson this was the ultimate corruption in a general Era of Corruption. It produced what became "the first principle" of Jacksonian Democracy, namely *"the majority is to govern."*[21] This doctrine Jackson announced in his first message to Congress and he repeated it at every opportunity. He brushed aside any and all intermediary agencies that stood between the people and their government—even those placed there by the Founding Fathers. To the people, he said, belonged the right "of electing their Chief Magistrate"; neither an electoral college nor the House of Representatives may alter their choice, nor was it ever meant that they should. Not to put too fine a point on it, Jackson was clearly on shaky historical ground in making this assertion—but make it he did. As far as he was concerned, absolutely nothing could block the execution of the popular will. For the experience of 1825 proved beyond all doubt, he insisted, that the more agencies are erected to execute the people's will the more it will be frustrated. And that must be prevented at all costs.[22]

Jackson placed his entire confidence in the wisdom of a virtuous people "to arrive at right conclusions," conclusions binding on all their representatives. That was the message carried by his speeches and public pronouncements to the Democratic party and the electorate. In asserting this principle he was subverting (consciously or not) republicanism and the constitutional system as devised by the Founding Fathers. For the perceived wisdom at the time insisted that a government had been established by the Constitution which distributed power among three branches of government and provided checks and balances to keep the branches equal and prevent any one of them from dominating the others. The language of the Constitution, according to this view, *is* the will of the people. Having spoken, the people are excluded from speaking again except through the difficult, if not impossible, process of amending the Constitution. The agency or branch of government that is given the final say on the meaning of the Constitution is the Supreme Court. And the Supreme Court is the most removed body from the people.[23]

This view Jackson totally rejected. Not only did he deny that the people may speak no more except by amending the Constitution, but he denied that the Supreme Court was the final interpreter of the meaning of the Constitution.[24] Jackson subscribed to another view. He maintained that the people remain active in the governing process. The people are *never* excluded from the power that is theirs by right. They never surrendered that right. And they exercise that right through the ballot box which all agencies of government (including the Supreme Court) must obey. A form of government, such as the one provided by the Constitution, does not divest the people of the right to self-government. It does not give the

Supreme Court, for example, the right to tell them what is or is not allowed under that form. "Forms of government," wrote George Sidney Camp in *Democracy*, a work published in 1841 and obviously written under the influence of Jacksonianism, "have been, for the most part, only so many various modes of tyranny. Where the people are everything, and political forms . . . nothing, there and there only is liberty."[25]

That was Jackson's philosophy precisely. The people govern. Their will must be obeyed. Majority rule constitutes the only true meaning of liberty. All of which subverts the earlier notion of republicanism which did indeed provide for intermediate agencies to refine and alter the popular will when it was deemed necessary, such as occurred in 1825.

The "constant celebration" of the people, therefore, is basic to Jacksonian Democracy.[26] And it was this celebration throughout Jackson's administration—a celebration the people enjoyed and acknowledged[27]—that steadily advanced the march toward greater democracy in the United States.

At one point Jackson himself made a stab at defining Jacksonian Democracy and listed many of its identifying marks. If the "virtuous yeomanry of Tennessee," he wrote as he struggled with the definition, would simply ask political candidates a few basic questions, they could distinguish true Democrats from "Whiggs, nullies & blue light federalists*" by the answers they received. The people, said Jackson, "ought to enquire of them, are you opposed to a national Bank—are you in favor of a strict construction of the federal and State constitution—are you in favor of rotation in office—do you subscribe to the republican rule that the people are the sovereign power, the officers their agents, and that upon all national or general subjects, as well as local, they have a right to instruct their agents & representatives, and they are bound to obey or resign—in short are they true republicans agreeable to the true Jeffersonian creed."[28]

Sovereign power resides with the people, declared Jackson, and that power applies to all national and local issues. Moreover, the people have a right to "instruct their agents & representatives" as to their will. It is not enough to say that once the people elect their representatives they have no further control of the governing process. For Jackson, they always retain control through the doctrine of instruction. He would take away from representatives the power or right to "correct" or alter the popular will.

Jackson would also deny the courts this power. But he made a distinction. He would allow the courts the right to review and interpret the *law* but he would not assign them ultimate authority in pronouncing "the true meaning of a doubtful clause of the Constitution" binding on all. The right to review and interpret the law may be "endured," he argued,

*Blue light Federalists supposedly signaled to the British fleet off the New England coast with blue lights during the War of 1812 to indicate a safe haven.

"because it is subject to the control of the majority of the people." But pronouncing the true meaning of the Constitution was altogether objectionable because "it claims the right to bind" the states and the people with bonds that no one can loose except by amending the Constitution, a difficult process at best. To allow the Supreme Court the ultimate authority to interpret the Constitution perpetuates an aristocratic rather than a democratic system of government because four persons (five today) can dictate to a nation, with or without popular consent. And that was intolerable. As Jackson said in his Bank veto, "The Congress, the Executive, and the Court must each for itself be guided by its own opinion of the Constitution." In a truly democratic state, he argued, the people ultimately decide the question of constitutionality. And they do it through the ballot box.[29]

In sum, then, Jackson took the position best articulated by Alexis de Tocqueville in his classic work *Democracy in America*. "The people reign in the American political world," wrote Tocqueville, "as the Deity does in the universe. They are the cause and aim of all things; everything comes from them, and everything is absorbed in them."[30]

And when Andrew Jackson talked about the "people" he knew precisely whom he meant. Over and over in his public and private statements the term "the people" was defined as "the farmers, mechanics, and laborers," or "the humble members of society," or "those who earn their living by the sweat of their brow." Certainly not businessmen, monopolists, emerging capitalists, or any other elitist group, as sometimes suggested by historians.[31] He repeatedly referred to the "working classes" of America as constituting "the people" and, to a very large extent, he meant laborers in the urban areas. For example, when Amos Kendall wrote him about a labor problem at the Navy Yard in Philadelphia, Jackson responded sympathetically to labor's complaint. It seems that the Navy Yard had problems obtaining good mechanics because the government demanded more than twelve hours per day from each worker and the mechanics would not work that long. The rate of pay was $2 per day for shipwrights, and in order to overcome the excessively long workday the Navy Yard had advertised that the rate per day would be increased to $2.50. But not a single mechanic applied because they had agreed "to a resolution that for a day's work they would labor only from 6 to 6." Other agencies in the Philadelphia area had acquiesced to this demand. "The government of the United States only holds out against it," Kendall told Jackson. "The concession of the richer classes was considered a triumph of the Democracy, and the Democracy here complain that the only opposition which exists, comes from an administration which relies on them for its support."

Kendall made his point as forcibly as possible: The working classes look to Jackson as their representative. In turn, the administration "relies on them" for support. "I think the point ought to be conceded," Kendall continued. "The demand of the workingmen that twelve hours shall constitute the working day, is not unreasonable. At Washington the extension of service in the Public Offices to ten hours is considered a hardship." What is to be gained in exacting more than twelve hours from the workingmen in the public service at Philadelphia? asked Kendall. In the first place, it has brought public service to a dead halt. In the second, "the democratic friends of the administration are disgusted and discouraged." I hope, he added, that the secretary of the navy will direct the Navy Board to comply with the wishes of the workingmen. "Concession will do much good; obstinancy will produce nothing but mischief . . . to the republican cause in this quarter."[32]

After Jackson read this letter he referred it to his secretary of the navy. But first he scribbled a note of instructions to the secretary: "If the Navy board have not been directed to order that the hours, from 6 oclock to 6 be agreed to as pr. my former, intimation that it may be forthwith adopted."[33] Clearly, then, Jacksonianism was not a movement of small businessmen. Jacksonian Democracy was more concerned with workingmen in places like the Philadelphia Navy Yard. This was confirmed in a long conversation a newspaper reporter had with the President on the subject. Jackson invariably "left upon the minds of all who have conversed with him," said the reporter, "a deep impression of his solicitude to see the laboring class of the country" freed from the burdens imposed by a business aristocracy. "He has expressed no sentiment in regard to other classes of society. . . . His motto is, Let labor have security, prosperity will follow—all other interests rest upon it, and must flourish if it flourishes." Contrast that statement with the opinion of Whigs, gloated the *Globe*. During the last congressional session, Daniel Webster said: *"Take care of the rich, and the rich will take care of the poor."* Webster denied making the remark, said Blair, but, "as the Indians say, he speaks with a forked tongue."[34]

The policy of the Jackson administration on labor was best defined in the *Globe*, taking its cue from a series of editorials in the Boston *Morning Post* and addressed directly "To All Democrats or Working Men." "If Democracy be the rule of your policy," the article read, "suffer no act to be passed . . . however it may promise local or personal advantage, if it tends in the smallest degree, to give *legal* advantages to *capital*, over *labor;* if it have that effect, it must necessarily increase the natural inequality in society; and finally, make two distinct classes: namely—masters and slaves."[35]

Editor Blair took great pains to identify Jackson personally with laborers, both here and abroad. European workers constantly look to the President as a champion of their cause, he said. "It must be gratifying to the Democracy of the United States to perceive that the laboring classes beyond the Atlantic—those who sigh for liberty—who pray for the privilege of turning their own toil to their own advantage, instead of having their substance devoured by lords, pensioners, and public creditors—look to the American Patriot President as the champion of those principles, through the propagation of which, under his auspices, they indulge the hope of deliverance for themselves and their children."[36]

But to return to the General's efforts to define Jacksonian Democracy: in addition to preaching majoritarian rule, Old Hickory cited strict construction of the Constitution as an essential article of faith. However much he himself subverted that doctrine, Jackson believed fundamentally in limited government and the necessity of keeping government spending to an absolute minimum. He also included opposition to a national bank and rotation in office as part of his creed. Rotation in office was simply his way of stating that the operation of government must be open to all. No elitism. No official class. Again, he himself may have failed to recruit from every social and economic class, but he insisted that democratizing the government be regarded as a cardinal doctrine of Jacksonianism.

Indeed, the General's views on holding office became even more democratic as he grew older. He proceeded from the premise that all offices —whether appointed or elected—must ultimately fall under the absolute control of the people. Appointed offices should be rotated, preferably every four years. Elected offices must be filled *directly* by the people. In keeping with this principle, Jackson tried to abolish the College of Electors in the selection of the chief executive by proposing a constitutional amendment. In addition, he said, the President should serve no more than a single term of either four or six years. Jackson advocated a single term in order to place the President beyond the reach of improper—"corrupting"—influences. Moreover, he believed that United States senators should be directly elected by the people. Also, their term should be limited to four years and they should be subject to removal. In Jackson's mind, the Senate was an elitist body of men committed to the principles of aristocracy and totally unrepresentative of the American people. Considering his long and bitter struggle with the upper house it is not surprising that he should feel so vehement. His thoughts on democratizing the Senate were conveyed to the electorate in the editorial columns of the *Globe*. "We say, then, to the People of the United States," wrote Blair, "is it not worthy of consideration to provide an amendment to the Constitution, limiting the senatorial term to four years and making the office elective by the People of the several States?"[37]

Interestingly, Jackson would also require federal judges to stand for election, and presumably he would include the justices of the Supreme Court once the Constitution had been properly amended. And he would limit judicial terms to seven years but permit reelection. By this time Jackson was so totally devoted to the democratic principle of officeholding that he could conceive of no better method of preserving freedom and ensuring justice for all. His remarkably advanced views were regarded by some as very radical—if not dangerous. The historian George

Bancroft interviewed Jackson on the subject and recorded some of the President's opinions. "He thinks every officer should in his turn pass before the people, for their approval or rejection," wrote Bancroft. "In England the judges should have independence to protect the people against the crown," said Jackson. But not in America. "Here the judges should not be independent of the people, but be appointed for not more than seven years. The people would always re-elect the good judges."[38]

Jacksonian Democracy, then, stretches the concept of democracy about as far as it can go and still remain workable. Obviously, Jackson himself was far ahead of his times—and maybe further than this country can ever achieve.

It should be noticed in reading Jackson's attempt at defining his brand of democracy that he said nothing about slavery, Indian removal, tariffs, or internal improvements—although his opposition to internal improvements might be implied by his strict constructionism. As to slavery, there has been much misunderstanding among modern historians about the position of Jacksonian Democrats on this issue. Contrary to wide belief, Democrats were not committed to the preservation of slavery—at least not as Jacksonians, however they may have felt about the issue individually and personally. True, they abhorred abolitionists. They regarded them as malcontents who, like aristocrats, feared the people and the kind of government that majoritarian rule produced. Abolitionists decried the demise of their Republic—just like all other elites—and blamed the demise on the rise of democracy. They therefore sought to create as much trouble as possible in order to discredit the democracy and bring about the restoration of their "elitist" rule. So the slavery question, as far as Jackson and his friends believed, was simply a blind to create trouble in order to prostrate the democracy.

Nullifiers aided and abetted the abolitionists, according to the Democrats, for the same reason and objective. These two groups of malcontents were linked together to produce havoc, and out of that havoc would ultimately rise to power "blue light federalists" in the north, consisting of monopolists, bankers, and wealthy businessmen, and nullifiers in the south, who would be their counterparts and agents. "The universal courtesy and kindness extended to the abolitionists in Congress," wrote Blair in the *Globe*, ". . . by all the *would be thought* Hotspurs of the South, while their fury and frenzy is directed against the Democrats . . . who are fighting the battles of the South, against the fanatics of the North, are all signs to prove the identity of political design between the nullifiers and abolitionists in every branch of federalism."[39]

Jacksonian Democracy did not represent a defense of slavery. Jacksonian Democrats believed they were defending the notion of majority rule and that the abolitionists and nullifiers and Whigs abhorred the notion of democracy and entered any sort of political alliance to discredit the new political system. The abolition question, wrote Martin Van

Buren, was a vicious device "of evil disposed persons to disturb the harmony of our happy Union through its agency."[40] Besides, slavery was not a matter for the government to concern itself—not if it expected to preserve "the harmony of our happy Union." The right of an individual to his private property without interference by the federal government was basic to the whole concept of freedom. For the government to legislate abolition would strike at the very foundation of American principles and institutions. Everyone knew this. Why, then, would abolitionists continue their agitation against slavery except that they were "evil disposed persons" with evil designs upon "our happy Union"?

To a large extent, therefore, Jackson and his friends equated all things in terms of the emerging democracy. Wherever they saw a linkage or connection that might be interpreted as a conspiracy against majority rule they instantly raised their voices in protest and alarm. Another example was their reaction to the increasing incidence of urban violence during the Jacksonian age. Again, the enemies of democracy were accused of inciting the violence to restore elitist rule. "Aristocrats, ever ready to take every unfair advantage of our situation," reported the *Globe*, "seize on these occurrances [of urban violence] as so many proofs that man is not capable of self-government and that the theory of a Republic where men will be equal is founded in error and can never be reduced to successful practice."[41] The Whigs constantly complained about the rising rate of crime and city violence and claimed it started when Jackson came to power. They said that the presence of this brawler and duelist in the White House, supported by the ignorant masses, served to sanction violence as a legitimate response in public discourse and argument. Violence can be terminated by putting down the democracy. Once the democracy goes, Jackson and his "reforms" go with it.

The leadership of the Democratic party not only believed this theory, they preached it. The Whigs blame every evil in the country on the rise of democracy, they said. Edwin Croswell, editor of the Albany *Argus*, the mouthpiece of Van Buren's political machine, the Albany Regency, explained their thinking to George Bancroft. "The Tory leaders labor to convey the impression that the modern tendency to violence & to the disregard of the law," he wrote, "arises from too great an infusion of the democratic spirit, & from the character & example of the Executive. . . . It is important . . . that the public mind . . . should be disabused on the subject; & that the excesses of the day sh'd be traced to their true source,—the revolutionary speeches, sundry harangues, threatened assassinations, and defiance & violation of law, by the Bank & its party leaders & agents, of the Tory school, in & out of Congress, during the memorable Panic season."[42]

It is instructive that Croswell traced the true cause of every evil in society—at least as far as Democrats saw it—to "the Bank & its party leaders & agents." Jacksonians not only vilified the Bank at every oppor-

tunity, they also warned against the power of money to corrupt government, betray the people, and jeopardize liberty. "Money is power," Jackson had said, and when controlled by a business elite it will inevitably
destroy the democracy. Even in his speech to Tennesseans at Columbia,
the President swiped at the "moneyed aristocracy." Never "can we hope
to see our domestic relations entirely tranquilized," he declared, as long
as the bankers and industrialists can unite the "heterogeneous elements
of discord into one common foe to the principles of republicanism."
They would concentrate power in the federal government, he went on,
to promote the interests of the wealthy and subvert the rights of the
people.[43]

Equally malignant in "undermining the purity and complicating the
simplicity of our virtuous Government," according to Jackson, was "the
paper system." This wretched business, he said, "has introduced a thousand ways of robbing honest labour of its earnings to make knaves rich,
powerful and dangerous." Also, "it seems to me that one of the greatest
threatners of our admirable form of Government, is the gradual consum-
ing corruption, which is spreading and carrying stockjobbing, Land job-
bing and every species of speculation into our Legislature, state and
national."[44] In writing these words, Jackson almost seemed to have a
sense of what would happen to the country after the Civil War.

Because Jackson explained and demonstrated his brand of democracy
everywhere he went—from the White House levees to the huge receptions that welcomed him from town to town, to the chance encounters
with individuals that occurred from time to time—he contributed significantly to the ever growing acceptance of his principles and political faith.
For example, it was during his trip back to Washington from his sojourn
in Tennessee when one of these "chance encounters" took place. A
young man by the name of John Stetson Barry had just reached Frostburg, Maryland, a short distance from Cumberland, where the National
Road began, on his way to Wheeling. He had heard that President Jackson was in the neighborhood and to his surprise, on arriving at Frostburg,
he found the General's carriage at the door of the local tavern. Barry and
the other members of his coach entered the tavern and discovered the
President "quietly seated in a chair & smoking a Dutchman's pipe 'of
goodly length.'" As soon as he saw the party enter the room, Jackson
"arose, shook hands with us, politely enquiring concerning our health."
Everyone was amazed. The Hero appeared so unremarkable, so ordinary,
so much like everyone else. He just seemed like an "old gentleman,"
dressed plainly, greeting everyone courteously, and going about his business with no pretension or suggestion of self-importance. And he was the
President of the United States!

Just at that moment a drunken Irishman staggered up to the President
and demanded to be introduced. His conversation, recounted Barry in his
diary, "excited no little laughter."

"Gineral, how old are ye?" demanded Paddy after the introductions had been completed.

Jackson showed no sign of offense or amusement. He answered as though the question was the most natural and proper in the world.

"If I live till the 18th of March next I shall be 70."*

"Gineral," Paddy persisted, "folks say you are a plaguy proud fellow, but I do not see as you are."

The group snickered its amusement. But again Jackson responded in a very straightforward manner.

"It is like a great many other things folks say of me," he replied, "there is no truth in it."

Just at that moment came the announcement that the stagecoach was ready to start and the group reluctantly departed, "leaving the paddy & the Gineral to their confab." But the idea of the President of the United States and a drunken laborer sitting in a public place and conversing informally struck the entire group as a sign of the uniqueness of American life and institutions, "a striking picture of *democracy*." There could be no doubt that, in some remarkable and marvelous way, the average American, the "common man," had been admitted into the mainstream of the nation's political life.[45]

---

*Barry must have heard wrong. Jackson would be seventy on March 15, not the eighteenth.

CHAPTER 23

Texas

THE PRESIDENT RETURNED TO WASHINGTON EARLY on October 1 after another triumphal swing up the Ohio valley, journeying much of the way aboard the steamboat *Marietta,* because of the poor condition of his horses, and nearly suffocating with the heat and "muskettoes." Wherever his boat stopped along the route, "immense crowds" appeared to welcome him. When he arrived at Cincinnati at 6 A.M. on September 19 no notice of his coming had been announced beforehand, but within a few hours the word of his presence spread through the city and he "was surrounded by at least 3000." His departure also produced spontaneous demonstrations with much cheering and flag waving as the boat sailed away. Only one incident marred the trip. As he approached Portsmouth, Ohio, another large crowd assembled. It was decided to fire the town's only cannon, an ancient piece that had been little used in the past few years. Suddenly, during the loading, the cannon exploded and killed three persons and mortally wounded a fourth. "This melancholy event filled me with pain," Jackson related to Sarah, "I could only as an evidence of my regrets give something to two widows which the sad catastrophe had deprived of their husbands—one was a lad whose brains were blown away—*doleful event.*"[1]

Otherwise the trip was one long triumphal progress. What pleased the Old Hero particularly was his conviction that these demonstrations forecast a stunning Democratic victory in the coming presidential election. "I have no doubt of every republican state in the Union going for Van Buren & Johnson," he wrote soon after his arrival at the White House. Kentucky, Ohio, Pennsylvania, and Maryland will support our ticket, he predicted, and Van Buren "will get every state in the Union but Massachusetts, Vermont, & South Carolina I believe."[2]

347

Jackson enjoyed his new role as political campaigner since he no longer suffered the restraint imposed by political practice in the early nineteenth century, which frowned upon candidates campaigning on their own behalf. As a matter of fact he originally planned a more elaborate swing through the western states on his way back. His excuse—not that he really needed one—was his desire to see the Niagara Falls. Then he would link up with Van Buren in New York and maybe parade down to Washington together, sharing the receptions along the way. Such a tour was certain to draw valuable support for the Democratic ticket from eastern and coastal states.[3]

But these plans evaporated at the last moment. Originally, Donelson, Charles J. Love, and Dr. Gwinn intended to accompany the President from Tennessee. But Donelson's wife, Emily, became quite ill and her husband refused to leave her until he had a better sense of the prognosis. She suffered from tuberculosis, and just prior to her husband's departure she started bleeding "from the lungs" and the hemorrhaging "continued 30 hours before it was stopped." So Jackson postponed his departure from the Hermitage in the hope that Emily would rally and that Donelson could accompany him to the Falls. But Emily did not rally. She grew weaker and more feverish as she suffered through the terminal stages of her disease. Finally Jackson had to leave Tennessee without Donelson. Duty required his presence at the capital. "I detained as long as my official duties would permit," the President wrote Van Buren, "and was obliged to travel without him." By that time it was too late to travel to the Falls and those plans were canceled.[4]

When he finally arrived in Washington on October 1, Jackson hoped to find a letter from Donelson giving him the latest news. "In this I was mistaken, & spent the night in melancholy gloom & in fore bodings of unpleasant information from our dear Emily." The next day the anticipated letter arrived. It carried the worst possible news. Donelson had despaired of Emily's life. "With painful sensations," Jackson told his nephew, "I . . . read the melancholy information of her continued ill health & forebodings of the result of her disease." Although the fever had left her and the hemorrhaging had ceased, she remained very weak and "has those symptoms of pulmonary disease, 'a kind of stupor,' " which indicated that the end was very near.[5]

Jackson tried to console his nephew.

> I trust in the mercy of a kind and superintending providence that he will restore her to health & bless her dear little children with her kind superintending care they so much need at their present tender years, & prolong her life to be a comfort to you in your declining years. But my dear Andrew, should providence will it & call her hence you must summon up all your fortitude to meet the melancholy event, keeping in mind how necessary your life becomes to your dear children, when the duty of a mothers care for her children devolves on the father & unites in him the duty of the mother & the father both. Still I have a hope that as the hemirage has ceased

& the fever checked she will soon recover, for which present to her my affectionate regards with my prayer for her speedy recovery & your safe arrival soon here, with all your dear little ones.[6]

The valiant Emily willed to stay alive. She rallied for a time and appeared to be recovering. In fact her condition improved to such an extent that Donelson felt he could return to Washington and wind up his business at the capital. The most pressing business, apart from anything he did for the President, was the validation of forty thousand patents. Since the President had no official secretary—one was not formally approved by Congress until 1861—Jackson provided Donelson with a position in the Land Office which had only minor responsibilities, such as signing patents, and which left the Major relatively free to assist his uncle with presidential business. So Donelson planned to return to Washington, clear his desk, and then return home by way of Philadelphia, where he would buy needed furniture for his new house at Tulip Grove, immediately adjoining the Hermitage.[7]

When Donelson arrived at the White House on October 20, Jackson falsely convinced himself that Emily had passed the crisis and would soon recover completely. He promised the dying woman that her husband "will be with you the first moment after he can close this absolute necessary duty" of signing the forty thousand patents, which would "be lost unless he can . . . sign them." But he worried about Donelson. The separation was a terrible strain on the Major and he worked under considerable pressure, all the while distracted and apprehensive about the condition of his wife. "I pity the majors situation," Jackson told Van Buren, "—her loss would unman him, & be a lamentable bereavement to her family."[8]

Donelson expected to leave Washington for home in late November, but Jackson's own illness delayed his departure. The young husband felt he could not desert his uncle when there was so much pressing business, such as the annual message to Congress, and he postponed his departure until December 3. When Jackson felt well enough he wrote to Emily to explain what had happened. He urged her to accept her suffering in the spirit of Christian resignation. "My dear Emily—this chastisement by our Maker we ought to receive as a rebuke from him, & thank him for the mildness of it—which was to bring to our view, & that it may be always before us, that we are mere tenants at will here. And we ought to live daily so as to be prepared to die; for we know not when we may be called home. Then let us receive our chastisements as blessings from God."[9]

Once the work on the message had been completed, and Jackson improved in health, Donelson rushed home. "With what regret that I should have been the cause of your detention from her of one day," Jackson lamented in a letter to his nephew. "I shall hope you have reached her in due time to have prevented her anxiety for your presence." But on the night of December 16 the General had an "extraordinary dream . . . that adds much to my anxiety on her account," he wrote. "I hope that you reached home on the night of the 12th or morning of the 13th . . . but my fears are hightened from my extraordinary dream—if providence has called her hence I am persuaded she has a happy immortality—still I hope our . . . redeemer has spared her." Each day thereafter the President waited impatiently for the mail, anxious to receive news that Donelson had arrived home in time to strengthen and comfort his wife. All the while he felt guilt and remorse and crushing sorrow.[10]

On December 15, Donelson wrote to Jackson from the Ohio River near Troy. He still had a way to go before reaching home. "O how I regret your unfortunate detention," the President moaned in reply. He cared so deeply for the Donelson family that he tormented himself with accusations for increasing their burden.[11]

Emily Donelson died at twelve noon on December 19, 1836. She was only twenty-eight years of age. During her last days she lay propped up in bed by the window of her bedroom where she hoped to see her returning husband. Each day she stared at the empty road and prayed for one last glimpse of her beloved. When she died Donelson was still a two-day journey away. Emily's mother refused to bury the young girl until her husband had returned. When he finally arrived the scene of reunion was one of staggering grief.[12]

Jackson was absolutely shattered when he received the news. *My dear Andrew,*" he wrote on December 31, "Through judge Grundy, I have this moment recd. the sad and melancholy intelligence, that our Dear Emily is no more, that she died on the 19th instant." Jackson could barely keep his pen steady as he wrote. Some of his words cannot be easily deciphered.

> I have no language in which I can express to you my grief at this mournful & sudden bereavement to us all, but particularly to you, & your dear little ones. I can only say to you, that I, with my whole household, unite in a tender of our heartfelt condolence on this mournful occasion. Would to god I had been there. I was fearful from my dream that her god had called her hence, & from not hearing from you, my fore bodings increased, & are now realised.
>
> My dear Andrew, we cannot recal her, we are commanded by our dear Saviour, not to mourn for the dead, but for the living. I am sure from my dream that she is happy, she has changed a world of woe, for a world of eternal happiness, & we ought to *prepare,* as we *too,* must soon follow. peace to her manes. it becomes our duty to submit to this heavy bereavement with due submission, & control our human passions, submit to the will of god who holds our lives in his hand & say with humble & contrite hearts, "The lords will be done on earth as it is in heaven."[13]

So profoundly grieved was Jackson that he penned a second letter of condolence to Donelson a week later. "What hightens my sorrow," he wrote, "is that providence in his unscruteable ways deprived you from reaching our dear Emily in time." But we must humbly submit to this as well, he said. "It becomes now your duty to live for the benefit of your dear little ones a double duty has devolved on you . . . to take care of them."14

Donelson resigned as Jackson's private secretary long before returning to Tennessee and the President replaced him with his own son, appointing Andrew under the sixth section of the General Land Office Act of 1836. Andrew and Sarah had arrived in Washington in late October to help the old man pack and prepare for his final return to the Hermitage. But it can be imagined how useful Andrew was to the President. "Andrew does all he can to ease me," the General reported, "and does much better than I had a right to calculate from his inexperience, but this will make him a man of business."15

The loss of Donelson as private secretary bothered Jackson considerably. As early as October he complained that the missing Donelson placed a great burden upon him, particularly now that he was winding down his administration. And his "incessant labour" at the public business meant he took little exercise, and this, he said, "has made medicine & the lancet" periodically necessary.16

The press of business got worse throughout the fall of 1836, for a number of public matters deeply concerned him. For one thing, he thought of a Farewell Address. Since he had always been compared to the "Immortal Washington," more so than any other previous President, it was not presumptuous of him to consider issuing a parting address to his countrymen. Indeed, it was expected. And like Washington, he turned to one of his principal advisers to shape his thoughts into the appropriate language. He wrote to Chief Justice Taney on October 13 and asked him to write something "as a means of rendering a last service to my country." What he had in mind, he said, was "a plain & honest expression of the principles which have given direction to my public course" and a review of the measures that sprang from these principles.17

Not that he wanted Taney to compose the address outright. Just a request that he "throw" some of his thoughts on paper as to the topics to be considered. It should emphasize throughout "our *glorious Union,*" he said, and how he strove to protect it against the "multiplied schemes" of "ambitious & factious spirits." He was especially anxious to warn against sectional jealousies and rivalries. Of course, the "dangerous power" of the Bank had to be included as well as the "dangerous tendency of privileged monopolies generally" and those aristocrats who wished to "adulterate the currency." Jackson wondered aloud about the appropriate time to release such an address. Should it go to Congress with his annual message or wait until the close of the session when the committees of both houses attended the President to ask if he had any further communication for them? "My mind inclines to the latter mode," he conceded.18

Taney immediately conveyed his delight that Jackson planned a Farewell Address and agreed that it should be the last act of his political life and not part of an annual address or mixed up in any way with the ordinary business of government. It should, he said, be devoted exclusively to "those great and enduring principles upon which our institutions are founded." Taney concluded by saying that he would provide any service connected with the composition of the piece "with real pleasure."[19]

There was another public matter on Jackson's mind throughout the fall of 1836. It was a problem he had lived with for years. The problem was Texas. The President had long coveted Texas as an essential component of his dream of empire. He took the position that it was part of the Louisiana territory and therefore had been acquired through purchase by the United States in 1803. The acceptance of the Transcontinental Treaty with Spain in 1819, which relinquished Texas in exchange for other considerations, was something Jackson deplored and denounced. He blamed the loss of Texas on John Quincy Adams, for having negotiated this "dismemberment" of the American empire.[20]

Once Mexico gained independence from Spain there were several attempts by the United States to acquire Texas—to "reannex" it. Each effort failed. Meanwhile Americans in increasing numbers—and with Mexican encouragement and approval, it should be noted—crossed the border and took up residence in Texas. For the next ten years relations between the two countries deteriorated rapidly. The cupidity of the United States was plain to all. Worse, the ministers sent by the United States to Mexico lacked finesse, patience, understanding, or appreciation of Mexican character and national sense of pride and honor. Undoubtedly, the worst one was Jackson's appointee, Colonel Anthony Butler. The President nominated Butler on Van Buren's recommendation and his own desire to select a minister who had firsthand knowledge of Texas.

Jackson's paramount objective with respect to Texas—indeed, his only objective—was its acquisition. He authorized Butler to sound out the Mexicans and gave him a catalog of reasons why such a transaction served Mexico's best interests.[21] Thus, Butler began his mission burdened by an objective that would take more skill, subtlety, diplomacy, and tact than he—or probably anyone else in the country—could provide. He was astonished upon his arrival in Mexico City to read in the government-controlled newspaper that the object of his mission was the purchase of Texas. And the newspaper named the price: $5 million. So the Mexicans knew what Butler was about when he arrived and they resented it deeply.[22]

Almost immediately the Mexicans pressured Butler to come to terms on a precise boundary separating Mexico from the United States. Although the Transcontinental Treaty fixed the boundary at the Sabine River, thus tucking Texas securely inside Mexico, the border had never been surveyed and no one knew which branches of the river were involved in the boundary. Jackson wanted the line drawn at the desert or Grand Prairie west of the Nueces River in order to gobble up Texas. And he was willing to pay handsomely. For reasons best known to himself, Old Hickory claimed (wrongly) that the Nueces was a branch of the Sabine. If the Mexicans rejected this line, he advised his minister, then he was willing to accept (grudgingly) the Lavaca River, next the Colorado, and then the Brazos.[23]

In 1828, Butler's predecessor, Joel Poinsett, signed a treaty with Mexico providing for a survey of the border by a joint American-Mexican commission. But it had never been done, and the deadline for the survey had lapsed. The secretary of state, Louis McLane, therefore urged Butler to renew the business of establishing the boundary as well as to seek recognition of damage claims by American citizens against Mexico.[24] But Butler never seriously gave much mind to the secretary of state. He rather regarded himself as Jackson's personal emissary and only felt bound by what the President instructed him to do.[25] For this improper behavior— as well as the appointment in the first place—Jackson bears chief responsibility.

Although the Mexicans wanted the boundary question resolved, Butler hemmed and hawed and made it pretty obvious that it could not be negotiated until the future of Texas had been settled. And he tried one trick after another to cajole the Mexicans into surrendering the province. Nothing worked. All the while the Mexican officials fumed over American arrogance and presumption. The Jackson administration was accused of fostering American emigration into Texas for the purpose of seizing it.

As late as August, 1833, Butler still thought he could snatch Texas from Mexico, and he said so to McLane.[26] Earlier, he told Jackson that "I will succeed in uniting T———to our Country before I am done with the Subject or I will forfeit my head."[27] The President practically begged him to do as he promised. "If you succeed it will be a lasting feather in your cap. . . . *Bring it to a speedy issue if you can.*" But Butler failed—again and again. Not much later his dispatches sounded very discouraged. Frustrated and angry, he turned desperate. He had the audacity to suggest to the President that "no other mode is left us but to occupy that part of the Territory lying west of the Sabine." Dispatch troops and seize it, he urged.[28]

Before Jackson could respond to this outrageous proposal, Butler wrote again and recommended that they stoop to bribery. "I have just had a very singular conversation with a Mexican," he began, and this Mexican is shrewd and intelligent and holds a high official station and "has much influence with the Presidt. Genl. St. Anna." In their initial conversation the two men actually discussed the financial terms of the bribe. "Have you command of Money?" the Mexican asked Butler. "Yes, I have money," came the quick reply. The price will come high, the

Mexican continued, maybe half a million or more. The Mexican himself required two or three hundred thousand dollars, Butler reported, but "there are others amongst whom it may become necessary to distribute 3 or 4 Hundred thousand more." The Mexican then asked Butler straight out: "Can you command that Sum?" The minister assured him there would be no problem.[29]

Jackson virtually invited this attempt at bribery. When Butler first went down to Mexico the President told him that he "scarcely ever knew a Spaniard who was not the slave of averice, and it *is not improbable* that this *weakness* may be *worth a great deal to us.*"[30] In Jackson's defense, it should be said that he was talking about the frauds in Florida, not a way of conducting diplomacy. Still, to a scoundrel like Butler, the letter surely sounded like an invitation to commit bribery. He actually wrote on the back of it: *"Gen Jackson. Remarkable communication."*[31] These people, Butler subsequently told Jackson, are "selfish, corrupt, utterly unprincipled. Any of them may be successfully appealed to through their Cupidity."[32]

In any event, Jackson's eyes registered his disbelief when he read Butler's letter detailing his interview with this highly placed Mexican. "I have read your confidential letter with care, and astonishment," Jackson replied, ". . .—astonishment that you would entrust such a letter, without being in cypher, to the mail." Astonishment in that you so construed my instructions as to believe that they "authorized you to apply to corruption, when nothing could be farther from my intention than to convey such an idea." You were supposed to fix a boundary, negotiate a commercial treaty, procure lasting peace and friendship, and obtain Texas "as far west as the Grand Desert" for a maximum of $5 million. All I wanted was the cession unencumbered by fraudulent Spanish grants, said Jackson, such as we had in Florida. The Mexicans could use the money to buy back the grants, not line their pockets. "All the U.S. is interested in," Jackson reiterated, "is the unincumbered cession, not how Mexico applies the consideration."[33]

Jackson should have pulled Butler out of Mexico the moment he read this letter. But he was too involved in other affairs, notably the removal of the deposits from the BUS, and could not give the matter the attention it deserved. Besides, more than anything else, he had a passion for Texas and sincerely believed that Butler would somehow gratify it. So he let Butler off with a warning not to get into a position where *"these shrewd fellows"* could accuse him of bribery. Stick to your instructions, Jackson lectured him. "Let us have a boundery without the imputation of corruption, & I will hail you welcome with it here—*none else.*"[34]

Butler was not only a scoundrel, he was a stupid scoundrel. He responded to Jackson's letter—this time using a cypher, albeit a thirty-year-old outmoded cypher, for certain key words—and said that the President's cautions to him showed "how little you know of mexican character. I can assure you Sir that bribery is not only common and familiar in all ranks and classes, but familiarly and freely spoken of." In effect, he was dismissing the President's instructions and insisting that bribery must be applied if they expected to gain Texas.[35]

By this time Jackson had completely lost patience with Butler. And not a moment too soon. He instructed Secretary McLane to inform the minister that he should conclude an agreement for extending the time for running the boundary and then return home. But Butler compounded his stupidity with arrogance. He next proposed that he head a filibustering expedition to seize Texas. "If you will withdraw me from this place," he wrote, again partially in cypher, "and make the movement to possess that part of Texas which is ours, placing me at the head of the country to be occupied, I will pledge my head that we have all we desire in less than six months without a blow."[36]

Jackson moaned in disbelief as he read the letter. Then he picked up his pen and wrote the following note on the cover sheet of the letter: "A. Butler: What a scamp. Carefully read. The Secretary of State will reiterate his instructions to ask an extension of the treaty for running boundary line, and then recall him, or if he has recd. his former instructions and the Mexican Govt. has refused, to recal him at once."[37]

By this time Butler was far beyond obeying the instructions of the secretary of state. Or Jackson either. He simply supposed—probably correctly—that if he could win Texas he would be forgiven everything. So he chose a different tack. He proposed coming to Washington to talk with the President personally. After only one hour's conversation, he said, he could return to Mexico with every prospect of completing his mission to everyone's satisfaction.[38] Permission for his return was granted, although Butler did not reach Washington until June, 1835.

The minister got his interview with the President upon his return, and he also spoke with the new secretary of state, John Forsyth. Again Butler emphasized the need to bribe the Mexican officials. He produced a letter which he handed to Jackson from Father Ignacio Hernández, the confidant of Mexico's President, General Antonio Lopez de Santa Anna, and the confessor of Santa Anna's sister. For a sum of $500,000, Father Hernández assured Butler that the affair could be concluded expeditiously and successfully.[39]

Jackson winced. He wanted no part of this unsavory business and brought the interview to a close as quickly as possible. Butler was formally told in writing that although still anxious to acquire Texas the President "is resolved that no means of even an equivocal character shall be used to accomplish it." Forsyth stated further that the President had lost confidence in the negotiations but was willing to allow them to continue if they could be completed in time to place the results before the next session of Congress. Butler was also authorized to offer Mexico an additional $500,000 if the boundary could be extended to cede San Francisco Bay to the United States. It was Jackson's old and haunting dream of empire.[40]

When left alone in his study the President again picked up the Hernández letter and examined it. Then he reached for his pen and endorsed it: "Nothing will be countenanced by the executive to bring this government under the remotest imputation of being engaged in corruption or bribery."[41]

Butler returned to Mexico and for the next several months maintained a total silence. With Congress about to reconvene, with no further word from Butler, and with Mexico at last demanding Butler's recall because of his intrigues, the President finally acted. On November 9, 1835, the secretary of state notified Butler to return to Washington. But the minister paid no attention. Instead, he wrote directly to Jackson, as he had always done, and said that he had too much at stake to leave empty-handed. Besides, Forsyth's instructions were vague and contradictory, he declared. "If you say that in December I must cease acting as the Representative of the U. States on this question, you shall be obeyed strictly, yet I shall not *return* as Mr. Forsyth says, on the contrary I shall remain and continue my efforts for a private association of Individuals. I have labored at this Negotiation too long, and have its success too deeply at heart, to omit struggling so long as there is a fair prospect of success." Butler made good his promise. Even after he received a further note from Forsyth informing him that the President was nominating Powhattan Ellis as his replacement for the Mexican mission, Butler stayed on and further damaged Mexican-American relations.[42]

Perhaps it was always impossible to settle the Texas question amicably since Mexico objected so strenuously to dismemberment. Perhaps no one possessed the skill to bring about the acquisition of this valuable province. But certainly the Jackson administration botched the diplomacy necessary for any settlement, and the President himself deserves much of the blame. He should never have appointed Butler in the first place; then he should have replaced him early on, especially when he realized that his minister was a scoundrel. Jackson's fumbling only increased Mexican suspicion and hostility toward American rights and claims. The Mexicans felt certain that the United States was encouraging filibustering expeditions in Texas, violating the neutrality laws, and arming men to stir up revolution. It was a sorry diplomatic record and stands in marked contrast to the many diplomatic triumphs the Jackson administration achieved in Europe.

Jackson's mismanagement also discouraged the Texans. As the inability of the United States to acquire the province became clear, as the intention of the Mexican government to centralize control over all parts of the Republic also became obvious, thus diminishing Texan home rule, and as the grievances of the Texans met indifference and contempt, a war party quickly emerged in Texas that won the active support and encouragement of many Americans. The consequence was immediate. A war for independence flashed into the open in October, 1835, and then roared to a climax when the President of the Mexican Republic, General Santa Anna, marched into Texas at the head of a six-thousand-man army. Texas independence was proclaimed on March 2, 1836; General Sam Houston assumed command of the Texan army and defeated Santa Anna at the Battle of San Jacinto on April 21, 1836. Santa Anna himself was captured and forced to sign a treaty (later repudiated) recognizing Texan independence.

The United States maintained a position of neutrality during the hostilities in accordance with the Neutrality Act of 1818. Jackson attempted to enforce this neutrality by ordering the district attorneys to prosecute violators but his order was generally disregarded. It was impossible to curb a population that wildly applauded the cause of independence.[43] "We have barely room to congratulate every man who has Anglo-Saxon blood in his veins," exulted the Washington *Globe*, "on the redemption of our brethren in Texas from Spanish power. The retributive justice which has so suddenly overtaken Santa Ana, was nearer at hand than we anticipated; but it did not reach him soon enough."[44]

The question of American neutrality was brought into sharp focus by the behavior and action of one of the nation's leading frontier generals. Edmund Pendleton Gaines, commanding along the border separating the United States from Texas, requested permission from the secretary of war on March 29, 1836, to move his troops across the border, ostensibly to quell Indian frontier raids. In response, he was told that he must not attempt to seize Mexican territory in his operations against Indians and that if a crossing did in fact become obligatory he was to advance no further than Nacogdoches.[45] But these instructions lacked precision. In any event, Gaines believed he had authority to invade Texas, and in June he crossed the Sabine River and occupied Nacogdoches.

The Mexican minister to the United States, Manuel Eduardo de Gorostiza, who had just been presented to President Jackson, vigorously protested the invasion and later carried his protests to the newspapers and the rest of the diplomatic community. He was so convinced of American duplicity and treachery that he eventually asked for his passports.[46] Gorostiza "is laboring to degrade you & the nation in the eyes of foreign countries & in the pages of history," charged Frank Blair in a letter to Jackson, "and bring upon our character as a people the infamy of the Carthagenians."[47]

Relations between Mexico and the United States then began to deteriorate very rapidly. On Tuesday, June 28, 1836, at a regular cabinet meeting, the secretary of the navy, Mahlon Dickerson, reported that he had received a message from Commodore Dallas describing the "indignities" which the American consul and residents at Tampico had suffered at the hands of the Mexican authorities. These same authorities also refused to permit American armed vessels in the vicinity to receive water or to have their officers go ashore. Furthermore, they threatened to put to death all Americans at Tampico in retaliation for the capture of Santa Anna by the Americans at San Jacinto.

The moment Dickerson finished his report the old chief "broke out in his most impassioned manner." Without stopping to inquire of the other members what their advice on the matter would be—which was his usual procedure—the President lashed out in a frightening display of Jacksonian passion.

"Write immediately to Commodore Dallas," he barked, "& order him to *blockade* the harbour of Tampico, & to suffer nothing to enter till they allow him to land and obtain his supplies of water & communicate with the Consul, & if they touch the hair of the head of one of our citizens, tell him *to batter down & destroy their town & exterminate the inhabitants from the face of the earth!*"

The cabinet members sat looking at each other in a near state of shock.

Jackson turned to Forsyth. "Have you rec^d any information on this subject?"

Forsyth shook his head.

"Then let the Secy of the Navy furnish you the papers," the Hero ordered, "& do you write immediately to Mr. Gorstiza informing him of the orders we have given to Commodore Dallas, & that we shall not permit a jot or tittle of the treaty to be violated, or a citizen of the United States to be injured without taking immediate redress."[48]

Jackson worked himself into a grand passion. Indeed, it was one of his grandest. Attorney General Butler, who recorded the scene the very next day, was stupefied by Jackson's behavior. He had never seen the President react so violently before. Moreover, he was stunned by the rapidity with which the General barked out his orders. The decisiveness and speed with which he acted totally amazed the attorney general.

Much of the passion was genuine in this instance. Jackson always reacted furiously when he thought that the rights of American citizens or the dignity and sovereignty of the nation had been violated in any way by a foreign power. The rights of this country and its citizens would be respected by the rest of the world, he stormed, as long as Andrew Jackson sat in the White House.

Although this incident did not produce the extermination of the inhabitants of Tampico, United States–Mexican relations continued to slide dangerously toward a violent confrontation. What hastened the slide was the behavior of the Texans. They were doing everything possible to win American recognition of their independence and eventual annexation. To achieve these goals the Texas government sent a veritable squadron of special commissioners to Washington, and their names and numbers changed constantly over the next ten months. They comprised a powerful lobby in Washington and immediately set about winning American support for their new status. They succeeded in gaining from the Senate a resolution recommending recognition when Texas established a civil government, and on July 4—it "being the great anniversary of the independence of this, our native country," wrote one of the Texas commissioners—the House of Representatives endorsed the resolution.[49]

As the commissioners arrived in Washington they were all cordially received by Jackson. And he made it very plain to them in conversation that he was "favorably disposed" toward their objectives. During one of these conversations, shortly before dinner was called, the President turned to Special Commissioner Samuel Carson and said: "Is it true, Mr. Carson, that your Government has sent Santa Anna back to Mexico?"

Carson admitted that Santa Anna was indeed expected to sail for Mexico to assist in winning ratification of the treaty recognizing Texas independence.

"Then I tell you, Sir, if ever he sets foot on Mexican ground, your Government may whistle; he, Sir, will give you trouble, if he escapes, which you dream not of."

Then there would be war, said Carson.

"Where is your means, Sir, to carry on an offensive war against Mexico?"

"In the enthusiasms of the American people, their devotion to the cause of Liberty and the ways and means, to defray the expenses of the War," responded Carson.

Jackson looked sour. His great concern was how the rest of the world would see American intervention. He desperately wished to acquire Texas, but he was fearful of taking action himself, "lest the censures of the world, or at least the civilized world might fall upon him." However, before the President could respond to Carson's remark, dinner was announced and the conversation broke off.[50]

The possible annexation of Texas had already begun to trouble Jackson on a number of grounds. His sympathy and desire, along with his great friendship with Sam Houston, were well-known. Without doing a thing, he was already suspect of aiding and abetting the Texas revolutionaries. Then abolitionists accused him of plotting to grab Texas in order to swell the size of the slavocracy. But that was ridiculous. Jackson's passion for Texas had nothing to do with slavery. He wanted Texas for reasons of national pride and national security.

Yet, what would the rest of the world say, if he actively intervened and moved to advance the cause of Texas separation from Mexico? What would they think? Normally, Jackson would not trouble himself for a moment about the opinion of Europeans—"I do precisely what I think just and right," he always said—but, in this instance, the United States had a treaty with Mexico, and the annexation of part of the Mexican Republic would be seen around the world as a gross violation of the "law of nations." It would constitute a dishonorable and brutal act of aggression, and not even Jackson could deny that. When Stephen F. Austin wrote the President an impassioned plea for assistance, shortly after the victory at San Jacinto, Jackson endorsed the back of it: "The writer does not reflect that we have a treaty with Mexico, and our national faith is pledged to support it. The Texians before they took the step to declare themselves Independent, which has aroused and united all mexico against them ought to have pondered well, it was a rash and premature act, our nutrality must be faithfully maintained. A.J."[51]

And there were other considerations. Jackson was already suspected of complicity in bringing about the Texas revolution. He was accused of hatching the plot with his old friend Sam Houston, to rob the Mexicans of Texas. It was a natural suspicion and soon had documentary support. And although the charge was totally false, it did make Jackson all the more cautious about charging ahead with annexation.[52]

Also, he had the "damned" abolitionists to worry about. They would exploit any issue to exacerbate feelings between the north and south. Once again slavery would become a ploy to undermine the democracy of the nation and win the restoration of aristocratic rule. Unquestionably, then, the Texas question posed a possible threat to the Union, and that slowed Jackson down to a crawl.

Another consideration was the impact of sectional rivalry over the issue on the presidential election. Van Buren's election must not be jeopardized. Under no circumstances must a Whig succeed to the presidency. The democracy itself would suffer a terrible reversal if Van Buren was defeated.

When the Texas commissioners arrived in Washington they made it absolutely clear that they were intent upon annexation and that they also expected the United States to meet a number of conditions. Naturally, they wanted their land titles guaranteed and slavery recognized. They also expected the assumption of Texas debts by the United States, since the new republic was in dire financial straits. They explained this to the secretary of state, John Forsyth, who passed the information along to Jackson.[53] Forsyth frankly informed the commissioners that he was not sympathetic with their mission but "that he knew the annexation of Texas to the U. States was a favorite measure of Genl' Jackson whenever it could be done with propriety."[54]

That was it exactly. The Hero wanted Texas and wanted it very badly, but it must be done "with propriety." So when the commissioners called on him to press their case, Old Hickory put them off. He told them that he had sent a secret agent to Texas "to prosecute various inquiries as to our situation, internal, Civil and Political," reported the commissioners, "and that nothing conclusive would be done until Said commissioner was heard from."[55] The secret agent was a man named Henry R. Morfit, who, in due course, reported to the President that he had his doubts about the Texans sustaining themselves against an outside enemy. The country was too sparsely settled and the inhabitants lived at great distances from each other. The defense of such an area would be impossible.[56]

All of which further slowed Jackson's natural desire to forge ahead with annexation. He used the occasion of his return to the Hermitage during the summer of 1836 to get away from Washington and leave the Texas business in the capable (if unsympathetic) hands of his secretary of state.[57] In the meantime, General Santa Anna wrote to Jackson—courtesy of General Houston—and appealed to him to assist in his release and the resolution of the conflict between Texas and Mexico. "Let us establish mutual relations, to the end that your nation and the Mexican, may strengthen their friendly ties," he begged.[58]

Jackson felt that his situation was very delicate, one that would not allow a wild display of expansionist zeal. So he responded to Santa Anna with great care. He also wrote to Houston. To his longtime friend, he reported rumors that Santa Anna was about to be tried by a military court and shot. This would be monstrous, Jackson exclaimed. "Nothing *now* could tarnish the character of Texas more than such an act at this late period. It was a good policy as well as humanity that spared him . . . his person is still of much consequence to you, he is the pride of the Mexican soldiers and the favorite of the Priesthood. . . . Let not his blood be shed unless it becomes necessary by an imperative act of just retaliation for Mexican massacres hereafter. this is what I think, true wisdom and humanity dictates."[59]

To Santa Anna, Jackson wrote a sympathetic letter that regretted that he could do nothing for the Mexican chief. "Your powers ceased with your capture," he said, "therefore until the existing Government of Mexico ask our friendly offices between the Contending parties, Mexico and Texas, we cannot interfere, but should Mexico ask it, our friendly offices will, with pleasure, be afforded to restore peace and put an end to this inhuman warfare at whose acts of barbarity and massacre has occasioned every christian people and humanity to shudder and condemn."[60]

In another effort to maintain this delicate balance, Jackson addressed the matter of General Gaines's presence across the Sabine. There had been a great outcry over this invasion in the opposition newspapers. It was a "War in Disguise!" stormed the *National Intelligencer.* Gaines's invasion "being as direct an advance against the Mexican forces as if instead of a treaty of perpetual peace and friendship with Mexico there existed a war of extermination between the two countries."[61] Even Democrats were appalled. As loyal an aid as Amos Kendall registered his chagrin. Of Gaines's invasion, he told Jackson, "I cannot but regret this movement, unless there are more conclusive reasons than I have heard of." Whatever happens, "I would wish our *government* . . . to maintain such an attitude as not only to be right but to appear so before the world." He was certain, he said, "that a large portion of our own people and the people of other nations generally will pronounce it wrong. Our *people* are already considered responsible for the warfare carried on against Mexico in Texas, and that sentiment will gain strength, day by day, throughout the world. . . . For the acts of our people, the *nation* is responsible; for the acts of the government, that responsibility is increased in the eye of the world ten fold."[62]

The good opinion of the world was something Jackson passionately cared about, particularly since it involved a matter of honor. Throughout the entire spoliations controversy he had repeated to France that her position was seen by the rest of the world as unjust. Now there was danger that the United States would also be seen in that light and Jackson could not abide such criticism, especially since such criticism would be totally justified. A democratic society must not be guilty of such transgressions, no matter how beneficial the end result might be. The time will come, Kendall predicted, "when Mexico will be overrun by our Anglo Saxon race, nor do I look upon it as a result at all to be deplored. I believe it would lead to the amelioration and improvement of Mexico herself; but as guardians of the peace and interests of the United States we are not permitted to go to war through philanthrophy or a design to conquer other nations for their own good."[63]

This letter had a profound impact on Jackson. After he read it he picked up his pen and jotted down the words: "to be answered." And he responded almost immediately. The view you have taken, he said to Kendall, "is certainly a Just view, & one which you will find I have adopted. I have determined to maintain a strict neutrality."[64] He had already taken several important actions. When Gaines first decided to occupy Nacogdoches he (Gaines) called on the governors of the surrounding states to provide him with additional troops from their militias. The governors pounced on the opportunity to share the glory of the Texas invasion. But Jackson put a stop to it. He countermanded Gaines's requisition in an Executive Order dated August 7, 1836, notified the governors of Tennessee, Kentucky, Mississippi, and Louisiana to discharge whatever men had been mustered for the operation, and directed that no troops should be moved unless ordered directly by the War Department.[65] As for the seizure of Nacogdoches, that was another matter. The entire area around the Sabine was under dispute and the United States had been begging without success to run the boundary line. Now that Texas had declared its independence, the United States must contend with two countries for the settlement of this boundary. Under the circumstances, therefore, "our troops" must protect "our interests" during this period of transition. Besides, the Mexican minister in Washington had been notified of this action "and acquiesced in by him."[66]

To Gaines, the President made it absolutely clear that "ours is a state of strict neutrality in reference to the struggle of Texas for independence: and you as the commander of our forces on that frontier must religiously observe and maintain it." Should the Indians disturb the peace of the frontier or endanger the lives of American citizens, then he might take action. "You must be careful however not to be deceived by the evidence on which you act. Unless the necessity exists . . . occupation of an advanced post beyond our limits must be avoided."[67]

Jackson's determination to ensure American neutrality in the present situation, buttressed by Morfit's pessimistic report about the limited resources of the Texans to repel attack and the President's mounting concern that his intentions would be misinterpreted at home and abroad, convinced Old Hickory that the decision about recognizing Texas should be initiated by Congress. Besides, Congress held the constitutional power to declare war and since the acknowledgment of the independence of Texas might lead to war with Mexico, "I think it most congeniel with the principles of our government," he said, to leave the question "to Congress, as the proper power, being in session to advise, upon the propriety of acknowledging the Independence of Texas."[68]

It is remarkable how Jackson could use the Congress when it suited his need. But he felt he had to proceed very carefully. What he planned to do was send "extracts" from Morfit's report to Congress and then submit a special message on the question. This he did on December 21, 1836.

The message was brief. It assured Congress that no action had been taken to recognize Texas independence. It fretted over possible misunderstanding if premature recognition was accorded the new nation. In the past, the United States had recognized all de facto governments when the clearest evidence existed of their permanence. The whole world knew, Jackson declared, that this country avoids all interference in the internal affairs of other nations. "Public opinion here is so firmly established and well understood in favor of this policy that no serious disagreement has ever arisen among" us.[69]

With regard to Texas, he continued, it was true that the Mexican civil authority had been expelled, its invading army defeated, the chief of state captured, and all Mexican power to control Texas annihilated. Still, "an immense disparity of physical force on the side of Mexico" existed, and the new chief of state, Anastasio Bustamante, was preparing a fresh invasion to recover the lost dominion. These circumstances "require us to act on this occasion with even more than our wonted caution." Some Americans felt that Texas "[is] a part of our property" and were reluctant to abandon this claim; most Texans were emigrants from this country and wished admission in our Union.[70]

Having warned of the need for caution, these last few words now seemed to be building to a call for recognition. Old Hickory, the expansionist, was about to revert to his true colors. But then came the surprise. Instead of leaving it to Congress to decide, he advised against "a too early" recognition since it would be seen around the world as a self-serving device to take over Texas. "Prudence," he charged, dictates "that we should stand aloof" for the moment, at least until Mexico herself, or one of the great foreign powers, should recognize Texas first. Or until the lapse of time and the course of events should prove that the Texans could maintain their separate sovereignty and uphold their government. Then, neither Mexico nor any foreign power could complain of our course. In this manner we would pursue our historic policy, one that had "secured to us respect and influence abroad and inspired confidence at home."[71]

Many people were stunned. It was hard to believe that Andrew Jackson was the author of this milksop. He had seemingly turned his back on Texas, on the province he had desperately hungered to possess for years. In submitting this message, Jackson may have been talked into it by Amos Kendall.[72] More probably, he consented to its composition because his mind was filled with fears—fears for the Union and for the course of American democracy. He was particularly worried about appearances, that recognition would look like "a preconceived arrangement" concocted to precede annexation.[73] He worried about what the rest of the world would say. He worried what it might produce in terms of sectional jealousy and hostility. He worried that abolitionists and other malcontents would use it to tear the Union apart. He still wanted Texas—desperately. But under present circumstances it was best to allow a less interested nation to make the first move toward recognition. Then it would be time enough for the United States to act.

William Wharton, the recently appointed minister from Texas to the United States, said the message "surprized every body. It has pleased no party 'en masse' except perhaps the abolitionists."[74] Everyone tried to figure Jackson's motivation: some said he deliberately delayed recognition so that his successor, Van Buren, would get the credit for it and the glory;[75] others suspected a treaty in progress by which Mexico would surrender Texas in due course; and still others predicted the early arrival of Santa Anna in Washington, at which time he would recognize Texas, followed by a guarantee of a treaty of independence by the United States.[76]

Santa Anna was indeed on his way to Washington. Sam Houston had set him free in the hope that he would talk with Jackson and assist in the resolution of the diplomatic problems involving recognition. Santa Anna's release also provided the advantage of getting rid of an embarrassing presence. Once out of Texas, Santa Anna was expected to keep Mexico in turmoil for years. So Houston freed him, presented him with a handsome horse, and pointed him (under escort) toward Washington.

General Santa Anna arrived in the American capital on January 17, 1837. As soon as it could be arranged he went to see General Jackson. The two men provided a marked contrast. Jackson, still recovering from a recent hemorrhage attack, looked wan and pale. Not exactly feeble—for on such occasions he mustered great presence to impress visitors with the dignity of his office—but from time to time he needed support and he rested at every opportunity. Still his face and general appearance exuded great strength. Here was a powerful personality trapped inside a broken and feeble frame. Santa Anna, on the other hand, looked rested and relaxed despite his long trip. He thoroughly enjoyed the notoriety that accompanied his arrival in the capital. Depicted in the press as a fire-breathing monster who ate children, he delighted in showing himself off as a gracious and cultivated man of impeccable manners and dress.[77] Swarthy, stolid looking, with heavy features, he still managed to appear elegant. A strong chin, a mouth slightly dropping, and black hair plastered across his head made him appear the very personification of Mexican pride and bearing.

The two men shook hands when they met in the White House on Thursday, January 19, 1837. "General Andrew Jackson greeted me warmly," Santa Anna recorded, "and honored me at a dinner attended by notables of all countries."[78] After the official greeting and reception, the two generals met again the following day and sat down for a long and "free conversation."[79] It was very informal. Jackson was dressed in his old calico robe, smoking his long-stemmed pipe. They talked mainly about the possibility of a treaty between their two countries which would permit an extension of the boundary of the United States to include Texas.

"If Mexico will recognize the independence of Texas," President Jackson said to his guest, "we will indemnify your country with six million pesos."

Santa Anna's eyes grew bright. A slight smile crossed his face. But then he grew cautious.

"To the Mexican Congress solely," he replied, "belongs the right to decide that question."[80]

This was Santa Anna's brief version of the interview. In writing his autobiography he obviously presented himself in the most favorable light. But Jackson provided a different version of the meeting. And his account was written up in a memorandum shortly after the interview. Furthermore, it is supported by an unsolicited letter written by Frank Blair a few years later.[81] According to Jackson, the Mexican general proposed the cession of Texas for a "fair consideration." Old Hickory supposedly replied that the United States could do nothing about a cession until "the disposition of the Texians" was resolved. "Until Texas is acknowledged Independent," said the American, "we cannot receive her minister or hold any correspondence with her as a nation." And since Santa Anna could not speak for the Mexican government, continued Jackson, "we can only instruct our minister at Mexico to receive any proposition her government may make on the subject—Until we hear her views we cannot speak to Texas."[82]

It was at this point that Jackson outlined a proposal to his guest by which the United States, under certain conditions, might extend her border to include Texas and northern California, in effect to run "the line of the U.States to the Rio grand—up that stream to latitude 38 north & then to the pacific including north California." As compensation he would offer $3½ million. "But before we promise anything," Jackson continued, "Genl Santana must say that he will use his influence to suspend hostilities."[83]

This is when Santa Anna may have spoken about the right of the Mexican Congress to decide the question. In any event, Jackson hastened to state that "this proposition is made to meet the views of the Genl, and not by the U. States to acquire Territory or take advantage of the disturbed state of Mexico." What he wanted most of all was to "secure peace & tranquility on our respective borders & lay the foundation of a permanent tranquility between the U.S. and Mexico."[84]

Blair, who was present during the entire interview, could never forget the conversation between the two generals—nor the "lecture" Jackson gave Santa Anna. "No man ever gave another a better lesson of patriotism and public virtue than Santa Anna received from you," Blair wrote, "not only in words, but in the example he saw before him of simplicity, probity and power."[85]

What was so instructive about the exchange between these two unlikely protagonists was the continuing desire of Jackson for Texas but only under the most legitimate and acceptable circumstances. It was very important to Jackson that the rest of the world see any exchange of territory as an honorable and proper transaction.

And so the interview between Jackson and Santa Anna ended on a polite but indefinite note. When the Mexican's stay in Washington ended after a round of farewell receptions, President Jackson provided him with a warship to take him to Vera Cruz. Santa Anna had nothing but praise for his host, and Old Hickory apparently thought the Mexican a very likable gentleman.[86]

Jackson discussed this conversation with William Wharton, the Texan minister. When the President mentioned a possible treaty with Mexico, Wharton protested. Texas independence, achieved through her own military prowess, was an accomplished fact. He therefore denied in toto the right of Mexico to sell Texas or make a treaty that in any way bound Texas without her consent.

As he listened, Jackson became quite agitated. He admitted Wharton's argument and swore that he would "*perish* before he would be guilty of any injustice to Texas, or attempt to bind her against her consent." Wharton said that it was "truly humiliating" to be even nominally sold after all his country had gone through in winning its independence. True, Jackson answered, but the wound to Texas "pride was only in name, in sound, not in substance." He then went on to repeat that he would never agree to a treaty without Texas consent.

Wharton interrupted. The recognition of Texas independence by the United States, he declared, must be a condition to any treaty. And this must come first. Only then could Texas be an equal. Recognition must be achieved during this session of Congress, he protested, otherwise the people of Texas would view a refusal "as evidencing a coldness and illiberality, not to say injustice" on the part of the Jackson administration.[87]

Jackson sighed. Such recognition would kill any prospect of a treaty with Mexico, for it would constitute an open declaration that Mexico no longer held any jurisdiction over Texas.

Recognition would not furnish Mexico with a serious complaint, Wharton insisted. But annexation would. Annexation would be a just and serious cause of war.

This tense conversation ended with Wharton again protesting that recognition must be a condition. Then the United States, Texas, and Mexico might conclude a tripartite treaty.[88]

Much of what Wharton said impressed the feeble President. Yet Jackson was concerned about the sectional antagonisms recognition could raise and what the abolitionists would say and do. At one point, as a means of quieting sectional rivalry, Jackson suggested to Wharton that Texas must claim California in order "to paralyze" the opposition of the north and east to annexation.[89] What a great and powerful nation that would make. It was his old dream of American empire—a nation sweeping across a continent to the Pacific Ocean.

Over the next several weeks Jackson moved closer toward recognition. The obvious and passionate desire of the Texans to be annexed—on this point Wharton was particularly eloquent each time he spoke to the President[90]—coupled with the mounting evidence of support for such expansion by the American people weighed heavily on Jackson's mind. He recognized and accepted the inevitability of the acquisition. Why, then, resist it or make it more difficult? If "the virtue of the people" dictated such a move, why should the disapproval of foreign nations disturb him?[91]

During the second week of February, 1837, Jackson met again with Wharton and with Memucan Hunt, who had been commissioned a special representative to assist the negotiations. In the course of their conversation, Jackson suddenly and unexpectedly burst out with a passionate announcement of his desire for the immediate recognition of Texas independence. The two men leapt at him. Would he act on this, they asked, and send another message to Congress and urge recognition?[92]

Jackson looked glum. He slumped into his seat. The passion dissipated. No, he said, it would be inappropriate for him to go back to Congress with still another message on the same subject after only a few weeks. The matter rested with Congress. It was up to the members to decide the question. Andrew Jackson, nearing the age of seventy, was a sick and tired old man, bordering on the pathetic. Only dimly now did he hear the din of battle.

Fortunately for this dying administration, the Congress responded to the prodding of the Texas commissioners and ministers, to the vocal cries for annexation heard around the country, and probably to their own secret desires. On February 28, the House of Representatives passed a series of resolutions appropriating the funds necessary for formal recognition and directed that an agent be sent to Texas by the President. The following day, on March 1, the Senate, by a vote of 23 to 19, recommended to the President the formal recognition of Texas.[93]

On Friday, March 3, the day before his administration would end, Jackson summoned Wharton and Hunt to the White House. On their arrival he announced to them that he had "consummated" the recognition of the Senate and the diplomatic appropriation bill of the House by nominating Alcée La Branche of Louisiana to be chargé d'affaires to the Republic of Texas. This nomination had already gone to the Senate. With Congress only hours away from adjournment, the three men waited up to see if it would be acted upon. Near midnight word came that the Senate had confirmed La Branche as chargé.

Jackson graciously asked his guests to join him in a glass of wine. The three men stood, smiled at each other, and raised their glasses in a toast: Texas![94]

CHAPTER 24

Jackson Triumphant

ON SATURDAY EVENING, NOVEMBER 19, 1836, while working in his study on his last annual message to Congress, President Andrew Jackson was seized with a violent fit of coughing. He had come down with a bad cold just a few days before and he found there was nothing he could do to ease his discomfort. So he just disregarded it, as he usually did, and kept working. And coughing. Then it happened. He hemorrhaged—and it was massive. Major Donelson, who had recently arrived from Tennessee, was with him at the time and recognized the seriousness of what was happening. Without a moment's delay he summoned the President's physician, Dr. Hunt.

As soon as he arrived, the doctor followed standard procedure. He bled the President and then administered a preparation of salt. The hemorrhaging stopped. Nearly unconscious from the enormous loss of blood, Jackson was carried to his bed. Some of the servants began to wail that the end was near. Indeed, Old Hickory looked ashen and Donelson knew that it was a very bad attack.[1]

The next morning the President complained of a pain in his side. But this was nothing unusual. That particular pain was chronic. Just then he started bleeding again, only not as profusely as the night before. When the doctor arrived, Jackson was "cupped and blistered" and for the remainder of the day he suffered excruciating pain. By evening, his condition was critical. "Uncle was very sick," reported Donelson to his family. So the doctor bled him again and drew "upwards of 60 ozs. blood." Which meant, Jackson later wrote, that "I lost in less than 48 hours, by the lancet & otherwise upwards of 70 ozs. of blood."[2] When the doctor and his assistants had finished with him the President was nearly lifeless.

How he survived it nobody knew. Even Jackson later admitted that 60 ozs. of blood "for a man of my age was a great deal, and of course has left me very much debilitated, so much so that I fear I will be compelled to confine myself closely to my room."[3]

By some miraculous means, Jackson passed the crisis during the night of November 21. Later, the servants joked that he simply made up his mind to go on living, and that was the end of it. Jackson himself had a different explanation. "A kind Providence, who holds our existence here in the hollow of his hand," decreed that he would survive. It was divine will.[4] But Jackson had come as close to death as that is possible and still pull through. For the next several days he just lay on his bed in a state of semiconsciousness. Once they stopped bleeding him he began to regain his strength. But it was slow. For weeks later he was very debilitated and listless. "Great care must be taken of him to prevent a return of the hemmoraghe," wrote Donelson, "and keep him free from cold, or it will be difficult for him to get thro the winter."[5] In the mornings Jackson suffered from shortness of breath which slowly improved over the course of the day. He was placed on a very strict diet, not that he cared particularly about what he ate. "I live on mush & milk," he admitted, "—this I find necessary, and I have frequently to take salts to remove costiveness & fever—I rest badly at night, and have some times to attend to too much business in the day."[6] But Jackson guarded himself well. He remained confined to his room for over two months. Between the first seizure and the last day of his administration on March 4, 1837, Jackson left his bedroom and went downstairs a total of four times.[7] Of course, he dared not venture outdoors. The possibility of catching cold was too risky, and Jackson was forever catching cold—even in the middle of summer. "Some days I feel like I would get out my room soon," he wrote in mid-January, "when the next I am worse still I trust to a kind providence that he will prolong my life & permit me to reach home Nevertheless I find myself very feeble & my cough in the morning very severe."[8]

It was because of the President's physical breakdown that Donelson was delayed so long in returning to his dying wife. That plus the necessity of finishing the presidential message before Congress reconvened on December 5. "He remained with me three days longer than I wished him," the guilt-ridden President moaned, "to aid me in compleating my message."[9] But as soon as he was conscious of what was happening around him and could gather sufficient strength to make his wishes known, Old Hickory begged his nephew to return to Tennessee. He did not stop hounding Donelson until he saw him depart the White House. And, as the young man raced to get home in time to see his wife, Jackson pursued him with letters filled with remorse for being "the cause of your detention from her." He was getting better, he assured Donelson, although he still had some bad days. "I am quite unwell yesterday," he wrote on December 6, "but having taken medicine, it has relieved me from a seveer pressure of the breast, pain in my side, & shoulder by bringing off the flime [phlegm] I am weak, but I will this morning get my message from my mind, & endeavour to be quiet for a few days—The Congress met yesterday—quorums in both Houses."[10]

Jackson's particular concern for this document was the fact that it would be his last State of the Union message. As such it was very important to him. He wanted to sum up his administration in a manner that would be instructive to the Congress and the American people. It was intended as a special statement. Not a farewell—that was yet to come— but as one to mark the end of his public career and of the generally happy conditions existing throughout the country. Jackson labored long and hard on it. Propped up in a sickbed, his spectacles resting on the top of his head when not in use, he corrected the final version before it was sent down to the Congress.

This eighth annual message was dated December 5, 1836, the very day the Congress reassembled to begin the second (short) session of the 24th Congress. After congratulating the country on its continued prosperity and its success in maintaining peace and cordial relations with foreign nations, Jackson proceeded immediately to the ordinary business of such messages. He reviewed foreign affairs, he elaborated on the strength of the economy, and noted that the Treasury would have a surplus of nearly $42 million (it required only $32 million to run the country in 1836), which would be distributed to the states. But he warned against an un-necessary accumulation of public revenue. "No people can hope to per-petuate their liberties who long acquiesce in a policy which taxes them for objects not necessary to the legitimate and real wants of their Govern-ment," he said. To require people to pay taxes in order to return it to them again "is sporting with the substantial interests of the country." At the moment, he declared, the surplus is distributed to the states, but something better needs to be devised. To distribute it among the people would be worse. "It would be taking one man's property and giving it to another." In terms of taxes, people contribute unequally; to distribute this money on an equal basis would be unjust. And to make the govern-ment the instrument of this "odious principle" would change the charac-ter of the government as designed by the framers of the Constitution.[11]

The question of finance occupied a good part of this last message. In passing, Jackson flatly asserted that the Founding Fathers always in-tended a currency consisting of "precious metals." The BUS betrayed this intent, he said, and substituted itself for the mint of the United States. This banking system robbed the laboring classes of their wages and contributed to the livelihood of speculators. "It was in view of these evils, together with the dangerous power wielded by the Bank of the United States and its repugnance to our Constitution, that I was induced to exert the power conferred upon me by the American people to prevent the continuance of that institution." He hoped that Congress in the future would continue the good work he had started by legislation designed to discourage the further use of paper in any negotiations involving the federal government.[12]

As another example of his good fight against the paper system Jackson explained the need for issuing his Specie Circular. "By preventing the extension of the credit system it measurably cut off the means of speculation and retarded its progress in monopolizing the most valuable of our public lands." The Circular tended to keep the public lands open to settlers who could buy the land at government prices rather than being forced to pay the "double or triple prices" demanded by speculators. The President stated that much good would be accomplished if the Congress restricted the sale of public land to actual settlers at "a reasonable reduction of price, and to limit the quantity which shall be sold to them."[13]

Turning to the Indian question, Jackson first noticed the ongoing war against the Seminoles and Creeks. He said he hoped the Seminole War could be ended soon but admitted that there existed an "urgent necessity" for further appropriations to halt the hostilities. Fortunately, the Creek War had gone better. "The unconditional submission of the hostile party was followed by their speedy removal to the country assigned them west of the Mississippi."

With respect to Indian removal generally—"founded alike in interest and humanity," pontificated Jackson—it may be said to have been "consummated" by the conclusion of the treaty with the Cherokees. But he warned against leaving it at that. I again invite your attention, he said, to "the importance of providing a well-digested and comprehensive system for the protection, supervision, and improvement" of the Indians. It was not enough to send them west. That was only the beginning. The true test of the "humanity" of the white man would be shown in the protection and help provided for all the tribes. "The best hopes of humanity in regard to the aboriginal race, the welfare of our rapidly extending settlements, and the honor of the United States are all deeply involved in the relations existing between this Government and the emigrating tribes."[14]

Indian removal was not the only success Jackson reported. He presented a highly gratifying picture of the condition of the Post Office Department. Its revenues had increased by 13 percent and showed a surplus of more than half a million dollars. "The Department has been redeemed from embarrassment and debt," he gloated.[15]

Always a politician, Jackson closed his message by turning to the great body of American citizens and expressing his gratitude to them for their encouragement and support during the "many difficult and trying scenes" of his public career. His efforts, he declared, had not always ended in success but he was persuaded that whatever errors he had committed would "find a corrective in the intelligence and patriotism of those who will succeed us." For the rest he would leave all to "that beneficent Being to whose providence we are already so signally indebted for the continuance of His blessings on our beloved country."[16]

It was not a terribly impressive message. It showed the strain that had permeated the White House over the past several weeks. The *Globe* called it a narrative of how "the President has labored to maintain the great principles and useful policies which he learned in the school of our revolutionary age."[17] Even the *National Intelligencer* was indulgent. The editors found less to fault than in any of his previous messages. Not that they were happy with every part of it, but at least it had neither "the tone of assumption and arrogation or of the vindictive spirit too often of late years discernible in the executive messages." It was not quarrelsome. The old warrior was laying down his arms and quietly leaving the scene. "We have in this message no claim of prerogative power for the executive; no assertion of his right to construe the Constitution and the laws as he understands them; no intimation of contingent purposes of coercion in the reference to any foreign powers; no denunciation of popular indignation against those who have ventured to question the infallibility of executive wisdom." As always, complained other Jackson critics, the worst part related to the BUS. "Bad temper and worse logic" inform his statements, they said. And he mangles facts.[18]

But almost everyone excused the President for whatever fault they found in the message. Either they accounted for the blemishes by his dreadful health or they reckoned them the last feeble gasps of a battered fighter who should be allowed to depart with the sounds of glory still ringing in his ears. "To hold the President accountable for this long and labored tirade," wrote one, "or for the conglomeration of crudities about a currency of the precious metals . . . would be a refinement of justice. In the present state of his health we are very sorry the President is known to be incapable of such labor and we dare to hope . . . that he would, had he been able to give it a careful perusal, have expunged three fourths of the whole discussion."[19]

But if the message, like his health, was less than satisfactory, and if it marked a low point in Jackson's presidency, the subsequent weeks from the end of December to the close of his administration on March 4, registered a definite upswing in his personal and political fortunes. First off, his health showed a dramatic improvement, even though he was still very weak and remained confined to his bedroom for nearly four months. But the event that really uplifted his spirit was the long-awaited news that his friend and heir apparent, Martin Van Buren, had been elected the eighth President of the United States. The wait had been interminable. As late as early December he still did not know the final results. Since there was no national election day—that came in 1845—each state chose a date that seemed most convenient, and some states did not open their polls until late November.

Throughout the long period of suspense, Jackson maintained his faith in the "virtue and wisdom of the people" and reassured Van Buren in practically every letter he wrote that "the political horison is brightening" and that the people would stick to good old "jeffersonian Democratic republican principles."[20] Not until the final week in November did it seem certain that Van Buren had squeezed out a victory. Although the Magician had been denounced in the south as an abolitionist, vilified in the north as a southern sympathizer, and ridiculed in all sections of the country as Jackson's hand-picked tool who would jump at Old Hickory's bidding, Van Buren amassed a total of 764,198 popular votes, which was slightly more than a bare majority. More important, he tallied 170 electoral votes, which represented 15 states. There was a marked increase in voting in the south, which helped Van Buren, and a slight falling off in some Middle Atlantic and New England states. The combined Whig popular vote reached 736,147, which represented 49.1% of the total. In the electoral college the several Whig candidates polled 124 votes from ten states, of which Harrison got 73 (Vermont, New Jersey, Maryland, Kentucky, Ohio, and Indiana), Judge White took 26 (Georgia and Tennessee), Webster received 14 (Massachusetts), and Willie P. Mangum obtained 11 votes from South Carolina, where the electors were appointed by the legislature.[21]

"We are to be cursed with Van Buren for President," groaned Thurlow Weed, the Whig boss of New York. "This certainly only makes me hate [him] the more cordially." How could the electorate do it, he muttered. "I have no confidence in a People who can elect Van Buren President. Depend upon it, his Election is to be the 'beginning of the end.' "[22]

Jackson, naturally, was jubilant. He was too ill at the time to celebrate properly but the news cheered him considerably. Like Samuel J. Tilden of New York, the President regarded Van Buren's victory as an incredible achievement. "Considering the game that was played against him," wrote Tilden, "the combination of discordant & powerful factions, the multiplicity of candidates, enlisting in their favor local & sectional interests, artfully calculated to divide & to prevent an election by the people; I must regard such a majority [of electoral votes] over the whole of them as a more triumphant victory than receiving ⅔ or ¾ of all the votes against a single candidate."[23]

Jackson's only real disappointment was Tennessee's abandonment of good old Democratic principles in favor of the great apostate and stool pigeon, Hugh Lawson White.[24] He even went public with his denunciation of White. "This, and many recent developments of character," Jackson ranted, "shew that Judge White under strong temptation has a lax code of morals for himself; and his remarkable readiness to invest pretexts to cover the naked and palpable selfishness of his late tergiversations and multiplied inconsistencies, shews, that he need not tax the invention of his subordinate instruments for falsehoods to suit his exigencies." This unwarranted and mean-spirited attack was published in virtually every newspaper in the country in early January, 1837, and showed the depth of Jackson's resentment and bitterness over what White had done.[25]

Jackson had tried desperately to transfer his towering popularity to Van Buren, particularly in Tennessee, and he had failed. Jackson was so singular a national figure that his presence actually distorted the normal operation of politics over the last dozen years. Once that presence was removed, the political game could resume a more normal and regular rhythm. Much as he tried, Jackson could not transfer his popularity, not even in Tennessee—and this probably was a good thing. More than anything else, the presidential election of 1836 demonstrated that a two-party system could function once again—that is without Andrew Jackson as a candidate. Now, instead of the electorate responding pro or con to Jackson personally, they responded more to the issues as well as the individual candidates. Banking, specie payments, distribution, tariff, and internal improvements had a better chance of being decided on their own intrinsic merits.

Jackson's life constituted a passionate trajectory through American politics and the American psyche. He was a unique figure. His stepping down from office, therefore, had a beneficial effect on American political life. It helped to restore the two-party system, and nowhere was the restoration more apparent than in the south, where one party had ruled unopposed for more than a decade. Jackson was too grand a figure for normal politics. He cut too wide a swath across the political landscape. In many places, he and he alone was the issue. Now, with his approaching retirement to the Hermitage, a more normal political operation could emerge. According to one historian, a new political era began in 1836, and a genuine two-party system between opposing political groups committed to differing ideologies and issues commenced.[26]

Fortunately for Jackson, that new era did not mean the defeat of the Democratic party. That would have been unbearable. A defeat was probably impossible, given Jackson's role in so many of the issues that confronted the American people in 1836. In fact, some thought that the victory was Jackson's third electoral triumph with the American people —or fourth, if the election of 1824 was "properly" interpreted.[27]

The election of 1836 also included electoral votes from two new states in the Union. Not since 1821, when Missouri entered the Union, had a new state been added. For the last fifteen years the American nation had consisted of twenty-four states. Then in 1836–1837 Arkansas and Michigan were admitted, one slave and one free, thereby maintaining the balance between the north and south. It had long been Jackson's intention to bring these two territories into the Union as quickly as possible. Not only was this progressive attitude in line with Jeffersonian republicanism but it made good politics. For a Democratic administration to engineer admission just prior to a presidential election practically guaranteed additional electoral votes. A new state showed its gratitude by voting for the party that sponsored its admission. And these additional votes for Van Buren could make a difference in blocking the efforts of the Whigs to throw the election into the House of Representatives. In addition to everything else, the admission of Arkansas and Michigan meant four new Democratic senators who could be expected to assist in cleansing the upper house of its "Whiggish" manners and conduct.

Arkansas came in first. Its admission went off with relative ease and occurred officially on June 15, 1836. But the Michigan admission proved more difficult because of a dispute between Michigan and Ohio over an elongated wedge-shaped slice of land running ten miles wide at the mouth of the Maumee River at the western tip of Lake Erie. A veritable "war" broke out between Ohio and Michigan, sometimes called the Toledo War, which produced more sound and nonsense than anything else. Jackson warned the Michigan territorial governor against exacerbating the difficulty, but the governor disregarded him and arrested several Ohio officials who ventured into the disputed territory. Jackson promptly removed the disobedient governor. Subsequently, the arrested Ohioans were released. In an effort to find a compromise, Michigan was promised the Upper Peninsula if it would relinquish its claim to the Toledo strip, but the Michigan legislature had no desire for the desolate Upper Peninsula and summarily rejected the offer. However, when it became known that the Treasury surplus would be distributed to states—not territories —and that Michigan stood to gain nearly half a million dollars as a state, all objections to the compromise proposal immediately vanished. Claims to the Toledo strip were abandoned, both houses of Congress passed a bill to admit Michigan, and President Jackson signed it on January 26, 1837. The admission of Arkansas and Michigan brought Martin Van Buren six additional electoral votes for President.[28]

Of far greater immediate concern to the Democratic political leaders in 1836 was the failure of the electorate to select a Vice President. Van Buren's running mate, Richard M. Johnson, failed to receive a majority. Virginia, still resenting the decision of the convention to bypass William C. Rives, gave its vote to William Smith. South Carolina and Georgia supported John Tyler, as did Tennessee. Consequently, Johnson received only 147 electoral votes as against 77 for the Whig candidate, Francis Granger, 47 for John Tyler, and 23 for Smith. Which meant that the election must go to the Senate for decision. Happily, the Senate was now safely Democratic and on February 8, 1837, by a vote of 33 to 16, Richard M. Johnson was elected Vice President of the United States.[29]

The present strength of the Democrats in the upper house encouraged them to plan a whole series of actions to bolster the administration. Our friends in the Senate, reported Silas Wright, Jr., of New York "called for our usual meetings that we might avail ourselves of our majority." At these meetings "we always agreed and always acted unanimously," he added.[30] Consequently, Senator Benton laid plans to bring about the passage of a resolution to "expunge" the censure of the President passed by the Senate in 1834 to vent its outrage over the removal of the deposits. Year after year Benton had sought to win Senate approval for his resolution. "The condemnation of the President," he said on one occasion to a packed house, only hastened the conspiracy of the BUS "to effect the most wicked and universal scheme of mischief which the annals of modern times exhibit. . . . President Jackson had done more for the human race than the whole tribe of politicians put together; and shall he remain stigmatized and condemned for the most glorious action of his life?"[31]

Most Democrats around the country agreed that the time had arrived to expunge the record. "The people have called for it, in language not to be mistaken," wrote Chief Justice Taney, "& justice demands that it should be done." Certainly it should be done before Jackson left office, as a kind of parting gift by a grateful nation for his many contributions and services to the American people. "I trust it will be made the great & leading topic day by day," said Taney, "until the good work is accomplished."[32]

As long as the Whigs held a majority in the Senate it was impossible to alter the record. But each year Democratic strength in the upper house increased and each year Benton was back at his stand demanding passage of an expunging resolution. It was now the last session of the last term of Jackson's administration. The present Democratic majority in the Senate almost guaranteed passage of such a resolution, and Benton had no intention of missing his chance. As Benton liked to point out to his fellow senators, the people of the United States had already expressed their will with respect to the censure. Some of the senators who had voted for it, he said, had themselves been voted out of office; others had been instructed by their state legislatures to rescind the censure or resign.[33] Of course Clay, Calhoun, and Webster "easily maintained themselves" against the obvious will of the people "but the mortality fell heavily upon their followers."[34]

On the second day of the session Benton announced to the Senate his intention of moving an expunging resolution and forcing it to a decision. In the past he had never asked for a decision because he did not have the votes. He merely took the opportunity to give a speech which he knew would "go to the people." But the Whigs, conscious of their own strength, always demanded a vote in order to reject the motion. Now, said Benton gleefully, "these dispositions were reversed." So, on December 26, the third anniversary of the day on which Clay introduced the censure, Benton offered the resolution to expunge it.[35]

> Resolved, That the said resolve [of censure] be expunged from the journal; and, for that purpose, that the Secretary of the Senate, at such time as the Senate may appoint, shall bring the manuscript journal of the session 1833 '34 into the Senate, and, in the presence of the Senate, draw black

lines round the said resolve, and write across the face thereof, in strong letters, the following words: "Expunged by order of the Senate, this —— day of ——, in the year of our Lord 1837".[36]

In support of his resolution Benton delivered one of his great efforts in a long history of superb oratorical performances. He decried the wrongs inflicted on the President and regaled his audience with the catalog of blessings Jackson had won for the people. "Imagination has been exhausted in her efforts to deck him with revolting and inhuman attributes," he said. "Tyrant, despot, usurper; destroyer of the liberties of his country; rash, ignorant, imbecile; endangering the public peace with all foreign nations; destroying domestic prosperity at home." Then he refuted these charges as he cited the many instances of public good brought by the Jackson administration. Even his use of the veto, Benton argued, strengthened the constitutional system. "From President Jackson, the country has first learned the true theory and practical intent of the constitution, in giving to the Executive a qualified negative on the legislative power of Congress. Far from being an odious, dangerous, or kingly prerogative," this power was nothing more than a replica of the veto power vested in the tribunes of the people by the ancient Romans.[37]

For the eight years of his two administrations, Benton boomed, President Jackson "has stood upon a volcano, vomiting fire and flames upon him." I saw him in these dark moments, the senator continued, "and never did I see his confidence in the ultimate support of his fellow-citizens forsake him for an instant. He always said the people would stand by those who stand by them; and nobly have they justified that confidence! That verdict, the voice of millions, which now demands the expurgation of that sentence, which the Senate and the bank then pronounced upon him, is the magnificent response of the people's hearts to the implicit confidence which he then reposed in them."[38]

Because the opposition understood Benton's strategy in raising the question at this time, they fully intended to fight the expunging resolution every foot of the way. Clay, Calhoun, and Webster prepared detailed speeches which they hoped would rouse their colleagues and win ultimate defeat for the resolution. Anticipating this concerted attack, Benton gathered the Democratic senators on the night of Saturday, January 14, at Boulanger, a famous restaurant of the time, where they caroused until midnight and planned their strategy. Nothing must be left to chance. Everything had to be organized. It required "all the moderation, tact and skill of the prime movers to obtain and maintain the union upon details," recorded Benton, and all the "winning resources of men like Silas Wright, Allen of Ohio and Linn of Missouri" to reach a consensus. Not that they disagreed about the expurgation, only the "mode" it would take. When they finally worked out the "details" of their agreement, each senator pledged himself to it and that there would be no adjournment of the Senate until it was passed. The following Monday, January 16, was the day set to call up the resolution. Expecting a long night of debate, Benton arranged to have "an ample supply" of cold hams, turkeys, beef, pickles, wines, and hot coffee in a certain committee room near the Senate chamber where members could refresh themselves and withstand the long ordeal.[39]

On Monday the motion was taken up at the precise hour the Democrats had planned. The great triumvirate—Clay, Calhoun, and Webster— watched silently and did not participate in the opening round of debate. Others substituted, including a new recruit, Judge Hugh Lawson White. Then, as darkness approached and the immense chandelier was lighted, illuminating the chamber in a blaze of color, a huge crowd filled every seat in the galleries, lobbies, and even on the Senate floor itself. "The scene became grand and impressive." Parties of four and six sauntered to the committee room to snack and chat, but always keeping an eye peeled to what was happening on the floor. "The night was wearing away: the expungers were in full force—masters of the chamber—happy—and visibly determined to remain."[40]

Calhoun rose. The battle was at last joined. He stared at the presiding officer for a moment and then he began. The Constitution says a journal shall be kept, he said in a soft voice. If you expunge, how can it be kept? "It does the very thing which the constitution declares shall not be done." His voice grew louder. And why is this unconstitutional thing being done? he asked. "It is by dictation from the White House. The President himself, with that vast mass of patronage which he wields, and the thousand expectations he is able to hold up, has obtained these votes of the State Legislatures; and this, forsooth, is said to be the voice of the people! No, sir. It is the combination of patronage and power to coerce this body into a gross and palpable violation of the constitution."[41]

Henry Clay followed. "The decree has gone forth," he announced. "The deed is to be done—that foul deed which, like the blood-stained hands of the guilty Macbeth, all ocean's waters will never wash out." The censure is to be expunged. "And when you have perpetrated it, go home to the people, and tell them what glorious honors you have achieved for our common country. Tell them that you have extinguished one of the brightest and purest lights that ever burnt at the altar of civil liberty. . . . Tell them that, henceforth, no matter what daring or outrageous act any President may perform, you have for ever hermetically sealed the mouth of the Senate. . . . And if the people do not pour out their indignation and imprecations, I have yet to learn the character of American freemen."[42]

Clay was good, and he knew it. It was a great misfortune that the country never received the full benefit of his magnificent talents. The presidency was forever denied him, and all on account of a "corrupt bargain" engineered to thwart the purpose and ambition of General Andrew Jackson.

Webster spoke last. He rose slowly as if physically burdened by the question about to be put. He was not as passionate as Clay or Calhoun, probably because he had suffered "no personal griefs" at the hands of Old Hickory. His protest, therefore, was brief and moderate. He would not stand in the way of the inevitable. "That cause, which has been powerful enough to influence so many State legislatures," he said, "will show itself powerful enough . . . to secure the passage of the resolution here. . . . This scene we shall behold; and hundreds of American citizens . . . will behold it also: with what feelings I do not undertake to say." He let out a long sigh—and then sat down.[43]

Midnight approached. No one left the chamber, and it was packed. Tensions mounted. Finally, one Whig senator walked over to Benton and said: "This question has degenerated into a trial of nerves and muscles. It has become a question of physical endurance; and we see no use in wearing ourselves out to keep off for a few hours longer what has to come before we separate. We see that you are able and determined to carry your measure: so call the vote as soon as you please. We shall say no more."[44]

So when Webster sat down there was a long silence. No one rose. Then someone called the question. The presiding officer, King of Alabama, ordered a vote. Forty-three senators were present, five absent. In favor of Benton's resolution to expunge, 24; opposed, 19. Among those voting in favor were Benton, Buchanan, Grundy, Linn, Rives, Tallmadge, and Wright; those against, Calhoun, Clay, Crittenden, Webster, and Hugh Lawson White.

After the chair announced the results of the vote, Benton rose and asked that the order to expunge be executed. It was so ordered. And at that precise moment the Whigs walked out of the chamber to demonstrate their disapproval. Asbury Dickens, the secretary of the Senate, then took down the original manuscript journal of the Senate and opened it to the condemnatory sentence of March 28, 1834. As the secretary proceeded to draw a square of broad black lines around the censure and write the words of expunging, a storm of hisses and boos, groans and catcalls rose from the left wing of the circular gallery. They were right over the head of Senator Benton.

Benton sprang to his feet. "Bank ruffians! Bank ruffians!" he cried. "Seize them, sergeant-at-arms! . . . Let them be taken and brought to the bar of the Senate."

The ringleader was seized and that action intimidated the others. Once order was restored the process of expunging was performed in quiet. The secretary completed drawing the lines around the censure. Then across its face he wrote: "Expunged by order of the Senate, this 16th day of January, in the year of our Lord 1837."[45]

When the "ceremony" ended, Benton took the pen used by the secretary to expunge the journal and on the next day sent his little son with it to Jackson. The old man was deeply touched. "I sincerely thank you for this precious *Pen,*" he wrote in return, "... and as this *pen* has been only used in this righteous act, so it shall be preserved with many other precious relics for further use, carefully kept by me during life, and shall by my last *will* and *testament* be bequeathed to you as its rightful heir—not only as its rightful heir, but as an evidence of my high regard, and exalted opinion of your talents, virtue and Patriotism."[46]

Andrew Jackson was indeed pleased by this "just sentence of the senate," a sentence, he liked to say, that had been ordered by "the voice of millions of freemen."[47] Not only did he keep the pen but also the many letters that congratulated him "on this proud & noble triumph." These were "precious relics" to him, a tribute, said Thomas Hart Benton, "to his invincibility."[48]

Jackson gave a "grand dinner" for the expungers, as they were called, and their wives. He was still too weak from his recent illness to do more than greet these heroes and express his pleasure and gratitude over their action. Then he walked over to Benton, the "head-expunger," and led him to his own chair at the head of the table before withdrawing to his sickroom. The company celebrated for several hours.

So ended the Bank War. The censure was expunged, the insult withdrawn. It was the "crowning mercy" of his civil career, declared Benton, just as New Orleans had been of his military life.[49]

CHAPTER 25

Life in the White House

WHEN ANDREW JACKSON, AS THE SEVENTH PRESIDENT of the United States, first moved into the White House on March 10, 1829, the mansion looked far different than it did when he left it. He completely altered its outward appearance. First of all there was no north portico in 1829, and without it the pediment looked naked. Second, the general appearance of the House can be described only as shabby. The mansion did not always get the attention it required to maintain its stately air. Inside, the East Room had never been decorated or completed. It was a big unpainted space, used mainly to accommodate overflow crowds at social gatherings, and therefore added to the general unfinished appearance of the House. And the residence had few modern comforts. No running water, for example. Two water closets were serviced by rainwater from tin cisterns built in the attic. All other water came from two wells situated in the breezeways between the House and the east and west wings.[1]

By the time Jackson moved into the White House, after it had nearly been wrecked by an exuberant crowd celebrating his inauguration, most of the worst damage had been repaired or replaced. But Jackson had more ambitious plans for the House and even before his inauguration had begun to discuss them with a congressional committee, chaired by Stephen Van Rensselaer of New York. His most immediate problem, of course, was the daily operation of the mansion, and here he relied on the Donelsons for their assistance. Emily Donelson, who said she wanted to make the House a "model American home," served as surrogate First Lady, and despite her youth she proved very efficient.[2]

The actual management of the White House first fell to Antoine Michel

Guista and his wife. Guista had worked for President John Quincy Adams and stayed on during Jackson's first administration. Apparently he did not get on well with Old Hickory and much preferred the Adamses as employers, in whose service he had first met his wife. In fact Jackson took violent exception to Guista's habit of bringing food—cakes, pies, bread, and other delicacies—to the Adamses whenever he visited them. That was Jackson-food going down the gullets of the Adamses, and the General resented every mouthful. But Guista proved indispensable in the beginning. He not only managed the huge House but he kept the books, did the marketing, and supervised the other servants. Jackson, of course, brought a number of black servants with him, and the presence of these slaves helped cut costs. But the needs of the presidential family, consisting usually of a dozen or so people, required the employment of a large staff, running from eighteen to twenty-four persons, and these servants had to be housed, fed, clothed and, in some instances, paid. For example, when Guista left, Jackson advertised for a cook. The previous cook had left Jackson's employ without giving notice, despite a written contract. The President paid him $35 per month during the summer, even though most summers the cook had little to do since the family was either at the Rip Raps or back home in Tennessee. During the congressional session the pay was higher by $5 or $10. Still the cook "hoodwicked" Jackson. He ran a boardinghouse for members of Congress on the side and did not come to the White House until after 2 P.M.—the family normally dined between 3 P.M. and 4 P.M.—leaving the arduous task of preparing the main meal to an assistant, a black man whom the President had hired. Jackson never discovered the deception. Not "until we had like to have went without our dinner today" did he learn what had been going on and that the cook had quit. This occurred just as the nullification crisis mounted. Poor Jackson searched for a new cook at the same moment he prepared his proclamation to the people of South Carolina. "Can a good cook be got in Philadelphia," he asked John Pemberton. "If so engage him thro a friend for me." He was willing to pay $40 or $45 per month during the congressional session. Also, "I want a man to live in the house, & spend all his time at his business. Until I get one I will have to get all my dinners from a confectioners."[3]

According to the census of 1830 there were twenty-four servants working for Guista, which was a very large number for the nineteenth-century White House, although not nearly as large as the number Jackson normally employed to run the Hermitage. By 1833 the hired staff was reduced considerably for financial reasons and the balance made up with slaves. According to a list of the President's servants prepared around 1833 or 1834, the White House staff consisted of the following: a house steward and housekeeper, a butler, a doorkeeper, an "odd man," a cook, an assistant cook, two sculleries, a housemaid, a staff maid, two laundry maids, two messengers, a valet, a coachman, and a footman.[4] This list did not include gardeners, stablemen, porters, and the like. The full staff for the House and grounds probably ran as high as ten additional employees.

When the family first moved into the White House in 1829, Jackson took the southwest corner of the second floor for his bedroom and a room at the other end of the corridor for his office. Across the hall from his bedroom, on the northwest side, the Donelsons occupied a suite of rooms for themselves and their small family. Donelson also had a small office (which he always kept locked) on the northeast corner almost opposite Jackson's office. Between Donelson's office and bedroom, Major Lewis and Ralph Earl found quarters.

The "Circular Green Room" on the second floor was probably used by Emily to receive callers and as a room where the ladies would congregate after dinner to talk and have coffee. Next to this circular room, on the southeast side, was the "audience room" where Jackson received petitioners, guests, and other callers. The next room, today's Lincoln Room, served as Jackson's office, which was also used for cabinet meetings. Here the President kept his books and papers. Maps decorated the walls. A rubber-faced oilcloth covered the floor. The window had silk curtains crowned with gilded-eagle cornices which Jackson had purchased. The last room, at the corner, was a narrow chamber and contained one of the two White House water closets.[5]

To separate the office area on the second floor from the family quarters, Jackson installed glass doors. Thus, when official callers came to see the President they used the staircase off the entrance hall (James Hoban, the architect of the White House, called it the "back stair"), while the family used the grand staircase at the west end of the transverse hall. The servants used the small stairwell off the porter's room.

Jackson changed the interior and exterior design of the White House almost from the first moment he arrived. Indeed, the exterior design of the House was completed by Jackson. Within weeks of moving in, he commenced building the north portico and it was brought to completion in September, 1829. The north portico altered considerably the overall appearance of the White House. It added character and distinction to the building. It clothed what looked naked and provided just the right touch of grandeur. The portico is in the Greek Revival style that was so popular at the time and which Jackson himself copied in rebuilding the Hermitage after the fire in 1834. This colossal colonnade, ironically, heralded the arrival of the new democratic age to America.

Jackson initiated other exterior changes around the House and grounds. First, there was the addition on the grounds of a stable building. The existing stable at the end of the west wing of the White House contained only eight stalls, hardly enough for Jackson's needs and the needs of his western friends and family. The plans for the new stable building were possibly drawn by Jackson himself, but it was erected by the Washington builder William P. Elliott.[6] It was placed outside the arched gate (the entrance to the south grounds from Pennsylvania Avenue) and was constructed of clay bricks. It included a porch supported by six round columns. Accommodations for two coaches and several smaller carriages, along with stalls for the animals, a feed room, hay loft and quarters for coachmen and grooms were provided. The whole was stuccoed over and painted. It was ready for use in September, 1834.

The old stable in the west wing was then converted into service rooms. Wooden floors were laid, partitions erected, and the walls plastered and whitewashed. Dairy cows had also been kept in the west wing. Jackson had them transferred to the stable (or possibly a separate building near the stable), and the milk was stored beneath the north portico of the White House, which was convenient to the kitchen.

Of paramount importance was the introduction by Jackson of running water into the mansion. Previous Presidents were served by two wells located in the breezeways between the mansion and the wings. In the spring of 1833 an engineer named Robert Leckie was assigned the task of piping water in iron pipes from Franklin Square directly into the White House. The work went quickly and was completed by the middle of May. A very elementary system, it used pumps, reservoirs, and fountains. But it provided water at only two or possibly three places in the mansion: the basement corridor; the butler's pantry, which had a marble sink; and possibly the kitchen. A brass cock or hydrant capped each pipe. Very soon thereafter—late 1833 or early 1834—a "bathing room" was installed to take advantage of this running water. The room had a hot bath, a cold bath, and a shower bath, and was equipped with large copper boilers for heating the water. The location of this room is uncertain, but most probably it was placed in the basement, if not the east wing.[7]

Considerable work on the White House grounds was begun in 1833 and continued until 1835. Jackson himself took a direct hand in this operation and worked closely with Owsley, the White House gardener, and James Maher, the public gardener, who had charge of all public grounds in the federal District. Whether Jackson actually planted the magnolia trees near the west stairway to the south portico, as is generally believed, is now open to question since a daguerreotype exists of the south lawn taken during President Polk's administration, which does not show any trees in the area whatsoever.[8] Whether Jackson planted these magnolias or not, they are known as the Jackson magnolias and presently shade the President's bedroom windows.

What can be documented are the other changes to the grounds undertaken by Jackson. Grading was begun on the south grounds and garden paths were marked out and topped with gravel. More important, the north front of the White House grounds was refenced. Jackson wanted

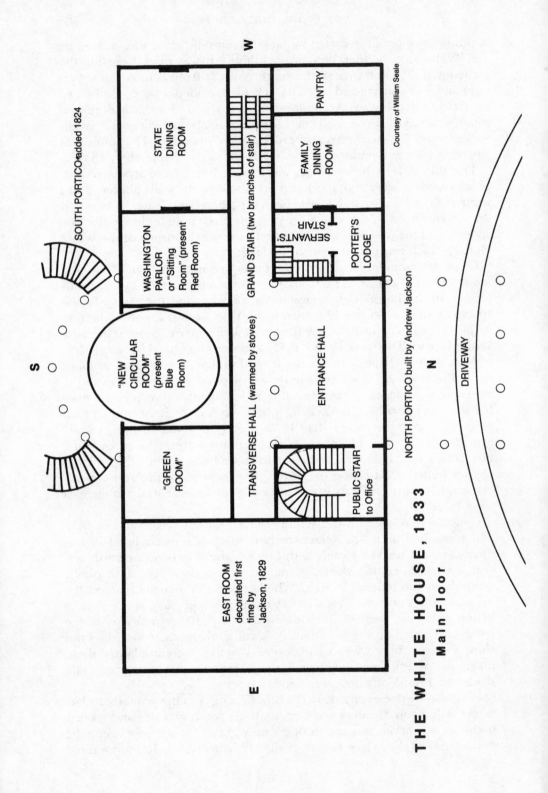

THE WHITE HOUSE, 1833
Main Floor

Courtesy of William Seale

SOUTH PORTICO added 1824

STATE DINING ROOM

WASHINGTON PARLOR or "Sitting Room" (present Red Room)

"NEW CIRCULAR ROOM" (present Blue Room)

"GREEN ROOM"

EAST ROOM decorated first time by Jackson, 1829

GRAND STAIR (two branches of stair)

PANTRY

FAMILY DINING ROOM

SERVANTS' STAIR

PORTER'S LODGE

TRANSVERSE HALL (warmed by stoves)

ENTRANCE HALL

PUBLIC STAIR to Office

NORTH PORTICO built by Andrew Jackson

DRIVEWAY

S

W

N

E

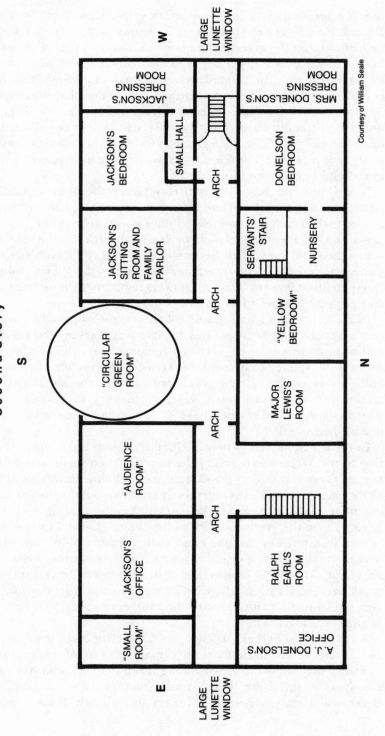

THE WHITE HOUSE, 1833
Second Story

S

W

N

E

LARGE LUNETTE WINDOW

JACKSON'S DRESSING ROOM

MRS. DONELSON'S DRESSING ROOM

SMALL HALL

JACKSON'S BEDROOM

DONELSON BEDROOM

ARCH

JACKSON'S SITTING ROOM AND FAMILY PARLOR

SERVANTS' STAIR

NURSERY

ARCH

"CIRCULAR GREEN ROOM"

"YELLOW BEDROOM"

ARCH

"AUDIENCE ROOM"

MAJOR LEWIS'S ROOM

ARCH

JACKSON'S OFFICE

RALPH EARL'S ROOM

"SMALL ROOM"

A. J. DONELSON'S OFFICE

LARGE LUNETTE WINDOW

Courtesy of William Seale

the configuration of the driveway and the gates at the north front radically altered. He directed the building of a parapet wall and iron railings. And he insisted that the gates and piers be moved wider apart than they had been. He made so many changes in the plans for the fence drawn up by William Nowland, the Commissioner of Public Buildings, that Nowland complained that the President had more than doubled the original cost of the fence.[9] When completed the fence ran the entire length of the north facade and it framed the White House "with a lacy though orderly line of black" rails. The main gate was widened and the driveway leading to the north portico was fixed in its present position and laid over with gravel and edged with footpaths.[10]

Jackson was the first President to separate the ornamental from the edible plantings on the White House grounds. The kitchen garden was moved to the southwest and fenced since it was intended for the exclusive use of the President, and the old ornamental garden in the southeast was redesigned and expanded. Letters written during Jackson's administration speak repeatedly of vegetables and fruit in the White House. They rarely mention flowers. The only flowers regularly seen were made of wax and protected under glass domes.

Jackson also built a hothouse, probably on the ruins of Latrobe's Treasury fireproof. The fireproof was a single-story rectangular building that had been attached to the Treasury building and originally intended to connect the White House with the Treasury. Remodeled by Jackson, the hothouse or orangery, as it was usually called, contained a tall central section for large plants and was flanked by glass-roofed wings that stretched out on either side. By 1836 this orangery was in full use. It was demolished in 1859.[11]

By the use of his veto power, Jackson also made an important contribution to the White House and its grounds. When the Treasury building burned there was talk by the Committee on Public Buildings of lumping all the executive buildings together in one giant building (since all the old executive buildings were inadequate) and either placing it on Lafayette Square or on the grounds south of the White House. Either would have been a disaster. On the one hand such a giant would have ruined the Square; on the other, it would have destroyed the southern vista from the President's House. Jackson vetoed both. He placed the Treasury building in its present location when he drove his cane into the ground and announced his decision. He also had the entire length of Pennsylvania Avenue macadamized.

As mentioned earlier, Jackson has been criticized for destroying the view of the White House from the Capitol because of the location of the Treasury building—the view running down Pennsylvania Avenue. Actually, Jackson saved the White House from "a far worse fate." The architectural vista planned by L'Enfant had already been destroyed by

George Washington, who placed the executive mansion to the north, "pulling it to the very edge of the Avenue's frame where it was barely visible." President Jefferson was so offended by the way the White House "shrank back" from the axis that he cut off what little view existed with a curving driveway and dense plantings. At least Jackson gave Pennsylvania Avenue its architectural terminus with "democratic grandeur" in the form of the Treasury's colossal portico and breathtaking Ionic columns.[12]

Of the White House's interior design, Jackson's most important change occurred in the East Room. This was an immense room that had not been decorated. Architecturally, it had been completed in 1818. It had a frieze running all around, but nothing else. The plaster on the walls was unpainted; and the mantels were all temporary. Because of the size of the room—eighty feet by forty—it handled overflow crowds from the entrance and transverse halls when the mansion was opened for presidential levees on New Year's Day and the Fourth of July. Jackson turned over the task of decorating the room to Major Lewis. And Lewis, after being assigned, meant to make the East Room not only modern but splendidly Jacksonian.[13]

Lewis demanded "an air of thundering grandeur" for the East Room, something he believed appropriate to General Jackson. That meant gilt everywhere—and sumptuous color. There was a huge arched doorway leading into the room. Lewis wanted it decorated so that it literally became an "arch of triumph" through which President Jackson would enter ceremoniously from the hall to greet his adoring public. The mise en scène became a grand setting for the Hero of New Orleans. Indeed, as finally decorated, it was a magnificent and opulent room. The great arch was no longer an archway. It now blazed with gilded sun rays and twenty-four golden stars emblematic of the states. It seemed to some like the portal for a temple through which only a deity might pass.[14]

The room itself contained four fireplaces with mantels faced with "Egyptian" black marble. Three enormous sunflowers in plaster-of-paris were affixed to the ceiling and from them hung three immense chandeliers of gilded brass and cut glass. Each chandelier held eighteen oil burners and fonts with glass shades. On the walls were attached rows of matching sconces or "Bracket Lights" holding five oil lamps each, and heavily gilded globe and astral lamps were placed at every darkened and convenient spot around the room. A lemon-colored wallpaper provided a bright background and it was trimmed with cloth borders of blue velvet.[15]

A relatively new convenience appeared in the Jacksonian age which Lewis took immediate advantage of in decorating the East Room, namely the furniture warehouse. Heretofore, for household furnishings, it had been necessary to shop at many places and frequently to have the artisans come to the White House and set up shop to provide all the necessary furnishings for any of the rooms. Now, "thanks to modern business methods," Lewis furnished the East Room by making one stop at the Philadelphia warehouse of Louis Veron, who stocked practically everything needed to decorate a house: lamps, tables, chairs, beds, sofas, curtains, stoves, carpets, washbowls, kitchen appliances, and so forth. A principal virtue in shopping at the warehouse was the amount of money that could be saved, for Jackson had made a great issue during his election campaign about the extravagances of the White House.

To commence the decorating, Lewis purchased from Veron a series of wide and high French plate mirrors in gilded frames and these were hung from the four walls of the East Room. Each was positioned directly opposite another, and the reflections carried the eye to an infinite distance. This effect was extremely popular in America throughout the nineteenth century. At the windows, silks of bright yellow and imperial blue were arranged in "luxuriant Grecian drapery," hanging from cornices topped by gilded eagles.[16] The cornices themselves were decorated with a line of golden stars.

What furniture remained in the East Room from the days of James Monroe and John Quincy Adams was reupholstered or replaced with new furniture from the Veron warehouse. A mahogany table with black marble top was positioned under each chandelier. Lamps with glass globes, all held high by classical female figures, rested on the tables. Along the walls, pier tables were located which helped divide the lines of chairs and sofas scattered around the room. A five-hundred-yard Brussels carpet in blue and yellow decorated the floor. This carpet alone cost $1,058.25. On crowded occasions, three Imperial rugs were laid to take the wear and tear of the mob. In deference to masculine need, twenty spittoons were strategically positioned.

At night, with all the lamps lighted, the East Room dazzled the eye. The sheen of the curtains, the black marble against a yellow wallpaper, the many surfaces of gilt metal, and the explosion of sunbursts around the room combined into a handsome setting for the majestic presence of General Andrew Jackson. The martial boldness of the blues and yellows never appeared tawdry or overpowering. The light never glared. It shimmered in the watery glass of the chandeliers.[17] As certain White House rooms today represent particular Presidents—the Lincoln bedroom, for example—the East Room in the nineteenth century belonged to Andrew Jackson. Unfortunately, it is all gone, destroyed by a wrecking crew in 1950.

The initial bill for the East Room furnishings, now preserved in the White House archives, came to $9,358.27. The L. Veron & Co. of Philadelphia submitted the bill on November 25, 1829, and it included the following items:

Three 18 light cut-glass chandeliers	$1,800.00
Three sets heavy bronzed chain and hooks for same	75.00
One 3 light center lamp supported by figures	65.00
Two astral lamps for round table	65.00
Four pair light mantel lamps with drops	356.00
Four pair vases, flowers and shades, fine paintings	200.00
Eight 5 light bracket lights, bronzed and gilt	300.00
Four bronzed and steel fenders, new style	120.00
Four sets fire brasses with pokers	40.00
Four pair chimney hooks	12.00
Four astral lamps on pier tables	100.00
Four pair vases, flowers, and shades	120.00
Three round tables, black and gold slabs	335.00
Four pier tables with Italian slabs	700.00
Four mantel glasses, rich gilt frames, French plates, 100 by 58 inches	2,000.00
Six blue and yellow window curtains	630.00
One large window curtain	210.00
Five hundred yards fine Brussels carpet and border	1,058.25
Four Imperial rugs	68.00
Twenty-four arm chairs and four sofas, stuffed and covered, mahogany work entirely refinished, and cotton covers	600.40
Ornamental rays over the door	25.00
Eighty-four gilt stars	17.50
White curtains inside the blue and yellow	75.00
Twenty spittoons	12.50
Total	$8,984.65

Not listed were the costs for "bunches" of artificial flowers, candlesticks, tea trays, extra-cut lamp glasses, and wicks.

Jackson also purchased mirrors and other furniture for the Green Room and the state dining room, and a $1,200 oilcloth for the transverse hall on the ground floor. He repapered his own bedroom, the public dining room, the private dining room, the sitting room, the Green Room, and the New Circular Room. He also bought a piano made of rosewood for $300. And to think that John Quincy Adams was excoriated during the presidential election of 1828 for his reputed extravagances in purchasing furniture for the White House!

Because Jackson drew enormous crowds wherever he went—he was surely the nation's first genuine celebrity—great numbers of people came each day to the White House and demanded a personal interview. Obviously this was not always possible. So Major Lewis hung a large portrait of Jackson over the mantel on the west wall of the entrance hall. The General was dressed in military blue with more braid and stars than the

East Room itself—if that was possible. Indeed, it seemed to complement the East Room. One way or another visitors got a glimpse of their Hero when they came to the White House. And they loved the portrait because it symbolized Jackson as defender of American liberty and democracy.[18]

In addition to the East Room furnishings, Jackson also purchased a considerable amount of silver service, china, and cut glass. He also imported French porcelains and fine silks. The French sterling silver plate cost $4,308.82 and consisted of 36 spoons, 36 forks, 36 knives, 4 sweetmeat spoons, 2 sugar spoons, 48 tea and coffee spoons, 8 small spoons, and 2 mustard spoons. The service also included 2 soup tureens, 4 vegetable dishes, 2 sauce boats and plates, 8 large and 12 small round plates and 6 oval plates, 2 baskets, 18 bottle stands, 12 skewers, 1 large and 1 small coffeepot, 1 cream jug, 1 fish knife, 8 double salts and 2 mustard stands, 36 tablespoons, 60 table forks, 8 long gravy spoons, and 2 soup ladles. In addition there were 60 table knives with silver handles, 36 dessert knives with silver handles and blades, another 36 knives with silver handles and steel blades, 3 large carving knives and forks (2 of which were made of silver), 11 silver ladles, and 2 trunks to contain the whole. "Ordinary" kitchen utensils numbered between 10 and 15 dozen.

Jackson also purchased a 440-piece dinner set of French china, "made to order, with the American eagle." It cost $1,500 and included 32 round and 32 oval dishes, 6 dozen soup plates, 20 dozen flat plates, 4 long fish dishes, 12 vegetable dishes with covers, 8 sugar covers and plates, 6 pickle shells, 6 olive boats, and 4 octagonal salad bowls. The President also bought a 412-piece dessert set for $1,000 which was made to order and designed "in blue and gold with eagle." This set contained 6 stands for "bonbons," 12 sweetmeat compotiers on feet, 6 round sugars and covers, 6 large fruit baskets on feet, 4 ice cream vases and covers with inside bowls, 18 dozen plates, 6 Greek form cups and saucers, 4 oval sugar dishes, and 4 cream jugs.

Between the furniture, silver, china, cut glass, silks, and porcelain, Jackson spent approximately $45,000. For someone who constantly preached economy and retrenchment in government, he hardly practiced it when making purchases for the White House.

To some extent the amount of china and silver service bought was necessitated by the size and number of Jackson's "levees," receptions, and dinners. His levees grew enormously during his two terms in office because invitations were not required and practically everyone in the city (and especially visitors) wanted to see him and clasp his hand. These levees were usually held (but not regularly) on Thursdays between the hours of 6 and 8 P.M. and on New Year's Day and the Fourth of July between the hours of 12 noon and 3 P.M. Mobs crowded into the House whenever they were announced. "Some thousands had arrived there, before us," reported one man, "of all ages and sexes and shades and colors and tongues and languages. There met the loud and whiskered representative of kingly legitimacy, with the plumed and painted untamed native of the western forest. The contrast was interesting and amusing." The company at Jackson's levees reminded one man of "Noah's ark—all sorts of animals, clean and unclean." Even the "rag-a-muffins of the city" gained entrance by climbing through the windows of the East Room. The marshal of the city and his deputies tried their best to keep them from entering by the front door, "but 'the boys' were too clever for them and got in by the windows!"

In the midst of the mob, "tall and stately," stood the commanding figure of the venerable President. The guests approached him, took him by the hand, either bowed or curtsied, and spoke a greeting. Then they moved on to give place to others "to participate in the same privileges." Among the "dense mass of gazing and wondering spectators" were diplomats "in their gold coats," officers in uniform, ladies in the latest finery, laborers, "rag-a-muffins," clerks, shopkeepers, and Indians "in war-dress and paint" with "plums" stuck in their hair. "Bonnets, feathers, uniforms and all, it was rather a gay assemblage," said one reporter.[19]

One of the most magnificent of these levees involved the celebrated "Jackson cheese." The idea of presenting President Jackson with a mammoth cheese originated with Colonel Thomas S. Meacham of Sandy Creek, Oswego County, New York, in the fall of 1835. He began on a modest scale—only a 500-pound cheddar—and for five days turned the milk of his 150 cows into curd which was then poured into a great hoop. But the hoop looked skimpy when he finished, so he decided to add to the cheese and when he had finished it, the monster weighed 1,400 pounds. It was four feet in diameter and two feet thick. The cheese was encircled by a "national belt," representing all the states, and on it were inscribed the words, "Our Union, it must be preserved." A team of twenty-four gray horses drew the flag-draped wagon which bore the behemoth and carried it on a triumphant journey to Washington, where it was formally presented to President Jackson. Apparently, the President kept it in the vestibule of the White House where it was cured for nearly two years. Then he directed that an invitation in the form of a public notice in the *Globe* be extended to all citizens to come to the mansion between 1 and 3 P.M. on February 22—Washington's birthday—to sample the magnificent cheddar. It was one of the great levees of all time. The President, cabinet members, Congress, diplomats, "the court, the fashion, the beauty of Washington," and, of course, "the People" (with a capital "P" as the *Globe* always wrote it) all attended. "Mr. Van Buren was there to eat cheese; Mr. Webster was there to eat cheese; Mr. Woodbury, Colonel Benton, Mr. Dickerson"—all of them eating cheese. "All you heard was cheese; all you smelled was cheese." The carpets were slippery with cheese, pockets were filled with balls of the stuff, and the very air for half a mile around was permeated with the aroma of cheese. The mob demolished the mammoth cheddar within two hours and left only a few scraps to grace the presidential table.

Because of his failing health the General was forced to receive this adoring crowd seated in a chair in the oval reception room. Still, he welcomed them "with his usual . . . dignified courtesy." Sarah Jackson, "dressed in full court costume," stood by his side and performed the honors of her station with "a grace and amenity which every one felt, and which threw a bloom over the hour." After a while the President was forced to retire and Martin Van Buren acted as host in his place.[20]

In addition to the levees, Jackson gave weekly dinners for department heads, congressmen, diplomats, and other distinguished guests. At first these dinners were very ordinary; later, they became sumptuous. David Campbell told his wife about one dinner at the White House in 1829 which Van Buren, the secretary of the navy, the postmaster general, Lewis, the Donelsons, Mary Easton, and two young gentlemen attended. "The dinner was as plain a one and as *badly* cooked as you ever sat down to," wrote Campbell. "Shall I describe it? It consisted of one dish with a piece of the side of bacon and greens—two or three ducks and turtle soup and a tongue all boiled to rags. Then ice cream—jelly—orange and almonds. *That's the whole.* The wine was good." Campbell thought that the Tennessee ladies were not up to Washington society and, unfortunately, had left the management of the dinner to a French cook who had no great regard for Jackson.[21] Once the President got rid of the French cook and employed Joseph Boulanger, a Belgian, as chef, and once Emily Donelson, the First Lady, became more comfortable with her new surroundings, the dinner parties improved most noticeably.

John R. Montgomery, a lawyer from Pennsylvania, recounted a formal dinner at the White House in 1834 that attested to some stunning changes. The table "was very splendidly laid and illuminated," he said. A large chandelier of thirty-two candles hung over the middle of it and all the piers and mantels glittered with numerous candles. "The first course was soup in the French style; then beef bouille, next wild turkey boned and dressed with brains; after that fish; then chicken cold and dressed white, interlaided with slices of tongue and garnished with dressed salad; then canvass back ducks and celery; afterwards partridges with sweet breads and last pheasants and old Virginia ham." For dessert, Montgomery reported jelly and small tarts in the Turkish style, blanche mode and kisses with dried fruits, preserves, ice cream and oranges and grapes. With the meal, sherry, port, Madeira, champagne, claret and Old Cherry were served.[22] It was a gargantuan feast.

At a more modest dinner party of a few invited guests, the atmosphere was more relaxed. The son of a prominent Ohio judge recalled one such occasion in December, 1834. He arrived at the White House at 3 P.M., the usual hour for the family evening supper. He was ushered into the Washington Parlor (the present Red Room), where he met two other guests.

The President and Major Donelson then joined the group and after fifteen to thirty minutes of conversation the steward announced dinner and the party crossed the hall into the family dining room. The five gentlemen seated themselves, Jackson gave the blessing, and then the servants descended, "one to every man." The first course was beef—all kinds: roast beef, corned beef, boiled beef, and "beef stake." When the beef was consumed the plates were removed, and new plates set for the fish course. For each dish came a new plate. During the entire meal a variety of appropriate wines were served. After the meal the company returned to the Washington Parlor where they had coffee and where they talked until about seven o'clock, when the guests departed.[23]

Dinner guests invariably commented most favorably about the liquid refreshments served by the President. Indeed, Jackson began a true wine cellar at the White House. Racks for bottles and barrels were constructed along the walls of an area beneath the state dining room. This was the area that later became the map room, where Franklin D. Roosevelt and Winston Churchill frequently met. The location was secured with heavy wooden bars during Old Hickory's tenure to keep out thieves. It stored hard liquor of many varieties, wine and beer.

Obviously, a touch of elegance—if not majesty—graced the presidential mansion during Jackson's residence. Still, he never forgot that the House belonged to the people and that he was their "steward."[24] To him this meant that anyone at virtually any hour could walk into the mansion to see the President and shake his hand. One foreign visitor was stunned to find no guard at the White House. A porter opened the front door when he knocked, a single servant ushered him into a large parlor, and Old Hickory interrupted what he was doing to greet the visitor and chat with him for a few minutes. But, presumably, that was what a democracy was all about: ready access to the powers of government. "I need hardly say," wrote this particular foreigner, "that my reception seemed to me to be exactly what it ought to have been from the chief magistrate of such a republic, easy, unaffected, and unreserved, and at the same time not wanting in dignity."[25]

Caleb Cushing, a young Massachusetts politico, planned to tour Europe, and he decided to visit Washington before leaving the country and pay his respects to General Jackson. When he arrived at the White House the President was having tea, so Cushing was escorted to the Washington Parlor to wait. The room was grandly furnished, he noted in his diary. Over the chimney "was a large pier glass" or mirror, and on the mantel rested a handsome French clock in which a Roman general on one side and the Roman standard on the other supported the timepiece. A full-length portrait of George Washington hung "on the back side of the room" (hence the name), with a piano directly under it. A matching "pier glass" hung from another wall, under which stood a table with a bust marked "Chloris." A round table of a single marble slab occupied the center of the room. Chairs with crimson damask seats and backs and a matching sofa were located at appropriate places.

Suddenly President Jackson strode into the room. He addressed Cushing by name, "took my hand in a friendly manner, & requested me to be seated." Cushing apologized that he had no other purpose for his call than to pay his respects before his departure for Europe, and the President replied that "he was very happy to see me & that had he known I was below he should have asked me to take tea with him." Then the two men chatted "very freely & sociably, until, thinking I had staid long enough, I rose & said I was aware his time was precious, & that I would not intrude any longer upon it & thanked him for the honor of the interview, & took leave." Jackson assured him that the honor was his and accompanied Cushing to the front door and said goodbye.

Cushing was absolutely awestruck. The President's manner was very pleasing, he wrote, "unpretending, easy. Nothing of the courtly air of Van Buren but *plain* & simple—frank bearing." Cushing said he had ample opportunity to observe Jackson's "air & gait. His step was quick & firm," he commented, "& the only indication of age in his form was a habitual stoop, which is said to be independent of his age." He looked thoughtful, Cushing commented, "as though he had much on his mind."[26]

Even visitors of a more critical bent came away impressed by the old man. Alexander H. Stephens of Georgia dropped in to see Jackson during a brief tour of Washington and took great exception to the President's language.

"What is the news from Georgia Mr. Stephens?" was Jackson's opening query.

"Nothing more than some little Indian Disturbances," answered Stephens.

"What in the name of God is General Howard doing?" the President retorted.

Stephens noted in his journal that although their conversation lasted twenty minutes or so, Jackson hardly spoke a sentence without uttering "by God" or "by the Eternal" or "in *the name of God!*" And they were simply discussing Indian affairs and mail delivery in Alabama.

"In the name of God," Jackson continued, "how big a place is Columbus."

Four or five thousand, came the response.

"In the name of God . . . is it possible that in so large a place as that men cant be found to rescue the mail of the U.S. Sir I have a communication from the P.M. at Co stating that the mail stage has been attacked by a party of Indians . . . and that he had offered $200 Dollars reward to any person or persons who would bring it into Columbus. And in the name of God was it possible that it is so large a place as that none had been offered to bring in the mail from a few Indians? etc."

Stephens was rather shocked by this monologue. Was this really the

President of the United States? The figure before him was "dressed plainly with a ruffle shirt—rather dirty—and with loose slippers." Still, Stephens admitted later, he felt the magnetic pull of this irresistible force. "He has great energy," Stephens marveled, despite his age and poor health, "and does not falter in the least. And upon the whole I was very favorably impressed."[27]

Stephens did not realize that Jackson could shed the trappings of common men very quickly and assume the air and grace of majesty to dazzle the most critical. On one occasion, James Buchanan, just back from Russia, arranged to present a "Lady E from England" to the President. He attempted to engineer the meeting according to his experience with royalty. He called on Jackson an hour before the interview to give him a few pointers and found the President in old clothes, feet on his desk, enjoying his corncob pipe. Horrified, Buchanan reminded the General that his visitor was a woman of high rank and accustomed to all the "refinements" of good society.

Jackson favored Buchanan with one of his withering stares. "Jeemes Buchanan," he said, as he drew the pipe from his mouth, "when I went to school I read about a man that I was much interested in. He was a man who minded his own business and he made a large fortune at it."

Buchanan withdrew as quickly as possible. He dreaded what would happen when Lady E arrived. A short time later he escorted the lady to the White House. "What was his surprise when Jackson descended to the coach in person, faultlessly arrayed, escorted the distinguished visitor to the House, and entertained her for an hour with such grace and courtesy that she declared she had never met a more elegant gentleman in all her travels."[28]

The accessibility of the President to virtually all callers frequently caused problems. The front door was routinely unlocked by the steward in the morning and locked again at sundown. As a consequence all sorts of people walked into the White House at almost any hour of the day. On Friday, April 17, 1835, an intruder gained access to the upper floor of the residence and during the night tried to enter Jackson's bedroom. The noise awakened the President (always a light sleeper), who demanded to know who was there and what he wanted. The intruder called out that he had lost his way and was simply trying to get out of the House. The commotion awakened other members of the family, who immediately presumed that another assassination attempt was in progress. They seized the intruder, but since he had no weapons they decided that theft, not murder, was his object. He was a day laborer, reported the *Globe* a few days later, who had "got into the house with a view to plunder but missed . . . his way and his object." Since it was night the "poor fellow ended up locked in the stables for safe keeping until he could be turned over to a magistrate the next morning." When morning came, however, the thief had disappeared. He escaped through a window which was thought to be too high for anyone to reach the ground safely.[29]

The family was deeply disturbed by the incident and fearful that there might be other intrusions. "I trust that in the future," Donelson wrote to his wife, "Uncle will never forget to lock his door when he retires to bed. After the attempts which have been made upon his life he should not neglect such precautions as will never permit another to escape immediate and exemplary punishment."[30]

Intruders were not always after plunder. Frequently they were ordinary citizens who simply wanted to see President Jackson, shake his hand, and tell him how devoted they were to his administration and his principles. Sometimes they wanted a lock of his hair or to demonstrate a talent for him, such as singing or dancing or performing tricks. One man by the name of Nicholas J. Ash ascended from the mall near the White House in a balloon to honor the President. On the day of the "performance" General Jackson was too ill to leave his room and so he watched the balloon ascend from his window on the second floor. As Ash rose into the blue sky he waved two American flags in Jackson's general direction and shouted huzzas to the glory of the Hero of New Orleans.[31]

Admirers frequently asked for a lock of Old Hickory's hair and he sometimes obliged. On one occasion, Mrs. Baily, an old woman who had served the cause of the Revolution, requested a lock and he sent it "as a memento of my recollection of her true patriotism, & love of our democratic system of government—and her aid, given to our cause in our revolutionary struggle for independence and liberty."[32]

Both the high and low approached the great democrat. Even Princess Victoria of England expressed a wish to have his autograph. Jackson graciously provided it and availed "himself of the occasion to offer her Royal Highness his best wishes for her happiness & prosperity."[33]

Frequently Old Hickory was asked to stand as godfather for newborn male infants about to be christened with the name "Andrew Jackson." He always declined the honor of attending the rites but told the parent that "[I] depend upon you to explain to him, with this injunction of his godfather that when he arrives at the years of manhood he will always be found sustaining the eagle of his country from the insults or grasp of a foreign foe, and the still more dangerous enemy, the intestine Traitor."[34]

Invariably, the President was waylaid on his way to church. He attended the First Presbyterian Church of Washington and rented pew no. 6, for which he paid $32.50 per annum.[35] His seat, noted one overseas traveler, was in "nowise distinguished from the others in the church. Nothing struck me more than seeing him mixing in the passage of the church with the rest of the congregation as a private individual, and conversing with such of them as he knew on going out, without the slightest official assumption." The great democrat bowed to one and all, obviously "not an ungenteel man," wrote this commentator, "in manner and appearance."[36]

By the time his administration ended Jackson attended church services regularly, unless he was too ill to leave the White House. Although he remained a passionate and excitable individual throughout his life, he seemed more restrained, more philosophic, as he grew older, and more introspective. He even lauded the worth of intellectual pursuits. "Seek wisdom," he wrote on one occasion, "—her ways are pleasantness and peace—makes smooth the path of life, and leads to a happy immortality."[37]

Naturally, the routine of White House life centered on the President, but more particularly it centered on the condition of his health. If his health permitted he took daily horseback rides. Often he interrupted his daily schedule to take an afternoon walk, on which he was usually accompanied by Ralph Earl. He would set out from the White House, cross President's Square in a northwest direction toward Katorama, and then circle around. Jackson also liked to ride down the Potomac on a steamboat and sometimes went to Mt. Vernon to visit with the family of George Washington.

During his second term in office Old Hickory laid the cornerstone of Jackson City, a new community located on the Virginia side of the Potomac River, just opposite Washington. There was a great parade to mark the occasion, and it was expected that the new development would become a thriving suburb. But the President failed to get a bridge built across the Potomac to make Jackson City more accessible to Washingtonians, and in a short time the place reverted to its original settlers: the frogs.

Over a period of years, as his health declined and the press of business increased, Jackson's excursions outside the White House were sharply reduced. Not infrequently during his eight years in office he spent an entire day in his bedroom or study to attend the demands of his office. He worked hard at being President. He was driven by an oppressive sense of duty. He rose early and went immediately to business. Even when ill he usually managed several hours of work. One of the President's secretaries, Nicholas Trist, remarked that Jackson exhibited an "utter defiance of bodily anguish. He would transact business with calmness and precision, when he was suffering the acutest pain, and when he was so pitiably feeble that signing his name threw him into a perspiration." Jackson performed his duties as chief executive with a degree of devotion and commitment that nearly consumed him. "He could not be kept from work," declared Trist. If too ill to "work with his hands, he wore himself out with thinking."[38]

In addition to the normal paperwork associated with his office, Jackson kept up a vast correspondence with officials, friends, family, politicians, and assorted citizens that required him to pen from ten to twenty letters every day. And sometimes these letters went on from four to eight to twelve pages of handwriting. How he found the time for this exercise, considering the extent of his correspondence, is not easy to explain. Many letters end with the excuse that he simply did not have the time to go back over what he had written to correct mistakes. But the discipline required to write as much as he did was truly remarkable.

Each day the President saw many visitors. That, too, was part of the job. Some, like Blair, came daily to hear the presidential will. "From my daily habit of going to see you," Blair wrote him, "I am never easy till I pay a visit to your office."[39] The Kitchen Cabinet dropped in regularly. The "parlor" cabinet met the President every Tuesday, unless emergencies dictated more frequent meetings. Jackson also read a great deal: official documents for the most part, and correspondence. Like all good politicians, he read the newspapers, but few books. A check of the Library of Congress shows that Jackson did not borrow a single book from the Library either as President or senator. Nor did Donelson, Lewis, or Trist take out any books for him.[40] Van Buren borrowed none, either. Kendall took out Elliott's *Laws of Indiana* and apparently never returned it. Taney borrowed books as chief justice, all of them Supreme Court reports. By contrast it is interesting to note that President Abraham Lincoln borrowed books ranging from poetry to drama to history to the science of war.[41]

However, Jackson did read from his wife's prayer book each day. Trist remembered going to the President's bedroom one night to get final instructions about the disposition of some letters and finding Jackson in his night clothes but not yet in bed. The General was sitting at a little table with his wife's miniature before him, reading from Rachel's prayer book. This miniature was always worn "next to his heart, suspended round his neck by a strong, black cord," except in the evening when he removed it as he read his prayers. "The last thing he did every night, before lying down to rest," said Trist, "was to read in that book with that picture under his eyes."[42]

Before preparing to retire each night, Jackson liked nothing better than to sit by the fire with his family, smoking his pipe, and reminiscing with Donelson or Lewis or Earl about his early exploits in Tennessee. Seated in a comfortable armchair, wearing a long, loose-fitting coat, and puffing away at his pipe, the President "recited incidents of the revolutionary struggle, of the late war, and of the Creek and Seminole campaigns" and even "the origin of his cognomen of 'Old Hickory.' "[43]

Life in the White House during Jackson's administration more often than not revolved around the presence of many young children and babies. Jackson's grandchildren and the Donelson children formed the core to which were added other visiting youngsters from time to time. Parties were regularly given in their honor. An invitation to the little Woodburys, McLanes, Blairs, Macombs, Pleasantons, and others in the neighborhood summoned them to the White House to mark one occasion or another. One such invitation read:

The children of President Jackson's family request you to join them on Christmas Day,
at four o'clock P.M., in a frolic in the East Room.

Washington, December 19

To this particular party a number of adults were also invited, including the Vice President, several foreign ministers, Mrs. James Madison, who brought along her grandniece, Addie Cutts, and Cora Livingston, the daughter of Edward Livingston. During the frolic such games as blind man's buff, puss in the corner, and forfeits were played. Then, as a band struck up with the "President's March," the little guests marched into supper. Afterward, they had a snowball fight. The snowballs, made of cotton, were stacked on a table. A gilt gamecock, with head erect and outstretched wings, sat atop the mound. When the children had exhausted themselves they were lined up to take their leave. One by one they bowed or curtsied to the President. "Good night, General," they piped. The old soldier beamed. Dolley Madison, who stood by his side, exclaimed: "What a beautiful sight it is! It reminds me of the fairy procession in the 'Midsummer Night's Dream!' "[44]

Jackson also enjoyed entertainments. Apart from dinner parties and levees, most of the White House entertainments consisted of musicales. Celebrated artists, like visiting dignitaries, all came to visit the Hero. Dancers, singers, actors, and painters sometimes mixed with heads of departments and diplomats at White House receptions. Jackson himself was not a man of the theater and rarely witnessed a stage performance in Washington. But when Fanny Kemble made her debut, the President went to see her. She was particularly noted for her Juliet, played opposite her father, Charles Kemble, the Romeo. They also appeared together in *School for Scandal.* [45]

Fanny visited the White House for a formal "presentation" and recorded her impressions of its occupant. Like everyone else she was immediately struck by his dignity and bearing, his simple and quiet manner. She described him as a "good specimen of a fine old well-battered soldier." They talked mostly about South Carolina. He playfully suggested that the recent disturbances in the south had their origin in the "scribblings" of a certain lady. Kemble allowed that if this was true then "the lady must have scribbled to some purpose." By the end of their conversation, which lasted only about a quarter of an hour, Kemble confessed her admiration of Jackson's "firmness and decision of character." She knew little of American politics, she said, "but firmness, determination, decision, I respect above all things," particularly in a statesman. And this trait Jackson possessed in generous amounts. Although he had been accused of being obstinate, she thought that obstinacy was far better than weakness in a ruler and that Jackson "sins on the right side of the question."[46]

If Jackson neglected the theater as a vehicle of relaxation and enjoyment, he compensated for it by spending a great deal of time at the racetrack. As a longtime and successful horsebreeder, he took an active interest in the care and training of horses and got out to the National Race Course as often as the affairs of state allowed. And until his illness restricted his movements toward the end of his administration, he used to visit the White House stable every morning to inspect his horses and tend to their grooming.[47] On one occasion he decided to go to the racetrack to watch the timing in trial runs and he took Van Buren with him. On their arrival the horses were brought out and saddled for the gallop. Suddenly, one of the horses reared, requiring two men to hold the animal before he could be mounted. Ever the man in charge, Jackson started firing orders at the grooms. Finally he turned to the trainer and said: "Why don't you break him of those tricks? I could do it in an hour."

When the running began, the timer took his position below the judges stand while Jackson and Van Buren remained on their mounts in the rear of the stand, which was safe, but commanded an excellent view of the entire track. The General was still issuing orders. "Why don't you take your position there," he shouted at the timer as he pointed to the place the timer intended to occupy in due course; "you ought to know where to stand to time a horse." The timer did as he was told without uttering a word. "Nobody ever jawed at Old Hickory when he was in one of his ways," he said later.

Again the difficult horse reared and Jackson started shouting. "Hold him, Jesse!" he cried to the jockey. "Don't let him break down the fence. Now bring 'em up and give 'em a fair start." At the same time all this was happening, Van Buren had left his safe position at the rear of the stand and ridden almost onto the track. Jackson saw him. "Get behind me, Mr. Van Buren," he called, "they will run over you, sir." Like the timer, Van Buren said nothing and did as he was told.[48]

This story about Van Buren quickly got out during the presidential election of 1836 to illustrate how dependent he was on Jackson for his place and for protection from his political enemies. And everyone thought it was an extremely amusing story—even Democrats, and those who should have known better. For Jackson could never resist taking charge of any situation in which he found himself. He simply dominated every activity he entered. And that included conversations. "He was the most fluent, impressive and eloquent conversationalist I ever met," remembered one man, "and in any company took the lead in conversation. Nobody ever seemed disposed to talk where he was."[49] People attended him to hear whatever he had to say and on any subject he had in mind.

Coupled with his "take-charge" disposition was Jackson's protective sense. Paternalistic to a fault, he treated everyone equally: as dependents, requiring his help and protection. Whether it was children, women, friends, neighbors, family, or his country—especially his country—Old Hickory assumed a personal responsibility for their safety and honor, and none complained. Indeed, it was part of his enduring appeal—it still is. Andrew Jackson was one of the few genuine heroes to grace the presidency. He was courageous and strong. And he was indomitable. The American people always believed that as long as General Andrew Jackson lived, the democracy was safe.

CHAPTER 26

Farewell

As HIS ADMINISTRATION WOUND DOWN, Jackson's personal satisfaction over his political triumphs in Congress and around the country brought a glow of intense pleasure to his face, despite his illness. And during the early months of 1837 the American people seemed more determined than ever to demonstrate to him their abiding affection and trust. In a special way he was their President, the very embodiment of their democratic ideals.

At his last levee in the White House, held on February 22, Washington's birthday, the public realized that this might be their last opportunity to see the great man. Even the Whig newspapers commented on the turnout and what it signified. The Washington *National Intelligencer* reported that an "immense throng" attended this last levee, "all anxious to avail themselves of . . . testifying their respect and veneration of the great and good old man." A remarkable statement for a Whig journal. An unusually large number of children also appeared among the company, the paper said, "brought by their parents for the purpose of carrying the recollection through future years of having touched the hand and have been welcomed by the kindly smile of President Jackson."[1]

On the morning of this last levee, a committee of citizens from New York appeared at the White House to present to the Hero the beautifully finished phaeton made from the timbers of the old frigate *Constitution*, or, as it was more popularly called, "Old Ironsides." The carriage was presented by Mr. Daniel Jackson, speaking for the committee, who told the President that the gift was meant to signify the country's "grateful appreciation of the many benefits you have conferred upon our country." The General was deeply touched. He accepted it with the "deepest sense of gratitude," he said in response. It meant a great deal to him because it came from New York, "the great emporium of our rising nation—a city which has so often welcomed, honored and contributed to support me." In bearing the "live oak of 'Old Ironsides' of which it is composed," Jackson continued, the phaeton will constantly remind me "of the glorious battles and the storms which that gallant vessel rode out in triumph while carrying abroad over the great deep the constellation of republican stars which she has never struck to the enemy." The heroic men who shed their blood on her decks in the cause of liberty, he said, will be remembered by all who see this carriage. "As such I will take care that it be preserved."[2]

This ceremony constituted a final act of homage by all the people. In presenting something of priceless value to the President, the New York committee hoped it would bespeak the nation's eternal gratitude. It was one of the most gratifying events of Jackson's entire administration. On both sides, the symbolic nature of the gift was recognized and duly noted.[3]

During these final weeks, other gifts poured into the White House, many of which conveyed a symbolic message. One such gift particularly pleased the old man. A "humble" laborer of Brooklyn sent him a hat that he made with his own hands, and Jackson acknowledged it by saying, "I shall wear [it] with prouder feelings than I would a crown."[4]

As agreeable and gratifying as these final gestures by the American public were to their revered leader, Congress could always upset and annoy him with its antics and "imbecilities." Of particular difficulty—and an issue that had mounted in intensity over the last few years—was the question of slavery. Abolitionists stepped up their campaign to exterminate the "peculiar institution," and since there was nothing the federal government could do about it in the states, the abolitionists agitated for the Congress to ban the slave trade and eliminate slavery in the District of Columbia. Many Jacksonians, like the President himself, saw the issue as a blind to hide Whiggish opposition to the administration and the continued democratization of American institutions. Some, like Blair, considered it a ploy to revive the BUS. None of the Jacksonians believed that concern for black people motivated these agitators. The motive of abolitionists was political. It was personal and it was antidemocratic.[5]

Events moved to a showdown of sorts with the presentation in the House of Representatives of the first abolitionist petition on December 16, 1835. Representative James H. Hammond of South Carolina, one of Calhoun's messmates, jumped to his feet when it was introduced and moved that it not be received. After a long and nasty debate that lasted six weeks and drove members to come to the chamber armed with knives, the House moved to table the petition. Finally, it passed a resolution in May, 1836, introduced by a committee chaired by Henry L. Pinckney of South Carolina, which declared that any interference with slavery in the District of Columbia was inexpedient, and in the states unconstitutional.

It also directed that all petitions, memorials, resolutions, and the like, relating in any way to slavery or its abolition, "be laid upon the table," without "either being printed or referred . . . and that no further action whatever shall be had thereon."[6] The adoption of the Pinckney resolution, with its so-called gag rule, inaugurated a running battle over the next several years between the abolitionists and their opponents. John Quincy Adams, the representative from Braintree, Massachusetts, led the attack on the gag rule, and he sometimes engaged in a shouting match with the Speaker over what he called the flagrant violation of the constitutional rights of his constituents. Democrats in the House hooted derision at him for his outrageously partisan and self-serving tactics. He cared nothing for the issue involved, they charged, and only raised a fuss because it would disturb the Democracy and even the score with Jackson.[7] The shouting and screaming that went on during these exchanges embarrassed most of the congressmen in the chamber. It was truly disgraceful.

By and large, the Democrats regarded all discussion in Congress of the slave question—whether emanating from abolitionists and their partisan friends in the north, or the extremists of the south—as essentially antiadministration and ultimately antidemocratic. And they were not far from the mark. The heat generated during the debates was unquestionably aimed, as one of its objectives, at damaging Jackson's relations with the people. And, by linking the President and his party to the slave question, the extremists on both sides of the question hoped to discredit democratic rule and everyone associated with it.

When the second session (the short session) of the 24th Congress convened in December, 1836, the slavery issue tagged right along. Incredibly, Speaker Polk ruled that the Pinckney resolutions of the previous session had expired, and that unleashed another verbal storm. Before the gag rule could be reinstated the entire House drained itself in an acrimonious debate that only served as a vehicle to assault Jackson and his administration.[8]

The old man was livid. He denounced the pious talk about liberty and the evils of slavery as nothing more than a "conspiracy" to disrupt the people's business, prevent legislation, impede the growth of democracy, and pummel him for championing populist causes. The tumult in the House particularly provoked him. It gave democracy a bad name. And everybody knew it. "Congress is getting on badly," he stormed, "no leader in the House of Representatives & the minority does with the majority as they did last year." Polk should have provided leadership, he grumbled. Instead, he repeatedly tumbled into the traps laid for him by the Whigs and frequently engaged in useless arguments with John Quincy Adams over parliamentary questions of order.[9]

Much of Jackson's chagrin over the disarray in Congress was revealed in editorials in the *Globe*. Again and again the newspaper argued that the disorder represented Whiggish contempt for popular rule.[10] Even though they had lost the presidential election in the fall they would not accept the verdict of the people as final. "Rule or ruin" is their motto, Blair insisted. And so here was the extraordinary sight of southern nullifiers and northern abolitionists cooperating with one another to destroy the democratic system.[11] "The universal courtesy and kindness extended to the abolitionists in Congress, especially J. Q. Adams, [Francis] Granger and [William] Slade by all the *would be thought* Hotspurs of the South, while their fury and frenzy is directed against the Democrats, the friends of Mr. Van Buren who are fighting the battles of the South, against the fanatics of the North, are all signs to prove the identity of political design between the nullifiers and abolitionists in every branch of federalism."[12] Then, when John Q. Adams began his contentious arguing with the Speaker, "snarling and quarreling," shouting and bickering, in a most irresponsible and "un-Adams-like" manner, his motives aroused dark suspicions among those who watched and listened to him. "He means," simply and solely, "to produce irritation," argued the *Globe*, "throw the House into disorder, and if he failed in everything else to waste the day in taking appeals from the decision of the Speaker on the rules of the House." This was the "mischievous course" of his dastardly behavior. This man who had been repudiated by the American people in 1824 and 1828, who had once told Congress not to be "palsied by the will of their constituents," was now speaking in the name of his constituents to take his revenge for his defeat in 1828 by making a mockery of democratic procedure.[13]

The slavery question was not the only issue the Whigs "dragged" into Congress to assault the administration. They demanded an investigation of Jackson's alleged misuse of the patronage. Henry A. Wise of Virginia introduced a resolution to refer the matter to a special committee which he would chair. At the same time another committee was formed to examine "the curious and strange" relationship of Reuben M. Whitney to the Treasury Department and the deposit banks. Fortunately for the President, both committees contained Democratic majorities and their subsequent reports exonerated the administration of any improper behavior.[14]

Jackson was disgusted by all this "circus" behavior. "They let Wise play them off like the shewman does his puppets," he wrote to Donelson, "by long resolutions calling upon the Heads of Departments and myself to answer criminating questions of violating the law instead of calling on them to support the charge, all of which if true, would be grounds of impeachment." He said he wanted to call upon Wise, Peyton, Bell, Underwood, and Pickens, his accusers in the House, and Calhoun, White, and Ewing of Ohio in the Senate, "to declare on oath what knowledge of fraud they have found in the Departments, upon which they have based their resolution." He simply could not believe that such things happened in this country, that spite and vindictiveness could hold forth without penalty or punishment. "Is it not strange," he added, "that a committee of congress would permit such a spanish inquisition as this, in a country of laws—the call is to answer questions to criminate ourselves, and if not answered, then the cry would be, their refusal is an evidence of guilt."[15]

The demand that Jackson "criminate" himself by supplying information about the alleged abuses and corruptions charged against his administration was sent to him by Wise on January 24. Jackson boiled. He responded within two days and told Wise rather emphatically what he thought of his "despicable" tactics. Wise did not ask him to answer to any specific charge, he scolded. Nor to explain any alleged abuse, nor request information as to a particular transaction. Rather Wise was assuming that the administration was guilty of the alleged charges and was now calling upon that administration "to furnish evidence against themselves!" This was simply monstrous. "You resort to generalities even more vague than your original accusations, and in open violation of the constitution and of that well established and wise maxim, 'that all men are presumed to be innocent until proven guilty, according to the established rules of Law.' " Wise expected the President and the department heads "to furnish the evidence to convict ourselves." Well, sir, the department heads might respond as they pleased, provided they did not take time from their public duties, but Jackson would order them to attend to their responsibilities "in preference to any illegal and unconstitutional calls for information, no matter from what source it may come." For myself, he continued, "I shall repel all such attempts as an invasion of the principles of justice, as well as of the constitution; and I shall esteem it my sacred duty to the people of the united states, to resist them as I would the establishment of a spanish inquisition."[16]

Jackson concluded his response by reminding Wise that he and his associates had an obligation to come forward and "testify before God and our Country" if they had any knowledge of specific acts of wrongdoing. Their evidence might then be evaluated according to the canons of law and a verdict rendered. But if they made no charge and offered no proof for their accusations, "you and your associates must be regarded by the good people of the United States as the authors of unfounded calumnies."[17]

On the final day of the session the committee gave its report and, having a majority of Democrats, completely exonerated Jackson. All the investigation accomplished, as Jackson had predicted, was to "leave the junto [of Wise, Bell, Peyton, White, and company] covered with disgrace."[18]

The Congress generated other problems for Jackson in these final months of his term. First off, a number of Whig senators were anxious to force the cancellation of the Specie Circular. They held that it drained specie from eastern cities to satisfy demand in the west, where most of the land was being sold. Such an imbalance was certain to provoke financial disaster, they argued. Senator Ewing of Ohio led the attack on the Circular and even questioned its legality. He offered a resolution in the Senate on December 14, 1836, rescinding the Specie Circular.

Thomas Hart Benton rose to the defense. He saw this latest Whig maneuver as just another scheme by Nicholas Biddle to influence legislation. As for the predictions about the fiscal safety of the country, Benton argued that there could be no safety for federal revenues "but in the total exclusion of local paper" from every branch of the government engaged in the collection of the revenue: post office, land office, and custom house. Only gold and silver provided protection. After forty years of wandering in the "wilderness of paper money," he said as he waxed biblical, the country had at last reached the haven of sound, constitutional currency. There was $75 million of specie in the country with the prospect of increasing that amount by $10 or $12 million over the next four years. With three branch mints about to begin operations in the spring, he continued, the total restoration of the gold standard now seemed assured. All of which, Benton concluded, attested to the "success of President Jackson's great measures for the reform of the currency."[19]

Jackson himself was deeply concerned over the state of the nation's finances and the rampant speculation in land that continued even after his Circular went into effect. At one point he considered the possibility of setting up a bank in the District of Columbia based on "real banking principles" of deposit and exchange and nothing more. But this consideration never got beyond the talking stage.[20]

The Whig motion to repeal the Specie Circular as a means of righting the financial imbalance in the country and halting the dangerous exercise of executive despotism began winning support from some members of the Democratic party,[21] especially southern Democrats who harbored many peeves against Jackson, most recently the accession of Van Buren to the presidency. William C. Rives, long a friend of both Jackson and Van Buren but deeply humiliated by his failure to win the vice presidential nomination, chose to break with the administration over the Circular issue. He formally notified his Democratic friends of his desertion from the ranks by proposing an amendment to Ewing's resolution that would rescind Jackson's Circular by requiring all debts owed by the government to be paid in specie or the *notes* of specie-paying banks. The denominations of these notes might not drop below a prescribed minimum, but over the next four years they would rise from five to twenty dollars.

Jackson reacted violently when he heard about Rives's amendment. He even considered leaving his sickroom to attend to this "rebellion." First of all, he regarded Ewing's resolution as a censure of the President for performing his "sworn duty" to protect the revenue and the security of the deposit banks. And Rives's amendment, he said, constituted an implied censure and presumed a power for Congress to recognize the paper issues of state banks as part of the currency of the United States and receivable as public dues. These horrors Jackson could never abide. "These are two things I cannot admit or approve," he declared. As for Rives, what could Jackson say. "Mr. Rives course is a strange one." It had occasioned a split among "our friends" in the Senate. "I fear it springs out of jelousy." He professed to espouse hard money and strict construction but his amendment did not comport with those professions. "I would yield much to my friends and particularly now as I am going out of office and I may say out of life, but I have the great republican principles to sustain." The Constitution must be preserved. It must be protected and defended. "I have to maintain a consistancy of character in all my acts to make my administration beneficial to republicanism." Wearily, he fretted over the failure of Democratic leadership and the division that seemed to be breaking out within the Senate among the members of his party. But he remained optimistic. After all, he still had the ultimate weapon in his veto power. "I therefore hope my friends will reject Mr Ewings resolution and do by law what is expected by the amendment, which you will see I cannot approve if sent to me, with justice to myself or the people of the United States." Basically, the matter was a simple one, he contended. There was no currency but gold and silver in any transaction by the government. "This is the currency of the U.S. established by the constitution."[22]

It came as a rude shock to Jackson that the Ewing/Rives proposal passed the Senate on February 10 by the lopsided vote of 41 to 5. It had been neatly steered around Silas Wright's Committee on Finance and placed in the hands of the Public Lands Committee. The Ewing proposal had been a resolution, but the committee reported out a bill which rescinded the Specie Circular, without naming it, by allowing the receipt of bank bills in payment of all dues owed the government. Wright and Benton opposed the bill to the bitter end, but they had few supporters.[23] The final vote was nearly unanimous—and deeply disheartening to the old chief. Clay and Webster, along with Buchanan, Rives, and Tallmadge, voted for it. But Calhoun abstained. He was unprepared to explain his reasons but since he believed the state of the currency "incredibly bad," he expected "an explosion" to occur at any moment. As far as he was concerned, it hardly mattered what the Senate did.[24]

The House, still faltering from ineffectual leadership, also passed the bill by a vote of 143 to 59. The Democratic leadership even failed to win approval for an amendment that would have restored to the Treasury secretary a measure of control over what money could be received for the payment of public dues. House passage of the bill came two days before the end of the session and went to the President for his approval.[25]

Jackson vetoed it. The bill came to him on Thursday, March 2, at 2 P.M. It was only one day short of the constitutional dissolution of the Congress and two days shy of the conclusion of Jackson's administration. There was so much about the bill that Jackson found "confusing" that he referred it to his attorney general for an opinion. Butler got back with his reply the following day at 5 P.M. In essence the attorney general agreed that the bill was ambiguous on many points and in the future would "be a subject of much perplexity and doubt." This simply confirmed the President's own opinion and added to his determination to kill the bill. Since the session was only hours away from termination, Jackson could have pocket vetoed the bill without assigning any reason for his action. Instead, he pocket vetoed it but wrote a brief message dated "March 3, 1837 —11:45 P.M.," in which he declared that because he had no time to expatiate on the problems of the bill he was enclosing the attorney general's opinion in order that his reasons for withholding approval might be better understood. The message was never sent to Congress but deposited in the State Department.[26]

So Jackson's last official act was a slap at Congress. He struck down their handiwork even though a majority of both houses belonged to the Democratic party. "The firmness of the President," recorded one admiring senator, "again saved the country from an immense calamity."[27] Perhaps.

Jackson also administered a personal rebuke to an individual senator. John C. Calhoun had given a speech in the Senate on February 4 in which he blamed the administration for the unchecked speculation in land rampant throughout the west and producing financial havoc. As reported in the *Congressional Globe,* a weekly put out by Blair and begun with the second session of the Twenty-third Congress in December, 1834, Calhoun's speech sounded like an outright accusation of malfeasance. "Was it not notorious," Calhoun cried, "that the President of the United States himself had been connected with the purchase of public lands?" A day or so later Blair worsened the report by declaring that Calhoun had also accused several members of the cabinet and the President's nephew of borrowing money to speculate in land for a quick profit.[28]

Jackson erupted into a furious fit of temper. Leave it to that "villain" to lie and twist the truth to serve his demagogic purposes. The President seized his pen and hurriedly poured out a succession of demands, challenging Calhoun to offer evidence in support of his accusations so that the President might be tried for high crimes, or else to retract them. The letter vehemently denied Calhoun's charges. "The imputations you have cast upon me," Jackson wrote, "are false in every particular." The accusations were nothing more than the offspring "of a morbid imagination or of sleepless malice." Two affidavits supporting the President's contention accompanied the letter.[29]

Calhoun rose in the Senate on February 9 to respond, and he not only repeated his charges but added new ones. In particular, he accused Jackson of a breach of senatorial privilege. What right did the President have to tell him what he might or might not say in Congress? None whatsoever, the irate senator answered himself. "I, as legislator, have a right to investigate and pronounced upon his conduct," he declared. "I, as a Senator, may judge him; he can never judge me." Acting for all the world like a "Roman tribune" challenging the imperial Caesar, Calhoun savaged Jackson as a would-be emperor and warned of a dire future for the liberties of the Congress and the American people.[30] But the Democratic majority in the Senate sat stony-faced and said nothing. After all, they knew who was the real tribune of the people. And his name was certainly not John C. Calhoun.

The end of the congressional session at midnight on March 3, 1837, brought the Twenty-fourth Congress to an inglorious end. Brawling among themselves and bickering on occasion with the chief executive, they left the Capitol strewn with unfinished business and uncomplete legislation.[31]

Andrew Jackson's tenure also ended, but his record provided far greater satisfaction. Indeed his eight years in office were soon described as marking an important era in the history of the American people, an era punctuated by reform and progress, an era in which the course of democracy noticeably advanced. "In coming time," declared the Chicago *Democrat,* "when history shall have recorded his glory it will be mentioned with pride, by those whose youthfulness have prevented them from yet figuring on the stage of action, that 'I was born in the Age of Jackson.' "[32]

More than anything else, most commentators agreed, Andrew Jackson had created a new presidential style. To be sure, not everyone liked or admired his style, but they admitted its unique character. To his friends, the Jacksonian presidential style reflected and embodied the popular will, and this identification with the Democracy meant that the President could assume a more appropriate position in a modern society, namely head of state and leader of the nation. Furthermore, to support the President in achieving his program and to help him implement his vision of the future, a party organization grounded in Jeffersonian republicanism had been established on a mass basis and committed to the doctrine that the people shall rule.

None of the previous Presidents acted upon, much less articulated, the notion that the President was elected by the people of the entire nation. Andrew Jackson established that contention. None previously claimed that the President was "more representative of the national will than the Congress." Old Hickory did. None argued superiority of a particular branch of the federal government. None tried to substitute his opinion for that of Congress, except where constitutionality was involved. Jackson did it regularly—or at least whenever he believed the public good required it. He is, therefore, the first modern President in American history, the first to conceive himself as the head of a democracy.

There were many specifics to Jackson's accomplishments as President. He saved the Union and put down nullification. That above all was his crowning achievement. Almost as important was his unique success in paying off the national debt. Such an achievement endeared him to conservatives forever, a feat that required "reform retrenchment and economy," just as he promised to provide at the start of his administration. As for "reform," Jackson did indeed root out a considerable amount of corruption within a reorganized bureaucracy. More than that, he provided the American people, according to a recent study on the subject, with one of the most honest and least corrupt administrations in the early history of this nation.[33]

The moral tone and level of honesty in any administration is set by the President himself. If he is lax or indifferent—or corrupt himself, as has happened in a few instances—scandal inevitably occurs. But if, like Jackson, the chief executive sincerely cares about the degree of honesty to be maintained by his administration, then the chances are extremely good that his term in office will be relatively free of corruption.

Among his other accomplishments, Jackson also acquired an enormous territory from the Indians extending farther than the combined states of Massachusetts, New Hampshire, Vermont, Connecticut, Rhode Island, New Jersey, and Delaware. Americans today may flinch at that achievement, in view of the human suffering it involved among Indians, but Americans of the Jackson era recorded it with pride. More important, removal probably did ensure the survival of several southern tribes.

Jackson also hurled a corrupt national bank into oblivion and, despite the reservations of some historians, the destruction of that money power helped advance the progress of American democracy. Under Old Hickory a ten-year truce over the tariff was reached and the internal improvements craze, which in Jackson's mind threatened constitutional safeguards, was halted. The sovereign status and national rights of the United States in foreign affairs improved during Jackson's tenure, as witness the many most-favored-nation treaties he concluded and the many nations who finally acknowledged and paid the legitimate debts they owed to this country. Jackson's successful efforts at expanding American markets abroad through these negotiated treaties was a significant factor in the economic boom of the 1830s. The formulation of a vigorous and flexible diplomacy, therefore, combined with favorable international conditions, provided one triumph after another in foreign affairs.

But there were failures, too. Jackson's appointments were generally wretched, although many of them, it should be noted, were the recommendations of Van Buren. However extraordinary his success at reform, he nonetheless appointed Samuel Swartwout who stole more money than all the crooks in his predecessor's administration put together. In the area of appointments Jackson made one mistake after another, but enough has already been said on this subject to make the point. Surprisingly, Jackson did not always exercise effective leadership of the Congress and the nation—for example, his failure to win passage of the Verplanck tariff bill, his failure to prevent the election of John Bell as Speaker, and his fumbling efforts in the mail delivery and Texas questions. Distractions, for the most part, explain these failures—distractions because of bad health, or his total concentration on other problems like the Bank or the Force Bill, or his concern for the safety of the Union. Moreover, Jackson's inability to provide a better banking system to replace the BUS, his simplistic ideas about specie, and his arbitrary intrusion into land speculation did not serve his country well. And, most of all, his ruthless determination to expel the Indians from their land blinded him to the infinite pain he inflicted upon a helpless people. He always believed his policy of removal was undertaken to save the Indians from inevitable extinction, as it did, but he failed to provide the adequate means for a safe and humane removal. Toward the end of his administration he was more devoted to their relocation beyond the Mississippi River than to their welfare or their survival.

On balance, though, Andrew Jackson served the American people very well. He preserved the Union, strengthened the presidency, and advanced democracy. The people prospered, and they enjoyed peace and the respect of the entire world.

Jackson himself was not only conscious of his record as President and concerned about the ultimate judgment of history, but he wanted to explain to the American people, as his last official act as their representative, what he had been about during his eight years in office, and the principles that motivated his actions. Like President George Washington, he proposed to issue a Farewell Address and had enlisted Chief Justice Taney in its composition. He wanted to emphasize "our *glorious Union*" and warn the nation that "ambitious and factious spirits," like the nullifiers and abolitionists, were ever ready to dissolve it and produce anarchy for their own selfish ends. Most particularly, he worried about sectionalism. "Sectional jealousies, the sectional parties, and sectional preferences" gave the malcontents a decided advantage by which they could "disturb and shake our happy confederacy," he said.[34]

From the copy of the address in the Jackson papers, written in Taney's hand and virtually identical to the published version, it is clear that the chief justice was the principal, if not the sole, writer of the President's Farewell Address. Issued on March 4, it began by thanking the American public for the "many proofs of kindness and confidence" which they had tendered him throughout his career. It was with "the deepest emotions of gratitude," he said, that he acknowledged the unbroken confidence with which the electorate had sustained him in every trial. We have now lived under the Constitution for fifty years, he went on, during trying periods of war and peace, and "we have passed triumphantly through all these difficulties." It was no longer a question of whether the country could survive under its present form of government. It had demonstrated the success of the experiment, that in a union of states there was the brightest hope of freedom and happiness for the people. "At every hazard and by every sacrifice this Union must be preserved."[35]

Still, there were dangers. There had been systematic efforts to sow the seed of discord between the several sections, especially north and south, and place party divisions upon geographical distinctions in order to foment controversy over "the most delicate" issues upon which many people could not speak "without strong emotion." Jackson was obviously speaking of slavery. In just a short time it had become the means by which disappointed and ambitious men hoped to pull the Union apart. The dissolution of the Union, he sighed, was now spoken of as possible or even likely. And such a tragedy could only occur if "artful and designing men" were allowed to inflame "the natural jealousies of different sections of the country. . . . The history of the world is full of such examples, and especially the history of republics."[36]

Be not mistaken, he warned. Once the fabric of Union was torn it might never be repaired. "If the Union is once severed, the line of separation will grow wider and wider, and the controversies which are now debated and settled in the halls of legislation will then be tried in fields of battle and determined by the sword." Worse, once the fabric was torn, it would be rent again and again. The result would be catastrophic. "This great and glorious Republic would soon be broken into the multitude of petty States, without commerce, without credit, jealous of one another, armed for mutual aggression, loaded with taxes to pay armies and leaders, seeking aid against each other from foreign powers, insulted and trampled upon by the nations of Europe, until . . . they would be ready to submit to the absolute dominion of any military adventurer and to surrender their liberty for the sake of repose."[37]

To preserve the Union unimpaired it was absolutely necessary that the laws be faithfully executed in every part of the country. "Every good citizen" must stand ready to put down all attempts at unlawful resistance to the law. And when oppressive laws are legislated, "then free discussion and calm appeals to reason and to the justice of the people" would not fail to right the wrong. All other remedies would provoke disruption and turmoil. Any government that cannot enforce its own laws within its own "sphere of action" would cease to be a government.

But government needs more than coercive powers. Its foundation must rest on the "affections of the people" and in the security it gives to life, liberty, and property. There must be "fraternal attachment" among the citizens of all the states in wanting to promote the happiness of each other. Hence, citizens of each state must avoid wounding "the sensibility or offend the just pride" of citizens of every other state and "frown" on those who disturb the tranquillity of their political brethren in other sections of the country. In a nation as large as this one there were bound to be differences of opinion on all kinds of subjects and issues. "But each State has the unquestionable right to regulate its own internal concerns according to its own pleasure." All efforts "to cast odium" upon the institutions of any state and all measures calculated to disturb the rights of property or the peace of any community "are in direct opposition to the spirit in which the Union was formed, and must endanger its safety." Weak men, Jackson contended, will persuade themselves that their efforts at disruption are undertaken "in the cause of humanity and . . . the rights of the human race." But be not deceived. "Everyone, upon sober reflection, will see that nothing but mischief can come from these improper assaults upon the feelings and rights of others."[38]

Clearly, Jackson worried not only about the extremists of the south, who would nullify federal law to prevent the execution of distasteful legislation, but also the abolitionists of the north, who, in the name of humanity, would assault slavery, the "delicate" institution of the south, and thereby hazard the future of the Union.

Free government can survive, Jackson went on, only when justice is faithfully observed. And that depends on the virtue of the people and "a lofty spirit of patriotism." Under our free institutions, all may prosper and gain happiness without infringing the rights of others. "Justice—full and ample justice—to every portion of the United States should be the ruling principle of every freeman, and should guide the deliberations of every public body, whether it be State or national."[39]

Of course, it is well known that there are those among us, said the President, who desperately wish to enlarge the powers of the general government, who seek to assume authorities not granted by the Constitution. If these efforts were not resisted every time they appeared and put down, then there would be "but one consolidated government." Only by confining the action of the central government strictly to its delegated powers and by maintaining the full vigor of the rights and sovereignty of the states could the nation's liberty and safety be ensured. The most "susceptible" abuse is the taxing power. Congress has no right to take money from the people, Jackson lectured, except to execute a specific power; and if they raise more than is necessary it is an abuse and therefore "unjust and oppressive." "Many powerful interests are continually at work" to raise taxes beyond the need of public service. Tariff interests, such as wealthy manufacturers, had succeeded in adding to the burden of the agricultural and laboring classes of the country. Corporations and monopolies advocated special considerations to increase their profits and they found support among "designing politicians" who curried their favor to increase their own influence. "There is but one safe rule, and that is to confine the General Government rigidly within the sphere of its appropriate duties."[40]

As long as Jackson and Taney kept to higher principles about the Union and the limits of federal power, the address spoke nobly and interestingly. But, unfortunately, once the taxing power had been broached, the discussion wandered off into paper currency, banks, monopolies, exclusive privileges and the like, about which the President had nothing particularly worthwhile to say for this special occasion. Still, these were the things he worried about and which he thought constituted a real danger to the welfare and happiness of the American people. He warned that the people must watch the government constantly or risk the loss of their liberty. "Be watchful in your States as well as in the Federal Government," he advised. "The power which the moneyed interest can exercise" can be applied on the local as well as the national level. The moneyed power may seem more confined on the state level, nevertheless over time it will gather its strength and move "with undivided force to accomplish any object it may wish to attain." No one is safe from this menace whose vigilence slackens.

> The planter, the farmer, the mechanic, and the laborer all know that their success depends upon their own industry and economy, and that they must not expect to become suddenly rich by the fruits of their toil. Yet these classes of society form the great body of the people of the United States; they are the bone and sinew of the country—men who love liberty and desire nothing but equal rights and equal laws, and who, moreover, hold the great mass of our national wealth. . . . But with overwhelming numbers and wealth on their side they are in constant danger of losing their fair influence in the Government. . . . The mischief springs from the power which the moneyed interest derives from a paper currency which they are able to control, from the multitude of corporations with exclusive privileges . . . which are employed altogether for their benefit; and unless you become more watchful in your States and check this spirit of monopoly and thirst for exclusive privileges you will in the end find that . . . the control over your dearest interests has passed in the hands of these corporations.[41]

The sovereignty of the country rests with you, Jackson reminded the American people. "To you everyone placed in authority is ultimately responsible. It is always in your power to see that the wishes of the people are carried into faithful execution, and their will, when once made known, must sooner or later be obeyed." As long as the people remain "uncorrupted and incorruptible," as long as they remain watchful and jealous of their rights, the nation is safe, the government secure, "and the cause of freedom will continue to triumph over all its enemies."[42]

Here, then, was Jackson's legacy, as best he could articulate it; here his understanding of the meaning of the Democracy that bore his name: The people are sovereign; their will is absolute; liberty survives only when defended by the uncorrupted.

Jackson next turned to the principles he deemed most appropriate for the conduct of foreign affairs. Friendly relations must be maintained with all nations, he agreed, and the calamity of war must be avoided by every honorable means. Frankness, sincerity, justice, and impartiality in our behavior toward all countries were the instruments to achieve these ends. But collisions with other powers were bound to occur from time to time and we should be well prepared to assert our rights if the use of force should ever become necessary. Preparedness—that was the key. Then, remarkably, he did not demand the strengthening of the army. The navy was our true line of defense, he said, and should be our first service. Our long coastline, with its many indented bays and deep rivers leading into the interior, as well as our extended and ever increasing commerce, "point to the Navy as our natural means of defense." It would be relatively inexpensive, he added, to increase the size of the navy and more useful in peacetime. Its strength could be improved each year without overburdening the people. "It is your true policy." And the strengthening of the navy should begin in this season of peace and an overflowing Treasury. When this was done and our navy sufficiently powerful we need not fear that we would be rudely insulted or needlessly provoked into a hostile action. "We shall more certainly preserve peace when it is well understood that we are prepared for war."[43]

Then he closed. The progress of the United States, Jackson said, had surpassed the most sanguine hopes of the Founding Fathers. We were prosperous, numerous, gaining in knowledge and all the useful arts, and had no longer any cause to fear danger from abroad. Our strength and power were well-known throughout the civilized world.

> You have the highest of human trusts committed to your care. Providence has showered on this favored land blessings without number, and has chosen you as the guardians of freedom, to preserve it for the benefit of the human race. May He who holds in His hands the destinies of nations make you worthy of the favors He has bestowed and enable you, with pure hearts and pure hands and sleepless vigilance, to guard and defend to the end of time the great charge He has committed to your keeping.
>
> My own race is nearly run. . . . I thank God that my life has been spent in a land of liberty and that He has given me a heart to love my country with the affection of a son. And filled with gratitude for your constant and unwavering kindness, I bid you a last and affectionate farewell.[44]

It was a moving and fitting close, not only to this address but to an exciting, frequently turbulent, but always fascinating administration.

As he signed his name to the final page of the manuscript and put it aside, Old Hickory nodded his satisfaction. He genuinely liked what Taney had written. It said everything he wanted, and parts of it had real power and sweep. He hoped it might find a place alongside Washington's Farewell Address as an inspiration for the American people.

Not everyone appreciated Jackson's address, of course. The Whigs snorted at his presumption and yawned over his tiresome arguments about banking and money. Some were especially critical. "Happily it is the last humbug which the mischievous popularity of this illiterate, violent, vain, and iron-willed soldier can impose upon a confiding and credulous people," commented the New York *American* when the address was published.[45]

After Jackson signed his message, his son, Andrew, entered the room to collect the sheets and send them off to be printed. Taney and Secretary Forsyth stood nearby during the final moments of this ceremony. A few minutes later, Senator William Allen, the newly elected senator from Ohio, was announced. Sometimes called "Earthquake" Allen on account of his powerful voice, he had come to pay his respects, and Jackson greeted him warmly. Then the President turned to the others and said: "Gentlemen, I think the occasion will warrant me in breaking over one of my own rules. Let us drink a little Madeira." The wine was brought. Jackson took a small glass, which was one of the few he had touched for several months on account of his illness. He then set down his glass, lighted his cob pipe, took several puffs, and turned to watch the face of a tall, old-fashioned clock that stood in one corner. It was five minutes to midnight. Slowly, the minute hand moved toward twelve o'clock. The silence in the room was almost painful. Suddenly, the sharp, clear bell of the clock struck the hour. At that moment, Jackson turned to his friends and said: "Gentlemen, I am no longer President of the United States, but as good a citizen as any of you." Quickly, he added: "I am very glad to get away from all this excitement and bother."[46]

After his company left him, the old man took down Rachel's Bible and read for a while. When his head began to ache he put the book aside and climbed into bed. The White House was dark and quiet. For all intents and purposes the presidency of Andrew Jackson was over.

CHAPTER 27

"Well Done Thou Faithful Servant"

As OLD HICKORY HAD HOPED, March 4, 1837, proved to be a bright and sparkling day. Indeed a "lovely day of brightest sunshine," reported the *Globe,* one to "gladden every heart." Bathed in this sunshine, Jackson would stand proudly before an adoring crowd on the portico of the Capitol "to witness the glorious scene of Mr Van Buren, once rejected by the Senate, sworn into office, by chief Justice Taney, also being rejected by the factious Senate."[1] What a perfect conclusion to his administration.

Both Van Buren and Taney were overnight guests in the White House prior to the inauguration, and their presence gave the old man much pleasure and comfort.[2] Having them as guests seemed to extend and expand the satisfaction he felt over the triumph all three of them shared.

At noon, March 4, the newly acquired phaeton stood gleaming in the sun at the entrance of the White House, waiting to receive its illustrious passengers. The phaeton had one seat but accommodated two persons. There was a "high box" for the driver in front bordered with a deep "hammercloth." The unpainted wood was highly polished and on each side was a representation of Old Ironsides under full sail.[3] Within moments the Old Hero descended from his bedroom, greeted the guests waiting for him in the foyer, saluted Van Buren in an appropriate manner, and headed for the phaeton. The President and President-elect took their places in the carriage, which was drawn by Jackson's four iron-grey horses decked out in fancy brass-mounted harnesses. A splendid escort of cavalry and infantry preceded the coach as it pulled away from the White House and headed down Pennsylvania Avenue toward the Capitol. An excellent band also accompanied the entourage and filled the air with martial music.

An immense crowd jammed the square on the east front of the Capitol but parted to permit the phaeton to enter the area and circle through the archway under the portico where it came to a halt in front of the portico steps. The two men alighted, Jackson first, followed by the President-elect. The tall, emaciated-looking Hero drew himself to his full height as he stepped from the carriage. He towered over the balding, corpulent Little Magician who stood beside him. Then they began to mount the stairs of the east portico, and suddenly "cheers of unanimous greeting rose from the surrounding people" and were repeated again and again in loud bursts.[4] These cheers were obviously directed at the departing President, for they "were repeated with an effecting emphasis when the whitened head of the toil-worn General was seen for the first time since his sickness, and probably for the last time, rising above the rest as he ascended the portico of the Capitol." The adoring crowd watched that cadaverous form as it reached the top of the stairs and disappeared inside the building, cheering as though to recall him to their presence. Poor little Van Buren was out of sight and virtually out of mind.

The two men moved quickly to the Senate chamber, which was crowded with cabinet officers, the Supreme Court justices, the military, and the diplomatic corps. Richard Mentor Johnson, the new Vice President, took the oath of office, whereupon Jackson, Van Buren, Taney, and the other dignitaries walked back to the east portico where a wooden rostrum had been erected over the steps. As they reemerged from the building, the crowd broke into applause.

The tall, erect, and commanding-looking General dominated the scene. He stood perfectly still for several moments as he stared out over that vast sea of men, women, and children. Then he bowed before them. The great democrat bowed low to the people, as he usually did in such circumstances. The crowd shivered with delight as he slowly pulled himself back to his full height and then turned and took his seat. "A murmur of feeling" swept over the people as they watched him.[5] At this point Van Buren advanced and read his inaugural address, a production that took at least an hour to get through. Toward the end of this marathon, Van Buren paid particular note of his "illustrious predecessor." "I know that I can not expect to perform the arduous task with equal ability and success," he said. "For him I but express with my own the wishes of all, that he may yet long live to enjoy the brilliant evening of his well-spent life."[6]

Following the address, the oath of office was administered by Chief Justice Taney, and many in the crowd, particularly the politicians, did not miss what the *Globe* called the "sublime spectacle" of a President who had been denounced by the Senate as a despot watching the inauguration of a man who had been recalled by the same Senate from a foreign mission as unworthy, and who was taking his oath from a chief justice who, in turn, had been rejected by the Senate as unfit for the office of secretary of the Treasury. Only in America! Only "in this great and happy Republic." The *Globe* noticed with pleasure that Clay and Webster (not Calhoun, however) had the class and style to attend the ceremonies and from their looks "seem to have caught the contagion of the fine day and glowing patriotism that surround them."[7]

Cheers erupted from the crowd as Van Buren kissed the Bible after taking the oath and Jackson strode toward him and shook his hand. Then the band played "Hail to the Chief." The crowd hushed almost at once when they saw Old Hickory begin to descend the steps and head for his phaeton waiting below. "This vast crowd remained riveted to their places, and profoundly silent," recorded Thomas Hart Benton. "It was the stillness and silence of reverence and affection; and there was no room for mistake as to whom this mute and impressive homage was rendered. For once, the rising was eclipsed by the setting sun."[8]

About halfway down the stairs the Old Hero halted, possibly to steady himself or to take one last look at his countrymen. As he did so, the crowd exploded in a volley of "acclamations and cheers bursting from the heart and filling the air." They could no longer restrain themselves. It was, said Benton, "the affection, gratitude, and admiration of the living age, saluting for the last time a great man."[9]

Jackson bowed once again. Uncovered, and with a look of "unaffected humility and thankfulness," he gestured in mute signs his deep appreciation for this demonstration of love and veneration. Benton choked up. "I was looking down from a side window," he wrote, "and felt an emotion which had never passed through me before." I have seen many inaugurations, he went on, but they all struck me as pageants, "empty and soulless." This one was different. This was real. "A man and the people": he laying down power; they acknowledging for "unborn generations" a collective vote of thanks for lifting the nation to a new level of freedom and democracy.[10]

The ex-President hurried down the remaining steps. As the cries of the multitude sounded in his ears, combined with the booming salute from the cannons at the nearby navy yard, Jackson rode back to the White House in his phaeton with the new President beside him. All along the route the people waved and shouted at the two men, and each responded in his own personal style. Jackson tried not to be too conspicuous since this day really belonged to Van Buren, but the people seemed determined to make this a farewell ceremony as well as an inauguration.

By the time the phaeton pulled up at the mansion the Old Hero was totally exhausted. He had to be helped to his room to rest. But it was a grand climax to a full and exciting two terms in office, crowned with the cheers and plaudits of a happy and prosperous people. It would have been unthinkable for Andrew Jackson to exit on a quiet note. However he departed, the moment needed to be wrapped in excitement. And it was. For the rest of his life the Old Hero remembered with tears in his eyes the affection poured out to him by the people on the occasion of his permanent retirement from public life.

But he still had one last duty. Before he could slip away and rest he needed to put in an appearance at the reception to be given in the East Room, where crowds of people and the diplomatic corps would attend to pay their respects to the old and new Presidents. So, after a brief period of rest, he descended to the East Room to honor his obligation. The reception, as it turned out, attracted a large throng. Fortunately, no near riot ensued, as had occurred in 1829. The diplomatic corps, headed by its dean, Señor Don Angel Calderon de la Barca, the Spanish minister, tended their congratulations to Jackson in a formal ceremony at the beginning of the reception. Speaking in French, the minister praised the former President for his successful efforts in preserving the harmony between the American Republic and the governments represented by the assembled diplomats. The prepared statement was gracious and cordial, and Jackson responded in similar vein. "I thank God," he said, "that my country, during my administration of its affairs, has maintained its peaceful relations with yours, and I feel assured that they will long endure, under the general conviction that reciprocal justice is the duty of nations in their intercourse with each other." Even in leaving office he did not waste the opportunity of reminding Europe that only so long as she treated the United States with the respect and justice it deserved could there be lasting peace.[11]

These formalities ended, Jackson then greeted the "thousands" who had jammed their way into the White House. But before long he began to tire and he was forced to retreat to his room to rest. Later on, he dined with Van Buren but retired early to guard his strength for the long journey home to Tennessee.[12]

For months the family had been gathering up their belongings and packing them off to Nashville, and Jackson personally had seen to the transportation of his papers and correspondence. He was anxious to get away, anxious to remove himself from the theater of political action so that his successor could function without his disturbing presence. Besides, he needed to get home and attend to his personal affairs, for he felt he bordered on financial ruin. He exaggerated, of course, but his affairs did indeed need immediate attention. "I carried $5000 when I went to Washington," he wrote. "I returned with barely $90 in our pocketts." It took a little doing to finance the trip home. "The burning of my house and furniture has left me poor," he said.[13]

The American public soon learned of Jackson's financial distress. It came out when several newspapers reported that he had made a "killing" at the White House and returned to Tennessee with close to a quarter of a million dollars in his wallet. The *Globe* labeled the report a contemptible lie and said that Jackson had left Washington with barely enough money to make it home.[14]

Not until Tuesday, March 7, was the former President ready to leave the White House. By that time he had quite recovered from the ordeal of the inauguration. Since putting aside the "cares of state," he looked rested, buoyant, and happy. "The General exhibited an alacrity and gayety of spirit," reported Frank Blair, that had not been seen since his recent illness. "He told one merry story after another, rallied his friends, and, on proposing a match to a bachelor of his Cabinet, whose eyes were filled with tears, told him that it was his habit to take care of his friends."[15] A select corps of friends, along with his old cabinet, gathered at the White House on Tuesday morning to say goodbye. For the journey home, Jackson would be accompanied by his immediate family; Ralph Earl, the painter; and Dr. Thomas Lawson, an army physician whom Van Buren asked to accompany the ex-President. After handshakes all around the General departed the White House for the last time. Van Buren escorted him to his carriage and accompanied him to the railroad depot. It was decided that the Hero should ride the railroad "for the sake of ease and comfort . . . until he reaches his private carriage which awaits him where the railroad connects with the macadamized National road." Before they separated Van Buren was overheard to promise to visit Jackson at the Hermitage. The old man nodded and smiled. Then he shook hands with the President and boarded the train.[16]

In slow and easy stages the Hero paraded across the countryside. The railroad took him to the western terminus of the Baltimore and Ohio at Ellicott's Mills, Maryland, where he transferred to his carriage, which was to convey him to Wheeling. In the old family coach, Jackson and Sarah occupied the back seat, while Andrew and Dr. Lawson took the front. The "little pet" and her brother Andrew III, together with their nurses, Gracie and Louisa, and Ralph Earl trailed immediately behind in a chartered stagecoach.[17] The journey was tedious but improved considerably when Speaker James K. Polk and his wife caught up with them after getting a late start from Washington.

The roads proved extremely bad and by the time they reached Flintstone, Maryland, on March 11, Jackson was complaining about them, even though some of them were relatively new. "We arrived here this morning," he told Blair, "over bad roads, altho a turn pike, nothing appurtaining to it but the toll gates, all the metal having disappeared, and the road cut up by the heavy wagons—still we are moving on with as much expedition as the kind greetings of my friends and fellow citizens will permit."[18]

Those "kind greetings" frequently took the form of mass rallies. Mobs congregated wherever he appeared and nearly everyone wanted to touch him or speak to him. "From the time I left you," he told Van Buren, "I have been literally in a crowd. Such assemblages of my fellow citizens I have never before seen on my passage to, or from, Washington." And that was saying a great deal, considering the many demonstrations he experienced over the past eight years, each of them sometimes numbering from five to seven thousand people.[19] In one town where the party stopped, a laurel wreath was brought and placed on the embarrassed (but delighted) Hero's head. Children were handed to him to fondle and kiss. Frequently, a parent would call out, "His name is Andrew Jackson," whereupon the General would give the child a silver half dollar and say to the parent: "This is our country's eagle. It will do for the little one to cut his teeth on now, but teach him to love and defend it." Before he got home, Jackson supposedly distributed one hundred and fifty of these half dollars.[20]

The number and size of these "greetings" grew as he journeyed west. There were receptions, dinners, parades, public gatherings of one kind or another, and, after a while, they began to tire the ancient warrior. "I assure you," he informed Blair, "altho nothing gives me more pleasure, or can add more to my gratitude, than the approbation of my fellow citizens, retireing from office as I am, still my strength, and feeble health will not permit me to receive their congratulations as I ought."[21] But he did his best. Somehow he always found the strength to meet one more crowd and shake one more hand. At Wheeling, several thousand people congregated at the dock to wish him "happiness thro life & a happy immortality" as he boarded the steamboat to descend the Ohio River. Jackson was staggered by the number of people in attendance. Indeed, he said, it was "one of the most numerous assemblages of my fellow citizens I have ever witnessed on any occasion—more numerous it is thought by Col Polk & the ladies than that at Washington on the 4th of March."[22]

At Cincinnati, where the Hero arrived on Saturday, March 18, at 5 P.M., another huge mob assembled. They came to see "the greatest man of the age, ANDREW JACKSON. They are the democracy," reported the Cincinnati *Republican* on March 20, "assembling for the last time, perhaps, to look upon, and take by the hand, the brave defender and protector of his country." As soon as they spotted the Hero the crowd started screaming. Salute guns boomed, the military presented arms, and the Cincinnati Band played "patriotic and national airs." How wonderful that this "greatest man of the age," chorused the Democratic press, should be so honored with these massive demonstrations. There had never been "greater spontaneous honors conferred before on a man seeking the repose of retirement." And their message was always the same: " 'Well done thou good and faithful servant' has been echoed and re-echoed, from the Potomac to the Mississippi," said the Louisville *Advertiser* on March 21.[23]

At Louisville, which Jackson reached on March 20 aboard the *Fayette*, the Hero debarked to dine with thirty distinguished officials and the members of his party at a local hotel. Outside the hotel the mob refused to disperse and waited until he finished his meal in order to escort him back to the steamboat. When the ship finally moved down the river the city band played "Home, Sweet Home," amid a chorus of huzzas.[24]

The steamboat descended the Ohio to the mouth of the Cumberland River. Jackson and his party then transferred to another boat and ascended the Cumberland to Nashville, which they reached at noon on Friday, March 24. "A vast assemblage of neighbors and fellow citizens gave [the ex-President] a splendid and cordial public reception." They refused to be outdone by the receptions accorded the Hero in other places and states. Dr. James Overton delivered an address of welcome to which Jackson responded with a prepared statement. "I embrace you, sir," he said, "and those in whose behalf you have addressed me, with the fervor of an old friend, who is anxious to renew his former relations, and to manifest in the walks of private life, how dearly he values the privilege of being numbered with you, one of the sovereign people of free and happy America."[25]

If Jackson was prepared for the welcome in Nashville—and he obviously was—he was totally oblivious to what was waiting for him ten miles away near his home at the Hermitage. There, in the cedars near Lebanon, a crowd patiently watched for him, with old men and boys drawn up to provide a special welcome. When Jackson's carriage finally appeared they started cheering. The Hero climbed out of his coach. Judge Campbell stepped forward and read another welcome. Jackson replied with a few oft-repeated phrases of appreciation. The old men offered a salute which visibly moved the General. Then Andrew Ewing spoke a welcome which ended with something to the effect that "the children of his old soldiers and friends welcomed him home, and were ready to serve under his banner." Suddenly Jackson began to tremble. His entire body shook and tears streamed down his creased cheeks. The reference to the children was more than he could bear.

"I could have stood all but this," he stammered, "it is too much, too much!"

The crowd surrounded him and for the next several minutes there was a general outburst of tears and laughter and happy reunion.[26]

When the ex-President had regained his composure he returned to his carriage and rode the short distance to the Hermitage. Home at last. He sighed and coughed and felt strangely exhilarated. "I reached home on the 25th instant," he wrote to Van Buren on March 30, "somewhat improved in strength, but with a very bad cough, increased by cold taken on board the Steam Boat." Even though it was nearly a week later when he wrote to Van Buren, the General could still hear the echoes of the salutes that hailed him along every mile of his journey home. "The approbation I have recd. from the people on my return on the close of my official life, has been very gratifying to me. I have been every where cheered by my numerous democratic republican friends, and many of the repenting Whigs with a hearty welcome, 'and well done thou faithful servant.' This is truly the patriots reward, and a source of great gratification to me, and will be my solace to the grave."[27]

In this letter Jackson thanked Van Buren for sending Dr. Lawson to accompany him home. The good doctor stayed only two days at the Hermitage and then returned to Washington. At this point the old man seemed compelled to review his administration for his successor, as though to remind him of certain truths. What emerged was a reaffirmation of republicanism, as Jackson understood it, and his abiding commitment to the needs of *"the people, the working classes."* I was challenged during my entire administration, he said, "by the combined talents, wealth, and power of the whole aristocracy of the union, aided . . . by the money monopoly, U.S. Bank, with its power of corruption." That he had triumphed over this villainy, "shews the virtue and power of the sovereign people." You, too, will triumph, Jackson assured the new President. "Fearlessly pursue your principles" and the people will sustain you against all apostates, demogogues, and ambitious and designing men.[28]

One thing deeply concerned him: the safety of the deposit banks in the west and south. The planters were deeply in debt and paying bankers and brokers exorbitant interest rates for cash. A number of banks had already failed, with losses totaling tens of millions of dollars. Banks around the country were suspending specie payments. Runs on the banks in New York City alone had reached over $2 million.

The suspension of specie payments clearly signaled the start of a severe economic recession, one long predicted in some quarters, that eventually deepened into a depression. If the Panic of 1837, as the dreadful debacle of the late 1830s came to be called, had a point of origin it undoubtedly came on March 17, 1837 (almost two weeks after the start of Van Buren's administration), when one of the largest dealers in domestic exchanges, I. and L. Joseph of New York, went bankrupt. The immediate cause of this failure was the collapse of the New Orleans cotton market, and since the company had extensive dealings with banks, mercantile establishments, and commercial enterprises, the bankruptcy set off a chain reaction that dragged down hundreds of businesses. Foreign bankers and merchants liquidated their American holdings in an effort to escape involvement, but the economic collapse proved to be a worldwide phenomenon and everyone suffered sooner or later. As the price of specie rose sharply it created a run on banks, and these establishments were therefore forced to suspend specie payments to avoid instantaneous collapse. For the next several months one bankruptcy followed another. The "happy and prosperous" country that Jackson had turned over to Van Buren seemed suddenly on the verge of total disaster.[29]

Jackson watched these events unfold during the early weeks of the

Panic and fretted over the safety of the deposit banks. He feared the "money monopoly" would drive them under. The speculators want more paper, Jackson warned, for the more their "raggs" depreciate the easier they can pay their debts. They wanted the Specie Circular suspended. But, said Jackson, the people were happy with it. Everywhere he traveled on his journey home, he found the Circular popular, except among speculators and gamblers. So, before doing anything about suspending the Circular, he instructed the President, "await the memorials from *the people, the working classes.*" It was the working classes who would sustain the administration, not the money men. Rely on them, check the paper mania and its corrupting influence, *"and the republic is safe, and your administration must end in triumph."* [30]

Always the reference to *"the working classes."* Again and again he mentioned them in his letters at this time, particularly his letters to Van Buren and the other leaders of the Democratic party. If we take principle as our guide and the public good our end, he said in one such letter, "the people, the real working classes, *the great bone and sinew of this nation"* will support us. Just as they had supported him during his administration, they would support Van Buren in this time of crisis. [31]

And his concern for labor was not prompted simply by politics—to win their electoral fealty. Jackson himself was anxious that labor prosper financially. Repeatedly he admonished his friends that unless "labor prospers, commerce and manufacturers must languish and the country be distressed. This is a government of the people, for their happiness and prosperity, and not for that of a few, at the expense of the many." [32]

Jackson's regard for the working classes reached the point where he invariably credited them for whatever triumphs the democracy realized. They constituted the very essence of the democracy, he said. It was their virtue and patriotism that protected the nation against the corruption of the wicked money power. "I am delighted with the honorable rally of the democracy, the labouring classes, in the City of New-York," he wrote on one occasion. "They have done their *duty well,*—have given evidence of their virtue & patriotism, and that they will never surrender their liberty to the mony King or *bow the Knee to Ball* [Baal]. It has been a noble stand against the corrupt money power, and let the result be as it may, it affords ample proof that the peoples eyes are opening to the corruption of the times—the danger of their liberties from the mony power, and their determination to resist it. . . . Fear not, the people may be deluded for a moment, but cannot be corrupted." [33]

According to Jackson, the panic conditions that developed during the spring of 1837 (especially the suspension of specie payments) were directly attributable to the greed of wealthy capitalists, who had fattened themselves so rapidly during the last several years that they were now called "millionaires," a new term in the American lexicon. "This is the new name given to merchants who deal in millions instead of hundreds and thousands," commented the *Globe*. "We glanced yesterday at the mischief which their immense credits and monopoly of business had brought on the government and the community by the suspension of specie payments."[34] The suspension of specie payments, therefore, worked to the economic advantage of these millionaires, argued Jackson and his friends, and this explained how and why it was brought about. Paper satisfied their gluttony, so they banished specie.

The Whigs, obviously, argued quite the reverse. They blamed everything on Jackson. Specifically, they faulted the Specie Circular as the cause of the Panic. "Every man who has become embarrassed by his own extravagant & improvident speculations," Van Buren declared, "relieves himself from self reproaches by laying his misfortunes at the door of the Treasury order."[35] And the danger was not simply the fear that pressure would be exerted on Van Buren to suspend the Circular, but that a renewed effort would be mounted to recharter the BUS. The alarm was real and was relayed to the Hermitage. Jackson was told by Blair that "distress" committees had already invaded the White House to plead with the President for recharter. Blair sighed for the days when Old Hickory still stalked the corridors of the mansion to say to these miscreants, "go to work," or "go to Nick Biddle for relief" as he had done in 1834.[36]

Jackson worried over this information. He worried the more when he learned that Nicholas Biddle had gone to see Van Buren and had been received with civility. And he especially worried over the rumors that English bankers would soon join Biddle in a great "conspiracy" to control the finances of both the United States and Britain. "The present is an important crisis in our national affairs," Jackson cried. "The attempt by Biddle and the Barings, to take into their keeping the management of the currency, both in England and America, is too alarming to every true republican." He deluged the administration with pleas to stand fast. Stick to principles, he thundered, retain the Specie Circular in full force, and the people, "the real working classes," will support you. But if the administration listened "to Biddle and his satelites," and yielded to the pressure he and his "corrupt mercenary merchants" had created in order to bring about "the destruction of the labour of the country," then it would fall.[37]

Van Buren did stand fast. "We mean never to strike the Specie flag," the secretary of the Treasury told Jackson, and they would make no further deposits of federal money in banks that had suspended specie payments.[38] The old man almost wept when he read this letter. On the back of it he penned the words: "The Executive firm, never will strike the specie flag. This is right, it is due to the laboring classes."[39]

Van Buren personally reassured the General. He was under enormous pressure and much harassed but he knew his duty. "My situation has been one of peculiar delicacy and difficulty," he wrote, "but all will, I hope, go well in the end. You cannot form an adequate idea of the dreadful state of the money market in New York."[40] It soon became obvious that Van Buren would have to call the Congress into special session to meet this crisis. If nothing else, the Deposit Act would have to be radically altered.

The Deposit Act of 1836 prohibited the government from depositing its funds in any bank that suspended specie payment, so when the banks suspended in the spring of 1837 the secretary of the Treasury, Levi Woodbury, was required by law to stop all payments of government money to these banks. This meant, in effect, that the Treasury became its own depository. Clearly, this situation could not continue. The Deposit Act would have to be repealed or substantially revised. Certainly the distribution provision of the act needed to be repealed.[41]

Van Buren finally decided to call a special session of Congress for the first Monday in September to address the crisis. Only three times previously had the Congress been summoned to special session, and all three had involved wartime emergencies.

When he learned of these plans and problems, Jackson tried to cheer the President. He offered practical political advice. And this to the Master Magician! You have a splendid issue, he prompted, in the reported course of Biddle and the Barings. Coupled with the efforts of the Whigs to drain the country of specie for the benefit of the Bank of England, it "is a theme that will arouse the people from Main to Louisiana and hurle the whigs from the confidence of the people."[42] Another thing. Prepare yourself. "Have your plans all matured." Write your message for the special session as far ahead of time as possible, show it to select congressmen as they arrive in Washington so they "may take the lead, and carry out your views in one solid phalanxs." This is what Jackson himself had done regularly and it spared him much grief.[43] The General was certain that if Van Buren showed courage and determination, enforced the Specie Circular, and protected the deposit banks, then the Panic would pass. "It is like the colera," he said, "it sweeps off the dissapated and of irregular habits, and when the epidemic has destroyed all those it will leave a healthy state in the mercantile community and restore to our country good morals." In short order, the "shin plasters," those small notes the banks were presently issuing in the emergency, would be swept away. Jackson really detested the shin plasters. "The outrageous course pursued by the broken Banks" in printing these notes "has aroused and are arousing the people, *the labouring people,* against the whole paper credit system."[44]

To meet the financial emergency and ensure a metallic currency which would free the government from all connection with paper-issuing banks, Jackson offered the President a program of recovery involving three steps: First, he advised a reduction of the tariff to the real needs of the government, with duties paid in gold and silver coin. Second, he would assign the collection and disbursement of all government funds to agents of the Treasury. Finally, he said, "let all disbursements be in gold and silver coin. This will circulate it . . . to the laborers . . . all over the Union, and in the space of one year it will be in the hands of the laborer of our country . . . and the paper credit system cannot then be wielded to the great injury of labour and to bankrupt the Union, as it now is, and rob the government of its revenue."[45]

Jackson's suggestion of divorcing the government from the banks was the course ultimately adopted by the Van Buren administration in proposing the Independent Treasury System. The idea did not originate with Jackson. Several congressmen in the past had recommended it, and Roger Taney discussed it in his report during the panic session of 1834. In the present crisis Jackson thought that divorce was the only answer to the nation's fiscal plight. In any event, he said, some plan should be formulated before Congress reconvened in special session and the administration's friends were informed of it so "that they may be prepared to act in concert, and carry them through." Make certain, he added, that "men of the first talents and energy" chaired the committees of Finance and the Post Office. Then the administration would have a "great and glorious triumph . . . which will put down the arristocracy and their paper credit forever."[46]

As the economic situation throughout the country steadily worsened, Jackson increasingly interpreted the problem as a simple conflict between the wealthy few and the laboring many. Greed versus virtue. Shin plasters versus specie. Once the administration makes clear that a paper system is forever dead, he said, the economy will be righted "and the democracy of numbers will never have another contest with the aristocracy of the few." It was as simple as that. The object of government, he went on, is to prevent the "merchants and Banks and shavers and Brokers" from manipulating the currency for their private gain. "It is the great working class that deserves the protection from the frauds of the Banks" and only the federal government can provide it. I have always argued this point, he wrote. "My feeble voice" has long been raised "in favour of a metalic currency to cover the labour of our country; and as long as pulsation beats, it will continue to support this system."[47]

The deepening depression in the nation frightened everyone—including Jackson. And his own personal situation had been made worse by the poor management of his farm during his absence. When he arrived at the Hermitage he was literally without cash. He found the corn cribs and hay lofts empty, his blooded stock in wretched order, and his cattle in very poor condition. Furthermore, his house needed additional repairs, particularly the roof. Still he did "not owe any man one cent," and that was no small blessing. Nor was he responsible for any debts except for some slaves which his son and Donelson had bought. To be free of debt meant more to Jackson than anything else, something he had tried without success to drum into the head of his witless son. "altho I have but little money," he proudly declared, there were no obligations outstanding.[48]

To get through the next several months, Jackson was forced to sell three of his "fine young well blooded stud colts." Most of his horses were in bad shape, except these colts. He realized, of course, that it might be difficult to find a buyer in these distressed times, but he hoped for the best. "I will give a bargain," he promised.[49]

The problem of restoring his farm to proper management and financial stability took all of Jackson's skill and patience, and still he was constantly hampered by his uncertain health and poor weather. He tried to experiment with wheat from Egypt, but the unusually dry and cold spring ruined it. "We will again try it by sewing in the fall," he said. His nephew, Major Donelson, who lived across the road, also struggled, and because the Major had a brood of motherless children to feed, his situation appealed strongly to the generous and emotional Jackson. "D'r Andrew," he wrote, "I heard you say that your means to buy corn was exausted. Inclosed I send you half of my present means."[50]

On top of everything else Jackson had to contend with poor health: his feebleness, a persistent cough and cold, the recurring pain in his side, and his excruciating headaches. Worse, he suffered a painful fall that curtailed his activities shortly after arriving home. And his vision got worse. Although it gave him no pain, his right eye troubled him "by a white something approaching the sight." He treated it, as he did all his eye ailments, with a weak solution of sugar of lead.[51] Frequently, he suffered from insomnia and his earaches often matched his headaches in their intensity.[52] Sometimes there was nothing for him to do but remain in bed until he felt better or simply got tired of lying around in his room. On his good days he enjoyed nothing so much as inspecting every operation of his plantation. He said he amused himself by "riding over my farm and visitting my good neighbours."[53] After breakfast he would ride his old white horse, Sam Patch, to inspect his stock and then visit his friends. Invariably he would take his "little pet," Rachel. When she was very young she rode before him; later she rode in back. This striking couple would stop and talk to the slaves, "always kindly and gently," remembered Rachel, and the slaves would give "three loud cheers for 'old master.' "[54] Jackson only went out for short distances on a good day, he said. Quite often, he went to see Donelson and his children because his nephew was "so depressed in spirits" on account of Emily's death. He felt he had an obligation to try to encourage the unfortunate man.[55] In his weakened condition family deaths and illness hit Jackson very hard. When any of the Donelsons died, especially a young one, he could barely compose himself. "It was such a sudden shock," he wrote about John Donelson's death in September, 1837, ". . . for a moment our philosophy fled, and we were unmanned. . . ."[56]

Jackson was constantly interrupted by the arrival of visitors. Everyone in the vicinity seemed compelled to journey to the Hermitage and pay their respects. And he cordially greeted one and all. "General Jackson's manner is so easy and familiar," recounted one gentleman, "that every-body is perfectly at home in his company." The Hermitage, this gentle-man admitted, "is almost constantly thronged with company." No one was turned away. "Everything is calculated to make the stay of those who call, agreeable and pleasant." They were even invited to stay for dinner which "was a plain and substantial repast." And at these dinners the General always proposed the same toast: "Our absent friends," he would say.[57]

At the end of the day, just before sunset, Jackson walked alone to the tomb of his wife in the garden. Although she had been dead nearly ten years she was still a vital part of his life. When he returned from the garden he would read or attend to his voluminous correspondence. Then, just before retiring, he would conduct family prayers, first reading a chapter from the Bible, next distributing a hymn which all joined in singing, and finally kneeling in prayer. When prayers were concluded, Sarah and the children would leave the room and Jackson's son and his manservant, George, who always slept in his room, assisted him into bed. The children then returned with their mother to bid him goodnight. Finally, Rachel would stand tiptoe on the top of a three-step ladder and lean over and kiss him. Jackson would then place his hand most tenderly on Rachel's head as he kissed her. "Bless my baby," he would say. "Bless my little Rachel. Goodnight."[58]

CHAPTER 28

To Join the Church

BESIDES HIS WIFE, RACHEL, ANDREW JACKSON had one other grand passion: horses. Virtually all his life the General had bought, bred, sold, raced, and loved horses. Few pleasures meant as much to him. His first great horse, Truxton, was purchased from Major John Verell of Virginia and was judged by Jackson to be among the best distance runners in the country. The four-mile heats were Truxton's true contest, but he had beaten such five-mile racers as Jack-of-Clubs and Greyhound. Most notably he beat the celebrated Plowboy, owned by Joseph Ervin, on April 3, 1806. But another contest between the two horses, which culminated in a duel between Jackson and Charles Dickinson, was better remembered. Truxton's total winnings netted Jackson at least $20,000, and the stud fees added even more. The stud fee Jackson normally charged was "300 pounds of good merchantable seed cotton or $18 in cash." This champion produced a great line of horses which the General proudly advertised. Young Truxton, an even larger horse than his sire, was advertised in the Nashville *Whig* in 1822 as standing 16 hands 1 inch high.[1]

Jackson owned two other notable horses during his early career: Doublehead and Pacolet. The latter, standing 15½ hands high, dapple grey and foaled in 1806, cost Jackson $3,000, but the animal amply repaid him by winning a great number of races and siring many horses and mares famed for their running and their offspring. Several other horses, including Indian Queen, Stump-the-Dealer, and Decatur, were among Jackson's prized runners; and, according to the General, his grey stud colt, Bolivar, was "one of the purest blooded horses in America . . . better than any that can be got in Virginia now."[2]

The racing of his horses became almost as important to Jackson as raising and training them. Sometimes it became an obsession. His horses must win. They must perform to perfection. When several of his prize colts were defeated by Captain Jessie Haynie's Maria, Jackson went to extraordinary lengths to find a horse that could beat her. He matched Pacolet against Maria but lost. He then bought Tam O'Shanter, a distinguished horse from South Carolina, to best the Haynie racer, and later went to Georgia and Kentucky to find likely contenders. All in vain. It amused the local breeders that General Jackson, who had conquered the Indians, defeated the British, annihilated the Bank, and outpolled Adams and Clay, could not beat Haynie's Maria. When Haynie at last offered to match his horse against any in the world, from one- to four-mile heats, for $5,000, Old Hickory finally admitted defeat. "Make the race for $50,000," he reportedly said to Haynie, "and consider me in with you. She can beat any animal in God's whole creation."[3]

In his younger days Jackson spent much of his time at the racetrack and was instrumental, along with a number of other men, in founding the first Jockey Club in Nashville.[4] He knew a great deal about the sport of horseracing and was wary of every trick to effect the outcome of a race. He admonished one famous jockey against anything underhanded. He did it playfully. "Now, Simon," he said, "when my horse comes up and is about to pass you, don't spit your tobacco juice in his eyes, and in the eyes of his rider, as you sometimes do."

The jockey was not intimidated by the famous man. "Well, *Gineral,*" he replied, "I've rode a good deal agin your horses, but [with an oath] none were ever near enough to catch my spit."[5]

After his return to the Hermitage, following his two terms as President, the General pretty much abandoned his racetrack interests. "I give over any attention to colts and the turf," he told the Reverend Hardy M. Cryer. He said he intended to keep up his blood stock on his farm but that would be the extent of it.[6] No more racing, no more plans to acquire champions to grace his stable. He simply had no time for "colts and the turf." He was far too busy running his plantation, for every aspect of its management engaged his interest and concern.

Fortunately, the depression did not hit the agricultural areas of the country as hard as it did the commercial. Cotton, for example, still commanded a world market, and Jackson managed to grow enough of it during his first year home to get him through a very difficult time. At first it was touch and go. The spring was dry and cold and the cotton seed lay in the ground for eight weeks without germinating. Jackson agonized over it. He had six acres of meadow sown shortly after his return and he watched it almost every day. "Not one blade up," he groaned, "and I am fearful all the seed is lost. It looks like a famine and no cotton this year." Then, in June, the rains came—and they never seemed to stop. The grass grew so fast it nearly choked out his cotton. But his slaves worked fast under Jackson's supervision so that he expected "as in times of old, full corn cribs and barns." By midsummer he boasted 150 acres of "fine oats" and 275 acres of corn "that now promises well. Thus when you visit," he told Blair, "we will be able to give you plenty of good milk, butter and good mutton."[7]

Despite the depression and the uncertainty of weather, Jackson always expressed confidence that "providence" would see him through any difficulty or emergency. Even when the corn was cut down by an unexpected frost and the seeds lay rotting in the ground, he did not despair. "These are bad prospects," he admitted, "but I trust that providence will provide for us, *'for he does all things well.'* " The following spring he started over again, planting early to get a good crop and make a better sale.[8]

In straightening out his affairs and getting his plantation back on a paying basis, Jackson was forced to sell his lots in Florence, Alabama, at whatever price they would bring. Still, he anticipated a brighter future. Through "industry and economy" and aided by "a kind providence" he expected to scratch out a modest "support." But it took concentrated effort and careful management. Considering all the calls on his time from politicians and friends, it is quite amazing how efficiently he attended to all his responsibilities. Sometimes these political summonses resulted from some action or decision of his taken during his presidency—Indian removal, for example. That problem commanded hours of his time. The new secretary of war, Joel R. Poinsett, consulted him about it repeatedly, and Jackson was particularly concerned that everything be done to guarantee the ultimate survival of the Cherokees. He also fretted over the continuing war against the Seminoles in the swamps of Florida. He pledged to gather "a corps that will put a speedy end to this expensive and shamefully prolongued war." And he succeeded in helping to raise a battalion of five companies of Tennessee volunteers numbering about 500 men. He told Poinsett that 3,000 regulars and two companies of spies should be enough to crush the Seminoles. "Find where their women are," he again counseled, capture them, and the war would end in a month. "Why it is that their deposit for their women have not been found I cannot conjecture." This war, he muttered angrily, has been "disgraceful . . . to the american character and its army."[9]

A year later when Jackson spotted what he thought was a scheme by John Ross, Principal Chief of the Cherokees, to postpone removal for another two years, he ranted at the President. He predicted that such postponement would ruin the administration and give comfort to the southern Whigs. Any delay in removal invites disaster, he asserted.[10] But he was immediately reassured. Van Buren had no intention of delaying removal two years. Rather he expected to complete it within that time. Unfortunately, Poinsett had been ill and his public statement on the subject included an ambiguous phrase that could be misinterpreted. "It was an unfortunate expression," Jackson was told.[11]

Still the old man fretted over Ross's delaying tactics and urged that

General Scott start moving the Cherokees by September 1. "He must not give a day, or Ross & his coadjutors will endeavour to postpone the removal to the meeting of Congress, & get up another excitement."[12]

Even when not asked for a comment on national issues, Jackson readily provided one when he felt so inclined. He watched the progress of events in Washington with undiminished interest and regularly signaled his concern, pleasure, apprehension, or whatever else he felt to the Democratic leadership. The moment the mail arrived at the Hermitage "his first inquiry was for the daily Washington newspapers, and the letters bearing the postmark of the capitol." Indeed, said Blair, Old Hickory "knew more of our affairs at the Hermitage, than we did in Washington."[13] For example, when a new Democratic newspaper, the *Madisonian,* was founded in Washington, edited by Thomas Allen, the General snapped to attention and sounded an immediate alarm. The paper was committed to a soft-money policy and soon became the organ of the Conservative wing of the Democratic party (which Jackson called the "no party party"[14]) led by Senators Nathaniel Tallmadge of New York and William C. Rives of Virginia. These Conservatives supported a pro-Bank policy as well as paper money. Jackson caught the drift of this new sheet straight off and soon flooded the mails with his cries of concern. The *Madisonian,* he told Blair, "is a *viper,* in the hypocritical disguise of *friend,* to the administration, and is intended to sting it, by dividing the republicans, and to undermine, and destroy you." The *Globe* should take note of this snake and crush it to death before it could sink its fangs into the body politic.[15]

But the viper struck before anyone knew what was happening. After Congress convened on September 4, the Conservatives in the House of Representatives worked out a deal with the administration whereby they agreed to support James K. Polk for Speaker but in return got Thomas Allen as printer for the House in place of Blair. As far as Van Buren was concerned, Blair was a "minor sacrifice."[16]

Blair went wailing to Jackson. He did not know of Van Buren's involvement in his ouster as printer and presumed that all the disaffected in Congress were punishing the administration through him. Allen "has plaid the Bell game on you," Jackson replied, "and has been made public printer by a union of some of our pretended friends with the opposition, therefore I suppose I may say that you are really *Bellised."* Van Buren better watch out, he added, or he too may be "Bellised" at the next election.[17] But Jackson's analysis of what had happened missed the mark totally; all it did was reveal the depth of his resentment toward Bell, who had gravely undermined the General's influence in Tennessee as well as in Washington.

Blair closeted himself with several senators, including Benton, and passed along Jackson's admonitions about protecting the Democratic party from vipers.[18] But the most remarkable thing that had happened lately, reported Blair to Jackson, was the desertion of John C. Calhoun from the ranks of his Whig friends. That worthy was now supporting the President! Obviously, said Blair, Calhoun feels he can aid the administration because "there is *no longer danger of its being too popular with the people!!!*"[19]

The return of Calhoun to Democratic ranks sent the Hero howling another cry of warning. He neither trusted the South Carolinian nor believed him loyal to the Union. "Be careful of *Cateline,*" he shot back, "he may be useful *but don't trust him.*"[20]

What had prompted the sudden shift by Calhoun was the call by the President, in his message for a special session, to legislate an Independent Treasury—a "divorce" or subtreasury bill, as it was more commonly called—which would require the public money to be managed by government officials without the aid of banks. This would apply to the collection, safekeeping, and transfer and disbursement of the funds. One of the measures connected with this system postponed the deposit of the fourth installment of the surplus revenue with the states. Calhoun strongly advocated this divorce plan,[21] but in providing support for the Independent Treasury he exacted a price. On September 18 he introduced an amendment which specified that the system accept three-fourths of the government's obligations in bank notes for 1838, one half in 1839, one quarter in 1840, and specie alone from 1841 onward.[22] Ultimately, the Senate passed the Independent Treasury on October 3, but the House, where at least a dozen Conservatives held the balance of power between the Democrats and Whigs, defeated it on October 14.[23]

Van Buren wrote to General Jackson soon after and explained what had happened. He thought they had done as well as could be expected under the circumstances.[24] The failure of the divorce bill to win passage in the House, plus the devastating defeat for the Democrats in the fall election in New York, where the Whigs took 101 out of 128 seats in the Assembly,[25] comprised a double-barreled defeat and the harbinger of worse defeats to come. Still, Van Buren tried to be cheerful. "We . . . will get over this as we have those which preceded."[26]

On a brighter note the President inquired about arranging for Jackson's biography. He wanted to inform George Bancroft, whose *History of the United States,* volume one, had just appeared, that he could undertake the task and could have Jackson's private papers. "He is precisely the man" for the job, said Van Buren. "A root and branch Democrat and the best writer in the U. States."[27]

Jackson was very anxious to assist the composition of his biography. He had always shown a deep concern for the historical record and the need to report accurately the events of his turbulent administration. He wanted the people to know how steadfast he had been in protecting the liberty of the American people and advancing their democratic institutions throughout his prolonged battle with the aristocracy. As a matter of fact he had discussed the matter on several occasions with Kendall and Blair and had gotten a commitment of sorts from Roger Taney to write a history of his administration.[28] As for an authoritative biography, he had already spoken to Kendall about writing it and had promised to give the postmaster general his papers. Naturally, Jackson was delighted to hear of Bancroft's interest. But he had made a promise. "I cannot do any thing to injure the feelings, or mar the prospects of Mr. Kendall," he replied to Van Buren, but should Kendall assent to giving the papers to Bancroft, then "I will yield them with pleasure, as it is the wish of my friends."[29] Jackson also wrote to Blair and asked him to discuss the matter with Kendall as "it is now too delicate a subject for me to open with him." See what he wants to do, the old man directed, but assure him that I have every confidence in his "talents and integrity." If, because of his health, he chose to relinquish his claim, then Blair was to inform Van Buren and ask him to notify Bancroft that the papers would be forwarded as soon as they could be processed. Jackson planned to have Blair take charge of all his papers and select those essential for the preparation of a biography. The General had the utmost confidence in the editor and had already determined to surrender his papers to Blair upon his death.[30]

Blair spoke to both Kendall and Bancroft and then informed Jackson that Bancroft had no intention of writing a biography but merely wanted the papers "to fill that niche in his history" which Old Hickory had dominated so totally. Kendall, on the other hand, fully intended to proceed with a biography and planned to contact Jackson about it in the near future.[31]

As for Blair himself, it was very important to him that he maintain his close association with the former President and that the "whole world" know it. As long as he maintained this relationship, both he and his newspaper were safe from jealous rivals. Indeed he kept a pile of Jackson's recent letters on a table in his home so that they were immediately spotted by all who visited him. When "friends ask if I've heard from you," he said, "I point to the bundle and now and then read a strong paragraph to the shivering, to warm them up and strengthen their faith." He met Taney on the street one day "and put your last letter in his hand to make him jealous" since it praised Blair's contribution to the success of Jackson's administration. "I am afraid to let the Magician see it, lest he take it in his head, that I have supplanted him in your heart."[32]

Like Blair, Van Buren understood the need to maintain close ties with the former President, so much so that he stoutly resisted any executive move that might remotely appear to be a repudiation of Jackson's policies. When the General was informed that the President hesitated about removing some of Jackson's appointees, lest the action be "construed with unkindness," the Hero immediately sent word to Van Buren "to use his Scissors and cut off all officers of my appointment who have become apostates and conservatives and are using their power against his administration."[33]

Jackson abhorred the Conservatives. Even the name itself bothered him. *"I detest the word and name,"* he snorted, "and all who adheres to them!" Conservatives believe "the people unfit to govern themselves . . . and I have no doubt but the people will view this junto in the proper light and discard them from their confidence." They would resurrect the BUS and institute another paper system. "You know I hate the paper system, and believe all Banks to be corruptly administered, there whole object to make money and like the Aristocratic Merchants if money can be made alls well, regardless of the injury to the people or the Government."[34]

Jackson's fighting spirit had not diminished in the slightest since his return home, and that spirit was sorely missed in Washington. Van Buren showed firmness as chief executive, but not like Jackson. Not like the old chief. Blair told the General that there was not one person whom he had left behind in Washington who did not sigh every now and then and say: "How I should like to have the old chief back again." That included Van Buren, said the editor—especially Van Buren. As for Blair himself, so accustomed to meeting with President Jackson each day, "I need not say that I miss you much," he wrote, "when I stroll about the walks, where I was once so happy in your invigorating conversation, in your cordial, kind, indulgent countenance and confidence."[35]

Jackson stroked Blair with a gentle hand. *"Do your duty,* come weal or come wo," he urged. "The people with one voice" cry out for specie and the divorce of the government from all banks. They must be heard and Blair must be their instrument. "Lash those conservatives and traitors with the pen of gall and wormwood—let them feel—no temporising."[36]

So, although separated by nearly a thousand miles from the seat of government, Jackson continued to play an active and vigorous role in national affairs.[37] His presence was constantly felt, especially at Democratic conventions and meetings involving policy decisions. The old man threw himself wholeheartedly into the battle in Congress over the Independent Treasury and regularly hounded Democratic Congressmen to support the divorce bill. The battle—and he always called it a battle—reinvigorated him because it reminded him of his own earlier struggles to get his programs through Congress. Indeed he saw the fight as the same old contest for liberty, the same "battle . . . between the aristocracy of the few against the democracy of numbers, etc." Nothing ever changed. "All who wish to hand down to their children that happy republican system bequeathed to them by their revolutionary fathers, must now take their stand against this consolidating, corrupting money power, and put it down, or their children will become hewers of wood and drawers of water to this aristocratic ragocracy. . . . Every lover of freedom and of our republican system must now put on his armor, and boldly meet this daring and insidious foe." To party leaders in Pennsylvania, New York, Ohio, and other key states he appealed for their support in winning passage for an Independent Treasury.[38]

Only his fragile health slowed him down occasionally, but it took a severe attack to immobilize him. One such occurred early in January, 1838. For two nights and days, he reported on January 16, "I never closed my eyes, part of which my head was much affected, with occasional delirium." Normally Jackson would have been bled immediately, but because of the "delirium" it was postponed. When the delirium left him Jackson called for the lancet and after the bloodletting he claimed he felt much better. "My ears, and head had swollen to an alarming degree—my head broke out all over in soars, which I have no doubt was favorable."[39] A month later he suffered another "hemorrhage equal to that I experienced at the City in November 1836."[40] At one point he himself "despaired of surviving." But somehow he pulled through, although he remained confined to his room for nearly a month afterward. Then he sustained several more physical shocks. First came "an inward fever and costiveness," followed almost immediately by an attack of dysentery which "broke out with great violence" and left him prostrate. But, he reported, "if it leaves my bowels in regular order, this effort of nature will prove very beneficial to me." In addition to everything else, Jackson's eyesight deteriorated very markedly over the next several years—he may have developed cataracts—and at times he could barely see well enough to write. Still he refused to allow these infirmities to get the better of him. As he said, fortunately "I am under my own roof with my little family and the peaceful shades of the Hermitage."[41]

These rude interruptions only temporarily diverted his attention. Despite persistent weakness, Jackson returned to his desk within days of an attack and scratched out letter after letter commanding the Congress to pass the subtreasury and free the nation from the "iniquitous burden" of a depreciated paper. "Justice demands this," he scolded, "and if congress fails to do it, the people, the sovereign people, will speak in a voice of thunder to their representatives." If only the House had better leadership, he moaned. "I would to god there were in the lower House a Benton, a Buchannon, a Walker & a Write &c &c to sustain with their talents the principles so ably sustained in the Senate and then the bill would be carried." The trouble arises because some congressmen care more for money than anything else. They "profess patriotism but have more love of money than of country."[42]

One of the scenes transpiring in the House to engage Jackson's close attention involved the "antics" of John Quincy Adams. The former President had at last found an issue that would immortalize him, namely the right of abolitionists to memorialize Congress to end slavery and the slave trade in the District of Columbia and the territories of the United States. The swelling of his popularity in many unlikely districts around the country only encouraged his daring and further sharpened his prickliness in debate. Violating the rules of the House with abandon and showing contempt for the gag rule that sought to silence him, Adams was repeatedly and futilely called to order by the Speaker, much to the amusement of the Whigs and the fury of southerners. Early in the session Adams presented petitions against the annexation of Texas and argued that the Texas Revolution was little more than a revolt against the emancipation of slaves in Mexico. The hapless Speaker finally ordered Adams to take his seat and the anti-Texas petitions, which the former President sought to read into the record, were all tabled by a vote of 127 to 68.[43]

At the Hermitage a feeble and debilitated skeleton carefully read the details of Adams's performances as described in the newspapers. "From his proceedings in congress," Jackson wrote, "he appears demented, and his actings and doings inspire my pity more than anger." What particularly caught the General's attention and piqued his anger was the "reckless depravity" of Adams in reading to the House one of Jackson's letters, marked "*Strictly Confidential,*" which Old Hickory claimed had been stolen from him. "I mean to make him responsible as accessory to the theft after the fact at least, and make him give up the theaf or hold him responsible as the Burglar."[44]

The letter was written by Jackson on December 10, 1830, to William S. Fulton, the then secretary of the Arkansas Territory. It came about because a certain Dr. Robert Mayo had had a conversation with Sam Houston about a possible rebellion in Texas to be organized in the United States, and Mayo had relayed this information to Jackson. Quite properly, Jackson notified Fulton to keep a careful eye on the border and inform him of any untoward movements[45] but added that he had doubts about the accuracy of his information. Jackson then returned Mayo's letter to its writer but inadvertently—or so Mayo later claimed—enclosed a copy of his letter to Fulton. Both letters were later turned over to Adams, who immediately assumed that Jackson's letter to Fulton was the original and that the General had changed his mind about sending it. Thus, through duplicity, argued Adams, Jackson connived in furthering Houston's Texas plot, for he knew beforehand what was likely to happen and did nothing about it. Actually the letter proved quite the opposite. As several friends commented, it was distinguished for its "probity, patriotism and perfect propriety."[46]

To Jackson, Adams was nothing more than a "hypocrite" and had been all his life. His present behavior in Congress over the abolition petitions (as though Adams really cared about the slaves) only confirmed it. "Humanity and charity toward him, would say," Jackson concluded, "that he must be demented, if not, then he is the most reckless and depraved man living."[47]

Demented or depraved, Adams was not going to escape Jackson's wrath for receiving "stolen" property to serve his political ends. The General composed a letter which excoriated Adams for not returning the letters and thereby "acquit yourself of all agency in purloining them." You know the criminal law well enough, Jackson rasped, that when one is found possessing stolen property he is held "the reputed thief" until he accounts satisfactorily for the manner in which he received it. But instead of mailing this letter directly to Adams, the Hero sent it to Blair with a request that he publish it so that Adams's behavior and purpose would be publicly condemned. In the meantime Major Lewis went to Mayo and demanded to know how he came into possession of the letter to Fulton. Mayo replied that both came to him legitimately through the mails. Jackson refused to believe this account and called Mayo a liar. He said it was impossible for him to have mistakenly inserted one letter with another and not be conscious of it.[48]

After reading Jackson's blistering lecture to Adams, Blair advised him to withdraw it. The editor was reluctant to engage Adams in a newspaper controversy and provide the "infamous old Scoundrel," as he called him, with space in his newspaper to vent his venomous wrath. Leave him to our friends in Congress, Blair counseled Jackson, who will nail his ears to a pillory. "You have no reason to vex yourself about it, however," he added, "for while he convinced everybody he deserved the Pillory, he convinced them also that you deserved the Presidency from which you kicked him."[49]

Jackson accepted Blair's recommendation and agreed to withdraw his letter, but he again insisted that Mayo stole the letter: stole it either from the files of the War Department or "from my table whilst I [had my back turned]." He will lie, Jackson grumbled. "The truth is not in him."[50]

And so it went throughout the summer of 1838: controversy, slander, accusations—most of which went nowhere. To top it off, Congress again failed to enact the Independent Treasury. Worse, and much more immediate and personal, Jackson's farm suffered a severe drought. For ten weeks there was no rain, and the corn dried up and the tender vegetable sprouts wilted and died. By the middle of August everything was "burnt up." It was impossible to sow turnips and Jackson expected a very poor cotton crop. "But the Lords will be done," he relentlessly reminded his family. The Christian has no choice but to submit to divine chastisements. They prepare him for eternity. "We who are frequently visited by this chastening rod, have the consolation to read in the scriptures that whosoever he chasteneth he loveth, and does it for their good to make them mindful of their mortality and that this earth is not our abiding place; and afflicts us that we may prepare for a better world, a happy immortality."[51]

Jackson was not only chastened by drought and the specter of possible starvation but bodily scourges as well. Throughout the summer he hemorrhaged regularly and he endured debilitating headaches and a constant pain in his side. Sometimes a threatened hemorrhage was averted by "the application of the lancet and Cathartics"; most times they took their natural course and after the hemorrhage subsided he was freely bled. "I have a great dificulty of breathing," he told Blair in mid-August, "and has lost by the lancet and cupping a great deal of blood within the last week." Surely he was a living phenomenon. He must have been to have survived such periodic and massive losses of blood.[52]

One happy event of the summer occurred on July 15. It was a Sunday, and on that day General Andrew Jackson joined the Presbyterian Church. The act of joining had been in his mind for many years since both his wife and mother ("for whose memory he has great respect," commented the officiating clergyman[53]) were members of the Presbyterian Church. Also, he had promised his wife to join but had postponed it because he felt that a public display of his religion would be tagged hypocritical. He would be accused of joining the church "for political effect." So he put off this "public act" until he had retired "when no false imputations could be made that might be injurious to religion."[54]

He consulted the Reverend James Smith, who officiated at the Hermitage Church, which Jackson had built for Rachel in 1823, and admitted he felt more "identified" with the Presbyterian Church than with any other.[55] Typically, however, he advised the clergyman that he did not hold to certain doctrines of the church. Although a Presbyterian of the old school, Jackson had absorbed some distinctly "Arminian" views. "I believe," he said at one point, "that every man has a chance for his own salvation." But what about the doctrine of election? Jackson dismissed it. As a matter of fact, on one occasion, he had a discussion of the subject with "an old clergyman named Bain" during which Bain declared himself a "firm believer" in the doctrine of election. The General listened in silence for several minutes. "Brother Bain," he finally responded, "do you mean to tell me that when my Saviour said 'Come unto me, all ye who labor and are heavy laden,' he didn't mean what he said?" Brother Bain said no more, and that ended the discussion on the doctrine of election.[56]

Another matter that kept him from joining the church, Jackson said, was his firsthand knowledge that a Presbyterian elder had once sworn to a lie—possibly having to do with the Eaton affair—and this "lie was on record." But the Reverend Smith was not put off by these reservations nor deterred from his determination to get Jackson to make good on his promise to join the church. He allowed that the General had "been much exercised on the subject of religion" since his return from Washington. He also noticed that the old man had made "the Bible the man of his council," reading it every day and conducting prayer services in the evening. "The last time I prayed in his family," reported Reverend Smith, "the old gentleman wept like a child, and at the close left the room."[57]

As to doctrinal matters, Smith discovered that Jackson knew nothing of "regeneration." Indeed, this may have been the nub of the General's difficulty, for Sarah Jackson complained to the minister that in middle Tennessee, Presbyterian clergymen would not baptize the children of those parents who had not joined the church. This was not the practice in Philadelphia, she protested. The Reverend Mr. Barns of Philadelphia, under whom she was raised, had baptized all her children except the last and she now found to her horror that she could not locate a clergyman who would perform the rites.

Smith took pity on the woman. Since she was a good Christian he decided after questioning her to baptize her youngest child. Smith discussed the matter with the Reverend Dr. John Todd Edgar, pastor of the First Presbyterian Church of Nashville, and related what he planned to do. Edgar demurred. Apparently he had been playing an elaborate game over a period of time in the hope of catching the souls of both Sarah and the General. Edgar had been one of the clergymen who refused to baptize the youngest member of the family, and "had made her joining the church a sina qua non in relation to his baptising her child." Edgar was working on the fears of the mother that if her child died he would go to purgatory instead of heaven.[58]

Sarah conveyed her anguish and fears to Edgar on one of his many visits to the Hermitage. She also said that perhaps she was too great a sinner herself to join the church.

Jackson overheard the remark. "You a sinner?" he cried, "why you are all purity and goodness! Join Dr. Edgar's church, by all means."[59]

Then one Sunday as Edgar preached on the interposition of Providence in human affairs—a matter of irrefutable truth in Jackson's private canon—and seeing the old gentleman come alive to his words, Edgar began sketching the career of a "hypothetical" man who had escaped the hazards of the wilderness, war, the attack of Indians, the invasion of his country, the vicissitudes of political strife, and the determination of an assassin. How can such a man pass through all these scenes unharmed, said the clergyman, and not see the protecting hand of Providence in his deliverance?

Jackson stirred in his pew. When the service ended he was deep in thought. He brooded all the way home. He spent the greater part of the day and evening in meditation and prayer. Part of the time he conversed with Sarah about joining the church and together they knelt and prayed. After she left him he was still too agitated to sleep and so he continued praying and meditating. At dawn, "a great peace fell upon him."[60]

Dr. Edgar visited him shortly thereafter. Jackson told him of his experience and how he had undergone what might be called a "conversion."[61] Thereupon he asked to be admitted to the church along with his daughter-in-law.

Edgar questioned him about his conversion. Most of the answers met an approving nod of the head. Finally Edgar asked the most important question of all.

"General, there is one more question which it is my duty to ask you. Can you forgive all your enemies?"

The question came as a shock. For a moment the General stood silent. The two men stared at one another.

Jackson breathed deeply. His eyes glittered.

"My political enemies," he said at last, "I can freely forgive; but as for those who abused me when I was serving my country in the field, and those who attacked me *for* serving my country—Doctor, that is a different case."

Edgar rejected the argument. There was no difference, he replied. Christians must forgive all. This was absolute. Without a general amnesty for all his enemies, Andrew Jackson could not join the church.

The stricken man sighed. There was a "considerable pause." Then Jackson spoke again. Upon reflection, he began, he thought he could forgive all who had injured him, even those who reviled him for his services to his country on the battlefield.

Edgar smiled his approval. He left the room to inform Sarah. A moment later the woman rushed into the room and embraced the old man. There was a flood of tears and the two remained locked in each other's arms for many moments.[62]

All of which makes a pretty story. It is essentially Edgar's story, told many years later, and probably embroidered to cover up Edgar's own connivance in Jackson's admission into the church. A different account was left by the Reverend Mr. Smith and recorded at the time Jackson actually took communion and joined the church. In fact Smith was much distressed by the way it came about. "To be honest and candid," he wrote, "I *do regret* that General Jackson joined the church when he did and as he did." It seems that Smith had decided to go ahead and baptize the youngest Jackson child despite Edgar's demurral. Edgar pretended to go along with this decision and offered his aid at the sacramental meeting. On Saturday, July 14, the day before the intended meeting, Smith took ill and Edgar advised him to stay home since he was obviously "about to have a billious attack" and should not expose himself. Meanwhile Edgar went to the Hermitage. That night, in the Hermitage church, Edgar preached "on the depravity of the human heart" and so offended Jackson that the old gentleman objected *"strenuously"* to the sermon. It looked as though Edgar had allowed the General to slip through his fingers after all.

Despite his illness, Smith managed to struggle to his feet and ride out to the Hermitage. "I took an immense store of the all powerful Brandroth pills," he said, "& on Sabbath morning was on my legs; So off I went." When he arrived at the Hermitage he "found that the old business of baptising the child was brought up." Edgar pulled no punches. Purgatory yawned for the child who died unbaptized. Think upon that, he thundered.

Sarah wilted. The old man said nothing. But apparently Edgar's words found their mark.[63]

On Sunday, July 15, 1838, the Hermitage church was jammed with parishioners. Servants standing outside the church pressed their faces against the glass of the windows. The regular sabbath services commenced and at their conclusion, General Andrew Jackson rose in his place to announce he desired to join the church. He further declared his belief in its doctrines, and his resolve to obey its precepts.[64] Also requesting admission were his daughter-in-law and a "beloved niece."[65] And so Andrew Jackson was formally admitted into the Presbyterian Church and received communion. "To see this aged veteran, whose head had stood erect in battle, and through scenes of fearful bearing, bending that head in humble and adoring reverence at the table of his divine Master, while tears of penitence and joy, trickled down his careworn cheeks, was indeed a spectacle of most intense moral interest."[66]

Indeed, recorded the Reverend Smith, "it was an affecting scene to see the old man at the Lord's table, but, but, but I fear Edgar has that to answer for. I would not have to do for the Hermitage & all its concerns & inmates, but I judge not this however. I would not have accepted General Jackson into our church. *Strictly confidential.*"[67]

For the remainder of his life General Jackson acted the role of true believer. It was a faith more uniquely his own than anyone might recognize in the Presbyterian Church—he could never accept the notion of an "elect" chosen by God, for example, because it offended his democratic soul—but it would have been most uncharacteristic of him had he submitted totally to all the precise teachings of his church. Still he attended services regularly—as regularly as his health allowed—and he read a portion of the Bible each day, along with biblical commentaries and the hymn book. Before he died he read through "Scott's Bible" twice. Each night he read prayers in the presence of his family and servants, and sometimes he offered short homilies of his own.[68] A delightful if apocryphal story has it that after Andrew Jackson died one of his slaves was asked if he thought the General had gone to heaven. The man thought a moment and replied, "If General Jackson wants to go to Heaven who's to stop him?"

CHAPTER 29

Silver Jubilee

As a loyal and certified Presbyterian, Jackson understood the trials and tribulations Christians must sometimes suffer on account of their faith. "Whosoever he chasteneth he loveth," Jackson repeatedly declared. In that event Old Hickory must have felt especially beloved because he said he was "frequently visited by this chastening rod."[1] Then, on September 16, 1838, he sustained a deep, personal grief when his old friend and traveling companion Ralph Earl suddenly died.

Earl had been ill only a few days. Indeed, he seemed to be recovering and had assured Jackson that his medicine had taken effect and that he was feeling better and had a good pulse. Then, about twenty hours before he expired, his hands grew extremely cold and nothing could warm them back to a normal temperature. On Sunday he died, said Jackson, "without a groan."[2]

Earl's death shocked Jackson terribly. Not only was it sudden and unexpected but it left him bereft of a trusted friend, a "good and honest man." In letter after letter the General referred to Earl's devotion and his willingness to travel with the ex-President whenever he was needed. "I have now no one to go with me," the old man wailed; I must travel alone. Jackson said nothing of Earl's many portraits and alluded only briefly to the disposition of the "painting apparatus." Death had come so quickly that "it was too late to talk with him on the subject of his worldly affairs."[3] All Old Hickory could do was bemoan his great loss and speculate on the few days and hours left to his own life. "I must soon follow him," he wrote, "and hope to meet him and those friends who have gone before me in the realms of bliss thro the mediation of a dear redeemer, Jesus Christ." Those who worked with Jackson in the White House and knew

448

the depth of his friendship with Earl commiserated with him. Blair admitted "a sort of fraternal affection" for Earl and allowed how the two of them used to regard the President as "a common Patron." They virtually made a joke of it. "Poor Earl, in his facetious way," wrote Blair, "frequently spoke of our relationship, saying that he, was the *King's Painter* and I the *King's Printer.*"[4]

Jackson suffered many other blows from the "chastening rod" during the remainder of 1838. The million and more dollar defalcation of Samuel Swartwout came to light and the revelation of this scandal mortified Jackson. He had appointed Swartwout to office "against a powerful influence," he said, and had done so because he had "great confidence in his honesty, honor and integrity."[5] Now the wretched man had escaped to Europe leaving Jackson's great boast of reform a subject of scorn and derision. *"O tempora O mores,"* was Jackson's feeble cry.[6] Swartwout ought to be dragged back from Europe and incarcerated for life, he said, or "hung" if the laws permitted it.[7] What made it even sadder was the fact that Swartwout's great theft gave credence to Whig propaganda that Old Hickory introduced a "spoils system" into national life. The fact that he had reformed the government through his reorganization of every department and had conducted one of the least corrupt administrations in American history was all but forgotten—even by future historians.

Jackson also hemorrhaged a great deal during these days of trauma. Indeed he was so weak from the loss of blood during Earl's illness that he had to drag himself upstairs to visit his friend in his bedroom.[8] Then he seemed to be going blind. He "measurably" lost the sight in his right eye—something that occurred, he noted, without the least bit of pain— and the vision in his left eye dimmed considerably, so much so that he found it difficult to write intelligibly and "cause me to write but little."[9]

He was also embarrassed by a request that he obtain a *noli prosequi* against Lieutenant Robert B. Randolph, who had assaulted him on a steamboat in 1833. He had always adhered to his mother's advice, he said, "to indict no man for assault and battery or sue him for slander," and so he refused to interfere. He said he would have no gratification or pleasure were Randolph to be fined or imprisoned. He therefore asked Van Buren, if Randolph were found guilty, to pardon him and remit the fine. "A pardon might have a good effect upon society," he added.[10]

And, in view of the catastrophic drought, his harvest was particularly bad. "We have neither potatoes, turnips, nor cabbage, and our corn and cotton not half crops," he admitted.[11] Even so, his thirty-year-old son took it into his head to purchase an extensive plantation in Mississippi in the hope of building a great landed estate that would add immeasurably to the family's prosperity. Andrew had just become the father of a second boy, Samuel, and he may have felt compelled to do something significant on his own.[12] The General tried not to oppose his son or dash his hopes with criticism, although he worried about the enterprise and the ability of Andrew to handle it. Jackson did offer suggestions, however, "but these are only hints for your consideration only."[13] In any event Andrew visited Mississippi and on November 20, 1838, agreed to purchase the Halcyon Plantation, an 1185.69-acre estate on the Mississippi River in Coahoma County, from Hiram G. Runnels for $20 per acre. Five thousand dollars was due on March 1, 1839, the balance of the $23,713.80 to be paid in four equal and annual installments each year thereafter. By a verbal agreement with General Jackson, however, the seller consented to postpone each payment one year.[14]

About the only pleasant events to occur at the Hermitage in the fall of 1838 were the visits of Mrs. Frank Blair and her daughter, Lizzie, in September, and Amos Kendall, who arrived a little later to begin research for the biography he had agreed to write.[15] In their talks together Jackson and Kendall relived many exciting scenes of the General's administration. Each relished particular moments. Ultimately the General loaned Kendall a large number of his papers and requested that he deposit them with Blair when he had no further use for them. Presumably these papers would form the core of the projected biography. But Kendall never completed the work. After publishing seven of the projected fifteen numbers (or volumes) of approximately thirty pages each and bringing the biography down to the end of the Creek War in 1814, Kendall became involved in other matters and lost interest in the project.[16] Then, instead of turning the manuscripts over to Blair, he retained some of them in his home and packed the rest in two trunks. His son-in-law, William Stickney, later discovered the trunks and turned them over to the Blair family.[17]

As the two men reminisced, one overriding sentiment was expressed again and again: Jackson's absolute and abiding faith and confidence in the virtue of the people. Despite the grave economic crisis facing the nation (and other dangers[18]), the ex-President placed his total trust "in the virtue of the real people, the great working class, that whenever they have time to reflect, will decide well, and to the safety and perpetuity of our happy republican system."[19] And more and more Jackson identified the "people" as the "working class," the farmers, mechanics, and laborers of the nation. This was the "true democracy" of America. They were the people he knew and appreciated and who appreciated him. This was the democracy that nullifiers and abolitionists sought to destroy. In a letter to Blair, written shortly after Kendall's departure, he continued his reminiscing. "The aid you gave me in my administration, in the most trying times, will not be soon forgotten by me—not whilst I live. There was no temporizing with either; trusting as we did to the virtue of the people, *the real people*, not the politicians and demagogues, we passed through the most responsible and trying scenes, sustained by the bone and sinew of the nation, *the laborers of the land*, where alone, in these days of Bank rule, and ragocrat corruption, real virtue and love of liberty is to be found."[20]

In addition to *"the real people,"* Jackson placed his full reliance on a "just and kind providence," despite the many blows rained upon him. Blair marveled at Jackson's faith. "Your doctrine of faith in providence and the people is with you, a sort of experimental philosophy. You have never found either to fail you, through a most eventful life. . . . And indeed I cannot but think we have your luck with us still, else it would have been impossible to have withstood such a general treachery of Banks and political Leaders."[21]

President Van Buren also decided to visit Jackson at the Hermitage in 1838 and possibly improve his own standing in the south. The General heartily approved the idea and suggested a route that would permit a wide swing through the southeast and southwest. He even offered to meet the President in Memphis and escort him to Nashville. But James K. Polk, who planned to run for governor of Tennessee at the next election, balked at the prospect of a presidential visit. He feared it might be interpreted as outside interference in state affairs and thereby injure his gubernatorial chances. Van Buren turned to Jackson for advice and got a typical answer. "I am unable to say how far the view of Col. Polk may be correct, as my course have been always to put my enemies at defience, and pursue my own course."[22] But that was not Van Buren's course. He avoided putting his enemies at "defience" at all hazard. So, with a certain amount of regret, he canceled his proposed tour.

One of the President's current problems—aside from the economy— over which he felt he could use additional popular support, was the status of relations with Great Britain. Relations had deteriorated very rapidly over the past few months on account of Canada. The Canadians had rebelled against British rule in 1837 and Americans quickly translated their sympathy for the rebel cause into outright aid. Arms were shipped across the border, and one route across the Niagara River employed a small steamboat, the *Caroline,* to transport illegal supplies. Canadian loyalists responded by seizing the *Caroline,* firing it, and setting it adrift in the river. One American died in the operation. To add to the worsening relations between the United States and Canada a virtual war broke out between farmers and lumberjacks who disputed the land grants along the Aroostook River bordering Maine and New Brunswick. This "Aroostook War," as it was called, threatened to escalate into a full-scale military operation. Something approaching hysteria gripped the nation as Americans demanded the invasion and liberation of Canada. Fortunately, the firm hand of President Van Buren eventually brought the crisis under control. He sent General Winfield Scott with an army to pacify the border and requested the governors of New York and Vermont to summon their militias and restore order.[23]

Naturally Jackson followed these events in the newspapers with keen interest and regularly offered the President his advice. He was especially concerned over the border conflict and the possibility of Britain turning it to the disadvantage of the United States. In fact he was prepared to respond to any military summons his country might make, despite his age and disabilities. Not that he desired war. But the very thought of defending his country had a beneficial effect on his general health. It exhilarated him. "I have been taking one bottle of the matchless sanative which has improved my health very much," he told Francis Blair, "and I feel enstrengthened appetite that another will cure me and if a British war should ensue which god forbid I will be able to face their army in the field."[24]

And he would have been formidable, even though feeble and half blind. He came alive in moments of crisis. Indeed, a recent unpleasantness involving several of his slaves demonstrated again how quickly he could gird his strength to meet an emergency. It seems there was a Christmas holiday dance in which a great deal of drinking, dancing, and musicmaking took place. Then fighting broke out. One fight started when Alfred, a slave belonging to Jackson, "cryed out he was the best man in the House"; and another occurred when Frank, the fiddler, was asked to stop playing until a fire could be built in the fireplace. A general melee resulted involving from forty to one hundred "drunken hords of Negroes," according to the General. Sticks were brandished and rocks thrown. One rock hit Frank in the head, "knocked out his brains and killed him." Four of Jackson's slaves—Alfred, George, Squire, and Jack—were arrested and charged with the homicide even though nearly a hundred persons were involved.[25]

Jackson was incensed. He immediately pronounced his slaves innocent —not because he knew what had happened; rather because he knew no one else had a clear sense of what had occurred. His slaves were arrested before any testimony was taken from any of the many witnesses to the tragedy. Stockley Donelson, Jackson's nephew, had obtained a warrant against the four slaves. Because Stockley had turned Whig, the General saw the action as political revenge, a cruel and vindictive display of spite. He "expostulated with Stockly" before the warrant was obtained but after consulting with another "turncoat" nephew, William Donelson, Stockley demanded the warrant.

Jackson raged. He swore he would win the freedom of his slaves no matter the cost. Now that they had been arrested, he shouted at Stockley, "the magistrate was bound to hear their defence, that it was a constitutional right, that all men by law presumed to be innocent until guilt was proven." "All men" included slaves under this constitutional guarantee, according to Jackson, an interpretation Stockley did not seem to appreciate.[26]

Relentlessly, Old Hickory worked to prove his slaves' innocence. Daily he attended the proceedings in which testimony was given. He took notes at these proceedings and requested a copy of the minutes in order to study them and make recommendations for the defense. All together to defend the four men he spent $1,000, which he was obliged to borrow.[27]

And he succeeded. One slave was acquitted by the grand jury. The other three were tried and declared innocent by a jury, which took only two minutes to reach its verdict—"to the great mortification and disgrace of my two Nephews, Stokely and William Donelson," declared Jackson after hearing the verdict. He pronounced the nephews "worthless Whig scamps."[28]

Between this victory in court and the regular application of the "matchless sanative" medicine, Jackson practically felt like a new man in the spring of 1839. He recommended the "sanative" to one and all. Indeed, many consulted him about their medical problems for he seemed to be a walking miracle. For example, Blair wrote him about Randolph Harrison's difficulty with dysentery and what might be done to combat it. Harrison was very anxious to learn Jackson's remedy. The General replied that after suffering acutely for five years with the malady and "trying every remedy prescribed by the most eminent physicians," he finally found relief in Dr. Flood's "burnt brandy" cure.

> The Brandy is prepared thus. Warm the Brandy in a cup, set it on fire, then placing as much loaf sugar as will sweeten it upon a fork, hold the sugar in the blaze of the Brandy untill it is disolved, let the brandy continue to burn as long as it will. Take a wine Glass of this in the morning and another when going to bed, and a little brandy toddy in the middle of the day if Col. Harrison chooses—his diet rice and milk, coffee, and any other food easy of digestion—this cured me, and he must recollect the old adage, "that if burned brandy wont save him nothing can." This I have no doubt will cure him.

No doubt. Unfortunately, Harrison died before the prescription could be gotten to him. But Blair assured Jackson that if it had arrived in time it would have surely cured him.[29]

When Mary Coffee Hutchings, the wife of Jackson's former ward, Andrew Jackson Hutchings, became seriously ill with tuberculosis and suffered violent pains in the small of her back, the General immediately placed his medical expertise at the husband's service. If the application of "camphire" has not been done, he wrote, have it applied at once. "This has often relieved me," he added. "Be careful to keep her bowells open with epsom or Harrodsburgh salts. Should this fail to relieve then apply a bag of hot ashes to the effected part, as hot as she can bear. this has relieved me of the most acute pain, supposed to proceed from an effection of the spinal morrow."[30] As for the tuberculosis, Jackson told his former ward to get two bottles of the "matchless sanative" which "will, I think, remove all symptoms of consumption." One drop in a teaspoon of warm milk, followed immediately by a wine glass of milk, was the way it should be administered. "I pray you to loose no time in getting it." The cost for this elixir: only $2.50 a bottle. When young Hutchings informed

Jackson of his wife's death in early December, 1839—she died just as Jackson's letter with its information of a cure was being written—the old man tried to console his friend. "What a glorious death she has died," he wrote. "She is taken from this world of tears and sorrow, and she now lives in the bosom of her Savior, in a happy and glorious immortality."[31]

Despite Mary's illness and death, Jackson remained reasonably cheerful. His generally buoyant mood was heightened by the success of the Democratic party in the fall elections, especially Polk's gubernatorial victory and the subsequent election of Blair and his partner, John Rives, as the public printer to the House of Representatives after Congress convened in December, 1839.[32] To add to his joy, Jackson was formally invited to attend special celebrations scheduled in his honor at New Orleans to commemorate the twenty-fifth anniversary of the Battle of New Orleans on January 8, 1840. This "silver jubilee" meant a great deal to Jackson and he later gave thanks that he had lived to see it happen. He fully expected the anniversary to rank with the Fourth of July as a national holiday, and he always noted whether suitable celebrations were conducted in Washington to acknowledge the importance of the event. Unquestionably he wanted to attend the jubilee—invitations came not only from New Orleans and Louisiana but the state of Mississippi—but he worried about the expense, the weather, and his uncertain health. An overland trip to Memphis might trigger a hemorrhage and he feared that an episode such as the one he suffered on his tour of New England in 1833 might prove fatal. A good excuse to go was the need to take his cotton to New Orleans, except that the water level of the Cumberland River was very low in early January. "I cannot bear to borrow or travel as a pauper," he complained to Andrew J. Donelson. Added to all this, he said in a mood of self-pity, "I have no one to go with me, was I inclined to go." Still the President strongly urged his attendance, and Jackson appreciated that the pageant might give impetus to the Democratic cause "by which alone can our republican system be perpetuated." So he invited Donelson to come to his house and talk it over and help him make up his mind.[33]

Two things finally convinced him to make the journey: the "good" it would do the public for him to be present at New Orleans; and the belief that it would help relieve his son from his "present embarrassments." Once again Andrew had found himself in deep financial straits. As usual it was a combination of debts owed for merchandise he could live without and his readiness, despite his father's warnings, to stand as surety for the debts of others. In the first instance Andrew had purchased a carriage in Washington and the note for $550 was two years overdue. Major William B. Lewis had guaranteed the note and the Washington Bank of the Metropolis now called upon him to honor his commitment. Andrew J. Donelson learned of the arrangement and informed Jackson. The old man was appalled, not only because he did not know about the debt but because he had just passed through an unpleasant exchange of letters with Lewis over his suggestion that Lewis resign his government position and return to Tennessee in order to avoid being "rotated" out. The exchange of letters did neither man any credit, but fortunately they avoided a quarrel and ended the exchange with a mutual pledge of continued friendship.[34] Now Jackson was forced to apologize for his son's delinquency. If only he had known about the debt before he left Washington, the General wrote, "and instead of wasting all my means to relieve him from other foolish as well as useless debts this would have been met. Now it is beyond my means."[35]

Andrew's other obligation was more serious. He had guaranteed liabilities for Albert Ward, a prominent Nashville citizen whose father was one of Jackson's oldest friends. Then, when Ward suffered financial collapse, his creditors sought legal judgments against all those who had agreed to stand security for repayment. And Andrew was among this number. Poor Andrew, moaned his father. "Wards creditors is tareing his property to pieces, by executions, principally Bank debts kept secrete from the world now made known by judgts., and leaving the securities for other debts to suffer. How unjust this is!" Again and again Jackson had warned his son against such involvements. Again and again Andrew paid no heed. Yet each time the son blundered the father forgave him, commiserated with him over the injustice of it all, and then proceeded to find the means to meet the obligations. "I would always sacrifice property," the General declared, "than the credit of my adopted son or myself."[36]

To rescue his son and "clear ourselves of debt and be freemen once more," Jackson decided upon a number of actions. In such emergencies the old man made quick decisions, so quick in fact that they reminded one man, who interviewed him at this time, "of the lightning's flash. . . . His almost intuitive quickness to discern *the very thing to be done,* caused slower minds to mistake prompt execution for reckless precipitancy." Indeed, on all subjects, said this reporter, quick perceptions and "dauntless presence of mind . . . distinguished this great man."[37] In any event, to meet this new emergency, Jackson first decided to accept the Mississippi and Louisiana invitations and attend the celebration at New Orleans on January 8. On his way down the river he would stop off and see Albert Ward in Memphis where "I will endeavour to have full security for you," he told his son. Then he planned to see Hiram G. Runnels, from whom Andrew had purchased the Halcyon Plantation, "and plaice yr. contract with him on such basis that will enable the proceeds of the farm to meet it." In addition he would ship his cotton down the river—low water or no—and borrow against it to meet the most pressing debts and finance his trip.[38]

Jackson also borrowed $3,000 from William Nicholas and assigned it to Andrew to cover the debts. The loan against the cotton was used to pay for the carriage and a piano that Andrew had recently purchased. At this time Andrew was overseeing his property in Mississippi and Jackson planned to inspect this plantation during his trip—one more reason for going to New Orleans.[39]

Aside from financial considerations, one other factor convinced Jackson to make the arduous journey, despite his uncertain health. He sincerely believed that he could personally advance the cause of democracy by going to New Orleans. "My whole life has been employed to establish & perpetuate, our republican system," he wrote to President Van Buren in explaining the motivation behind his trip; and "if I should die in the effort, it cannot end better than endeavouring to open the eyes of the people, to the blessings we enjoy, and to the corruption of the opposition, and the continued struggle of the aristocracy, aided by the mony power, to put down the sovereignty of the people, & usurp the government." What must be established above all else, he insisted, is the "true principle that a majority ought & must rule."[40] By going to New Orleans, Jackson could demonstrate by word and action his belief in this "true principle." Surely, then, "the blessing of a kind providence," he concluded his letter to Van Buren, "will give victory to the democracy."[41]

So, Jackson literally took his life into his hands to go to New Orleans to fulfill his commitment.[42] He set out with Major Donelson on Christmas eve with the object of getting to Memphis by the first of January. It was to be his first public appearance in nearly three years. Because of the low level of the Cumberland River they were forced to go overland part of the distance. The roads were rough and in some places covered with snow. At times Jackson was very uncomfortable, but he kept moving. The first day they traveled 29 miles, the second 40, the third 29, and the fourth 27, each day riding from morning to night without stopping. On December 28 they reached the mouth of the Cumberland River, where they boarded the steamboat *Gallatin* and headed down the Ohio toward the Mississippi. Floating ice filled the river and a twenty-four-hour snowstorm forced the boat to seek shelter at night. Through it all Jackson's health held out. He was determined to get to New Orleans.[43]

On his way down the Mississippi River Jackson stopped off to inspect the Halcyon Plantation. Although he had time for only a partial inspection of the property, he was well pleased with it. He especially liked its location and told Sarah that he thought "a great deal of mony" could be made by supplying wood to steamboats plying the river. Accordingly, he instructed the overseer to keep a ready supply of wood on the riverbank. He thought it might be a good idea to send some men from the Hermitage to cut wood. Ten hands could cut twenty cords of wood a day, he wrote, and that was worth thirty dollars "in cash" when sold.[44]

The state of Mississippi sent a steamboat to pick up Jackson and take him to Vicksburg, which was the designated staging area for the final descent to New Orleans. But then, on the way down, he suffered another hemorrhage. It happened just before the boat reached Pittsburgh. Still he never flinched. "I have long found that complaining never eased pain,

I therefore put on a calm face." The only relief was provided by the application of common salt. He should have rested but so many distinguished guests came on board to see him that he never got to bed before eleven o'clock. He was in agony and no one knew it. "I was determined to go through or fail in the struggle."[45]

At Vicksburg the General debarked and traveled to Jackson, Mississippi, where he stayed two nights and a day in the hope of getting some rest. Still no relief. Too many people demanded to see him and there was nothing he could do or say to put them off. For the remainder of his trip he found no respite from the penalty of his popularity. He "struggled against pain and sickness for ten days and nights," he reported, "still providence, as usual, took care of me."[46]

The delay at Vicksburg was required so that the General's arrival in New Orleans could be precisely timed to fall on the exact day of the anniversary. The arrangements committee had gone to considerable trouble to orchestrate the pageant so as to generate as much excitement and drama as possible. Parades, dinners, fireworks, speeches, wreath laying, the dedication of a monument, visits to the battlefield, and a ceremony at the cathedral were all scheduled during the festivities. And Jackson cooperated to the fullest despite his fatigue and pain. He played his role to perfection.

Returning to the steamboat at Vicksburg, Jackson proceeded on his journey as scheduled. Four steamboats convoyed his ship on the final leg of its run. These ships were crowded with soldiers and other passengers. With "cannons firing and colors streaming," the convoy arrived at New Orleans on Wednesday morning, January 8. Thirty thousand spectators, according to one report, jammed the levee and the streets leading to it, and when the "gallant old chief" stepped foot upon the shore at 10 A.M., they exploded in a "chorus of enthusiastic cheers." All hats came flying off and were "waved vigorously at the General." Those without hats waved handkerchiefs. "Huzza! Huzza! Huzza!" they cried. "JACKSON! JACKSON! JACKSON!" It was "Vox Populi, vox dei," enthused one reporter, "and none can prevail against it."[47]

The mayor came forward and welcomed the Hero in a handsome address that could scarcely be heard. Jackson stood perfectly still throughout the address. Several spectators later reported that "the old General looks somewhat the worse for age, but is still remarkably active and hearty for one of his years." Then a procession formed. Old Hickory was led to a barouche, drawn by four white horses, and the "Legion and Washington Battalion" positioned itself around the open carriage. But the people themselves joined the escort as it moved slowly along Canal Street to the state house. *"Amid a sea* of human heads" the majestic Hero sat in his coach ramrod straight, "with his silver locks uncovered," returning the salute of the spectators with a wave of his hand. The balconies, windows, doors, and rooftops of houses were crammed with "ladies fair" who fluttered their handkerchiefs at the General. Each wave "never failed to meet with a response from the gallant veteran." The "pride, pomp and circumstance of war was forgotten" in this stupendous outpouring of affection and gratitude. "Truly, he was a spectacle worthy of the veneration of the people, who owe so much to him."[48]

When the barouche arrived at the state house the Hero alighted and walked to the chamber of the legislature, where he met officers of the army and militia, the heads of the state and treasury departments, judges and legislators. He was introduced to each one in turn and at the end of this reception the assembled officials gave him a long, noisy ovation. He returned to the barouche and the procession proceeded down Canal to Chartres Street into the Place d'Armes. Even English merchants standing on the balconies doffed their hats and bowed to "the conqueror of the *elite* of their own brave battalions."[49]

At the Place d'Armes the volunteers, cavalry, and infantry stood at attention on three sides of the square, and Jackson received their salute as he passed before each line. Then he entered the cathedral, where a "Te Deum" was sung and the Abbé delivered "a thrilling oration," first in English and then in French. Judge Watts followed with a speech so spirited and animated that despite "the sanctity of the place, there were passages in this speech which called forth the strongest bursts of applause —indeed, we believe no American could have listened unmoved to similar language on such an occasion."[50]

Following the services in the cathedral it was intended "to march the old hero" to the battleground—the Plain of Chalmettes—to lay the cornerstone of a monument to commemorate the victory, "but the fatigue of the day was too much even for the iron frame of Old Hickory, enfeebled as it had been by sickness, and broken by the hardships of war." He begged off, and no one seemed to mind except the thousands who waited there in vain. Instead he retired to the "splendid apartments" prepared for him at the French Exchange on St. Louis Street. As his carriage moved through the streets the mob pressed closer to get a better look at him. Never had there been "so grand a moral spectacle presented in America," said one, "as that of thirty or forty thousand people being almost willing to risk their lives merely to get a look at the brave old General." Even Whigs capitulated. "We, in our individual capacity," commented one, "are among those who have politically opposed General Jackson in thought, word and deed . . . still we yesterday forgot the politician and thought only of the man—welcomed him as the 'Hero of New Orleans' and the fearless defender of his country, and were willing to forget aught else."[51]

Upon his arrival at the French Exchange the General entered the saloon where the surviving veterans of the great Battle were waiting to greet him. General Jean B. Plauché, who commanded the Orleans battalion during the engagement, addressed his chief "in a few short but thrilling words." Jackson responded in the same spirit and then retired to his apartment for a few hours rest. That evening he attended the St. Charles theater, which "was crammed from the pit to the dome," where an anthem, especially composed for the occasion, was sung. Mr. J. M. Field came to the front of the stage to deliver "a poetical address" which he had written himself. Old Hickory, he said, had returned "to bless the children of the sires he saved." Then the entire audience of two thousand sang "Hail Columbia." Twice the General rose in his place to "acknowledge the enthusiastic cheering of the multitude." At the conclusion of "Hail Columbia," the Hero left the theater amid the "prolonged cheers" of a delirious audience. It was a glorious ending to an exciting and emotional day. What made it so stirring was the "animation, the joy, the enthusiasm that glowed in every countenance."[52]

"I remember Gen. Washington's arrival in Philadelphia in 1798, I saw Lafayette here in 1825, I have beheld many exhibitions of the kind," wrote one observer, "but never one like that of last Wednesday." Indeed partisan and foe both agreed that this celebration marked a "supreme" moment in American history. "New Orleans has won some fame for the brilliance of her military displays," commented one Whig newspaper, "but the parade of yesterday exceeded anything of the kind we have ever achieved."

More than anything else, the festivities celebrated free government— or so Old Hickory kept telling the crowds. Jackson used every opportunity to extol the people, their virtue, their incorruptibility. By right, he cried, the majority must rule. Government must listen. "All must bow to public opinion."[53]

So ended the commemoration of the silver jubilee of the Battle of New Orleans. But it took a physical toll. The totally exhausted Hero staggered homeward as soon as he mustered his strength. Some wondered if he would make it.

Along the way he was obliged to stop off in Mississippi to receive the honors of the state for his victory over the Indians as well as over the British. At the capitol Governor McNutt gave a "grand levee" in the General's honor, but the weakened man lasted only an hour and a half before retreating to his quarters. Naturally, everyone wanted to shake his hand, but when "they looked upon his feeble frame, bending and tottering," they recoiled to see him so broken by disease and hardship. They almost feared to get too close lest he disintegrate at their touch.[54]

While in Mississippi Jackson arranged to meet Hiram Runnels, who sold the Halcyon property to Andrew, and got him to agree to an extension of the note due him for one year. So the trip produced a number of advantages, just as Jackson had anticipated. In fact he said he was "truly pleased" with the journey despite the physical hardship. Still he faced a a long and difficult homeward journey. For ten days and nights the crew struggled against the ice in the Mississippi River. Thanks to the energy of the captain and his crew and the "smiles of a kind and gracious providence," they reached Nashville safely on Saturday, February 1. An immense crowd of friends and neighbors, along with the entire legislature, met Jackson on his arrival, and they insisted on a formal ceremony of welcome. The General felt very poorly, his weakened condition aggravated by a cold he caught aboard the steamboat, but he suffered through the welcome with no loss of dignity or amiability. The following day he returned to the Hermitage.[55]

Without question, by 1840, Andrew Jackson had achieved a new status with the American people. He had always been a symbol—a symbol of the enduring strength of a free people—but now he seemed more like a luminous fixture of a glorious past. Somehow the greatness of America evolved because Andrew Jackson lived. American democracy, as it had developed over the past few decades, appeared to many as nothing more than Jackson's lengthened shadow.

Long before he died Old Hickory was a legend, and his home virtually a shrine—"the democratic shrine."[56] More and more visitors came like pilgrims to see him. No one visited Nashville without driving out to pay their respects to General Jackson. "The Hermitage is almost constantly thronged with company," reported one man, and everyone was received with cordiality and respect, no matter their station. Even in retirement Jackson always conducted himself "as the servant of the people." And his admonition to every citizen who visited him was the same: The people "ought & must rule."[57]

With favored groups Jackson might reminisce about his exploits in the Creek War or—his greatest pride—the Battle of New Orleans. To others he might comment on national or international issues. On one occasion, Dr. William A. Shaw visited Jackson. Shaw positively idolized the Hero. They got to talking about world politics and at one point Jackson predicted with remarkable prescience that Russia would become the "great eastern rival of the United States of America, rising *pari passu* with her." He anticipated no further trouble with Great Britain, despite the long history of enmity that had once existed between the two countries. "The next great war we have will be with Russia," Jackson predicted.

And what will be the result, Shaw asked.

"We will beat them, sir," Jackson responded; "we can whip all Europe with United States soldiers. Give me a thousand Tennesseans, and I'll whip any other thousand men on the globe!"

To the day he died Andrew Jackson remained a flag-waving, fire-breathing superpatriotic nationalist. A Union man to the marrow of his bones, said Shaw, "he loved his whole country, without sectional bias."

Jackson reminisced the night away talking to Shaw, and as he did so, he grew more and more dreamy. Then, all of a sudden, he paused and turned to Shaw as though he had thought of something quite unique.

When he finally spoke again he quoted Shakespeare. "There is a tide in the affairs of men," he said, "which, taken at the flood, leads on to fortune."

Shaw just listened.

Then, as though he understood these words for the first time, Jackson murmured: "That's true, sir, I've proved it during my whole life."[58]

CHAPTER 30

Beaten But Not Conquered

ANDREW'S DEBTS MOUNTED. EVERY TIME Jackson seemed to turn around there was another creditor with extended hand. The extent of his son's indebtedness unraveled very quickly once Andrew's involvement with Ward's bankruptcy became known. Worried creditors feared for their loans and presented their claims. At first Jackson thought the debts totaled no more than $6,000, apart from the mortgage on the Halcyon Plantation. But that figure soon doubled. And went higher. More than $15,000 in obligations was dumped into Jackson's lap, "ten thousand of which," said the General, "he has been swindled out of by endorsements and securityship."[1]

Poor Jackson. He was seventy-three years of age and dying as fast as he could get on with it—or so he said; still he suffered one jolting blow after another from the "chastening rod." If only Andrew had confided in him. "If he had only let me know of the amount of the whole debts I would have saved both his and my own feelings but this he did not do." The prodigal son finally broke under the strain. Andrew collapsed and took to his bed. The pressure of these debts, said his father, "was praying on his mind and I believe brought upon him his sickness and then the relapse. it far exceeded his calculation by one hundred percent, but I have struggled to meet it, and every dollar I could raise since I come from Washington has been applied to his use."[2]

To meet these crushing and unexpected obligations Jackson sold every bit of property he owned in Alabama. He instructed his nephew and former ward, Andrew J. Hutchings, to put up his remaining lots in Florence and sell them in a public auction if a private sale could not be arranged. Jackson hoped to realize $500 for three lots, but all Hutchings

462

could get was $240.³ He also put up for sale the Hunter's Hill property and said he was willing to take $14,000 provided the buyer put down a $6,000 deposit. He did not sell this property until December 10, 1842, when he received $12,000 for it from Mrs. Elizabeth E. Donelson. Over a two-month period the General paid "upwards of twelve thousand dollars in actual cash" to clear the obligations, and still they kept turning up. There seemed to be no end to them. After a while, and not unexpectedly, Jackson began to suspect a conspiracy, a political conspiracy bent on destroying him. "I have been greatly distressed in mind and feeling," he wrote. "Every Whigg that he was indebted to has either sued or warranted him." They took all of Jackson's cash, leaving him, as he said, "without active funds until our crops come in."⁴

Even though Jackson drew renewed strength from this adversity—it stirred his combative spirit—the flesh showed the strain. He suffered regularly from intense headaches, a stabbing pain in his side, and fits of violent coughing which usually triggered a hemorrhage. As a matter of fact, on the average, he now hemorrhaged once a month. But he seemed to have abandoned the lancet as a regular procedure each time he bled. Instead he took the "matchless sanative." Since the hemorrhages were less severe (though more frequent) he credited the medicine with improving his condition. "I have no doubt of its entire eficasy in preventing Hemorhage," he wrote. He took the sanative every day when ill with a glass of wine or toddy (not milk, as he prescribed for ladies) one hour before each meal. "It creates an appetite, promotes digestion, and in a few days," he told young Hutchings, who was himself dying from tuberculosis, "you will find yourself gaining strength."⁵

Political adversity also reinvigorated the old man. In view of the deep economic depression over the past several years he knew that the Democratic party had a fight on its hands to bring off Van Buren's reelection, but he never lost confidence in the people. "When the people, the real working people are oppressed and cursed by a depreciated paper and the Banks, bankers, speculators and swindlers fattening at the expense of the labourer," they will assert themselves at the ballot box and pledge themselves anew to "real Democratic and republican principles."⁶ Still he appreciated how unpopular Van Buren had become, particularly in the south, and therefore advised the party to jettison Richard M. Johnson as Vice President and substitute James K. Polk as its candidate. He had nothing against Johnson personally, despite the furor over the Kentuckian's private life, but he understood its disastrous impact politically. "I like Col. Johnston but I like my country more, and I allway go for my Country first, and then for my friend."⁷ He was certain that Polk could win Tennessee, Alabama, Mississippi, and Louisiana for the ticket, and maybe Virginia, the Carolinas, Georgia, and even Kentucky. But the party needed to run the strongest man possible with Van Buren, he lectured, one that would "not be a dead weight." If nominated by the Baltimore

Convention, Johnson would hang like a millstone around Democratic necks, he said. "Take the strongest say I, regardless of men. . . . We must be united and adopt the Motto, Everything for principle and nothing for men."[8] One important reason for Jackson's desire to elevate Polk was his even stronger desire to "rescue" Tennessee from the likes of "Bell, White & Co," and he really seemed to think that Polk could do it. Almost as much as he wanted Van Buren's reelection, Jackson hungered for White's defeat and humiliation.[9]

But the Democratic nominating convention meeting at Baltimore on May 5, 1840, chose to play the "Whig game" and leave the nomination of a Vice President to the states in the hope that it would draw strength to their presidential candidate, Martin Van Buren. Thomas Hart Benton told Jackson that Silas Wright, Jr., and a number of other friends in Congress preferred to duck the issue rather than face a floor fight between the Polk and Johnson forces at the convention. But Jackson was appalled by this reaction and wrote and told Van Buren so. He said it gave him "much pain" to learn that the second slot would be left vacant for each state to fill as it chose. "We are to have a hard battle," he reminded the President, "and to ensure success there must be union, and to produce this the Baltimore convention must . . . select a man upon whom the whole republicans—the whole democrats can rally. . . . There must be no maiden modesty on this subject—we require unity & energy & with it all is safe." In his reply Van Buren wistfully pointed out that he was not General Andrew Jackson and could not tell the convention what to do, all of which the old Hero was forced to concede. "Having done what I conceive my duty to patriotism & my country," Old Hickory declared, "I cheerfully submit to whatever the Baltimore convention may do."[10]

What made the election all the more precarious was the action of the Whig party in nominating General William Henry Harrison for the presidency instead of Henry Clay. Harrison was a military hero of sorts and appeared to have voter appeal. At least that was the way Whig politicians read his returns in the 1836 contest. So instead of going for a two-time loser in Clay, they opted for a military hero in an effort to "out-Jackson" the Democratic party. To bolster their ticket even further the Whigs nominated John Tyler of Virginia for Vice President. Tyler was a strong states' rights southerner who had deserted the Democratic party on principle because he abhorred the tactics and program of Andrew Jackson. For Van Buren it was a lethal combination and no one saw this more clearly than Old Hickory himself. "By the Eternal god," he moaned, it was the same struggle they had been waging for the last ten years. The Whigs would stop at nothing "to put down . . . the republican system, and on its ruins to establish an aristocracy built upon the great corrupting power of a combined mony system—and to rule the people by its corruption . . . and destroy the liberty, & sovereign power of the people."[11]

To make matters worse, the Congress still stumbled along its purpose-

less course and failed to enact the Independent Treasury bill. Three years
had passed without significant legislation on banking. The Democrats
were outmarshaled and outmaneuvered. They have no leader, Jackson
stormed, and are "cursed with a weak and imbecile speaker. *They deserve
this.*"[12] These Democrats should "be shot as deserters from their posts
on the lines of the enemy," he told Francis Blair, if they failed again to
pass the bill during the present session of Congress. So intense were
Jackson's feelings as he wrote these words that he began to hemorrhage.
Fortunately no wholesale slaughter of congressmen was necessary, as he
had demanded, for on July 4, 1840, the Congress finally passed the bill
creating the Independent Treasury System. "The Whiggs whipt," Jackson exulted, "so it goes *all well.*"[13]

One incident that really sent Jackson's blood coursing was the personal
appearance of Henry Clay in Nashville in August, 1840, to deliver a
political address on behalf of the Harrison-Tyler ticket. Clay received a
warm welcome—which must have infuriated Jackson—and took particular delight in needling the "illustrious captain" who lived not far away.
Clay never failed to mention Jackson's military renown and then followed
it by enumerating his disasters as President. In particular Clay noted in
his Nashville speech how many of the General's appointees ended up as
defaulters. Everyone knew about Samuel Swartwout, of course, but Clay
insinuated that Edward Livingston was also a defaulter. He weakly excused the former President by suggesting that Jackson probably "did not
sufficiently reflect" upon these appointments as he should have.

Jackson was livid when he read the speech. His administration had set
a standard for honesty, he contended, which no corrupt slanderer could
demean. He quickly penned a reply which was published in the Nashville
Union.

> . . . Mr. Clay was appointed Secretary of State . . . with recommendations
> for character and fitness not more favorable than those produced to me by
> the citizens of New York in behalf of Mr. Swartwout. Mr. Clay, too, at the
> time of his own appointment to that high office, it will be recollected, was
> directly charged throughout the Union with having bargained for it, and by
> none was this charge more earnestly made than by his present associates
> in Tennessee, Messr. Bell and Foster.
> Under such circumstances how contemptible does this demagogue ap-
> pear, when he descends from his high place in the Senate and roams over
> the country, retailing slanders against the living and the dead.[14]

It was a smashing response. It was nicely calculated to do Clay as much
injury in Tennessee as possible. But because of Jackson's reference to the
"corrupt bargain"—a charge that never went away—Clay felt compelled
to respond in print. He insisted that he had spoken of the ex-President
in his speech in respectful terms only to be assaulted with "insinuations
and gross epithets . . . alike impotent, malevolent, and derogatory." Still,

"they have fallen harmless at my feet," he wrote, "exciting no other sensation than that of scorn and contempt."[15]

Jackson's public outburst won the plaudits of Democrats, however. Both Taney and Blair wrote letters of congratulations, and both expressed indignation at Clay's "harsh and cruel" attack on the memory of Edward Livingston.[16] Mrs. Livingston was deeply hurt by the false accusation and thanked Jackson for his vigorous defense. "I never forget a friend, or abandon one," he replied. "Your dear departed husband deserved my friendship" and carried it to his grave. "When that roaming lying demagogue, Clay, attempted to slander his memory, it was my duty, well knowing the abominable falshood that this stump orator had pronounced against the dead, to come forth with the truth and crush the base defamer at a blow—This was my duty."[17]

Throughout the summer and into the early fall of 1840, the Whigs demonstrated how much they had learned from the Democrats about winning elections by mounting a "boozy" campaign of nonsense and merriment. This was the Log Cabin campaign for "Tippecanoe and Tyler, Too," complete with hard cider, rolling balls, coonskin hats, and other paraphernalia to "enlighten" the mind of the electorate. A gallant soldier, a veteran Indian fighter, "Old Tip" Harrison was palmed off as a veritable Andrew Jackson in Whig clothing. "Van, Van, the used up man," on the other hand, was an effete easterner, whose perfumed side-whiskers and fashionable clothing proclaimed him an "aristocratic" dandy.[18]

Old Hickory fumed over this desecration of the political process. Not unexpectedly, he saw the log cabins and cider kegs and rolling balls as further examples of Whig contempt for popular rule, as a renewed campaign against the democracy. "The attempt by their mummeries to degrade the people to a level with the brute creation has opened the peoples eyes,—it is saying to them in emphatic language, that they are unfit for self government and can be led by hard cider, Coons, Log cabins and big balls, by the demagogues, as can the lowering herd be, by his keeper and a baskett of salt." Still he maintained his unshakable trust in the "moral and virtuous portion of our Citizens—the great labouring classes." Once they were aroused by the designs of aristocrats and apostates to raise "a monied King to rule . . . & make the labour of our country Hewers of wood & drawers of water to its power" then "I have no fear of the result in Novbr. next."[19]

The mention of apostates in this letter no doubt referred to Tyler. But it also referred to two men who had been closer to Jackson and whose "betrayal" wounded him far more than Tyler's. John Eaton had returned from his mission to Spain with the announcement that he was unwilling to support Van Buren's reelection. That came as quite a shock for Jackson, who had risked his own reputation and administration in support of his old friend. Eaton came home, said the General, "an ulogiser of Harrison." The other apostate was General Richard Keith Call, whose failures in the Seminole War had earned Jackson's wrath. Deeply hurt by this criticism, Call deserted to the Whigs.[20]

Because of the mounting success of the Whig campaign to sell "Old Tip" as a man of the people, Jackson felt obliged to do more than sit at home and pen letters and directives to his friends and newspaper editors around the country. He decided to hit the campaign trail. He ached to speak to the American people directly and disabuse them of Whig propaganda. He never wanted for invitations to speak at dinners or barbecues, but in the past he had always kept a discreet distance between himself and such flagrant politicking. But now he appreciated the grave danger to the Democratic cause, to Van Buren, and to the principles that he had helped articulate and advance. Besides, he needed above everything else to recapture Tennessee from the Whigs. So when he was invited to a "free barbecue" at the town of Jackson in the western district of his state, he jumped at it. "I am determined to make the attempt particularly when I see that Genl. Call and Major Eaton, have apostatised and taken the field with the piebald opposition of abolitionists, antimasons and blue light federalist." It meant risking his health, he told Van Buren, but "I cannot die in a better cause than in perpetuating our republican system." If "providence" is about to chastise this nation, he went on, no "greater curse" is possible than the election of William Henry Harrison. Within four years, said Jackson, "every feature of our democratic system would be trampled under foot."[21]

So Old Hickory set about showing the electorate what a real "man of the people" looked like during the final days of the campaign. Besides Jackson, Tennessee, he journeyed to Williamson, next Rutherford, and then Davidson. He toured the western part of Tennessee rather extensively and gave short speeches in praise of the Democratic ticket. Mostly he condemned the Whig party as a conspiracy to deprive the people of their right to self-rule. He predicted that Whig victory would result in a new mammoth bank with dukes and lords of England as stockholders.[22]

Jackson was very pleased with his efforts as a campaigner. He noted with what respect and attention the electorate listened to him. Here were the real people, he said, the working classes of America, not the aristocrats and the "moneyed" elite. "Instead of riot and brawling I never saw more order and decorum in a church. These are the signs of reason reassuming its umpire, and when this is the case, democracy must and will triumph."[23]

At the "great congregation of people" held at Jackson, Tennessee, on October 8, Old Hickory saw fit to address the problem of abolitionism. Since he had noticed that the question had been frequently raised of late,[24] he decided to alter his text and address this question head on and tell the people exactly what he thought. Although Major Donelson helped him to write most of the speech, the section on the abolitionists came directly from the mind and pen of Old Hickory himself.[25]

After a long "People's Address," delivered by the chairman of the proceedings and which enshrined Jackson next to Washington and Jefferson in the nation's pantheon, the old man slowly advanced to the speaker's stand, nodded an acknowledgment of the applause, adjusted his spectacles and began to read his prepared speech. The crowd listened carefully to each word. "It affords me unspeakable pleasure to be able to meet you on this occasion," he began. "It is probably the last time that I shall have it in my power to exchange salutations with you—the last opportunity that I shall have to thank you personally for the many proofs you have given me of your respect for my character and services." There was a slight murmur of dissent from the crowd but Jackson paid it no heed and continued reading. He spoke of his youth, of his commitment to republicanism, and of his faith in the people. "My earliest impressions imbibed in our revolutionary struggle were that the people . . . were the only safe depository of power." He paused at this point and looked out over his audience. Then he reiterated his fears that "the federal party" under the Whig banner would in short order subvert "the spirit of our institutions" if they defeated the Democratic ticket in 1840. We are yet to see, he rumbled, whether we can successfully resist "the many schemes" of those who would disrupt our harmony as states bound together in a perpetual Union.

Having prepared his audience for his principal subject, Jackson immediately launched into an attack upon the abolitionists. "Look, I pray you," he pleaded, "at the efforts which are making to array one section of the Union against the other. It is in this aspect that the movements of the abolitionists become fearful and portentous." Maybe they were motivated by "real philanthropy" in advocating their cause, but they had been manipulated in a "false direction" by those who were intent upon the resurrection of the "doctrines of the Federal party." Not a single abolitionist, as far as he knew, supported the principles of the Democratic party. Their influence had been channeled to advocate a national bank, a system of internal improvements at war with the rights of the states, and a protective tariff calculated to multiply the "sources of discord between the various sections of the Union." Even though a majority of the people had repudiated these doctrines, he said, there were those who would dismiss the dictates of the electorate and foist upon them the rule of the "moneyed elite."

As far as Jackson was concerned the only point worth mentioning with respect to the abolitionists was the fact that they were being used—used politically—for an ignominious cause. Abolitionists were intent upon subverting the democracy, he said, and that was wrong and had to be prevented. Worse, they would tear the Union apart to achieve their goal.

"The election of Mr. Van Buren is essential to the preservation of republican principles," Jackson argued. If you cast your ballots for him, "your republican system is perpetuated"; but if you vote for Harrison, "the chosen candidate of the apostate republicans, the abolitionists, and the Hartford Convention federalists, and your constitutional liberties are perhaps gone forever, and may end like that of ancient republics."

"Then I say to you, go to the polls like independent voters," he cried in his best political voice, "bearing in mind the blood, the treasure, the days of toil . . . it cost your revolutionary fathers to procure and bequeath to *you* the invaluable boon of those blessings of liberty which we enjoy; and which every obligation we owe to posterity binds us to hand down to them unimpaired." Go to the polls on November 3, he commanded, "go, I say, looking steadfastly at the stars and stripes," on the banner of your country's glory, and give your votes like freemen to that candidate you believe is "pure, undeviating" and sworn to republican doctrine. And when you do, he declared, "your liberty is safe." You will snatch the republican system from certain defeat, a disaster conceived by Federalists, apostates, and abolitionists to raise upon the ruins of our Constitution "a great consolidated government based upon the combined moneyed power of England and America, and make the laboring and producing classes of our country, 'hewers of wood and drawers of water' for their own aggrandisement."

Remember the fate of ancient Rome, he said in conclusion. Remember that by corruption she lost her liberty. Can anyone who values his freedom vote for a man who when asked for his principles insults you with the reply, "I will answer no questions coming either from friend or foe"? Can you vote for such a "*mum* candidate"? "I answer for you that none worthy to be free can do so."[26]

As Jackson stepped away from the rostrum he again apologized for the feebleness of his health which made it difficult for him to do justice to the great purpose of this meeting. He hoped, however, that everyone heard him. And with that he returned to his seat.

Because of the importance of his remarks, Jackson's speech was republished throughout the Union; and, indeed, his campaigning won national attention.[27] Not only were his remarks about abolitionists carefully noted but the moral overtones about a money power robbing the laboring classes of the country also won attention.

The Whigs responded as best they could. Because Van Buren's lifestyle produced mockery and undisguised contempt during this freewheeling campaign, Jackson's extravagance in the White House was also faulted. As a matter of fact he had spent a great deal of money both entertaining and refurbishing the residence. But he could not abide any intimation that the people's money had been spent improperly to satisfy his "aristocratic" tastes. He immediately wrote to William B. Lewis in Washington for documentation so that future historians would know that out of the money appropriated by Congress in 1829 to repair the furniture in the White House, a good $9,000 of it went into finishing the East

Room.[28] But Jackson should not have worried. No one really ever suspected him of stealing. He was scrupulously honest. And he paid his debts —even on his deathbed he made provision for their liquidation—despite the fact that most of them belonged to his son.[29]

Because he had campaigned so intensely, General Jackson was totally unprepared for the crushing electoral defeat sustained by the Democratic party in the presidential election. All during the campaign Jackson sneered at the log cabin tactics of the Whigs and assured his friends that the people would resent such shenanigans. Even when the defeat in Pennsylvania and the likely defeat in New York were reported, Jackson did not lose faith. "I do not believe one word of it," he told Van Buren. "I trust in a kind providence that he has not so early doomed us to fall by bribery, and corruption."[30]

But fall the Democrats did. And it was a mighty fall. Nearly two and a half million voters went to the polls, attracted by the excitement of the contest and their agitation over economic conditions. It was a jump from 57.8 percent in 1836 to 80.2 percent in 1840. When all these votes were counted, Harrison took 52.9 percent of them, or 1,275,612, while Van Buren captured 46.8 percent, or 1,130,033. This was bad enough, but the electoral count was worse. Harrison won 19 states for 234 electoral votes, and Van Buren took 7 states for a total of 60 votes.[31] A third-party candidate, James Birney, ran on an abolition ticket, called the Liberty party, and got 0.3 percent of the vote, or 7,053. What made the Democratic defeat so devastating was the length and breadth and depth of the Whig victory. Not only did the Whigs win states in every section of the country—indicating that the two-party system was now national at long last—and win every large state except Virginia, but they also captured the Congress. In the House the Whigs took 133 seats as against the Democrats 102; in the Senate the Whigs held 28 and the Democrats 22 seats.[32] Presumably the Whigs could now govern the nation according to "blue light federalist" principles, and dismantle all of Jackson's reform programs.

The Hero was devastated. "Corruption, bribery and fraud has been extended over the whole Union," he wailed. It was enough to shake the spirit of any man. Not Old Hickory, however. "The democracy of the United States have been shamefully beaten," he told Van Buren in an effort to comfort the defeated candidate, *"but I trust, not conquered."* As always he reaffirmed his faith in the virtue of "the unbought people of this Union" who will crush the Federalist notion that the electorate are incapable of self-government and must be ruled by a moneyed elite. The ultimate triumph of democracy, he said, depends on "the virtue of the great working class" who will resist being "ruled by the combined mony power of England and The Federalists of this Union." They will drive this "corrupt" pack back to "their native dunghills."[33]

Despite Jackson's limited but significant efforts in the campaign, despite the more vigorous involvement of such heavyweights as Benton, Wright, Buchanan, Polk, Grundy, and other Democrats—all organized under the masterful direction of Amos Kendall, who resigned as postmaster general to manage the campaign and edit an *Extra Globe*—Van Buren and his party went down to humiliating defeat. And the principal reason was the depression. Probably nothing and nobody could have overcome that liability. Too many men lost jobs. Too many bankruptcies occurred throughout Van Buren's administration. In short, too much economic hardship permeated the entire country. To some extent the "locofoco" policies of the Democrats also alienated voters. Locofocos got their name because they used "locofoco" matches to light candles during a New York meeting when conservative Democrats turned off the gas lights. Locofocos opposed corporations, monopolies, and imprisonment for debt. They also abhorred slavery, although they were not abolitionists. They favored specie and free trade, and condemned banks as the agents of corruption and elitism. Regarded as "radicals" by many, they were accused of advancing ideas and policies that delayed the economic recovery of the nation.[34]

For Jackson, the defeat of the Democratic party involved much greater implications than a political turnabout. To him it meant the possible scuttling of his economic reforms and the return of the money power bent on curbing the democratic thrust he had provided the nation.[35] He was certain that Clay would attempt to repeal the Independent Treasury and substitute a new national bank. And that, he said, had to be prevented at all costs. So Jackson campaigned among his many political friends and newspapers editors, urging them "to open the eyes of the American people to the danger with which they are now surrounded." Only then would their friends in Congress rally to the republican standard and protect the doctrines of their party. Only then would they resist "the corrupt doings of this wicked combination" to resurrect a national banking system. Only then would they "sit like brave men" and "die at their posts before they will deliver up the ship to the enemy."[36]

Jackson received a tremendous boost in his campaign to arouse the American public when in 1841 the Bank of the United States in Philadelphia went bankrupt and closed its doors. After the Bank's charter expired in 1836, Biddle had kept the Philadelphia branch operating by winning incorporation in Pennsylvania as a state bank at a cost of nearly $6 million. It was a terrible price to pay, particularly with a major depression in the offing, but Biddle had little choice. Then he borrowed heavily in Europe, which was another mistake; finally, he tried to corner the cotton market, but when cotton prices plummeted he was forced to draw on the Bank's credit until it disappeared. To maintain solvency, Biddle resorted to some questionable practices and thereby squandered what little remained of his prestige and reputation. Investors shed the Bank's stock; its price fell to $19 (it had once commanded well over $100) "but is really believed to be worth nothing," said one man.[37] On January 4, 1841, the remaining stockholders appointed a committee to investigate the condition of the Bank, and the report issued on April 4, 1841, exposed "frauds of a most stupendous and alarming character." With credit and reputation gone, the once mighty BUS closed its doors and in the process "brought ruin upon thousands." Wrote one man: "The Widow and the Orphan for whom these gentlemen professed so much feeling and sympathy have been fleeced by them in the most unmerciful manner."[38]

Nicholas Biddle had long since resigned as president, submitting his resignation two years earlier. The stockholders sued him for nearly a quarter of a million dollars, and later he was arrested on charges of criminal conspiracy. The court, however, subsequently exonerated him, although he was plagued by litigation virtually to the day he died.[39]

Around the country the Democratic press let out a cheer for Old Hickory, who had long warned of the Bank's nefarious operations and the certainty of its eventual demise. Even some Whigs credited Jackson with a measure of wisdom in identifying the hydra's wickedness and saving the federal government from its effects. "Many of your former enemies," the Hero was told, "who denounced you bitterly for the removal of the public deposites from that bank are now giving you great credit for your extraordinary caution and foresight in relation to that measure." As for Biddle, once the idol of the elite, he was now scorned by all honest and honorable men as though he were "a dangerous reptile."[40]

Jackson naturally rejoiced over this vindication. He felt like a prophet. Indeed, he was much given to prophesying during the last years of his life, particularly in political affairs. And he always reminded his correspondents of their accuracy when they proved true. But one event far beyond Jackson's powers to predict, and more startling than the collapse of Biddle's bank, occurred on Saturday, April 3, 1841, when President William Henry Harrison died suddenly.

Harrison had been in office hardly a month, and he had recently won confirmation of his cabinet and called a special session of Congress. He seemed healthy enough, but then he caught cold, ate and drank "enormously" to combat it, and succumbed to pneumonia. He was the first President to die in office.[41]

Jackson could barely disguise his delight when he heard the news. Predictably, he read Harrison's untimely death as a happy omen for the democracy. He praised "providence" for saving the nation from Whig misrule. "A kind and overuling providence has interfered to prolong our glorious Union and happy republican system which Genl. Harrison and his cabinet was preparing to destroy under the dictation of the profligate demagogue, Henry Clay." Jackson was sure that they planned to increase the debt, raise the tariff, and revive a national bank. All of which, Old Hickory said, "by the death of Harrison is blown sky high." Our happy system of republicanism is preserved, he exulted. *The Lord ruleth, let our nation rejoice.*[42]

The day following Harrison's death, John Tyler took office as President, and both parties waited anxiously to see what he would do. For Tyler was not a Whig. He could best be described as a states' rights Virginian. He had deserted the Democratic party on account of Jackson's vigorous exercise of presidential power, an exercise that Tyler felt had clearly violated the Constitution and threatened the liberty of the country. Ostensibly, he deserted because of the nullification controversy, although that was probably more excuse than reason. But now he sat in Jackson's chair and instead of serving as an acting President he said that he would be the actual President, exercising all the powers of his office.

Frank Blair worried that the new President would feel an obligation to keep Harrison's cabinet and allow Henry Clay to direct the government. "I fear that Tyler is such a poor weeping willow of a Creature," he told Jackson, "that he will resign all to the audacious depravity of the political black-leg." But Old Hickory was not so fearful. Naturally, he expected Clay to attempt another bank and to raise tariff rates, but he felt certain that Tyler's speeches and actions in the past committed him incontrovertibly to states' rights, and that he would oppose these monstrosities. "He cannot without abandoning all these professions of republican principles," argued the General, "sanction by approval any of these measures." And, said the Hero, under no circumstances could Tyler approve another bank bill without "perjuring" himself before the entire country. He was already on record as declaring the matter a violation of the Constitution. "How then can a President under such a solemn obligation approve a law creating a Bank without wilfull and corrupt perjury." He has the veto, said Jackson; he will use it.[43]

Although Blair continued to fret, claiming Tyler threw out "ambiguous voices" like a ventriloquist, Jackson reassured him that such ambiguity could not last long in the White House and that he "will have to unmask his principles." Besides, he said, there is a divine hand guiding the American people and protecting their "glorious Union."[44]

But more than anything else Jackson came to believe in the strength and power and perpetuity of democracy. That was the real hand protecting the "glorious Union." An experiment that had begun in 1789 as a republic, based on consent but providing safeguards against the exercise of absolute control by a majority, had evolved into a democracy. Under Jackson the concept of freedom became identified with majority rule. The system was now one in which elected officials were obliged to represent the people and execute their wishes. Perhaps Jackson said it best when he wrote: "The people are the government, administering it by their agents; they are the Government, the sovereighn power."[45]

CHAPTER 31

A Fading Taper

THE "BLACK-LEG" WASTED NO TIME IN LAUNCHING his national program. As soon as the special session of Congress convened on the last day of May, Henry Clay began engineering a repeal of the Independent Treasury, the creation of a new national bank, and a higher tariff. Audacious and autocratic, he soon earned the title "Dictator." Had he ever won the presidency, he surely would have out-Jacksoned Jackson as an autocrat.[1] Almost immediately he proposed a fiscal bill that established a central bank like the old BUS in the District of Columbia with power to establish branches within consenting states. Shortly thereafter a land bill, combining Clay's distribution plan with preemption, was also introduced. This bill permitted a squatter on government land to purchase 160 acres without competing for it. Ten percent of the proceeds from these sales would go to the state in which the land was located, the rest was to be distributed to all the states. However, should tariff rates exceed 20 percent, as they soon did, distribution would be suspended.[2]

When word of this intended legislation reached the Hermitage, along with the dictatorial manner of the "black-leg" in attempting to ram it through Congress, the General lost none of his confidence that the nation would somehow escape this corruption and folly. "Clay will not get his Bank bill passed," he predicted. "Tyler will veto it." And mark me, Jackson continued, when this happens those two worthies will be at "dagger's points" and the heterogeneous mass of unprincipled men who constitute the Whig party will "burst asunder" as though driven by the four winds of heaven. There will "scarcely be a wreck left behind," he concluded.[3]

Jackson radiated confidence. Part of his bright tone and happy spirits during the late spring and early summer of 1841 resulted from his improved state of health. The hemorrhages had diminished and he coughed less. Of course he knew that these remissions were temporary and that at any moment he could be prostrated by a sudden attack. Indeed, one morning in early July, Jackson sat down to breakfast and, he said, "as I was raising the fork to my mouth I was struck. Like as it was a thunderbolt through my left breast and shoulder." The pain was excruciating. Then a second shock bolted him to his feet. Aid was quickly summoned and when he regained his breath, "the lancet was applied but no blood could be obtained until my right arm was immersed in very hot water." For eight hours, he told Frank Blair, "I suffered more pain than through all my life." He mended very slowly from this apparent heart attack, with "frequent returns of pain." What surprised him most of all, however, was the steadiness of his nerves, even though "I am much debilitated in body and a perfect skeleton."[4]

The news of Jackson's latest collapse frightened his many friends in Washington, who were all certain he could never survive it. They were dumbfounded when he "fooled" them again and pulled through. They were so surprised that they congregated at Blair's house and demanded to see the familiar scrawl of his most recent communication so "that they might read in the characters of your autograph," Blair told him, "the assurance of the continuation of your powers." Even John C. Calhoun and Francis Pickens—mark that!—came and expressed their "satisfaction" over the General's recovery. Blair said that he felt much inclined to "throw the veil of oblivion" over the past and take Calhoun's "present powerful agency" in fighting the money power as more than "indemnity" for his past misdeeds.[5]

Jackson agreed. Always the practical politician, he never refused a proffered hand of support when accompanied by obvious indications of sincere contrition. "I am happy to learn that Mr. Calhoun is got right; god send that he may continue so. . . . If Mr. Calhoun remains firm, I am sure I will not throw the least shade over him, *to err is human, to forgive divine.*"[6]

But that black-leg, "that roaming, lying demagogue, Clay," to him forgiveness was not extended, not while he still persevered in his abominable scheme to revive the monster bank. And the black-leg almost succeeded. On August 6, 1841, Congress passed the fiscal bank bill and sent it to the President. Tyler waited the full ten days permitted by the Constitution and then vetoed the bill on August 16.[7]

The Democrats cheered. A number of them wrote to Jackson and thanked him—as though he were responsible for Tyler's action—"that the torrent of Federalism has been turned back." "None of us forget you," wrote one. Everywhere, at every public turn and corner, wherever "old fashioned Democrats" gathered together, a cry could be heard: "It will do Old Hickory's heart good when he hears of the Veto." One "old

Jacksonian," when he heard of Tyler's act, burst out, "Egad, he has found one of old Jackson's pens and it wouldn't write any way but plain and straitforward."[8]

Old Hickory was indeed gratified by the veto. "The whole republican democratic party will sustain him throout the union," he said of Tyler. But he had long predicted a presidential veto of the bill and took exquisite pleasure in pointing this out to his friends. But more needed to be done, he said. He wanted Tyler to veto the distribution bill because it was "a palbable violation of the Constitution."[9]

The Whigs were enraged over the veto and some of them blamed Clay because he had acted so arbitrarily and had refused for a time to accede to any of the President's objections to the bill. So they quickly constructed a new bill which they hoped would overcome the President's objections. And they wrote it without Clay's involvement. Still Tyler would have none of it. On September 9 he vetoed again. However, it is quite possible that this second veto was more a political act intended to assist the formation of a new party based on states' rights that would rally behind Tyler and reelect him in 1844.[10]

Unfortunately, Tyler did not follow through and veto the distribution bill or the repeal of the Independent Treasury. Jackson was deeply disappointed by these failures. If the Whigs fail to repeal the distribution law, he predicted, "the people will shew them that they are the sovereign power, and will soon return them . . . to their native dunghills, as wicked & corrupt servants." The Whigs, led by Henry Clay, he said, are determined to create an awesome national debt—it had already ballooned to $13.5 million by 1842—and the American people will never suffer a national debt in time of peace. "It allway endangers a Republican government by increasing arristocracy," he wrote, "which is allway dangerous to liberty."[11] As for the repeal of the Independent Treasury, he felt that Tyler erred in not vetoing it. Had the President "posponed" the repeal until some other fiscal system had been adopted and "vetoed that act *of abomination and corruption,*" the distribution bill, then Tyler would have been "the most popular man in the Union, and would have raised for himself a fame as durable as a monument of brass."[12] Instead, Tyler waffled both ways and only succeeded in disgruntling both sides. Jackson's confidence in Tyler's "democratic and state right principles" remained high but he wished that the President had a better understanding of the government's obligations to business and labor.

> The duty of the government is to leave commerce to its own capital and credit as well as all other branches of business, protecting all in their legal pursuits, granting exclusive privileges to none. Foster the labour of our country by an undeviating metalic currency for its surpluss, allways recollecting that if labour is depressed neither commerce or manufactures, can flourish, as they are both based upon the production of labour, produced from the earth, or the mineral world. It is unjust then by Legislation to

depress labour by a depreciated currency with the idea of prospering commerce etc. which is in reallity injured by it.[13]

Only when bankers and merchants and industrialists are left to operate on their own capital and credit, without any interference or assistance from the government, can there be true harmony within the economic sector of society. The government must protect all in equal measure, said Jackson, *"granting exclusive privileges to none,"* and "we will then have purity of Legislation by Congress and not before."[14]

Tyler is surrounded by a cabinet, the General declared, that "has no stability of principle, and in heart, hates every thing that wears the appearance of democracy."[15] Again and again Jackson expressed his concern for democracy at this critical time because Whigs, abolitionists, and nullifiers hated it with a passion and wanted to discredit it in order to revive privilege and aristocracy.

Tyler's vetoes worked marvelously for the Democrats, for they split the Whig party from top to bottom. The entire cabinet, with the exception of the secretary of state, Daniel Webster, resigned. On the day Congress adjourned its special session, a large body of Whig congressmen issued an address that read Tyler out of the party.

All of which Jackson received with intense satisfaction. "Federalism with its cooneries and modern Whigeries is down forever," he wrote, "and our republican system will long endure."[16] This upswing in political affairs somewhat compensated for his sagging personal and fiscal problems, problems that grew more severe with each passing month.

Last year's cotton crop had been a failure and the price of land as well as cotton was abysmally low. Jackson even considered selling some of his slaves—he claimed to have "one hundred and fifty odd negroes, old and young large and small"—but if he sold at this time it would be "at a great sacrafice."[17] He also had to contend with his son's debts and incompetence. Andrew was now a man of thirty-three years, but he continued to behave like an irresponsible child, hell-bent on squandering a fortune. He ended up losing everything Jackson left him, including the Hermitage.[18]

At the moment, the General desperately needed cash and so he was forced to borrow once again. He therefore authorized William B. Lewis, who still held his government position in Washington, to negotiate a loan of $6,000 for six years from David Henshaw, late collector of Boston, who had heard reports of Jackson's "pecuniary embarrassments" and contacted Lewis with an offer of $8,000 or $10,000 to relieve the Hero of *"immediate* pressure."[19] Unfortunately, as it turned out, Henshaw could loan the money only for two years, which was too short a time period to suit Jackson's needs. Meanwhile, General Jean B. Plauché, veteran of the New Orleans campaign, insisted on the "honor" of lending his old commander $6,000, although it meant mortgaging his own property to make the loan. He asked for no guarantee, not even a signature. But at Jackson's insistence he finally agreed to accept a note signed jointly by father and son. He said he did not wish to lose "the only opportunity which has ever presented itself of being agreeable to you." So Jackson took the loan —indeed, he had little choice—and when Plauché subsequently provided a letter of credit for $7,000 the grateful Hero declined the additional funds.[20]

It annoyed Jackson that his "pecuniary embarrassments" had become generally known, particularly because they were distorted by the Whig press to ruin his credit. He insisted he was not "broke" and that these individual arrangements meant he could retain his property.[21]

Word of Jackson's financial distress reached as far away as Peru, where the chargé, James C. Pickett, read about it and immediately proposed to Frank Blair that the General's friends pay off all the debts. He authorized Blair to include him in any such arrangement and to let him know the size of his obligation. "I mention this only," Blair told Jackson, "to give you proof how much you are loved by men whom you have probably forgotten." As for cash, Blair continued, "I can lend you as much as you want." The government owed him and his partner, John C. Rives, $20,000, and as soon as the appropriation bill passed—and he expected it to pass very soon—he could oblige Jackson for as much as $10,000.[22]

The old man was overwhelmed. It was said that he burst into tears when he received Blair's offer.[23] He admitted that he was under considerable pressure and had already sacrificed some valuable property.[24] If Blair could lend him $10,000 for three or four years he would gladly pay 6 or 7 percent interest. It will be secured in such a way, he promised, that neither life nor death "nor all the calamities that may befall a nation, or individuals, except earthquakes," could jeopardize the principal and interest.[25] "I need not say to you," the Hero gushed, "that act of liberality and friendship, has overwhelmed my heart with gratitude to you." For his seventy-fifth birthday on March 15, 1842, it was no doubt the best birthday present he could possibly receive.[26]

Jackson secured the loan with a mortgage on the Halcyon Plantation and for "thirty odd negroes." In the event of his "early" death, he also added a codicil to his will "making all my property real personal or mixed, subject to the payment of this debt." Jackson and his son agreed to start paying the interest on March 4, 1843, and a third of the principal on March 4, 1844. Another third would be paid on March 4, 1845, and the remaining principal and interest on March 4, 1846.[27] Jackson received the money in Treasury notes on May 31, 1842, and in gratitude he sent Blair's daughter a filly out of one of his blooded mares which he called "Miss Emuckfau" after his celebrated victory over the Creek Indians.[28]

As a further means of assisting Jackson, a number of his friends in Congress, led by the senator from Missouri, Dr. Lewis F. Linn, agreed to sponsor a bill to restore to him the $1,000 fine plus interest and costs imposed on him in New Orleans in 1815 by Judge Dominick Hall. This, said Senator Benton, was "by way of expunging that sentence from the judicial records of the country."[29] Jackson was characteristically very sensitive about the fine. He had paid it in 1815 and, over the years, had stubbornly refused every offer by private individuals to refund it. The fine was a smear on his otherwise shining military record at New Orleans, he said, imposed by a tyrant who denied him his constitutional right of self-defense, and Jackson wanted the United States government to repudiate Hall's action so that future military officers would know that their government protected them "from the Tyranny and oppression of vindictive judges."[30]

The introduction of the Linn proposal in the Senate touched off a partisan free-for-all between Whigs and Democrats. The Whigs said they were willing to refund the fine (rather than risk the political consequence of an outright refusal) but they insisted that it be done "by special grace," implying the justice of the charges against Jackson and the propriety of Hall's fine. So they amended Linn's measure, whereupon the Democrats properly and promptly killed the entire bill. "You judge rightly of my feelings," Jackson wrote to Blair, "when you say I would not touch one cent of the money under that odious and insulting amended bill, and those who proposed the amendment, if they possessed any honorable feelings knew that I would starve before I would be fed upon their *especial grace* and at the expense of my honor and my fame. . . . When I approach Congress it is to demand justice, not to beg it. I only appeal to my god for acts of special grace, not to man."[31]

Jackson was terribly depressed by the antics of Congress, not simply because the members had denied him the justice he deserved but because their debates and actions at times verged on the bizarre and the dangerous. John Quincy Adams, for example, was up to his old tricks again. He introduced into the House a petition from forty-six Massachusetts citizens that Congress adopt measures to dissolve the Union. He asked that the document go to a select committee to draft a response explaining why the petition ought not be granted. Many Democrats regarded this spite as the willful ploy of a crazy old man who ought to be censured. He desired nothing more than to stir up trouble in Congress, they said, and pitch the nation into sectional strife. Adams may have considered his motion a grand joke to make some dubious point about the freedom of petition but in point of fact he deliberately raised tensions between sections that could endanger the life of the Union.[32]

Jackson shook his head in dismay. "What disgraceful scenes in congress," he wrote. "Is Mr Adams demented, or is he perversely wicked. Both, I think, and Adams ought to be confined to a hospital."[33]

The General also watched with a sense of foreboding the portentous events transpiring in Rhode Island. Early in 1841 Thomas W. Dorr led a rebellion against the state's franchise law of 1724 which restricted the suffrage to property holders. He and his supporters framed a People's Constitution, abolished limited franchise, and set up a new government with Dorr as governor. They successfully stormed the arsenal at Providence, whereupon martial law was declared by state officials under the old colonial charter. Eventually the Dorr rebellion was put down and Dorr himself seized and sentenced to life imprisonment.[34]

As far as Jackson was concerned these events in Rhode Island only provided additional proof that an aristocracy stood ready to strike down any movement or activity that bore the slightest "appearance of democracy."[35] Over and over in his letters he reiterated the inevitability and absolute justice of majority rule.

> The people of Rhode Island will triumph as they ought in Establishing their republican constitution and that state will hoist the republic banner and democracy will triumph there. Surely it cannot be that the U. States will aid the aristocracy of Rhode Island to continue the charter of charles the 2nd when bound to gurantee the Republican form of Government to every state in the Union. If the President should be weak anough to order a regular force to sustain the charter against the peoples constitution a hundred thousand of the sovereign people would fly to the rescue to sustain the peoples constitution, as it would be an act by the Executive, hostile to the principles upon which our republican government is based. The people are the sovereign power and agreable to our system they have the right to alter and amend their system of Government when a majority wills it, as a majority have a right to rule.[36]

As Jackson predicted, democracy eventually triumphed. Dorr was released by an act of the Democratic legislature after a year in prison and electoral reforms were engrafted upon a more equitable constitution.

All of these political and financial woes sharply aggravated Jackson's physical condition. Throughout the winter and spring of 1842 he suffered constant pain in his head and ears, and his eyesight got worse. For the next three years he continued to go downhill gradually but steadily, and it was all rather sad. "I am like a taper," he wrote. Just as it is about to flicker out it will suddenly "blaze up again for a time." But, as Blair reminded him, strength of spirit more than compensated for "the want of bodily vigor. Your life is of the soul, more than the body."[37]

About the only bright moment during the spring of 1842 was the visit to the Hermitage of Martin Van Buren. The ex-President decided to take a fence-mending political swing around the country in preparation for the 1844 presidential contest and nothing could serve his political designs better than a visit with the Hero of New Orleans to receive the General's blessings on his campaign. Jackson advised him to come via Mobile and New Orleans and thereby "have a birds eye view of the vally on the Mississippi." Van Buren planned to make the tour in company with James K. Paulding, the writer and former secretary of the navy.[38] Although he first planned to take his son, Martin, the plans were eventually changed.

Van Buren arrived in Nashville with his party on April 25, 1842, and was received with more enthusiasm than might have been expected, considering all the criticism heaped on him during the last campaign. Jackson himself was delighted with the reception. "Instead of a dwarf dutchman, a little dandy who you might lift in a bandbox," he wrote, "the people found him a plain man of middle size, plain and affable."[39] The ex-President proceeded directly to the Hermitage where Old Hickory warmly greeted him. He stayed several weeks and during his visit received many marks of Jackson's "benevolent kindness and unbounded hospitality." The General had hoped to accompany his guest on the next leg of his tour—at least as far as Columbus, Ohio—but continued "debility from sickness" and "great afflictions in my head & ears" forced him to forgo this "pleasure."[40] When Van Buren reached Lexington, Kentucky, he was met by Henry Clay, who "respectfully and kindly" inquired about Jackson's health. Clay had himself resigned from the Senate to prepare for the presidential canvass in 1844.[41]

The General's sense of well-being improved considerably when President Tyler vetoed the so-called Little Tariff Bill on June 29. This measure extended the rates of the Compromise Tariff of 1833 for one month beyond July 1 at which time, under the provisions of that act, the rates would have been reduced to 20 percent. The purpose of the extension was to ensure the distribution of the proceeds from the sale of public lands among the states. The veto further alienated Tyler from the Whig party, but Jackson credited him with taking the just and proper course of action. The General said he now lived for the day "when Whiggery, with all its evils, will be troden down, and democracy over the whole Union triumphant."[42] So pleased was he with Tyler's performance as President that he wrote him on August 18 and congratulated him on preserving the principles of republicanism which they both revered. Tyler's response was delayed because of the death of his wife, but his eventual reply conveyed his sincere appreciation for Jackson's understanding and support. "The plaudits of the multitude," Tyler wrote, "have now received the endorsement of the sage in his closet, and I shall with renewed resolution continue to so battle under the principles which distinguished our republican forefathers, believing that it is only by doing so that the blessings of civil liberty can be handed down to a remote posterity." He hoped Jackson would write as often as his health would permit and said he would be flattered to receive any suggestions from him "relative to the conduct of public affairs."[43]

The sage—as many, like Tyler, now called Jackson—was less pleased with the outcome of the Webster-Ashburton Treaty, which at long last settled the northeast border between Maine and Canada. Something like 12,000 square miles had been in dispute and this treaty arranged a settlement by which the United States received approximately 7,000 square miles. Jackson felt the nation had been cheated. He called it an "odious" treaty. Not only was it "disgraceful, but humiliating to our National character and humbling us in dust and ashes." This treaty was less favorable by almost 900 square miles from the one awarded by the King of the Netherlands in 1831. At the time William P. Preble, U.S. minister to the Netherlands, argued against accepting the award. So, too, had Jackson's cabinet. "I yielded to this recommendation," the sage declared, "but sincerely have I regretted it since. . . . But it has passed away, and our country is now to be humbled by a disgraceful treaty." At least, he said, if the St. John River had been designated as the boundary line there would have been some "resiprosity in it."[44]

More satisfactory to him was the recovery of the Democratic party in the fall elections of 1842, particularly in New York, Ohio, and Pennsylvania. He predicted a great victory in 1844 and the continued spread of democracy around the country. "How I rejoice in the results of the late Election," he wrote to Blair. "Whiggery is done and Clay will now *surely* retire to Ashland and take care of his *short horned Durhams, cut his corn stalks and repair his fences.* He is really a *dead Coon.*"[45]

Increasingly, throughout the closing months of 1842, Jackson concerned himself with the approaching presidential election. He was totally committed to Van Buren as the Democratic candidate and he assured his little friend that all the gossip about his endorsing Calhoun or anyone else was just so much idle talk. "I have . . . said, that the candidate of the democracy must be selected by a national convention fresh from the people, and may he be whom he may, the democracy must unite upon him." He hoped that person would be Martin Van Buren, "the people having now been convinced," he told the Magician, "that you were slandered & defrauded out of your election." "Frauds the most dire," he rumbled, "calumnies the most unfounded & vile and humbugery, most disgraceful to our national character"—these were the causes of Van Buren's defeat, and they "have demorolised our citizens over our whole country."[46]

Jackson felt he must make a public statement to assist Van Buren in the approaching election, and he figured it could be "done without giving any room for an attack upon me by interfering in the election." He asked Donelson for help in the composition of the statement and, as usual, provided the necessary guidelines to what he wanted written. Say something "such as this," he wrote: "Martin Van Buren, the states man, patriot, and pure republican allway sustaining the constitution agreable to the powers expressly granted to the general government, and protecting the reserved rights to the states, & to the people—he deserves the confidence of the democracy of these United States—he has never proved false to them."[47]

The General also hoped that his friend James K. Polk would complete the Democratic ticket. Already some communities in southern states had proposed his name for the second slot in their local meetings. Regrettably, Polk had been defeated the previous year for reelection as governor of Tennessee by "Lean Jimmy" Jones, a clownish incompetent who nonetheless had learned all the right political lessons from the Log Cabin campaign and worked them into a 3,000-vote margin of victory. Jackson was outraged by the "apathy of the Democracy" in permitting such nonsense to transpire. "Govr. Polk deserves the thanks of the Democracy of the whole union," Jackson pointedly remarked to Van Buren, "he fought the battle well & fought it alone."[48]

A Van Buren–Polk ticket struck Jackson as a shrewd balance that would excite the approval of the "Democracy of the union" and bring victory in 1844. He doubted that he would live to see another inauguration, but if he did and Van Buren was elected, "I would cheerfully go on," he wrote, "take my constitution carriage and take him in it, to the capitol to be inaugurated." One reason for his doubts about surviving until March 4, 1845, apart from his usual run of hemorrhages and the like, was the fact that he sustained a bad accident when a "careless driver" upset the carriage in which he was riding with Major Donelson and his new wife, Elizabeth Martin Randolph. Because of his "debility," Jackson was the only passenger to sustain any real injury, and had the horses taken fright, "not one of us could have escaped death," he told Blair, "or great injury." He was a tough old bird, even though battered and worn and over seventy-five years of age. "Providence still protects me," he chuckled.[49]

Blair said that the accident reminded him of the time when they sailed down the Chesapeake Bay on their way toward the Rip Raps with George Washington Parke Custis, the grandson of Martha Washington. A storm threatened and Custis remarked that he feared he could never make his annual trip down the Bay without some disaster taking place. Old Hickory turned to him, a quizzical look on his face. "My good friend," the General said, "you never travelled with me." Custis immediately presumed that Jackson was comparing himself to Julius Caesar, who, when warned by a pilot about putting out to sea in a storm, replied: "Why do you fear, you carry Caesar." But that had not been Jackson's intent at all. He simply believed in his own good "luck" to see him through any emergency. He believed in himself and in his destiny.[50]

The strong likelihood that Jackson's days were numbered—something the old man had been anticipating for decades at least—prompted Blair to query him about his will, particularly the disposition of his papers. At length Jackson agreed to place the entire corpus of his papers in Blair's safekeeping and he drew up a new will dated September 1, 1842. This superseded the one executed on September 30, 1833. In his will the General said that he desired to be buried next to his "dear departed wife" in the vault prepared in the garden of the Hermitage. He wanted all his just debts paid out of his estate—and he named the $6,000 debt to Plauché and the $10,000 due Blair and Rives. He bequeathed the Hermitage to his son, along with all his slaves except for two boys whom he gave to his grandsons and four female slaves whom he left to Sarah. This last bequest recognized Sarah's "great kindness to me on all occasions, and particularly when I have been sick, and greatly debilitated she has watched over me with great kindness."[51]

Not a single slave did Jackson free, not even his own manservant, George. True, manumission was incredibly difficult in Tennessee by the 1840s; but for a man who cared so deeply about freedom he had no conception that it might apply to black people. In that respect he resembled many of his contemporaries. In view of his background, temperament, and experience, perhaps it is expecting too much to presume that he could move beyond the accepted standards of his time and location and accord justice to his servants. He probably would have been offended —if not outraged—had anyone recommended such action to him.

His other bequests involved some of his prized possessions. To Andrew J. Donelson he left the elegant sword given him by the state of Tennessee, and to his grandnephew, Andrew J. Coffee, he gave the sword presented by the rifle company of New Orleans. Another sword presented by the citizens of Philadelphia went to his grandson and namesake. The gold box presented by New York and the large silver vase given by the ladies of Charleston, South Carolina, his native state, were left in trust to his son "with directions that should our happy country not be blessed with peace . . . he will at the end of the war . . . present each . . . to that patriot residing in the city or state from whence they were presented, who shall be adjudged by his countrymen to have been the most valient in defence of his country and her rights." It was not a war between the states that Jackson anticipated in making this bequest. Rather he worried that Great Britain would create trouble on one pretext or another in order to humiliate the United States. The recent "odious" treaty was a case in point in which this country paid dearly in lost territory. But there were other events to indicate that a war might be brewing. The *Creole* incident, for example, in which slaves mutinied aboard an American ship and gained their freedom by sailing it into a British port; and the *Carolina* incident. "To cap the climax," he said, "an entangling alience with great britain to surpress the slave trade, *by a fleet of eighty guns,* which will cost us at least half a million per annum—and this to insult France our friend —and abandoning our independence by an entangled allience with great Britain." And what should we do about it? We should demand restoration of the slaves seized aboard the *Creole,* he responded, or obtain an "ample indemnity"; we should inform the British that "we will make reprisals" in the future and that "we are determined to sustain our nations rights & independence at all hazzards." Such strong language and measures will give us peace, he insisted; "a temporising policy will at last lead to war." So, if and when the war came, Jackson wanted his prizes to be awarded to those patriots who had displayed the greatest valor in defending the country and her rights.[52]

The final article of Jackson's will disposed of the pistols given him by General Lafayette. These pistols had been presented to Lafayette by George Washington and Colonel William Robertson, and Jackson now bequeathed them to Lafayette's son. In conclusion, he named his son as executor. The will was witnessed by Marion Adams, Richard Smith, and Thomas J. Donelson.[53]

Jackson revised this will ten months later when, on June 7, 1843, he added another bequest to recognize his high regard for General Robert Armstrong, who had fought with him at the Battle of Enotachopco Creek during the Creek War.[54] To Armstrong he left his case of pistols and the sword he had worn throughout his military career. His walking canes "and other relics" he left to his son to be distributed to relatives who were his namesakes, beginning with "my esteemed nephew" Andrew J. Donelson, who was to be given first choice. This June 7 revision also added two more witnesses: Elizabeth D. Love and Robert Armstrong.[55]

Not much later while walking in the garden with Major Lewis, Jackson informed his friend that he was leaving his entire estate, with small exceptions, to his son. Knowing the son's incompetence, Lewis objected as tactfully as possible, suggesting that part of the property ought to be left to Sarah and the children in order to protect them from Andrew's mismanagement.

"No," responded Jackson after a long pause, "that would show a want of confidence. If *she*"—pointing with his cane to the tomb in the garden —"were alive, she would wish him to have it all, and to me her wish is law."[56]

Nothing was said in either will about Jackson's papers, probably because they lacked monetary value and because their disposition had already been settled. Kendall was supposed to come to the Hermitage at this time to pick them up but he could not leave Washington because he was involved in a lawsuit over a fraudulent claim by two postal contractors during his tenure as Jackson's postmaster general. Instead he sent his wife's nephew, James A. McLaughlin, to the Hermitage to examine and arrange the papers for Kendall's future use in preparing Jackson's biography. The General agreed to this switch in plans and offered his friend any help he could in fighting the lawsuit. Your "stern and unflinching honesty," he wrote, "saved millions of the money of the government from the rapacious hands of contractors."[57]

McLaughlin arrived at the Hermitage early in December, 1842. But even before his arrival, Jackson had begun selecting the documents which he felt would be useful in reconstructing his life. He was particularly diligent in sorting out the materials relating to his quarrel with John Sevier, the North Carolina land frauds, his "affray" with the Bentons, his duel with Dickinson, and the materials dealing with various aspects of his military career. Unfortunately, he had no maps or diagrams of his New Orleans campaign, nor any early likenesses of himself or Rachel. They had been burned in the fire. But he promised Kendall to work up plans of his principal battles with the Indians "in such form as you can understand it." His aide during the Creek War, Major John Reid, kept a journal of all his military operations, he said, but "it is lost, and a great Loss it is to the history of my operations against the Indians and British in the late war."[58]

The Jackson family was quite taken with young McLaughlin and the General said he was "much pleased" with his diligence and attention to the difficult task of sorting through a huge mass of manuscripts. McLaughlin worked "from breakfast to bed time" and soon gathered piles of material which were boxed and shipped to Kendall. Unfortunately these documents said little about Jackson's private life and Kendall requested that the General take pen in hand and write down some of his earliest recollections. McLaughlin helped. Several times he interviewed Jackson about particular events and wrote them up in narrative form and sent them to his uncle. Out of these reminiscences and narratives came new documents describing the General's early experiences during and immediately following the Revolution.[59]

Once Kendall received this material and began writing his biography he had many questions to ask about specific events, and he wrote the General or McLaughlin almost daily.[60] Jackson obliged as much as his health allowed and even assisted in the preparation of a map of the Waxhaw settlement which showed the location of his birthplace, various Revolutionary War battlegrounds, and the spot where Jackson was imprisoned during the War.[61] McLaughlin remained at the Hermitage for three months and came away deeply impressed by the hardship and suffering that characterized much of Jackson's life. He marveled at the General's powers of survival. "What a picture of patience, courage and endurance of hardship does this scene afford!" he wrote to Kendall in relating the numerous times Jackson crossed the wilderness between Knoxville and Nashville after his arrival in Tennessee. Some of these exploits defied belief.[62]

Kendall advised McLaughlin to use the opportunity in Nashville to interview some of the participants in the events of Jackson's early life, particularly Generals William Carroll and Robert Armstrong. McLaughlin followed through on these instructions, but Carroll refused to cooperate, apparently intending to write his own book of reminiscences. "He is a complete old gossip," wrote McLaughlin to Kendall, "all talk and no action."[63]

Jackson assisted in obtaining some of General John Coffee's military papers. Alexander Coffee sent two bundles of his father's papers to Jackson, almost all of which dealt with the Creek War and the Battle of New Orleans. Practically all of these were forwarded directly to Kendall.[64] Because Jackson was extremely reluctant to hazard these papers to the vagaries of the United States postal system under his frank, he importuned any friend headed for Washington to deliver a bundle to Kendall. On one occasion, J. G. Harris, editor of the Nashville *Union*, carried a trunk load of the General's papers to Washington.[65] Before he was done, Old Hickory had conveyed an enormous collection of his manuscripts, running into the thousands.

Kendall busied himself writing the biography throughout the winter of 1842–1843, and in February publicly announced that he intended to publish a life of General Andrew Jackson in fifteen or more numbers. This biography, he said, carried the approbation of Old Hickory himself, who had placed in his hands books and papers, both private and public. It was Kendall's intention to bring out the first number in May and then, if his health permitted, to issue a number each month thereafter.[66]

Kendall was unable to keep to his schedule. Not until the following October, 1843, did he issue the first number and present Jackson with a copy.[67] Six additional numbers appeared at irregular times thereafter before Kendall tired of the work or became preoccupied with other matters, such as his later involvement with Samuel F. B. Morse's telegraph company. He never got any further than the conclusion of the Creek War in 1814. Worse, he used virtually none of the rich manuscript material in his possession. Almost all of the dozen odd citations which appeared in the text came from several small volumes of "Letters and Orders" containing copies of military letters and general orders. It was a phenomenal waste of resources and added little to the story of Jackson's life currently available in the Reid and Eaton biography.[68]

Jackson read at least five (and possibly all seven) numbers of the work before he died. From time to time he noted errors that had crept into the text and informed Kendall of them.[69] After Kendall abandoned the biography he neglected to turn the papers over to Blair as Jackson had directed him to do. Blair was therefore obliged to ask Andrew, Jr., to write to Kendall and prod him into compliance. By that time Blair and Kendall had had a falling out, and ceased corresponding. The difficulty began during the initial writing of the biography. Gossips distorted irritations, which soon produced bitter words. For one thing Kendall never felt adequately compensated for his role in founding the *Globe,* and after he began the publication of his own Washington newspaper, the *Expositor,* the two editors became rivals for the printing patronage. Then, too, Kendall said he would support Tyler if the presidential election in 1844 turned into a Tyler versus Clay contest, rather than the expected Van Buren versus Clay, and Blair responded by saying he would have nothing to do with "prostitutes" who followed in Tyler's train.[70]

Jackson tried to mediate between the two men because both were his friends and both had served him well. Without taking sides he urged the two men to close their ears to the "poison" of "secrete busy bodys" who would delight in causing a breach between them. *"Let it die,"* he pleaded, *"and rest in oblivion."*[71] He begged them to have a personal interview and calmly discuss the matter. As usual, Jackson ultimately saw the dispute as a conspiracy against himself. "There are evil spirits at work secretely to put down the Globe," he told Blair, "and whatever pretext may be held forth the real secrete cause is, that the Globe has sustained me; and Mr Van Buren, carrying out the same principle." These "evil spirits" planned to manipulate the quarrel in order to crack the democracy, divide the party, and punish Andrew Jackson. As for supporting Tyler, the General tended to agree with Blair's position—at least temporarily. He would not exclude Tyler forever from the party. "We are all willing that Mr. Tyler should retire from his administration with credit for his good acts," he said, "but not to make him head of the Democratic church until he gives evidence of real repentance for his course in 1840."[72]

Blair and Kendall ran into one another at Dr. Linn's place. There was an awkward moment, but then the two men shook hands. "To gratify your wishes upon the subject," Blair wrote Jackson, "I would sacrifice any motive, however strong, which might urge me to pursue a controversy with him."[73] But the handshake did not repair the torn friendship and the two men never completely reconciled, much to Jackson's intense regret.

The developing estrangement between his two friends was not the only misery Jackson suffered during 1843. His health continued its downward trend and he remained confined to his room throughout the entire winter. Later he suffered attacks of "billous collic, and coloramorbis," which, he told Major Lewis, "nearly carried me hence."[74] His financial situation also deteriorated and he was obliged to ask Blair and Rives to postpone for a year the installment of their loan to him due in May, 1844. "Note that this indulgence is only asked if it can be done without injury or inconvenience to you, *not else.*" He offered to loan Blair a family of ten slaves to make it up to him. So desperate was he for cash that he instructed Andrew J. Donelson to sell some of his prize horses for ridiculously low prices. He offered one filly for $400 but reckoned that "she is worth really $1000 to a sportman."[75]

But worse than the condition of his health and pocketbook were the blows of the "chastening rod" that struck down several loved ones. Over the last few years Jackson lost a favorite ward, a loyal friend, and a grandchild. Andrew Jackson Hutchings, Jr. was the first. He died of tuberculosis on January 15, 1841, aged twenty-eight years, despite the "matchless sanative," and other remedies prescribed by "Dr." Jackson. Hutchings's death surely caused the General intense grief. In the past few years the old man had grown very close to his former ward, and he wrote to him frequently in much the same tone he once wrote to his good friend John Coffee. Toward the end Jackson tried desperately to help the young man, and the thought of all the tragedy and disappointments Hutchings suffered during his short life, especially the loss of his young wife, no doubt heightened Jackson's sorrow.

The loss of his friend and staunch supporter in Congress, Dr. Lewis F.

Linn, senator from Missouri, was another blow. His death, wrote the General, "has thrown me into a gloom for several days." But the worst and most devastating tragedy came with the death of Andrew's and Sarah's fifth child, Robert Armstrong Jackson. This was the second of their children to die. Another son, Thomas, was born prematurely on August 18, 1841, and died the same day.[76]

Robert Armstrong Jackson was sickly from birth, suffered constantly from colic, and died on November 11, 1843, barely four months and twenty-three days old. The end was frightful. It was, said Jackson, "the first time in my life that I witnessed the pangs of a mother being separated from a darling child from her breast." What made it worse was the absence of the child's father in Mississippi. The full brunt of this terrible tragedy fell directly on the aged Hero. "It was the most distressing scene I ever witnessed," he said. He wept throughout most of the night.[77]

CHAPTER 32

"We Must Regain Texas"

IF THE YEAR 1843 ENDED IN TRAGEDY the new year began on a note of triumph. After years of wrangling, the Whigs accepted the unique place Jackson had come to occupy in the affections of the American people and withdrew their objections to the bill to restore to the "Sage of the Hermitage" the fine imposed on him by Judge Hall in 1815. Although Dr. Linn had died a few months earlier, his place in the drive for restitution was assumed by C. J. Ingersoll of Pennsylvania, once an important lawyer for Biddle during the Bank War. No humiliating amendments were added to the bill to outrage Jackson and force him to refuse the money. It was a straightforward bill of restitution and included both the principal and interest. It passed the House on January 8, the anniversary of the Battle of New Orleans, by a vote of 158 to 28. The selection of this date was prearranged by Ingersoll, Wright, and Benton.

Jackson was very gratified. "I feel grateful to my friends in the House of Representatives," he wrote, "for doing me that Justice to which I was entitled by wiping from my memory that unjust imputation bestowed upon it by a wicked & corrupt Judge." Not much later the Senate approved the bill on February 10 by a vote of 30 to 16. "Will you have the goodness," Jackson asked Blair, "to present my good wishes to Col King, Benton, Allen, Wright, Walker, Buchanan and Dawson and all my democratic friends in the Senate and the House of Representatives, being too many to enumerate, do not forget to present my gratitude to the Honble C. J. Ingersol for his disinterested and unsolicited labour." But above all else, he felt especially grateful to the American people. "The democracy has produced this Justice to me," he wrote.[1]

Blair agreed. The bill, he said, was "wrung from a reluctant Tory senate by the voice of people. . . . Some poor devils skulked, some apologized, some denied the rights of instruction yet felt their consciences so mollified by the force of public opinion, that they voted for it against their convictions and wishes!!"[2]

The instant the bill was handed to Tyler, he signed it. Then he penned a letter of congratulations to Jackson in which he said that the legislation offered new evidence of the high esteem which the country placed on his manifold and invaluable services. Nothing now remained to "sully, in any degree, the glory of the memorable defence" of New Orleans.[3]

The entire nation—except for the dwindling few whose hatred for Jackson would yield him nothing—applauded the action. Like the Hero, they took enormous pride in the victory over the British at New Orleans and resented anything that tended to tarnish it. The action by Congress, they agreed, honored both the nation and the Hero himself.

Across Broadway in New York City a banner was stretched.

> ### JUSTICE TO THE BRAVE
> Judge Hall's
> Sentence on
> **GENL JACKSON**
> Repudiated by the
> Nation
> Feb. 14th 1844[4]

On Tuesday evening, February 27, 1844, Jackson received a check from the Treasurer of the United States for $2,732.90, representing the principal and the interest which had accrued since 1815. The draft was drawn on New York—"it is the best money that the Government has," observed Major Lewis—and Jackson immediately sent $600 of it to Blair to apply to the interest on his loan and another $20 which he asked to be converted into four half eagles of American gold in order to purchase an "outfit" for Lizzie Blair's filly, Miss Emuckfau, who was in foal by Priam.[5]

Jackson received more good news when Blair told him that he and Rives would be happy to extend the deadline for the repayment of their loan. Jackson thanked him profusely. Staving off these financial crises year after year, he said, was beginning to sink him into his grave. Had it not been for the incessant rains, which destroyed half his cotton crop at the Hermitage and a quarter of it at the Halcyon Plantation, he would have found some way to meet his obligation—or so he said. About 120 bales had been lost in toto. Just one good crop and a decent market price, he wistfully wrote, and I will meet all my obligations and free Andrew from debt. But it all depended on "providence."[6]

A few weeks later, while Jackson was propped up in bed recovering from his latest "bleeding," a young gentleman appeared at the door of the Hermitage. His name was William D. Miller and he was the private secretary of General Sam Houston, president of the Texas Republic. Among his belongings he carried a long letter from his employer to Old Hickory. It was a reply to a letter Jackson had written him months before, and in it Houston admitted his willingness to cooperate in achieving the immediate annexation of Texas by the United States.[7]

Jackson had always desired the annexation of Texas, however feeble his efforts of achieving it during his final years as President. It was part of his earlier dream of empire, to extend the nation across what once had been Spanish North America. Like Florida at an earlier time, Texas threatened American security if dominated by foreign powers. Apart from everything else, Jackson desired Texas in order to guarantee this nation's safety. "The safety of the republic being the supreme law, and Texas having offered us the key to the safety of our country from all foreign intrigues and diplomacy," the Sage wrote to Blair, "I say accept the key . . . and bolt the door at once."[8]

And Jackson did not hesitate to state his views publicly whenever the opportunity arose. Thomas W. Gilmer of Virginia had written a letter published in the Baltimore *Republican* of January 10, 1843, urging the annexation of Texas on account of Great Britain's growing interest in the area, and Representative Aaron V. Brown of Tennessee sent a copy to Jackson and asked for his opinion. The General speedily obliged. He insisted that Texas belonged to the United States under the Louisiana Treaty and had been shamelessly surrendered by John Quincy Adams in the Florida Treaty. He also declared that if Great Britain allied herself with Texas—which already seemed in train—she could then move "an army from canady, along our western frontier," march through Arkansas and Louisiana, capture New Orleans—he always fretted over the possible loss of New Orleans—"excite the negroes to insurrection," "arouse the Indians on our west to war," and "throw our whole west into flames that would cost oceans of blood & hundreds of millions of money to quench, & reclaim. . . . Texas must be ours; our safety requires it." With the passage of time Jackson became more shrill and chauvinistic. "We must regain Texas," he exploded at Major Lewis, *"peaceably if we can, forcibly if we must."*[9]

Jackson kept up his contacts with the heads of state of both Texas and Mexico. To Santa Anna, recently restored to power, he sent several letters, usually requesting (successfully) the release of some imprisoned American.[10] With Sam Houston, he had always maintained a close friendship, and Houston invariably addressed him as *"Venerated Friend."* Indeed at one point Houston wrote: "To you General, I feel myself *vastly* indebted for many principles, which I have never abandoned thro' life. One is a holy love of country, and a willingness to make every sacrifice to its honor and safety! Next a sacred regard for its constitution and laws, with an eternal hostility and opposition to all Banks!"[11]

The Tyler administration was also anxious to affect annexation. Adding Texas to the Union not only accorded with Tyler's own personal desire and that of his new secretary of state, John C. Calhoun,[12] but it was seen as a political triumph of such dimensions as to guarantee Tyler's reelection. But therein lay the danger. Because Van Buren Democrats worried that immediate annexation could eliminate their candidate from the race, some of them opposed bringing Texas into the Union at this time. Consequently, the Tyler administration saw only one solution to the problem: enlist the venerable Hero of New Orleans in the cause for annexation.

The task of approaching Old Hickory was assigned to Robert J. Walker, senator from Mississippi. A wisp of a man, weighing hardly 100 lbs., Walker breathed expansionism as a holy cause. As such he made an ideal go-between. "I write you confidentially and in haste," was the opening sentence of Walker's letter to Jackson. "I think the annexation of Texas depends *on you.*" And this could be your "crowning act." It seems, he said, that Houston believed that a treaty made with the present administration would fail because the Democrats would vote against it. Would you therefore write to Houston and disabuse him of this idea, said Walker. Any delay in the process of annexation can lose us Texas forever.[13]

Jackson agreed. He wrote several letters to Houston in January, 1844, in which he predicted that if annexation succeeded "your name & fame" would be enshrined among the greatest chieftains of history. He also forwarded Walker's letter, after receiving it, and pointed out how "sanguine" Walker was about winning confirmation. "You know you can rely on my friendship & I say to you that such a treaty made under your administration will be doing more for the prosperity & permanent happiness of Texas . . . than any other act of your life."[14]

Houston's response was delivered by his private secretary, William D. Miller, less than two months later. In a long, rambling letter the Texas President worried over past diplomatic fumblings and stressed his success in dealing with the powers of Europe, particularly Great Britain. "Texas with peace could exist without the U. States," he declared; "but the U. States cannot, without great hazard to the security of their institutions, exist without Texas." Be that as it may, Houston understood the importance of the "U. States" to Texas and he at length admitted as much by announcing in his letter that a special minister had been appointed to meet with the chargé at Washington and "to consummate the work of annexation" with dispatch. Miller would serve as the secretary to a "Secret Legation" at Washington. He warned, however, that if ratification failed in the Senate, Texas "would seek some other friend" in the family of nations.[15]

After reading Houston's letter carefully Jackson turned to Miller and assured him that annexation would indeed move with dispatch once the treaty was signed. He therefore hoped that the secretary would reassure

Houston on that point when next he wrote him. Furthermore, to assist Miller in Washington, as well as advance the treaty negotiations, Old Hickory handed him a confidential letter of introduction to Senator Walker in which Jackson advised Walker to give the young man his confidence. "The present golden moment to obtain Texas must not be lost," he declared, "or Texas might from necessity, be thrown into the arms of England and be forever lost to the United States." Then England would unite Oregon to Texas and the consequences would be catastrophic. "How easy would it be for great Britain to interpose a force sufficient to prevent emigration to California from the United States & supply her garrison from Texas."[16]

Thus it was not only Texas that Jackson felt the United States must acquire to ensure her protection, but Oregon and California as well. It was his old dream of empire.

> The important question, the Oregon and annexation of Texas, are now all important to the security and the future peace and prosperity of our union, and I hope there are a sufficient number of pure american democrats to carry into effect the annexation of Texas, and extending our laws over Oregon. No temporising policy or all is lost . . . *Oragon*, and Texas which was ours, *and must be* ours, or the safty of the south and west is put in Jeopardy.[17]

As for California, there could be no doubt of its attraction to the British, according to Jackson. "Need I call your attention to the situation of the United States," he lectured Walker, "England in possession of Texas, or in strict allience offensive & defensive, and contending for California." Thus we must not lose this opportunity to regain Texas or we may have to go to war with Great Britain to safeguard the American west. He ended by asking about their chances for success. "Pleas say to me can you command thirty five votes to ratify the treaty in the Senate. If you can then all is safe."[18]

Jackson enclosed Houston's letter with his letter of introduction and told Walker to use it in any manner that he thought would promote "the security, happiness, and prosperity of both Texas and the U. States." I know you will use it "prudently," he added—and "benefically."[19]

Miller could spare only a few hours and therefore refused Jackson's invitation to stay the night at the Hermitage. So the General had only a short time to scratch out a quick note to Major Lewis—"the confident of Mr. Tyler," according to Jackson[20]—which he asked Miller to deliver. Again, he wanted to broaden the young man's contacts in Washington as far and as quickly as possible. In this note he advised Lewis to speak to Walker and also to ask to see Houston's letter.[21]

Straightaway, Jackson informed Houston of his action and said they were moving on annexation as rapidly as possible. All his influence would be exerted to this end. What they were trying to do was prevent Great

Britain from getting an "ascendency over Texas," he wrote, for then "she would form an iron Hoop around the United States, with her West India Islands that would cost oceans of blood, and millions of money to Burst assunder." They were also planning to keep the treaty secret, once it was drawn up, until it was sent to the Senate for ratification. "This prevents that arch fiend, J. Q. Adams, from writing memorials and circulating them for signatures in the opposition to the annexation of Texas, and to prevent the ratification of the Treaty, and giving time for all the abolition and Eastern Federal papers, to fulminate against it before this wretched old man can circulate his firebrands, and memorials against the ratification of the treaty, it will be ratified by the Senate."[22]

A few weeks later Lewis talked with Walker and read the Houston letter, which he pronounced "capital," so good in fact that he thought it ought to be read in the Senate in executive session whenever a treaty was signed. Walker asked Lewis to inform Jackson that he was positive that a treaty would win immediate ratification. He felt he had the necessary 35 votes. But Lewis doubted it. "There seems to be a great unwillingness that Messrs. *Tyler* and *Calhoun* shall have the credit of consummating this great and long desired measure."[23]

These doubts were also conveyed to Jackson by Miller after he arrived in Washington. He was concerned not only about the Democrats but the Whigs as well, since many of them feared what immediate ratification might do to the candidacy of Henry Clay. Unfortunately, neither Clay nor Van Buren, the two probable presidential candidates, had committed themselves publicly on the question. At the moment, therefore, it looked as though the chances for ratification in the present session of Congress were dim. "Much, very much, my dear General, I am well assured," Miller told Jackson, "depends upon your continued efforts." And if Texas is spurned by the mother, he warned, "she may look to a better reception from the grandmother."[24]

Jackson refused to believe that Democratic senators—men of principle and virtue—would concern themselves about who would reap the merit of something that was so important to the safety of the nation. Such men, he scolded, "have no patriotism, or love of country, and ought to be publickly exposed" and returned to "their own native dunghills, there to rest forever." Tell Walker, he instructed Lewis, to push the treaty, and if it was defeated in the Senate then arouse "some of our members" to introduce "a bill and have it passed thro Congress accepting of the tender, and annexing Texas to this Union." Jackson obviously meant a "joint resolution." "This will be both legal and constitutional," he added. Any senator who votes against a treaty is a traitor. This subject involves national security, *"the perpetuation of our republican system, and of our glorious Union."*[25]

As he wrote, Jackson grew more agitated. On such issues the old fire could still burn with all the old intensity. His hand was steady as the pen dug into the paper. The look of a "chafed lion" still radiated from his eyes. But he paid a price in physical discomfort. "I am now suffering much," he admitted. "A severe and continued pain in my side, shortness of breath and costiveness, and I have wrote this with great labour."[26]

On April 12, 1844, a treaty of annexation was signed by the representatives of Texas and the United States. Almost immediately, President Tyler conveyed the news to Jackson. "For the part my dear Sir, that you have taken in this great matter," wrote Tyler, "you have only added another claim to the gratitude of the country."[27] Ten days later it was submitted to the Senate for ratification.

Although Jackson had actually played only a very small part in getting the treaty signed, his role was nonetheless important. The Sage's influence, on both sides, carried enormous weight.

When the treaty went to the Senate it was accompanied by a letter written by the secretary of state, John C. Calhoun, to the British minister to Washington, Richard Pakenham, in which the secretary raised the dread issue of slavery. He contended that the treaty had been signed to protect American slavery from British efforts at interfering in Texas to bring about universal abolition. The action of the United States was intended to block that "reprehensible" effort.

Major Lewis groaned when he read the letter. Calhoun has placed annexation "*exclusively* upon the ground of *protection* of *Slavery* in the *Southern States!*" he complained to Jackson, and the Democratic senators from the nonslaveholding states are furious "because it would be death to them, politically, if they were to vote for the Treaty based on such principles." Calhoun should have placed it "upon broad *national* principles—avoiding everything of a local or sectional nature." These negotiations have been "injudiciously managed," he concluded.[28]

But Blair claimed to know Calhoun's diabolical purpose. The secretary means to kill the treaty with his letter to Pakenham, the editor informed Jackson, for it will "drive off every Northern man from the reannexation" and give him "a pretext to unite the whole South upon himself as the Champion of its cause." He schemes to dissolve the Union, said Blair, create "a Southern Confederacy" as the only means of winning Texas, and thereby "make himself the great man of this fragment which he expects to tear from the embrace of our glorious Govt."[29]

When Jackson read Calhoun's letter to Pakenham he was forced to agree with all of Blair's conclusions. The General called it a foolish and weak letter because it deliberately introduced the slavery problem "to arouse the Eastern states against the annexation of Texas. The power of the states over slavery was not necessary by him then to have been brought into view." Why should he bring it up—unless, of course, he wants to kill the treaty. Like abolitionists, the nullifiers had one goal, and that was the disruption of the Union. "How many men of talents," Jackson wearily wrote, "want good common sense."[30]

Between Calhoun's "deliberate" mismanagement of the ratification process, and "that arch fiend, J. Q. Adams" and his squads of memorial-writing abolitionists, the Union stood in great jeopardy, and it was agreed among the Democratic leadership that only someone like Andrew Jackson could counteract their efforts and rescue the cause of annexation. What Old Hickory thought on any issue influenced large segments of the American electorate, but when the issue involved national security it assumed even greater importance. So it was deemed vital to let the American people know that General Jackson was absolutely convinced that the acquisition of Texas "is all important to the safety of N. Orleans . . . and the real safety of our western frontier, to our revenue, and commerce . . . [and presents] to us the key that Locks out all these threatening evils." Democratic editors in every state published suitable quotations from his correspondence and public statements, and his letter to Aaron Brown was widely circulated. "You will have perceived from the Globe," Blair wrote Jackson on May 2, "that . . . I endeavoured to give impulse to your views and wishes in regard to Texas." Proannexation Democrats everywhere imitated Blair's example.[31]

Unfortunately, the widespread dissemination of these views came too late—at least as far as the principal presidential contenders were concerned. On April 27, 1844, the Washington *National Intelligencer* published a letter written by Henry Clay in Raleigh, North Carolina, on April 17—the very day the treaty of annexation was signed—opposing the acquisition of Texas. He regarded annexation as dangerous to the country in that it might trigger a war with Mexico, excite passions over slavery within the Union, and prove financially disastrous because the Texas debt of approximately $10 million would have to be assumed by the United States.

Jackson's published views on the question would never have influenced Clay in any shape or form—except in a perverse way, perhaps—but they surely would have halted Martin Van Buren dead in his tracks before releasing his own letter opposing annexation. The Van Buren letter, interestingly enough, appeared in the *Globe* on the exact day that Clay's appeared in the *Intelligencer*. Since both candidates obviously hoped to avoid making Texas an issue in the election, and since both met together in Kentucky during Van Buren's tour in 1842, it can be assumed that the two men came to an understanding about the issue and agreed to declare their opposition when the time seemed propitious.[32]

As might be expected, Van Buren's letter was prudent and circumspect and intended to offend no one. It came to be written when William H. Hammet, an unpledged delegate to the Democratic nominating convention, asked Van Buren for his opinion on Texas. At first the cagey Magician suspected a trap. But when he learned that the request was legitimate he replied to Hammet and confessed his opposition to annexation on the grounds that it would provoke sectional rancor and possible war with

Mexico. But, he continued in a typical Van Buren balancing act, if the public overwhelmingly favored annexation then he would accede to their wishes and go along. At the moment, however, he felt he must state his honest position and declare against acquisition.

When Van Buren released his letter he certainly knew Jackson's general attitude on the subject, but he said he was compelled to take his stand in view of Calhoun's Pakenham letter that tied Texas inexorably to slavery. Other nations may resort to "aggression and conquest," he declared, but this nation is regulated by "reason and justice."[33] Obviously, then, Calhoun had scored exactly as he planned.[34]

Jackson shuddered when he read the "Hammet letter." "I have shed tears of regret," he admitted. "I would to god I had been at Mr. V. B. elbow when he closed his letter. I would have brought to his view *the proper conclusion.*"[35] When word of Clay's "Raleigh letter" first arrived in Nashville on May 4, he told Major Lewis, the democracy burst into cheers. They pronounced Clay "a dead political Duck." Then, in the evening, Van Buren's Hammet letter reached the city and the prostrated southern Whigs came alive again. They say they can support Clay after all, even though they abhor his Texas position. "There is great excitement here at present on this subject," Jackson wrote. Everyone sensed the danger. "I am . . . mortified at Mr. V. B. letter," he said. It "makes my tears flow with regret."[36]

If only Van Buren had closed his letter by "observing that he had no way of Judging of the truth of the prevailing rumors of Foreign interference by which our safety as a nation" was jeopardized, Jackson said. Then Democrats might have wriggled out of their predicament about nominating him for President. They could set the facts before him and then hope he would repudiate the Hammet letter. As it was, all they could do was either find another candidate or pass a resolution at the nominating convention stating that the majority of Americans desired annexation. Since "Mr. V.B. has said in his letter whenever a majority of people declare their voice for it he would approve it," perhaps then they could go ahead and nominate him with the understanding that he would reverse himself. "Some such plan must be adopted," he told Blair, "or the democracy of the south and west" will desert the party.[37]

Almost immediately after reading the Hammet letter, Jackson wrote to Van Buren and very bluntly told him that "the die was cast," and in view of his annexation position "it was impossible to elect him," as impossible as it would be "to turn the current of the Mississippi." It was very painful for Jackson to write these words, but he felt he must speak the truth.[38]

If Van Buren could not be elected, did that mean finding another presidential candidate? But who could the Democrats nominate to run in his place? Tyler was out of the question as far as many Democrats were concerned; even the southern Whigs had long ago deserted him for Clay. And his feeble efforts to form a third party had come to nothing. Calhoun

was mentioned by some southern Democrats, but too many others, especially in the north, could not abide him, and he eventually withdrew.
Other possibilities included Lewis Cass, James Buchanan, Richard Johnson, Levi Woodbury, and Thomas Hart Benton.

Benton might have made a good choice, except that he too opposed
the treaty of annexation as a criminal attempt to dismember Mexico. And
he publicly stated his opposition in speeches on the Senate floor and in
a letter printed in the *Globe* on April 29.[39] This announcement by his old
friend also "mortified" Jackson, and he predicted that the democracy in
Missouri would punish Benton. A better presidential candidate on all
accounts was Silas Wright, Jr., of New York, but he steadfastly refused to
consider a nomination. He was fanatically loyal to his friend and chief,
Martin Van Buren, and bent all his energies to winning the nomination
for the Magician.[40]

All this left Jackson with but a single candidate: James K. Polk of
Tennessee—except that Polk was slotted for the vice presidency. Just
when it crossed anyone's mind that Polk might be shifted to the first
position is not certain. It probably occurred to Polk himself in late 1843
(if not sooner), and he was no doubt encouraged to consider a higher
calling by the letters he received from Robert Armstrong, S. H. Laughlin,
Cave Johnson, Gideon Pillow, and others. Certainly Jackson had been
working vigorously for Polk for the past few years, albeit his object was
the vice presidency, at least in the beginning. Polk was told in late December, 1843, that "the old chief is bestirring himself more in his correspondence with the proper parties than you are aware of."[41] At what point the
Old Hero bestirred himself to seek the presidency for Polk cannot be
pinpointed to a specific day, but it certainly came no later than the
moment he read the Hammet letter.

In fact it might have come at least six months earlier. When Polk lost
the gubernatorial race in August, 1843, because he had linked his campaign with Van Buren's presidential drive, and when he subsequently lost
control of the state convention in November after the Calhoun crowd in
Tennessee took over the Democratic party and chose anti–Van Buren
delegates to the national convention in Baltimore, both he and Jackson
surely read the writing on the wall: Van Buren could never carry a southern state that also had a strong Whig party, not Tennessee, Kentucky,
Georgia, Virginia, North Carolina, or Louisiana. Even in Mississippi—a
one-party state—the democracy was badly split over a possible Van Buren
nomination. And all of this had transpired long before the annexation
issue. The Hammet letter simply sealed Van Buren's doom throughout
the south.

To anyone who had watched the course of political events over the last
few years it had become increasingly obvious that Van Buren could not
hold the party together, that his nomination in 1844 would drive away
several segments of the Democratic organization, especially in the south

and west. Certainly the Tyler and Calhoun forces would never support his nomination. And there were many others around the country who either disliked Van Buren personally or blamed him for past mistakes and misguided policies.

Andrew Jackson not only watched but studied the course of political events, especially in Tennessee. Trouncing the Whigs meant everything to him. Another defeat was intolerable. In that case someone other than Van Buren was needed to head the national Democratic ticket if the party was to remain reasonably cohesive to defeat Clay in the approaching election. But where to turn? Certainly not to Tyler, nor Calhoun, Cass, or Buchanan. Might Polk be a realistic possibility? As it turned out, when Cave Johnson of Tennessee—a principal Polk manager in Washington, with whom Jackson kept in reasonably close contact—suggested to Silas Wright that he, Wright, accept the nomination, the New Yorker turned around and, after refusing it point blank, said that James K. Polk was "the only man he thought the Northern democrats would support if Van B. was set aside."[42]

The Hammet letter gave Jackson the excuse necessary to set Van Buren aside. It had to be done—something he had known many months before —but at least now it could be done with a measure of grace and justification.

It was at this point that the Sage summoned Polk to the Hermitage. The General directed both Donelson and Robert Armstrong to invite Polk to his home.[43] Two simultaneous summonses brought Polk immediately, and he arrived in Nashville from his home in Columbia on Sunday, May 12. He consulted with Armstrong and some other friends upon his arrival, and then on Monday rode out to the Hermitage.

As Polk and Armstrong approached the General's home they met Andrew J. Donelson on his way into town, bearing another public letter on annexation which Jackson had just composed and which was intended for publication in the Nashville *Union*. The letter was dated May 13 and was written in response to the Van Buren and Benton letters. In it Jackson disclaimed any other motive in making this statement than the interest of his country. Not politics. Certainly not presidential nominations. Nothing but a desire "to give to this country the strength to resist foreign interference." For it cannot be doubted, Jackson wrote, that if Texas failed to gain admittance into "our confederacy" she would be driven into alliances with European powers of "a character highly injurious and probably hostile to this country." He then proceeded to dispute Van Buren's various arguments against annexation and outlined the sort of language he would use with Mexico, once acquisition was accomplished, to explain our needs and intent. As for the method of acquisition, he had no preference: either ratification by the Senate or a joint resolution by both houses of Congress. Then, having kicked out the supports under Van Buren's brief, he closed with an affectionate salute to the New

Yorker, explaining away the Hammet letter as something resulting from outdated information. "Circumstances are so far altered as to give a new aspect to the whole question," Jackson said.[44]

After reading the letter, Polk and Armstrong convinced Donelson to hold up delivering the letter and join them in returning to the Hermitage. Together they hurried to the General's study. They found the Sage "cool and collected," which was quite usual in moments of difficulty or crisis. He held a long conversation with Polk and told him that Van Buren and Benton had "cut their own throats politically." He said he did not know whether Van Buren could now be nominated and doubted that he could win southern and western support even if nominated. Certainly Tennessee would never support him. With a deep sigh, Jackson again expressed his regret over this "fatal error which *Mr. V. B.* has committed," but since he was a realistic politician he knew there was no point fretting over it. "It is done," he said with finality, and now "the convention must select some other as the candidate." As soon as Van Buren realized that the people rejected his position, Jackson continued, he would withdraw. I fervently hope so, he added. "The candidate for the first office," he declared in a strong voice, "should be an annexation man, and from the Southwest." You! he said, looking directly at Polk. "He openly expresses . . . the opinion," the startled Polk later wrote, "that I would be the most available man; taking the Vice-Presidential candidate from the North."[45]

Who but Andrew Jackson could be this audacious? Who but the Hero of New Orleans could set aside the ostensible candidate of most Democrats and declare a relative unknown as the next presidential nominee of the Democratic party?

Yet his choice made sense. All of the other candidates carried severe liabilities in one form or another. Not one of the others could unite the party. Many of them would distract it, excite passions and antagonisms, and rend the party into several warring factions. Only Polk, in Jackson's astute political mind, could unite the democracy. He stood for all the principles and reforms[46] Old Hickory had sought to advance during his eight years in office. He also advocated annexation. And he came from the southwest.

Standing before the old chief, Polk sputtered a protest. He had never aspired so high, he said. "In all probability the attempt to place me in the first position would be utterly abortive," he added. Still, one never knew. Lightning might strike. In reporting this conversation with one of his managers scheduled to attend the Democratic convention, Polk conceded that "in the confusion which will prevail" at Baltimore "there is no telling what may occur." The wary, extremely cautious Polk therefore placed himself in the hands of his friends at the convention. "They can use my name in any way they may think proper," he said.[47]

As heady and exciting as the prospect of succeeding to the presidency may have been to Polk at the time Jackson conferred upon him his recognition as "the most available man," he was shrewd enough to reckon that the odds in his favor at this late date were less than overwhelming, despite Old Hickory's endorsement. That gave him pause. Although he certainly said and did everything he thought appropriate to advance his availability, at the same time he did not wish to overstep himself and risk losing the vice presidency, just in case the first slot went to someone else. He was particularly concerned about offending Van Buren, and therefore he told his convention managers to conduct themselves in such a manner as to avoid jeopardizing his chances for second place.[48]

For this reason Polk probably prevailed upon Jackson to tone down his letter, intended for publication in the *Union,* as regards Van Buren's unavailability now that the Magician had revealed his opposition to immediate annexation. In fact he much preferred that Jackson suppress the letter altogether. But the old man would not hear of it. He insisted on having his say, and having it before the convention met. Nonetheless, in deference to Polk's concern, he probably deleted a few sections that focused upon the need to substitute another presidential candidate.[49]

On May 16, the Nashville *Union* published Jackson's letter. A week later the paper posted a list of six names, headed by Polk, who were selected as the most likely to win nomination if Van Buren should withdraw.

By this time Polk was certain that Van Buren's withdrawal as a candidate was "not only possible, but I think probable." In which case, he told his managers at the convention, "I see no reason why my friends should not make the effort [to obtain the nomination for me]. It will require judgment and delicacy in managing the matter," he added.[50]

At about the time Polk wrote this letter, the Tennessee delegation left home for the Baltimore convention. Most, if not all, of them—and specifically Andrew J. Donelson, who was a delegate—knew Jackson's sentiments on the nomination, and they were prepared to convey them to delegates from other states at the appropriate time.[51] They needed to exercise "judgment and delicacy," just as Polk had said. They also needed a little luck.

In the meantime the Whig party held its nominating convention on May 1, four days after the publication of Clay's Raleigh letter, and nominated the Kentuckian anyway. It nominated him by acclamation. As his running mate, the convention chose Senator Theodore Frelinghuysen of New Jersey.

The Democrats met on May 27. Through the astute maneuvering of Robert J. Walker, Jackson's contact with the Tyler administration on the Texas question, the two-thirds rule was adopted. First adopted at the 1832 convention, this rule required approval of two-thirds of the delegates for any candidate to win nomination. Its adoption at the 1844 convention proved disastrous to the friends of Van Buren, for they had a clear majority of delegates but lacked two-thirds. The friends of all the other candidates, therefore, supported the rule as the only means of blocking the Magician's selection. But the Polk managers avoided any sign of disloyalty to Van Buren throughout the contest over the two-thirds rule. They wisely reckoned that once Van Buren started to lose delegates, Polk would make an attractive alternate to all the New Yorker's friends.[52]

The convention balloted seven times. Van Buren scored well on the first ballot—he had more than a majority but not two-thirds—but lost ground rapidly thereafter. Lewis Cass was the greatest gainer on all the subsequent ballots but he, too, failed to win two-thirds. For the Van Buren men the situation became desperate. They strongly resisted the Cass nomination because they regarded Cass as the prime mover in the anti–Van Buren drive. Soon cries for adjournment were heard but no one paid much attention. Fistfights broke out. Then someone called out the name, "Andrew Jackson," and moved that he be declared unanimously nominated. And on that happy, if impossible, note the convention adjourned for the day.[53]

Embittered and angry, the Van Buren men blamed the Cass forces "totally and exclusively" for the demise of their candidate. The resentment swelled each hour. Eventually all of it was turned to Polk's advantage through the efforts of Gideon J. Pillow, one of Polk's floor managers; George Bancroft, the historian and soon to become secretary of the navy; and Benjamin F. Butler, the attorney general under both Jackson and Van Buren.[54] These men worked through the night to reverse the trend toward Cass, and when the convention reconvened the next day they won Polk's nomination for the presidency on the ninth ballot by a unanimous vote. As the balloting ended, the delegates exploded into wild shouts of approval. Not only had they found an acceptable candidate, but they had escaped a deadlock that could have split the party and guaranteed defeat at the polls.

The convention next chose Silas Wright for the vice presidency and when his refusal shot back over the new telegraph wires from Washington, they chose George Dallas of Pennsylvania—a kinsman of Robert Walker—in his place. A "platform" proposed by Walker to the resolutions committee was adopted. Among other things taken from the canon of Jacksonian Democracy about banks, tariffs, debts, and internal improvements it also called for the "reoccupation of Oregon and the reannexation of Texas at the earliest practicable period."[55]

As the telegraph tapped out the news of these momentous events, Andrew J. Donelson dashed to his desk to scribble a quick letter to his uncle to notify him of their victory. "The dark sky of yesterday has been succeeded by the brightest day democracy has witnessed since your election," he enthused. "Polk has been unanimously chosen by the convention. . . . The moment his nomination was made every difference of opinion seemed to disappear."[56] Jackson, too, was overjoyed when he heard the good news. He sincerely regretted the necessity of Van Buren's withdrawal, but the good of the nation required it. A few weeks earlier he had written to Benjamin F. Butler, manager of the Van Buren forces at the convention, to tell him in his now familiar figure of speech that "you might as well, it appears to me, attempt to turn the current of the Mississippi, as to turn the democracy from the annexation of Texas." Now he wrote to Butler to thank him for his efforts on Polk's behalf. We all know, he said, that Van Buren is governed by "the will of the people" and would have come around on Texas eventually, "yet it may be best that a concession was made to the feelings of others in order to secure the harmony & consent of action necessary to bring the whole party into the field against the Federal schemes of Mr. Clay." Polk is "sound," he continued, and "deeply regrets" the circumstances which necessitated the postponement of Van Buren's nomination. Still, the people have been well served by what transpired in Baltimore.[57]

Jackson was especially happy over the resolution concerning Texas and Oregon, although he felt that annexation should not be a party question "but a national one." Once Texas is absorbed into the country, he said, and "our laws extended over Orragon," then "the perpetuation of our glorious Union" will be "as firm as the Rocky mountains, and put to rest the vexing question of abolitionism, the dangerous rock to our Union, and put at defiance all combined Europe, if combined to invade us."[58]

Polk proved to be an extremely shrewd strategist during the campaign. The first thing he did was declare publicly that he would not seek a second term in office. This had the effect of pulling the party together by encouraging the defeated rivals to support the ticket in hopes of inheriting the Democratic leadership four years hence. Moreover, it was "rotation" with a vengeance, a highly "orthodox Jacksonian tenet," and the old man loudly applauded Polk's action. This public disavowal of a second term, the General said, proved the wisdom of nominating him, and it will surely unite the entire democracy—as, indeed, it did.[59]

Polk also demonstrated uncommon good sense in guiding the campaign by making excellent use of Jackson. It was important to him that Tyler withdraw from the race and the task of talking him into it was assigned to Old Hickory. The General first approached his quarry through Major Lewis and John Y. Mason, Tyler's secretary of the navy. Through these men, Jackson told Tyler that if he expected to leave the presidency with any prospect of future service he must withdraw now. Otherwise his refusal would benefit no one but Henry Clay, and the democracy would never excuse him for that misdeed. Because of his stand on the Bank and the annexation of Texas, Jackson said, Tyler had earned the gratitude of all true Democrats, and his retirement would certainly add to his popularity and enhance his reputation.[60]

Still Tyler hesitated. He favored Polk's election over Clay but said he would not withdraw until the Democratic press—and, in particular, Blair's *Globe*—stopped assailing him and, as a second condition, until he had genuine assurances that he and his friends would be treated as allies and equals by their Democratic brethren.[61] To fulfil this second condition, Robert J. Walker felt that a private letter from Polk to Tyler and a public one from Jackson were essential. Naturally, it was presumed that Jackson would prevail upon Blair to stop attacking the President.

As soon as Polk learned of Tyler's demands he dispatched his friend General Gideon J. Pillow to the Hermitage to gain Jackson's assistance. Polk felt uneasy about writing a private letter himself or making any pledge and he wanted Jackson to do it for him.[62] But the Hero agreed to go along only halfway. He wrote to Lewis and told him to assure Tyler that he (the President) and his friends would be *received as brethren . . . all former differences forgotten.*" But the Sage steadfastly refused to write a public letter. It would be seen as a "corrupt bargain," he said, just like the one Clay and Adams engineered in 1825. As for Blair, the General signaled him to back off. "I have but one remark," he told the editor, "—support the cause of Polk and Dallas and let Tiler alone." The order was immediately carried out. The *Globe* ceased its attacks and Blair pledged "to do nothing to drive off Tyler & his office holders." Meanwhile, Lewis showed Jackson's letter to the President. Tyler pondered the arguments advanced and then a few days later wrote to the General and announced his decision. "Your views as to the proper course for me to pursue in the present emergency of public affairs," he said, "has decided me to withdraw from the canvass." He officially withdrew in a public announcement on August 20.[63]

Although Jackson immeasurably advanced Polk's presidential prospects throughout the campaign, he failed to overcome the opposition to annexation in Congress. On June 8, to no one's surprise, the Senate rejected the Texas treaty by the vote of 35 to 16. The Whigs and northern Van Buren men combined to kill it, but the blame for the defeat was laid directly at the door of the secretary of state, John C. Calhoun, whose Pakenham letter deliberately and foolishly linked Texas to slavery. Blair assured Jackson that Calhoun willfully contrived to keep Texas out of the Union in order "to make it a means of seperation between the slave holding and non Slave-holding States and part of a New Confederacy of the former."[64]

Jackson seethed over the rejection. "Has America become craven," he rasped, "that we as an independent nation cannot adopt measures for the security and prosperity of our whole Union. . . . Away with such craven hearted Senators, Traitors to the best interests of our country, and to our Glorious Union, and they will soon be spurned from the confidence of every true American."[65]

The Hero immediately contacted Houston. He wrote "as patriotic a letter as I could dictate," he informed Blair. He naturally fell back on his proposal of a joint resolution by Congress to get around the "craven" act of a "traitorous" Senate. He was prepared to take almost any action to prevent the loss of Texas which he felt would threaten the security of the nation and ultimately lead to war. Other Democrats calculated more radical measures, and some southerners plotted to convert a mass Democratic rally, already planned for Nashville on August 15 to launch the presidential campaign, into a sort of southern convention to demand annexation or threaten secession. Again poor old Jackson was carted out to help stave off this chaos, and he was prevailed upon to write letters urging northern Democrats to attend the rally in order to prevent southern hotheads from fomenting talk of secession.[66]

The "great, great Mass meeting of the democracy," as Jackson called the rally, attracted many leading Democrats to Nashville in mid-August. Naturally they all trooped out to the Hermitage to pay homage and, if lucky, to receive a blessing on their future ambitions and plans. To one and all the Hero reiterated his old familiar cry: *"The Union must be preserved!"*[67]

With such an admonition few Democrats were prepared to raise the banner of secession in Jackson's home town, and so the meeting went off handsomely. It ended, reported the General, "much to the honor and the increase of the democratic cause. . . . I think I may safely say that it has added to the least of the democratic gain of one thousand votes."[68]

For the remainder of the summer and fall—indeed, thoughout the entire campaign—Jackson took an active part in promoting the candidacy of James K. Polk. He wrote vigorous letters to all parts of the country, many of which went straight into the newspapers.[69] Polk also asked the General to write again to Sam Houston and urge him to hold out against European pressure to enter an alliance that would guarantee Texas's independence. To date Houston had not answered Jackson's appeals because he was not yet certain what his next move would be. He wished to stand uncommitted in case Texas should be obliged to pursue a course of national independence.[70]

Tyler also asked for Jackson's assistance on the Texas matter. The American chargé in Texas had died, and the President wanted to appoint Andrew J. Donelson as his replacement. Aside from questions of ability, Donelson was chosen not only because he knew Houston personally, but "over all," Tyler explained to Jackson, because he is "a member of your family and in your close confidence. This I doubt not will have a controuling influence with Genl. Houston and incline him . . . to pause ere he declares against annexation." Jackson was asked to use his influence to win Donelson's acceptance of the post, which he did, and also aid with the ongoing negotiations to bring Texas into the Union.[71]

Tyler apparently planned to attempt to win annexation through a joint resolution of both houses of Congress. At least that was Jackson's hope, and he complained throughout the summer that the friends of Texas in Congress had not introduced such a resolution the moment the treaty failed in the Senate. "It appears to me," he grumbled, "that this *great and important* question was lost sight of for President making." Indeed, the question was deeply interwoven with "President making," so much so that the British minister in Washington, Richard Pakenham, advised Lord Aberdeen in London to ease the pressure on Texas about a guaranteed independence because it might injure Clay's chances in the election. The governments of England and France, he counseled, had everything to gain by Clay's victory in the fall election and therefore the European powers should avoid anything that might jeopardize it.[72]

The Democrats immediately picked up on Clay's attractiveness to the "crowned heads" of Europe. Every one of those monarchs desires his election, they argued, because they wish to subvert our republican system of government. Polk represents the people, just like Jackson, they declared, while Clay represents the aristocracy. Democrats had dubbed Polk "Young Hickory," out of "affection for you," Jackson was told, to emphasize his association with the Sage and to encourage him to imitate the virtues and statesmanship of the great man. Of course, the Whigs ridiculed this propaganda, especially the claim that Polk represented the democracy. "Who is James K. Polk?" they contemptuously asked. Nothing but a "blighted burr that has fallen from the mane of the warhorse of the Hermitage."[73]

The election proved to be extremely close. A third candidate was put forward by a Liberty party, formed to bring about the abolition of slavery. This party named James G. Birney to head the ticket and he undoubtedly attracted votes away from Clay in crucial states. Polk won by a count of 170 electoral votes to 105. But the popular vote was much closer—1,337,243 to 1,299,062[74]—and Polk squeezed ahead of Clay by a 1.4 percent margin. "A mere *Tom Tit,*" has triumphed over the "old Eagle," snorted John Q. Adams. "The partial associations of Native Americans, Irish Catholics, abolition societies, liberty party, the Pope of Rome, the Democracy of the sword, and the dotage of a ruffian are sealing the fate of this nation, which nothing less than the interposition of Omnipotence can save."[75]

Indeed most observers, including the foreign press, saw the election as a victory of an "adventurous democracy" over the "respectable classes," a victory of workers, farmers, slaveowners, the foreign born, and the partisans of Texas. "Nothing can withstand the Democracy of this Country," complained a New York stockbroker. It had advanced too far and too long under the direction of that "ruffian" in the Hermitage.[76]

The argument that the election of 1844 was a mandate for the annexation of Texas has long been put to rest. It is far more probable that voters favored annexation because they were Democrats, not that they voted Democratic because they desired Texas. The Democratic party was the majority party, consisting mainly of laborers and farmers and the foreign born. It was a party with little appeal to the "respectable classes," although any number of "respectable" men supported it. This majority held together behind Polk—ample proof that his nomination was a wise move on the part of the Democratic leaders—and might have dissolved had Van Buren headed the ticket.[77]

The splendid news of Polk's victory arrived at the Hermitage with the booming of cannon in Nashville on November 15. "I thank my god," the old man declared, "that the Republic is safe & that he had permitted me to live to see it, & rejoice." In letter after letter for the next several weeks Jackson repeated the phrase: "The Republic is safe." He had lived to witness Clay's third attempt and third defeat to win the presidency and with him the defeat of Whiggery and coonery and aristocracy. "The glorious result of the presidential election has rejoiced every democratic boosom in the United States," he wrote to Andrew J. Donelson, now the American chargé in Texas, "and as to myself I can say in language of Simeon of old, 'Let thy servant depart in peace, as I have seen the solution of the liberty of my country and the perpetuity of our Glorious Union.'"[78]

Only one result of the election disappointed him—and that result rankled. Tennessee voted for Clay by a mere 113 votes. It so infuriated Old Hickory that he automatically assigned the reason for it to "the vilest frauds that have ever been practised."[79]

The effort Jackson expended to win Polk's election was tremendous—and important. But again he paid for it. He forced himself to write each day, which meant he had to be propped up in bed. He hemorrhaged a great deal and suffered from chills and fever. Between "the lancet to correct the first, and calomel to check the second, I am greatly debilitated," he said. He complained almost daily of "shortness of breath" and found that a few steps down the corridor from his room left him panting and close to fainting. No longer could he leave the house; no longer had he sufficient breath to walk to the gravesite of his beloved Rachel. Soon after the election he was confined totally to his own room.[80]

Jackson knew he was dying and yet he could not let go. Regaining Texas was his single concern. To that end he wrote regularly to Donelson in Texas, he prodded Polk, and he sent a steady stream of advice to members of Congress and to Frank Blair for use in his *Globe.* In fact Polk came to see the Hero within ten days after learning of his election and the two men talked at length about ways of acquiring Texas. The President-elect stayed at the Hermitage for several days and in a vigorous round of talks that raised the spirits of the old man he agreed to dump the Tyler cabinet in toto and select a new one in which every prospective member would be required to sign a statement disavowing presidential ambitions. Earlier Jackson had taken it upon himself to survey the Democratic leaders in Washington to learn "what effect it would produce by changing *entire* the present cabinet." The Hero also wanted Polk to retain the *Globe* as the administration paper and find a place for William B. Lewis, both of whom would be useful "to ferret out and make known to you all the plotts and intrigues Hatching against your administration."

Kendall, too, needed employment and Jackson suggested sending him to Spain. That meant removing Washington Irving, but Old Hickory had no problem on that score. "There can be no delicacy in recalling Erwin," he told Polk. "He is only fit to write a Book and scarcely that, and has become a good Whigg."[81]

Polk listened to all this advice and did not raise serious objections. Nor did he commit himself. As he later told Cave Johnson, "I intend to be *myself* President of the U. S." As for keeping the *Globe* as the administration paper, the President-elect was not enthusiastic. Blair had never accorded him much attention in the past and Polk thought a better arrangement might be one in which Blair would sell his interest in the *Globe* to Thomas Ritchie of the Richmond *Enquirer.* Jackson was aghast when he heard this proposal and tried to talk Polk out of it. "I pledge myself for Blair and you will be shielded, and if attacked well defended by the Globe. Ritchie is a good Editor but a very unsafe one. He goes off at half bent, and he does great injury before he can be set right."[82]

At different times Jackson and Polk also discussed what to do with John C. Calhoun. He could not be dismissed so easily since Polk needed all the support he could get, especially in view of the close election. It was essential to hold the party together and include even those Democrats who sometimes strayed from the fold. Jackson finally suggested sending the South Carolinian to Britain. "England is the place for him," Old Hickory impishly announced, "there to combat with my Lord Aberdeen, the abolition question."[83] Sometimes the old man revealed a dry but delightful sense of humor.

But all these questions, important as they were, paled by comparison to the Texas problem. Jackson could not rest easy until he knew that it had been satisfactorily resolved. Once Congress reconvened in December, the General charged after its members with demands that they pass a joint resolution for immediate annexation and thereby execute the will of the people as mandated by Polk's election.[84] At the same time he kept his nephew, Andrew J. Donelson, informed of all developments, instructing him on what he thought should be brought to the attention of the Texas officials. "This you will have to bring to their view," he wrote in one letter concerning the "secret designs" of Britain to reduce Texas to a colony. "Remember, the word reannex," he added, "this hold forth," namely the right of the United States to Texas under the Louisiana Purchase of 1803. As for the Florida Treaty of 1819 which renounced Texas, that was a "nullity, not having the approbation of France and the citizens of Louisia," no matter what "that old scamp, J. Q. Adams" says about it.[85]

Early in the congressional session a joint resolution was introduced for immediate annexation. This resolution required only a simple majority in both houses. The friends of Calhoun and the Tyler administration insisted on a resolution that vindicated the rejected treaty with all its connotations about slavery. They also demanded a provision requiring that the United States absorb the Texan debt. Again, many voiced doubts as to whether Calhoun and his allies really wanted the resolution to pass, arguing that they actually preferred the dissolution of the Union.[86] The House took up the resolution first, and, after a lively debate, passed it on January 25, 1845. Obviously many congressmen believed with Jackson that the people had expressed their view on the subject and wanted Texas admitted to the Union posthaste.

In the House version of the joint resolution, Texas would be admitted as a state, her debt and public lands would remain her own, four additional states could be carved from her territory, but slavery would be prohibited in any of these states if they extended north of the Missouri Compromise line of 36° 30'. Still many northerners disliked this version because it seemed to ensure the spread of slavery into a new area. That meant rough sledding through the Senate. Thomas Hart Benton, who opposed immediate annexation without Mexico's consent, changed his position after receiving instructions from the Missouri legislature. He withdrew his original bill which required Mexico's consent and substituted one that authorized the President to appoint five commissioners to negotiate all the terms of annexation with the Texas government.[87]

Jackson thoroughly disliked Benton's original bill and notified his friends in Washington that it was an insult to Texas and would be spurned out of hand. But the second bill had his wholehearted support. He "rejoiced" over Benton's conversion and predicted that "he will be hailed again by the democracy of the U. States as their champion & leader." Moreover, Benton proved himself a true Jacksonian Democrat. He abided by the will of the people as expressed to him in Polk's election and the instructions from the Missouri legislature. "Say to the Col. for me," Jackson wrote, "that the course intimated is the only proper course, and one which the authorities of Texas will promptly embrace, and he will be hailed over the whole Union as the flag bearer of Texas into the Union. *Be it so.*"[88]

Jackson's enthusiasm was shared by other Democrats, especially those northern senators who disliked the House bill. As expected, the *Globe* seconded Jackson's support for Benton's effort, and the Texas representative in Washington said he preferred the Senate bill over the House resolution.[89] At this point Polk arrived in Washington to prepare for his inauguration on March 4. "He is for Texas, Texas, Texas," reported Senator Willie P. Mangum of North Carolina, "& talks of but little else."[90] And that about settled the matter, especially when a compromise was worked out between the House and Senate versions of the resolution by leaving the choice of alternatives to the President. On February 27 the amended compromise was introduced into the Senate by Robert J. Walker and barely squeezed through by a vote of 27 to 25. It was supported by every Democratic senator along with three southern Whigs.[91]

The following day the House approved the amended measure. Tyler signed the resolution on March 1, 1845, just three days before he was scheduled to leave office. Then on Sunday, March 2, he sent a messenger to Texas offering annexation under the terms of the House resolution.[92]

"Texas is ours," cried the democracy. What a "happy result," enthused Blair in a letter to Jackson written moments after the House agreed to the compromise. "I congratulate you, Dear General, on the success of the great question which you put in action."[93]

Ten days later the feeble voice in the Hermitage replied: "I not only rejoice, but congratulate my beloved country Texas is reannexed, and the safety, prosperity, and the greatest interest of the whole Union is secured by this . . . great and important national act."[94]

CHAPTER 33

"We Will All Meet in Heaven"

BEFORE PRESIDENT-ELECT POLK LEFT FOR HIS INAUGURATION in Washington he had several interviews with Jackson at the Hermitage. The last one took place on January 30, and during their conversations they discussed Polk's intended cabinet. It was a nicely balanced group that Polk suggested in terms of geography and political associations and the General awarded it his full approval. When Polk finally departed the Hermitage on Friday morning, January 31, he knew he would most probably never see his old chief again. Their farewell was both affectionate and heartfelt. As they shook hands, Jackson said he was confident that his protégé would "fearlessly carry out all his principles" and "keep all cliques at a distance."[1]

Jackson conveyed the news of the appointments in confidence to several friends in Washington. He especially liked Polk's declared intention of requiring every member of his official family to renounce "in writing" all presidential ambitions. In the General's mind that idea accorded perfectly with the basic principles of Jacksonian Democracy.[2]

By the time Polk reached Washington, however, political circumstances among the various Democratic factions had changed considerably and Polk—always astute and sometimes unscrupulous[3]—adjusted to them by radically altering the cabinet selections he had named at the Hermitage. When Jackson learned about them he was not at all happy with some of the changes and he made no effort to disguise his disappointment. He even commented at one point that the new secretary of state, James Buchanan—who incidentally gave a very ambiguous answer to Polk's demand for a renunciation of presidential ambition—was a moral lightweight. Worse, Polk failed to reward Amos Kendall, which sent that

512

worthy into the telegraph business where he became a millionaire. The President also dismissed Major Lewis. Indeed, Lewis knew nothing of his dismissal until his replacement suddenly appeared at his desk one morning and informed him that he had been "rotated" back to Tennessee. Presumably, "national security" could be jeopardized in some way since Lewis's daughter was married to the French minister.[4]

About the only action by Polk to win Jackson's complete approval was the President's inaugural address, particularly the statement that the American claim to Oregon was "clear and unquestionable." The area had long been in dispute and during the last presidential campaign there were some who felt it should be seized right up to its northernmost limits. The cry "Fifty-four forty or fight" had stirred nationalists in every state. As far as Jackson was concerned, the problem over Oregon had resulted because of the failure of Daniel Webster in concluding the Webster-Ashburton Treaty with England in 1842. "Had Mr. Webster had an ounce of American feeling in him, when negotiating on the North Eastern boundery," Jackson carped, "he would have put this matter to rest, when Asburton proposed to stop the line at the Rockey Mountains." If, instead, Webster had said: "No Sir, we carry it out to the Pacific agreable to the Treaty of 1783, or our negotiation is at an end," England would have capitulated because she was engaged in war with China and the "Afinghams" [Afghans] and because of her problems with Ireland. So she has kept Oregon, he said, "as a nest egg" to provoke war with us whenever she believes she can benefit from it.[5]

When the British reacted sharply to the President's statement with thinly disguised threats of war, Jackson counseled Polk to stick to his guns. "This is the rattling of British drums to alarm us," he wrote, "and to give life to . . . blue light federalists and abolitionists . . . and give strength to the traitors in our country." Deny their claims, he urged, and restate our right to extend our laws over Oregon and populate it with our people. During the presidential campaign, Jackson continued, "I gave a thousand pledges for your energy and firmness, both in *war* and in *peace.*" Do not waver from this pledge. Do not temporize. "Dash from your lips the council of the timid." Ask nothing but what is right and permit nothing that is wrong. "War is a blessing compared with national degradation." Besides, the way to avoid war is to take a "bold and undaunted front. . . . England with all her Boast dare not go to war."[6]

Rest easy, Polk responded. The "blustering manners and tone of defiance" by the British, he wrote, is probably intended "to test our nerves. We stand firmly and boldly on our rights." We desire peace, but we are also prepared to maintain our rights "at any hazard."[7]

Jackson breathed easier when he read this letter. The White House at last had a master sitting at the executive desk. The General would have been even more pleased had he been able to read a statement by Polk's editorial spokesman in Washington less than a month later that a "corps of properly organized volunteers . . . would invade, overrun and occupy Mexico" in the event that Mexico resisted American expansionist claims in the west. "They would enable us not only to take California, but to keep it."[8] It would seem that Polk was intent on fulfilling Jackson's earliest dream of empire for the American nation: the dream of acquiring "all Spanish North America."

This last exchange of letters with Polk occurred as the General's health worsened dramatically. "My disease has assumed an alarming type of dropsy," Old Hickory told Young Hickory, "how soon this with my other combined afflictions may take me off, that all-wise god . . . only knows. I am ready to submit to his will with calm resignation."[9] He also submitted with resignation to the continued deterioration of his financial health. "Poverty stares us in the face," he admitted. The price of cotton had continued very low, so low in fact that "it yields at present nothing to the grower." He had raised a bountiful crop at the Hermitage but it brought only $1,300 on the market. Worse, a flood destroyed half the crop at the Mississippi plantation. The wood at this plantation was worth "an immense fortune," according to Jackson, and if Andrew had only "obayed my advice, and attended to the wood instead of pushing the cotton," they would have cleared themselves of debt.[10] The General reluctantly concluded that he must sell the Mississippi property, and he asked William B. Lewis in Washington to help him find a buyer. "I fear my son has not sufficient energy to conduct such establishment at a distance," he confessed to Lewis, and since "you are in the thoroughfare of the rich farmers" you can render an enormous service. "Aid me in getting a purchaser," he pleaded, "and I will die happy."[11]

Lewis knew how reluctant Jackson was to sell this property, and indeed Andrew actively opposed it. So he showed the General's letter to Blair, who immediately wrote to his friend and offered his aid. "Now, my Dear General, you must not permit such matters to afflict you while I have means to prevent it." Whatever Jackson needed he would raise. Meanwhile, the General was to forget the interest on the loan now due.[12]

When this letter arrived at the Hermitage Jackson was working with Sarah on their accounts. He read the letter to her and both of them burst into tears. The Hero poured out his thanks "for this deinterested offer of such liberality and friendship." He reckoned that if Blair and Rives could spare $7,000 it would "consolidate our whole debts" into their hands. And they would be repaid, he promised, without question. "Mr. A. Jackson jnr has pledged himself that he will not create another debt, of one dollar untill he is clear of his present incumbrances." "Mr. A. Jackson jnr" happened to be away in Mississippi when Sarah and her father-in-law estimated the amount they needed. When he returned a few weeks later he mentioned a few other debts he had recently incurred and his father was forced to ask Blair and Rives to raise the loan to $8,000.[13]

Rives reconfirmed Blair's pledge. After all, where would they be if

Jackson had not plucked them out of obscurity. "Mr. Blair and myself are indebted to you for *all we are worth.* Some might think that we are indebted to the *people* for it. In answer to such a thought, I say, if ANDREW JACKSON had not *endorsed* us, the people would not have *supported* us."[14]

Under the circumstances it can be imagined how distressed Jackson must have been when his son brought him a rumor that Polk intended to replace the *Globe* as the administration's newspaper organ, a rumor that had been floating around for some time. It was said that Samuel H. Laughlin, editor of the Nashville *Union,* had bought an interest in the *Madisonian* and that he had gone to Washington to become the administration's spokesman. "This if true," said the old man, "would be one of the most fatal steps for Col. Polk that could be taken. . . . It would split the democracy to pieces." Jackson relayed these rumors to the President and begged him to keep the *Globe* as his mouthpiece.[15]

Polk replied that the rumors were utterly without foundation. "No such thing was thought of." But Polk quibbled. He was only talking about Laughlin's taking over the *Madisonian* and making it the administration's organ. The President frankly admitted that there was no newspaper in Washington that "sustains my administration for its own sake." The *Globe,* he said, "does not look to the success or the glory of my administration" so much as it does the interests and wishes of "certain prominent men" in the Democratic party. Moreover, in the course of the last fifteen years, Blair had incurred "the hostility of certain other men" through his hard-hitting editorials—Calhoun for one, although Polk did not mention him by name—and because of these editorials it was impossible for Blair to command the support of the entire party. Since the Democrats were badly fragmented between the friends of the administration, Van Buren, Cass, Calhoun, and others, the President's greatest task was holding it all together. And Blair would be a hindrance toward that end. To be blunt, Polk wanted someone else to assume editorial direction of the *Globe,* such as Thomas Ritchie or Andrew Jackson Donelson, in order to help him unite the democracy.[16]

Late in March Polk summoned Blair to the White House and informed him that he must retire as editor of the *Globe.* If he did not go quietly, the President said, a new administration paper would be founded.[17] At first Blair was tempted to stand his ground and fight, but he quickly realized that a contest with the administration would surely end in his own ruin and the ruin of the Democratic party. Besides, he had grown weary of political strife.[18] It had taken its toll. So Blair capitulated. Ritchie agreed to assume command of the paper—Donelson refused it—and when he offered to purchase the *Globe,* Blair agreed if Jackson and Van Buren approved.[19]

Jackson was devastated. He knew how important it was to hold the Democratic party together but he vehemently denied that the way to do it involved sacking Frank Blair. Jackson wrote Polk a "long candid and friendly" letter in which he told the President that he had gotten some pretty "bad advice" and that he ought to have had enough "good sense" to see through it. The General assured him of Blair's "firm support" and insisted "that the Globe has the confidence of more of the democratic members of Congress than any paper in the Union." He predicted "the destruction of the democratic party" if Polk found another editor. "I am very sick," Jackson told Blair, "exausted by writing to Polk."[20]

The letter to the President was so strong that Polk probably burned it.[21] Still Polk did not budge and on April 12, 1845, the *Globe* was sold to Ritchie and John P. Heiss, publisher of the Nashville *Union,* the Hero having given his approval of the sale a few weeks earlier. On April 14, Blair and Rives publicly announced their departure in the *Globe,* and urged all Democrats to rally behind the President. The *Globe* ceased publication on Wednesday, April 30, and the next day it appeared under a new name, the Washington *Union.*

So the great Democratic organ that Jackson had called into existence disappeared over night. And with it ended one of the most dynamic and tempestuous eras in American history. The Jacksonian revolution had "run its course" and a new generation prepared to administer its legacy. The idealism of democracy and the passion for reform no longer aroused the American people in quite the same way as they had when Andrew Jackson resided in the White House. Sectional jealousy and economic rivalry had replaced them.[22]

"How loathsome it is to me to see an old friend laid aside," Jackson moaned in commenting on Blair's ouster, "principles of Justice to friendship forgotten, and all for the sake of *policy.*" When Jackson thought of the numerous times Blair had defended him when he himself was too engaged or too ill to undertake the task himself, he blessed the day he had met the tiny man. "How grateful I am for such a friend as Mr. Blair," he said.[23] At Polk he wagged his finger in disdain and regret. "My dear friend the movement was hasty," he lectured, "and as I think badly advised and I pray my god that it may not result in injury to the perfect unity of the democracy."[24]

Jackson congratulated Blair on the manner and grace with which he closed down the *Globe.* "You have done your duty to this great party," he told his friend. "You have left it united & prosperous, and I pray god it may so continue—my voice whilst I can speak will be to keep it firmly united, as I know yours will."[25] Much had been sacrificed for the party by both men—now more than ever. But the sacrifices were worth it to Jackson, even though they sometimes inflicted great personal pain.

The closing down of the *Globe* meant that Jackson lost his public defender. He was very jealous of his reputation and quick to take offense over any criticism. Moreover, he was extremely concerned about history's final verdict on his career.

"Doctor, what do you think will be my fame with posterity?" he asked his Presbyterian minister friend, Dr. Edgar. "I mean, what will posterity blame me for most?"

The minister thought a moment and then wondered about the number of his removals.[26] Perhaps they were a bit excessive.

The General shook his head. The facts would not justify such a complaint, he said.

The minister quickly changed the subject by asking him what he would have done with Calhoun and the other nullifiers had they persisted in their intransigence.

"Hung them, sir, as high as Haman," was the immediate reply. "They should have been a terror to traitors to all time, and posterity would have pronounced it the best act of my life."[27]

Since leaving the White House Jackson had been criticized for his many failures, character defects, lapses of judgment, and all-around misrule as chief executive. Each time these attacks appeared in print, Blair rushed to Jackson's defense. Even now with John Quincy Adams quoting his diary to prove that Jackson acquiesced in the surrender of Texas in the Florida Treaty of 1819, the *Globe* spoke up for Old Hickory in its final issues and dismissed Adams's claims as pure fabrication. "I feel greatly indebted to my friend Mr. Blair," Jackson remarked to Van Buren at one point, "for the defence of my character and the castigation he has given to that old scamp John Q. Adams who makes statements contradicted by the recorded history of the times and diaries, to prop up his utter falsehoods, as it regards myself."[28]

This final brawl between Adams and Jackson earned neither one any merit. How different the attitude between John Adams and Thomas Jefferson in their old age. Somehow the country seemed nastier than it had been a few decades before. Elegance and gentility had disappeared.[29]

So now the *Globe* was gone. And the old man sorrowed. In the future who would defend him against the scamps who might try to defame him?

He knew he had only a few months to live and yet he concerned himself over his stature in history. Since the beginning of the year the shortness of breath had become so acute that he thought at times he would suffocate. Early in April his feet and legs swelled. Then his hands and abdomen. He looked awful. "It may be," he wrote, "that my life ends in dropsy, all means hitherto used to stay the swelling has now failed to check it. I am fully prepared to say the Lord's will be done."[30]

A friend visited him and in the course of their conversation mentioned that he looked very weak and infirm. "Yes," the Hero replied, "I feel my time is approaching, but I am prepared to die—when the Angel of Death comes I shall say with pleasure—march on, I'll follow."[31]

At about the time he celebrated his seventy-eighth birthday on March 15, 1845, Jackson received a letter from Commodore Jesse Duncan Elliott, who offered him a sarcophagus for his personal use which had been brought from Palestine and was believed to have been made for the

Roman Emperor Severus. To think that anyone could imagine this crusty old democrat lying for eternity in an emperor's coffin! Jackson graciously declined the honor. "I cannot consent that my mortal body shall be laid in a repository prepared for an Emperor or a King—my republican feelings and principles forbid it—the simplicity of our system of government forbids it." Every monument erected in this country for our statesmen and heroes, he continued, "ought to bear evidence of the economy and simplicity of our republican institutions and the plainness of our republican citizens, who are sovereigns of our glorious Union, and whose virtue is to perpetuate it." Virtue is the bedrock of republicanism, and "true virtue cannot exist where pomp and parade are the governing passions. It can only dwell with the people, the great laboring and producing classes, that form the bone and sinew of our confederacy."[32]

Right to the very end of his life, Jackson extolled the laboring class as the vital core of democracy. Not business-oriented plutocrats. Not a cadre of aspiring entrepreneurs. But "the great laboring and producing classes." Long ago he had declared his faith and trust and abiding commitment in the mass of American workers and farmers and he had transformed that commitment to the highest level of participation in the political process.

In refusing the sarcophagus, Jackson explained that he had already prepared a "depository" for his mortal remains beside that of his beloved wife. "Without any pomp or parade," he would sleep beside Rachel "until the last trumpet sounds to call the dead to judgment, when we, I hope, shall rise together."[33]

But while he still drew breath, however labored, the Old Hero kept up a lively interest in the running of his plantation and the running of the nation. He wrote letters practically every day in his own hand, and there was no loss of intellectual vitality or strength. His handwriting showed few signs of physical difficulty. Although his body deteriorated rapidly, Jackson still willed to survive.

Isaac Hill was one of the General's last visitors "from back East." He was appalled by what he saw. A bloated shell stared up at him. "If it were any other man," Hill wrote, "I could scarcely suppose he would live a week." For the past four months Jackson had not taken his customary meals with the family, he reported. Throughout the day the General sat in a well-constructed easy chair, with his writing materials, miniature Bible, and hymn book. As soon as the daily mail arrived Jackson demanded the Washington newspapers and those letters bearing the postmark of the capital. "With all his bodily weakness," said Hill, "his intellect seems to have been brightened and matured by time."[34]

Dozens of other visitors came regularly to see Old Hickory in these final months of his life. They wanted the privilege of boasting that they had seen Andrew Jackson face to face before he died. On May 29, for example, a crowd of thirty trooped through his bedroom. "All were admitted," wrote an observer, "from the humblest to the most renowned, to take the venerable chieftain by the hand and bid him farewell."[35]

The Hero radiated graciousness, although he could barely hold his head up. He apologized for his weakness and thanked one and all for visiting him. General Jesup, commander during the Second Seminole War, called and was distressed by how ghostly the Hero looked. He asked Jackson how he felt and what the future might hold.

Old Hickory could barely move. The swelling of his body practically immobilized him. "Sir," the dying man croaked, "I am in the hands of a merciful God. I have full confidence in his goodness and mercy.... The Bible is true.... I have tried to conform to its spirit as near as possible. Upon that sacred volume I rest my hope for eternal salvation, through the merits and blood of our blessed Lord and Saviour, Jesus Christ."[36]

Although Jackson's religious faith naturally intensified at this time, it actually had been a fixture of his life for several decades. His dependence on Providence, his Christian acceptance of sorrow and tragedy, his belief in repentance and salvation through the merits of Christ—all these had long constituted his basic religious faith and did not change during his final years. Even when he joined the church there was no perceptible alteration in his behavior or thinking except that he now received communion on a regular basis. Since he could no longer leave his room, he usually asked his daughter-in-law to invite the minister to return home with her after services in order to allow him to "partake of the sacred feast."[37]

As the days passed in late spring 1845 Jackson's bloated condition worsened. "I am a blubber of water," he said. The swelling now extended to his face and his suffering was quite acute. He could not lie down. Indeed he had not been able to lie down for the past six months. He had to be propped up with pillows in his bed at night and in his armchair during the day. In addition he had great difficulty breathing, although his cough had nearly disappeared.[38] "My dear Andrew," he wrote to Donelson, "what may be my fate god only knows. I am greatly afflicted, suffer much.... I [am] swollen from the toes to the crown of my head, and in bandages to my hips." In addition he suffered a return of acute diarrhea accompanied by constant nausea. "How far my god may think proper to bear me up under my weight of afflictions," the Hero said, "he only knows."[39]

Each morning the family was surprised to find that he had survived another night. Then they had him moved to his armchair. During the day he usually dressed in an old-style snuff-colored coat with a high stiff collar, presidential and dignified to the end. A coverlet was thrown over him from chest to toe and a servant boy stood near by fanning him to keep off flies and other insects. There was "a look of death" about him, reported visitors. His once falcon eye seemed "sunken and rayless," his countenance "languid and insignificant."[40] Jackson's appearance was so distorted throughout the spring that when George P. A. Healy, a young American painter, arrived at the Hermitage to execute a portrait of the General, he was frustrated in his efforts to get a respectable likeness. Healy, who resided in Paris, had been sent to America by the king of France, Louis Philippe, to paint the portraits of Jackson and twelve of the most distinguished revolutionary patriots.[41] The king wanted Jackson's portrait to hang in his gallery beside that of George Washington. The twelve others would surround these two notables. The best Healy could do, as it finally developed, was to copy one of Earl's portraits and retouch it in places. "The upper face of the General struck him to day as very peculiar," reported Judge Catron in a letter to Sarah, but "by retouching it in the General's presence . . . he thought he could satisfy the general and his friends, as well as his employer."[42] When Healy finished the portrait and showed it to Jackson the old man was extremely pleased with it and in a tone of uncommon graciousness said it was the best likeness that had been done of him. "I feel very much obliged to you, sir, for the very great labor and care you have been pleased to bestow upon it."[43]

By the time Healy finished the portrait Jackson was "a perfect Jelly from the toes to the upper part of my abdome, in any part of which a finger can be pressed half an Inch and the print will remain for minutes." Also, his bowels seemed to be disintegrating. Between his gastrointestinal problems and his colitis, he experienced excruciating "bowell complaints, several passages with gripping daily, with a severe attack of piles."[44] By this time the family had taken up a death watch. They hovered about him throughout the day, until about nine o'clock at night when they would take their leave, except for the few who rotated to watch by his side. As each member approached him to say good night he would kiss them, bless them, and bid them farewell as though he might never see them again. "My work is done for life," he would murmur.[45]

Each new day he struggled to "discharge every duty" he felt obliged to fulfill. That had been a guiding principle throughout his entire life. If nothing else there was always his enormous correspondence. But sometimes his pain was so intense that he lay motionless throughout the entire day. "Yet, in the midst of the worse paroxysm of pain, not a murmur, not even a groan escaped his lips." Still his suffering etched itself clearly on his bloated face.[46]

Sarah Jackson or her widowed sister, Marion Adams, who lived with the family since her husband's death, constantly attended the dying man throughout the day. His granddaughter, Rachel, who was now twelve years of age, visited him frequently. Whenever she entered his bedroom the General would look at her with "peculiar affection." The child was said to have "all the lovely and amiable qualities" of her namesake.

Sometimes Jackson's strength seemed to return and he would talk at length about Texas and Oregon or political conditions within the country. He said he was happy that the nation seemed fixed on a democratic course and "that the rights of the laboring classes were respected and protected." "Give them an honest government, freedom from monopolies, and privileged classes," he would storm with some of his old vigor and enthusiasm; "give them . . . hard money—not paper currency for their hard labor, and all will be well."[47]

On Sunday, June 1, 1845, the General asked his family to invite the Reverend Mr. Lapshy and Dr. Curry to visit him after services. It was very important to him. "This is apparently the last Sabbath I shall be with you," he ventured. For the rest of the morning he remained very quiet. When the clerics arrived Jackson brightened and talked with them at length upon "religious subjects." He was "calm & resigned and said that he was ready to go whenever his divine master thought fit to take him, that he suffered a great deal of bodily pain, but the Lords will be done." The clergymen nodded appreciation of his Christian fortitude and acceptance of divine providence. Then they gave him Holy Communion. It was a "solemn scene," said his son.[48]

The Hero closed his eyes for a long moment after receiving communion. When at last he opened them he again "referred to his death & felt confident it was not far distant—but that he had no fears of it." He looked at his visitors most intently. "When I have suffered sufficiently," he said very slowly and deliberately, "the Lord will then take me to himself—but what are all my suffering compared to those of the blessed Saviour, who died upon that cursed tree for me, mine are nothing." With that Old Hickory began praying. The Hero of New Orleans, the terror of Indians, Spaniards, British soldiers, politicians, and other assorted "scamps," lay on his deathbed praying with fervor and deep conviction.

From that moment on, reported his son, something very strange and marvelous happened. Andrew Jackson never again mentioned his suffering, "not a murmur was ever heard from him—all was borne with amazing fortitude—he spent much of his time in secret prayer, as was evident from the movements of his lips & hands."[49]

Not that his suffering escaped the attention of his family. They watched every movement he made and quickly responded to any sign of distress. In fact the very next day he began to swell alarmingly and his physician, Dr. John H. Esselman, was summoned immediately from Nashville. An operation was performed, Jackson was "tapped," and "much water was taken from his abdomen."[50] This provided immediate relief but totally prostrated the poor man. Indeed, the number of surgical procedures performed on Jackson during his lifetime approaches the astronomical.

That night his suffering was very great. An anodyne was administered to help him sleep but it had little effect. Early the next morning Doctors Robertson and Waters arrived from Nashville to consult with Esselman, who had remained the night, and they agreed that nothing more should be done except to "conform to the General's temporary wants."[51]

On Thursday, June 5, Jackson again talked at length about the comfort of the Christian religion. "What blessed promises," he murmured, "are those in the Portuguese hymns." And then from memory he recited the following:

> "When thro, the deep waters I call thee to go
> The rivers of wo shall not thee overflow."[52]

After that—unbelievably—he rallied. The next day he said he felt "pretty comfortable," which brought smiles to the faces of the family; but then he added: "I shall not long be with you." He asked that Major Lewis and Judge Campbell assist his son in making his funeral arrangements. "I wish to be buried in a plain, unostentatious manner," he said. Then he jabbered on about Texas and praised the conduct of Sam Houston. As for Oregon, he had confidence that Polk would acquire it without resorting to war. "If not," he declared, "let war come. There will be patriots enough in the land to repel foreign aggression . . . to maintain sacredly our just rights and to perpetuate our glorious constitution and liberty, and to preserve our happy Union."[53]

What he did worry about was fraud and corruption in the government, the very thing that had started him on the road to the White House twenty years before and had prompted him to initiate a program for "reform retrenchment and economy." So saying he called for pen and paper and in a steady hand that showed no trace of his impending death he wrote:

(confidential)

Hermitage
June 6th 1845

James K. Polk
president of the
United States—

My dear Sir,
    Your letter of the 12th ultimo *(confidential)* has been received—Be assured my friend that it is truly gratefull to learn from you that you have a united & harmonious Cabinett—May it so continue to exist through your administration, is the prayer of your friend. . . . I am informed thro a channel in which I have a right to confide, and is a man of much truth himself—That the late Secretary of the Treasury, for the short time, he was at the head of it [George M. Bibb], made ninety thousand dollars, by arangements with the two brokers Banks of Newyork where large sums of the public mony was deposited, & other deposit Banks in N.York. Enquire cautiously amonghst the clerks in the city of Washington, by which you will find a key that may unlock the door to a proper enquiry—But an enquiry by the Whiggs, are prepared for you should Mr. Walker [the present secretary of the treasury] have the folly to have any thing to do with either of these abominable projects—I say to you put yr veto upon them both, or you & your secretary will be blown sky high—And what cares those corrupt speculators for you, or his character if they ever get hold

of the cash—I can write no more—friendship has aroused me to make this attempt—yr friend

Andrew Jackson[54]

This was the last letter Jackson wrote, although he franked a letter for Andrew the following day to Thomas F. Marshall of Kentucky. Unfortunately his Polk letter went undelivered for five months.[55] Andrew had mislaid it.

After writing to the President, the General broke out in a cold clammy sweat, evidence "of death approaching," reported his son. Jackson talked very little after that. He seemed to know the end was near. Later in the evening Dr. Esselman came to see what he could do to "check his bowels but to no purpose." Because of mounting water in his chest the old man had increased difficulty in breathing. He asked the doctor to remain with him, "aware that his dissolution was near at hand." He rested for the remainder of the evening without uttering a word.[56]

Despite his prediction, the Hero did live to see another Sabbath—June 8—a hot, bright day. His servants, George and Dick, had just propped him in his armchair when Dr. Esselman entered his room to check his condition. "I immediately perceived that the hand of death was upon him," recorded the doctor. He summoned the family and Andrew then dispatched a servant to fetch Major Lewis. Shortly thereafter, "nature seemed to give way & the general fainted."

"He is gone," announced Dr. Esselman.[57]

The family stared at the figure for a moment and then moved him back into his bed. But the old warrior still had life in him. Slowly he opened his eyes. He spoke, and the sound of his voice startled everyone in the room. He asked to see his grandchildren. Quickly they were hurried into the room and everyone crowded around his bed.

Jackson turned to Sarah first and thanked her for all her kindness, especially during his long illness. Next he said farewell to Marion Adams and after her, his adopted son. Finally he said goodbye to his grandchildren and then the children of Mrs. Adams. One by one he took them by the hand and kissed them and blessed them. He told them that they had good parents and that they must all be obedient children. They must all "keep holy the Sabboth day and read the New Testament."[58]

Still alert, his mind incredibly clear, he noticed that two children were missing, a grandson and one of Mrs. Adams's sons. When told that they were attending Sunday school he asked that they be summoned. When they arrived in his bedroom Jackson kissed and blessed them.

By this time most of his servants had either gathered in the room or congregated at the windows. With such an audience, all tears, he could not resist lecturing them, both family and servants. He delivered, said Dr. Esselman, "one of the most impressive lectures on the subject of religion that I have ever heard." He spoke "with calmness, with strength, and, indeed, with animation." He also spoke at length—at least half an hour. He confessed his implicit faith in the Christian religion, the hope of salvation as revealed in the Bible, his great anxiety that they should all "look to Christ as their only Saviour." Then he turned to his servants. They must do their duty, he declared. "As much was expected of them according to their opportunities," he said, "as from whites." They "must try and meet him in heaven," he commanded.[59]

Major Lewis arrived about 2 P.M. The old man smiled. "Major," he said, "I am glad to see you. You had like to have been too late." He gave Lewis messages for Houston, Blair, Benton, and others. He sent them his farewell. After that he lapsed into a long silence.[60]

At four o'clock the General appeared to be sinking rapidly. His son approached the bed and took the old man's hand. "Father," he whispered, "how do you feel,—do you know me."

The figure stirred. "Know you—yes," came the reply. "I would know you all, if I could but see—bring my spectacles."

His eyeglasses were brought to him and adjusted to his head.

"Where is my Daughter & Marion," he asked. When he saw them he spoke again. "God will take care of you for me. I am my God's. I belong to him, I go but a short time before you, and I want to meet you all in heaven, both white & black."[61]

Everyone in the room burst into tears. The servants standing outside on the porch also cried out and wrung their hands. Jackson seemed startled by the sobbing.

"What is the matter with my Dear Children," he said, "have I alarmed you? Oh, do not cry—be good children & we will all meet in heaven."[62]

Those were Jackson's last words. He fixed his eyes on his granddaughter, Rachel, as though "invoking the blessings of heaven to rest upon her." His breathing was so gentle that it was difficult to know whether he was still alive. Major Lewis supported his head to help him breathe. At six o'clock, after "one slight convulsion," General Andrew Jackson, the seventh President of the United States, expired, aged seventy-eight years, two months, and twenty-four days. The long years of suffering had ended. "Thus died the greatest and best man of the age, or, perhaps of any age," said Dr. Esselman.[63]

It has long been assumed that the immediate cause of Jackson's death was heart failure as evidenced by dropsy. But recently doctors have suggested that his death resulted from nephrotic kidneys caused by amyloidosis. This disease usually follows many years of infection. Certainly Jackson suffered a massive edema of the entire body during his last illness which, according to medical science, is not usual in congestive heart failure—at least not when the patient has suffered intermittent fluid retention over such a long period of time as Jackson did. Perhaps no single cause of death can ever be assigned. Jackson suffered from so many illnesses—respiratory and gastrointestinal, on top of which he regularly poisoned himself with calomel and mercury—that after a long and valiant struggle his body simply gave out.[64] It could no longer respond to his imperious will.

Immediately upon Jackson's death the news of it shot out across the countryside. No name was mentioned. "The Old Hero, the Old Roman, the Old Lion, the Great Captain is dead."[65] And everyone knew who that was. Literally moments after the warrior died, General Sam Houston and his young son arrived at the Hermitage to receive a final blessing. "He was there in time to grasp the hand of his friend, but it was cold in death." He fell to his knees, sobbing, and buried his face on Jackson's breast. After a moment Houston composed himself and drew the boy to his side. "My son," he said, "try to remember that you have looked upon the face of Andrew Jackson."[66]

The mayor of Nashville, P. W. Maxey, called a special session of the Board of Aldermen for Monday at 9 A.M., at which time it was resolved that a public meeting be held at the court house at 4 P.M. to arrange "suitable preparations" for the funeral of their "distinguished dead." At that public meeting Andrew Ewing and Sam Houston spoke to a very large crowd of people. Then resolutions were passed extolling the dead and directing that minute guns be fired during the funeral from ten until two, that the survivors of the General's army serve as pallbearers, that all business be suspended throughout the day of the funeral, and that citizens attending the funeral wear "ordinary garb to honor the request of the deceased."[67] In the meantime the family distributed a simple notice: "The friends and acquaintance of GEN. ANDREW JACKSON are invited to attend his Funeral at the Hermitage, on to-morrow (Tuesday) morning at 11 o'clock. Divine service by the Rev. Dr. Edgar. His death took place last evening at 6 o'clock."[68]

The body of the Hero was laid out in the parlor of the Hermitage with the face uncovered. Everyone wished to take one final look at this "greatest and best man of the age." The coffin was draped in black cloth with a silver plate in the form of a shield upon it bearing the name of "ANDREW JACKSON."[69]

Early Tuesday morning every conceivable vehicle in the neighborhood was pressed into service to carry the mourners to the Hermitage. Over two hundred carriages drove onto the grounds, to say nothing of the horses, and they filled the yard in front of the house and the surrounding woods. Something like three thousand people attended the service.[70]

At eleven o'clock the Reverend Dr. Edgar took a position on the front porch next to the parlor and preached a sermon taken from Revelation 7:13–14:

> 13th And one of the elders answered, saying unto me, what are these which are arrayed in white robes? And whence came they?

14th And I said unto him, sir, thou knowest. And he said to me, these are they which came out of great tribulation, and have washed their robes, and made them white in the blood of the Lamb.

William Frierson Cooper, who attended the services, said that Edgar's "sermon was nothing extraordinary." But when the minister spoke about Jackson himself he seemed to catch fire. "His remarks towards the close in relation to Genl Jackson, were very good," recorded Cooper. "He dwelt upon his private character, & upon his christian conduct. His audiences were deeply impressed. Verily, the tears started, unbidden, to my own eyes."[71]

The slaves, standing nearby in groups of fifteen and twenty, wept silently. When Edgar addressed them and spoke of Jackson's character there was a great "gush of grief," wrote one reporter, "and I, as usual, sent forth my shower."[72]

After the eulogy the assembled mourners sang several hymns: "Why Do We Mourn Departed Friends," "Why Should We Start & Fear to Die," "I Would Not Live Always," and "How Firm a Foundation Ye Saints of the Lord."[73]

While these hymns were being sung, the body was laid in a customary coffin, which coffin was placed in a second one of lead and the top carefully soldered. Then Jackson's remains were slowly carried to the mausoleum in the garden to rest beside his wife's as he had directed.[74]

As the coffin was lowered into the ground, another hymn was sung. Apparently, before he died, the General had decreed that no "dirt" must be thrown on top of his remains, so the coffin was lowered into an open vault that was lined with limestone and brick. At the bottom of the vault, four feet below the level of the ground, a slab of limestone was placed over the coffin and inscribed with the words: "GENERAL ANDREW JACKSON."[75]

The Reverend Dr. Edgar intoned the words of Psalm 90 as the grave was closed. Three volleys of musket, fired by the Nashville Blues in uniform, concluded the service. Off in the distance could be heard the firing of minute guns and the mournful tolling of church bells.

News of Jackson's death moved across the country very rapidly. Immediately, newspapers bordered their columns in black; flags flew at half-mast; public offices were "decorated in sable crape"; and the toll of church bells "and the sound of the salute guns from every armed position" announced "that mourning is in the land." Eulogies were preached in pulpits, lecture halls, and newspapers. Sometimes they came from the most unlikely places. The Charleston *Mercury*, for example, acknowledged his towering presence in American life. "Standing over his grave few men will deny him the praise of patriotism; none, the distinction of greatness; and we do neither so abound with Heroes or with Patriots, that one can think of his final removal without deep and poignant regret. Who shall fill that mighty space where his shadow stands?" Speaking before the New-York Historical Society, Daniel Webster called Jackson a man of "dauntless courage, vigor, and perseverance," who, on several occasions, as President, had shown "wisdom and energy."[76]

When President Polk heard the sorrowful news he promptly closed government offices and directed military personnel to wear mourning for six months. He ordered a solemn funeral ceremony of commemoration on June 27, and citizens of Washington voluntarily suspended business to attend and witness the rites. On the appointed day, the funeral procession formed at President's Square at one o'clock and marched up Pennsylvania Avenue to the Capitol. It stretched one mile in length. In its ranks rode or walked the President, heads of departments and bureaus, the judiciary, the diplomatic corps, the authorities of the District, the military, "numerous ASSOCIATIONS—citizens and strangers." On reaching the east front of the Capitol the crowd heard a prayer by the Reverend Mr. Sprogle and a two-hour oration by George Bancroft, the noted historian and secretary of the navy. Bancroft extolled Jackson's long career in a handsome and moving address. "He was the servant of the people," said Bancroft of Old Hickory. "In discipline stern, in a just resolution inflexible, he was full of the gentlest affections, ever ready to solace the distressed, and to relieve the needy, faithful to his friends, fervid for his country. Indifferent to other rewards, he aspired throughout his life to an honorable fame, and so loved his fellow-men, that he longed to dwell in their affectionate remembrance. Heaven gave him length of days, and he filled them with deeds of greatness."[77]

Virtually every city and community throughout the country produced similar processions and commemorations. In Baltimore, reported one newspaper, "the ceremonies were unsurpassed by those of any city of the Union, in taste and arrangement, the comparative numbers and appropriate display, in short in every particular to render the pageant imposing and expressive of the occasion." Chief Justice Roger B. Taney officiated and he seemed shaken by this outpouring of affection and reverence. In Philadelphia, the Vice President of the United States, George M. Dallas, not only led the procession but pronounced the eulogy.[78]

But one of the most imposing and impressive ceremonies occurred in New York City on June 24. Although the weather was extremely warm, an immense crowd turned out to honor the Hero. They began gathering in the streets at daybreak even though the start of the rites was scheduled for 2 P.M. The procession formed on Grand Street and then turned into the Bowery and headed for City Hall Park. The numbers of organizations and societies that demanded to walk in the procession stunned and delighted the committee on arrangements. Everyone seemed to feel a desperate need to participate in this public tribute to Andrew Jackson.

Thirteen divisions marched in this parade. The first division consisted entirely of military personnel, among whom were the Light Guard, Independence Guard, Tompkins Blues, Washington Guard, and the National Guard. In the second division came the officiating clergy, ex-President Martin Van Buren, Governor Silas Wright, Jr., Secretary of War William L. Marcy, General of the Army Winfield Scott, and his aides, members of the court of errors, and officers of the army and navy.

Then followed a "funeral Urn," escorted by a guard of U.S. Marines and troops from Governor's Island. The Urn was borne on an open cart, draped in black, and drawn by four white horses, also caparisoned in black. A groom walked behind the cart leading a riderless horse, both arrayed in mourning. Spectators standing on the sidewalks openly wept as the Urn passed by. The pallbearers, twenty-eight in number, followed in carriages arranged in a double line, and these included the most distinguished citizens from New York City, Brooklyn, and Jersey City.

The next division comprised such dignitaries as foreign ministers and consuls, who were escorted by the City Guard. These gentlemen, "in rich uniforms," rode in carriages and were accompanied by the U.S. Marshal and his deputies, the collector of the port and officers of the customhouse, magistrates, members of the bar, police, sheriff and deputies. Then came the president, faculty, and students of Columbia University, "cum multis aliis," reported the press.[79]

The fifth division consisted of the Tammany Society, "the democratic republican committee, the American republican general committee, ward committees," and other Democrats. The "Empire Club" marched in this division and escorted a large vehicle, draped in mourning, "on which was a tomb in imitation of white marble," bearing the simple inscription "JACKSON." This was followed "by grooms with lead horses, richly caparisoned, but all their housings dressed in mourning."

The remaining divisions included Odd Fellows, literary groups, civic clubs, benevolent societies, and workingmen's associations. Many of them carried "beautiful banners, insignias &c, dressed in deep mourning."

Among all the marching societies and organizations none presented a more imposing appearance or attracted greater attention than the members of the Fire Department, "who turned out in great force." The firemen were dressed in black, their banners and trumpets shrouded in mourning. These "ordinary citizens," commented the press, these urban workers, by their numbers and obvious devotion, bespoke the "love of millions" for Old Hickory.[80]

The route of the procession was "crowded with an immense throng, while door steps and windows" and even rooftops were jammed with spectators. Most mercantile establishments were closed for the day and all flags flew at half-mast. Bells throughout the city were tolled from 2 P.M., when the procession began, until the last division reached the Park. At the same time minute guns were fired from the Battery, Tompkins

Square, and Brooklyn Heights. The procession, which was formed six abreast, took three hours to pass a given point.[81]

At City Hall a crowd estimated at six thousand gathered in front of an improvised stage to hear an oration delivered by Benjamin F. Butler, the former attorney general. The ex-President, the governor, the secretary of war, and the twenty-eight pallbearers, along with clergymen and a large choir from the Sacred Music Society, sat on the stage to listen. After a "solemn and appropriate prayer" by the Reverend Mr. Krebs, Butler walked to the center of the platform and addressed the crowd.

"Andrew Jackson," he began, "upon whose bed of sickness and suffering have been so intently fixed the filial and solicitous regards of the millions of Americans, is no more. His great soul has ascended to its Author; his venerable form has sunk into the grave. To that grave, with swelling hearts, and tearful eyes, and sad funeral rites, a nation is repairing. We have come to it to-day. While we linger within its sacred precincts, the praises of the hero we reverenced, the magistrate we have honored, and the man we loved, rise instinctively to our lips. To their free utterance affection prompts, duty enjoins, nature compels us. It is fitting, it is right that such tributes should be paid to those who, in council or in camp, have advanced the glory of their country and the welfare of their kind."[82]

Despite the heat of the day and the size of the crowd, the oration "was listened to with great attention by the vast assemblage." Indeed it was a very moving address and deeply affected all those who heard it. At its close a dirge composed for the occasion was sung by the Sacred Music Society, accompanied by "an excellent band." The proceedings closed with a blessing delivered by the Reverend Dr. Wainwright.

From the moment the procession began until the conclusion of Butler's oration, the funeral commemoration took six hours. It was an endurance, but the people felt a need to participate to the very end in order to testify to their love and devotion for this great man. Around the country similar expressions accompanied every ceremony that marked Jackson's passing. Most testified with tears. A few struggled to find appropriate words. The number of literary efforts to commemorate his death surpassed anything attempted for previous Presidents or heroes. All attested to the nation's staggering loss:

> Weep, Columbia, weep!
> Breathe once again the note
> Of sorrow, stern and deep,
> Wide o'er the land to float,—
> He rests—the Hero-Sage
> His earthly toils are o'er,
> And History's golden page
> Shall wait for him no more.[83]

At length one sovereign artist found the language to express what Andrew Jackson had meant to his generation. In *Moby Dick,* Herman Melville paid everlasting tribute to the fallen hero:

"Men may seem detestable . . . but man, in the ideal, is so noble and so sparkling . . . that over any ignominious blemish in him all his fellows should run to throw their costliest robes. . . . But this august dignity I treat of, is not the dignity of kings and robes, but that abounding dignity which has no robed investiture. Thou shall see it shining in the arm that wields a pick or drives a spike; that democratic dignity which, on all hands, radiates without end from God; Himself! The great God absolute! The centre and circumference of all democracy! His omnipresence, our divine equality!

"If, then, to meanest mariners, and renegades and castaways, I shall hereafter ascribe high qualities, though dark; weave round them tragic graces; . . . if I shall touch that workman's arm with some ethereal light . . . then against all mortal critics bear me out in it, thou just Spirit of Equality, which hast spread one royal mantle of humanity over all my kind! Bear me out in it, thou great democratic God! . . . Thou who didst pick up Andrew Jackson from the pebbles; who didst hurl him upon a warhorse; who didst thunder him higher than a throne! Thou who, in all Thy mighty earthly marchings, ever cullest Thy selectest champions from the kingly commons; bear me out in it, O God!"[84]

To such an invocation of Jackson on behalf of the democratic ideal, one can only say, Amen, O God, Amen.

Notes

Abbreviations and Short Titles Used in the Notes

Adams, *Memoirs*	Charles Francis Adams, ed., *Memoirs of John Quincy Adams* (Philadelphia, 1874–1877), 12 volumes.
AHR	*American Historical Review*
AJ	Andrew Jackson
ASPFA	*American State Papers, Foreign Affairs*
ASPIA	*American State Papers, Indian Affairs*
ASPMA	*American State Papers, Military Affairs*
Bassett, *Jackson*	John Spencer Bassett, *The Life of Andrew Jackson* (New York, 1916).
Bemis, *Adams*	Samuel Flagg Bemis, *John Quincy Adams* (New York, 1956), 2 volumes.
Benton, *Thirty Years View*	Thomas Hart Benton, *Thirty Years View* (New York, 1865), 2 volumes.
Calhoun Papers	W. Edwin Hamphill et al., eds., *The Papers of John C. Calhoun* (Columbia, 1963–), 14 volumes.
CHS	Chicago Historical Society
CUL	Columbia University Library
Duane, *Narrative and Correspondence*	William J. Duane, *Narrative and Correspondence Concerning the Removal of the Deposites and Occurrences Connected Therewith* (Philadelphia, 1838).
DUL	Duke University Library
Freehling, *Prelude to Civil War*	William W. Freehling, *Prelude to Civil War: The Nullification Controversy in South Carolina, 1816–1836* (New York, 1965).
Hamilton, *Reminiscences*	James A. Hamilton, *Reminiscences of James A. Hamilton* (New York, 1869).
HL	Huntington Library

Hone, *Diary*	Allan Nevins, ed., *The Diary of Philip Hone, 1828–1851* (New York, 1927), 2 volumes.
HUL	Harvard University Library
Jackson, *Correspondence*	John Spencer Bassett, ed., *The Correspondence of Andrew Jackson* (Washington, D.C., 1926–1933), 6 volumes.
JAH	*Journal of American History*
James, *Jackson*	Marquis James, *The Life of Andrew Jackson* (Indianapolis and New York, 1938).
JPP	Jackson Papers Project, Hermitage, Tennessee
JRDF	John R. Delafield Foundation, New York, N.Y.
JSH	*Journal of Southern History*
Kendall, *Autobiography*	William Stickney, ed., *The Autobiography of Amos Kendall* (Boston, 1872).
Latner, *Presidency of Jackson*	Richard B. Latner, *The Presidency of Andrew Jackson: White House Politics, 1829–1837* (Athens, Ga., 1979).
LC	Library of Congress
LHA	Ladies'Hermitage Association,Hermitage,Tenn.
McLemore, *Franco-American Relations*	Richard A. McLemore, *Franco-American Diplomatic Relations, 1816–1836* (University, La., 1941).
Manning, *Diplomatic Correspondence*	William R. Manning, *Diplomatic Correspondence of the United States, Inter-American Affairs* (Washington, D.C., 1933), 12 volumes.
MHS	Massachusetts Historical Society
ML	Pierpont Morgan Library, New York, N.Y.
Munroe, *McLane*	John A. Munroe, *Louis McLane: Federalist and Jacksonian* (New Brunswick, 1973).
MVHR	*Mississippi Valley Historical Review*
NA	National Archives
NYHS	New-York Historical Society
NYPL	New York Public Library
NYSL	New York State Library
Parton, *Jackson*	James Parton, *The Life of Andrew Jackson* (Boston, 1866), 3 volumes.
PHS	Historical Society of Pennsylvania, Philadelphia, Pa.
Polk Papers	Herbert Weaver et al., eds., *Correspondence of James K. Polk* (Nashville, 1969–), 5 volumes.
PUL	Princeton University Library
Remini, *Jackson*	Robert V. Remini, *Andrew Jackson and the Course of American Empire, 1767–1821* (New York, 1977); *Andrew Jackson and the Course of American Freedom, 1822–1832* (New York, 1981).
RG	Record Group
Richardson, *Messages and Papers*	J. D. Richardson, *Compilation of the Messages and Papers of the Presidents* (Washington, D.C., 1908), 20 volumes.

RUL   University of Rochester Library

Schlesinger, *Age of Jackson*   Arthur M. Schlesinger, Jr., *The Age of Jackson* (Boston, 1946).

Sellers, *Polk*   Charles G. Sellers, Jr., *James K. Polk, Jacksonian, 1795–1843* (Princeton, 1957); *James K. Polk, Continentalist, 1843–1846* (Princeton, 1966).

SHC   Southern Historical Collection, University of North Carolina, Chapel Hill, N.C.

THM   *Tennessee Historical Magazine*

THQ   *Tennessee Historical Quarterly*

THS   Tennessee Historical Society

TSL   Tennessee State Library, Nashville, Tenn.

Tyler, *Letters and Times*   Lyon G. Tyler, *The Letters and Times of the Tylers* (Richmond, 1884–1896), 3 volumes.

Van Buren, *Autobiography*   John C. Fitzpatrick, ed., *Autobiography of Martin Van Buren* (Washington, D. C., 1920).

Webster Papers   Charles M. Wiltse et al., eds., *The Papers of Daniel Webster* (Hanover, N.H., 1974–), 5 volumes.

Weed, *Autobiography*   Harriet H. Weed, ed., *Autobiography of Thurlow Weed* (Boston, 1883).

White, *Jacksonians*   Leonard D. White, *The Jacksonians: A Study in Administrative History, 1829–1861* (New York, 1954).

White, *Memoir*   Nancy N. Scott, ed., *Memoir of Hugh Lawson White* (Philadelphia, 1856).

Wiltse, *Calhoun*   Charles M. Wiltse, *John C. Calhoun* (Indianapolis and New York, 1949), 3 volumes.

WSH   State Historical Society of Wisconsin, Madison

WUL   Washington University Library, St. Louis, Mo.

YUL   Yale University Library

CHAPTER 1

1. J. D. Steele, Manuscript Journal, HL; AJ to Donelson, October 5, 10, 1832, Donelson Papers, LC; AJ to Andrew Jackson, Jr., September 30, 1832, William K. Bixby Collection, WUL.

2. For details of the 1832 presidential election, see Remini, *Jackson*, II, 374ff; for Jackson's mounting problems with South Carolina and Georgia, see ibid., 275ff and 381ff. The quotation, which Jackson repeated many times in different places, is taken from AJ to Poinsett, January 24, 1833, in Jackson, *Correspondence*, V, 11.

3. The quotations and descriptions are taken from the following travelers' accounts: Michel Chevalier, *Society, Manners and Politics in the United States* (Boston, 1839), pp. 267, 269–270, 271–272, 299; Francis Grund, *Aristocracy in America* (London, 1839), pp. 107–111; Captain Frederick Marryat, *A Diary in America* (London, 1839); J. S. Buckingham, *America* (London, 1841), p. 53; Captain Basil Hall, *Travels in North America in the Years 1827 and 1828* (Philadelphia, 1829); Thomas Hamilton, *Men and Manners in America* (Philadelphia, 1833), I, 14; Harriet Martineau, *Society in America* (New York, 1837), I, 29–31, 210ff; and Frances Trollope, *Domestic Manners of the Americans* (London, 1832), pp. 416–419.

4. On the changing role of women in American society, see Mary P. Ryan, *Womanhood in America* (New York, 1975); Nancy F. Cott, *The Bonds of Womanhood* (New Haven, 1976); and Barbara Welter, "The Cult of True Womanhood, 1820–1860," *American Quarterly* (1966), XVIII, 151–174.

5. On American industrialization, see Douglass C. North, *Economic Growth in the United States, 1790–1860* (New York, 1961); John R. Commons et al., *A Documentary History of American Industrial Society* (Cleveland, 1910); and Thomas C. Cochran, *Frontiers of Change: Early Industrialism in America* (New York, 1981).

6. On the transportation revolution, see George Rogers Taylor, *The Transportation Revolution, 1815–1860* (New York, 1951); Ronald E. Shaw, *Erie Water West: A History of the Erie Canal, 1792–1854* (Lexington, Ky., 1966); Carter Goodrich et al., *Canals and American Economic Development* (New York, 1961); Archer B. Hulbert, *The Cumberland Road* (Cleveland, 1904); and Philip D. Jordan, *The National Road* (Indianapolis, 1948).

7. Some of the better studies of American railroading include John F. Stover, *American Railroads* (Chicago, 1961); Albert Fishlow, *American Railroads and the Transformation of the AnteBellum Economy* (Cambridge, Mass., 1965); and Edward Hungerford, *The Story of the Baltimore and Ohio Railroad, 1827–1927* (New York, 1928).

8. On the growth of cities, see Richard C. Wade, *The Urban Frontier: The Rise of Western Cities, 1790–1830* (Cambridge, Mass., 1959); David T. Gilchrist, ed., *The Growth of the Seaport Cities, 1790–1825* (Charlottesville, Va., 1967); and Sam Bass Warner, Jr., *The Urban Wilderness: A History of the American City* (New York, 1972).

9. See Joseph G. Rayback, *A History of American Labor* (New York, 1959); and Walter Hugins, *Jacksonian Democracy and the Working Class* (Stanford, 1960).

10. Studies of American science and technology include Roger Burlingame, *March of the Iron Men, A Social History of Union through Invention* (New York, 1938); George H. Daniels, *American Science in the Age of Jackson* (New York, 1968); Walter B. Kaempffert, ed., *A Popular History of American Invention* (New York, 1924); and Bernard Jaffe, *Men of Science in America* (New York, 1958).

11. There are several classic studies of the cultural advances achieved in Jacksonian America, among them O. B. Frothingham, *Transcendentalism in New England* (New York, 1876); Francis O. Matthiessen, *American Renaissance* (New York, 1941); and Van Wyck Brooks, *The Flowering of New England* (New York, 1936). A more modern study is Russel B. Nye, *Society and Culture in America* (New York, 1974).

12. See Richard P. McCormick, *The Second American Party System: Party Formation in the Jacksonian Era* (Chapel Hill, N.C., 1966).

13. The best of William Leggett's editorials for the New York *Evening Post* can be found in Theodore Sedgwick, Jr., ed., *A Collection of the Political Writings of William Leggett* (New York, 1840), pp. 71ff, 83ff, 140ff.

14. Trollope, *Domestic Manners of the Americans*, pp. 155ff.

15. On reform, see Arthur Bestor, *Backwoods Utopias* (Philadelphia, 1950); Clifford S. Griffin, *The Ferment of Reform, 1830–1860* (New York, 1967); Arthur M. Schlesinger, *The American As Reformer* (Cambridge, Mass., 1951); and Alice Felt Tyler, *Freedom's Ferment* (Minneapolis, 1944).

16. For Jackson as symbol, see John William Ward, *Andrew Jackson: Symbol of an Age* (New York, 1955).

17. Remini, *Jackson*, II, 387. Jackson's apprehension is expressed in a number of letters at this time. See, for example, AJ to Joel Poinsett, November 7, 1832, Poinsett Papers, PHS.

CHAPTER 2

1. Van Buren to AJ, November 18, 1832, Van Buren Papers, LC.

2. For the background of Jackson's problems with South Carolina and Georgia, see Remini, *Jackson*, II, 275ff and 380ff.

3. Edwin Miles, "After John Marshall's Decision: *Worcester* v. *Georgia* and the Nullification Crisis," *JSH* (1973) XXXIX, 539.

4. Isaac Southard to Samuel Southard, December 24, 1832, ibid., p. 534 note.

5. B. F. Butler to Wilson Lumpkin, December 17, 1832, Gratz Collection, PHS; Miles, "After John Marshall's Decision," p. 534.

6. Kendall to Van Buren, November 2, 10, 1832, Van Buren Papers, LC.

7. AJ to Poinsett, December 2, 1832, Poinsett Papers, PHS.

8. Kendall to Van Buren, November 10, 1832, Van Buren Papers, LC.

9. E. Tilden to Samuel J. Tilden, December 17, 1832, Tilden Papers, NYPL; George M. Dallas to AJ, December 6, 1832, in Jackson, *Correspondence*, IV, 496.

10. AJ to Van Buren, November 18, 1832, ibid., p. 489.

11. Lewis to Overton, November 23, 1832, Claybrooke Collection, THS.

12. Richardson, *Messages and Papers*, II, 1157, 1160.

13. Ibid., p. 1161.

14. Richard B. Latner, "The Nullification Crisis and Republican Subversion," *JSH* (1977) XLIII, 30.

15. Richardson, *Messages and Papers*, II, 1162.

16. Ibid.

17. Ibid., pp. 1162–1169.

18. Private Memorandum of A. Jackson, Jackson Papers, LC.

19. *State Papers on Nullification* (Boston, 1834), pp. 29–31.

20. Poinsett to AJ, November 24, 25, 29, 1832, Jackson Papers, LC.

21. AJ to Poinsett, December 2, 1832, Poinsett Papers, PHS.

22. Freehling, *Prelude to Civil War*, p. 266.

23. Parton, *Jackson*, III, 458–459.

24. Ibid., p. 459.

25. Ibid., p. 447.

26. *Globe*, March 28, 1833; C. C. Clay to Henry Gold Thwaites, December 29, 1832, Miscellaneous C. C. Clay Papers, LC. For a full discussion of Adams's career as congressman, see Bemis, *Adams*, II, 221ff.

27. Davy Crockett, *An Account of Colonel Crockett's Tour* . . . (Philadelphia, 1835), p. 65.

28. The best account of the nullification controversy is Freehling, *Prelude to Civil War*, but the author is at great pains to prove that slavery is the hidden reason motivating these events and I think he overstates his thesis. Paul H. Bergeron, "The Nullification Controversy Revisited," *THQ* (1976) XXXV, 263–275, and "Tennessee's Response to the Nullification Crisis," *THQ* (1973) XXXIX, 23–44, raises serious questions about Freehling's thesis. My own views on the issue can be found in chapters 22, 26, and 28.

29. C. C. Clay to Henry Gold Thwaites, December 29, 1832, Miscellaneous C. C. Clay Papers, LC.

30. Private Memorandum of A. Jackson, Jackson Papers, LC. See also the *Globe*, January 8, 1833.

31. J. F. H. Claiborne, *Life and Times of General Sam Dale* (New York, 1860), p. 178.

32. Private Memorandum of A. Jackson, Jackson Papers, LC.

33. Adams, *Memoirs*, VIII, 503.

34. See Kendall's draft in Jackson Papers, LC; AJ to Livingston, December 4, 1832, Livingston Papers, JRDF.

35. Ibid.; Parton, *Jackson*, III, 466.

36. Ibid.

37. AJ to Livingston, December 4, 1832, Livingston Papers, JRDF. This is the original document and it is in Jackson's handwriting. A copy in the hand of Nicholas Trist is in the New York Public Library and a copy of this copy, with a few small errors, is printed in Jackson, *Correspondence*, IV, 494–495.

38. Livingston's importance in the composition of the proclamation should not be underestimated, however. "It is you who have struck the Goliah in the forehead, and I am unwilling that it should be left an historically uncertain whether your success contributed or not to the death-blow." George Dallas to Edward Livingston, April 4, 1833, Livingston Papers, JRDF. The same sentiments were expressed by Daniel Webster. "I find every where, a high & grateful feeling of respect entertained towards yourself," he told Livingston, "for the part you universally understood to have been performed by you, in regard to measures, so necessary to the honor & well being of the Government, & which have manifested so high a degree both of patriotism & talent." Webster to Livingston, March 21, 1833, Livingston Papers, JRDF.

39. AJ to Livingston, Friday at night, December 7, 1832, Livingston Papers, JRDF.

40. Parton, *Jackson*, III, 467.

41. Levi Woodbury to William Plumer, January 6, 1832, Miscellaneous Woodbury Papers, NYHS.

42. Richardson, *Messages and Papers*, II, 1203–1204.

43. Ibid., p. 1206.

44. Ibid., p. 1211.

45. John Van Buren to Martin Van Buren, January 2, 1833, John Van Buren Papers, private collection, copy in author's possession; AJ to Maunsel White, December 22, 1832, California State Library, San Francisco, copy JPP.

46. Richardson, *Messages and Papers*, II, 1213.

47. Kenneth M. Stampp, *The Imperiled Union: Essays on the Background of the Civil War* (New York, 1980), p. 33. The Supreme Court case referred to is *Texas v. White*. My argument about Jackson and the perpetuity of the Union follows closely the analysis by Professor Stampp and I am extremely indebted to him for his invaluable interpretation.

48. Richardson, *Messages and Papers*, II, 1213.

49. Stampp, *The Imperiled Union*, p. 34.

50. AJ to Maunsel White, December 22, 1832, California State Library, San Francisco, copy JPP.

51. Richardson, *Messages and Papers*, II, 1215.

52. Ibid., p. 1217.

53. Ibid., pp. 1217–1218.

54. Ibid., p. 1219.

CHAPTER 3

1. Clay to Francis Brooke, December 12, 1832, in Calvin Colton, ed., *The Private Correspondence of Henry Clay* (Boston, 1856), p. 345; Richard Rush to Edward Livingston, December 18, 19, 1832, Livingston Papers, JRDF; Van Buren to AJ, December 22, 1832, Van Buren Papers, LC.

2. AJ to Joel Poinsett, December 9, 1832, Poinsett Papers, PHS; AJ to Van Buren, December 22, 1832, Van Buren Papers, LC; AJ to William M. Berryhill, December 25, 1832, Jackson Papers, THS.

3. AJ to Coffee, December 14, 1832, Coffee Papers, THS.

4. AJ to Van Buren, December 15, 1832, in Jackson, *Correspondence*, IV, 500–501.

5. George McDuffie to Nicholas Biddle, December 25, 1832, Biddle Papers, LC.

6. Poinsett to AJ, December 17, 1832, J. R. Ervin to Poinsett, December 25, 1832, AJ Papers, LC.

7. AJ to Lewis Cass, December 17, 1832, in Jackson, *Correspondence*, IV, 502; AJ to Cass, January 7, 1833, Hurja Collection, THS.

8. Rush to Livingston, December 19, 1832, Livingston Papers, JRDF.

9. James O'Hanlon to AJ, December 20, 1832, AJ Papers, LC; Freehling, *Prelude to Civil War*, p. 275.

10. *State Papers on Nullification* (Boston, 1834), pp. 184–201; Parton, *Jackson*, III, 471.

11. Cass to Scott, January 26, 1833, in *ASPMA*, V, 160–161.

12. O'Hanlon to AJ, December 20, 1832, AJ Papers, LC.

13. Freehling, *Prelude to Civil War*, p. 282.

14. See the Washington *Globe*, November–December, 1832–1833, and especially November 29, December 3, 1832, January 2, 8, March 2, 28, 1833.

15. AJ to Van Buren, December 23, 25, 1832, Van Buren Papers, LC.

16. Van Buren to AJ, December 27, 1832, Van Buren Papers, LC; John Van Buren to Martin Van Buren, January 2, 1833, John Van Buren Papers, private collection, copy in author's possession.

17. Poinsett to AJ, January 7, 16, 20, 27, 28, 30, 1833, AJ Papers, LC; AJ to Poinsett, February 7, 1833, Poinsett Papers, PHS.

18. Silas Wright to Van Buren, January 13, 1833, Van Buren Papers, LC; Parton, *Jackson*, III, 472.

19. AJ to Van Buren, January 13, 1833, in Jackson, *Correspondence*, V, 3.

20. AJ to Blair, August 12, 1841, AJ Papers, LC. In a letter to Van Buren, Mahlon Dickerson said that it was generally understood that the bill was "drawn by your *Pet* McLane." January 11, 1833, Van Buren Papers, LC.

21. *House Report*, No. 14, 22d Congress, 2d Session, p. 21; Levi Woodbury to William Plumer, January 6, 1832 [but more probably 1833], Miscellaneous Woodbury Papers, NYHS.

22. Wright to Van Buren, January 13, 1833, Van Buren Papers, LC; *Globe*, March 2, 1833.

23. Latner, *Presidency of Jackson*, p. 150; Munroe, *McLane*, pp. 368–369.

24. Richardson, *Messages and Papers*, II, 1183–1184.

25. Ibid., pp. 1192–1193; Freehling, *Prelude to Civil War*, p. 285.

26. Richardson, *Messages and Papers*, II, 1194.

27. Ibid., pp. 1194–1195.

28. Macon to AJ, August 26, 1833, September 25, 1833, in Jackson, *Correspondence*, V, 171–172, 208. Jackson initiated this correspondence when he read in a Norfolk newspaper a letter by Macon which said that the proclamation was as contrary to the Constitution as nullification. "What principles are advanced," Jackson asked him, ". . . contrary to the doctrines avowed by the republican party with which you & I have so long acted." August 17, 1833, Jackson Papers, LC.

29. AJ to Macon, September 2, 1833, in Jackson, *Correspondence*, V, 177–178.

30. Macon to AJ, August 26, 1833, ibid., p. 172.

31. Munroe, *McLane*, p. 370.

32. Erastus Smith to John M. Niles, January 4, 1833, Gideon Welles Papers, LC.

33. Calhoun to Armistead Burt, January 16, 1833, in *Calhoun Papers*, XII, 15; Wright to Azariah C. Flagg, January 19, 1833, Flagg Papers, NYPL.

34. Poinsett to AJ, January 20, 22, 27, 28, 1833, Jackson Papers, LC; AJ to Poinsett, January 16, 1833, Poinsett Papers, PHS.

35. AJ to Poinsett, January 24, 1833, Poinsett Papers, PHS.

36. Alfred Balch to Livingston, January 20, 1833, Livingston Papers, JRDF.

37. *Globe*, May 1, 1833; Paul Bergeron, "Tennessee's Response to the Nullification Crisis," *JSH* (1973), XXXIX, 23–44. See also Bergeron, "The Nullification Controversy Revisited," *THQ* (1976), XXXV, 263–275.

38. Latner, *Presidency of Jackson*, p. 151.

39. Balch to Livingston, January 20, 1833, Livingston Papers, JRDF; Churchill C. Cambreleng to Van Buren, no date, Van Buren Papers, LC.

40. Van Buren, *Autobiography*, p. 547.

41. AJ to Van Buren, January 25, 1833, Van Buren Papers, LC.

42. Freehling, *Prelude to Civil War*, p. 288.

43. Wright to Flagg, January 14, February 2, 1833, Michael Hoffman to Flagg, January 15, 1833, Flagg Papers, NYPL. See Clay's reaction in his letter to Francis Brooke, January 24, 1833, Miscellaneous Clay Papers, DUL.

44. The *Pennsylvania Inquirer* of January 25, 1833 provided what Webster called "an account of the result of divers conversations between Mr Clay & Mr Calhoun, &c, &c." Webster to Edward Everett [January 26, 1833], in *Webster Papers*, III, 209. The quote in the text is taken from Hoffman to Flagg, January 20, 1833, Flagg Papers, NYPL.

45. Tyler to John Floyd, January 22, 1833, in "Original Letters," *William and Mary College Quarterly Historical Magazine* (1912), XXI, 11. Apparently the report of the dinner got into all the newspapers. See Charles Miner to Webster, February 4, 1833, in *Webster Papers*, III, 210.

46. "The state of things here is in every sense horrible," wrote Senator Wright to Flagg, January 20, 1833, Flagg Papers, NYPL. Freehling, *Prelude to Civil War*, p. 286.

47. Wiltse, *Calhoun*, II, 189.

48. Wright to Flagg, January 19, 1833, Flagg Papers, NYPL; *Register of Debates*, 22d Congress, 2d Session, 519–553.

49. Ibid., pp. 553–587; Benjamin F. Perry, *Reminiscences of Public Men* (Philadelphia, 1883), p. 45; Wiltse, *Calhoun*, II, 194. For a variation of the Randolph anecdote, see Merrill D. Peterson, *Olive Branch and Sword—The Compromise of 1833* (Baton Rouge, 1982), p. 63.

50. AJ to Poinsett, February 17, 1833, Poinsett Papers, PHS; Norman Brown, "Webster-Jackson Movement for a Constitution and Union Party in 1833," *Mid-America* (1964), XLVI, 147–171, is an excellent account of the abortive alliance between Jackson and Webster.

51. *Register of Debates*, 22d Congress, 2d Session, p. 688; Webster to Joseph Hopkinson [February 21, 1833], in *Webster Papers*, III, 219.

52. Benton to Van Buren, February 16, 1833, Van Buren Papers, LC.

53. Van Buren to AJ, February 20, 1833, Van Buren Papers, LC.

54. Thomas Ritchie to William Rives, January 6, 1833, Rives Papers, LC; Tyler to Tazewell, February 2, 1833, in Tyler, *Letters and Times*, I, 448; Freehling, *Prelude to Civil War*, p. 287.

55. When Van Buren talked this way, Jackson simply turned a deaf ear. If Jackson responded to this letter, and I suspect that he did, Van Buren destroyed it. There is no trace of it in either the Van Buren Papers or the Jackson Papers.

56. King to Van Buren, January 9, 1833, Van Buren Papers, LC; Michael Hoffman to Flagg, February 25, 1833, Flagg Papers, NYPL; Cambreleng to Van Buren, no date, Van Buren Papers, LC.

57. Clay to Francis Brooke, January 17, 1833, in *The Works of Henry Clay*, Calvin Colton, ed. (New York, 1904), V, 347; Cambreleng to Van Buren, February 5, 1833, Van Buren Papers, LC; Wiltse, *Calhoun*, II, 184.

58. Calhoun's biographer, Charles M. Wiltse, says that the South Carolinian rejected the Verplanck bill because it would be "too hard on the manufacturers," for no peace was possible with "total victory for either side." Wiltse, *Calhoun*, II, 184–185. Calhoun's remarks and speeches, both in and out of Congress, can be found in *Calhoun Papers*, XII, 40–140.

59. Hoffman to Flagg, February 25, 1833, Flagg Papers, NYPL; Albany *Argus*, February 26, 1833.

60. Granger to Weed, February 19, 1833, Granger Papers, LC.

61. *Register of Debates*, 22d Congress, 2d Session, pp. 462–478; Munroe, *McLane*, pp. 373–374.

62. *Register of Debates*, 22d Congress, 2d Session, pp. 473–478; White, *Memoir*, pp. 299–300.

63. AJ to Grundy, February 13, 1833, Whiteford R. Cole Collection, TSL.

64. Gulian C. Verplanck voted against Blair. He opposed Jackson's Bank policy and particularly disliked Blair's anti-BUS editorials in the *Globe*.

65. Hoffman to Flagg, February 20, 1833, Flagg Papers, NYPL.

66. T. J. Randolph to Rives, February 21, 1833, Rives Papers, LC.

67. Clay to Biddle, March 4, 1833, Biddle Papers, LC; Parton, *Jackson*, III, 484; Brown, "Webster-Jackson Movement," pp. 148, 150. For Clay's efforts to draw Webster into his "arrangement," see Clay to Webster, February 5, March 2, 1833, in *Webster Papers*, III, 211, 221–222.

68. *Register of Debates*, 22d Congress, 2d Session, pp. 697–701, 715–716; Hoffman to Flagg, February 25, 1833, Flagg Papers, NYPL; Munroe, *McLane*, p. 374.

69. Benton, *Thirty Years View*, I, 309, 310.

70. *Register of Debates*, 22d Congress, 2d Session, pp. 694–716.

71. Ibid., p. 1903.

72. AJ to Poinsett, March 6, 1833, Poinsett Papers, PHS.

73. Wright to Flagg, February 25, 1833, Flagg Papers, NYPL; Wiltse, *Calhoun*, II, 193.

74. AJ to Poinsett, March 6, 1833, Poinsett Papers, PHS.

75. Macon to Van Buren, March 2, 1833, Van Buren Papers, LC; George Dallas to his mother, March 2, 1833, Miscellaneous Dallas Papers, NYHS. Calhoun said the Force Bill was an act to "repeal the Constitution." Calhoun to William C. Preston, no date, in *Calhoun Papers*, XII, 37.

76. *State Papers on Nullification*, pp. 230, 274.

77. AJ to Coffee, April 9, 1833, Coffee Papers, THS.

78. Bergeron, "Tennessee's Response to the Nullification Crisis," p. 23. Some statistical support for this argument as it applied to South Carolina is provided by Bergeron in "The Nullification Controversy Revisited," pp. 263–275. His conclusions are buttressed by data provided for Cumberland County, North Carolina, by Harry L. Watson in his book *Jacksonian Politics and Community Conflict* (Baton Rouge, 1981). Watson concludes that during the 1830s in Cumberland County most political questions centered on economic issues and the preservation of liberty, "but usually not with slavery per se" (p. 319).

79. Wright to Van Buren, January 13, 1833, Van Buren Papers, LC; AJ to Van Buren, January 13, 1833, in Jackson, *Correspondence*, V, 3.

80. AJ to Reverend Andrew J. Crawford, May 1, 1833, ibid., p. 72. This opinion was shared by others, namely that at the bottom of the nullification

controversy "lurked a settled design to dissolve the Union and set up a Southern Confederacy." Only the "disaprobation" of other southern states caused its abandonment at present. B. F. Perry to Webster, April 1, 1833, Webster Papers, New Hampshire Historical Society.

81. Freehling, *Prelude to Civil War*, p. 293.

82. Ibid.

83. The most recent study of the compromise is Merrill D. Peterson, *Olive Branch and Sword—The Compromise of 1833* (Baton Rouge, 1982).

84. AJ to Poinsett, November 12, 1844, Jackson Papers, ML.

85. AJ to Amos Kendall, October 7, 1844, Jackson Papers, DUL, copy JPP.

86. A. Davezac to Livingston, April 3, 1833, Livingston Papers, JRDF.

CHAPTER 4

1. Adams, *Memoirs*, VIII, 533.

2. Descriptions are provided by the Washington newspapers, *National Intelligencer, Telegraph,* and *Globe,* March 4, 5, 6, 1833.

3. E. S. Davis to Webster, March 27, 1833, Webster Papers, LC.

4. Draft of Inaugural Address in Jackson's hand, no date, Jackson Papers, LC.

5. Ibid.

6. Ibid.

7. Ibid.

8. Hone, *Diary*, I, 89.

9. Ibid., p. 88.

10. Ibid., pp. 88–89.

11. *Globe*, March 6, 1833, *National Intelligencer*, March 5, 1833. John Q. Adams said the address was "brief, and full of smooth professions." *Memoirs*, VIII, 535.

12. Hone, *Diary*, I, 89.

13. AJ to Coffee, March 16, 1833, Coffee Papers, THS.

14. AJ to Hutchings, April 18, 1833, Hutchings Papers, Dyas Collection, THS.

15. AJ to Hutchings, November 3, 1833, ibid.

16. AJ to Coffee, March 16, 1833, Coffee Papers, THS.

17. Holtzclaw to AJ, March 6, 1833, Lewis to AJ, April 21, 1833, in Jackson, *Correspondence,* V, 30, 61–65; AJ to Maunsel White, December 22, 1832, California State Library, San Francisco, copy JPP.

18. AJ to Lewis, April 29, 1833, in Jackson, *Correspondence,* V, 66; AJ to Van Buren, April 25, 1833, Van Buren Papers, LC.

19. AJ to Andrew Jackson, Jr., April 8, 1833, Jackson Papers, LC; AJ to Coffee, March 17, 1833, Coffee Papers, THS.

20. AJ to Polk, December 16, 1832, Polk Papers, LC.

21. He purposely loaned out millions, said Jackson, to avoid paying the debt and thus "gain power . . . and force the Government . . . to grant it a new charter." AJ to Duane, June 26, 1833, Jackson Papers, LC.

22. Biddle to C. A. Wickliffe, December 6, 1832, Biddle Papers, LC. See also Private Memorandum of A. Jackson, March, 1833, Jackson Papers, LC. For background to the Bank War, see Ralph C. H. Catterall, *The Second Bank of the United States* (Chicago, 1903); Thomas Govan, *Nicholas Biddle* (Chicago, 1959); and William B. Smith, *Economic Aspects of the Second Bank of the United States* (Cambridge, 1953).

23. *House Report* No. 121, 22d Congress, 2d Session, pp. 42ff; *House Journal*, 22d Congress, 2d Session, p. 450; Munroe, *McLane*, pp. 379–380.

24. Ibid., p. 384; Kendall, *Autobiography*, p. 375; AJ to Taney, March 12, 1833, in *Maryland Magazine of History*, IV, 297; Private Memorandum of A. Jackson, March, 1833, Jackson Papers, LC.

25. John T. Sullivan, Peter Wager, and Henry D. Gilpin (government directors of the BUS) to AJ, April 8, 1833, in Jackson, *Correspondence*, V, 54.

26. AJ to Livingston, March 19, 1833, Livingston Papers, JRDF; Private Memorandum of A. Jackson, May, 1833, Jackson Papers, LC.

27. For background, see Munroe, *McLane*, pp. 304ff, and Remini, *Jackson*, II, 336ff.

28. The *Globe* said that "a person accidentally passing" discovered the blaze. April 1, 1833.

29. *Globe*, April 1, 15, 1833; Munroe, *McLane*, p. 383.

30. Material provided to the author by the Office of the Secretary of the Treasury, December, 1980; *Globe*, April 1, 1833.

31. McLane to AJ, May 20, 1833, in Jackson, *Correspondence*, V, 77–101; Munroe, *McLane*, p. 386.

32. "There are some strong points in this view—all ably discussed," Jackson wrote as an endorsement to McLane's response, in Jackson, *Correspondence*, V, 101.

33. "Notes on Treasury Opinion" [May, 1833], ibid., pp. 102–104.

34. George M. Dallas to Livingston, April 4, 1833, Livingston Papers, JRDF.

35. AJ to Van Buren, December 6, 17, 1831, Van Buren Papers, LC.

36. *Globe*, July 20, 1832; Munroe, *McLane*, pp. 363–367.

37. AJ to Van Buren, September 16, 1832, Van Buren Papers, LC; McLane to Van Buren, August 11, 1832, in Van Buren, *Autobiography*, p. 572.

38. Ibid., p. 594; Munroe, *McLane*, p. 357.

39. Taney to Van Buren, March 3, 1860, in *Maryland Historical Magazine* (1915), X, 15–16.

40. Roger B. Taney, "Roger B. Taney's 'Bank War Manuscript,'" Carl B. Swisher, ed., *Maryland Historical Magazine* (1958), LIII, 234.

41. AJ to Van Buren, November 25, 1832, in Van Buren, *Autobiography*, p. 595.

42. Ibid., p. 596.

43. The father was still alive in 1832 but no longer active as a newspaper editor.

44. AJ to Van Buren, November 25, 1832, in Van Buren, *Autobiography*, p. 596.

45. In a memorandum written a year later, Levi Woodbury said that Duane's appointment was brought about by McLane. Levi Woodbury, "Levi Woodbury's 'Intimate Memoranda' of the Jackson Administration," Ari Hoogenboom and Herbert Ershkowitz, eds., *Pennsylvania Magazine of History and Biography* (1968), XC, 510.

46. The entire discussion of the responsibility for the appointment can be traced in Van Buren, *Autobiography*, pp. 592–599.

47. Parton, *Jackson*, III, 486.

48. Duane, *Narrative and Correspondence*, pp. 2–4.

49. McLane to AJ, May 20, 1833, Jackson Papers, LC.

50. Livingston to AJ, and AJ to Livingston, May 29, 1833, Webster to Livingston, May 18 [sic], 1833, Livingston Papers, JRDF.

51. AJ to Cora Livingston Barton, June 4, 1833, Livingston Papers, JRDF.

CHAPTER 5

1. For Jackson's account of what happened, see Memorandum, May, 1833, Notes on Lt Randolph's conduct, in Jackson's handwriting, Jackson Papers, LC; also AJ to Coffee, May 11, 1833, Coffee Family Papers, LC; and *Globe,* May 13, 1833.

2. AJ to Coffee, May 11, 1833, Coffee Family Papers, LC.

3. Ibid.

4. Donelson to Coffee, May 14, 1833, Donelson Papers, LC.

5. AJ to Van Buren, May 12, 1833, Van Buren Papers, LC; *Memoirs of General Andrew Jackson,* compiled by a citizen of western New York (Auburn, N.Y., 1845), p. 171; Parton, *Jackson,* III, 486–488; Donelson to Coffee, May 14, 1833, Coffee Papers, THS.

6. AJ to Van Buren, May 12, Van Buren Papers, LC.

7. A bench warrant from the circuit court was issued against Randolph but he avoided the process-server. AJ to Van Buren, May 19, 1833, Van Buren Papers, LC.

8. Randolph was implicated in the discrepancies in the accounts of navy purser John Timberlake, Peggy Eaton's first husband. Randolph took over as acting purser after Timberlake's suicide and shortly thereafter deposited several thousand dollars in a Boston bank. To avoid criminal prosecution he surrendered the money. He was court-martialed and dishonorably discharged from the navy by direction of the President. Randolph claimed that he had been "unjustly" treated by Jackson. *House Document,* No. 116, 21st Congress, 1st Session. AJ to Van Buren, December 4, 1838, Van Buren Papers, LC.

9. John Campbell to David Campbell, May 12, 1833, Campbell Papers, DUL.

10. Fletcher Green, "On Tour with President Andrew Jackson," *New England Quarterly* (1963), XXXVI, 210–211.

11. Donelson to Emily Donelson, June 22, 1833, Donelson Papers, LC.

12. *Globe,* March 15, 1833; Green, "Tour with Jackson," p. 212.

13. *Niles Weekly Register,* April 6, 1833.

14. Ibid., April 13, 1833.

15. Van Buren to Marcy, May 3, 1833, Van Buren Papers, LC. For more of Van Buren's efforts to arrange the tour, see his letter to AJ, May 16, 1833, Van Buren Papers, LC.

16. AJ to Van Buren, June 6, 1833, Van Buren Papers, LC.

17. Ibid.

18. Kendall to Van Buren, June 9, 1833, Van Buren Papers, LC.

19. Ibid.

20. Duane, *Narrative and Correspondence,* pp. 6–7.

21. Kendall, *Autobiography,* p. 377.

22. Duane, *Narrative and Correspondence,* p. 7.

23. Ibid., p. 9.

24. Ibid.

25. *Globe,* June 7, 1833.

26. AJ to Andrew Jr., June 6, 1833, Jackson Papers, LC; *Globe,* June 8, 1833.

27. Manuscript Journal of a young Irishman touring the United States, May 27–November 15, 1833, HL.

28. *Niles Weekly Register,* June 8, 1833; *Globe,* June 8, 1833.

29. *Globe,* April 24, 1833. For the Black Hawk War, see Ellen M. Whitney, comp. and ed., *The Black Hawk War: 1831–1832* (Springfield, Ill., 1970–1975).

30. Black Hawk, *Autobiography* (Rock Island, Ill., 1833), pp. 116–117; *Globe,* April 27, 1833.

31. Frances A. Kemble, *Journal* (London, 1835), II, 157, 159.

32. Journal of a young Irishman, HL.

33. *Niles Weekly Register,* June 15, 1833.

34. Ibid.

35. Ibid.

36. Ibid.

37. *Globe,* June 12, 14, 1833; Munroe, *McLane,* p. 390.

38. *Globe,* June 17, 18, 1833.

39. John B. Moses and Wilbur Cross, *Presidential Courage* (New York, 1980), p. 40.

40. Parton, *Jackson,* III, 489.

41. Ibid.

42. AJ to Andrew Jr., June 10, 1833, in Jackson, *Correspondence,* V, 109.

43. *National Intelligencer,* June 20, 1833.

44. *United States Telegraph,* June 14, 1833; *National Intelligencer,* June 18, 22, 1833.

45. AJ to Andrew Jr., June 10, 1833, in Jackson, *Correspondence,* V, 109.

46. Hone, *Diary,* I, 94.

47. Ibid., p. 95.

48. Ibid., p. 96; Green, "On Tour with Jackson," p. 218.

49. The only other mishap at this time occurred during the firing of a salute to Jackson. A seaman on a revenue cutter lost both hands and eyes and was taken immediately to the hospital for treatment. A fund was established for his benefit, to which Jackson contributed $50. Donelson to Washington Irving, June 13, 1833, in *Niles Weekly Register,* July 27, 1833.

50. Seba Smith, *Life and Writings of Major Jack Downing* (New York, 1834), p. 216; Parton, *Jackson,* III, 489–490.

51. Hone, *Diary,* I, 96–97; John Nivens, *Gideon Welles* (New York, 1973), p. 157.

52. New York *Standard,* June 13, 14, 1833; New York *American,* June 13, 15, 18, 1833.

53. AJ to Andrew Jr., June 14, 1833, in Jackson, *Correspondence,* V, 109.

54. *Niles Weekly Register,* July 27, 1833.

55. Parton, *Jackson,* III, 490.

56. McLane to Van Buren, June 4, 1833, in Van Buren, *Autobiography,* pp. 601–602.

57. Ibid.; Munroe, *McLane,* pp. 392–393.

58. New York *Journal of Commerce,* June 15, 1833; Trenton, New Jersey, *True American,* June 14, 1833.

59. *National Intelligencer,* June 20, 1833. The tavern bill is given in *Niles Weekly Register,* July 27, 1833.

60. AJ to Andrew Jr., June 17, 1833, in Jackson, *Correspondence,* V, 110.

61. Niven, *Welles,* p. 158.

62. *Globe,* June 29, 1833.

63. Josiah Quincy, *Figures of the Past from the Leaves of Old Journals* (Boston, 1883), p. 297.

64. Ibid.

65. Ibid., pp. 297–298.

66. Ibid., p. 298.

67. Ibid., p. 299.

68. *Niles Weekly Register,* July 27, 1833.

69. Quincy, *Figures of the Past,* pp. 300–301.
70. Donelson to Emily Donelson, June 24, 1833, Donelson Papers, LC.
71. Quincy, *Figures of the Past,* p. 302.
72. AJ to Duane, June 26, 1833, in Jackson, *Correspondence,* V, 111–113.
73. AJ to Duane, June 26, 1833, ibid., 113ff, 128.
74. Adams, *Memoirs,* VIII, 546–547.
75. Ibid., p. 546.
76. Quincy, *Figures of the Past,* p. 303; Parton, *Jackson,* III, 492.
77. Quincy, *Figures of the Past,* p. 305.
78. Ibid., pp. 306–307.
79. Parton, *Jackson,* III, 492.
80. Quincy, *Figures of the Past,* p. 307.
81. Ibid., pp. 308–309.
82. Ibid., p. 309.
83. *Niles Weekly Register,* July 6, 1833.
84. Quincy, *Figures of the Past,* p. 309.
85. *National Intelligencer,* July 2, 1833.
86. Quincy, *Figures of the Past,* p. 310.
87. Ibid., p. 311.
88. Ibid., p. 312.
89. Ibid.
90. Donelson to Emily Donelson, June 24, 1833, Donelson Papers, LC.
91. *Niles Weekly Register,* July 6, 1833.
92. Portland *Courier,* June 20, 1833.
93. *Niles Weekly Register,* July 6, 1833.
94. Ibid.
95. Ibid.
96. Ibid.
97. Ibid.
98. Quincy, *Figures of the Past,* p. 315.
99. William B. Lewis to Edward Livingston, November 18, 1833, Livingston Papers, JRDF.
100. Adams, *Memoirs,* IX, 6.
101. Ibid., 4.
102. Lewis to Livingston, November 18, 1833, Livingston Papers, JRDF.
103. *Niles Weekly Register,* July 22, 1833.

CHAPTER 6

1. AJ to Coffee, May 3, 1833, Coffee Papers, THS.
2. AJ to Donelson, August 5, 1833, Donelson Papers, LC.
3. *Globe,* September 8, 1832.
4. Duane, *Narrative and Correspondence,* p. 39.
5. AJ to Duane, June 26, 1833, in Jackson, *Correspondence,* V, 112.
6. Duane to AJ, July 10, 1833, Jackson Papers, LC.
7. AJ to Duane, July 12, 1833, Jackson Papers, LC. A few days later Jackson sent Duane a point-by-point refutation of the secretary's argument. "I . . . regret to find . . . [that you have] greatly misapprehended" [my] opinions. AJ to Duane, July 17, 1833, Jackson Papers, LC.
8. Duane, *Narrative and Correspondence,* p. 57.
9. Kendall, *Autobiography,* p. 378.
10. Duane, *Narrative and Correspondence,* p. 84.

11. Kendall, *Autobiography*, p. 379.

12. Ibid.; Duane, *Narrative and Correspondence*, pp. 84–95.

13. Memorandum in Jackson's handwriting [July, 1833], Jackson Papers, LC.

14. Kendall to AJ, July 19, 1833, Jackson Papers, LC.

15. Roger B. Taney alerted his Baltimore banking friends to Kendall's coming. Taney to Thomas Ellicott, July 24, 1833, Taney Papers, LC.

16. Kendall to Duane, July 28, August 10, 27, 1833, NA; Treasury Department Report, July 23, 1833; Reports of Amos Kendall, Including Correspondence with Banks, NA.

17. Kendall to Niles, October 2, 1833, Niles Papers, Connecticut Historical Society, Hartford, Connecticut. See also Kendall to J. Delafield, December 24, 1834, Miscellaneous Papers, NYHS; and A. C. Flagg to Woodbury, November 3, 1834, Woodbury Papers, LC.

18. He had some trouble along the way, however. A few banks refused to offer security. "Those not offering security where others do offer," he wrote, "will, I think, be thrown out of competition." Kendall to Thomas Ellicott [?], August 3, 1833, Taney Papers, LC.

19. Kendall to AJ, August 14, 1833, Jackson Papers, LC.

20. Ibid.; Kendall, *Autobiography*, p. 383.

21. Kendall to AJ, August 14, 1833, Jackson Papers, LC.

22. AJ to Robert J. Chester, August 8, 1833, in Jackson, *Correspondence*, V, 149.

23. Parton, *Jackson*, III, 493, provides an anecdote on this point.

24. AJ to Van Buren, July 24, 1833, Van Buren Papers, LC.

25. Van Buren to AJ, July 24, 1833, Van Buren Papers, LC.

26. E. Whittlesey to John W. Taylor, October 10, 1833, Taylor Papers, NYHS.

27. Wright to Flagg, August 8, 1833, Flagg Papers, NYPL.

28. Nathaniel Niles to William Rives, July 23, 1833, Rives Papers, LC.

29. AJ to Van Buren, August 16, 1833, Van Buren Papers, LC.

30. Blair to Van Buren, August 17, 1833, Van Buren Papers, LC.

31. Reuben Whitney to Blair, August 12, 1833, Blair-Lee Papers, PUL.

32. AJ to Andrew J. Hutchings, November 3, 1833, Hutchings Papers, Dyas Collection, THS; AJ to Hutchings, September 6, 1833, Jackson Papers, THS; AJ to Mary Coffee, August 15, 1833, Coffee Papers, THS; William B. Lewis to AJ, May 3, 1833, Jackson Papers, LC.

33. AJ to Mary Coffee, August 15, September 15, 1833, Coffee Papers, LC. "Learn never to repine at the acts of providence," he instructed Andrew Hutchings, "he holds our lives in the hollow of his hand—he has given it & he has the right, and the power to take it away at his good pleasure & shews the propriety of all living so that we are always prepared to die." AJ to Hutchings, Hutchings Papers, Dyas Collection, THS.

34. AJ to Mary Coffee, August 15, September 15, 1833, Coffee Papers, THS; AJ to Donelson, August 5, 1833, Donelson Papers, LC; AJ to Hutchings, September 15, 1833, Hutchings Papers, Dyas Collection, THS.

Later Jackson was asked to provide an inscription for Coffee's tomb. He composed one with the aid of his various friends and secretaries and said that he hoped it would meet with the family's wishes and the "faithfull character of the deceased." With but few minor modifications it was inscribed on the tombstone:

"Sacred to the Memory
of
General John Coffee

who departed this life on the 7th day of July, 1833, aged sixty-one years. As a husband, parent, and friend, he was affectionate, tender and sincere. He was a brave, prompt and skillful general, a disinterested and sagacious patriot, an unpretending, just and honest man. To complete his character religion mingled with these virtues her serene and holy influence and gave him that solid distinction among his fellow men which detraction cannot sully nor the grave conceal. Death could do no more than remove so excellent a being from the theatre he so much adorned in this world, to the bosom of the God who created him and who alone has the power to reward the immortal spirit with exhaustless bliss." AJ to John D. Coffee, December 24, 1834, in Jackson, *Correspondence*, V, 314–315, and footnote 2.

35. Blair to Van Buren, November 13, 1859, in Van Buren, *Autobiography*, p. 607.

36. Jackson paid his hotel bill at the Rip Raps with a check for $395.75 drawn on Biddle's Bank. The bill included board for himself, his son and daughter, Earl, Emily Donelson and her three children, and five servants. Part of this bill included the cost of many gallons of wine and hard liquor. Champagne, claret, Madeira, port, brandy, gin, whiskey, and six bottles of olives totaled $128. The hotel graciously declined to charge him for the company Jackson entertained during his stay. See Jackson, *Correspondence*, V, 168–169. After their return to Washington, Sarah and Andrew Jackson, Jr., continued on to the Hermitage.

37. Van Buren to AJ, September 4, 1833, ibid., p. 181.

38. Ibid.

39. Government Bank Directors to AJ, August 19, 1833, in *Senate Documents*, 23d Congress, 1st Session, Document No. 2.

40. AJ to Van Buren, September 8, 1833, Van Buren Papers, LC. The two-thirds refers to the vote needed in Congress to override his veto.

41. AJ to Tilghman A. Howard, August 20, 1833, in Jackson, *Correspondence*, V, 165–166.

42. Ibid.

43. This sentiment was substantiated by a report he received in August from the government directors of the BUS. Directors to AJ, August 19, 1833, in *Senate Documents*, 23d Congress, 1st Session, Document No. 2. This report, Jackson said later to Congress, established beyond all question that the BUS "had been actively engaged in attempting to influence the elections of the public officers by means of its money." Richardson, *Messages and Papers*, II, 1249.

44. AJ to Van Buren, September 8, 1833, Jackson Papers, LC.

45. Van Buren to AJ, September 11, 14, 1833, Jackson Papers, LC.

46. AJ to Van Buren, September 8, 1833, Van Buren Papers, LC.

47. *National Intelligencer*, September 26, 1833; Duane to AJ, July 22, 1833, in Duane, *Narrative and Correspondence*, p. 90.

48. Letters to Banks, September 26, 1833, Treasury Department, NA.

49. Duane, *Narrative and Correspondence*, p. 96.

50. Ibid., pp. 90, 92–94; Munroe, *McLane*, p. 402.

51. Duane, *Narrative and Correspondence*, p. 97.

52. Ibid., pp. 97–98.

53. AJ to Van Buren, September 15, 1833, Van Buren Papers, LC.

54. AJ to Taney, September 15, 1833, Jackson Papers, LC.

55. Ibid.

56. Duane, *Narrative and Correspondence*, pp. 98–99; Munroe, *McLane*, p. 402; Carl Swisher, *Roger B. Taney* (New York, 1935), p. 231.

57. Duane, *Narrative and Correspondence*, p. 99.

58. Ibid., pp. 99, 100; Statement by Levi Woodbury on removal of the deposits dated September 18, 1833, Woodbury Papers, LC; Private Memorandum, Jackson Papers, LC.

59. Duane, *Narrative and Correspondence,* p. 100.

60. Blair to Van Buren, November 13, 1859, in Van Buren, *Autobiography,* p. 608; AJ to Lewis [September, 1833], Jackson Papers, ML; AJ to Taney, September 15, 1833, Jackson Papers, LC.

61. Taney to AJ, September 17, 1833, Jackson Papers, LC.

62. AJ to Van Buren, September 19, 1833, Van Buren Papers, LC.

63. Paper Read to the Cabinet, September 18, 1833, in Jackson, *Correspondence,* V, 192–203.

64. Ibid., p. 198.

65. Ibid., pp. 198–199, 203.

66. Duane, *Narrative and Correspondence,* p. 100.

67. Ibid.

68. Parton, *Jackson,* III, 505–506.

69. Duane, *Narrative and Correspondence,* pp. 100–101.

70. Ibid., pp. 102–103.

71. November 2, 1833.

72. Duane, *Narrative and Correspondence,* p. 107; AJ to Van Buren, September 23, 1833, Van Buren Papers, LC.

73. Private Memorandum Book of A. Jackson, Jackson Papers, LC.

74. AJ to Van Buren, September 23, 1833, Van Buren Papers, LC.

75. Parton, *Jackson,* III, 501.

76. Blair to Van Buren, November 13, 1859, in Van Buren, *Autobiography,* p. 608.

77. Ibid.

78. Duff Green to John Floyd, November 20, 1833, Floyd Papers, LC.

79. AJ to Van Buren, September 24, 1833, in Van Buren, *Autobiography,* pp. 603–604.

80. Munroe, *McLane,* p. 404.

81. Parton, *Jackson,* III, 502.

82. September 26, 1833.

83. AJ to Van Buren, September 25, 1833, in Van Buren, *Autobiography,* p. 604.

CHAPTER 7

1. AJ to Colonel Anthony Butler, October 1, 1833, in Jackson, *Correspondence,* V, 213.

2. Taney to Woodbury, September 25, 1833, Woodbury Papers, LC.

3. The Bank of America was the exception, but the objections (which were political) were soon withdrawn. Kendall, *Autobiography,* p. 387.

4. AJ to Van Buren, September 29, 1833, Van Buren Papers, LC; Kendall, *Autobiography,* pp. 387–388.

5. Letters to Banks, September 28, 1833, Treasury Department, NA; Frank Otto Gatell, "Secretary Taney and Baltimore Pets," *Business History Review* (1965), XXXIX, 205–227, for a full discussion of the problems of pet banking as seen through the operations of the Baltimore pet.

6. AJ to Van Buren, September 26, and Van Buren to AJ, September 28, 1833, Van Buren Papers, LC.

7. AJ to Van Buren, September 29, 1833, Van Buren Papers, LC.

8. Gatell, "Spoils of the Bank War: Political Bias in the Selection of Pet Banks," *AHR* (1964), LXX, 36.

9. Executive discretion in the selection of the pet banks was terminated by congressional action in 1836.

10. AJ to Van Buren, September 23, and Van Buren to AJ, September 26, 1833, Van Buren Papers, LC.

11. AJ to Van Buren, September 23, 1833, Van Buren Papers, LC.

12. *Globe,* October 26, 1833.

13. Van Buren to Butler, November 8, 1833, Butler Papers, PUL. On Butler, see Arthur A. Ekirch, Jr., "Benjamin F. Butler of New York: A Personal Portrait," *New York History* (1977), LVIII, 47–68.

14. Van Buren to Butler, November 8, 1833, Butler to Harriet Butler, November 14, 1833, Butler Papers, PUL.

15. AJ to Van Buren, November 19, 1833, Van Buren Papers, LC.

16. AJ to Van Buren, October 5, 1833, in Jackson, *Correspondence,* V, 216.

17. Biddle to Joseph Hopkinson, February 21, 1834, Biddle Papers, LC. See also Taney to Van Buren, June 30, 1860, Van Buren Papers, LC.

18. AJ to John Donelson Coffee, Coffee Papers, Dyas Collection, THS.

19. Taney to Ellicott, October 23, December 13, 1833, Taney Papers, LC; John M. McFaul, *The Politics of Jacksonian Finance* (Ithaca, 1972), p. 60.

20. Taney to Ellicott, September 28, 1833, Taney Papers, LC.

21. *National Intelligencer,* October 2, 1833.

22. Ibid., September 21, October 2, 4, 16, November 2, 1833.

23. George C. Dromgoole to Edward Dromgoole, January 8, 1834, Dromgoole Papers, SHC. Amos Kendall marked the beginning of this political battle with the reaction of Henry Clay when Clay wrote: "But the time has arrived, which I long ago apprehended, when our greatest exertions are necessary to maintain the free institutions inherited from our ancestors. Yes, gentlemen, disguise is useless; the time is come when we must decide whether the Constitution, the laws, and the checks which they have respectively provided, shall prevail, or the will of one man have uncontrolled sway. In the settlement of that question I shall be found where I have ever been." Henry Clay to friends, October 14, 1833, in Kendall, *Autobiography,* p. 391.

24. Green to John Floyd, November 20, 1833, Miscellaneous Floyd Papers, LC.

25. Ibid.; Tyler to Tazewell, December 3, 1833, in Tyler, *Letters and Times,* I, 480.

26. E. Whittlesey to John W. Taylor, October 10, 1833, Taylor Papers, NYHS; Webster to Stephen White, December 21, 27, 1833, in *Webster Papers,* III, 289, 296–297.

27. AJ to Lewis, November 7, 1833, Jackson Papers, ML.

28. Hill to Woodbury, October 5, 1833, Woodbury Papers, New Hampshire Historical Society.

29. Van Buren to AJ, October 12, 1833, Van Buren Papers, LC.

30. Hill to Woodbury, October 5, 1833, Woodbury Papers, New Hampshire Historical Society.

31. Biddle to William Appleton, January 27, 1834, Biddle Papers, LC. See also Taney to Van Buren, June 30, 1860, Van Buren Papers, LC.

32. Hamilton to Van Buren, December 30, 1833, Van Buren Papers, LC; Charles A. Davis to Biddle, January 27, 1834, Biddle Papers, LC; James Van Alen to Van Buren, January 27, 1834, Van Buren Papers, LC; John Tyler to Mrs. Tyler, February 17, 1834, in Tyler, *Letters and Times,* I, 485; Jacob Barker to Van Buren, February 25, and Jesse Hoyt to Van Buren, January 29, 1834, Van Buren Papers, LC; Levi Lincoln to Webster, January 11, 1834, in *Webster Papers,* III, 308–309.

33. AJ to Andrew Jr., October 11, December 1, 2, 22, 1833, Jackson Papers, LC; AJ to Sarah, October 6, 1833, Jackson Papers, HL.

34. Ibid.

35. Lewis to Livingston, November 18, 1833, Livingston Papers, JRDF. See also AJ to John Forsyth, January 7, 1834, Donelson Papers, LC. For Cass's correspondence with Gayle, see *Globe* for October and November, 1833; *National Intelligencer*, October 30, 1833.

36. Van Buren to Hamilton, December 8, 1833, in Hamilton, *Reminiscences*, p. 266; Adams, *Memoirs*, IX, 41; Lewis to Livingston, November 18, 1833, Livingston Papers, JRDF.

37. Parton, *Jackson*, III, 549–550.

38. C. W. Lawrence to George Newbold, February 9, 1834, Newbold Papers, NYHS.

39. Parton, *Jackson*, III, 549–550.

40. Ibid., p. 553.

CHAPTER 8

1. Lewis to James A. Hamilton, September 22, 1833, in Hamilton, *Reminiscences*, p. 266.

2. Lewis to Livingston, November 18, 1833, Livingston Papers, JRDF.

3. For an excellent biography of this outstanding but underestimated statesman who died prematurely, see John A. Garraty, *Silas Wright* (New York, 1949).

4. Van Buren, *Autobiography*, pp. 673–675.

5. Ibid., p. 678; Irving H. Bartlett, *Daniel Webster* (New York, 1978), p. 141. See also Calhoun to Samuel D. Ingham, December 28, 1833, in *Calhoun Papers*, XII, 195.

6. Bartlett, *Webster*, p. 142; Van Buren, *Autobiography*, p. 678.

7. AJ to Blair, November 30, 1833, Jackson Papers, LC; Latner, *Presidency of Jackson*, p. 184.

8. Sellers, *Polk*, I, 213, 276.

9. Adams, *Memoirs*, IX, 32.

10. They included Horace Binney of Pennsylvania, Richard H. Wilde of Georgia, and Benjamin Gorham of Massachusetts.

11. *Globe*, September 30, October 21, 28, November 18, 25, December 2, 1833; Wright to Flagg, January 3, 1834, Flagg Papers, NYPL; Samuel T. Tilden to his father, March 22, 1834, Tilden Papers, NYPL.

12. Benton, *Thirty Years View*, I, 374; Parton, *Jackson*, III, 537.

13. AJ to Blair, November 30, 1833, Jackson Papers, LC.

14. Richardson, *Messages and Papers*, II, 1239–1240.

15. Ibid., p. 1244.

16. Ibid., p. 1247.

17. Ibid., p. 1248.

18. Ibid., p. 1249, 1250.

19. Ibid., pp. 1251–1252. On racism during the early nineteenth century, see Reginald Horsman, *Race and Manifest Destiny* (Cambridge, Mass., 1981).

20. Richardson, *Messages and Papers*, II, 1252, 1254.

21. Ibid., pp. 1287, 1288.

22. Benton, *Thirty Years View*, I, 374–379, 385–392.

23. Ibid., p. 373; *Senate Documents*, 23d Congress, 1st Session, Document No. 2.

24. Jackson was very proud of this paper. He sent a copy to his son at the Hermitage. "I wish you to preserve it & file it at home. The history of my

administration will be received with interest years after I am dead, & I trust will be the means of perpetuating our happy union & our liberties with it." AJ to Andrew Jackson, Jr., October 11, 1833, AJ Papers, LC.

25. *Register of Debates*, 23d Congress, 1st Session, pp. 23–37.

26. Benton, *Thirty Years View*, I, 400.

27. Sellers, *Polk*, I, 214.

28. AJ to Polk, December 18, 1833, Polk Papers, LC; Sellers, *Polk*, I, 215.

29. AJ to Polk, December 18, 1833, Polk Papers, LC.

30. Richard Wilde to Verplanck, December 24, 1833, Verplanck Papers, NYHS.

31. Ibid.; Wright to Flagg, December 11, 1833, Flagg Papers, NYPL.

32. Wilde to Verplanck, December 24, 1833, Verplanck Papers, NYHS.

33. *Register of Debates*, 23d Congress, 1st Session, p. 1175.

34. Benton, *Thirty Years View*, I, 423.

35. *Register of Debates*, 23d Congress, 1st Session, pp. 84–85. For a superb account of this Panic session see Schlesinger, *Age of Jackson*, pp. 103–114.

36. *Register of Debates*, 23d Congress, 1st Session, pp. 84–85, 94.

37. Parton, *Jackson*, III, 542.

38. AJ to Andrew Jr., February 16, 1834, Jackson Papers, LC.

39. AJ to William Findlay, August 20, 1834, in Jackson, *Correspondence*, V, 285.

40. Parton, *Jackson*, III, 542; Benton, *Thirty Years View*, I, 411.

41. *Register of Debates*, 23d Congress, 1st Session, p. 220.

42. Webster to Edward Everett [December 13, 1833], in *Webster Papers*, III, 284; Webster to Biddle, December 21, 1833, Biddle Papers, LC.

43. Robert V. Remini, *Andrew Jackson and the Bank War* (New York, 1967), p. 140; Benton, *Thirty Years View*, I, 409.

44. See, for example, Senator Isaac Hill's speech in *Register of Debates*, 23d Congress, 1st Session, p. 791.

45. AJ to Lewis Cass, January 29, 1834, in Richard B. Morris, "Andrew Jackson, Strikebreaker," *AHR* (1949), LV, 61.

46. Ibid., p. 66.

47. A. Rencher to Charles Fisher, February 11, 1834, Fisher Papers, SHC.

48. J. S. Barbour to James Barbour, January 22, 1834, Barbour Papers, NYPL.

49. Kendall, *Autobiography*, p. 416. "I entertain no doubt," wrote Calhoun, "that the administration will be overthrown. . . . Its majority in the House is gradually giving away. You may put down the whole South as lost to the powers that be." Calhoun to Christopher Vandeventer, January 25, 1834, in *Calhoun Papers*, XII, 229.

50. Samuel Bell to Joseph Blount, February 27, 1834, Autograph File, HUL.

51. Biddle to Joseph Hopkinson, February 21, 1834, Biddle Papers, LC.

52. Ralph C. H. Catterall, *The Second Bank of the United States* (Chicago, 1903), pp. 306–307.

53. *Globe*, January 21, 23, 28, February 4, 6, 11, 13, 1834.

54. Webster to Biddle, February 12, 1834, Biddle Papers, LC; Remini, *Bank War*, p. 161.

CHAPTER 9

1. *Register of Debates*, 23d Congress, 1st Session, pp. 829–832.

2. Henry R. Stanton, *Random Recollections* (New York, 1886), pp. 205–206.

3. Tyler to Tazewell, December 25, 1833, in Tyler, *Letters and Times*, I, 482; Van Buren to John Van Buren, January 29, 1834, Van Buren Papers, LC.

4. Van Buren, *Autobiography*, pp. 675–676.

5. Mrs. Smith to Mrs. Kirkpatrick [1834], in Gaillard Hunt, ed., *The First Forty Years of Washington Society* (New York, 1906), p. 352.

6. Clay to Francis Brooke, March 23, 1834, in Henry Clay, *The Works of Henry Clay*, Calvin Colton, ed. (New York, 1904), I, 383.

7. AJ to Henry Horn, February 16, 1834, Jackson Papers, LC.

8. Robert Lyttle to Blair, March 5, 1834, Johnson to Blair, June, 1835 [?], Blair-Lee Papers, PUL; Van Buren to AJ, July 25, 1834, Van Buren Papers, LC.

9. C. Lawrence to George Newbold, April 1, 1834, Newbold Papers, NYHS; Woodbury to Nathaniel Niles, February 26, 1834, Woodbury Papers, LC; R. H. Wilde to Verplanck, February 22, 1834, Verplanck Papers, NYHS.

10. Johnson to Blair, no date, Blair-Lee Papers, LC.

11. AJ to Hamilton, February 2, 1834, in Hamilton, *Reminiscences*, p. 270; Sellers, *Polk*, I, 220–221.

12. Butler to Olcott, March 20, 1834, Olcott Papers, CUL.

13. Richardson, *Messages and Papers*, II, 1011; for Jackson's position, see also AJ to Van Buren, March 30, 1837, Van Buren Papers, LC. On political parties, see Arthur M. Schlesinger, Jr., ed. *History of U.S. Political Parties* (New York, 1973); Roy F. Nichols, *The Invention of American Political Parties* (New York, 1967); and Richard Hofstadter, *The Idea of Party* (Berkeley, 1969).

14. Hone, *Diary*, I, xii, II, 629; Dixon Ryan Fox, *Decline of Aristocracy in the Politics of New York* (New York, 1919), p. 367; and E. Malcolm Carroll, *Origins of the Whig Party* (Durham, 1925), p. 123. Webster first used the term in a letter to Benjamin G. Welles, April 15, 1834, in *Webster Papers*, III, 339–341.

15. *Globe*, April 12, 21, 22, 1834; Richmond *Enquirer*, April 21, 1834.

16. *Globe*, April 21, 22, November 8, 1834.

17. June 26, 1834.

18. *National Intelligencer*, March 18, 1834; Tyler to Dr. Henry Curtis, March 28, 1834, in Tyler, *Letters and Times*, I, 491. An important article on the Whig party is Lynn L. Marshall, "The Strange Stillbirth of the Whig Party," *AHR* (1967), LXXII, 425–444. For party ideology, see Daniel Walker Howe, ed., *The American Whigs: An Anthology* (New York, 1973), and *The Political Culture of the American Whigs* (Chicago, 1979).

19. March 28, 1834.

20. Ibid. According to Van Buren, when writing his *Inquiry into the Origins and Course of Political Parties in the United States* (New York, 1867), the only effect on farmers and laborers of the Hamiltonian program was to increase the antagonism "between those who live by the sweat of their brow and those who live by their wits." Pp. 177ff.

21. Aaron Ward to John Sing, March 22, 1834, Miscellaneous Papers, NYHS.

22. Glyndon G. Van Deusen, *The Jacksonian Era, 1828–1848* (New York, 1959), pp. 96–97. See also Van Deusen, "Some Aspects of Whig Thought and Theory in the Jacksonian Period," *AHR* (1958), LXIII, 305–322. Historiographically, it has been very fashionable in the last thirty years to dispute the social and economic differences between Whigs and Democrats. See, for example, Lee Benson, *The Concept of Jacksonian Democracy: New York as a Test Case* (Princeton, 1961). Frankly I find these efforts unpersuasive—that is, when they suggest that as many rich men can be found in the Democratic as in the Whig party. For what I think is a very insightful examination of one of the essential differences between Whigs and Democrats, see Major L. Wilson, *Space, Time, and Freedom: The Quest for Nationality and the Irrepressible Conflict* (Westport, Conn., 1974).

23. Clay to Francis Brooke, March 23, 1834, in Clay, *Works*, I, 383.

CHAPTER 10

1. A. Rencher to Charles Fisher, February 11, 1834, Fisher Family Papers, SHC; Benton, *Thirty Years View*, I, 421.

2. Cambreleng to Edward Livingston, March 16, 1834, Livingston Papers, JRDF.

3. Aaron Ward to John Sing, March 22, 1834, Miscellaneous Papers, NYHS.

4. AJ to Sarah Jackson, February 18, 1834, Facsimile in Jackson Papers, LC; Cambreleng to Livingston, March 16, 1834, Livingston Papers, JRDF.

5. AJ to Sarah Jackson, February 18, 1834, Facsimile in Jackson Papers, LC.

6. Donelson to Livingston, March 7, 1834, Livingston Papers, JRDF.

7. AJ to Sarah Jackson, January 5, 1834, in Jackson, *Correspondence*, V, 239.

8. AJ to Andrew Jr., November 16, 1833, Jackson Papers, LC.

9. Ibid.

10. He died of lockjaw. Linda Bennett Galloway, "Andrew Jackson, Jr.," *THQ* (1950), IX, 195–216, 306–343.

11. AJ to Andrew Jr., December 22, 1833, Jackson Papers, LC.

12. AJ to Andrew Jr., February 12, 16, March 9, 1834, Jackson Papers, LC.

13. AJ to Andrew Jr., February 12, 16, March 9, April 6, 1834, Jackson Papers, LC.

14. Andrew Jr. to AJ, January 25, 1834, Jackson Papers, LC.

15. AJ to Andrew Jr., February 12, 1834, Jackson Papers, LC.

16. AJ to Andrew Jr., February 16, 1834, Jackson Papers, LC.

17. AJ to Andrew Jr., March 16, 1834, Jackson Papers, LC.

18. AJ to Andrew Jr., March 26, April 6, 1834, Jackson Papers, LC.

19. Ibid.

20. Maunsel White to AJ, April 18, 1834, in Jackson, *Correspondence*, V, 261.

21. AJ to Andrew Jr., April 20, 1834, Jackson Papers, LC.

22. *Globe*, February 4, 18, 1834; Thomas Hamilton, *Men and Manners in America* (London, 1833), II, 135–142.

23. J. R. Montgomery to his daughter, Letitia, May 25, 1834, in James, *Jackson*, pp. 668–669.

24. Ibid.

25. AJ to Sarah Jackson, January 5, 1834, in Jackson, *Correspondence*, V, 239; AJ to Sarah Jackson, March 25, 1834, Jackson Papers, THS; Andrew Jr. to AJ, January 25, 1834, AJ to Andrew Jr., April 15, 1834, Jackson Papers, LC. Van Buren later agreed to act as the child's godfather.

26. George Dallas to Livingston, April 27, 1834, Livingston Papers, JRDF.

27. Benton, *Thirty Years View*, I, 411–415. See also Calhoun to J.E. Colhoun, February 8, 1834, in *Calhoun Papers*, XII, 231–232.

28. *Register of Debates*, 23d Congress, 1st Session, 386–387.

29. Benton, *Thirty Years View*, I, 421; Van Buren to John Van Buren, February 10, 1834, Van Buren Papers, LC.

30. Benton, *Thirty Years View*, I, 424.

31. Parton, *Jackson*, III, 554.

32. These resolutions were modified from time to time, right up to the moment they were voted upon. Benton, *Thirty Years View*, I, 423.

33. To add further insult, Clay suggested that the signers of the memorials be counted and added to the yeas and nays, anticipating that the weight of

public opinion could be added to the senatorial condemnation. Clay estimated that well over one hundred thousand Americans had expressed their dismay over the presidential order of removal. He was mistaken. Ibid.

34. AJ to Kendall, April [1834?], de Coppet Collection, PUL.

35. Ibid.; R. H. Wilde to Verplanck, May 1, 1834, Verplanck Papers, NYHS.

36. *Globe*, March 31, 1834.

37. Ibid., April 3, 19, 1834.

38. *National Intelligencer*, April 19, 1834; Richardson, *Messages and Papers*, II, 1289.

39. Ibid., pp. 1291-1293, 1299, 1301.

40. Ibid., pp. 1304, 1306-1309, 1301, 1304, 1305.

41. Ibid., p. 1311.

42. Ibid.

43. Ibid., pp. 1311-1312.

44. *National Intelligencer*, April 19, 1834.

45. Ibid.

46. Quoted ibid., May 6, 1834.

47. Daniel Webster, *The Writings and Speeches of Daniel Webster* (Boston, 1903), VII, 139, 143, 144, 145, 147.

48. Ibid., p. 139.

49. Richmond *Enquirer*, April 21, 1834; Joel Poinsett to Livingston, June 5, 1834, Livingston Papers, JRDF.

50. *Globe*, May 12, 1834.

51. *Register of Debates*, 23d Congress, 1st Session, p. 1646.

52. For background of this congressional caucus and the election of 1824–1825, see Remini, *Jackson*, II, 25–36, 74ff.

53. *Globe*, April 19, 1834.

54. R. H. Wilde to Gulian C. Verplanck, May 1, 1834, Verplanck Papers, NYHS.

55. Ibid.

56. Richardson, *Messages and Papers*, II, 1312–1313.

57. *Register of Debates*, 23d Congress, 1st Session, pp. 1394–1395.

58. Ibid., pp. 1397–1398; Wiltse, *Calhoun*, II, 222.

59. *Register of Debates*, 23d Congress, 1st Session, p. 1375.

60. Nathan Sargent, *Public Men and Events* (Philadelphia, 1875), I, 347.

CHAPTER 11

1. C. W. Lawrence to George Newbold, February 9, 1834, Newbold Papers, NYHS; AJ to Van Buren, January 3, 1834, Van Buren Papers, LC.

2. Kendall to Thomas Ellicott, April 15, 1834, Taney Papers, LC.

3. Van Buren to Theodore Sedgwick, February 18, 1834, Sedgwick Papers, MHS.

4. *Globe*, February 11, 1834.

5. AJ to Tilghman A. Howard, August 20, 1833, in Jackson, *Correspondence*, V, 166.

6. AJ to Van Buren, January 3, 1834, Van Buren Papers, LC; Silas Wright to Azariah C. Flagg, January 4, 1834, Flagg Papers, NYPL; Resolutions of the 4th Democratic Ward, New York City, January 29, 1834, Van Buren Papers, LC.

7. On the "doctrine of instruction," see the *Globe*, November 10, 1835; White, *Memoir*, p. 301; Sellers, *Polk*, I, 218. The point made by White is confirmed

in AJ to R. M. Barton, May 14, 1834, Jackson Papers, ML.

8. Taney, "Bank War Manuscript," Taney Papers, LC; Joseph Hopkinson to Biddle, February 11, 1834, Biddle Papers, LC; R. H. Wilde to Verplanck, February 22, 1834, Verplanck Papers, NYHS.

9. Some even thought it originated with Amos Kendall. Silas M. Stilwell to Biddle, February 1, 1834, Biddle Papers, LC.

10. Wright to Flagg, January 4, 1834, Flagg Papers, NYPL; John A. Garraty, *Silas Wright* (New York, 1949), p. 116.

11. Benjamin F. Butler to Thomas W. Olcott, March 20, 1834, Olcott Papers, CUL.

12. AJ to Governor Wolf, February, 1834, in Jackson, *Correspondence*, V, 243.

13. Jabez D. Hammond, *History of Political Parties in the State of New York* (New York, 1852), II, 441.

14. Van Buren to Marcy, March 31, 1834, Van Buren Papers, LC.

15. Van Buren to David E. Evans, February 13, 1834, Van Buren Papers, LC; Greene to Levi Woodbury, March 14, 1834, Woodbury Papers, LC.

16. Sellers, *Polk*, I, 219–220.

17. Ibid., p. 221; *House Committee Reports*, 23d Congress, 1st Session, No. 312.

18. Ibid.; Private Memorandum of A. Jackson, Jackson Papers, LC.

19. *Register of Debates*, 23d Congress, 1st Session, pp. 3474–3477

20. Sellers, *Polk*, I, 222.

21. AJ to John D. Coffee, April 6, 1834, Coffee Papers, THS; AJ to Andrew Jr., April 6, 1834, Jackson Papers, LC; Butler to Olcott, June 19, 1834, Olcott Papers, CUL.

22. *National Intelligencer*, June 14, 1834.

23. Webster to Samuel Jaudon, August 2, 1834, in *Webster Papers*, III, 358–359.

24. Sellers, *Polk*, I, 222.

25. Biddle to J. G. Watmouth, May 2, May 10, 1834, Biddle Papers, LC; Rives to Woodbury, May 26, 1834, Woodbury Papers, LC.

26. The report was requested by James Polk.

27. *House Committee Reports*, 23d Congress, 1st Session, No. 422.

28. Ibid.

29. Ibid.; Taney to Ellicott, May 23, 1834, Taney Papers, LC.

30. *Globe*, April 21, 1834.

31. Ibid., July 1, 1834.

32. AJ to Van Buren, August 8, 1834, Van Buren Papers, LC.

33. *Globe*, July 1, 1834.

34. Ibid., August 8, 1834.

35. AJ to Governor William Findlay, August 20, 1834, in Jackson, *Correspondence*, V, 286.

36. *Globe*, July 1, 1834.

37. June 26, 1834.

38. August 16, 1834.

39. *Globe*, August 6, 1834; AJ to Woodbury, July 3, 1834, Woodbury Papers, LC.

40. Van Buren to John Van Buren, June 22, 1834, Van Buren Papers, LC.

41. Quoted in Sellers, *Polk*, I, 233.

42. *National Intelligencer*, September 20, 1834.

43. Munroe, *McLane*, p. 426.

44. Tyler to Dr. Henry Curtis, March 28, 1834, in Tyler, *Letters and Times,*

I, 491; *Register of Debates*, 23d Congress, 1st Session, pp. 1420–1423.

45. Supposedly some senators said they would vote for Taney for any other office but Treasury, including State, if Jackson would nominate him. But Taney supposedly replied that "he will not receive *a favor* at their hands." Butler to Harriet Butler, June 25, 1834, Butler Papers, NYSL.

46. *Globe*, June 24, 25, 1834.

47. Butler to Harriet Butler, June 25, 1834, Butler Papers, NYSL.

48. *Globe*, June 30, 1834.

49. AJ to Edward Livingston, June 27, 1834, Livingston Papers, JRDF.

50. AJ to John D. Coffee, June 1, 1834, Coffee Papers, THS.

51. *Globe*, June 25, 1834.

52. *Senate Executive Journal*, IV, 426–429.

53. Jackson sent a letter of regret to Rives over his decision to resign and expressed "the hope that you will permit me to think of you for some public station" in the future. AJ to Rives, February [22], 1834, AJ Papers, LC.

54. Butler to Harriet Butler, June 17, 1834, Butler Papers, NYSL; Francis Wayland, *Andrew Stevenson* (Philadelphia, 1949), p. 101.

55. Biddle to Webster, May 28, 1834, Biddle Papers, LC.

56. AJ to Polk, May 18, 1834, Polk Papers, LC.

57. *Register of Debates*, 23d Congress, 1st Session, 4368–4373; Mangum to Bell, June 15, 1835, Bell to Mangum, July 2, 1835, in *THM* (1917), III, 198–200.

58. Sellers, *Polk*, I, 242.

59. AJ to John D. Coffee, June 1, 1834, Coffee Papers, THS.

60. *National Intelligencer*, June 10, 1834; *Register of Debates*, 23d Congress, 1st Session, 2075–2076.

61. Butler to Harriet Butler, June 17, 19, 1834, Butler Papers, NYSL.

62. Van Buren, *Autobiography*, pp. 612–613.

63. Ibid.

64. Ibid., p. 613.

65. Van Buren to John Van Buren, June 22, 1834, Van Buren Papers, LC.

66. William Allen Butler, *A Retrospect of Forty Years* (New York, 1911), p. 79; Dallas to Edward Livingston, July 6, 1834, Livingston Papers, JRDF.

67. *Senate Executive Journal*, IV, 442.

68. *Niles Weekly Register*, July 1, 1834.

69. "Say to him [Benton]," Jackson instructed Major Lewis, "the people soon will vote him a golden medal for his conduct in the Senate." AJ to Lewis, July 26, 1834, Jackson-Lewis Papers, NYPL.

70. Dallas to Livingston, July 6, 1834, Livingston Papers, JRDF.

71. "The Jackson cause," said the *Globe*, September 5, 1832, "is the cause of democracy and the people, against a corrupt and abandoned aristocracy." Van Buren to Marcy, March 31, 1834, Van Buren Papers, LC; Richardson, *Messages and Papers*, II, 1011; AJ to Van Buren, March 30, 1837, Van Buren Papers, LC.

72. Van Buren to Rives, May 23, 1834, Van Buren Papers, LC.

73. Cambreleng to Livingston, July 30, 1834, Livingston Papers, JRDF.

74. The people believed him "honest and patriotic; that he was the friend of the *people,* battling for them against corruption. . . . They loved him as their friend." Nathan Sargent, *Public Men and Events* (Philadelphia, 1875), I, 347.

CHAPTER 12

1. Cambreleng to Livingston, July 30, 1834, Livingston Papers, JRDF; AJ to Lewis, July 15, 1834, Jackson Papers, ML. At first Martin Van Buren planned

to accompany Jackson to the Hermitage—he had been invited many times—but political conditions in New York canceled these plans. Van Buren to Mrs. Rives, May 23, 1834, Rives Papers, LC; Lewis to Van Buren, July 19, 1834, Van Buren Papers, LC.

2. AJ to Andrew Jr., July 15, 26, 1834, Jackson Papers, LC; AJ to Woodbury, July 15, 26, 1834, Woodbury Papers, LC.

3. Lewis to Van Buren, July 19, 1834, Van Buren Papers, LC; Lewis to AJ, July 25, 1834, Donelson Papers, LC.

4. Lewis to Van Buren, July 19, 1834, AJ to Van Buren, August 8, 1834, Van Buren Papers, LC; Donelson to Emily Donelson, July 26, 1834, Donelson Papers, LC.

5. Robert V. Remini, *Andrew Jackson and the Bank War* (New York, 1967), pp. 166–167; Dallas to Livingston, July 6, 1834, Livingston Papers, JRDF.

6. AJ to Blair, August 7, 1834, Jackson Papers, LC; AJ to Woodbury, August 15, 1834, Woodbury Papers, LC.

7. AJ to Blair, August 7, 30, 1834, Jackson Papers, LC.

8. Ibid.

9. AJ to Woodbury, August 15, 1834, Woodbury Papers, LC; AJ to Van Buren, August 16, 1834, Van Buren Papers, LC.

10. Nashville *Banner*, August 14, 1834, copy JPP; AJ to Van Buren, August 8, 16, Van Buren Papers, LC; Sellers, *Polk*, I, 245–246.

11. AJ to Van Buren, August 8, 16, 1834, Van Buren Papers, LC.

12. AJ to Findlay, August 20, 1834, in Jackson, *Correspondence*, V, 285–286.

13. Robert Burton to Polk, August 27, 1834, S. H. McLaughlin to Polk, September 9, 1834, Polk Papers, LC; Sellers, *Polk*, I, 253.

14. Van Buren to AJ, August 2, 1834, in Jackson, *Correspondence*, V, 278–279.

15. AJ to Andrew Jr., September 10, October 1, 1834, Jackson Papers, LC.

16. S. H. McLaughlin to Polk, September 9, 1834, Polk Papers, LC; AJ to Lewis, September 14, 1834, in Jackson, *Correspondence*, V, 292.

17. AJ to Andrew Jr., September 10, 1834, Jackson Papers, LC.

18. AJ to Andrew Jr., September 11, 1834, Jackson Papers, LC.

19. AJ to Andrew Jr., October 1, 11, 15, 1834, Jackson Papers, LC.

20. Armstrong to AJ, October 14, 1834, Donelson to AJ, October 14, 1834, in Jackson, *Correspondence*, V, 295–296; Andrew Jr. to Hutchings, November 20, 1834, Hutchings Papers, Dyas Collection, THS.

21. AJ to Harriet Butler, June 24, 1837, C. Norton Owen Collection, Glencoe, Illinois; Donelson to AJ, October 14, 1834, in Jackson, *Correspondence*, V, 296.

22. Ibid.

23. Andrew Jr. to Hutchings, November 20, 1834, Hutchings Papers, Dyas Collection, THS; Armstrong to AJ, October 14, 1834, in Jackson, *Correspondence*, V, 295.

24. Stockley D. Donelson to AJ, October 14, 1834, Armstrong to AJ, October 14, 1834, in Jackson, *Correspondence*, V, 295–297; Andrew Jr. to Hutchings, November 20, 1834, Hutchings Papers, Dyas Collection, THS.

25. AJ to Andrew Jr., October 23, 25, 1834, Jackson Papers, LC.

26. Ibid.

27. AJ to Andrew Jr., October 30, 1834, Jackson Papers, LC.

28. AJ to Andrew Jr., October 1, 15, 30, Andrew Jr. to AJ, October 13, 1834, Jackson Papers, LC.

29. Lewis to AJ, November 3, 1834, Jackson Papers, LC.

30. AJ to Andrew Jr., November 12, 1834, Jackson Papers, LC; AJ to Andrew Jr., December 7, 1834, Jackson Papers, HL.

31. Lewis to AJ, November 3, 1834, AJ to Andrew Jr., November 19, 1834, Jackson Papers, LC.

32. AJ to Andrew Jr., November 26, 27, 1834, Jackson Papers, LC. For some details of their trip see Lewis to AJ, November 16, 1834, Jackson Papers, LC.

33. AJ to Andrew Jr., December 7, 1834, Jackson Papers, HL.

34. Ibid.; Love to AJ, January 28, 1835, and Memorandum of Agreement for Rebuilding the Hermitage, January 1, 1835, in Jackson, *Correspondence*, V, 315–317, 322–323.

35. AJ to Andrew Jr., October 30, 1834, Jackson Papers, LC.

36. Estimates for Rebuilding the Hermitage, August 2, 1836, in Jackson, *Correspondence*, V, 414–415.

37. Itemized list of expenses, December, 1834, Jackson Papers, LC.

38. AJ to Andrew Jr., March 29, 1836, Jackson Papers, LC; Stanley F. Horn, *The Hermitage, Home of Old Hickory* (Richmond, 1938), p. 71.

39. Nicholas Gist to Blair, November 13, 1842, Blair Papers, LC. The expression "Sage of the Hermitage" never matched his more popular title "The Hero of New Orleans."

CHAPTER 13

1. Jackson's address to the foreign ministers, April 6, 1828, U.S. Presidents, A. Jackson Papers, NYPL; Richardson, *Messages and Papers*, II, 1006.

2. Denmark is one example. See statement in Jackson's handwriting to the Danish minister, 1833, Jackson Papers, LC.

3. *American State Papers, Naval Affairs*, IV, 154ff; James W. Gould, "Sumatra—America's Pepperpot, 1784–1873," *Essex Institute Historical Collections* (July, 1956), XCII, 203–251; John M. Belohlavek, "Andrew Jackson and the Malaysian Pirates: A Question of Diplomacy and Politics," *THQ* (1977), XXXVI, 19, 21, 22, 23. Jackson genuinely regretted the attack by Downes, and his displeasure was conveyed to the captain by the secretary of the navy. See Levi Woodbury to John Downes, July 16, 1832, Woodbury Papers, LC.

4. *National Intelligencer*, July 10, 1832; *Globe*, July 11, 1837, April 26, 1837; Richardson, *Messages and Papers*, II, 1114, 1138.

5. Van Buren, *Autobiography*, p. 419.

6. Ibid.

7. Dallas to Livingston, July 6, 1834, Livingston Papers, JRDF.

8. See Eaton to Buchanan, May 31, June 7, 1831, and Buchanan to Eaton, June 15, 1831, in James Bassett Moore, *The Works of James Buchanan* (New York, 1960), II, 174–176; Philip S. Klein, *President James Buchanan* (University Park, Pa., 1962), pp. 78–80. Secretary of State Livingston was ill at the time and so these negotiations were conducted by Eaton for Jackson.

9. Buchanan to AJ, September 10, 1831, Buchanan Papers, PHS.

10. Livingston to Buchanan, March 31, 1832, in *House Documents*, 33d Congress, 1st Session, No. 111.

11. Buchanan to Livingston, October 19/31, 1832, in Moore, *Works of Buchanan*, II, 253.

12. Joseph C. Baylen, "James Buchanan's 'Calm of Despotism,' " *Pennsylvania Magazine of Biography and History* (1953), LXXVII, 296ff.

13. Buchanan to Livingston, December 20, 1832, in Moore, *Works of Bu-*

chanan, II, 271–278. The czar, Buchanan told Jackson, "is one of the best of Despots." June 22, 1832, ibid., p. 199.

14. Buchanan to Livingston, December 20, 1832, ibid., p. 271; William B. Hatcher, *Edward Livingston: Jeffersonian Republican and Jacksonian Democrat* (Baton Rouge, 1940), p. 402.

15. AJ to Woodbury, March 7, 1834, Woodbury Papers, LC; Livingston to Van Buren, August 1, 1831, Van Buren Papers, LC.

16. Preble to Van Buren, January 17, 1831, Van Buren to AJ, September 23, October 14, 1832, AJ to Van Buren, December 17, 1832, Van Buren Papers, LC.

17. Parton, *Jackson,* III, 605.

18. AJ to Blair, August 7, 1842, Jackson Papers, LC. Too bad Jackson yielded, for the U.S. got considerably less under the Webster-Ashburton Treaty; had he remained firm, the Aroostook War would have been avoided altogether.

19. *Senate Documents,* 24th Congress, 1st Session, No. 414.

20. Roberts to Livingston, May 10, 1833, Edmund Roberts Papers, LC; Edmund Roberts, *Embassy to the Eastern Courts of Cochin-China, Siam, and Muscat* (New York, 1837), pp. 210–216.

21. Hunter Miller, ed., *Treaties and Other International Acts of the United States of America* (Washington, D.C., 1933), III, 755–758, 796–798.

22. H. M. Neiditch, "The Origins and Development of Andrew Jackson's Foreign Policy," Doctoral Dissertation, Cambridge University, 1977, pp. 210ff.

23. Livingston to Roberts, June 6, 1832, Roberts Papers, LC; Hatcher, *Livingston,* p. 403.

24. Livingston to William N. Jeffers, July 30, 1831, in Manning, *Diplomatic Correspondence, Central America,* III, 3–9; Miller, ed., *Treaties,* III, IV, passim; Van Buren to T. P. Moore, June 9, 1829, Department of State, Instructions, American States, XIV, 14, 19, NA.

25. The fullest account of this incident is Julius Goebel, *The Struggle for the Falkland Islands* (New Haven, 1927) but it lacks the wealth of U.S. government documents published a few years later and consequently its interpretation is badly distorted. A better account is Craig Evan Klafter, "United States Involvement in the Falkland Islands Crisis of 1831–1832," a paper written by a graduate student at the University of Chicago, 1982, and soon to be published by the *Journal of the Early Republic.* I am grateful to the author for permission to use his paper. See also Paul D. Dickens, "The Falkland Islands Dispute," *Hispanic American Historical Review* (1929), IX, 454ff.

26. *Senate Documents,* 32d Congress, 1st Session, No. 109; Livingston to Baylies, January 26, February 14, April 3, 1832, in Manning, *Diplomatic Correspondence, Argentina,* I, 3–14; Klafter, "United States Involvement in Falkland Crisis," p. 23.

27. "They must be taught a lesson," wrote Baylies to Livingston, August 19, 1832, in Manning, *Diplomatic Correspondence, Argentina,* I, 153–154; Francis Rawle, "Edward Livingston," in *The American Secretaries of State and Their Diplomacy* (New York, 1928), IV, 250–254.

28. Baylies to Livingston, September 26, 1832, April 23, 1833, in Manning, *Diplomatic Correspondence, Argentina,* I, 161–165, 180; Hatcher, *Livingston,* p. 410.

29. Miller, ed., *Treaties,* III, 653–659.

30. Howard R. Marraro, "John Nelson's Mission to the Kingdom of the Two Sicilies [1831–1832]," *Maryland Historical Magazine* (1949), XLIV, 154–155.

31. Ibid., pp. 159–160. For a discussion of American involvement in the

Mediterranean, see James A. Field, Jr., *America and the Mediterranean World, 1776–1882* (New York, 1969).

32. Dispatch in Jackson's handwriting, no date, Livingston Papers, JRDF.

33. *Senate Documents*, 22d Congress, 2d Session, No. 70; Marraro, "John Nelson's Mission," pp. 166–167; Howard R. Marraro, "Auguste Davezac's Mission to the Kingdom of the Two Sicilies, 1833–1834," *Louisiana Historical Quarterly* (1949), XXXII, 791–808.

34. For popular reaction to these diplomatic successes, see the *Globe*, July, August, 1833. For the incidents involving the freed slaves, see Livingston to Van Buren, December 5, 1831, Van Buren to Palmerston, February 5, 1832, in *Senate Documents*, 24th Congress, 2d Session, No. 174, and Livingston to Aaron Vail, February 26, 1833, Department of State, Instructions, Great Britain, XIV, 131, NA.

35. McLane to Van Ness, August 27, December 5, 1833, May 28, 29, 1834, Van Ness to McLane, November 28, December 21, 1833, February 18, 1834, in *Senate Documents*, 23d Congress, 2d Session, No. 147; Munroe, *McLane*, p. 412.

36. Ibid.

37. McLane to Livingston, August 6, 1833, Livingston Papers, JRDF.

38. Taney to Van Buren, April 9, 1860, Van Buren Papers, LC.

39. Livingston to Niles, February 8, 1833, Department of State, Instructions, France, XIV, 111, NA.

40. Broglie to Niles, March 26, 1833, Department of State, Diplomatic Dispatches, France, NA.

41. AJ to Van Buren, April 25, 1833, Van Buren Papers, LC.

42. Thomas P. Govan, *Nicholas Biddle* (Chicago, 1959), pp. 233–234.

43. McLane to Livingston, June 3, July 25, August 6, 1833, Livingston Papers, JRDF.

44. AJ to Van Buren, July 30, 1833, Van Buren Papers, LC.

45. Livingston to McLane, October 4, 22, 29, November 14, 22, 1833, Livingston Papers, JRDF; Livingston to Broglie, October 5, November 11, 1833, Broglie to Livingston, October 23, 1833, in *House Documents*, 23d Congress, 2d Session, No. 40.

46. Richardson, *Messages and Papers*, II, 1239–1240, 1241.

47. Ibid., p. 1240; AJ to Van Buren, April 25, 1833, Van Buren Papers, LC; McLane to Livingston, August 1, 1833, Livingston Papers, JRDF.

48. McLane to Livingston, December 11, 1833, Livingston Papers, JRDF; *Register of Debates*, 23d Congress, 2d Session, p. 112.

49. Livingston to McLane, October 13, 1833, Livingston Papers, JRDF.

50. *Globe*, May 9, 1833.

51. McLemore, *Franco-American Relations*, pp. 112–113; George M. Gibbs to Van Buren, April 2, 1834, Van Buren Papers, LC.

52. Livingston to McLane, April 3, 1834, Livingston Papers, JRDF.

53. Ibid.

54. Livingston to McLane, April 13, 1834, Livingston Papers, JRDF.

55. Livingston to McLane, April 3, 8, 13, 1834, Livingston Papers, JRDF.

56. Taney to Van Buren, April 9, 1860, Van Buren Papers, LC.

57. Ibid.

58. Ibid.

59. Ibid.

60. Ibid.

61. Van Buren later claimed that he strongly dissented from the opinion expressed by McLane in the cabinet meeting and although it might produce "momentary embarrassments" with both the President and McLane, he felt

obliged to convey it to Jackson. Van Buren, *Autobiography,* p. 612; Taney to Van Buren, April 9, 1860, Van Buren Papers, LC.

62. Ibid.

63. Rives to Van Buren, May 15, 1834, Van Buren Papers, LC. On Rives, see Raymond C. Dingledine, Jr., "The Political Career of William Cabell Rives," Doctoral Dissertation, University of Virginia, 1947.

64. Rives to Van Buren, May 16, 1834, Van Buren Papers, LC.

65. Van Buren, *Autobiography,* p. 612; Livingston to McLane, April 8, 13, 23, May 7, 9, 12, 1834, McLane to Livingston, May 17, 29, 30, 1834, Livingston Papers, JRDF.

66. AJ to Woodbury, May 25, 1834, Woodbury Papers, LC.

67. McLane to Livingston, May 30, 1834, in *House Documents,* 23d Congress, 2d Session, No. 40; Munroe, *McLane,* p. 421.

68. Sérurier to McLane, June 5, 1834, in McLemore, *Franco-American Relations,* p. 119.

69. McLane to Sérurier, June 27, 1834, ibid., p. 120.

70. See chapter 11 for further details.

71. Taney to Van Buren, April 9, 1860, Van Buren Papers, LC.

CHAPTER 14

1. AJ to Livingston, June 27, 1834, Livingston Papers, JRDF.

2. Ibid.

3. Livingston to AJ, June 23, 1834, Jackson Papers, LC.

4. Livingston to Rigny, July 25, 26, 29, 1834, Livingston Papers, JRDF.

5. Rigny to Livingston, July 31, 1834, Livingston Papers, JRDF.

6. Ibid.

7. AJ to Van Buren, October 27, 1834, Van Buren Papers, LC.

8. Livingston to Forsyth, August 4, 10, 1834, Livingston Papers, JRDF.

9. This was Jackson's understanding of what Sérurier had said to him. See Rives to Van Buren, October 14, 1834, Van Buren Papers, LC.

10. AJ to Van Buren, October 27, 1834, Van Buren Papers, LC.

11. AJ to Van Buren, October 5, 1834, Van Buren Papers, LC.

12. Rives to Van Buren, October 14, 1834, Van Buren Papers, LC.

13. AJ to Van Buren, October 27, 1834, Van Buren Papers, LC; Livingston to AJ, October 12, 1834, Jackson Papers, LC.

14. Sérurier to Rigny, October 22, 1834, in McLemore, *Franco-American Relations,* p. 127.

15. Sérurier to Rigny, November 29, 1834, ibid., p. 128.

16. Van Buren to Rives, October 23, 1834, Rives Papers, LC.

17. Livingston to Forsyth, November 22, 1834, in Richardson, *Messages and Papers,* II, 1349, 1350.

18. Wise, *Seven Decades of the Union* (Philadelphia, 1881), pp. 145, 146; E. B. Smith, *Francis Preston Blair* (New York, 1980), p. 49.

19. Richardson, *Messages and Papers,* II, 1319.

20. Ibid., pp. 1321–1322.

21. Ibid., p. 1323.

22. Ibid., pp. 1323, 1324.

23. Ibid., p. 1325.

24. Ibid., pp. 1325, 1326.

25. Ibid.

26. Taney to AJ, October 12, 1834, Jackson Papers, LC.

27. Richardson, *Messages and Papers*, II, 1327.

28. Remini, *Jackson*, II, 256.

29. Richardson, *Messages and Papers*, II, 1327.

30. Ibid., pp. 1327–1328, 1331, 1332, 1336.

31. Ibid., pp. 1332, 1337, 1340–1342.

32. For party reaction to the message, see *National Intelligencer*, December 4, 1834, and *Globe*, December 5, 1834.

33. Hone, *Diary*, I, 143.

34. *National Intelligencer*, December 4, 1834.

35. *Globe*, December 5, 1834.

36. Both Sérurier and Sir Charles Vaughan, British minister to the U.S., informed their countries that Jackson's message lacked his cabinet's support. Although the President enjoyed widespread public support on the issue, said Vaughan, he probably could not get Congress to take any decisive action at the moment. Vaughan to Palmerston, December 4, 20, 1834, in McLemore, *Franco-American Relations*, pp. 134–135.

37. *Globe*, December 17, 1834.

38. *Senate Documents*, 23d Congress, 2d Session, No. 40.

39. *Register of Debates*, 23d Congress, 2d Session, p. 216.

40. Memorandum, 1834, Clay Papers, LC.

CHAPTER 15

1. *National Intelligencer*, December 4, 5, 8, 1834; Hone, *Diary*, I, 143; AJ to Andrew Jr., December 4, 1834, Jackson Papers, HL.

2. Parton, *Jackson*, III, 580.

3. *Globe*, January 12, 1835.

4. A full account of the celebration, including many of the toasts, can be found in the *Globe*, January 14, 1835.

5. January 8, 12, 14, 1835.

6. AJ to Andrew Jr., December 4, 7, 1834, Jackson Papers, HL.

7. Ibid.

8. AJ to Andrew J. Hutchings, January 25, 1835, Hutchings Papers, Dyas Collection, THS.

9. AJ to Joseph Conn Guild, April 24, 1835, in Jackson, *Correspondence*, V, 338.

10. "Booth" to AJ, July 4, 1835, ibid., p. 355. A wordier threat from "Booth" to AJ, May 7, 1834, can be found in the Jackson Papers, CHS.

11. There are a great many books on the social reforms for the Jacksonian era. For a list of them, see *The Era of Good Feelings and the Age of Jackson, 1816–1841*, a bibliography compiled by Robert V. Remini and Edwin A. Miles (Arlington Heights, Ill., 1979), pp. 159–204.

12. Harriet Martineau, *Retrospect of Western Travel* (London, 1838), I, 161.

13. *Globe*, January 31, 1835; *National Intelligencer*, January 31, 1835; Tyler to Robert Tyler, January 31, 1835, Miscellaneous Papers, HL; Benton, *Thirty Years View*, I, 521. For further details of the attempted assassination, see Carlton Jackson, "—Another Time, Another Place—The Attempted Assassination of President Andrew Jackson," *THQ* (1967), XXVI, 184–190, and Richard C. Rohrs, "Partisan Politics and the Attempted Assassination of Andrew Jackson," *Journal of the Early Republic* (1981), I, 149–163.

14. Tyler to Robert Tyler, January 31, 1835, Miscellaneous Papers, HL.

15. Parton, *Jackson*, III, 582; Van Buren, *Autobiography*, p. 353.

16. Tyler to Robert Tyler, January 31, 1835, Miscellaneous Papers, HL; *Globe*, January 31, 1835.

17. He also mentioned members of the House and included such Democrats as Van Buren, Benton, and Judge White. Benton, *Thirty Years View*, I, 523. On the suspicion of a plot, see Webster to Jeremiah Mason, February 1, 1835, in *Webster Papers*, IV, 25.

18. Key to Taney, January 30, 1835, Miscellaneous Key Papers, LC; *Globe*, February 3, 4, April 13, 1835. The trial began at 9:30 A.M. and ended at 6 P.M. Most of the testimony concerned Lawrence's sanity. The jury took only ten minutes to reach its verdict.

19. AJ to Aaron Vail, April 16, 1835, Vail Collection, NYHS.

20. Benton, *Thirty Years View*, I, 524; McLaughlin to Donelson, March 1, 1835, Donelson Papers, LC. See also Webster to Jeremiah Mason, February 1, 1835, in *Webster Papers*, IV, 25.

21. Cambreleng to Livingston, December 11, 1835, Livingston Papers, JRDF.

22. *Register of Debates*, 23d Congress, 2d Session, p. 730; Benton, *Thirty Years View*, I, 554.

23. AJ to Livingston, March 10, 1835, Livingston Papers, JRDF; Samuel J. Tilden to Elan Tilden, March 8, 1835, Tilden Papers, NYPL. See also AJ to Major Rodney Church, April 27, 1835, Jackson Papers, LC, in which Jackson says that it was not up to him to inquire into the Senate's reasons for the action. That right belongs to the people, whose decisions, he said, are always honest and seldom, if ever, wrong.

24. The Whigs kept insisting that the message might be interpreted as a menace to France. See *National Intelligencer*, December 11, 1834.

25. Livingston to Forsyth, January 11, 1835, Livingston Papers, JRDF; Livingston to AJ, January 16, 1835, Jackson Papers, LC.

26. Livingston to Dallas, December 31, 1834, Livingston Papers, JRDF. Jackson probably felt the bill would fail. See Van Buren to Rives, January 25, 1835, Rives Papers, LC.

27. Livingston told Rigny that Jackson had used "moderate language" in his message. Livingston to Forsyth, January 14, 15, 1835, Livingston Papers, JRDF.

28. Ibid.

29. Livingston to Forsyth, January 14, 15, 1835, Livingston Papers, JRDF; McLemore, *Franco-American Relations*, p. 143; Livingston to AJ, January 16, 1835, Jackson Papers, LC.

30. Livingston to Rigny, January 29, 1835, Livingston Papers, JRDF.

31. AJ to Livingston, March 10, 1835, Livingston Papers, JRDF.

32. Adams, *Memoirs*, IX, 207, 217.

33. AJ to Rodney Church, April 27, 1835, Jackson Papers, LC.

34. Ward to Sing, February 20, 1835, Miscellaneous Sing Papers, NYHS. See also Calhoun to Bolling Hall, February 21, 1835, in *Calhoun Papers*, XII, 500.

35. Livingston to AJ, January 31, 1835, Jackson Papers, LC.

36. Van Buren to Mrs. William C. Rives, December 12, 1834, Rives Papers, LC.

37. Forsyth to Livingston, March 5, 1835, Livingston Papers, JRDF; Forsyth to Livingston, February 13, 1835, in Richardson, *Messages and Papers*, II, 1348–1349.

38. Van Buren to Livingston, March 8, 1835, Livingston Papers, JRDF.

39. AJ to Livingston, March 10, 1835, Livingston Papers, JRDF; Livingston to Donelson, February 5, 1835, Donelson Papers, LC. Some members of the

cabinet thought that Livingston should have left France immediately on learning of Sérurier's recall, but Jackson disagreed with them. Woodbury to Livingston, March 17, 1835, Livingston Papers, JRDF.

40. McLemore, *Franco-American Relations,* pp. 151–152; Hatcher, *Livingston,* p. 443.

41. Livingston to AJ, April 12, 16, 1835, Jackson Papers, LC.

42. Livingston to Forsyth, April 19, 1835, Livingston Papers, JRDF.

43. Ibid.

44. Livingston to Broglie, April 25, 1835, Livingston to Forsyth, April 19, 1835, Livingston Papers, JRDF. For an explanation of Sérurier's note to Forsyth, see Livingston to Forsyth, April 23, 1835, Livingston Papers, JRDF.

45. Livingston to Forsyth, April 19, 1835, Livingston Papers, JRDF.

46. Livingston to Forsyth, April 23, 1835, Livingston Papers, JRDF.

47. *Globe,* May 30, 1835; *National Intelligencer,* May 30, 1835; Adams, *Memoirs,* IX, 238.

48. Ibid.; Rives to Van Buren, June 2, 1835, Van Buren Papers, LC; *National Intelligencer,* May 29, 1835.

CHAPTER 16

1. AJ to Andrew J. Hutchings, March 24, 1835, Hutchings Papers, Dyas Collection, THS; AJ to Dr. E. Breathitt, March 30, 1835, Jackson Papers, LC.

2. AJ to Andrew Jr., April 14, 1835, in Jackson, *Correspondence,* V, 335–336.

3. Jackson seems to have had a fixation about this problem, the psychological meaning of which should be left to experts in the field to explain.

4. AJ to Andrew Jr., April 5, 14, 15, 23, 1835, AJ to Dr. E. Breathett, March 30, 1835, Jackson Papers, LC; AJ to Hutchings, March 24, 1835, Hutchings Papers, Dyas Collection, THS; AJ to Lewis, April 27, 1835, Jackson-Lewis Papers, LC. Today at the Hermitage can be seen a mahogany medicine chest fitted with seven bottles, some of which contain remnants of medicine such as ipecac (to induce vomiting) and rhubarb (a purgative).

5. AJ to Dr. Philip Syng Physick, May, 1835 [?], in Jackson, *Correspondence,* V, 342.

6. AJ to Andrew Jr., April 14, 1835, ibid., p. 335; Donelson to Livingston, April 13, 1835, Livingston Papers, JRDF.

7. AJ to Andrew Jr., April 23, May 2, 1835, Jackson Papers, LC.

8. AJ to Andrew Jr., April 14, May 2, 9, 1835, Jackson Papers, LC.

9. *Extra Temperance Recorder,* December, 1834, PHS. The amount of alcohol consumed in the United States during the early nineteenth century was staggering. For particulars, see William J. Rorabaugh, *The Alcoholic Republic* (New York, 1980).

10. AJ to Dr. E. Breathitt, March 30, 1835, Jackson Papers, LC.

11. Pope to AJ, February 19, 1829, in Jackson, *Correspondence,* IV, 8.

12. The details of Jackson's mishandling of his cabinet appointments can be found in Remini, *Jackson,* II, 159ff.

13. Kendall, *Autobiography,* p. 337.

14. *Niles Weekly Register,* May 18, 1833.

15. *House Report,* 23d Congress, 2d Session, No. 103; *Senate Documents,* 23d Congress, 1st Session, No. 422.

16. Ibid., pp. 31–33. See also Senator Thomas Ewing's report of January 27, 1835, in *Senate Documents,* 23d Congress, 2d Session, No. 86.

17. *House Document,* 23d Congress, 2d Session, No. 103, pp. 50–51.
18. Kendall to AJ, August 21, 1834, Jackson Papers, LC.
19. Kendall to AJ, November 24 [1834], Jackson Papers, LC.
20. Kendall, *Autobiography,* pp. 332–335. Kendall was confirmed on March 15, 1836.
21. Ibid., p. 335.
22. Ibid., p. 336.
23. Taney to Van Buren, May 12, 1835, Van Buren Papers, LC.
24. Some idea of these rules can be gleaned from the rules Kendall imposed as Fourth Auditor:

> 1. Every clerk will be in his room, ready to commence business at nine o'clock, A.M. and will apply himself with diligence to the public service until three o'clock, P.M.
> 2. Every clerk will hold himself in readiness to discharge any duty which may be required of him in office hours or out.
> 3. Newspapers or books must not be read in the office . . . nor must conversation be held with visitors.
> 4. Gambling, drunkenness, and irregular and immoral habits will subject any clerk to instant removal.
> 5. The acceptance of any present or gratuity . . . will subject any clerk to instant removal.

The others are printed in Kendall, *Autobiography,* p. 319.
25. Ibid., pp. 337, 340; Kendall to Caleb Butler, May 13, 1835, Kendall Papers, LC.
26. *Senate Documents,* 24th Congress, 1st Session, No. 1, p. 389.
27. White, *Jacksonians,* p. 275.
28. *Senate Documents,* 24th Congress, 1st Session, No. 1, pp. 391–392.
29. Kendall, *Autobiography,* p. 340.
30. Ibid., p. 342.
31. White, *Jacksonians,* p. 280.
32. Ibid., pp. 274–276; Kendall, *Autobiography,* p. 344.
33. Kendall to Caleb Butler, May 13, 1835, Kendall Papers, LC; AJ to Kendall, July 19, 1835, in Jackson, *Correspondence,* V, 356.
34. For these guidelines, see Remini, *Jackson,* II, 184ff.
35. See ibid., p. 199, for details. On the operation of the bureaucracy, see Matthew A. Crenson, *The Federal Machine: Beginnings of Bureaucracy in Jacksonian America* (Baltimore, 1975).
36. *Senate Documents,* 23d Congress, 2d Session, No. 108.
37. "Outline of principles," February 23, 1829, Jackson Papers, LC.
38. AJ to Woodbury, May 21, 1835, Woodbury Papers, LC.
39. Note of charges against clerks, May 21, 1835, Jackson Papers, LC. See also AJ to Kendall, May 21, 1835, in Jackson, *Correspondence,* V, 351–352.
40. AJ to Joseph Conn Guild, April 24, 1835, ibid., p. 340.
41. Lloyd M. Short, *The Development of National Administrative Organization in the United States* (Baltimore, 1923), pp. 15ff.
42. For the reorganization of the State Department, see Munroe, *McLane,* p. 408.
43. White, *Jacksonians,* p. 535. On the Land Office, see Malcolm Rohrbough, *The Land Office Business* (New York, 1968).
44. Nathan Sargent, *Public Men and Events* (Philadelphia, 1875), I, 282; *Register of Debates,* 23d Congress, 2d Session, pp. 219–231; *Senate Journal,* 23d Congress, 2d Session, p. 79; Wiltse, *Calhoun,* II, 257; Benton, *Thirty Years View,* I, 557; *Calhoun Papers,* XII, 415ff.
45. *House Document,* 28th Congress, 1st Session, No. 45.

46. AJ to Guild, April 24, 1835, in Jackson, *Correspondence*, V, 340.

47. Sidney H. Aronson, *Status and Kinship in the Higher Civil Service: Standards of Selection in the Administrations of John Adams, Thomas Jefferson, and Andrew Jackson* (Cambridge, 1964), passim.

48. Parton, *Jackson*, III, 212, 220.

49. Richardson, *Messages and Papers*, II, 1011–1012.

50. White, *Jacksonians*, p. 566.

CHAPTER 17

1. Ellen Hanson to AJ, March 12, 1835, in Jackson, *Correspondence*, V, 330.

2. AJ to Hanson, March 25, 1835, ibid., p. 333.

3. Donelson to Livingston, April 13, 1835, Livingston Papers, JRDF.

4. AJ to Hutchings, June 30, 1835, Hutchings Papers, Dyas Collection, THS; AJ to Donelson, May 2, 12, 1835, Donelson Papers, LC. For the early history of the Whig party, see E. Malcolm Carroll, *Origins of the Whig Party* (Durham, 1925).

5. David Campbell to William B. Campbell, April 8, 1835, David Campbell Papers, DUL.

6. AJ to Hutchings, June 30, 1835, Hutchings Papers, Dyas Collection, THS.

7. A full discussion of the background of White's candidacy can be found in Sellers, *Polk*, I, 253ff. See also White, *Memoir*.

8. AJ to Balch, February 16, 1835, and AJ to Guild, April 24, 1835, in Jackson, *Correspondence*, V, 327–328, 338, 339. The idea that White's candidacy was intended to destroy the administration is also stated in Donelson to Livingston, April 13, 1835, Livingston Papers, JRDF.

9. Ibid.; McLemore to AJ, April 6, 1835, Donelson Papers, LC. See also Calhoun to Francis W. Pickens, May 19, 1835, in *Calhoun Papers*, XII, 534–535.

10. AJ to Guild, April 24, 1835, in Jackson, *Correspondence*, V. 339; AJ to Hutchings, June 30, 1835, Hutchings Papers, Dyas Collection, THS; AJ to Charles J. Love, September 7, 1835, Jackson Papers, LC.

11. Leigh to Francis Brooke, August 16, 1835, Clay Papers, LC; Henry Martindale to J. W. Taylor, February 6, 1835, Taylor Papers, NYHS; memorandum, no date but obviously April 24, 1835, Jackson Papers, LC. See also Clay to Brooke, June 27, July 20, 24, August 19, 1835, Clay Papers, DUL.

12. AJ to Dr. E. Breathett, March 30, 1835, Jackson Papers, LC. See also AJ to Andrew Jr., April 23, May 2, 1835, Jackson Papers, LC; AJ to Polk, May 3, 12, 1835, Polk Papers, LC; AJ to Donelson, May 12, 1835, Donelson Papers, LC.

13. Poinsett to Livingston, December 15, 1834, Cambreleng to Livingston, December 11, 1834, Livingston Papers, JRDF. See also Henry W. Kinsman to Webster, January 18, 1835, Webster Papers, New Hampshire Historical Society; Martindale to John W. Taylor, February 6, 1835, Taylor Papers, NYHS.

14. Poinsett to Livingston, June 1, 1835, Livingston Papers, JRDF; AJ to Charles J. Love, September 7, 1835, Jackson Papers, LC.

15. AJ to Polk, May 12, 1835, Polk Papers, LC; Blair to AJ, May 19, 1835, Jackson Papers, LC.

16. AJ to Blair, May 20, 1835, Jackson Papers, LC. For details of Tennessee's "betrayal," see Donelson to Van Buren, September 25, 1835, Van Buren Papers, LC.

17. Sellers, *Polk*, I, 272; *National Intelligencer*, May 23, 1835.

18. New Hampshire *Patriot*, June 1, 1835.

19. Some Whigs hoped the convention would do to Van Buren what the

congressional caucus of 1824 did to Crawford. See Seward to Weed, March 11, 1835, Weed Papers, RUL.

20. The feud in Pennsylvania between Wolf and Muhlenberg, reported Thurlow Weed to William Seward, "is deadly." June 15, 1835, Seward Papers, RUL.

21. Poinsett to Livingston, December 15, 1835, Livingston Papers, JRDF.

22. Catron to AJ, March 21, 1835, Jackson Papers, LC.

23. New Hampshire *Patriot*, June 1, 1835.

24. Wright to Van Buren, May 22, 1835, Van Buren Papers, LC. Van Buren tried to comfort Rives and prevent a party split. Rives reassured him, but he was deeply offended. "Certainly on my part," Rives wrote in response, "nothing shall be wanting to allay every feeling of dissatisfaction which may have arisen on my account, & to promote, by whatever means may be in my power, that hearty Republican concert which is so necessary to the ascendency of the principles for which we have contended." Van Buren to Rives, May, 1835, Rives to Van Buren, June 2, 1835, Van Buren Papers, LC. Rives later deserted to the Whig party.

25. Joel Silbey, "Election of 1836," in Arthur M. Schlesinger, Jr., ed., *History of American Presidential Elections, 1789-1968* (4 vols.; New York, 1971), I, 584.

26. The full address is carried ibid., and the quotations in the text can be found on pp. 619, 629, 633-634.

27. See series of articles entitled "The Aristocracy" in the *Globe*, August 1, 5, 15, 1835.

28. *Globe*, July 8, 1835; AJ to Polk, August 3, 1835, Polk Papers, LC.

29. Lewis to AJ, May 3, 1835, Jackson Papers, LC.

30. AJ to Donelson, July 7, 20, 24, August 1, 1835, Donelson Papers, LC.

31. Freehling, *Prelude to Civil War*, p. 340.

32. Ibid., p. 341. See also Frank Otto Gatell, ed., "Postmaster Huger and Incendiary Publications," *South Carolina Historical Magazine* (1963), LXIV, 193-201.

33. Freehling, *Prelude to Civil War*, p. 341.

34. Kendall to Postmaster of Charleston, August 4, 1835, in *Niles Weekly Register*, August 22, 1835.

35. Kendall to AJ, August 7, 1835, in Jackson, *Correspondence*, V, 360.

36. Ibid., AJ to Kendall, August 9, 1835.

37. Ibid. For a full discussion of this phenomenon, see Leonard L. Richards, *"Gentlemen of Property and Standing": Anti-Abolition Mobs in Jacksonian America* (New York, 1970).

38. AJ to Kendall, August 9, 1835, in Jackson, *Correspondence*, V. 360-361.

39. White, *Jacksonians*, pp. 518-519.

40. Richardson, *Messages and Papers*, II, 1395.

41. Calhoun to S. D. Ingham, December 27, 1835, in *Calhoun Papers*, XII, 12-13, 22-28; White, *Jacksonians*, p. 520. Kendall had a controlling hand in the drafting of this legislation.

42. Freehling, *Prelude to Civil War*, p. 346.

43. For the Leggett quotation, see White, *Jacksonians*, p. 519.

44. AJ to Dickerson, June 6, 1835, Jackson Papers, LC.

CHAPTER 18

1. *Globe*, June 26, July 13, 1835.

2. A copy can be found in Richardson, *Messages and Papers*, II, 1397-1403.

3. *Globe*, July 10, 1835; *National Intelligencer*, June 26, July 3, 1835; Dallas to Livingston, July 6, 15, 1835, Livingston Papers, JRDF.

4. Livingston to Forsyth, June 21, 1835, in Vincent P. Carosso and Lawrence Lader, eds., "Edward Livingston and Jacksonian Diplomacy," *Louisiana History* (1966), VII, 247; Livingston to AJ, June 22, 1835, Jackson Papers, LC.

5. Richard Rush to Livingston, June 27, 1835, Livingston Papers, JRDF; Livingston to Forsyth, June 29, 1835, in Richardson, *Messages and Papers*, II, 1403; Livingston to AJ, July 11, 1835, Jackson Papers, LC.

6. Livingston to Forsyth, June 29, 1835, Forsyth to Livingston, June 30, 1835, in Richardson, *Messages and Papers*, II, 1403–1404; Dallas to Livingston, July 6, 1835, Livingston Papers, JRDF.

7. Forsyth to Barton, June 28, 1835, in Richardson, *Messages and Papers*, II, 1412.

8. AJ to Kendall, July 19, 1835, in Jackson, *Correspondence*, V, 357.

9. The full background to the Barry and McLean appointments can be found in Remini, *Jackson*, II, 164–165.

10. All the particulars about these Supreme Court appointments can be found in Henry J. Abraham, *Justices and Presidents: A Political History of Appointments to the Supreme Court* (New York, 1974), pp. 87ff.

11. Carl B. Swisher, *Roger B. Taney* (New York, 1935), p. 314; Webster to [Gales and Seaton], [March 8, 1835], in *Webster Papers*, IV, 36. See also Paul A. Freund, ed., *History of the Supreme Court of the United States:* Volume IV, *The Challenge of Jacksonian Democracy: The Marshall Court, 1826–1835*, Gerald Gunther, ed. (New York, 1974). *National Intelligencer*, March 10, 1835.

12. Benton to Van Buren, June 7, 1835, Van Buren Papers, LC.

13. Livingston to Davezac, December 16, 1835, Livingston Papers, JRDF.

14. AJ to Lewis, February 28, 1842, Jackson-Lewis Papers, NYPL.

15. Dallas to Livingston, July 6, 1834, Livingston Papers, JRDF; Adams, *Memoirs*, IX, 244.

16. AJ to Woodbury, July 17, 1835, C. V. Fox Papers, NYHS; AJ to Woodbury, July 28, 1835, Woodbury Papers, LC.

17. Account with F. M. Boykin, August 16, 1835, in Jackson, *Correspondence*, V, 362.

18. Dickerson to Livingston, August 13, 1835, Livingston Papers, JRDF.

19. *National Intelligencer*, August 12, 1835; *Globe*, August 19, 1835.

20. Dickerson to Livingston, August 13, 1835, Livingston Papers, JRDF. See also *National Intelligencer*, August 14, 1835.

21. An excellent account of this phenomenon is Michael Feldberg, *The Turbulent Era: Riot and Disorder in Jacksonian America* (New York, 1980).

22. *National Intelligencer*, August 15, 1835.

23. Narrative of Nicholas Trist, in Parton, *Jackson*, III, 606–607.

24. Editorial reprinted in *Globe*, August 22, 1835.

25. Ibid.

26. Ibid.

27. *National Intelligencer*, July 27, 1835.

28. *Globe*, August 25, 1835.

29. *National Gazette*, quoted in *Globe*, August 29, 1835. See also *Globe*, September 30, October 7, November 14, 18, 1837, and Albany *Argus* throughout the fall of 1837.

30. See, for example, Van Buren to Nathaniel Macon, February 13, 1836, Macon Papers, DUL. But there are many other examples.

31. This argument is particularly well developed in the *Globe* throughout 1835 and 1836. The editorials frequently showed the controlling hand of Jackson

in some of the particulars of the argument. Gerald S. Henig, "The Jacksonian Attitude Toward Abolitionism in the 1830s," *THQ* (1969), XXVIII, 42–56, demonstrates fairly convincingly that the Jacksonians feared abolitionism as a threat to the Union. See also John M. McFaul, "Expediency vs. Morality: Jacksonian Politics and Slavery," *JAH* (1975), LXII, 24–39.

32. *Globe*, August 19, 1835.

33. Parton, *Jackson*, III, 607. AJ to James Hamilton, Jr., June 29, 1828, in Jackson, *Correspondence*, III, 412, is taken out of context but it is a sentiment Jackson repeated many times during his administration. I find this quotation one of the simplest and best expressed of his views. *Globe*, September 30, 1835.

CHAPTER 19

1. AJ to Charles J. Love, September 7, 1835, Jackson Papers, LC.

2. This note was later published in the *National Intelligencer*, January 22, 1836. After Jackson saw Broglie's note he felt it was "polite" but "worthless." Donelson to Livingston, September 9, 1835, Livingston Papers, JRDF.

3. Ibid.

4. Ibid.

5. Instructions for Thomas P. Barton, September 14, 1835, Jackson Papers, LC.

6. Ibid.

7. Broglie to Barton, October 26, 1835, in Richardson, *Messages and Papers*, II, 1415.

8. Ibid., Barton to Broglie, October 24, 1835.

9. AJ to Kendall, October 31, 1835, in Jackson, *Correspondence*, V, 374–375.

10. AJ to Polk, September 15, 1835, Polk Papers, LC; AJ to Robert Armstrong, September 15, 1835, AJ to Grundy, September 24, 1835, in Jackson, *Correspondence*, V, 366, 367.

11. Sellers, *Polk*, I, 287–288, 291–292.

12. Donelson to Livingston, October 8, 1835, Dallas to Livingston, October 24, 1835, Livingston Papers, JRDF. Dallas was quoting from Shakespeare's *Hamlet*.

13. AJ to Kendall, October 31, 1835, in Jackson, *Correspondence*, V, 374.

14. Notes for the Annual Message, December 7, 1835, ibid., p. 377.

15. Ibid., pp. 377–379.

16. Donelson to Livingston, November 4, 1835, Livingston Papers, JRDF, indicates that Jackson saw Livingston toward the end of the month.

17. White was nominated by the Tennessee legislature on October 16, 17, 1835. The problem of getting the resolutions passed is described in Sellers, *Polk*, I, 288–292.

18. Ibid.; Benton, *Thirty Years View*, I, 569.

19. Sellers, *Polk*, I, 292ff, has a fine account of this election and deftly intertwines both national and state politics in his narrative.

20. Richardson, *Messages and Papers*, II, 1367, 1371ff, 1376.

21. Ibid., p. 1379.

22. Ibid.

23. Ibid., pp. 1379, 1380, 1381.

24. Ibid., p. 1384.

25. Ibid., pp. 1385, 1387.

26. Ibid., p. 1390.

27. Ibid., pp. 1390–1392, Jackson went on to describe the many efforts of the government to assist the Indians in adjusting to their new surroundings.

28. Ibid., pp. 1395, 1396.

29. Livingston to Davezac, December 16, 1835, Livingston Papers, JRDF.

30. McLemore, *Franco-American Relations*, p. 173.

31. Pageot to Forsyth, December 1, 1835, Forsyth to Pageot, December 3, 1835, in Richardson, *Messages and Papers*, II, 1418, 1419.

32. Pageot to Forsyth, December 5, 1835, ibid., p. 1420. "We are in a state of some excitement, about the French business," wrote Senator Webster. "The President is warm, & warlike, Mr. Van Buren more pacific; & on the whole, there is, as we learn, a good deal of division in the Cabinet." Webster to Mrs. Caroline Webster, January 10, 1836, in C. H. Van Tyne, ed., *The Letters of Daniel Webster* (New York, 1902), p. 198.

33. AJ to Livingston, December 31, 1835, Woodbury to Livingston, December 27, 1835, Livingston Papers, JRDF.

34. Hone, *Diary*, I, 184.

35. Parton, *Jackson*, III, 574–576.

36. Livingston to AJ, January 11, 1836, in Charles H. Hunt, *Life of Edward Livingston* (New York, 1864), pp. 428–429; *National Intelligencer*, January 11, 1836.

37. *Register of Debates*, 24th Congress, 1st Session, p. 163.

38. Richardson, *Messages and Papers*, II, 1408, 1411, 1412.

39. Benton, *Thirty Years View*, I, 594, 600; *Register of Debates*, 24th Congress, 1st Session, pp. 169ff.

40. This is described in McLemore, *Franco-American Relations*, pp. 177ff.

41. Note of Charles Bankhead, dated January 27, 1836, in Richardson, *Messages and Papers*, II, 1436–1437.

42. Forsyth to Bankhead, February 3, 1836, ibid., pp. 1439, 1440.

43. Message of February 8, 1836, ibid., p. 1433.

44. *National Intelligencer*, February 1, 1836; *Globe*, February 1, 1836.

45. Hone, *Diary*, I, 197.

46. McLemore, *Franco-American Relations*, p. 184.

47. Ibid., p. 187.

48. Bankhead to Forsyth, February 15, 1836, in Richardson, *Messages and Papers*, II, 1440.

49. Ibid., pp. 1435, 1436.

50. *National Intelligencer*, May 11, 1836.

51. Van Buren to Nathaniel Macon, February 13, 1836, Macon Papers, DUL. Van Buren himself was also congratulated. See Rives to Van Buren, February 19, 1836, Taney to Van Buren, March 8, 1836, Van Buren Papers, LC.

52. AJ to Livingston, February 27, 1836, Livingston Papers, JRDF.

53. Richardson, *Messages and Papers*, II, 1006.

54. Remini, *Jackson*, II, 283; Jackson's address to the foreign ministers, April 6, 1829, U.S. Presidents, A. Jackson, NYPL.

55. Rives to Van Buren, September 8, 1830, Van Buren Papers, LC.

56. Vail to Van Buren, January 22, 1835, Van Buren Papers, LC.

57. McLemore, *Franco-American Relations*, pp. 206–207.

58. Paul Varg, *United States Foreign Relations, 1830–1860* (Lansing, 1979), p. 91. However, Jackson told Livingston on February 27, 1836, that he assumed the first payment had already been made. Livingston Papers, JRDF. Richardson, *Messages and Papers*, II, 1446.

59. Benton to Woodbury [no date but the letter was received by Woodbury on February 16, 1836], Woodbury Papers, LC.

60. Livingston to AJ, February 16, 1836, Jackson Papers, LC.

61. AJ to Louise Livingston, May 26, 1836, Livingston Papers, JRDF. One additional reason for Jackson's loyalty to Livingston was the repeated kindnesses Livingston and his wife had shown to Rachel Jackson before her death. Louise Livingston even offered to assist Rachel in the selection of her wardrobe for her entrance into Washington society as First Lady. Rachel accepted the offer with profound thanks. "To serve me is viewed as an additional proof of that disinterested friendship which has always characterised the conduct of your family towards myself & the Genl." Rachel Jackson to Louise Livingston, December 1, 1828, Livingston Papers, JRDF. The letter is not written in Rachel's hand, nor was it composed by her.

62. *Globe*, January 19, 22, 1836; *National Intelligencer*, January 22, 1836; McLemore, *Franco-American Relations*, pp. 192, 199.

63. Memorandum Respecting A. Pageot, November 15, 1836, and Memorandum [November 15, 1836] in Jackson, *Correspondence*, V, 436–438, and footnote on p. 437.

64. AJ to Lewis, October 19, 1839, Jackson-Lewis Papers, NYPL.

65. Memorandum Respecting A. Pageot, November 15, 1836, in Jackson, *Correspondence*, V, 437. See Remini, *Jackson*, II, 292, 312, 315–316 for his problems with Branch.

CHAPTER 20

1. AJ to Van Buren, October 5, 1839, Van Buren Papers, LC.

2. Technically the Committee (upper house) and Council (lower house) of the Cherokee Nation controlled the annuities, though the Principal Chief might propose how they should be distributed. I am grateful to Professor Mary Young for this information. Two useful biographies of Ross are Rachel C. Eaton, *John Ross and the Cherokee Indians* (Menasha, Wis., 1914) and Gary E. Moulton, *John Ross, Cherokee Chief* (Athens, Ga., 1978).

3. Apparently Ross and Jackson had several meetings in Washington in 1834 and 1835. Later Jackson refused to see the Chief because he would not cooperate with removal. See Ross et al. to AJ, February 3, 1834, and Jackson's endorsement, Jackson Papers, LC.

4. Remini, *Jackson*, II, 275–278. As of 1833 no more than 400 Cherokees had removed since passage of the Removal Act. Hardin to Lumpkin, October 5, 1833, Wilson Lumpkin Papers, Georgia State Department of Archives, Atlanta, Ga.

5. Morris L. Wardell, *A Political History of the Cherokee Nation, 1838–1907* (Norman, Okla., 1977), p. 16. Jackson's relations with the Treaty party were rather good. See, for example, the Ridges' salutation to AJ, 1833, Texas State Library, Austin, Texas, copy JPP.

6. Mary Young's two excellent Carroll lectures, "Friends of the Indian," I and II, delivered at Mary Baldwin College, October 8–9, 1980, form the basis of much of the argument in this chapter dealing with the Cherokees. I am grateful for Professor Young's analysis and interpretation. The lectures were printed in pamphlet form by the College and are cited here with permission. Pages 6 and 26 of the pamphlet develop the point about a mixed-blood elite. I have also used Mary Young, "Indian Removal and the Attack on Tribal Autonomy: The Cherokee Case," in John K. Mahon, *Indians of the Southeast* (Gainesville, 1975), pp. 125–134, and her *Redskins, Ruffleshirts and Rednecks: Indian Allotments in Alabama and Mississippi, 1830–1860* (Norman, Okla., 1961). With respect to Jackson's attitudes, see also the fragment of a memorandum in Jackson's handwriting regard-

ing the treaty negotiated by John Eaton with the Cherokees on June 19, 1834, no date on the memorandum, Jackson Papers, LC, and the *Globe* editorials of June 3, 1834, June 22, 1835. The *Globe* constantly reminded its readers that Ross was a "white man, with a small intermixture of Indian blood." *Globe*, June 3, 1834.

7. AJ to Van Buren, October 5, 1839, Van Buren Papers, LC.

8. Eaton, *John Ross*, p. 83.

9. Ibid., pp. 83–84; Moulton, *John Ross*, pp. 60–61; Grace Steele Woodward, *The Cherokees* (Norman, Okla., 1963), pp. 178–179; Ross et al. to Cass, February 14, 25, 27, 28, 1835, Cass to Ross et al., February 16, 27, 1835, in *House Documents*, 23d Congress, 2d Session, No. 286. Professor Young does not feel that Ross's estimate of the value of the Cherokee Country East is "preposterous" because it takes into account the probable value of the gold mines in Georgia and North Carolina.

10. Memorial of the Cherokee Delegation, March 3, 1835, and Memorial and Protest of the Cherokee Nation, ibid. In this series see also documents 292 and 315. For other terms proposed by Ross, see Ross et al. to AJ, March 28, 1834, RG 46, E 327, 23 A-G6, NA. On the back of this petition, in Jackson's handwriting, are the words: "We are bound to extinguish for the benefit of Georgia the Indian tittle, & we cannot interfere with the sovereign powers of a state. As to exploring the country west, you may say to them we will ask for [an] appropriation [for] this purpose [and if] made, with a [condition ?] of sending the [Cherokee] nation there [we w]ill pay the [exp]ence of an exploring [p]arty but unless the [Na]tion agree all to go, it is useless." As to the offer of $5 million, both Jackson and the Senate honestly believed it was a generous offer in view of the estimated federal share from the sale of Cherokee lands.

11. *House Documents*, 23d Congress, 2d Session, No. 292; Moulton, *Ross*, pp. 62–63.

12. Young, "Friends of the Indian," II, 26. For provisions of the "draft treaty," see *House Documents*, 23d Congress, 2d Session, No. 292.

13. The Senate would not consider a treaty until ratified by the Cherokees themselves. See fragment of a memorandum in Jackson's handwriting, no date, Jackson Papers, LC.

14. *National Intelligencer*, March 14, 1835. See also *Globe*, March 28, 1835.

15. I am grateful to Professor Young for this estimate. Arrell M. Gibson, *The American Indian* (Lexington, 1980), p. 321, estimates over 8 million acres.

16. Mary Young, "The Cherokee Nation: Mirror of the Republic," *American Quarterly* (1981), XXXIII, 505. The "mirror" figure of speech is Young's.

17. Jackson's talk, 1835, Jackson Papers, LC. See a version of this talk in AJ to Cherokee chiefs, March 16, 1835, *Globe*, March 28, 1835.

18. Ibid., June 27, 1835.

19. *National Intelligencer*, December 1, 1835.

20. *Senate Documents*, 24th Congress, 1st Session, No. 120; Charles C. Royce, "Cherokee Nation of Indians," *Fifth Annual Report*, Bureau of American Ethnology (Washington, 1887), part 2, p. 281; Major Ridge, Elias Boudinot et al. to AJ, December 1, 1835, RG 46, E 357, 25A-F5, NA.

21. Eaton, *Ross*, p. 97.

22. Ibid., p. 100; Moulton, *Ross*, pp. 72–74; AJ to Van Buren, October 5, 1839, Van Buren Papers, LC; *Globe*, November 3, 1832, June 22, 1835. Again I wish to acknowledge the considerable help I had from Professor Young in understanding the conflict between Ross and Jackson over the question of Cherokee governance.

23. Reginald Horsman, "American Indian Policy and the Origins of Manifest Destiny," in Francis Paul Prucha, ed., *The Indian in American History* (New York,

1971), p. 25. See the *Globe,* October 19, 1836, for a reprint of some of Clay's letters to the Cherokees. See also *National Intelligencer,* November 2, 1836.

24. Young, "Indian Removal and Autonomy," p. 133. White even helped raise $10,000 for expenses for the Ross delegation. See Schermerhorn's letter in the *Globe,* August 20, 1836.

25. Mary Young, in her Carroll lecture, II, 26, calculated that ¹⁵/₁₆ths of the entire Nation opposed the treaty. In defense of Jackson's action it should be said that the Treaty party constantly assured him that "a majority of the people" of the Cherokee Nation gratefully approved the New Echota Treaty "and all are willing peaceably to yield to the treaty and abide by it." Major Ridge and John Ridge to AJ, June 30, 1836, RG 75, NA, copy JPP.

26. Young, "Friends of the Indian," II, 26.

27. This treaty, along with all other treaties mentioned in this chapter, can be found in Charles C. Royce, *Indian Land Cessions in the United States* (Washington, 1900).

28. Robert V. Remini, *Revolutionary Age of Andrew Jackson* (New York, 1976), pp. 111, 112, 113; James Mooney, *Myths of the Cherokees* (Chicago, 1972), pp. 130, 133; *Senate Documents,* 27th Congress, 3d Session, No. 219. See also Marion L. Starkey, *The Cherokee Nation* (New York, 1946); Thurman Wilkins, *Cherokee Tragedy* (New York, 1970); Grant Foreman, *Indian Removal: The Emigration of the Five Civilized Tribes* (Norman, Okla., 1966); and Henry T. Malone, *Cherokees of the Old South* (Athens, Ga., 1956). In any discussion of the Cherokee removal, Mary Young feels it is important to point out that Scott and others "were concerned about their reputation for humaneness, and probably even for the Cherokee. There just wasn't much they could do about it."

29. *Senate Documents,* 27th Congress, 3d Session, No. 219, 86. Jackson was repeatedly informed of the frauds against the Creeks and he sent General Sanford to investigate. But many Indians refused to testify before Sanford because of fear of arrest for old debts and deportation to the west. Creek Chiefs to AJ, August 25, 1835, RG 46, E 340, 24A-E6, NA.

30. Creek Chiefs to AJ, April 14, 1836, RG 233, E 281, HR 24A-F4, NA; *National Intelligencer,* July 12, 1836.

31. Angie Debo, *The Road to Disappearance* (Norman, Okla., 1941), pp. 98–102; Michael D. Green, *The Politics of Indian Removal: Creek Government and Society in Crisis* (Lincoln, 1982), pp. 184–185. The best account of the Creek War is Kenneth L. Valliere, "The Creek War of 1836: A Military History," *Chronicles of Oklahoma* (1979), LVII, 463–485.

32. Quoted in Grant Foreman, *Indian Removal: The Emigration of the Five Civilized Tribes* (Norman, Okla., 1966), p. 176.

33. AJ to Seminole Chiefs, February 16, 1835, in A Late Staff Officer [Woodburne Potter], *The War in Florida* (Baltimore, 1836), pp. 78–80. The response of the chief can be found ibid., pp. 51, 53. See also the talk of the friendly Seminole chiefs to AJ, February 7, 1836, RG 75, NA, copy JPP. It should be pointed out that the Treaty of Payne's Landing mandated removal only after a delegation of Seminoles visited their proposed destination in the west and then agreed to be removed there. The Indians later claimed that their delegation did not like the western country proposed for them but were threatened with abandonment in the west unless they signed an agreement of acceptance. Once back home they repudiated the agreement and claimed they signed under duress.

34. [Potter], *The War in Florida,* pp. 81–82.

35. John K. Mahon, *History of the Second Seminole War, 1835–1842* (Gainesville, 1967), p. 95.

36. Ibid., p. 91.

37. Ibid., p. 101.

38. The First Seminole War occurred in 1818, when Jackson marched into Florida to subdue the Indians and proceeded to seize the territory from Spain. See Remini, *Jackson*, I, 351ff.

39. AJ to Blair, July 28, 1840, private collection, copy JPP.

40. March 15, 1836.

41. AJ to Blair, July 28, 1840, private collection, JPP.

42. Charles Winslow Elliott, *Winfield Scott: The Soldier and the Man* (New York, 1937), pp. 325-327; Memorandum on the Florida Campaign, April [?], 1837, in Jackson, *Correspondence*, V, 468-471.

43. Call to AJ, May 30, June 1, 1836, and endorsements in *Senate Documents*, 23d Congress, 2nd Session, No. 278. On the military problems of fighting this war, see James Gadsden to AJ, August 25, 1836, Jackson Papers, CHS.

44. For another complaint about Jackson's behavior in this matter, see James Gadsden to AJ, July 16, 1836, Jackson Papers, CHS.

45. AJ to Call, May 25, 1836, in *The Collector* (December, 1907), p. 16, copy JPP.

46. Call to AJ, May 30, 1836, and endorsements, in *Senate Documents*, 23d Congress, 2d Session, No. 278. Jackson constantly urged his commanders to attack, even in the "sickly season," and their reluctance to take his advice infuriated him. See AJ to Jesup, August 3, 1836, private collection, copy JPP.

47. Butler to Call, November 4, 1836, in Clarence E. Carter, ed., *The Territorial Papers of the United States, Florida* (Washington, 1936-), XXV, 339-340; see also Memorandum, November 3, 1836, Jackson Papers, LC.

48. AJ to Call, November 1, 5, 1836, Jackson Papers, LC.

49. An excellent biography which traces the relations between the two men is Herbert J. Doherty, *Richard Keith Call: Southern Unionist* (Gainesville, 1961).

50. AJ to Jesup, November 5, 1836, private collection, copy JPP.

51. AJ to Butler, November 2 [1836], Butler Papers, NYSL.

52. Butler to Jesup, November 4, 1836, in Carter, ed., *Territorial Papers*, XXV, 341-342.

53. Mahon, *Second Seminole War*, pp. 214-218.

54. White to J. Knowles, February 15, 1837, in Carter, ed., *Territorial Papers*, XXV, 378.

55. See his Memorandum, in Jackson, *Correspondence*, V, 468ff; and AJ to Blair, July 28, 1840, private collection, copy JPP.

56. *Congressional Globe*, 25th Congress, 2d Session, pp. 42ff; Mahon, *Second Seminole War*, p. 244.

57. Ibid., p. 321, which cites the Indian Affairs Bureau, "United States, Indian Population and Land," March, 1963.

58. Royce, *Indian Land Cessions*, pp. 748-766. Chippewa, Ottawa, and Potawatomi Chiefs to AJ, no date, RG 46, E 339, 24A-D7, NA. Some of the appeals of these tribes to Jackson are very moving. "Your agent," pleaded a delegation of Potawatomi, Ottawa, and Chippewa chiefs to Jackson, "told us at the Treaty made at Chicago in 1833 that the country assigned to us west of the Mississippi was equally as good as the lands in Illinois. . . . Father—we have been deceived and we feel disappointed & dissatisfied. . . . There is scarce timber enough to build our Wigwams, and that some of our land is too poor for snakes to live upon. Our men are not accustomed to the Prairie. They have always lived in the woods." The date of this petition is probably March 10, 1835, RG 75, NA, copy JPP.

59. I am very grateful to Professor Ronald N. Satz for this information on the number of Indians removed. See his article "Indian Policy in the Jacksonian

Era: The Old Northwest as a Test Case," *Michigan History* (1976), LV, 81–82, note 38, and *American Indian Policy in the Jacksonian Era* (Lincoln, 1975), 97, 115, note 1. See also Report from the Office of Indian Affairs, December 1, 1836, *Senate Documents*, 24th Congress, 2d Session, No. 1, p. 420; and Statement Showing the Quantity of Lands Ceded by the Indian Tribes to the United States, December 1, 1836, Records of the Office of Indian Affairs, Miscellaneous Records, I, 300–301, II, 6–8, 90–100, RG 75, NA. From 1789 to 1838, approximately 81,282 Indians were removed beyond the Mississippi River. *House Documents*, 25th Congress, 3d Session, No. 347. I am grateful to Professor Francis Paul Prucha for this information.

60. Again and again Jackson wrote memorandums detailing the "advantages" of removal. "The Indians have been and are removing to a country selected for them fertile & productive beyond the Mississippi where they are living in plenty,—and happy under their own laws and customs, protected in their posessions, & safety, by the general government, whilst their former residence are filled in the new states, with an industrious, moral, and happy yeomanry." Frequently these memorandums were intended for Congress, either in an annual message or special message relating to removal. Memorandum, no date, Jackson Papers, LC.

61. Everyone knows what happened to the Yemassees, Mohicans, and Narragansetts. They are gone, wiped out. And there are other such tribes. President Jackson and his Democratic friends warned the Cherokees and the other southern tribes that extinction would be their fate if they refused to remove. Mary Young, in a recent paper entitled "Pagans, Converts, and Backsliders, All: A Secular View of the Metaphysics of Indian-White Relations," declares: "Though the Cherokee Nation West lost its national domain and jurisdiction two generations after the death of Andrew Jackson, Cherokee people today have a tribal identity, a living language, and at least three governmental bodies—the Cherokee Nation East, the Cherokee Nation West, and the Original Cherokee Community of Oklahoma. That's more than you can say of the Yemassee." Andrew Jackson was right after all. But what a price to pay.

CHAPTER 21

1. John Tyler to Robert Tyler, February 15, 1836, John Tyler to Mrs. Mary Tyler Jones, February 18, 1836, in Tyler, *Letters and Times*, I, 534ff.

2. *Senate Executive Journal*, IV, 520–522.

3. *Globe*, March 16, 1836.

4. March 19, 1836.

5. Francis F. Wayland, *Andrew Stevenson: Democrat and Diplomat, 1785–1857* (Philadelphia, 1949), p. 110.

6. See the *National Intelligencer*, for example, throughout the spring, 1836.

7. This opinion not only can be found in Jackson's correspondence at this time but appears frequently in the editorials of the *Globe*. See, for example, the issues of April 1, 16, November 10, 16, 18, 1835.

8. The quotation is taken from an editorial of the *Globe*, July 27, 1832, but it clearly represents Jackson's thinking. See Taney's correction of the editorial in his letter to Blair, July 31, 1832, Blair Papers, LC.

9. Richardson, *Messages and Papers*, II, 1013–1014, 1063, 1119.

10. Glyndon G. Van Deusen, *The Life of Henry Clay* (Boston, 1937), pp. 254, 288.

11. Ibid., pp. 254–255.

12. Richardson, *Messages and Papers*, II, 1284, 1285–1286.

13. Ibid., p. 1286.

14. Ibid., p. 1284.

15. Ibid., p. 1286.

16. Ibid., pp. 1287, 1288.

17. *Congressional Debates*, 22d Congress, 1st Session, 2853, 24th Congress, 2d Session, 373–374. Jackson believed that Clay's object was the revival of the BUS and he swore to prevent it. "I have my eye fixed upon the memoth of corruption (the Bank) and on Mr. Clays bill, which is intended to aid the monster in corrupting & bribing the states—*it shall not become a law, unless by the vote of two thirds.*" AJ to Livingston, February 27, 1836, Livingston Papers, JRDF.

18. Ibid.; *House Document*, No. 422, 23d Congress, 1st Session; Taney to Rives, April 16, 1836, Rives Papers, LC; Robert V. Remini, *Andrew Jackson and the Bank War* (New York, 1967), p. 169; Sellers, *Polk*, I, 225. See page 168 above for Jackson's proposals to reform the nation's currency and banking.

19. AJ to Woodbury, April 30, 1836, Woodbury Papers, LC.

20. Benton suggested that all the indemnity money coming from foreign countries ought to be obtained in gold. Benton to Woodbury, letter marked "received February 16, 1836," Woodbury Papers, LC.

21. AJ to Woodbury, June 13, 1836, Woodbury Papers, LC.

22. AJ to Woodbury, February 3, 1836, Woodbury Papers, LC; Robert V. Remini, *Andrew Jackson and the Bank War*, pp. 169–170.

23. Ibid.

24. Benton, *Thirty Years View*, I, 657–658; *Niles Weekly Register*, June 25, 1836; Remini, *Andrew Jackson and the Bank War*, pp. 170–171.

25. *National Intelligencer*, June 23, 1836.

26. "Proposed Veto of the Surplus Revenue Bill of 1836," June 20, 1836, in Jackson, *Correspondence*, V, 405, 406.

27. Ibid., pp. 407, 408.

28. Ibid., p. 409.

29. AJ to Kendall, November 24, 1836, Jackson-Kendall Papers, LC; AJ to Woodbury, July 3, 8, August 15, 1836, Woodbury Papers, LC.

30. Benton said that Van Buren's friends urged Jackson to sign the bill but opponents of it did not visit the President. Benton, *Thirty Years View*, I, 658.

31. Harry Scheiber, "Pet Banks in Jacksonian Politics and Finance, 1833–1841," *Journal of Economic History* (1963), XXIII, 202.

32. Richard M. Johnson to AJ, June 21, 1836, in Jackson, *Correspondence*, V, 409.

33. *National Intelligencer*, June 23, 25, 1836.

34. Benton, *Thirty Years, View*, I, 658; *National Intelligencer*, June 27, 1836; Dix to Flagg, August 20, 1836, Flagg Papers, NYPL.

35. *National Intelligencer*, June 27, 1836; *Globe*, July 16, 23, 1836.

36. *Globe*, September 17, 1836; Benton, *Thirty Years View*, I, 657.

37. Taney to AJ, June 27, 1836, in Jackson, *Correspondence*, V, 410.

38. Ibid. See also Jackson's memoranda, annual messages to Congress, pocket veto of the land bill and the like throughout his second administration, Jackson Papers, LC.

39. See *Globe*, October 1, 5, 8, 12, November 26, December 17, 1836.

40. Ibid., June 22, 1836.

41. Ibid., August 31, 1836; Benton, *Thirty Years View*, I, 677.

42. Ibid., p. 678.

43. AJ's memorandum to his cabinet, July 5, 1836, Jackson Papers, LC.

44. Benton, *Thirty Years View*, I, 676.
45. Ibid., p. 678.
46. Nathan Sargent, *Public Men and Events* (Philadelphia, 1875), I, 321.
47. Benton, *Thirty Years View*, I, 678.
48. Van Buren to AJ, August 5, 1836, Van Buren Papers, LC.
49. *National Intelligencer*, July 14, 15, 1836.
50. Quoted in *Globe*, July 20, 1836. The order of these objections has been rearranged to provide clarity.
51. Ibid., August 31, 1836, October 12, 1836.
52. Ibid., December 17, 1836.
53. Vanderpoel to Jesse Hoyt, December 6, 1836, in William L. Mackenzie, *Lives of Benjamin F. Butler and Jesse Hoyt* (Boston, 1845), p. 263.
54. *Globe*, October 1, 5, 8, 12, November 26, 1836. The Whigs were the most notable doomsayers and the *Globe* seemed to take delight in noting their predictions in order to ridicule them.

CHAPTER 22

1. AJ to Andrew Jr., March 29, 1836, Jackson Papers, LC; Eaton to AJ, April 12, 1836, in Clarence E. Carter, *The Territorial Papers of the United States, Florida* (Washington, D.C., 1956–1962), XXV, 273.
2. AJ to Henry Toland, January 9, 1836, DeCoppet Collection, PUL; AJ to Andrew Jr., November 2, 1834, Jackson Papers, LC; "Bill for Furnishing the Hermitage, January 2, 1836," "Estimates for Rebuilding the Hermitage, August 2, 1836," in Jackson, *Correspondence*, V, 382–383, 414–415.
3. *Globe*, July 13, 1836.
4. Ibid.; Donelson to Emily Donelson, July 17, 1836, Donelson Papers, LC. AJ to Andrew Jr., July 17, 1836, in Jackson, *Correspondence*, V, 414.
5. *Globe*, August 13, 1836.
6. Ibid. This was true in other states as well. See, for example, William F. Gordon to Tyler, January 15, 1836, in Tyler, *Letters and Times*, I, 529.
7. Sellers, *Polk*, I, 299.
8. "The People's Man," reprinted in *Globe*, July 20, 1836.
9. AJ to Kendall, August 5, 1836, A. G. Mitten Collection, Indiana Historical Society, Indianapolis. I am grateful to the Ladies Hermitage Association and the Jackson Papers Project for information and detailed plans of the building.
10. Stanley F. Horn, *The Hermitage, Home of Old Hickory* (Richmond, 1938), pp. 58ff.
11. Robert Armstrong to AJ, August 13, 1835, AJ to Andrew Jr., October 25, 1835, in Jackson, *Correspondence*, V, 361, 372; AJ to Andrew Jr., March 29, 1836, AJ to Dr. E. Breathitt, March 30, 1835, Jackson Papers, LC.
12. AJ to Andrew Jr., March 25, 26, August 23, 1836, Jackson Papers, LC.
13. AJ to Blair, August 12, 1836, Jackson Papers, LC; Donelson to Emily Donelson, June 22, 1836, Donelson Papers, LC.
14. AJ to Blair, August 22, 1836, Jackson Papers, LC.
15. Nashville *National Banner*, August 26, 1836, copy JPP.
16. *Niles Weekly Register*, September 10, 1836.
17. AJ to Blair, August 22, 1836, Jackson Papers, LC; AJ to Van Buren, August 22, 1836, Van Buren Papers, LC.
18. *Niles Weekly Register*, September 10, 1836, quoting the Richmond *Enquirer*'s account of the dinner.
19. Woodbury to AJ, August 19, 1836, AJ Papers, LC.

20. Columbia *Democrat*, August 29, 1836, quoted in the *Globe*, September 17, 1836.

21. Richardson, *Messages and Papers*, II, 1011.

22. Ibid.

23. The argument of this section follows closely along the lines of John William Ward's superb article "Jacksonian Democratic Thought: 'A Natural Charter of Privilege,' " in Stanley Coben and Lorman Ratner, eds., *The Development of an American Culture* (New York, 1983), pp. 58–79. I think this is one of the best statements of Jacksonian political thought in print.

24. See Jackson's Bank veto in Richardson, *Messages and Papers*, II, 1144–1145.

25. George Sidney Camp, *Democracy* (New York, 1841), pp. 161–162.

26. The phrase, and it is a good one, is Ward's. See "Jacksonian Democratic Thought," p. 73.

27. Nathan Sargent, *Public Men and Events* (Philadelphia, 1875), I, 347.

28. AJ to Donelson, May 12, 1835, Donelson Papers, LC.

29. These views, written by Blair, were expressed in the *Globe*, July 27, 1832, but they clearly carry Jackson's imprimatur. The two men discussed them at the time the Bank veto was written.

30. Alexis de Tocqueville, *Democracy in America* (New York, 1945), I, 58.

31. Richard Hofstadter is undoubtedly the leading spokesman of the "entrepreneurial" school of interpretation. See his *The American Political Tradition and the Men Who Made It* (New York, 1948), chapter 3; see also Bray Hammond, *Banks and Politics in America* (Princeton, 1957); Joseph Dorfman, *The Economic Mind in American Civilization* (New York, 1946), II, chapter 24; and Marvin Meyers, *The Jacksonian Persuasion* (Stanford, 1957).

32. Kendall to AJ, August 7, 1836, Miscellaneous Collection, New Jersey Historical Society.

33. Ibid., AJ's endorsement.

34. *Globe*, March 28, August 18, 1834.

35. Ibid., April 16, 1835.

36. Ibid., October 8, 1834. See also reprints of editorials in the *Globe* from other Democratic newspapers during 1834 and 1835.

37. Manuscript Ledger, George Bancroft Papers, MHS; *Globe*, April 1, 1834.

38. Manuscript Ledger, George Bancroft Papers, MHS.

39. *Globe*, January 28, 1837.

40. Van Buren to Nathaniel Macon, February 13, 1836, Macon Papers, DUL.

41. *Globe*, August 21, 1835.

42. Croswell to Bancroft, August 13, 1836, Bancroft Papers, MHS.

43. *Globe*, September 17, 1836.

44. AJ to Taney, October 13, 1836, Jackson Papers, LC.

45. John Stetson Barry, Manuscript Diary, CHS; Alfred Mordecai to Ellen Mordecai, March 4, 1830, Mordecai Papers, LC. "A striking picture of *democracy*" is taken out of context and actually refers to a similar scene in which Jackson participated at an earlier time.

CHAPTER 23

1. AJ to Andrew Jr., September 17, 19, 22, 23, 1836, Jackson Papers, LC; Louisville *Advertiser* quoted in *National Intelligencer*, September 27, 1836; AJ to

Sarah, September 22, 1836, Jackson Papers, ML; AJ to Van Buren, September 22, 1836, Jackson Papers, ML; AJ to Van Buren, September 19, 1836, Van Buren Papers, LC.

2. AJ to Donelson, October 2, 1836, Donelson Papers, LC. Vermont, New Jersey, Delaware, Maryland, Ohio, Indiana, and Kentucky went to Harrison; Georgia and Tennessee to White; and Massachusetts to Webster.

3. AJ to Van Buren, October 2, 1836, Van Buren to AJ, August 5, 1836, AJ to Van Buren, September 19, 1836, Van Buren Papers, LC.

4. AJ to Earl, September 23, 1836, Historical Society of York County, Pennsylvania, copy JPP; AJ to Van Buren, October 2, 1836, Van Buren Papers, LC.

5. AJ to Donelson, October 2, 1836, Donelson Papers, LC; AJ to Van Buren, October 2, 1836, Van Buren Papers, LC.

6. AJ to Donelson, October 2, 1836, Donelson Papers, LC.

7. AJ to Emily Donelson, October 31, 1836, Donelson Papers, LC.

8. AJ to Emily Donelson, October 21, 31, 1836, Donelson Papers, LC; AJ to Lucius J. Polk, October 16, 1836, Polk-Yeatman Papers, SHC; AJ to Van Buren, October 2, 1836, Van Buren Papers, LC.

9. AJ to Mary Polk, December 22, 1836, Private Collection, copy JPP; AJ to Emily Donelson, November 27, 1836, in Jackson, *Correspondence*, V, 439–440.

10. AJ to Donelson, December 6, 17, 27, 29, 1836, January 1, 1837, Donelson Papers, LC.

11. AJ to Donelson, January 1, 1837, Donelson Papers, LC.

12. Donelson to AJ, December 23, 1837, Jackson Papers, LC.

13. AJ to Donelson, December 31, 1836, Donelson Papers, LC.

14. AJ to Donelson, January 9, 1837, Donelson Papers, LC.

15. AJ to Donelson, December 27, 1836, Donelson Papers, LC.

16. AJ to Van Buren, October 2, 1836, Van Buren Papers, LC; AJ to Lucius Polk, October 16, 1836, Polk-Yeatman Papers, SHC. Andrew Jr. was appointed on July 4, 1836.

17. AJ to Taney, October 13, 1836, Jackson Papers, LC.

18. Ibid.

19. Taney to AJ, October 15, 1836, Jackson Papers, LC.

20. For details see Robert V. Remini, *Jackson*, I, 341ff.

21. Ibid., II, 289–290, 218–220.

22. Butler to Van Buren, January 10, 1829, in *House Executive Document*, No. 351, 25th Congress, 2d Session, p. 310.

23. Eugene C. Barker, "President Jackson and the Texas Revolution," *AHR* (1907), XII, 789, 794.

24. Munroe, *McLane*, p. 414.

25. Butler did manage to negotiate the Treaty of April 5, 1831, which reconfirmed the boundary line of 1819 and extended the time for the survey.

26. Butler to McLane, August 5, 1833, in Manning, *Diplomatic Correspondence*, VIII, 263.

27. Butler to AJ, January 2, 1833, Jackson Papers, LC.

28. Butler to AJ, September 26, 1833, Jackson Papers, LC.

29. Butler to AJ, October 28, 1833, Jackson Papers, LC.

30. Robert V. Remini, *Jackson*, II, 220.

31. Butler's endorsement to AJ to Butler, October 10, 1829, in Jackson, *Correspondence*, IV, 81.

32. Butler to AJ, October 28, 1833, Jackson Papers, LC.

33. AJ to Butler, November 27, 1833, Jackson Papers, LC. From his expe-

rience in Florida, Jackson knew the extent of the frauds that could be practiced on the U.S. government. See his memorandum [1835–1836], Jackson Papers, LC.

34. Ibid.

35. Butler to AJ, February 6, 1834, in Jackson, *Correspondence*, V, 245.

36. Munroe, *McLane*, p. 414; Butlrer to AJ, March 7, 1834, in Jackson, *Correspondence*, V, 251.

37. Ibid., pp. 251–252.

38. Butler to AJ, June 6, 1834, ibid., p. 269.

39. Hernández to Butler, March 21, 1835, in *House Executive Document*, No. 351, 25th Congress, 2d Session, p. 279.

40. Forsyth to Butler, July 2, 1835, State Department Instructions, Mexico, XV, NA.

41. AJ's endorsement to Hernández to Butler, March 21, 1835, in *House Executive Document*, No. 351, 25th Congress, 2d Session, p. 279.

42. Butler to AJ, no date [December, 1835?], Jackson Papers, LC; Joe Gibson, "A. Butler: What a Scamp!" *Journal of the West* (1972), XI, 246.

43. Barker, "Jackson and Texas Revolution," p. 804; *House Executive Document*, No. 74, 25th Congress, 2d Session, III, 3–4, 23; Ritchie to Van Buren, June 9, 1836, Van Buren Papers, LC. On U.S.-Mexican relations, see Eugene Barker, "The United States and Mexico, 1835–1837," *MVHR* (1914), I, 3–30.

44. *Globe*, May 18, 1836.

45. *House Executive Document*, No. 351, 256, 25th Congress, 2d Session, XII, 768, 24th Congress, 1st Session, VI, 32–33, 45, 48, 54.

46. *Senate Document*, No. 1, 24th Congress, 2d Session, I, 100. See also Blair to AJ, August 1, 1836, Jackson Papers, LC. For Gorostiza's complaints, see Barker, "The United States and Mexico," pp. 12–15.

47. Blair to AJ, August 1, 1836, Jackson Papers, LC.

48. Butler to Harriet Butler, June 29, 1836, Butler Papers, NYSL.

49. Carson to Burnet, July 3, 1836, in *Diplomatic Correspondence of the United States, American Historical Association, Annual Report* (Washington, 1907), I, 101, 102. See also Stanley Siegel, *A Political History of the Texas Republic, 1836–1845* (Austin, 1956), p. 44.

50. Carson to Burnet, July 3, 1836, in *Diplomatic Correspondence*, pp. 101, 102.

51. Parton, *Jackson*, III, 605; Austin to AJ et al., April 15, 1836, with endorsement, Jackson Papers, LC.

52. The accusation is well refuted, I think, in Barker, "Jackson and the Texas Revolution," pp. 797–803.

53. Collinsworth and Grayson to Burnet, July 15, 1836, in *Diplomatic Correspondence*, p. 110; Forsyth to AJ, July 15, 1836, Jackson Papers, LC.

54. Collinsworth and Grayson to Burnet, July 15, 1836, in *Diplomatic Correspondence*, p. 110.

55. Ibid.

56. Morfit's reports can be found in *Senate Document* No. 20, 24th Congress, 2d Session.

57. But Jackson kept himself informed of all developments. See Blair to AJ, August 25, 1836, Jackson Papers, LC.

58. AJ to Cass, August 31, 1836, William L. Clemens Library, University of Michigan; Santa Anna to AJ, July 4, 1836, in Jackson, *Correspondence*, V, 412.

59. AJ to Houston, September 4, 1836, ibid., p. 425.

60. AJ to Santa Anna, September 4, 1836, ibid., p. 426. Copies of his letters to Santa Anna, Gaines, and Houston were sent to Washington, along with a copy of the secret agreement between Santa Anna and the Texans. "This is not

to be made public," cautioned Jackson. AJ to Cass, September 5, 1836, Jackson Papers, LC.

61. July 26, 1836. See also the issues for August 1, 5, 6, 8, 1836.

62. Kendall to AJ, July 30, 1836, Jackson Papers, Chicago Historical Society.

63. Ibid.

64. AJ to Kendall, August 12, 1836, in Jackson, *Correspondence*, V, 420.

65. Richardson, *Messages and Papers*, II, 1453–1455.

66. AJ to Kendall, August 12, 1836, in Jackson, *Correspondence*, V, 420–421. See also Jackson's letters to Governor Newton Cannon of Tennessee, ibid., pp. 415–418.

67. AJ to Gaines, September 4, 1836, ibid., p. 424.

68. AJ to Kendall, December 8, 1836, Jackson Papers, LC.

69. Richardson, *Messages and Papers*, II, 1485.

70. Ibid., p. 1487.

71. Ibid., pp. 1487, 1488.

72. AJ to Kendall, December 8, 1836, Jackson Papers, LC.

73. Wharton to Austin, December 28, 1836, in *Diplomatic Correspondence*, p. 157.

74. Ibid., p. 158.

75. It was even suggested that Van Buren himself wrote the message. Ibid.

76. Ibid., p. 159.

77. Wharton to Rusk, February 16, 1837, ibid., p. 188.

78. Ann Fears Crawford, ed., *The Eagle: The Autobiography of Santa Anna* (Austin, 1967), p. 57; *Globe*, January 21, 1837.

79. Wharton to Thomas J. Rusk, February 16, 1837, in *Diplomatic Correspondence*, p. 187; *Globe*, January 21, 1837.

80. Blair to AJ, August 28, 1839, Jackson Papers, LC; Santa Anna, *Autobiography*, p. 57.

81. Blair to AJ, August 28, 1839, Jackson Papers, LC.

82. Memorandum, no date, Jackson Papers, LC.

83. Ibid.

84. Ibid.

85. Blair to AJ, August 28, 1839, Jackson Papers, LC.

86. Santa Anna, *Autobiography*, p. 57.

87. Wharton to Rusk, February 16, 1837, in *Diplomatic Correspondence*, pp. 190–191.

88. Ibid., pp. 191–192.

89. Wharton to Houston, January 24, 1837, ibid., pp. 193–194.

90. Wharton to Rusk, February 16, 1837, ibid., pp. 190–191.

91. Memorandum, no date, Jackson Papers, LC.

92. Wharton and Hunt to AJ, February 8, 1837, in *Diplomatic Correspondence*, p. 197.

93. *Congressional Globe*, 24th Congress, 2d Session, pp. 213, 219. Siegel, *Political History of Texas*, p. 77.

94. Wharton and Hunt to J. Pinckney Henderson, March 5, 1837, in *Diplomatic Correspondence*, p. 201.

CHAPTER 24

1. Donelson to Emily Donelson, November 20, 1836, Donelson Papers, LC.

2. Ibid.; AJ to Mary Polk, December 22, 1836, private collection, copy JPP.

3. Donelson to Emily Donelson, November 21, 1836, Donelson Papers, LC; AJ to Maunsel White, December 2, 1836, in Jackson, *Correspondence*, V, 440.

4. AJ to Emily Donelson, November 27, 1836, ibid., p. 439.

5. Donelson to Emily Donelson, November 27, 1836, Donelson Papers, LC.

6. AJ to Donelson, December 16, 1836, Donelson Papers, LC.

7. AJ to Nicholas P. Trist, March 2, 1836, Trist Papers, LC.

8. AJ to Donelson, January 9, 1837, Donelson Papers, LC. For public reports of Jackson's illness, see *Globe*, November 23, 1836.

9. AJ to Mary Polk, December 22, 1836, private collection, copy JPP.

10. AJ to Donelson, December 6, 1836, Donelson Papers, LC.

11. Richardson, *Messages and Papers*, II, 1459, 1460.

12. Ibid., pp. 1465, 1466, 1467, 1468.

13. Ibid., pp. 1468–1469.

14. Ibid., p. 1475.

15. Ibid., p. 1476.

16. Ibid., pp. 1478, 1479.

17. *Globe*, December 7, 1836.

18. *National Intelligencer*, December 7, 1836.

19. Ibid. Jackson's friends thought otherwise, of course, and said that the message made a strong impression on the public mind and would add to Jackson's stature as the great friend of the people. See, for example, Taney to AJ, December 8, 1836, Jackson Papers, LC.

20. AJ to Van Buren, August 22, September 19, 1836, Van Buren Papers, LC.

21. Svend Petersen, *A Statistical History of the American Presidential Elections* (New York, 1963), pp. 22–24; Joel Silbey, "Election of 1836," in Arthur M. Schlesinger, Jr., ed., *History of American Presidential Elections, 1789–1968* (4 vols.; New York, 1971), I, 595–599, 640.

22. Weed to Seward, October 25, November 25, 31, 1836, William H. Seward Papers, RUL.

23. Tilden to Elam Tilden, December 12, 1836, Tilden Papers, NYPL.

24. AJ to Maunsel White, December 2, 1836, in Jackson, *Correspondence*, V, 440.

25. AJ to Adam Huntsman, January 2, 1837, ibid., p. 447. This is not Jackson's usual language. It was obviously written by another, and although the copy in the Jackson papers is written in Andrew Jr.'s hand, it is more likely that Blair and/or Kendall actually authored it.

26. Silbey, "Election of 1836," p. 598.

27. For example, see Benton, *Thirty Years View*, I, 735.

28. For the early history of Arkansas, see Lonnie J. White, *Politics on the Southwestern Frontier: Arkansas Territory, 1819–1836* (Memphis, 1964), and Jack Scroggs, "Arkansas Statehood: A Study in State and National Political Schism," *Arkansas Historical Quarterly* (1961), XX, 227–244. On Michigan, see Ronald P. Formisano, *The Birth of Mass Political Parties: Michigan, 1827–1861* (Princeton, 1971), and Alec R. Gilpin, *The Territory of Michigan* (East Lansing, 1970).

29. Silbey, "Election of 1836," p. 600. For a biography of Johnson, see Leland W. Meyer, *The Life and Times of Colonel Richard M. Johnson of Kentucky* (New York, 1932).

30. Wright to Flagg, January 9, 1837, Flagg Papers, NYPL.

31. Benton, *Thirty Years View*, I, 645–646.

32. Taney to AJ, December 8, 1836, Jackson Papers, LC.

33. Benton, *Thirty Years View*, I, 717.

34. Ibid., p. 718.

35. Ibid.

36. Ibid., p. 719.

37. Ibid., pp. 721–722, 723–724.

38. Ibid., p. 726.

39. Ibid., p. 727.

40. Ibid., pp. 727, 728.

41. Ibid., p. 728.

42. Ibid., p. 729.

43. Ibid., p. 730.

44. Ibid.

45. Ben: Perley Poore, *Perley's Reminiscences* (Tecumseh, Mich., 1886), I, 142; Henry A. Wise, *Seven Decades of the Union* (Philadelphia, 1881), p. 143.

46. AJ to Benton, January 17, 1837, Jackson Papers, LC.

47. Ibid. Others agreed with Jackson's assessment. See, for example, Taney to AJ, January 27, 1837, Jackson Papers, LC.

48. Taney to AJ, January 27, 1837, with Jackson's endorsement, Jackson Papers, LC; Benton, *Thirty Years View*, I, 731.

49. Ibid.

CHAPTER 25

1. William Seale, manuscript "History of the White House," a work in progress, chapter II of Book III, p. 2. Dr. Seale kindly allowed me to read his manuscript and use whatever material on Jackson I found valuable. I cannot begin to express my appreciation to him for this noble act of scholarly friendship and generosity. Much of the information in this chapter, particularly concerning the White House and its operation, comes directly from Seale's work.

2. Pauline W. Burke, *Emily Donelson of Tennessee* (Richmond, 1941), I, 174.

3. AJ to John Pemberton, December 10, 1832, Pemberton Papers, PHS.

4. Statement, "White House Household," Jackson Papers, LC. In this document it is difficult to determine whether there are two messengers and one valet or two valets and one messenger.

5. Seale, "History of the White House," Book III, chapter II, p. 22.

6. Ibid., p. 46.

7. Ibid., pp. 51–52.

8. The daguerreotype I saw is in the White House collection. Granted that magnolias grow very slowly, still the picture was taken a good ten years after Jackson left the White House.

9. Seale, "History of the White House," p. 56.

10. Ibid.

11. Ibid., pp. 65–66.

12. Ibid., p. 68.

13. Ibid., p. 26. There was not $50 worth of furniture in the room when Jackson decorated it. Nathan Sargent, *Public Men and Events* (Philadelphia, 1875), I, 135.

14. Seale, "History of the White House," pp. 26–28.

15. Ibid., pp. 28–29.

16. Ibid., p. 29.

17. Ibid., p. 30.

18. The portrait was probably painted by Earl. It is uncertain what became of it.

19. *Report of the House Committee on Expenditures on the Public Buildings*, April 1, 1842, pp. 5ff. For an announcement and description of the levees, see *Globe*, December 31, 1834, and newspaper accounts in Esther Singleton, *The Story of the White House* (New York, 1907), I, 214–227.

20. *Globe,* February 22, 1837; *National Intelligencer,* February 22, 1837; *Niles Weekly Register,* February 25, 1837. "Register of the names of Citizens and amounts contributed" for the Jackson cheese, NYSL, copy JPP.

21. David Campbell to Mary Campbell, May 21, 1829, Campbell Papers, DUL.

22. John R. Montgomery to Letitia A. Montgomery, February 20, 1834, in *New York Times,* February 21, 1935, copy JPP. It is interesting to note that the *Times* published the letter about this feast during the height of the Great Depression.

23. Seale, "History of the White House," pp. 41–42.

24. Jessie Benton Frémont, *Souvenirs of My Time* (Boston, 1887), p. 98.

25. James Stuart, *Three Years in North America* (Edinburgh, 1833), II, 44–45.

26. Caleb Cushing, Manuscript Diary, LC.

27. Manuscript Journal of Alexander Hamilton Stephens, January, 1837, LC.

28. Statement, Donelson Papers, LC, copy JPP.

29. *Globe,* April 20, 1835.

30. Donelson to Emily Donelson, May 10, 1835, Donelson Papers, LC.

31. Seale, "History of the White House," p. 69.

32. AJ to Colonel Harris, editor of the Nashville *Union,* no date, CHS.

33. AJ to Victoria, March 12, 1834, Royal Library Collection, UK, printed "By gracious permission of Her Majesty, Queen Elizabeth II," copy JPP.

34. AJ to ?, February 19, 1837, in New York *Commercial Advertiser,* January 29, 1834.

35. Receipt, Jackson Papers, LC.

36. Stuart, *Three Years in North America,* II, 42, 43.

37. Memorandum, February 25, 1836, Jackson Papers, Missouri Historical Society, St. Louis, Missouri.

38. Parton, *Jackson,* III, 612.

39. Blair to AJ, July 30, 1836, Jackson Papers, LC.

40. Library of Congress, Receipt Books, Book B and D, LC.

41. Ibid. I am very grateful to John McDonough of the Manuscript Division, Library of Congress, for assisting me in obtaining this material.

42. Parton, *Jackson,* III, 602.

43. Nashville, *Union,* November 30, 1837, copy JPP.

44. Anne H. Wharton, *Social Life in the Early Republic* (New York, 1902), pp. 264–266.

45. Ben: Perley Poore, *Perley's Reminiscences* (Tecumseh, Mich., 1886), I, 194.

46. Frances Anne Butler Kemble, *Journal* (Philadelphia, 1835), II, 95–96, 96 note.

47. Poore, *Reminiscences,* pp. 190–191.

48. Balie Peyton, "Reminiscences of the Turf," in James Douglas Anderson, *Making the American Thoroughbred* (Norwood, Mass., 1916), pp. 243–245.

49. Ibid.

CHAPTER 26

1. *National Intelligencer,* February 25, 1837.

2. *Globe,* February 25, 1837.

3. Ibid.

4. AJ to W. H. Peck, March 4, 1837, Litchfield Historical Society, copy JPP.

5. See the many editorials in the *Globe* for January and February, 1837.

6. *Register of Debates*, 24th Congress, 1st Session, pp. 2756–2757.

7. Ibid., pp. 4050ff.

8. *Congressional Globe*, 24th Congress, 2d Session, pp. 108ff.

9. AJ to Donelson, January 11, 1837, Donelson Papers, LC; *Congressional Globe*, 24th Congress, 2d Session, pp. 349ff; Sellers, *Polk*, I, 312–316; Thomas Ritchie to Van Buren, February 11, 1837, Van Buren Papers, LC.

10. *Globe*, December 17, 1836.

11. Ibid.

12. Ibid., January 28, 1837.

13. Ibid., February 4, 1837.

14. *Congressional Globe*, 24th Congress, 2d Session, pp. 349ff, 380ff; Sellers, *Polk*, I, 316–317.

15. AJ to Donelson, January 24, 1837, Donelson Papers, LC.

16. AJ to Henry A. Wise, January 26, 1837, in Jackson, *Correspondence*, V, 453–454.

17. Ibid., p. 455.

18. AJ to Donelson, January 31, 1837, Donelson Papers, LC.

19. Benton, *Thirty Years View*, I, 696, 697, 698.

20. AJ to Kendall, November 24, 1836, in Jackson, *Correspondence*, V, 438–439.

21. For a detailed statement of the maneuvering occurring in Congress, see Wright to Flagg, January 9, 1837, Flagg Papers, NYPL.

22. AJ to Blair, January, 1837, Jackson Papers, LC; AJ to Donelson, January 11, 1837, Donelson Papers, LC.

23. Benton provides details of the debate in *Thirty Years View*, I, 694–707.

24. Ibid., p. 706; Wiltse, *Calhoun*, II, 301; *Register of Debates*, 24th Congress, 2d Session, pp. 21ff.

25. Ibid., pp. 562–563, 577ff; Benton, *Thirty Years View*, I, 706.

26. Richardson, *Messages and Papers*, II, 1501–1502 for the Message and pages 1502–1507 for Butler's paper.

27. Benton, *Thirty Years View*, I, 707.

28. *Globe*, February 6, 1837; *Congressional Globe*, 24th Congress, 2d Session, p. 315; Wiltse, *Calhoun*, II, 467 note 53.

29. AJ to Calhoun, February 7, 1837, in *Calhoun Papers*, XIII, 403–404.

30. *Register of Debates*, 24th Congress, 2d Session, pp. 755–760; Wiltse, *Calhoun*, II, 304.

31. Wright to Flagg, February 16, 1837, Flagg Papers, NYPL.

32. January 21, 1834.

33. Professor David Hackett Fischer was kind enough to share with me some of his conclusions about corruption within the administrations of the early Presidents. Much of his work is based on quantitative evidence. His study, soon to be published, is entitled *Corruption: Rhythms of Renewal and Decay in American History*.

There were many attempts by Democrats to enumerate the accomplishments of "Jackson's reign." One of the more interesting, detailed, and easily found is the effort by Amos Kendall, *Autobiography*, pp. 296–303.

34. AJ to Taney, October 13, 1836, Jackson Papers, LC.

35. Richardson, *Messages and Papers*, II, 1511, 1512.

36. Ibid., pp. 1512, 1513, 1514.

37. Ibid., p. 1515.

38. Ibid., pp. 1516, 1517.

39. Ibid.

40. Ibid., pp. 1518, 1519, 1520.

41. Ibid., pp. 1523, 1524–1525.

42. Ibid., p. 1525.

43. Ibid., p. 1526.

44. Ibid., p. 1527.

45. Quoted in Parton, *Jackson*, III, 627.

46. Ben: Perley Poore, Boston *Budget*, in *New York Times*, May 16, 1886, copy JPP.

CHAPTER 27

1. *Globe*, March 8, 1837; AJ to Nicholas Trist, March 2, 1837, Trist Papers, LC.

2. AJ to Taney, February 9, 1837, Jackson Papers, Maryland Historical Society.

3. Ben: Perley Poore, *Perley's Reminiscences* (Tecumseh, Mich., 1886), I, 199.

4. Benton, in his account, says the crowd stood mute, but his work was written many years later. *Thirty Years View*, I, 735. This account is taken from the report in the *Globe*, and the reporter wrote in the March 8, 1837, edition that the cheers were repeated many times.

5. N. P. Willis, *Prose Works* (Philadelphia, 1849), p. 569.

6. Richardson, *Messages and Papers*, II, 1537.

7. March 8, 1837.

8. Benton, *Thirty Years View*, I, 735.

9. Ibid.

10. Ibid.

11. *Globe*, March 7, 1837.

12. Ibid., March 8, 1837.

13. Endorsement in AJ's hand to Reverend A. D. Campbell to AJ, March 15, 1837, in Jackson, *Correspondence*, V, 465. It took his crop and salary, after paying his debts, to get the family home.

14. *Globe*, March 13, 1837.

15. Ibid., March 8, 1837.

16. Ibid., March 9, 1837.

17. Rachel Jackson Lawrence, "Andrew Jackson at Home: Reminiscences by his Granddaughter, Rachel Jackson Lawrence," *McClure's Magazine* (July, 1897), p. 792.

18. AJ to Blair, March 11, 1837, Jackson Papers, LC. See also AJ to William Noland, March 11, 1837, Miscellaneous Collection, Colonial Williamsburg Foundation, copy JPP.

19. AJ to Van Buren, March 22, 1837, Van Buren Papers, LC.

20. Rachel Jackson Lawrence, "Andrew Jackson at Home," p. 793. It is hard to imagine that a man who had less than $100 in his pocket would hand out so many half dollars. Yet little Rachel remembers that he did, and it strikes me as very probable. Jackson could be fatally generous at times.

21. AJ to Blair, March 11, 1837, Jackson Papers, LC.

22. AJ to Donelson, March 19, 1837, Jackson Papers, LHA; AJ to William Noland, March 11, 1837, Miscellaneous Collection, Colonial Williamsburg Foundation, copy JPP.

23. Nashville *Union*, March 24, 1837, copy JPP. News of his triumphal journey reached Washington even before Jackson boarded the steamboat at Wheeling. See Van Buren to AJ, March 20, 1837, Van Buren Papers, LC.

24. *Globe*, March 31, 1837, quoting the Louisville *Advertiser* of March 21.

25. Nashville *Union*, March 25, 1837, copy JPP; *Globe*, April 10, 1837.

26. Parton, *Jackson*, III, 630.

27. AJ to Van Buren, March 30, 1837, Van Buren Papers, LC.

28. Ibid.

29. On the panic, see Reginald C. McGrane, *The Panic of 1837* (Chicago, 1924); Samuel Resneck, "The Social History of an American Depression, 1837–1843," *AHR* (1935), XL, 662–687; and Peter Temin, *The Jacksonian Economy* (New York, 1969).

30. AJ to Van Buren, March 30, May 12, 1837, Van Buren Papers, LC; AJ to Blair, April 24, 1837, Jackson Papers, LC.

31. Ibid.; AJ to Van Buren, May 12, June 6, 1837, Van Buren Papers, LC; AJ to Blair, January 29, 1839, Jackson Papers, LC; AJ to Maunsel White, July 12, 1837, in Jackson, *Correspondence*, V, 499.

32. Ibid.

33. AJ to Van Buren, May 1, 1838, Van Buren Papers, LC.

34. April 26, 1837. See also the edition of April 25, 1837.

35. Van Buren to AJ, March 20, 1837, Van Buren Papers, LC.

36. Blair to AJ, May 1, 1837, Jackson Papers, LC.

37. AJ to Blair, April 18, 1837, Blair to AJ, April 23, 24, 1837, Jackson Papers, LC.

38. Woodbury to AJ, June 4, 1837, Jackson Papers, LC.

39. Ibid.

40. Van Buren to AJ, April 24, 1837, Van Buren Papers, LC.

41. McGrane, *Panic of 1837*, pp. 91–154.

42. AJ to Van Buren, May 12, 1837, Van Buren Papers, LC.

43. AJ to Van Buren, June 6, 1837, Van Buren Papers, LC.

44. Ibid.; AJ to Van Buren, May 12, 1837, Van Buren Papers, LC.

45. This program was written by Jackson to Kendall but shown to the President. In the meantime Jackson advised Van Buren to pay particular heed to Kendall, who, he said, possessed "a capacity and depth of thought, worthy to be listened to." AJ to Kendall, June 23, 1837, in Jackson, *Correspondence*, V, 489; AJ to Van Buren, June 6, 1837, Van Buren Papers, LC.

46. AJ to Kendall, June 23, 1837, in Jackson, *Correspondence*, V, 490.

47. AJ to Blair, July 23, 1837, Jackson Papers, LC; AJ to Maunsel White, July 12, 1837, in Jackson, *Correspondence*, V, 499.

48. AJ to Andrew J. Hutchings, April 4, 1837, Hutchings Papers, Dyas Collection, THS; AJ to Van Buren, May 12, 1837, Van Buren Papers, LC.

49. AJ to Hutchings, April 4, 1837, Hutchings Papers, Dyas Collection, THS.

50. AJ to Van Buren, August 7, 1837; AJ to Donelson, April 22, 1837, in Jackson, *Correspondence*, V, 504, 477.

51. AJ to Van Buren, June 6, 1837, Van Buren Papers, LC; AJ to Donelson, March 29, April 4, 1837, Donelson Papers, LC; AJ to Van Buren, August 7, 1837, in Jackson, *Correspondence*, V, 506.

52. AJ to Donelson, July 18, 1837, Donelson Papers, LC.

53. AJ to Blair, April 2, 1837, Jackson Papers, LC.

54. Rachel Jackson Lawrence, "Andrew Jackson at Home," pp. 793, 797.

55. AJ to Blair, April 6, 1837, Jackson Papers, LC.

56. AJ to Hutchings, September 6, 1837, Hutchings Papers, Dyas Collection, THS.

57. Letter of N. Lester, editor of the Columbus *Democrat* to T. A. S.

Doniphan, September 28, 1837, printed in Nashville *Union*, November 30, 1837, copy JPP.

58. Rachel Jackson Lawrence, "Andrew Jackson at Home," p. 793.

CHAPTER 28

1. The estimate of Truxton's winnings comes from a statement by AJ in *The American Farmer*, X, quoted in James Douglas Anderson, *Making the American Thoroughbred* (Norwood, Mass., 1916), p. 49. The information from the Nashville *Whig* is also taken from Anderson, p. 64.

2. Ibid., pp. 50, 55–56, 273.

3. Ibid., p. 262.

4. Ibid., p. 268.

5. Ibid., p. 269.

6. Ibid., p. 274. An undated statement of the "Pedigree of Blooded Stock —raised by Genl A. Jackson Hermitage" can be found in the Jackson Papers, LC.

7. AJ to Blair, May 11, June 5, July 9, 1837, Jackson Papers, LC.

8. AJ to Blair, May 11, 1837, Jackson Papers, LC; AJ to Hutchings, April 4, 1838, Hutchings Papers, Dyas Collection, THS.

9. AJ to Poinsett, August 27, October 14, December 13, 1837, Poinsett Papers, PHS.

10. AJ to Van Buren, June 1, 4, 1838, Van Buren Papers, LC; AJ to Blair, June 4, 1838, Jackson Papers, LC. Jackson also pointed out that in Georgia the Indian lands had already been sold and that the buyers had taken possession. In Tennessee, he said, three counties "are thickly settled by men" who wish to buy the land. Ibid.

11. Blair to AJ, June 16, 1838, Jackson Papers, LC; Van Buren to AJ, June 17, 1838, AJ to Van Buren, July 6, 1838, Van Buren Papers, LC.

12. AJ to Van Buren, July 6, 1838, Van Buren Papers, LC.

13. Letter of Isaac Hill to New Hampshire *Patriot* describing visit to the Hermitage, reprinted in the McMinnville, Tennessee, *Central Gazette*, April 18, 1845, copy JPP; Blair to AJ, October 13, 1837, Jackson Papers, LC.

14. AJ to Blair, September 6, 1837, in Jackson, *Correspondence*, V, 509.

15. Ibid., p. 508.

16. John Niven, *Martin Van Buren and the Romantic Age of American Politics* (New York, 1983), chapter XXIII.

17. Blair to AJ, September 9, 1837, AJ to Blair, September 15, 1837, in Jackson, *Correspondence*, V, 509, 511, 512. See also AJ to Van Buren, September 14, 1837, ibid., pp. 510–511.

18. *"He does not himself know, how right he is,"* declared Benton on hearing Jackson's admonitions. Blair to AJ, October 1, 1837, ibid., p. 514.

19. Ibid.

20. AJ to Blair, September 27, 1837, Jackson Papers, LC. Blair promised to remember the warning. Blair to AJ, October 13, 1837, Jackson Papers, LC.

21. Calhoun to James Edward Calhoun, September 7, 1837, in *Calhoun Papers*, XIII, 535–536.

22. Wiltse, *Calhoun*, II, 354–355.

23. *Congressional Globe*, 25th Congress, 1st Session, pp. 35–57.

24. Van Buren to AJ, October 17, 1837, AJ to Van Buren, October 24, 1837, Van Buren Papers, LC.

25. Jackson called it a "political tornado." AJ to James Buchanan, December 26, 1837, Buchanan Papers, PHS.

26. Van Buren to AJ, November 18, 1837, Van Buren Papers, LC.

27. Van Buren to AJ, October 17, 1837, Van Buren Papers, LC.

28. Actually it was Taney's intention simply to write a history of the Bank War. Taney to AJ, May 28, 1838, in Jackson, *Correspondence*, V, 551. That incompleted manuscript was published in an edited form by Carl B. Swisher as "Roger B. Taney's 'Bank War Manuscript,' " in *Maryland Historical Magazine* (1958), LIII, 126ff.

29. AJ to Van Buren, October 29, 1837, Van Buren Papers, LC.

30. AJ to Blair, October 31, 1837, Jackson Papers, LC.

31. Blair to AJ, November 29, 1837, Jackson Papers, LC.

32. Blair to AJ, February 11, 1838, Jackson Papers, LC.

33. AJ's endorsement to Blair to AJ, March 28, 1839, Jackson Papers, LC.

34. AJ to Blair, October 31, June 5, 1837, Jackson Papers, LC.

35. Blair to AJ, May 26, 1837, Jackson Papers, LC.

36. AJ to Blair, November 29, 1837, Jackson Papers, LC.

37. Jackson was so engrossed in politics that he fretted over poor Donelson, who had lost his appetite for the sport because of his recent bereavement. AJ to Blair, April 6, 1837, Jackson Papers, LC. On Jackson's continuing role as Democratic leader, see AJ to Van Buren, June 1, 1838, Van Buren Papers, LC. Van Buren's deference is only one indication of it.

38. AJ to Edward G. W. Butler [1838?], in Jackson, *Correspondence*, V, 524; see also Jackson's correspondence with Blair during 1837 and 1838 in the Jackson Papers, LC. AJ to Buchanan, December 26, 1837, Buchanan Papers, PHS.

39. AJ to Blair, January 16, 1838, Jackson Papers, LC.

40. AJ to Blair, February 26, 1838, AJ to Colonel Robert Armstrong, January 9, 1838, Jackson Papers, LC.

41. AJ to Van Buren, April 4, 1838, Van Buren Papers, LC; AJ to Hutchings, January 26, 1838, Hutchings Papers, Dyas Collection, THS; AJ to Blair, March 26, 1838, Jackson Papers, LC.

42. AJ to Blair, January 16, 1838, Jackson Papers, LC; AJ to William S. Fulton, December 26, 1837, Jackson Papers, HL.

43. Bemis, *Adams*, II, 362.

44. AJ to Van Buren, January 23, 1838, Van Buren Papers, LC; AJ to Blair, July 19, 1838, Blair to AJ, July 7, 1838, Jackson Papers, LC.

45. Jackson addressed this letter to the secretary, who was his friend and had served under him in Florida, rather than the governor of the Territory because he wanted to keep it private and not make it an official act.

46. AJ to Fulton, December 10, 1830, in Jackson, *Correspondence*, IV, 212–213 and footnote; Blair to AJ, July 7, 1838, Jackson Papers, LC.

47. AJ to Blair, July 19, 1838, Jackson Papers, LC.

48. AJ to Adams, July 21, 1838, in Jackson, *Correspondence*, V, 558–559; AJ to Blair, August 9, 1838, Jackson Papers, LC.

49. Blair to AJ, July 7, 1838, Blair to AJ, July 30, 1838, Jackson Papers, LC.

50. AJ to Blair, August 9, 1838, Jackson Papers, LC.

51. AJ to Hutchings, June 21, 30, August 2, 1838, Hutchings Papers, Dyas Collection, THS.

52. AJ to Blair, August 9, 15, 1838, Jackson Papers, LC.

53. Reverend James Smith to Reverend Finis Ewing [1838], Finis Ewing Papers, THS. This comment, gratuitous in the letter, undoubtedly expressed Jackson's true feelings toward his mother. Michael Paul Rogin's argument that Jackson hated his mother is quite mistaken, I think. See Rogin, *Fathers & Children:*

Andrew Jackson and the Subjugation of the American Indian (New York, 1975), pp. 39, 40, 43–44, 46, 50.

54. AJ to William P. Lawrence, August 24, 1838, in Jackson, *Correspondence*, V, 565.

55. Smith to Ewing [1838], Ewing Papers, THS.

56. Parton, *Jackson*, III, 633.

57. Smith to Ewing [1838], Ewing Papers, THS.

58. Ibid. All of the information in this account is taken from this source, and Smith specifically mentions purgatory. He does not say limbo.

59. Parton, *Jackson*, III, 644.

60. Ibid., p. 646.

61. This is Dr. Edgar's story, which he later told to Parton. He may have been attempting to justify his subsequent action in admitting Jackson to church membership.

62. Parton, *Jackson*, III, 647.

63. This entire account is taken from Smith to Ewing [1838], Ewing Papers, THS.

64. Parton, *Jackson*, III, 647.

65. Nashville *Whig*, July 20, 1838, copy JPP.

66. Ibid.

67. Smith to Ewing [1838], Ewing Papers, THS.

68. Parton, *Jackson*, III, 648; Rachel Jackson Lawrence, "Andrew Jackson at Home: Reminiscences by His Granddaughter, Rachel Jackson Lawrence," *McClure's Magazine* (July, 1897), p. 793.

CHAPTER 29

1. AJ to Hutchings, August 2, 1838, Hutchings Papers, Dyas Collection, THS.

2. AJ to Nicholas Trist, September 19, 1838, Trist Papers, LC; AJ to Hutchings, September 20, 1838, Hutchings Papers, Dyas Collection, THS; AJ to Blair, September 27, 1838, Jackson Papers, LC.

3. Ibid.; AJ to Hutchings, September 20, 1838, Hutchings Papers, Dyas Collection, THS; AJ to Trist, September 19, 1838, Trist Papers, LC.

4. AJ to Hutchings, September 20, 1838, Hutchings Papers, Dyas Collection, THS; Blair to AJ, October 19, 1838, Jackson Papers, LC.

5. AJ to Lewis, December 10, 1838, Jackson-Lewis Papers, NYPL. For details of the Swartwout swindle, see Remini, *Jackson*, II, 199.

6. AJ to Van Buren, December 4, 1838, Van Buren Papers, LC.

7. AJ to Blair, January 5, 1839, Jackson Papers, LC.

8. AJ to Blair, September 27, 1838, Jackson-Lewis Papers, LC.

9. AJ to Lewis, December 10, 1838, Jackson-Lewis Papers, NYPL.

10. AJ to Van Buren, December 4, 1838, Van Buren Papers, LC.

11. AJ to Blair, September 27, 1838, Jackson Papers, LC.

12. Linda Bennett Galloway, *Andrew Jackson, Jr., Son of a President* (New York, 1966), p. 59. Samuel was born June 9, 1837, and died September 29, 1863.

13. AJ to Andrew Jr., November 11, 1838, Jackson Papers, LC.

14. "Agreement for Purchase of Land," November 20, 1838, in Jackson, *Correspondence*, V, 571.

15. AJ to Andrew Jr., November 11, 1838, Jackson Papers, LC; Bassett, *Jackson*, p. 728.

16. It should be added that Kendall made very little use of the papers

Jackson had loaned him. Jackson's copy of Kendall's work can be found in the rare book room of the Library of Congress, the second volume of which contains a number of corrections in Jackson's handwriting.

17. Stickney and a man named William Terrell, a Washington newspaperman, discovered the trunks in Jackson Hall, the old *Globe* office in Washington. Terrell kept approximately 100 letters which he published in the Cincinnati *Commercial* in February, 1879. Most of these letters were later purchased by the Library of Congress. The bulk of Jackson's papers were inherited by Francis Blair's son, Montgomery, and later by Montgomery's children. In 1903 these papers were presented to the Library of Congress by the Blair family. In 1931 the Library of Congress purchased a large body of Jackson papers from a New York dealer. They are sometimes cited as Jackson Papers, second series. Presumably these were the papers that Kendall retained in his home, but how the dealer acquired them is unknown. The Jackson collection in the Library of Congress now totals well over 22,000 items.

18. In particular, controversies that had arisen with Great Britain. See below, this chapter, for the Canadian border difficulty.

19. AJ to Blair, May 2, 1839, Jackson Papers, LC.

20. AJ to Blair, January 29, 1839, Jackson Papers, LC.

21. Blair to AJ, May 20, 1839, Jackson Papers, LC.

22. AJ to Van Buren, March 4, 1839, Van Buren Papers, LC.

23. John Niven, *Martin Van Buren and the Romantic Age of American Politics* (New York, 1983), pp. 425ff., has an excellent account of the President's handling of the problem. See also Albert B. Corey, *The Crisis of 1830–1842 in Canadian-American Relations* (New Haven, 1941); Howard Jones, "Anglophobia and the Aroostook War," *New England Quarterly* (1975), XLVIII, 519–539; and Thomas LeDuc, "The Maine Frontier and the Northeastern Boundary Controversy," *AHR* (1947), LIII, 30–41.

24. AJ to Blair, April 20, 1839, Jackson Papers, LC.

25. AJ to John A. Shute, January 3, 1839, in Jackson, *Correspondence*, VI, 1, 2; AJ to Polk, February 11, 1839, Polk Papers, LC.

26. AJ to Shute, January 3, 1839, in Jackson, *Correspondence*, VI, 2.

27. Ibid.; AJ to Hutchings, May 20, 1839, Hutchings Papers, Dyas Collection, THS.

28. AJ to Polk, February 11, 1839, Polk Papers, LC; AJ to Blair, February 20, 1839, Jackson Papers, LC.

29. AJ to Blair, September 23, 1839, in Jackson, *Correspondence*, VI, 28; Blair to AJ, September 23, October 6, 1839, Jackson Papers, LC.

30. AJ to Hutchings, September 5, 20, 1839, Hutchings Papers, Dyas Collection, THS.

31. AJ to Hutchings, December 19, 1839, Hutchings Papers, Dyas Collection, THS.

32. Rives was office manager of the *Globe* and became a full partner in 1834. See Elbert B. Smith, *Francis Preston Blair* (New York, 1980), p. 49.

33. AJ to Donelson, December 10, 1839, Donelson Papers, LC.

34. See the exchange of letters between Jackson and Lewis in Jackson, *Correspondence*, VI, 18, 19ff, 29ff, 33ff, 36ff. Jackson comes off less well than Lewis in this exchange, I think, although Lewis runs on at great length about what is owed him for his past services.

35. AJ to Lewis, November 11, 1839, ibid., p. 40.

36. AJ to Hutchings, December 19, 1839, Hutchings Papers, Dyas Collection, THS; AJ to Reverend Hardy M. Cryer, February 5, 1840, in Jackson, *Correspondence*, VI, 49.

37. Quoted in Parton, *Jackson*, III, 633–634.
38. AJ to Andrew Jr., December 27, 31, 1839, Jackson Papers, LC.
39. Ibid.
40. AJ to Van Buren, December 23, 1839, Van Buren Papers, LC.
41. Ibid.
42. "Circumstances of a *private and imperious nature*," induced him to make this trip, AJ to Hutchings, December 19, 1839, Hutchings Papers, Dyas Collection, THS.
43. AJ to Andrew Jr., December 27, 1839, Jackson Papers, LC.
44. AJ to Sarah, January 4, 1840, Jackson Papers, LC.
45. AJ to Kendall, April 16, 1840, Jackson Papers, LC.
46. Ibid.
47. *Globe*, January 20, 22, 1840; *Niles Weekly Register*, February 1, 1840; Nashville *Union*, January 22, 1840, copy JPP.
48. *Niles Weekly Register*, February 1, 8, 1840; Nashville *Union*, January 22, 1840, copy JPP.
49. *Globe*, January 22, 1840.
50. Ibid.
51. Quoted in Nashville *Union*, January 22, 1840, copy JPP.
52. *Niles Wekly Register*, February 1, 8, 1840; *Globe*, January 20, 30, 1840.
53. Nashville *Union*, January 22, 1840, copy JPP; *Globe*, January 20, 30, 1840; AJ to Van Buren, March 30, 1837, Van Buren Papers, LC.
54. *Globe*, February 15, 1840.
55. AJ to Cryer, February 5, 1840, in Jackson, *Correspondence*, VI, 48.
56. Parton, *Jackson*, III, 632.
57. Nashville *Union*, November 30, 1837, copy JPP; AJ to Van Buren, December 23, 1839, Van Buren Papers, LC.
58. Quoted in Parton, *Jackson*, III, 634.

CHAPTER 30

1. AJ to Lewis, December 26, 1840, Jackson-Lewis Papers, NYPL.
2. AJ to Hutchings, August 3, September 11, 1840, Hutchings Papers, Dyas Collection, THS.
3. AJ to Hutchings, March 5, 18, May 1, 1839, Hutchings Papers, Dyas Collection, THS.
4. AJ to Donelson, February 19, September 8, 1840, Donelson Papers, LC; AJ to Hutchings, August 3, September 11, 1840, Hutchings Papers, Dyas Collection, THS. Jackson announced the sale of Hunter's Hill in the Nashville *Union*, March 30, 1840, copy JPP.
5. AJ to Hutchings, May 25, December 30, 1840, Hutchings Papers, Dyas Collection, THS.
6. AJ to Blair, April 9, 1840, Jackson Papers, LC.
7. AJ to Blair, February 15, 1840, Jackson Papers, LC.
8. AJ to Kendall, April 16, 1840, Jackson Papers, LC.
9. AJ to Blair, May 22, June 17, 1840, Jackson Papers, LC.
10. Benton to AJ, April 24, 1840, in Jackson, *Correspondence*, VI, 59; AJ to Van Buren, April 3, 29, May 21, 1840, Van Buren Papers, LC.
11. AJ to Van Buren, May 21, 1840, Van Buren Papers, LC. The same sentiment is expressed in AJ to Blair, May 22, June 17, 1840, Jackson Papers, LC.
12. AJ to Blair, May 22, 1840, Jackson Papers, LC. Robert M. T. Hunter of Virginia was elected Speaker on December 16, 1839.

13. AJ to Blair, June 17, 1840, Jackson Papers, LC; AJ to Donelson, July 9, 1840, Donelson Papers, LC. On the Independent Treasury, see David Kinley, *The Independent Treasury of the United States and Its Relations to the Banks of the Country* (Washington, 1910); James R. Sharp, *The Jacksonians Versus the Banks: Politics in the States After the Panic of 1837* (New York, 1970); and Richard H. Timberlake, "Independent Treasury and Monetary Policy before the Civil War," *Southern Economic Journal* (1960), XXVII, 92–103.

14. Both Clay's speech and Jackson's response were carried in the Nashville *Union*, August 19, 1840, copy JPP. AJ's notes on Clay's speech can be found in a memorandum dated August 17, 1840, Jackson Papers, LC.

15. Ibid.

16. Taney to AJ, September 4, 1840, Blair to AJ, September 10, 1840, in Jackson, *Correspondence*, VI, 71–72, 75.

17. AJ to Louisa Livingston, November 12, 1840, Livingston Papers, JRDF.

18. On the election of 1840, see Robert G. Gunderson, *The Log-Cabin Campaign* (Lexington, Ky., 1957).

19. AJ to Blair, September 26, 1840, Jackson Papers, LC; AJ to Kendall, June 2, 1840, in Jackson, *Correspondence*, VI, 63; AJ to Hutchings, August 3, 1840, Hutchings Papers, Dyas Collection, THS.

20. AJ to Hutchings, September 7, 1840, Hutchings Papers, Dyas Collection, THS.

21. AJ to Blair, September 26, 1840, Jackson Papers, LC; AJ to Van Buren, September 22, 1840, Van Buren Papers, LC.

22. Ibid.

23. AJ to Blair, September 26, 1840, Jackson Papers, LC.

24. Indeed, Jackson said it drew "the serious attention of the people here." AJ to Donelson, October 8, 1840, Donelson Papers, LC.

25. Ibid. The language and the ideas in the speech about abolitionists can be found in a number of Jackson's letters, all written before he gave the speech. See, for example, AJ to Hutchings, August 12, 1840, in which virtually the exact language of the speech is used. Hutchings Papers, Days Collection, THS.

26. Nashville *Union*, October 15, 1840, copy JPP.

27. It was during this tour that the General accidentally ran into Eaton. Both men behaved properly during the encounter and nothing embarrassing or untoward happened. Still, Jackson did not trust the Whigs. If they try to "make Whigg capital out of this meeting of ours," he wrote, "it shall be corrected." AJ to Donelson, October 8, 1840, Donelson Papers, LC.

28. AJ to Lewis, October 27, 1840, Jackson-Lewis Papers, NYPL.

29. By the end of summer 1840, Jackson came "within a few hundred dollars" of closing out Andrew's debts—or so he thought. AJ to Hutchings, August 3, September 11, 12, 1840, Hutchings Papers, Dyas Collection, THS; AJ to Andrew Jr., September 28, 1840, Jackson Papers, LC.

30. AJ to Van Buren, November 12, 1840, Van Buren Papers, LC.

31. Svend Petersen, *A Statistical History of the American Presidential Elections* (New York, 1963), pp. 18–27.

32. William N. Chambers, "The Election of 1840," in Arthur M. Schlesinger, Jr., Fred L. Israel, and William P. Hansen, eds., *History of American Presidential Elections* (New York, 1971), I, 681.

33. AJ to Van Buren, November 24, 1840, Van Buren Papers, LC; AJ to Kendall, January 2, 1841, in Jackson, *Correspondence*, VI, 88.

34. F. Byrdsall, *History of the Loco-Foco, or Equal Rights Party* (New York, 1842), pp. 13ff. See also Leo Hershkowitz, "The Loco-Foco Party of New York:

Its Origins and Career, 1835–1837," *New-York Historical Society Quarterly* (1962), XLVI, 305–329, and Jabez D. Hammond, *History of Political Parties in the State of New York* (New York, 1852).

35. AJ to Van Buren, November 24, 1840, Van Buren Papers, LC; AJ to Kendall, January 2, 1841, in Jackson, *Correspondence*, VI, 89.

36. Ibid.; AJ to Blair, June 27, 1840, Jackson Papers, LC.

37. Henry Horn to AJ, April 9, 1841, in Jackson, *Correspondence*, VI, 102.

38. Ibid.; Taney to AJ, April 24, 1841, ibid., p. 107.

39. Walter B. Smith, *Economic Aspects of the Second Bank of the United States* (Cambridge, Mass., 1953), pp. 200–201, 219–220, 226–227. Biddle died on February 27, 1844. An excellent biography of Biddle is Thomas P. Govan, *Nicholas Biddle* (Chicago, 1959).

40. Horn to AJ, April 9, 1841, in Jackson, *Correspondence*, VI, 102.

41. Blair to AJ, April 4, 1841, Jackson Papers, LC.

42. AJ to Blair, April 19, 1841, Jackson Papers, LC.

43. AJ to Blair, April 4, 19, May 31, 1841, Blair to AJ, April 11, 1841, Jackson Papers, LC.

44. AJ to Blair, May 31, 1841, Jackson Papers, LC.

45. AJ to Lewis, August 19, 1841, Jackson-Lewis Papers, NYPL.

CHAPTER 31

1. Glyndon G. Van Deusen, *The Life of Henry Clay* (Boston, 1937), p. 345.

2. *Congressional Globe,* 27th Congress, 1st Session, pp. 80ff.

3. AJ to Blair, July 17, 1841, Jackson Papers, LC.

4. Ibid.

5. Blair to AJ, August 2, 1841, Jackson Papers, LC.

6. AJ to Blair, August 12, 1841, Jackson Papers, LC.

7. Robert Seager II, *And Tyler Too* (New York, 1963), pp. 155–156; Oliver Perry Chitwood, *John Tyler: Champion of the Old South* (New York, 1939), p. 226.

8. Dabney S. Carr to AJ, August 18, 1841, in Jackson, *Correspondence*, VI, 119.

9. AJ to Lewis, August 19, 1841, ibid., pp. 120, 121.

10. Clement Eaton, *Henry Clay and the Art of American Politics* (Boston, 1957), p. 150; Seager, *And Tyler Too,* pp. 157–160; Chitwood, *John Tyler,* pp. 235–236.

11. AJ to William Gwin, January 11, 1842, Jackson Papers, LC.

12. Ibid.; AJ to Lewis, September 23, 1841, Jackson-Lewis Papers, NYPL; AJ to Donelson, September 9, 1841, Donelson Papers, LC.

13. AJ to Lewis, December 28, 1841, Jackson-Lewis Papers, NYPL.

14. AJ to Lewis, September 23, 1841, Jackson-Lewis Papers, NYPL.

15. AJ to Lewis, December 28, 1841, Jackson-Lewis Papers, NYPL.

16. AJ to Van Buren, November 25, 1841, Van Buren Papers, LC.

17. AJ to Lewis, August 19, 1841, in Jackson, *Correspondence*, VI, 119–120; AJ to Blair, February 3, 1842, Jackson Papers, LC. Donelson also suffered financially and asked Jackson to help him secure a loan. AJ to B. F. Butler, July 12, 1842, Jackson Papers, LC.

18. Within ten years of Jackson's death his son was close to $100,000 in debt. The state of Tennessee in 1856 purchased the Hermitage and 500 acres of adjoining land for $50,000, $2,000 of which was withheld for rent for a two-year period. Linda B. Galloway, *Andrew Jackson, Jr.* (New York, 1966), pp. 74, 75.

19. AJ to Lewis, August 19, 1841, in Jackson, *Correspondence*, VI, 120.

20. Plauché to AJ, June 1, December 21, 1841, ibid., pp. 115–116, 129.

21. AJ to Lewis, February 27, 1842, Jackson Papers, ML; AJ to Lewis, August 19, 1841, in Jackson, *Correspondence,* VI, 119–120.

22. Blair to AJ, January 18, 1842, Jackson Papers, LC.

23. Parton, *Jackson,* III, 640.

24. In addition to a crop failure Jackson suffered "a great mortality" among the blooded stock. AJ to Blair, February 24, 1842, Jackson Papers, LC.

25. AJ to Blair, February 3, 24, 1842, Jackson Papers, LC.

26. AJ to Blair, March 29, 1842, Jackson Papers, LC.

27. Ibid.

28. AJ to Lewis, June 2, 1842, Jackson-Lewis Papers, NYPL.

29. Benton to AJ, March 10, 1842, Jackson Papers, LC. For details of the fine, see Remini, *Jackson,* I, 310ff.

30. AJ to Blair, June 4, July 2, 1842, Jackson Papers, LC; AJ to Linn, March 12, June 2, 1842, in Jackson, *Correspondence,* VI, 143–146, 156–157; AJ to Donelson, June 1, 2, 1842, Donelson Papers, LC.

31. AJ to Blair, June 4, 1842, Jackson Papers, LC; AJ to Donelson [1842], Donelson Papers, LC. Those who had proposed the amendment to Linn's bill sought to discredit Jackson by quoting the testimony of New Orleans residents who had defended Hall's action at the time. But the Hero dismissed their testimony by impugning their bravery and loyalty. Besides, he said, they were in league with aristocratic Frenchmen who "hated any thing that wore the appearance of democracy." AJ to Linn, June 2, 1842, in Jackson, *Correspondence,* VI, 157. Jackson asked Donelson to assist him in the composition of the letter to Linn. "I want a costic but decorous criticism upon the conduct of the Whiggs incorporated in my letter to Doctor Linn," he said. AJ to Donelson [1842], Donelson Papers, LC.

32. Bemis, *Adams,* II, 427. Adams's biographers believe his fight over the gag rule was his finest hour.

33. AJ to Lewis, February 27, 1842, Jackson Papers, ML.

34. Schlesinger, *Age of Jackson,* pp. 410–413. See also Marvin E. Gettleman, *The Dorr Rebellion* (New York, 1973), and George M. Dennison, *The Dorr War* (Lexington, Ky., 1976).

35. This expression was used in another context but it conveyed Jackson's views precisely. AJ to Linn, June 2, 1842, in Jackson, *Correspondence,* VI, 157.

36. AJ to Blair, May 23, 1842, Jackson Papers, LC.

37. AJ to William Gwin, January 11, 1842, AJ to Blair, April 23, May 24, 1842, Jackson Papers, LC; AJ to Sam Houston, May 25, 1842, Jackson Papers, copy CHS; AJ to Kendall, June 18, 1842, in Jackson, *Correspondence,* VI, 159; Blair to AJ, May 24, 1842, Jackson Papers, LC.

38. AJ to Van Buren, February 22, 1842, Van Buren Papers, LC; Nashville *Union,* April 28, 1842.

39. AJ to Blair, May 23, 1842, Jackson Papers, LC.

40. AJ to Van Buren, June 3, 1842, Van Buren Papers, LC. Jackson's trip to Ohio was arranged in response to invitations from citizens of Cincinnati and Columbus but had to be canceled.

41. Van Buren to Jackson, May 27, 1842, Van Buren Papers, LC.

42. AJ to Kendall, June 18, 1842, in Jackson, *Correspondence,* VI, 159.

43. Tyler to AJ, September 20, 1842, ibid., pp. 167–168.

44. AJ to Blair, August 7, 1842, Jackson Papers, LC. See also AJ to Van Buren, September 15, 1842, Van Buren Papers, LC.

45. AJ to Blair, October 29, 1842, Jackson Papers, LC; AJ to J. George Harris, December 14, 1842, private collection, copy JPP.

46. AJ to Van Buren, August 16, 1841, September 15, December 15, 1842, Van Buren Papers, LC; AJ to Donelson, December 18, 1842, private collection, copy JPP.

47. AJ to Donelson, December 18, 1842, private collection, copy JPP.

48. AJ to Blair, August 12, 1842, Jackson Papers, LC; Sellers, *Polk*, I, 430ff.

49. AJ to Blair, October 19, November 25, 1842, November 2, 1843, Jackson Papers, LC.

50. Blair to AJ, November 13, 1842, Jackson Papers, LC. Jackson remembered this incident, too, and agreed with Blair's interpretation. AJ to Blair, November 25, 1842, Jackson Papers, LC.

51. AJ's will, September 1, 1842, private collection, copy JPP.

52. Ibid.; AJ to Van Buren, September 15, 1842, Van Buren Papers, LC; AJ to Gwin, January 11, 1838, Jackson Papers, LC.

53. AJ's will, September 1, 1842, private collection, copy JPP.

54. At that battle Armstrong was wounded and as he fell to the ground he called out: "My brave fellows, some may fall, but save the cannon." Jackson insisted in inserting this information into the will.

55. AJ's will, June 7, 1843, in Jackson, *Correspondence*, VI, 220–223.

56. Parton, *Jackson*, III, 649.

57. Kendall to AJ, September 19, 1842, Jackson Papers, LC; White, *Jacksonians*, pp. 38–39, 278–279; AJ to Kendall, September 29, 1842, in Jackson, *Correspondence*, VI, 170.

58. AJ to Cave Johnson, November 25, 1842, AJ to Kendall, December 12, 1842, ibid., pp. 179–180.

59. McLaughlin to Kendall, December 26, 1842, January 8, 1843, Kendall Papers, LC; Kendall to AJ, June 5, November 29, 1842, Jackson Papers, LC; AJ to Kendall, January 10, 1843, Jackson Papers, TSL; Sam B. Smith and Harriet C. Owsley, eds., *The Papers of Andrew Jackson* (Knoxville, 1980), I, 5–9.

60. Kendall to AJ, November 23, 29, 1842, Jackson Papers, LC.

61. A copy of this map is reproduced in volume I of this biography, p. 18. For information on the preparation of Kendall's biography, see the several letters in Jackson, *Correspondence*, VI, 213–219.

62. McLaughlin to Kendall, March 13, 1843, ibid., pp. 213–214.

63. McLaughlin to Kendall, February 24, 1843, Kendall Papers, LC.

64. AJ to Alexander D. Coffee, February 22, 1843, Coffee Papers, LC; Coffee to AJ, March 11, 1843, Jackson Papers, LC.

65. Harris to AJ, January 6, 1843, AJ to Blair, November 2, 1843, Jackson Papers, LC.

66. Kendall, *Autobiography*, p. 505; Kendall to AJ, March 19, 28, 1843, Jackson Papers, LC.

67. Kendall to AJ, October 21, 1843, Jackson Papers, LC.

68. John McDonough, *Index to the Andrew Jackson Papers* (Washington, 1967), p. xv.

69. AJ to Kendall, January 9, September 10, 1844, Jackson Papers, LC.

70. AJ to Blair, February 7, 1843, Jackson Papers, LC; and *Globe* editorials for April, May, 1843. On the quarrel see especially Kendall to AJ, January 27, 1843, Blair to AJ, January 7, 1843, Jackson Papers, LC.

71. AJ to Blair, January 11, 17, 1843, Jackson Papers, LC.

72. AJ to Blair, February 7, 1843, August 18, 1843, Jackson Papers, LC; AJ to Blair, December 15, 1843, Blair–Lee Papers, PUL.

73. Blair to AJ, February 18, 1843, Jackson Papers, LC.

74. AJ to Blair, March 20, 1843, Jackson Papers, LC; AJ to Lewis, September 12, 1843, Jackson-Lewis Papers, NYPL.

75. AJ to Blair, November 22, 1843, Jackson Papers, LC; AJ to Donelson, December 19, 1842, October 23, 1843, Donelson Papers, LC; AJ to Blair, August 11, November 22, 1843, Jackson Papers, LC; AJ to Donelson, October 15, 1843, Donelson Papers, LC.

76. AJ to Blair, October 31, 1843, Jackson Papers, LC; AJ to Lewis, August 19, 1841, Jackson-Lewis Papers, NYPL. Of the sons only Andrew III and Samuel lived to maturity. Andrew III born April 4, 1834, died December 17, 1906; Samuel born June 9, 1837, died September 29, 1863.

77. AJ to Lewis, November 16, 1842, Jackson Papers, ML; AJ to Blair, November 17, 1843, Blair to AJ, November 20, 1843, Lewis to AJ, December 4, 1843, Jackson Papers, LC.

CHAPTER 32

1. AJ to Lewis, January 18, 1844, Jackson-Lewis Papers, NYPL; AJ to Blair, January 19, February 24, 1844, Blair to AJ, December 25, 1843, Lewis to AJ, January 9, 1843, Jackson Papers, LC. The fullest treatment of the fine can' be found in Charles J. Ingersoll, *Gen. Jackson's Fine* (Washington, 1843), and A. Kendall, "General Jackson's Fine," *United States Magazine and Democratic Review* (January, 1843), XII, 58–77.

2. Blair to AJ, February 11, 1844, Jackson Papers, LC.

3. AJ to Lewis, February 27, Jackson-Lewis Papers, NYPL; Tyler to AJ, February 16, 1844, in Jackson, *Correspondence*, VI, 260.

4. Henry Lieberman to AJ, February 19, 1844, Jackson Papers, LC. Jackson received many congratulations from around the country. See Van Buren to AJ, February 21, March 8, 1844, Van Buren Papers, LC, and Taney to AJ, March 15, 1844, Blair-Lee Papers, PUL.

5. Lewis to AJ [1844], February 15, 1844, AJ to Blair, February 29, 1844, Jackson Papers, LC; AJ to Lewis, February 27, 1844, Jackson-Lewis Papers, NYPL.

6. AJ to Blair, February 23, 1844, AJ to Kendall, March 18, 1844, Jackson Papers, LC.

7. AJ to Lewis, February 27, March 11, 1844, Jackson-Lewis Papers, NYPL.

8. AJ to Blair [1844], Jackson Papers, LC.

9. AJ to Blair, March 5, 1844, AJ to Kendall, April 12, 1844, Jackson Papers, LC; AJ to Aaron V. Brown, February 9, 1843, in Jackson, *Correspondence*, VI, 201–202.

10. AJ to Santa Anna, February 27, 1843, March 1, 1844, ibid., pp. 212, 268; AJ to G. B. Semor, February 28, 1842, ML; Lewis to AJ, February 26, 1844, Jackson Papers, LC.

11. Houston to AJ, January 31, 1843, in Jackson, *Correspondence*, VI, 189.

12. After completing the negotiations for the Webster-Ashburton Treaty, Webster resigned and was replaced by Abel P. Upshur, who was accidentally killed in an explosion aboard the U.S.S. *Princeton*.

13. Walker to AJ, January 10, 1844, Jackson Papers, LC.

14. AJ to Houston, January 18, 23, 1844, private collection, copy JPP.

15. Houston to AJ, February 16, 17, 1844, in Jackson, *Correspondence*, VI, 261, 264–265.

16. AJ to Walker, March 11, 1844, Jackson Papers, CHS; AJ to Blair, March 5, 1844, Jackson Papers, LC.

17. Ibid. See also AJ to Blair, July 12, 1844, Jackson Papers, LC.
18. AJ to Walker, March 11, 1844, Jackson Papers, CHS.
19. Ibid.
20. AJ to Houston, March 15, 1844, private collection, copy JPP.
21. AJ to Lewis, March 11, 1844, Jackson-Lewis Papers, NYPL.
22. AJ to Houston, March 15, 1844, private collection, copy JPP.
23. Lewis to AJ, March 28, 1844, Jackson Papers, LC.
24. Miller to AJ, April 7, 1844, in Jackson, *Correspondence*, VI, 276, 277.
25. AJ to Lewis, April 8, May 3, 1844, Jackson-Lewis Papers, NYPL.
26. Ibid.
27. Tyler to AJ, April 18, 1844, in Jackson, *Correspondence*, VI, 279.
28. Lewis to AJ, April 26, 1844, Jackson Papers, LC.
29. Blair to AJ, May 2, 19, 1844, Jackson Papers, LC.
30. AJ to Blair, May 11, 1844, Jackson Papers, LC.
31. AJ to Blair, May 11, 1844, Jackson Papers, LC, contains Jackson's oft repeated warning of threatened perils. Blair to AJ, May 2, 19, 1844, Jackson Papers, LC. See editorials in April and May in the *Globe*, Albany *Argus*, and other Democratic newspapers.
32. Rodman W. Paul, *Rift in the Democracy* (Philadelphia, 1951), p. 38.
33. *Globe*, April 27, 1844.
34. Blair to AJ, May 2, 19, 1844, Jackson Papers, LC.
35. AJ to Blair, May 11, 1844, Jackson Papers, LC.
36. AJ to Blair, May 7, 1844, Jackson Papers, LC; AJ to Lewis, May 7, 1844, Jackson-Lewis Papers, NYPL.
37. AJ to Blair, May 11, 1844, Jackson Papers, LC.
38. AJ to Blair, March 10, 1845, Jackson Papers, LC. That Jackson wrote the letter mentioned in the text is confirmed in AJ to Blair, May 11, 1844, Jackson Papers, LC. However, the letter to Van Buren itself is missing from the Van Buren Papers, LC, which would tend to support the suspicion expressed in Volume II of this work (page 412, note 42) that some of Jackson's letters in the Van Buren collection may have been destroyed by Van Buren after Jackson's death.
39. It is reported in the newspapers, Jackson wrote, that after the debate on the annexation bill "Col Benton seized J. Q. Adams by the hand and said, 'we are both old men, we must unite and save the constitution.' Do my dear Mr. Blair inform me if this can be true, if it is, I want no better proof of his derangement." AJ to Blair, June 25, 1844, Jackson Papers, LC. Blair took a great deal of criticism for publishing Benton's letter. He explained his position in a letter to Jackson, September 9, 1844, Jackson Papers, LC.
40. AJ to Blair, May 7, 11, June 7, 25, 1844, Jackson Papers, LC; AJ to Lewis, June 28, 1844, Jackson-Lewis Papers, NYPL. John A. Garraty, *Silas Wright* (New York, 1949), gives the best account of the Wright–Van Buren relationship.
41. S. H. Laughlin to Polk, December 18, 1843, Polk Papers, LC.
42. Johnson to Polk, May 8, 1844, Polk Papers, LC.
43. Donelson to Polk, May 10, 1844, Armstrong to Polk, May 10, 1844, Polk Papers, LC.
44. Jackson to the editors of the Nashville *Union*, May 13, 1844, copy JPP.
45. Polk to Cave Johnson, May 4, 14, 1844, copies of which were provided me by the Polk Project editor at Vanderbilt University. They can also be found in "Letters of James K. Polk to Cave Johnson, 1833–1848," *THM* (September, 1915), I, 238–241.
46. Blair to AJ, November 7, 1844, Jackson Papers, LC.
47. Polk to Johnson, May 3, 1844, copy Polk Papers Project.
48. Polk to Johnson, May 13, 14, 17, 1844, copies Polk Papers Project.

49. Sellers, *Polk*, II, 73–74.

50. Polk to Cave Johnson, May 17 [14], 1844, copy Polk Papers Project.

51. Polk said that Jackson expressed his views quite openly on the matter. Polk to Johnson, May 14, 1844, copy Polk Papers Project.

52. The maneuvering to bring about the adoption of the two-thirds rule is fully described in Sellers, *Polk*, II, 76ff. It is obvious that some Van Buren men (westerners and southerners) supported the two-thirds rule or it would never have passed. And they probably supported it in order to bring about a deadlock and thereby win release from their pledges. Gideon J. Pillow in his letter to Polk, May 22, 1844, copy Polk Papers Project, shows how conciliatory the Polk men tried to be. "I think it now best," he wrote, "to use all our influence & power to *heal* the wounds of the party & re-unite it if possible & until that is done, say but little about the V.P."

53. Ibid.; Sellers, *Polk*, II, 91.

54. Ibid., p. 92.

55. Charles Sellers, "Election of 1844," in Arthur M. Schlesinger, Jr., Fred L. Israel, and William P. Hansen, eds., *History of American Presidential Elections* (New York, 1971), I, 772–774.

56. Donelson to AJ, May 29, 1844, in Jackson, *Correspondence*, VI, 296.

57. AJ to Butler, May 14, 1844, Van Buren Papers, LC; AJ to Butler, June 24, 1844, Blair-Lee Papers, PUL. This second letter is in Donelson's handwriting which explains the spelling and grammar.

58. AJ to Blair, June 7, 25, 1844, Jackson Papers, LC.

59. Sellers, *Polk*, II, 114; AJ to Blair, June 25, 1844, Jackson Papers, LC; AJ to Butler, June 24, 1844, Blair-Lee Papers, PUL.

60. AJ to Lewis, July 12, 1844, Jackson-Lewis Papers, NYPL; AJ to John Y. Mason, August 1, 1844, in Jackson, *Correspondence*, VI, 305–306.

61. Walker to Polk, July 10, 1844, Polk Papers, LC.

62. Jackson advised Polk against making such pledges. See AJ to Polk, July 26, 1844, Polk Papers, LC.

63. AJ to Lewis, July 26, 1844, in Tyler, *Letters and Times*, III, 144; AJ to Polk, July 26, 1844, Polk Papers, LC; AJ to Blair, July 26, August 29, September 9, 1844, Jackson Papers, LC; Tyler to AJ, August 18, 1844, in Jackson, *Correspondence*, VI, 315.

64. Blair to AJ, July 7, 1844, Jackson Papers, LC.

65. AJ to Lewis, July 12, 1844, Jackson-Lewis Papers, NYPL; AJ to Blair, July 12, 1844, Jackson Papers, LC.

66. AJ to Blair, August 15, 1844, Blair to AJ, August 4, 1844, Jackson Papers, LC; AJ to Lewis, July 12, 1844, Jackson-Lewis Papers, NYPL; Polk to Donelson, June 26, 1844, Donelson Papers, LC; Donelson to Polk, July 1, 1844, Polk Papers, LC; AJ to Houston, July 19, 1844, Andrew Jackson Houston Papers, copy JPP; Sellers, *Polk*, II, 116.

67. AJ to Lewis, August 15, 1844, Jackson-Lewis Papers, NYPL; AJ to Blair, August 29, 1844, Jackson Papers, LC.

68. Ibid.

69. Sellers, *Polk*, II, 139.

70. Polk to Donelson, July 22, 1844, Donelson Papers, LC; AJ to Polk, July 23, 1844, Polk Papers, LC; Donelson to AJ, December 28, 1844, Houston to AJ, December 13, 1844, Jackson Papers, LC.

71. Tyler to AJ, September 17, 1844, in Jackson, *Correspondence*, VI, 320.

72. AJ to Blair, September 19, 1844, Jackson Papers, LC; Pakenham's letter is quoted in Sellers, *Polk*, II, 132.

73. Quoted ibid., pp. 141–142.

74. Sellers, "Election of 1844," p. 861. Birney took 62,300 popular and no electoral votes.

75. Adams, *Memoirs*, XII, 103, 110.

76. Quoted in Sellers, *Polk*, II, 158.

77. Ibid., pp. 159, 160–161.

78. Jackson to Kendall, November 23, 1844, Jackson Papers, LC; AJ to Donelson, November 18, 1844, in Jackson, *Correspondence*, VI, 329; AJ to Donelson, December 2, 1844, AJ to Mrs. Elizabeth Donelson, November 14, 1844, Donelson Papers, LC; AJ to Kendall, November 23, 1844, Jackson Papers, LC.

79. AJ to Donelson, November 18, 1844, in Jackson, *Correspondence*, VI, 330; AJ to Blair, November 18, 1844, Jackson Papers, LC.

80. AJ to Blair, October 17, 1844, Jackson Papers, LC; AJ to Van Buren, February 10, 1845, Van Buren Papers, LC.

81. AJ to Polk, December 13, 1844, Polk Papers, LC; AJ to Lewis, December 18, 1844, Donelson Papers, LC; AJ to Kendall, November 28, 1844, Jackson Papers, LC.

82. Polk to Johnson, December 21, 1844, in "Letters of Polk to Johnson," *THM* (September, 1915), I, 254; Sellers, *Polk*, II, 167; AJ to Polk, December 13, 1844, Polk Papers, LC.

83. AJ to Polk, December 16, 1844, Polk Papers, LC.

84. Jackson was not alone in reading the election as a mandate from the American people to acquire Texas. Houston thought so, too. See Houston to AJ, December 13, 1844, Jackson Papers, LC.

85. AJ to Donelson, December 11, 1844, in Jackson, *Correspondence*, VI, 338; AJ to Blair, November 18, 1844, Jackson Papers, LC; AJ to Blair, February 8, 1845, Miscellaneous Manuscript Collection, YUL; AJ to Van Buren, February 10, 1845, Van Buren Papers, LC; AJ to Lewis, February 11, 1845, Jackson-Lewis Papers, NYPL.

86. Blair to AJ, January 3, 4, February 28, 1845, Jackson Papers, LC.

87. Blair to AJ, January 30, February 9, 1845, Jackson Papers, LC.

88. AJ to Lewis, January 1, 1845, Jackson-Lewis Papers, NYPL; AJ to Blair, January 21, 1845, Jackson Papers, LC; AJ to Blair, February 8, 1845, Miscellaneous Manuscript Collection, YUL.

89. *Globe*, February 13, 14, 1845; Blair to AJ, February 9, 1845, Jackson Papers, LC.

90. Mangum to T. R. Caldwell, February 20, 1845, in Henry T. Shanks, ed., *The Papers of Willie Person Mangum* (Raleigh, N.C., 1950), IV, 468.

91. Sellers, *Polk*, II, 208.

92. *Congressional Globe*, 28th Congress, 2d Session, pp. 362–363, 372; Robert Seager II, *And Tyler Too* (New York, 1963), p. 283; Oliver Perry Chitwood, *John Tyler: Champion of the Old South* (New York, 1939), pp. 360ff.

93. Blair to AJ, February 28, 1845, Jackson Papers, LC.

94. AJ to Blair, March 10, 1845, Jackson Papers, LC. Jackson learned the joint resolution had passed on March 5, 1845. AJ to Polk, March 6, 1845, Polk Papers, LC.

CHAPTER 33

1. AJ to Lewis, February 4, 1845, Donelson Papers, LC; AJ to Lewis, February 5, 1845, Jackson Papers, ML; AJ to Blair, February 8, 1845, Miscellaneous Manuscript Collection, YUL.

2. AJ to Lewis, February 4, 1845, Donelson Papers, LC.

3. Sellers, *Polk*, II, 208.

4. AJ to Lewis, February 28, 1845, in Jackson, *Correspondence*, VI, 375; AJ to Polk, April 11, May 2, 1845, Polk Papers, LC; AJ to Lewis, April 9, 10, 1845, Lewis to AJ, March 31, Jackson-Lewis Papers, NYPL; Sellers, *Polk*, II, 273. Lewis explained his removal to "personal dislike on the part of Polk and Cave Johnson" on account of "that old *sore* of 1834, about the speakership." Lewis to AJ, April 1, 1845, Jackson Papers, LC.

5. AJ to Lewis, September 17, 1844, Jackson-Lewis Papers, NYPL.

6. AJ to Polk, May 2, 1845, Polk Papers, LC.

7. Polk to AJ, May 12, 1845, Jackson Papers, LC.

8. Washington *Union*, June 2, 6, 1845.

9. AJ to Polk, April 11, 1845, Jackson Papers, LC; AJ to Van Buren, February 10, 1845, Van Buren Papers, LC.

10. AJ to Donelson [1845], Donelson Papers, LC; AJ to Lewis, February 12, 1845, Jackson-Lewis Papers, NYPL; AJ to Van Buren, February 10, 1845, Van Buren Papers, LC; AJ to Blair, March 3, 1845, Jackson Papers, LC.

11. AJ to Lewis, February 12, 1845, Jackson-Lewis Papers, NYPL. Twelve dollars per acre for all the land, he said, "will buy the place." AJ to Donelson, February 16, 1845, Donelson Papers, LC.

12. Blair to AJ, February 21, 1845, Jackson Papers, LC.

13. AJ to Blair, March 3, 1845, Jackson Papers, LC; AJ to Lewis, March 22, 1845, Jackson-Lewis Papers, NYPL.

14. John C. Rives to AJ, March 12, 1845, in Jackson, *Correspondence*, VI, 380.

15. AJ to Lewis, February 28, 1845, ibid., pp. 375–376, AJ to Lewis, March (?) 28, 1845, Robert Caldwell Collection, PUL.

16. Polk to AJ, March 17, 1845, Jackson Papers, LC.

17. Blair to Van Buren, March 29, April 11, 1845, Van Buren Papers, LC.

18. Sellers, *Polk*, II, 278; E. B. Smith, *Francis Preston Blair* (New York, 1980), p. 165.

19. AJ to Blair, April 7, 1845, Jackson Papers, LC.

20. AJ to Blair, April 4, 10, 28, 1845, Jackson Papers, LC; AJ to Polk, April 7, 1845, Polk Papers, LC.

21. Sellers, *Polk*, II, 280.

22. Ibid., p. 282.

23. AJ to Van Buren, February 10, 1845, Van Buren Papers, LC.

24. AJ to Polk, April 11, 1845, Polk Papers, LC.

25. AJ to Blair, April 10, 18, 20, May 3, 1845, Jackson Papers, LC.

26. Parton, *Jackson*, III, 669. This is what Parton reported, but it should be remembered that Parton was practically pathological on the subject of rotation and said that if Jackson's other acts had been perfectly correct this one failure was enough to condemn his administration.

27. Ibid., p. 670.

28. On this dispute see the exchange of letters with Lewis and Blair, in Jackson, *Correspondence*, VI, 359, 360, 362, 364, 367; AJ to Van Buren, February 10, 1845, Van Buren Papers, LC.

29. The Adams-Jefferson and the Adams-Jackson difference was commented on by a number of writers later on. See Parton, *Jackson*, III, 665, for one.

30. AJ to Blair, April 9, 1845, Jackson Papers, LC.

31. Columbia, Tennessee, *Democrat*, March 27, 1845, copy JPP.

32. AJ to Jesse Duncan Elliott, March 27, 1845, in Jackson, *Correspondence*, VI, 391.

33. Ibid., pp. 391–392.

34. Letter of Hon. Isaac Hill to the *New Hampshire Patriot,* April 4, 1845, copy JPP.

35. Diary of William Tyack, May 28–June 3, 1845, in Memphis *Commercial Appeal,* July 11, 1845, copy JPP.

36. Ibid.

37. Andrew Jr. to A.O.P. Nicholson, June 17, 1845, Miscellaneous Jackson Papers, NYHS.

38. AJ to Blair, May 3, 1845, Jackson Papers, LC; Esselman to Blair, June 9, 1845, in *Niles Weekly Register,* July 5, 1845.

39. AJ to Donelson, May 24, 1845, Donelson Papers, LC; AJ to Kendall, May 20, 1845, Jackson Papers, LC.

40. *Niles Weekly Register,* July 5, 1845.

41. Parton, *Jackson,* III, 672.

42. Catron to Sarah Jackson, May 19, 1845, in Jackson, *Correspondence,* VI, 409 note.

43. Diary of William Tyack, in Memphis *Commercial Appeal,* July 11, 1845.

44. AJ to Blair, May 26, 1845, Jackson Papers, LC.

45. Diary of William Tyack, in Memphis *Commercial Appeal,* July 11, 1845.

46. Ibid.

47. Ibid.

48. Andrew Jr. to Nicholson, June 17, 1845, Miscellaneous Jackson Papers, NYHS.

49. Ibid.

50. Ibid.; Esselman to Blair, June 9, 1845, in *Niles Weekly Register,* July 5, 1845.

51. Ibid.

52. Andrew Jr. to Nicholson, June 17, 1845, Miscellaneous Jackson Papers, NYHS.

53. Parton, *Jackson,* III, 676.

54. AJ to Polk, June 6, 1845, Jackson Papers, LC.

55. Prodded by Polk, who was very anxious to let the American people know that there had been no estrangement between himself and Jackson, Andrew searched and found the letter and sent it to Washington, where it was immediately published. Sellers, *Polk,* II, 282.

56. Andrew Jr. to Nicholson, June 17, 1845, Miscellaneous Jackson Papers, NYHS; Esselman to Blair, June 9, 1845, in *Niles Weekly Register,* July 5, 1845.

57. Ibid.; Andrew Jr. to Nicholson, June 17, 1845, Miscellaneous Jackson Papers, NYHS.

58. Ibid.

59. Esselman to Blair, June 9, 1845, in *Niles Weekly Register,* July 5, 1845; Elizabeth Donelson's pencil notations on the reverse side of Andrew J. Donelson to Elizabeth Donelson, May 20, 1845, Donelson Papers, LC.

60. Parton, *Jackson,* III, 678.

61. Andrew Jr. to Nicholson, June 17, 1845, Miscellaneous Jackson Papers, NYHS. This statement by Jackson is attested to by several other witnesses, including Elizabeth Donelson and Dr. Esselman. It was repeated in many newspaper accounts. Obviously, it had a profound effect on these witnesses.

62. Ibid.

63. Esselman to Blair, June 9, 1845, in *Niles Weekly Register,* July 5, 1845; Elizabeth Donelson's notations, Donelson Papers, LC; Andrew Jr. to Blair, June 10, 1845, Jackson Papers, LC.

Upon Jackson's death an inventory of his personal estate executed on August 4, 1845, revealed a large mansion (the Hermitage) with household furnishings, many of priceless value, on property of approximately 1,000 acres. In Wilson County he also left 50 acres of cedar timbers. In Mississippi the plantation consisted of 2,700 acres. Jackson also left 110 slaves at the Hermitage farm and another 51 on the Mississippi plantation, for a total of 161 slaves, "large and small." Between the two plantations he left 50 horses, some of them extremely valuable, 400 hogs, 180 sheep, and 100 cattle. Inventory of Estate presented in Davidson County Court by Andrew Jackson, Jr. executor, Wills and Inventories, XIII, 307, Davidson County, Tennessee, copy JPP; Account Book and Slave Register, 1845–1877, Hermitage, The Western Reserve Historical Society, Cleveland, Ohio, copy JPP.

64. John B. Moses and Wilbur Cross, *Presidential Courage* (New York, 1980), p. 66.

65. Journal and Letterbook of William Frierson Cooper, June 10, 1845, Cooper Family Papers, TSL.

66. Clarksville, Tennessee, *Jeffersonian*, June 21, 1845, copy JPP; James, *Jackson*, p. 786.

67. Nashville *Union*, June 12, 1845, copy JPP.

68. Jackson Papers, LC.

69. Jonesborough, Tennessee, *Sentinel*, July 19, 1845, copy JPP.

70. Nashville, *Union*, June 12, 1845, copy JPP.

71. Journal of William Frierson Cooper, Cooper Family Papers, TSL.

72. Jonesborough, Tennessee, *Sentinel*, July 19, 1845, copy JPP.

73. Andrew Jr. to Nicholson, June 17, 1845, Miscellaneous Jackson Papers, NYHS.

74. Journal of William Frierson Cooper, Cooper Family Papers, TSL.

75. On July 15, 1976, in the presence of representatives of the Ladies Hermitage Association, the top cover of Jackson's grave was removed, but the slab below ground level was not disturbed. What was observed is reported here. For other details of the funeral service, see Nashville *Union*, June 12, 1845, copy JPP.

76. Charleston *Mercury* quoted in *Niles National Register*, June 21, 1845; Webster's speech is quoted ibid., July 5, 1845.

77. Washington *Union*, June 16, 30, 1845.

78. *Niles National Register*, June 28, July 5, 1845.

79. Ibid.; New York *Evening Post*, June 25, 27, 1845.

80. Ibid.; Nashville *Union*, July 7, 1845, copy JPP.

81. New York *Evening Post*, June 27, 1845; *Niles National Register*, July 5, 1845.

82. Ibid.

83. *Memoirs of General Andrew Jackson*, compiled by a citizen of western New York (Auburn, N.Y., 1845), p. 141.

84. This is the concluding section of chapter 26, "Knights and Squires," in Herman Melville, *Moby Dick* (New York, 1851). I am grateful to Professor Todd Boli, who reminded me of this passage.

Bibliography

The vast corpus of materials at the Jackson Papers Project now numbers approximately 50,000 items. It is drawn from both private and public sources and consists of correspondence, memoranda, public documents, account books, legal and military papers, farm journals, and other miscellaneous materials. I was fortunate to participate in the formation of this collection. Not only did my own microfilm collection start the Project with all the Jackson correspondence available at the Library of Congress, but I traveled to virtually every major repository in this country to search for Jackson documents and had them copied and sent to the Hermitage. My travels on this mission also took me to London, Paris, Madrid, and Seville. The most important documents in this collection will be published in a letterpress edition, the first volume of which was issued in 1980 and covered Jackson's life from 1767 to 1803. A second volume, encompassing the years 1804–1813, is now nearing completion. A microfilm edition of the entire collection will also be issued in the near future.

I. Manuscripts

A. *Andrew Jackson*

The principal collection of the original Jackson manuscripts is located in the Library of Congress. This collection consists of roughly 22,500 items of various types (mostly correspondence), and they are kept in 269 volumes and 58 containers. The military papers take up 14 volumes and the map division of the Library has 11 additional items dealing with Jackson's military operations along the Gulf coast. John McDonough in his *Index to the Andrew Jackson Papers* (Washington, D.C., 1967) narrates the strange history of the collection, and how the papers were dispersed and later reassembled. But many Jackson letters turn up each year and autograph dealers do a rather brisk business in Jacksoniana. The Van Buren, Polk, and Blair Family papers in the Library of Congress also include a great many Jackson letters.

The Tennessee Historical Society in Nashville maintains over 10,000 pieces of

documentary material dealing with Jackson, Overton, Coffee, and other promi-
nent Tennesseans of the early nineteenth century. In addition, the Tennessee
State Library and Archives in Nashville has 1,500 Jackson items. And the Ladies'
Hermitage Association keeps a considerable collection of original Jackson documents, including his farm journal, account book, and personal library. Some 450
Jackson letters and miscellaneous material can be found in the Chicago Historical
Society, many of which are fragments of letters that Harriet Owsley cleverly
matched with fragments in the collection in the Library of Congress. The Andre
de Coppet Collection in the Princeton University Library is another important
depository of Jackson material.

The Alabama Department of Archives and History at Montgomery possesses
some 200 items relating to Jackson's career in East Florida. The Bibliotheca
Parsoniana in New Orleans contains material relating to the Battle of New Orleans. The William Clements Library at the University of Michigan has 33 Jackson
letters; the Duke University Library, 47 and recently (1983) purchased many
more; the Missouri Historical Society, 40; the New-York Historical Society, 21;
the Thomas Gilcrease Institute of American History and Art in Tulsa, 10; and the
Pierpont Morgan Library in New York City, 72. A very valuable collection of
Jackson correspondence with William B. Lewis, consisting of 254 items, and
sometimes called the Ford Collection or Jackson-Lewis Papers, is located in the
New York Public Library.

The Archivo General de Indias in Seville, Spain, contains a rich collection of
documentary material relating to Jackson, including many letters written by or to
the General. These items tend to be scattered in the collection, but Cuba, legajos
1795, proved most valuable. The Archivo General de Simancas and the Ar-
chivo Historico Nacional in Madrid, along with the Public Record Office in London, also yielded valuable documents.

B. *The Jackson Administration*

1. The President

The National Archives contains an enormous collection of manuscript documents dealing with the Jackson administration that relate to all the various departments and bureaus of the government. When I began my research many years ago
I was fortunate to be able to see and read the original documents themselves.
Lately, I find, researchers are asked to read them in microfilm and that is a very
long and tedious process. The State Department archives proved most useful,
especially the Appointment Papers, Diplomatic Dispatches and Instructions, Domestic Letters, and Notes to Foreign Legations. On Indian Removal I have relied
heavily on Record Group 75, the Records of the Bureau of Indian Affairs. Also
important were the Records of the War Department, Letters of the Secretary
Relating to Military Affairs, and Letters Sent to the President by the Secretary.
Recently, the National Archives published a *Guide to Records in the National Archives
Relating to American Indians* (Washington, 1982), and this publication can save a
researcher much time and effort in locating the documents relating to the Indians
and their removal.

2. The Vice President

There are good-size collections of manuscript materials on both of Jackson's
Vice Presidents. The largest collections of Calhoun material can be found at
Clemson College, South Carolina (approximately 2,500 items) and the South
Carolina Library in Columbia (about 3,500 items). Other collections are located
in the Library of Congress, and the Duke University Library. The Martin Van

Buren Papers, consisting of approximately 6,000 pieces, are deposited in the Library of Congress. Practically all of the Van Buren–Jackson correspondence can be found in this collection. Smaller holdings of Van Buren material are located in the New York State Library, the New-York Historical Society, New York Public Library, Massachusetts Historical Society, and the Columbia University Library.

3. The Secretary of State

Jackson's four secretaries included Van Buren, Livingston, McLane, and Forsyth. The Edward Livingston Papers are held by the John R. Delafield Foundation, and I would like once more to express my profound gratitude to John W. Delafield for permission to use these papers. The Louis McLane Papers were made available to John Munroe for the preparation of his distinguished biography of McLane, and copies of these papers are now located in the University of Delaware Library. A small collection of McLane material can be found in the Library of Congress. For John Forsyth there are very few items extant, unfortunately; they are located in the Georgia Department of Archives and History. The Library of Congress has Forsyth's diary, and about 100 items can be found in the Princeton University Library.

4. The Secretary of the Treasury

Samuel D. Ingham, Louis McLane, William J. Duane, Roger B. Taney, and Levi Woodbury served as secretary of the treasury during Jackson's administration. There are eleven boxes of Ingham material in the University of Pennsylvania Library. The rest is mostly scattered. A small collection of William J. Duane documents can be found in the Library of the American Philosophical Society. There are several hundred items of Roger B. Taney documents at Dickinson College, and approximately 100 items in the Maryland Historical Society. The Library of Congress has one box of Taney material, but the Carl Swisher Papers in the Library contain many copies of Taney letters. On Levi Woodbury, the Library of Congress has a large collection, running to 107 volumes and boxes. Much smaller collections of Woodbury material can be found in the New Hampshire Historical Society and Dartmouth College.

5. The Secretary of War

The three secretaries included John Henry Eaton, Lewis Cass, and Benjamin F. Butler. Unfortunately there is no real collection of Eaton material. Some of his letters are scattered throughout the various Jackson collections, but Peggy's manuscript autobiography is located in the Library of Congress. For Lewis Cass there are very substantial collections of his manuscript papers in the William L. Clements Library at the University of Michigan and the Burton Historical Collection in the Detroit Public Library. There are also a few items at the Central Michigan College Library and the Library of Congress. Benjamin F. Butler is represented by two relatively sizable collections, one in the New York State Library at Albany (6 boxes) and the other at the Princeton University Library (8 cartons).

6. The Secretary of the Navy

John Branch, Levi Woodbury, and Mahlon Dickerson served in this office. The John Branch Papers, consisting of approximately 4,000 items, are located in the Southern Historical Collection at Chapel Hill, North Carolina. A much smaller collection of Mahlon Dickerson Papers, representing about 1,000 pieces, can be found in the New Jersey Historical Society. An even smaller number of Dickerson manuscripts is deposited in the Rutgers University Library.

7. The Attorney General

There were three attorney generals: John M. Berrien, Roger B. Taney, and Benjamin F. Butler. The John M. Berrien Papers, comprising four volumes of approximately 1,500 items, are located in the Southern Historical Collection in Chapel Hill, with much smaller collections in the Georgia Historical Society and the Library of Congress.

8. The Postmaster General

William T. Barry and Amos Kendall were the postmasters during Jackson's administration. There is not much material on Barry. The Filson Club in Louisville, Kentucky, has one volume of papers, most of them copies; otherwise what manuscripts survive are scattered. For Amos Kendall, the Library of Congress has three volumes of materials, and the Massachusetts Historical Society has one box. A few of his letters can also be found in the New-York Historical Society. But the best place to find Kendall letters is the Blair-Lee Collection in the Princeton University Library. This is a very valuable collection for both Kendall and Blair. Since Blair was such an important figure in the Jackson administration, both as editor and member of the Kitchen Cabinet, perhaps it should also be mentioned that the Library of Congress has a very extensive collection of Blair Family Papers and in 1982 added to this number by acquiring many private letters between Blair and the members of his immediate family.

II. Additional Manuscript Collections

John Quincy Adams Papers (microfilm), MHS
Nathan Appleton Papers, MHS
Bailey Papers, MHS
John Bailey Papers, NYHS
P. P. Barbour Papers, NYPL
John Stelson Barry Ms. Diary, CHS
James Gordon Bennett Ms. Diary, NYPL
Bixby Collection, HL
Blair Family Papers, LC
Blair-Lee Papers, PUL
Gist Blair Papers, LC
Harmanus Bleecker Papers, NYSL
Sidney Breese Papers, Illinois State Library, Springfield
Brock Collection, HL
Jacob Brown Papers, MHS
Bryant-Godwin Papers, NYPL
Jacob Burnet Papers, LC
Armistead Burt Papers, DUL
Philip S. Butler Papers, LC
Cadwalader Papers, PHS
John Caldwell Papers, Illinois State Historical Society, Springfield
Robert Caldwell Collection, PUL
David Campbell Papers, DUL
Newton Cannon Papers, LC
Robert L. Caruthers Papers, SHC
Salmon P. Chase Ms. Diary, LC
Langdon Cheves Papers, South Carolina Historical Society, Charleston
Percy Childs Papers, NYPL
J. F. H. Claiborne Papers, SHC

C. C. Clay Papers, LC
Henry Clay Papers, LC
Claybrook Collection, TSL
John M. Clayton Papers, LC
Thomas G. Clemson Papers, Clemson College Library, Clemson, South Carolina
De Witt Clinton Papers, CUL; NYPL
Coffee Family Papers, LC
John Coffee Papers, THS and Alabama Department of Archives and History, Montgomery
Whiteford R. Cole Collection, TSL
Edward Coles Papers, PUL
Daniel P. Cook Papers, CHS
Cooper Family Papers, TSL
Andre de Coppet Collection, PUL
Richard K. Crallé Papers, Clemson College Library, Clemson, South Carolina
William H. Crawford Papers, LC
John J. Crittenden Papers, LC
Hardy M. Cryer Papers, THS
Caleb Cushing Ms. Diary, LC
George Dallas Papers, PHS
Moses Dawson Collection, LC
James M. Dickinson Papers, THS
John A. Dix Papers, CUL
Andrew J. Donelson Papers, LC
Lyman Draper Papers, WSH
Dreer Collection, PHS
George C. Dromgoole Papers, SHC
Henry W. Dwight Papers, LC
Ninian Edwards Papers, CHS
Jonathan Elliott Papers, LC
Powhatan Ellis Papers, LC
Jeremiah Evarts Papers, LC
Edward Everett Papers, MHS
Ewing Papers, THS
Thomas Ewing Papers, LC
Millard Fillmore Papers, Buffalo Historical Society
Fisher Family Papers, SHC
Azariah C. Flagg Papers, NYPL
John Floyd Papers, LC
Peter Force Papers, LC
C. V. Fox Papers, NYHS
B. B. French Papers, LC
Timothy Fuller Papers, LC
Gales & Seaton Papers, LC
Albert Gallatin Papers, NYHS; LC
Galloway-Maxcy-Markoe Papers, LC
Joshua R. Giddings Papers, Ohio State Archaeological and Historical Society, Columbus
Henry D. Gilpin Papers, PHS
C. W. Gooch Papers, University of Virginia Library, Charlottesville
Samuel Gouverneur Papers, NYPL
Governors' Papers, TSL
Francis and Gideon Granger Papers, LC

Simon Gratz Autograph Collection, PHS
Duff Green Papers, SHC; LC
Felix Grundy Papers, SHC
James Hamilton, Jr., Papers, SHC
James A. Hamilton Papers, NYHS
Charles Hammond Papers, Ohio Historical Society, Columbus
Jabez D. Hammond Papers, NYHS
James Hammond Papers, LC
Edward Harden Papers, DUL
Hardin Family Papers, CHS
William Henry Harrison Papers, LC
Benjamin Hawkins Papers, Georgia Department of Archives, Atlanta; LC
Paul Hamilton Hayne Papers, DUL
Robert Y. Hayne Papers, South Caroliniana Library, University of South Caro-
    lina, Columbia
James Heaton Papers, LC
David Henshaw Papers, LC
Isaac Hill Papers, New Hampshire Historical Society, Concord
Ethan Allen Hitchcock Papers, LC
N. P. Hobart Papers, LC
Michael Hoffman Papers, NYHS
Sam Houston Papers, LC
William Hunter Papers, LC
Hurja Collection, THS
Andrew J. Hutchings Papers, Dyas Collection, THS
Charles Jared Ingersoll Papers, PHS
Russell Jarvis Papers, LC
Thomas Jefferson Papers, LC
Andrew Johnson Papers, LC
William Jones Papers, LC
Elias K. Kane Papers, CHS
Amos Kendall Papers, LC
Francis Scott Key Papers, LC
Benjamin King Papers, LC
Rufus King Papers, NYHS
Lewis-Neilson Papers, PHS
William Lowndes Papers, LC
Wilson Lumpkin Papers, Georgia State Department of Archives, Atlanta
David Lynch Papers, LC
George McDuffie Papers, DUL
John McLean Papers, LC
Nathaniel Macon Papers, DUL
James Madison Papers, LC
William L. Marcy Papers, LC
Jeremiah Mason Papers, New Hampshire Historical Society, Concord
Virgil Maxcy Papers, LC
Henry Meigs Papers, NYHS
Return J. Meigs Papers, LC
A. G. Mitten Collection, Indiana Historical Society, Indianapolis
James Monroe Papers, LC; NYPL
Jacob Bailey Moore Papers, Harvard University Library
Alfred Mordecai Papers, LC
Marcus Morton Papers, MHS

Murdock Collection, THS
Newbold Papers, NYHS
Alfred O. P. Nicholson Papers, NYHS
C. M. Nielson Papers, LC
John Niles Papers, Connecticut Historical Society, Hartford
Nathaniel Niles Papers, LC
Norcross Collection, MHS
Thomas W. Olcott Papers, CUL
John Overton Papers, TSL
Daniel Parker Papers, LC
John Pemberton Papers, PHS
James L. Petigru Papers, LC
William Plumer Ms. Diary, LC; Miscellaneous Papers, NYHS
Joel Poinsett Papers, PHS
James K. Polk Papers, LC
Polk-Yeatman Papers, SHC
Worden Pope Papers, LC
Peter B. Porter Papers, Buffalo Historical Society
William Pitt Preble Papers, LC
John Randolph Papers, LC
John Reid Papers, LC
Thomas Ritchie Papers, LC
William C. Rives Papers, LC
Edmund Roberts Papers, LC
Rush Family Papers, PUL
Horace B. Sawyer Papers, LC
Henry Rowe Schoolcraft Papers, LC
Theodore Sedgwick Papers, MHS
John Sevier Papers, TSL
Samuel Seward Papers, NYSL
William H. Seward Papers, RUL
Shelley Family Papers, LC
Samuel Smith Papers, LC
Samuel L. Southard Papers, LC
Ambrose Spencer Papers, NYSL
J. D. Steele Ms. Journal, HL
Alexander H. Stephens Ms. Journal, LC
Stevenson Family Papers, LC
Henry R. Storrs Papers, NYHS
Tallmadge Family Papers, NYHS
Benjamin Tappan Papers, LC; Ohio Historical Society, Columbus
William Tappan Collection, LC
John W. Taylor Papers, NYHS
Jesse B. Thomas Papers, Illinois State Historical Library, Springfield
Smith Thompson Papers, LC
Samuel J. Tilden Papers, NYPL
Nicholas Trist Papers, LC
John Tyler Papers, LC
Vail Collection, NYHS
Van Ness Papers, NYHS
Stephen Van Rensselaer Papers, NYHS
Gulian C. Verplanck Papers, NYHS
James Wadsworth Papers, RUL

Robert J. Walker Papers, LC
Garrett Wall Papers, LC
George Walterston Papers, LC
Alexander Washburn Collection, MHS
Daniel Webster Papers, LC; New Hampshire Historical Society, Concord
Thurlow Weed Papers, RUL
Gideon Welles Papers, LC; Connecticut Historical Society, Hartford
Tappan Wentworth Papers, LC
Campbell P. White Papers, NYHS
Hugh Lawson White Papers, LC
Lewis Williams Papers, LC
James Winchester Papers, THS
Robert C. Winthrop Papers, MHS
William Wirt Papers, Maryland Historical Society, Annapolis
S. H. Witherspoon Papers, LC
George Wolf Papers, PHS
Bartlett Yancey Papers, SHC

III. PRINTED PUBLIC RECORDS

Printed public records are essential for Jackson's congressional career and his presidential administration. Those used most frequently include *House Journals, House Reports, House Executive Documents, Reports on the Finances, Senate Journals, Senate Documents, American State Papers,* the *Annals of Congress,* the *Register of Debates,* the *Congressional Globe, Congressional Directories,* and *Statutes at Large.* The presidential messages to Congress, vetoes, and other papers can be found in James D. Richardson, comp., *A Compilation of the Messages and Papers of the Presidents, 1789–1902* (10 vols., Washington, D.C., 1905).

IV. PUBLISHED CORRESPONDENCE, DIARIES, AUTOBIOGRAPHIES, AND MEMOIRS

John Spencer Bassett edited six volumes of *Correspondence of Andrew Jackson* (Washington, D.C., 1926–1935), publishing many of the best letters from the Jackson, Polk, and Van Buren collections in the Library of Congress, and from the Coffee Papers in Nashville and the Jackson-Lewis Papers in the New York Public Library. There is no other major publication of Jackson material, save for *The Papers of Andrew Jackson* (Knoxville, 1980), which have just begun to appear. Scholars of the Jacksonian era are fortunate in that all the leading figures but one are represented by comprehensive publication projects. These include Daniel Webster, John C. Calhoun, Henry Clay, and James K. Polk. Only Martin Van Buren is missing. As of 1983 the correspondence of Daniel Webster, which reaches the year 1843, has been published in five volumes; the Calhoun papers, which reach the year 1839, have been published in fourteen volumes; the Clay papers have arrived at the year 1827 in six volumes; and the Polk correspondence reaches 1843 in six volumes. These uncompleted projects must be supplemented with the following: Calvin Colton, ed., *The Private Correspondence of Henry Clay* (Cincinnati, 1856); Franklin Jameson, ed., *Correspondence of John C. Calhoun,* AHA, *Annual Report for the Year 1899* (Washington, D.C., 1900); Richard K. Crallé, ed., *The Works of John C. Calhoun* (6 vols., New York, 1854–1857); Fletcher Webster, ed., *The Private Correspondence of Daniel Webster* (2 vols., Boston, 1857) and *Writings and Speeches* (18 vols., Boston, 1903).

Among a tremendous number of printed primary sources, the following had particular value in the preparation of this biography: John C. Fitzpatrick, ed., *The Autobiography of Martin Van Buren*, AHA, *Annual Report for the Year 1918* (Washington, D.C., 1920); Charles Francis Adams, ed., *Memoirs of John Quincy Adams* (12 vols., Philadelphia, 1874–1877); Thomas Hart Benton, *Thirty Years View* (2 vols., New York, 1865); Reginald C. McGrane, *The Correspondence of Nicholas Biddle* (Boston and New York, 1919); James A. Hamilton, *Reminiscences of James A. Hamilton* (New York, 1869); William Stickney, ed., *Autobiography of Amos Kendall* (Boston, 1872); Henry T. Shanks, ed., *The Papers of Willie Person Mangum* (5 vols., Raleigh, N.C., 1950–1956); William J. Duane, *Narrative and Correspondence Concerning the Removal of the Deposits* (Philadelphia, 1838); William T. Barry, "Letters of William T. Barry," *William and Mary College Quarterly Historical Magazine* 1904–1905, XIII, 236–244, and 1905–1906, XIV, 19–23, 230–241; Charles F. Deems, *The Autobiography of Peggy Eaton* (New York, 1932); Charles H. Ambler, ed., "Unpublished Letters of Thomas Ritchie," *The John P. Branch Historical Papers of Randolph-Macon College* (1911, III, 199–252); Allan Nevins, ed., *The Diary of Philip Hone, 1828–1851* (2 vols., New York, 1936); Gaillard Hunt, ed., Mrs. Samuel Harrison Smith, *The First Forty Years of Washington Society* (New York, 1906); Nancy N. Scott, *A Memoir of Hugh Lawson White* (Philadelphia, 1856); Harriet A. Weed, ed., *Autobiography of Thurlow Weed* (Boston, 1883); Henry S. Foote, *Casket of Reminiscences* (Washington, D.C., 1874); John W. Forney, *Anecdotes of Public Men* (New York, 1873); Benjamin F. Perry, *Reminiscences of Public Men* (2 vols., Philadelphia, 1883, 1889); Ben: Perley Poore, *Perley's Reminiscences of Sixty Years in the National Metropolis* (Tecumseh, Mich., 1886); Nathan Sargent, *Public Men and Events* (2 vols., Philadelphia, 1875); and Henry A. Wise, *Seven Decades of the Union* (Philadelphia, 1881).

V. Travel Accounts

A number of European visitors have provided indispensable accounts of American society during the Jacksonian age. I have used the following with considerable profit: Harriet Martineau, *Society in America* (London, 1837), and *Retrospect of Western Travel* (2 vols., New York, 1838); Frances Trollope, *Domestic Manners of the Americans* (London, 1832); Michel Chevalier, *Society, Manners and Politics in the United States* (Boston, 1839); Francis J. Grund, *Aristocracy in America* (2 vols., London, 1839); Captain Frederick Marryat, *A Diary in America* (London, 1839); Thomas Hamilton, *Men and Manners in America* (Philadelphia, 1833); J. S. Buckingham, *America* (London, 1841); Captain Basil Hall, *Travels in North America in the Years 1827–1828* (Philadelphia, 1829); and Frances A. Kemble, *Journal* (2 vols., London, 1835).

VI. Newspapers and Periodicals

Albany *Argus*
Albany *Evening Journal*
Albany *Register*
Baltimore *Federal Republican*
Baltimore *Niles Weekly Register*
Baltimore *Patriot*
Boston *Columbian Centinel*
Boston *Daily Advertiser and Patriot*
Boston *Statesman*
Charleston *Courier*
Charleston *Mercury*
Charleston *Southern Patriot*

Chicago *Democrat*
Columbia, South Carolina, *Pendleton Messenger*
Columbia, South Carolina, *Telescope*
Cincinnati *Advertiser*
Cincinnati *Gazette*
Cincinnati, *Truth's Advocate and Monthly Anti-Jackson Expositor*
Fayetteville, North Carolina, *Observer*
Frankfort, Kentucky, *Argus of Western America*
Knoxville *Gazette*

Knoxville *Register*
Lancaster, Pennsylvania, *Journal*
Jackson, Tennessee, *Truth Teller*
Nashville *Constitutional Advocate*
Nashville *Gazette*
Nashville, *Impartial Review and Cumber-land Repository*
Nashville *National Banner*
Nashville *Republican*
Nashville *Republican Banner*
Nashville *Union*
Nashville *Whig*
New Haven *Journal*
New Hampshire *Patriot*
New York *American*
New York *Courier and Enquirer*
New York *Daily Advertiser*
New York *Enquirer*
New York *Evening Post*
New York *Journal of Commerce*
New York *National Advocate*
New York *Standard*
New York *Statesman*
New York *Tribune*
North American *Review*
Philadelphia *Columbia Observer*

Philadelphia *Democratic Press*
Philadelphia *National Gazette*
Raleigh, North Carolina, *Observer*
Raleigh, North Carolina, *Star*
Richmond *Constitutional Whig*
Richmond *Enquirer*
Richmond *Whig*
Rochester, New York, *Anti-Masonic Enquirer*
Trenton *True American*
United States Magazine and Democratic Review
Vermont Patriot
Washington, D.C., *Democratic Review*
Washington, D.C., *Globe*
Washington, D.C., *Kendall's Expositor*
Washington, D.C., *Journal*
Washington, D.C., *Madisonian*
Washington, D.C., *National Intelligencer*
Washington, D.C., *National Journal*
Washington, D.C., *Republican and Congressional Examiner*
Washington, D.C., *Union*
Washington, D.C., *United States Telegraph*

VII. SECONDARY SOURCES

It is impossible to list the many articles and books written about Jackson and his age that contributed to the writing of this biography. That list is simply too long. A few years ago I assisted Edwin A. Miles in putting together a list of all books and articles relative to the period 1816–1841. Entitled *The Era of Good Feelings and the Age of Jackson, 1816–1841* (Arlington Heights, Ill., 1979), it is a volume in the "Goldentree Bibliographies in American History" published by Harlan Davidson Publishing Corporation. It lists nearly 5,000 titles, and groups them under various headings, both chronological and topical. I would therefore refer readers to this publication for a reasonably complete listing to 1979 of publications on specific subjects.

However, I would be remiss not to single out special works that were invaluable in the writing of this biography. To begin with, I believe that there are two great works that deal specifically with Andrew Jackson: James Parton, *Life of Andrew Jackson* (3 vols., New York, 1861), and Arthur M. Schlesinger, Jr., *The Age of Jackson* (Boston, 1946). Parton's work, at once spirited and engrossing, is a critical study that vividly presents Jackson's character and personality in all their contrasting and contradictory moods. Little of great significance has been added to our knowledge about Jackson's character since Parton's biography first appeared, despite some heroic efforts to wrestle the old man onto a psychiatrist's couch and force him to admit to thoughts and acts of which he was totally innocent. Moreover, Parton provided pioneering research, and without his efforts we would know virtually nothing about the first twenty-one years of Jackson's life. But the biography does have serious flaws: the three volumes are uneven in merit; factual errors occasionally intrude; and Parton's relentless criticism of rotation distorts the purpose and direction of the Jackson administration. Still the work maintains itself as an important statement of Jackson's life and career. Few other biographies can compare to it in terms of scholarship and writing style. Marquis James, *The Life of Andrew Jackson* (2 vols., Indianapolis and New York, 1933, 1937), is excitingly written but is totally uncritical and presents Jackson simply as Hero and Patriot, not much more. John Spencer Bassett, *The Life of Andrew Jackson* (2 vols., New York, 1916), is a valuable work of scholarship but it is very thin on Jackson's early life and it is written in a lifeless and prosaic style.

Arthur Schlesinger's *Age of Jackson* marks the beginning of modern Jackson scholarship. It is a landmark study. It pointed research in a new direction and stimulated debate among historians for nearly a generation. To my mind it is one of the most valuable and insightful books ever written about the Hero. No other study has influenced my early thinking about Jackson and his age—with the possible exception of Alexis de Tocqueville's *Democracy in America* (2 vols., New York, 1945). Tocqueville's majestic and classic work continues to have a profound impact on the thinking of many Americans about their past, despite the protest of Edward Pessen, whose article, "The Egalitarian Myth and the American Social Reality: Wealth, Mobility, and Equality in the 'Era of the Common Man,' " *AHR*, 1971, LXXVI, 989–1034, has been described by one wag as a feeble effort to bury the noble Tocqueville in Brooklyn under a pile of tax receipts. It is difficult to take seriously anything Pessen writes about the era because his dislike of Jackson personally is so intense. It is rather remarkable—and instructive—that Old Hickory still has the power to arouse such fierce emotional responses from historians even though he has been dead nearly 150 years.

In terms of early biographies of Jackson, I found John Reid and John Henry Eaton, *The Life of Andrew Jackson* (Philadelphia, 1817), most valuable. It is especially important for the Hero's military career. There is a splendid new edition of this work, published in 1974 by the University of Alabama Press, which Frank L. Owsley, Jr., edited. Amos Kendall, *The Life of General Andrew Jackson* (New York, 1844), is a disappointment. Considering all the resources placed at the author's command, it is a spectacular failure. I am convinced that Augustus C. Buell, *History of Andrew Jackson* (2 vols., New York, 1904), is a fraud, and therefore I made a conscious effort to avoid it, despite its many delightful anecdotes and usable quotations. See Milton W. Hamilton, "Augustus C. Buell, Fraudulent Historian," *The Pennsylvania Magazine of History and Biography*, 1956, LXXX, 478–492. William Graham Sumner, *Andrew Jackson* (New York, 1882), tells a reader almost as much about the author as it does about its subject. What I particularly liked about the Sumner biography was that it alone, among the early biographies, offers a distinct point of view about Jackson and his era.

For Jackson's early career in Tennessee, Thomas Abernethy, *From Frontier to Plantation in Tennessee* (Chapel Hill, 1932), proved very helpful, despite the author's hostility toward Jackson personally. In chronicling Old Hickory's military career, I relied heavily on Frank L. Owsley's *Struggle for the Gulf Borderlands: The Creek War and the Battle of New Orleans, 1812–1815* (Gainesville, 1981), which I read in manuscript. Also useful were James F. Doster, *The Creek Indians and Their Florida Lands, 1740–1823* (New York and London, 1974); Robin Reilly, *The British at the Gates* (New York, 1974); Reginald Horsman, *The War of 1812* (New York, 1969); Wilbert S. Brown, *The Amphibious Campaign for West Florida and Louisiana* (University, Ala., 1969); Jane L. DeGrummond, *The Baratarians and the Battle of New Orleans* (Baton Rouge, 1961); and John K. Mahon, *The War of 1812* (Gainesville, 1972).

With respect to the Indians, in particular Jackson's attitude and behavior toward them, I have had the invaluable assistance of Professor Mary Young, who read the chapter on Indian removal in this volume and wrote several pages of criticisms and suggestions. Her comments plus her many articles cited in the footnotes and her important study *Redskins, Ruffleshirts and Rednecks* (Norman, 1961) form the core of my thinking about Jackson's relations with the Indians. I also wish to acknowledge my debt to two other studies: Ronald N. Satz, *American Indian Policy in the Jacksonian Era* (Lincoln, 1975); and Francis Paul Prucha, "Andrew Jackson's Indian Policy: A Reassessment," *JAH*, 1963, LVI, 299–322. Both works are essential to any investigation of Indian removal.

For the period following the War of 1812, I am indebted to George Dangerfield, *The Era of Good Feelings* (New York, 1952), and several superb biographies. Charles M. Wiltse, *John C. Calhoun* (3 vols., Indianapolis and New York, 1944–1951), is a treasure-house of information, attractively presented. Margaret L. Coit, *John C. Calhoun, American Portrait* (Boston, 1950), was a constant reminder of how biography should be written. Samuel F. Bemis, *John Quincy Adams and the Foundations of American Foreign Policy*, and *John Quincy Adams and the Union* (2 vols., New York, 1949, 1956), taught me to revere one of the nation's great statesmen even though Jackson thought Adams was a crazy old man. Harry Ammon, *James Monroe: The Quest for National Identity* (New York, 1971), is a solid piece of scholarship which treats a most difficult subject. I think there is an unattractive, if not dark side to Monroe's character which Ammon does not address. But what is presented is outstanding. Especially important—indeed, I kept both volumes within easy reach throughout the writing of this biography—were Charles Grier Sellers, Jr., *James K. Polk, Jacksonian, 1795–1843* (Princeton, 1957), and *James K. Polk, Continentalist, 1843–1846* (Princeton, 1966). It is to be hoped that Sellers will complete this exceptional biography in the near future. John Munroe's *Louis McLane, Federalist and Jacksonian* (New Brunswick, 1973) is another superb study whose attention to detail and completeness place it in the highest category of usefulness to all Jackson scholars. I was privileged to read John Niven's *Martin Van Buren and the Romantic Age of American Politics* (New York, 1983) in manuscript, and it is good to report that the Little Magician has at last found a biographer worthy of his stature and importance in American history. William N. Chambers, *Old Bullion Benton, Senator from the New West* (Boston, 1956), first taught me an appreciation for some of the twists in the Jacksonian position on hard money. And I have been everlastingly grateful to Chambers for another reason as well. His recommendation that I be invited to teach for a year at Columbia University changed the course of my life. Other helpful biographies include Wayne Cutler's doctoral dissertation (which I trust someday he will publish), "William H. Crawford: A Contextual Biography," University of Texas at Austin, 1971; and Glyndon G. Van Deusen, *The Life of Henry Clay* (Boston, 1937), and *Thurlow Weed, Wizard of the Lobby* (Boston, 1947).

On the rise of mass politics and the formation of the Democratic and Whig parties there are several outstanding works: Richard P. McCormick, *The Second American Party System: Party Formation in the Jacksonian Era* (Chapel Hill, 1966); Richard Hofstadter, *The Idea of a Party System* (Berkeley, 1969); and Ronald P. Formisano, *The Birth of Mass Political Parties: Michigan, 1827–1861* (Princeton, 1971). Lee Benson, *The Concept of Jacksonian Democracy: New York as a Test Case* (Princeton, 1961), provides an "ethnocultural" interpretation of Jacksonian politics.

The scholarly enthusiasm for the Jacksonian period triggered by the publication of Schlesinger's study produced a number of excellent monographs in intellectual history that sought to clarify the meaning of the age. John William Ward's *Andrew Jackson: Symbol of an Age* (New York, 1955) can only be described as brilliant. Equally compelling is Marvin Meyers, *The Jacksonian Persuasion* (Stanford, 1957). And I find Major L. Wilson, *Space, Time, and Freedom: The Quest for Nationality and the Irrepressible Conflict* (Westport, Conn., 1974), a most stimulating and valuable book.

For the Jackson administration as a whole the best of the modern studies is Richard Latner, *The Presidency of Andrew Jackson: White House Politics, 1829–1837* (Athens, Ga., 1979). The Bank War is surveyed in Robert V. Remini, *Andrew Jackson and the Bank War* (New York, 1967); Thomas P. Govan, *Nicholas Biddle: Nationalist and Public Banker, 1786–1844* (Chicago, 1959); and John M. McFaul, *The Politics of Jacksonian Finance* (Ithaca, 1972). I liked particularly William G. Shade, *Banks or No Banks: The Money Question in Western Politics, 1832–1865* (Detroit, 1972). Although Bray Hammond, *Banks and Politics in America from the Revolution to the Civil War* (Princeton, 1957), was written by a former member of the Federal Reserve Board who unquestionably knows a great deal about banking, I find the book totally wrong respecting Jackson's role and involvement in the Bank War.

On Jackson's system of rotation, otherwise known as the spoils system, I relied on two works: Leonard D. White, *The Jacksonians: A Study in Administrative History, 1829–1861* (New York, 1954), and Sidney H. Aronson, *Status and Kinship in the Higher Civil Service: Standards of Selection in the Administrations of John Adams, Thomas Jefferson, and Andrew Jackson* (Cambridge, Mass., 1964). The nullification controversy is best explained in William H. Freehling, *Prelude to Civil War: The Nullification Controversy in South Carolina, 1816–1836* (New York, 1965), although I am frank to admit that I disagree with the author's contention about the role of slavery in the controversy. On this point Paul H. Bergeron, "The Nullification Controversy Revisited," *THQ,* 1976, XXXV, 263–275, and Harry L. Watson, *Jacksonian Politics and Community Conflict* (Baton Rouge, 1981), are useful correctives. In writing the chapters on the controversy I borrowed heavily from Kenneth M. Stampp, *The Imperiled Union: Essays on the Background of the Civil War* (New York, 1980).

On foreign affairs very little outside two doctoral dissertations has been written by modern scholars. H. M. Neiditch, "The Origins and Development of Andrew Jackson's Foreign Policy," Doctoral Dissertation, Cambridge University, 1977, is excellent as far as it goes, but is limited in its coverage. Unfortunately this estimable dissertation is difficult to come by, and I am grateful to Craig Evan Klafter for lending me his microfilm copy. Douglas M. Astolfi, "Foundations of Destiny: A Foreign Policy of the Jacksonians, 1824–1837," Doctoral Dissertation, Northern Illinois University, 1972, is of little use. A few articles on foreign affairs can be found in learned journals. A study of foreign relations during Jackson's presidency is badly needed and one, in fact, may be under way.

In recent years scholars have concentrated on social history and the number of studies treating social development during the Jacksonian age is staggering. Some notable studies that I think illuminate our understanding include Rowland Berthoff, *An Unsettled People: Social Order and Disorder in American History* (New York, 1971); David J. Rothman, *The Discovery of the Asylum: Social Order and Disorder in the New Republic* (New York, 1971); T. L. Smith, *Revivalism and Social Reform* (New York, 1957); William J. Rorabaugh, *The Alcoholic Republic* (New York, 1980); Nancy F. Cott, *The Bonds of Womanhood* (New Haven, 1976); Leonard L. Richards, *"Gentlemen of Property and Standing": Anti-Abolition Mobs in Jacksonian America* (New York, 1970); Michael Feldberg, *The Turbulent Era: Riot and Disorder in Jacksonian America* (New York, 1980); Russel B. Nye, *Society and Culture in America* (New York, 1970); Thomas Dublin, *Women at Work: The Transformation of Work and Community in Lowell, Massachusetts, 1828–1860* (New York, 1979); Stephan Thernstrom and Richard Sennett, eds., *Nineteenth Century Cities: Essays in the New Urban History* (New Haven, 1969); and Peter R. Knights, *The Plain People of Boston, 1830–1860: A Study in City Growth* (New York, 1971).

Edward Pessen has written a great deal on social mobility, class, and wealth distribution for this period. His *Riches, Class, and Power Before the Civil War* (Lexington, Mass., 1973) relies heavily on quantification, but Richard Jensen, who knows about such things, reports that Pessen "misinterprets his own tables" and "draws the wrong conclusions." According to Jensen, numerous "analytical shortcomings" mar the book, including measurement techniques that are "crude." See Jensen's critical review of Pessen's work in the *Indiana Magazine of History*, 1974, LXX, 185–187. Still valuable in understanding the society of this era are the many accounts provided by foreign travelers, including Tocqueville, Trollope, Martineau, Grund, and Chevalier. Indeed, Tocqueville remains the surest and best key to unlocking the mysteries and wonder of Jacksonian America.

Index

617